The TALE

— of the —

TARDY OXCART

PUBLICATIONS BY CHARLES R. SWINDOLL

BOOKS

Active Spirituality
The Bride
Come Before Winter
Compassion: Showing We Care in a
Careless World
David: A Man of Passion and Destiny
Dear Graduate
Dropping Your Guard
Encourage Me
Esther: A Woman of Strength and Dignity
The Finishing Touch
Flying Closer to the Flame
For Those Who Hurt
God's Provision in Time of Need
The Grace Awakening
Growing Deep in the Christian Life
Growing Strong in the Seasons of Life
Growing Wise in Family Life
Hand Me Another Brick
Home: Where Life Makes Up Its Mind
Hope Again
Improving Your Serve
Intimacy with the Almighty
Joseph: A Man of Integrity and Forgiveness

Killing Giants, Pulling Thorns
Laugh Again
Leadership: Influence that Inspires
Living Above the Level of Mediocrity
Living Beyond the Daily Grind, Books I and II
The Living Insights Study Bible, General
Editor
Living on the Ragged Edge
Make Up Your Mind
Man to Man
Paw Paw Chuck's Big Ideas on the Bible
The Quest for Character
Recovery: When Healing Takes Time
Sanctity of Life
Simple Faith
Starting Over
Strengthening Your Grip
Stress Fractures
Strike the Original Match
The Strong Family
Suddenly One Morning
Three Steps Forward, Two Steps Back
Victory: A Winning Game Plan for Life
You and Your Child

MINIBOOKS

Abraham: A Model of Pioneer Faith
David: A Model of Pioneer Courage
Esther: A Model of Pioneer Independence

Moses: A Model of Pioneer Vision
Nehemiah: A Model of Pioneer
Determination

BOOKLETS

Anger
Attitudes
Commitment
Dealing with Defiance
Demonism
Destiny
Divorce
Eternal Security
Forgiving and Forgetting
Fun Is Contagious!
God's Will
Hope
Impossibilities
Integrity
Leisure
The Lonely Whine of the Top Dog

Make Your Dream Come True
Making the Weak Family Strong
Moral Purity
Our Mediator
Praise . . . In Spite of Panic
Portrait of a Faithful Father
The Power of a Promise
Prayer
Reflections from the Heart: A Prayer Journal
Seeking the Shepherd's Heart
Sensuality
Stress
This is No Time for Wimps
Tongues
When Your Comfort Zone Gets the Squeeze
Woman

SWINDOLL
LEADERSHIP
LIBRARY

The TALE

— of the —

TARDY

OXCART

And 1,501 Other Stories

CHARLES R. SWINDOLL

WORD PUBLISHING

NASHVILLE

A Thomas Nelson Company

THE TALE OF THE TARDY OXCART
Swindoll Leadership Library

Copyright © 1998 by Word Publishing, Inc. All rights reserved.

Published in association with Dallas Theological Seminary (DTS):
General Editor: Charles Swindoll
Managing Editor: Roy B. Zuck
The theological opinions expressed by the author are not necessarily the
official position of Dallas Theological Seminary.

The author expresses gratitude to all the copyright holders for permission
to include their works. For a complete listing of acknowledgments, see pg. 633

Library of Congress Cataloging-in-Publication Data

Swindoll, Charles R.
Tale of the tardy oxcart and 1501 other stories: a collection of stories, anecdotes, illus-
trations, and quotes / Charles R. Swindoll
p.   cm.—(Swindoll leadership library)
Includes bibliographical references.
ISBN 0-8499-1351-9 (alk. paper)
1. Christian life—Anecdotes.   2. Christian life—Quotations, maxims, etc.
I. Title.   II. Series
BV4517.S95   1998
251'.08—dc21
                                                        98-15088
                                                        CIP

Printed in the United States of America
99 00 01 02 03 04 05 BVG 9 8 7 6 5 4 3

Dedication

This book is dedicated,
with great admiration,
to all my colleagues in ministry,
especially those who work hard at
communicating God's truth
with accuracy, clarity, and practicality,
and therefore are in constant pursuit of
"just the right illustration"
to get the message across,
lest they clothe the
riches of Christ
in rags.

Alphabetical List of Topics

—M—

—N—

—O—

—P—

Introduction

I AM A PREACHER. I have been standing before congregations and various other audiences in and around America for more than thirty-five years. I have served in pastorates in Massachusetts, California, and Texas. My travels have also taken me up into Canada, down through Mexico and Central America, and beyond the great oceans of this world, from Alaska to Australia, from Maui to Mannheim, proclaiming the Good News of Jesus Christ. What an invigorating journey! Through all these experiences, nothing has given me greater satisfaction and fulfillment than communicating on my feet, regardless of the place I stood, as people listened to God's truth from His life-giving Word.

God gets all the praise and glory for this. After all, He is the One who distributes the gifts and the One who provides the insights, energy, and results. What a privilege it is to continue serving as a messenger of the King! I freely confess, my heart still skips a beat or two when I anticipate preparing and proclaiming His message. To this day, I've not lost the joy or the excitement connected with being one of His voices. I love the challenges as well as the changes preaching requires. To tell you the truth, I enjoy the *whole* experience, including all that goes into the preparation process. I do my own research, I dig into the Scriptures on my own, and I read widely on a regular basis. Those disciplines provide a major source of my enthusiasm; that's how the fire starts to build within me. But admittedly the crowning moment occurs when I have the privilege of standing and delivering. When the Spirit of God takes charge and honors the hard work of study and prayer and planning and thinking, it is rewarding beyond description. Nothing compares to that!

Through all the years and in all the places I have been engaged in this calling, I have learned the value of good illustrations. Interesting illustrations. Illustrations that grab the attention and clear the minds of those listening. Illustrations that open the windows, bringing light to truth. Under the general heading of illustrations, I would include stories, anecdotes, quotations, analogies, incidents, experiences, poems, songs, delightful moments, struggles I've endured, as well as humorous situations I've been in that, when later told, help make the truth come alive.

More times than I can count, I remember using such illustrations and watching God pry open the eyes and unstop the ears (not to mention soften the hearts) of others, many of whom were bound and determined not to give me even the time of day . . . until they were stabbed awake and compelled to listen. Those experiences have always thrilled me and sometimes amazed me. A well-chosen illustration can transform a hostile skeptic into an interested participant. I know; I've seen it happen.

Many who listen to our radio ministry, *Insight for Living,* write to tell me how much a particular example I used or story I told grabbed their attention and turned them around spiritually. Congregational members have said similar things. Truth, made clear through the use of just the right illustration, anecdote, story, or quotation is applied more quickly and remembered much longer. I've rarely been asked, "How did you come up with that outline?" or "When did those insights from that Scripture dawn on you?" But I have often heard, "Where did you get that illustration?" and even more often, "Can I have a copy of that example you used?"

Knowing the effectiveness and long-lasting benefits of illustrations, I have been doing what most preachers do: gathering them from every source imaginable, then using them for introductions, for clarification, for conclusions. My collection fills several file drawers, and the stack increases each year. You can appreciate my delight when I first found Solomon's remarks about this. "In addition to being a wise man, the Preacher also taught the people knowledge, and he pondered, searched out and arranged many proverbs. . . . [he] sought to find delightful words and to write words of truth correctly. The words of wise men are like goads, and masters of these collections are like well-driven nails; they are given by one Shepherd" (Eccles. 12:9–11 NASB).

If that doesn't describe the work of faithful and effective preachers, I don't know what does. Who can measure the persuasive goading of "delightful words" that have been pondered and searched out? Who better than a preacher has experienced the compelling impact of stories or examples that penetrate the surface of the soul and then hammer the truth home like "well-driven nails"? And best of all, when the biblical truths, thoughts, and ideas, mixed with just the right illustrations, are "given by one Shepherd"—the Lord Himself—who is more thrilled than the preacher, whose joy it is to communicate it to others?

In light of all this, it seemed only reasonable to pause from preaching long enough to unload my files and put into print the illustrations I have collected over these three-and-a-half decades. Since they have been of such help to me personally, perhaps others can benefit from them as well. If you find them useful, no one is more delighted than I.

A great deal of credit goes to Carol Martin, to whom I am indebted for her tireless effort and meticulous attention to detail. For years at her Insight for Living office she has reviewed my messages, locating so many of these illustrations, then more recently, at my request, categorizing and alphabetizing them in the order you find them in this book. Thank you, Carol, for your diligence, dedication, and determination to see this project to completion. I should also acknowledge the careful, sometimes tedious, work of Julie Meredith, who assisted me in securing the permissions from hundreds of sources. What a valuable contribution, accomplished with a splendid attitude of devotion and determination! Without both of you, this volume would have never been published.

Finally, let me state a needed disclaimer. In a work this large, full of illustrations from hundreds of different sources over the past thirty-five years, there is no way I could possibly give the proper credit to each original author, composer, or source. I have attempted to locate and then identify those who deserve the credit for specific material, but in some cases, I found myself unable to do so, much to my regret. Please accept my apologies, should you be one of those I should have named but did not. The omission was the result of oversight, time constraint, or some other inadequacy on my part, but in no way was it my attempt to claim ownership or credit that rightfully belongs to another. Having been quoted (and sometimes misquoted!) by others without being properly contacted for prior approval, I understand the feelings some of my unidentified sources may entertain—and I sincerely apologize ahead of time, lest there be any misunderstanding.

It is my hope and prayer that you who use this book will be able to glean a great deal of assistance from it, especially you who are looking for "just the right illustration" to enhance the message you plan to deliver. To borrow from Solomon, I hope you find them "like goads," a helpful collection of "well-driven nails" that allow you to cinch the truth in place.

—CHUCK SWINDOLL
Dallas, Texas

$\mathcal{A}a$

ABILITY

ABILITIES ARE LIKE tax deductions, we use them or we lose them.

—Sam Jennings, quoted in Lloyd Cory, *Quote Unquote*

THE SPRINGFIELD, OREGON, Public Schools newsletter published an article that caught my eye some time ago. As I read it, it struck me that I was reading a parable of familiar frustration in the Christian home and the body of Christ today.

Once upon a time, the animals decided they should do something meaningful to meet the problems of the new world. So they organized a school.

They adopted an activity curriculum of running, climbing, swimming, and flying. To make it easier to administer the curriculum, all the animals took all the subjects.

The *duck* was excellent in swimming; in fact, better than his instructor, but he made only passing grades in flying, and was very poor in running. Since he was slow in running, he had to drop swimming and stay after school to practice running. This caused his web feet to be badly worn, so that he was only average in swimming. But average was quite acceptable, so nobody worried about that—except the duck.

The *rabbit* started at the top of his class in running, but developed a nervous twitch in his leg muscles because of so much make-up work in swimming.

The *squirrel* was excellent in climbing, but he encountered constant frustration in flying class because his teacher made him start from the ground up instead of from the treetop down. He developed charley horses from overexertion, and so only got a C in climbing and a D in running.

The eagle was a problem child and was severely disciplined for being a nonconformist. In climbing classes he beat all the others to the top of the tree, but insisted on using his own way to get there. . . .

The obvious moral of the story is a simple one: Each creature has its own set of capabilities in which it will naturally excel—unless it is expected or forced to fill a mold that doesn't fit. What is true of creatures in the forest is true of Christians in the family. God has not made us all the same. It's OK to be you . . . so relax. Enjoy your own capabilities, cultivate your own style. Appreciate the members of your family or your fellowship for who they are, even though their outlook or style may be miles different from yours. Rabbits don't fly. Eagles don't swim. Ducks look funny trying to climb. Squirrels don't have feathers. Stop comparing!

—Charles R. Swindoll, *Growing Strong in the Seasons of* Life

BETWEEN THE GREAT THINGS we can't do and the little things we won't do, the danger is we shall do nothing at all.

ABORTION

A PROFESSOR IN A COLLEGE ETHICS CLASS presented his students with a problem. He said, "A man has syphilis and his wife has tuberculosis. They have had four children: one has died, the other three have what is considered to be a terminal illness. The mother is pregnant. What do you recommend?" After a spirited discussion, the majority of the class voted that she abort the child. "Fine," said the professor. "You've just killed Beethoven."

—*HIS* magazine, February 1984

FORMER SURGEON GENERAL C. Everett Koop says in his thirty-five years in medicine he has "never seen one case where abortion was necessary to save a mother's life."

—Bill Hybels, *One Church's Answer to Abortion*

IN APRIL 1971 a White House Conference on youth met at Estes Park, Colorado, to report on the influence of the mass media. Concern was voiced about the media's power being used to glorify violence, glamorize sin, and laugh at Christian faith and virtue. "It seems that Dr. Alan Guttmacher, director of Planned Parenthood World Population and a member of the board of directors of the Euthanasia Society of America, and his fellow creators of *Sesame Street* had planned twenty-six one-hour shows on 'health' for their 1974–1975 schedule. Dr. Guttmacher and spokesmen for a task force which advised on the 'family planning' segments, decided the word 'abortion' should be used constantly in sixteen of the twenty-six scheduled shows in order to 'detoxify' the viewing audience from cultural shock. Following this, they included a segment which involved a pregnant eight-year-old girl who would be denied an abortion by her mother. Not one pro-life representative was asked to take part in the planning sessions for these programs."

—Willard Aldrich, *The Battle for Your Faith*

ACCEPTANCE
(Also see *Forgiveness, Self-esteem*)

DURING HIS DAYS AS PRESIDENT, Thomas Jefferson and a group of companions were traveling across the country on horseback. They came to a river which had left its banks because of a recent downpour. The swollen river had washed the bridge away. Each rider was forced to ford the river on horseback, fighting for his life against the rapid currents. The very real possibility of death threatened each rider, which caused a traveler who was not part of their group to step aside and watch. After several had plunged in and made it to the other side, the stranger asked President Jefferson if he would ferry him across the river. The president agreed without hesitation. The man climbed on, and shortly thereafter the two of them made it safely to the other side. As the stranger slid off the back of the saddle onto dry ground, one in the group asked him, "Tell me, why did you select the president to ask this favor of?" The man was shocked, admitting he had no idea it was the president who had helped him. "All I know," he said, "is that on some of your faces was written the answer 'No' and on some of them was the answer 'Yes.' His was a 'Yes' face."

—R. Lofton Hudson, *Grace Is Not a Blue-Eyed Blond*

ACCEPTANCE MEANS YOU ARE VALUABLE just as you are. It allows you to be the real you. You are not forced into someone else's idea of who you are. It means your ideas are taken seriously since they reflect you. You can talk about how you feel inside, why you feel that way, and someone really cares. Acceptance means you can try out your ideas without being shot down. You can even express heretical thoughts and discuss them with intelligent questioning. You feel safe. No one will pronounce judgment on you even though they don't agree with you. It doesn't mean you'll never be corrected or shown to be wrong. It simply means it's safe to be you and no one will destroy you out of prejudice.

Gladys M. Hunt, quoted in *Eternity* magazine, October 1969

HOW MANY PRODIGALS are kept out of the kingdom of God by the unlovely characters of those who profess to be inside!

—Henry Drummond

I WAS TOLD A WONDERFUL STORY about Coach Tom Landry that illustrates the level of his Christian love and acceptance of others. Years ago, the late Ohio State coach, Woody Hayes, was fired for striking an opposing player on the sidelines during a football game. The press had a field day with the firing and really tarred and feathered the former Buckeye coach. Few people in America could have felt lower than he at that time; he not only lost control in a game and did a foolish thing, but he also lost his job and much of the respect others had for him.

At the end of that season, a large, prestigious banquet was held for professional athletes. Tom Landry, of course, was invited. Guess who he took with him as his guest? Woody Hayes, the man everyone was being encouraged to hate and criticize.

—Charles R Swindoll, *Hope Again*

The New Colossus
Not like the brazen giant of Greek fame,
With conquering limbs astride from land to land;
Here at our sea-washed sunset gates shall stand
A mighty woman with a torch, whose flame
Is the imprisoned lightning, and her name
Mother of Exiles. From her beacon-hand
Glows world-wide welcome; her mild eyes command
The air-bridged harbor that twin cities frame.
"Keep, ancient lands, your storied pomp!" cries she
With silent lips. "Give me your tired, your poor,
Your huddled masses yearning to breathe free,
The wretched refuse of your teeming shore.
Send these, the homeless, tempest-tost to me,
I lift my lamp beside the golden door!"

—Hazel Felleman, *Poems That Live Forever*

YOU EVER FEEL LIKE A FROG? Frogs feel slow, low, ugly, puffy, drooped, pooped. I know. One told me. The frog feeling comes when you want to be bright but feel dumb, when you want to share but are selfish, when you want to be thankful but feel resentment, when you want to be great but are small, when you want to care but are indifferent. Yes, at one time or another each of us has found himself on a lily pad, floating down the great river of life. Frightened and disgusted, we're too froggish to budge.

Once upon a time there was a frog, only he wasn't really a frog, he was a prince who looked and felt like a frog. The wicked witch had cast a spell on him and only the kiss of a beautiful maiden could save him. But since when do cute chicks kiss frogs? So there he sat, an unkissed prince in frog form. One day a beautiful maiden gathered him up and gave him a big smack! Zap!! There he was, a frog turned handsome prince and they lived happily after. So what's the task of the Christian? Kissing frogs, of course!

—Bruce Larson, *Ask Me to Dance*

THE MOST CONSISTENTLY ENDEARING human trait is warmth. Everybody responds to the person who radiates friendliness from a serene core. Such people are lovely to be around because they don't reject or belittle and, best of all, they bring out the best, most generous qualities in the people they encounter.

—Barbara Walters, *How to Talk with Practically Anybody about Practically Anything*

WILL ROGERS SAID, "I never met a man I didn't like." Someone added, "You never met my husband."

PHILIP YANCEY made an interesting observation. "It's easy to see why people like the sea gull. I've sat overlooking a craggy harbor and watched one. He exults in freedom. He thrusts his wings backward with powerful strokes, climbing higher, higher until he's above all the other gulls, then coasts downward in majestic loops and circles. He constantly performs, as if he knows a movie camera is trained on him, recording.

"In a flock, though, the sea gull is a different bird. His majesty and dignity melt into a sordid slough of in-fighting and cruelty. Watch that same gull as he dive-bombs into a group of gulls, provoking a flurry of scattered feathers and angry squawks, to steal a tiny morsel of meat. The concepts of sharing and manners do not exist among gulls. They are so fiercely competitive and jealous that if you tie a red ribbon around the leg of one gull, making him stand out, you sentence him to execution. The others in his flock will furiously attack him with claws and beaks, hammering through feathers and flesh to draw blood. They'll continue until he lies flattened in a bloody heap."

If we must select a bird to serve as a model for our society the sea gull is not the best choice. Yancey has suggested that we consider the behavior of geese, instead. Have your ever wondered why these remarkable birds fly in "V" formation? Science has recently learned that the flock actually travels up to 71 percent faster and easier by maintaining this pattern. The goose on the point of the "V" has the most difficult assignment, resulting from greater wind resistance. Thus, that lead position is rotated every few minutes in the air, which permits the flock to fly long distances without rest. The easiest flight is experienced at the two rear sections of the formation and, remarkably, the strong geese permit the young, weak, and old birds to occupy those less strenuous positions. It is even believed the constant "honking" of the flock is a method by which the stronger birds encourage the laggards. Furthermore, if a goose becomes too tired or is ill and has to drop out of the flock, he is never abandoned. A healthy bird will follow the ailing one to the ground and wait with him until he can continue in flight. This cooperation within the social order contributes greatly to the survival and well-being of the flock. . . . There are times it seems our society consists of 200 million solitary sea gulls, each huffing and puffing to do his own thing, but paying an enormous price in loneliness and stress for his individuality.

—James Dobson, *The Strong-Willed Child*

THE CHURCH IS TO BE a place of open affection. A man saw a book *How to Hug* and went to buy it. It was an encyclopedia volume covering subjects HOW–HUG.

—Ray Stedman, sermon *"Guilt to Glory,"* March 20, 1997

TONY CAMPOLO TELLS a true story of a Jewish boy who suffered under the Nazis in World War II. He was living in a small Polish village when he and all the other Jews of the vicinity were rounded up by Nazi SS troops and sentenced to death. This boy joined his neighbors in digging a shallow ditch for their graves, then faced the firing squad with his parents. Sprayed with machine-gun fire, bodies fell into the ditch and the Nazis covered the crumpled bodies with dirt. But none of the bullets hit the little boy. He was splattered with the blood of his parents and when they fell into the ditch, he pretended to be dead and fell on top of them. The grave was so shallow that the thin covering of dirt did not prevent air from getting through to him so that he could breathe.

Several hours later, when darkness fell, he clawed his way out of the grave. With blood and dirt caked to his little body, he made his way to the nearest house and begged for help. Recognizing him as one of the Jewish boys marked for death, he was turned away at house after house as people feared getting into trouble with the SS troops. Then something inside seemed to guide him to say something that was very strange for a Jewish boy to say. When the next family responded to his timid knocking in the still of the night, they heard him cry, "Don't you recognize me? I am the Jesus you say you love." After a poignant pause, the woman who stood in the doorway swept him into her arms and kissed him. From that day on, the members of that family cared for that boy as though he was one of their own.

—Anthony Campolo, *Who Switched the Price Tags?*

DAVID REDDING wrote about his personal experience with acceptance.

I remember going home from the Navy during World War II. Home was so far out in the country that when we went hunting, we had to go toward town. We had moved there for my father's health when I was thirteen. We raised cattle and horses. Some who were born on a farm regard the work and the solitude as a chore, but coming from town as I did then, made that farm home an Eden to me.

I started a little flock of Shropshire sheep, the kind that are completely covered by wool except for a black nose and the tips of the legs. My father helped them have their twins at lambing time, and I could tell each one of the flock apart at a distance with no trouble. I had a beautiful ram. The poor man next door had a beautiful dog, and a small flock of sheep he wanted to improve with my ram. He asked me if he could borrow the ram; in return he would let me have the choice of the litter from his prize dog.

That's how I got Teddy, a big black Scottish shepherd. Teddy was my dog, and he would do anything for me. He waited for me to come home from school. He slept beside me, and when I whistled he ran to me, even if he were eating. . . . And when I went away to war, I didn't know how to leave him. How do you explain to someone who loves you that you're leaving him and you won't be chasing woodchucks with him tomorrow like always?

So coming home that first moment from the Navy was something I can scarcely describe. The last bus stop was fourteen miles from the farm. I got off there that night about eleven o'clock and walked the rest of the way home. It was two or three in the morning before I was within a half mile of the house. It was pitch dark, but I knew every step of the way. Suddenly Teddy heard me and began his warning barking. Then I whistled only once. The barking stopped. There was a yelp of recognition, and I knew that a big black form was hurtling toward me in the darkness. Almost immediately he was there in my arms.

What comes home to me now is the eloquence with which that unforgettable memory speaks to me of my God. If my dog, without any explanation, would love me and take me back after all that time, wouldn't my God?

—David A. Redding, *Jesus Makes Me Laugh with Him*

DR. HUDSON ARMERDING, the former president of Wheaton College, sometime ago faced the dilemma of a particular problem brought on by prejudice. He stood before the student body that had packed the chapel and made an announcement that got everyone's attention.

Because of the ramifications of this problem with prejudice, the school was facing the possibility of a financial crunch. It seems as though a number of those who were heavy financial contributors to the college had been visiting the campus. And the word had spread that a number of the young men on campus were wearing their hair awfully long. And, in fact, a number of these Christian young men were now wearing beards. This had posed such a tremendous problem in the minds of those who gave heavily to the school that they were threatening to withdraw their support as some had already done. The student body sat quietly, anxiously awaiting the response of the administration.

Dr. Armerding began to scan the student body with his eyes. And he finally landed on one young man, whom he called by name, and asked him to stand to his feet. He did, reluctantly. And then the president said, "I want you to come and join me on the platform." He did, with greater reluctance. He stood there with long hair and a long beard. And Dr. Armerding, looking him straight in the face, said this, "Young man, you have long hair and a long beard. You represent the very thing that these supporters of the school are against. I want you to know that the administration of this school does not feel as they do. We accept you and we love you. We believe you are here to seek and to find the truth as it is in the Lord Jesus Christ."

With that, the president reached out his arms, drew the young man to himself, and publicly embraced him, at which time the entire student body stood to its feet, giving spontaneous acclaim to this brave president.

—Ray Stedman, *The Birth of the Body*

ACCOUNTABILITY

PERSONAL ACCOUNTABILITY is invaluable. Recently, I was encouraged to hear about a minister who meets once a week with a small group of men. They are committed to one another's purity. They pray with and for each other. They talk openly and honestly about their struggles, weaknesses, temptations, and trials. In addition to these general things, they look one another in the eye as they ask and answer no less than seven specific questions:

1. Have you been with a woman this week in such a way that was inappropriate or could have looked to others that you were using poor judgment?
2. Have you been completely above reproach in all your financial dealings this week?
3. Have you exposed yourself to any explicit material this week?
4. Have you spent time daily in prayer and in the Scriptures this week?
5. Have you fulfilled the mandate of your calling this week?
6. Have you taken time off to be with your family this week?
7. Have you just lied to me?

—Charles R. Swindoll, *The Bride*

SEVERAL YEARS AGO some church fellows recognized my spotless, white 1979 Volkswagen Superbeetle convertible run a red light. I was invited to meet my accusers at Randy's Coffee Shop for breakfast or face "exposure" to the media. Well, I was caught red-handed by the rascals, so I decided to show up at the coffee shop bright and early. I stuck a big sign on my shirt that read "Guilty as Charged." I walked up to the startled waitress at seven forty-five that morning and asked her to seat me at a table where several could join me. I told her I was meeting some Pharisees that morning. She put some menus down and walked away shaking her head. At eight o'clock sharp in they walked! When we all had a laugh at my sign, I turned it over. On the back I had written, "He who is without sin cast the first stone!" They bought my breakfast. If I live to be a ripe old age of 100, I doubt that I'll ever forget that whole episode. Every time I'm tempted to run a light, the incident comes back to haunt me . . . one of the many benefits of accountability!   —Charles R. Swindoll, *Dropping Your Guard*

DANIEL WEBSTER was asked, "What is the greatest thought that can occupy a man's mind?" He said, "His accountability to God."

—Abel Ahlquist, *Light on the Gospels*

BEHAVORIAL SCIENCES in recent years have expounded the simple truth that "behavior that is observed changes." People who are accountable by their own choice to a group of friends, to a therapy group, to a psychiatrist or a pastoral counselor, to a study group or prayer group, are people who are serious about changing their behavior, and they are finding that change is possible.

Studies done in factories have proven that both quality and quantity of work increase when the employees know they are being observed. If only God knows what I'm doing, since I know He won't tell, I tend to make all kinds of excuses for myself. But if I must report to another or a group of others, I begin to monitor my behavior. If someone is keeping an eye on me, my behavior improves.

—Bruce Larson, *There's a Lot More to Health Than Not Being Sick*

ACHIEVEMENT
(Also see *Ambition, Finish Line, Motivation, Success*)

OFTEN ONE SEEKS GREENER GRASS on the other side, only to find when he gets there it's not edible. Sometimes, however, it is. "If the grass is greener on the other side, you can bet their water bill is higher."

If you have accomplished all you planned for yourself, you've probably not planned enough.

—*Meggido Message,* quoted in Lloyd Cory, *Quote Unquote*

HAS THE ENEMY COME and swept away the trophies of remembrance of God's good hand on you? Focus on what has been achieved, not on what has not.

ARNOLD PALMER SAID, "The most rewarding things you do in life are often the ones that look like they cannot be done."

—Arnold Palmer, quoted in Lloyd Cory, *Quote Unquote*

THE GREAT COMPOSER doesn't set to work because he is inspired, he becomes inspired because he's working. Beethoven, Bach, and Mozart wrote with regularity that an accountant uses with figures. They didn't waste time waiting for inspiration.

—Ernest Newman, quoted in Lloyd Cory, *Quote Unquote*

THE SECRET OF ACHIEVEMENT is not to let what you're doing get to you before you get to it.

—Lloyd Cory, Quote Unquote

SIZE AIN'T GOT NOTHING TO do with it. If it did, a cow could outrun a rabbit.

—Junior Samples, TV program Hee Haw

BOY AT THE CHALKBOARD to his teacher: "I'm not an underachiever; you're an overexpecter."

THERE IS A DIFFERENCE between achieving something and inheriting something. For example, having a net worth of two million dollars that you've worked a lifetime for is achievement earned. If a young man simply inherits the fortune, there is more of a careless attitude toward money which he did nothing to earn.

PICTURE THE SCENARIO of two friends graduating. One goes to India as a missionary, the other becomes a successful businessman. Both get the announcement of a class reunion and while there compare lives. It would be easy for the missionary to think himself a failure. We need to clear the hurdle of comparison. True achievement for each one of us is listening to and obeying the voice that says, "Follow Me."

TEDDY ROOSEVELT BELIEVED, "Far better it is to dare mighty things, to win glorious triumphs, even though checkered by failure, than to take rank with those poor spirits who neither enjoy much nor suffer much because they live in the gray twilight that knows neither victory nor defeat."

—Charles R. Swindoll, Starting Over

TO KEEP WHAT HAS BEEN GAINED is not a smaller virtue than to make new acquisitions.

—John Calvin

AN ARTICLE in Newsweek titled "Advice to a (Bored) Young Man" sheds light on the life of one individual whose life was one of exploration and discovery.

Many people reading this page are doing so with the aid of bifocals. Inventor? Benjamin Franklin, age 79.

The presses that printed this page were powered by electricity. One of the first harnessers? B. Franklin, age 40.

Some are reading this on the campus of one of the Ivy League universities. Founder? B. Franklin, age 45.

Others, in a library. Who founded the first library in America? B. Franklin, age 25.

Who started the first fire department? B. Franklin, age 31.

Who invented the lightning rod? B. Franklin, age 43.

Who designed a heating stove still in use today? B. Franklin, age 36.

Wit. Conversationalist. Economist. Philosopher. Diplomat. Printer. Publisher. Linguist (he spoke and wrote five languages). Advocate of paratroopers (from balloons) a century before the airplane was invented. All this until age 84.

And he had exactly two years of formal schooling. It's a good bet that you already have more sheer knowledge than Franklin ever had when he was your age.

Perhaps you think there's no use trying to think of anything new, that everything's been done. Wrong. . . . Go do something about it.

—Ted Engstrom, *Motivation to Last a Lifetime*

FOR NINE LONG YEARS the record of the mile hovered just above four minutes. As early as 1945, Gunder Haegg had approached the barrier with a time of 4:01.4. But many people said the limits of physical capacity had been reached; it was impossible to break the four-minute barrier. But in 1954 Roger Bannister broke the tape at 3:59.4. And what was the result? Well, as soon as the myth of the "impossible barrier" was dispelled, the four-minute mile was attacked and pierced by many with apparent ease. In almost no time the four-minute achievement was bettered sixty-six times by twenty-six different runners! If one dismisses this as merely the power of competition, the point is missed. There was just as much competition before the four-minute mile was broken. What the succeeding runners discovered from Bannister was it can be done.

—Alan Loy McGinnis, *Bringing Out the Best in People*

CRIPPLE HIM, and you have Sir Walter Scott.

Lock him in a prison cell, and you have a John Bunyan.

Bury him in the snows of Valley Forge, and you have a George Washington.

Raise him in abject poverty, and you have an Abraham Lincoln.

Subject him to bitter religious prejudice, and you have a Disraeli.

Strike him down with infantile paralysis, and he becomes a Franklin D. Roosevelt.

Burn him so severely in a schoolhouse fire that the doctors say he will never walk again, and you have a Glenn Cunningham, who set the world's record in 1934 for running a mile in four minutes and 6.7 seconds.

Deafen a genius composer, and you have a Ludwig van Beethoven.

Have him or her born black in a society filled with racial discrimination, and you have a Booker T. Washington, a George Washington Carver, or a Martin Luther King, Jr.

Make him the first child to survive in a poor Italian family of eighteen children, and you have an Enrico Caruso.

Have him born of parents who survived a Nazi concentration camp, paralyze him from the waist down when he is four, and you have incomparable concert violinist, Itzhak Perlman.

Call him a slow learner, "retarded," and write him off as uneducable, and you have an Albert Einstein.

—Ted Engstrom, *The Pursuit of Excellence*

CBS CORRESPONDENT CHARLES KURALT uncovered an unforgettable story. He happened upon the Chandlers, a large black family in Prairie, Mississippi.

A long road took nine children out of the cotton fields, out of poverty, out of Mississippi. But roads go both ways, and this Thanksgiving weekend, they all returned. This is about Thanksgiving, and coming home.

One after another, and from every corner of America, the cars turned into the yard. With much cheering and much hugging, the nine children of Alex and Mary Chandler were coming home for their parents' fiftieth wedding anniversary.

Gloria Chandler: There's my daddy. (Gloria rushes to hug him.)

Gloria Chandler Coleman, master of arts, University of Missouri, a teacher in Kansas City, was home.

All nine children had memories of a sharecropper's cabin and nothing to wear and nothing to eat. All nine are college graduates.

Cooking the meal in the kitchen of the new house the children built for their parents four years ago is Bessie Chandler Beasley, B.A. Tuskegee, M.A. Central Michigan, dietitian at a veteran's hospital, married to a

Ph.D. And helping out, Princess Chandler Norman, M.A., Indiana University, a schoolteacher in Gary, Indiana. You'll meet them all.

But first, I thought you ought to meet their parents. Alex Chandler remembers the time when he had a horse and a cow and tried to buy a mule and couldn't make the payments and lost the mule, the horse, and the cow. And about that time, Cleveland, the first son, decided he wanted to go to college.

Alex Chandler: We didn't have any money. And we went to town; he wanted to catch the bus to go on up there. And so we went to town and borrowed two dollars and a half from her niece, and bought him a bus ticket. And when he got there, that's all he had.

From that beginning, he became Dr. Cleveland Chandler. He is chairman of the economics department at Howard University. How did they do it, starting on one of the poorest farms in the poorest part of the poorest state in America?

Princess Chandler Norman: We worked.

Kuralt: You picked cotton?

Norman: Yes, picked cotton, and pulled corn, stripped millet, dug potatoes.

They all left. Luther left for the University of Omaha and went on to become the Public Service Employment Manager for Kansas City. He helped his younger brother, James, come to Omaha University, too, and go on to graduate work at Yale. And in his turn, James helped Herman, who graduated from Morgan State and is a technical manager in Dallas. And they helped themselves. Fortson, a Baptist minister in Pueblo, Colorado, wanted to go to Morehouse College.

Fortson Chandler: I chose Morehouse and it was difficult. I had to pick cotton all summer long to get the first month's rent and tuition.

So, helping themselves and helping one another, they all went away. And now, fifty years after life began for the Chandler family in a one-room shack in a cotton field, now, just as they were sitting down in the new house to the ham and turkey and sweet potatoes and cornbread and collard greens and two kinds of pie and three kinds of cake, now Donald arrived—the youngest—who had driven with his family all the way down from Minneapolis. And now the Chandlers were all together again.

Alex Chandler (saying grace): Our Father in heaven, we come at this moment, giving thee thanks for thou hast been so good and so kind. We want to thank you, O God, for this, for your love, and for your Son. Thank you that you have provided for all of us through all these years. (Mr. Chandler begins weeping.)

Remembering all those years of sharecropping and going hungry and working for a white man for fifty cents a day and worrying about his children's future, remembering all that, Alex Chandler almost didn't get through his blessing.

Alex (continuing grace): In Jesus' name, Amen.

And neither did the others. (Family members wiping tears away.)

The Chandler family started with as near nothing as any family in America ever did. And so their Thanksgiving weekend might have been more thankful than most. (Chandler family singing "I'll Fly Away.")

"I'll Fly Away" is the name of an old hymn. It is Mr. Chandler's favorite. His nine children flew away, and made places for themselves in this country; and this weekend, came home again. There probably are no lessons in any of this, but I know that in the future, whenever I hear that the family is a dying institution, I'll think of them. Whenever I hear anything in America is impossible, I'll think of them.

—Charles Kuralt, *On the Road with Charles Kuralt*

IF I COULD WRAP all my father's counsel into one sentence, it would be "Get with it, son."

—Lorne Sanny of the Navigators

ADULTERY

(Also see *Immorality, Sin*)

DR. DONALD BARNHOUSE shares this story about a man falling into the temptation of lust with his secretary.

One day I was visited by a young man in his thirties, who had a personal problem. He told his story something like this: "I work for such-and-such a company, and I have a private office. Several months ago my secretary was absent and I had to use another girl. One day she brought papers for my perusal; she got too close, and when she leaned over my desk, she let her hair trail across my face. I fought it down, but after all, I am a man, and toward the end of the day I put my hand on her and she came right back to be kissed. Even while kissing her, I was visualizing my two children running to meet me and my wife standing in the door. I hated what I was doing, but I kept on. I had the greatest desire to push her from me, but I kept pulling her to me; my body was doing one thing and my mind was doing another.

"When I went home that night, I hugged my children so hard that one of them cried, and when we got him to laughing, I told them that it was because I loved them so much. I had tears in my eyes and my wife's eyes were shining. We all clung together in one of those moments that are indescribable. My wife was extremely happy, because I walked around the house that evening, touching familiar things that we had scrimped to buy, expressing my love for the home and for her, and before God I was never more true. Next day, the office intrigue began all over again. I was never more miserable in my life.

"Before a month had gone by I realized that my lust and my love were in a terrible battle. When I came home, there was everything I wanted in life. When I went to the office, the machine of my body seemed geared to something terrible that was purely mechanical, and which I wanted to get out of more than any fly ever wanted to get off flypaper. I heard my wife tell someone that I was becoming more and more of a homebody, and that all I wanted to do was stay at home. And it is true. I follow her around the house, talk with her in the kitchen where she is working, and watch her as she puts the children to bed.

"This morning, when I left the house, she told me that she thought she was the happiest woman in the world, because I showed so much that I loved her alone. I could hardly talk. In fact tears came to my eyes, and when I lifted a lock of her hair to dry them, I said to her, 'I love you more than life itself.' She cried and I crushed her to me until she screamed and smiled at the same time. Then I ran off to my train. But now what shall I do?"

With the husband's consent, I called the wife to my office and told her the story. Fear leaped to her eyes, but I reassured her. We took a taxi and went to his office. He was expecting us, and I stood by as they embraced and she said, "I know, I know, I understand, it's all right." Then I called the other girl into the office. The scene that followed typified the mortal struggle between the flesh and the spirit, both striving for the mastery of the body. But the wife was not striving; she knew that the mind, soul, and heart of her husband had never been away from her. She understood the glandular warfare of his body, and that his lust had sprung to life in response to the lure of strange flesh. She looked at him with complete understanding and love.

The secretary stood there speechless. I said to her, "She knows all about it. She loves him and he loves her completely; he has never had any thought toward you except one of animal lust. You were never wanted except physically, and you are not wanted at all from now on. Do you understand?" I asked her to wait in the hall while I prayed with the couple.

As I left, I saw the secretary dabbing at her eyes; I stopped and talked to her about her need of Jesus Christ.

—Donald Barnhouse, *Let Me Illustrate*

Sweet Peril

Alas, how easily things go wrong!
A sigh too much, or a kiss too long,
And there follows a mist and a weeping rain,
And life is never the same again.

—George MacDonald, *Best Loved Poems of the American People*

DURING THE RECENT SEX SCANDALS that rocked Capitol Hill, Dr. Sam Janus, professor at New York Medical College, said, "A safe bet would be that nearly half of the members of Congress were involved in affairs outside of marriage."

—J. Allan Petersen, *The Myth of Greener Grass*

I HAD AN INTERESTING EXPERIENCE in January 1990. I had been invited to speak in New Orleans at the Super Bowl breakfast sponsored by Athletes in Action. En route from Los Angeles to New Orleans, I had to change planes in another city. The connecting flight was packed, naturally, and there was a festive spirit on board since everyone was headed for Super Bowl XXIV. I noticed an empty seat behind mine . . . the only empty seat on the plane. Only minutes before we backed away from the terminal, one final passenger hurried on board. Her plane had been late in arriving, making it questionable if she could make her New Orleans connection. She did. As she hurried on, a bit harried, she immediately broke into a broad smile as her eyes met those of the man sitting next to the seat she would occupy. She didn't simply sit down— she fell into his arms as they kissed, giggled, and embraced for the next ten minutes.

My immediate thought was, Now there's a happily married couple! How wrong I was. They were both married . . . but not to each other. Because they sat right behind me, I got the full scoop. I must confess to some eavesdropping. Their carefully arranged plan was to rendezvous on the plane, then spend the weekend together in New Orleans. Their conversation, mixed with frequent kisses, included all kinds of comments about the fun they had in front of them, the intimate ecstasy of being together for a couple of nights, along with attending the Super Bowl. Both laughed and joked as they talked about how each other's mate knew nothing of it. I might add here that neither made any mention of the possible consequences—the loss of reputation, of the depression that was sure to follow, the possibility of unexpected pregnancy, the embarrassing humiliation when their mates (not if, but when) would find out. Why, of course not! This couple was on fire. Their full focus turned to the delightful time they would have together. They just couldn't talk about anything else.

All the while I'm sitting there in front of them, working on a chapter on sexual temptation, thirty-six inches behind me is a living illustration of lust in action. There flashed through my mind these words Solomon once wrote: "Stolen waters are sweet." No doubt about it. Unbridled, blinding lust is running over with the sweet ecstasy of sensual pleasure—at least for a weekend. Laughter, creativity, and excitement abound in such sexual escapades. It is not until later that the fog lifts and reality returns with its Monday-morning depression.

—Charles Swindoll, *Sanctity of Life*

A CALL FOR FIDELITY . . . is like a solitary voice crying in today's sexual wilderness. What was once labeled adultery and carried a stigma of guilt and embarrassment now is an affair—a nice-sounding, almost inviting word wrapped in mystery, fascination, and excitement. A relationship, not sin. . . . Sexual promiscuity has never been the established custom of any human society. . . . Sex, sex, sex. Our culture is near the point of total saturation. The cesspool is running over.

—J. Allan Petersen, *The Myth of Greener Grass*

AND IN CASE YOU NEED A REMINDER that God is serious about fidelity, I ask you to consider this true story. It could save you from some tragedy that could be just around the corner. The names are fictitious, but the story is true.

Clara and Chester's twenty-eight-year-old marriage was a good one. Not the most idyllic, but good. By now they had three grown children who loved them dearly. They were also blessed with sufficient financial security to allow them room to dream about a retirement home, so they began looking for one. A widower we'll call Sam was selling his place. They liked it a lot and they returned home to talk and to make their plans. Months passed.

Last fall Clara told Chester she wanted a divorce. He went numb. After all these years, why? How could she deceive him? How could she have been nursing such a scheme while they were looking at a retirement home? She said she hadn't been . . . not for that long. Actually, this was a recent decision now that she had found another man. Who? Clara admitted it was Sam, the owner of the house they were considering. She had inadvertently run into him several weeks after they had discussed the sale. They had a cup of coffee together; later the next week they went out to dinner. For several weeks they had been seeing each other privately and were now sexually involved. Since they were now "in love," there was no turning back. Not even the kids, who hated the idea, could dissuade their mother.

On the day Clara was to leave, Chester walked through the kitchen toward the garage. Realizing Clara would be gone when he returned, he hesitated, "Well, hon, I guess this is the last time . . ." and his voice dissolved as he broke into sobs. She felt awkward, so she hurriedly got her things together, backed out of the driveway, and never looked back. She drove north to meet Sam. Less than two weeks after she moved in with her new lover, Sam was seized with a heart attack and lingered a few hours. The following morning Sam died.

When it comes to morality, God is serious . . . as serious as a heart attack.

I have said for years that if God moved that swiftly in every case, most folks I know would think again before they started an affair. If God moved now like He did in the days of Ananias and Sapphira, I wonder if you'd have to build a morgue in the basement of every church.

—Charles R. Swindoll, *Sanctity of Life*

_____

THE FOLLOWING IS AN INCOMPLETE LIST of what you have in store after your immorality is found out.

- Your mate will experience the anguish of betrayal, shame, rejection, heartache, and loneliness. No amount of repentance will soften those blows.
- Your mate can never again say that you are a model of fidelity. Suspicion will rob her or him of trust.
- Your escapade(s) will introduce to your life and your mate's life the very real probability of a sexually transmitted disease.
- The total devastation your sinful actions will bring to your children is immeasurable. Their growth, innocence, trust, and healthy outlook on life will be severely and permanently damaged.
- The heartache you will cause your parents, your family, and your peers is indescribable.
- The embarrassment of facing other Christians, who once appreciated you, respected you, and trusted you, will be overwhelming.
- If you are engaged in the Lord's work, you will suffer immediate loss of

your job and the support of those with whom you worked. The dark shadow will accompany you everywhere . . . and forever. Forgiveness won't erase it.

- Your fall will give others license to do the same.
- The inner peace you enjoyed will be gone.
- You will never be able to erase the fall from your (or others') mind. This will remain indelibly etched on your life's record, regardless of your later return to your senses.
- The name of Jesus Christ, whom you once honored, will be tarnished, giving the enemies of the faith further reason to sneer and jeer.

—Charles R. Swindoll, *The Finishing Touch*

THE MONSTROSITY OF SEXUAL INTERCOURSE outside marriage is that those who indulge in it are trying to isolate one kind of union (the sexual) from all the other kinds of union which were intended to go along with it and make up the total union. The Christian attitude does not mean there is anything wrong about sexual pleasure, any more than about the pleasure of eating. It means that you must not isolate that pleasure and try to get it by itself, any more than you ought to get the pleasures of taste without swallowing and digesting, by chewing things and spitting them out again.

—C. S. Lewis, *Mere Christianity*

ADVENTURE
(Also see *Travel*)

IT HAD BEEN TOO LONG since Horace Walpole smiled. Too long. Life for him had become as drab as the weather in dreary old England. Then, on a grim winter day in 1754, while reading a Persian fairy tale, his smile returned. He wrote his longtime friend, Horace Mann, telling him of the "thrilling approach to life" he had discovered from the folk tale . . . how it had freed him from his dark prison of gloom.

The ancient tale told of three princes from the island of Ceylon who set out on a pursuit of great treasures. They never found that for which they searched, but en route they were continually surprised by delights they had never anticipated. While looking for one thing, they found another.

The original name of Ceylon was Serendip, which explains the title of this story—"The Three Princes of Serendip." From that, Walpole coined the wonderful word serendipity. And from then on, his most significant and valued experiences were those that happened to him while he was least expecting them.

—Charles R. Swindoll, *The Finishing Touch*

MAYBE IT'S TIME to make some new discoveries. Larry Walters did. The thirty-three-year-old truck driver had been sitting around doing zilch week in, week out, until boredom got the best of him. That was back in the summer of '82. He decided enough was enough; what he needed was an adventure. So, on July 2 of that year he rigged forty-two helium-filled weather balloons to a Sears lawn chair in San Pedro and lifted off. Armed with a pellet gun to shoot out a few balloons should he fly too high, Walters was shocked to reach 16,000 feet rather rapidly. He wasn't the only one. Surprised pilots reported seeing "some guy in a lawn chair floating in the sky" to perplexed air-traffic controllers.

Finally, Walters had enough sense to start shooting a few balloons, which allowed him to land safely in Long Beach some forty-five minutes later. The bizarre stunt got him a Timex ad as well as a guest spot on *The Tonight Show*. Ultimately, he quit his job to deliver motivational speeches. When asked why he did such a weird thing, Walters usually gave them the same answer: "People ask me if I had a death wish. I tell them no, it was something I had to do . . . I couldn't just sit there."

—Charles R. Swindoll, *The Finishing Touch*

ROBERT PERSIG, insightful author of *Zen and the Art of Motorcycle Maintenance* (don't let the title fool you), is a real believer in traveling free and relaxed—rather than cooped up in the "compartment" of a car. He talks a lot about the thrill of taking it all in while zipping along five inches above the asphalt blur beneath his feet. The man builds a real case for tasting and feeling and fully digesting a trip across the country, not just enduring monotonous miles, squinting through a Chevy windshield. He touches the "hot button" inside this Harley-ridin' sermonator! Isn't it about time you made plans to add some variety to your life?

—Charles R. Swindoll, *The Finishing Touch*

ADVERSITY

(Also see *Pain, Suffering, Trials*)

TOUGH DAYS. We all have them. Some are worse than others. Like the one the hard-hat employee reported on his accident form when he tried to be helpful:

When I got to the building I found that the hurricane had knocked off some bricks around the top. So I rigged up a beam with a pulley at the top of the building and hoisted up a couple barrels full of bricks. When I had fixed the damaged area, there were a lot of bricks left over. Then I went to the bottom and began releasing the line. Unfortunately, the barrel of bricks was much heavier than I was—and before I knew what was happening the barrel started coming down, jerking me up.

I decided to hang on since I was too far off the ground by then to jump, and halfway up I met the barrel of bricks coming down fast. I received a hard blow on my shoulder. I then continued to the top, banging my head against the beam and getting my fingers pinched and jammed in the pulley. When the barrel hit the ground hard, it burst its bottom, allowing the bricks to spill out.

I was now heavier than the barrel. So I started down again at high speed. Halfway down I met the barrel coming up fast and received severe injuries to my shins. When I hit the ground, I landed on the pile of spilled bricks, getting several painful cuts and deep bruises. At this point I must have lost my presence of mind, because I let go of my grip on the line. The barrel came down fast—giving me another blow on my head and putting me in the hospital.

I respectfully request sick leave.

—Michael Green, *Illustrations for Biblical Preaching*

ADVERSITY IS HARD on a man. But for everyone who can handle prosperity there are a hundred who can handle adversity.

—Thomas Carlyle

AN UNUSUAL EVERGREEN is the lodgepole pine that is seen in great numbers in Yellowstone Park. The cones of this pine may hang on the tree for years and years, and even when they fall they do not open. These cones can only be opened when they come in contact with intense heat. But God has a reason for planning them this way. When a forest fire rages throughout parks and forests all the trees are destroyed. At the same time, however, the heat of the fire opens the cones of the lodgepole pine; and these pines are often the first tree to grow in an area that has been burned by fire.

—Benjamin Browne, *Illustrations for Preaching*

UNCLE TOM had been wrenched from his old Kentucky home and put on a steamship headed for an unknown place. It was a terrible moment of crisis for Uncle Tom. Borham observes,

> Uncle Tom's faith was staggered. It really seemed to him that in leaving Aunt Chloe and the children and his old companions he was leaving God. Falling asleep, the slave had a dream. He dreamed that he was back again and that little Eva was reading to him from the Bible. He could hear her voice, "When thou passeth through the waters, I will be with thee, for I, the Lord thy God, the Holy One of Israel, I am thy Savior."
>
> A little later poor Tom was writhing under the cruel lash of his new owner. But the blows fell only on the outer man and not, as before, on the heart. Tom stood submissive, and yet the master named Legree could not hide from himself the fact that his power over his victim had gone. As Tom disappeared in his cabin and Legree wheeled his horse suddenly around, there passed through the tyrant's mind those vivid flashes that often send the lightning of conscience across the dark and wicked soul. He understood full well that it was God who was standing between him and Tom.

—F.W. Borham, *A Casket of Cameos*

A SHIPWRECKED MAN managed to reach an uninhabited island. There, to protect himself against the elements and to safeguard the few possessions he had salvaged, he painstakingly built a little hut from which he constantly and prayerfully scanned the horizon for the approach of a ship. Returning one evening after a search for food, he was terrified to find the hut completely enveloped in flames. Yet by divine mercy this hard affliction was changed into a mighty advantage. Early the following morning he awoke to find a ship anchored off the island. When the captain stepped ashore, he explained, "We saw your smoke signal and came." Everything the marooned man owned had to be destroyed before he could be rescued.

—Walter A. Maier, *Decision* magazine

A MOVIE WAS MADE about Jill Kinmont's 1955 experience titled *The Other Side of the Mountain.* She was a wonderful athlete destined for the Olympics but a skiing accident left her paralyzed. Unable to cope with this tragedy, her financé wouldn't marry her. Then a new love came into Jill's life, but he was killed in a plane crash. The story does not have a happy ending. Many things in life do not.

SOME DAYS when life is especially tough, think about these words:

The Valley of Vision

Lord, high and holy, meek and lowly,
Thou hast brought me to the valley of vision,
    where I live in the depths but see thee in the heights;
    hemmed in by mountains of sin I behold thy glory.

Let me learn by paradox
    that the way down is the way up,
    that to be low is to be high,
    that the broken heart is the healed heart,
    that the contrite spirit is the rejoicing spirit,
    that the repenting soul is the victorious soul,
    that to have nothing is to possess all,
    that to bear the cross is to wear the crown,
    that to give is to receive,
    that the valley is the place of vision.
Lord, in the daytime stars can be seen from the deepest wells,
    and the deeper the wells the brighter thy stars shine;
Let me find thy light in my darkness,
    thy life in my death,
    thy joy in my sorrow,
    thy grace in my sin,
    thy riches in my poverty,
    thy glory in my valley.

—Arthur Bennett, *Valley of Vision*

IF GOD PROMISED His servants an unbroken run of prosperity, there would be many counterfeit Christians. Don't be surprised at famine . . . it is permitted to root you deeper just as a whirlwind makes the tree grapple deeper roots into soil.

—F. B. Meyer, *Abraham*

WHEN THE HIGH SEAS are raging, it's no time to change ships.

—Leon Morris, *First Corinthians*

ADVICE

(Also see *Communication, Speech, Tongue*)

A PHYSICIAN FRIEND OF MINE in Fullerton was treating a woman in her mid-eighties who was in fairly good condition. She either walked very fast or jogged every day. He became quite concerned about her, even though her health was good, and he warned her about exerting herself. She heeded his advice and ceased most of her activity. Several months later he sat in the funeral parlor, attending her memorial service. Later he said to me, "You know, Chuck, I could cut my tongue out for ever having told her to be careful, to stop exerting herself. I doubt that I will ever give that advice again . . . especially to older people who are enjoying life as much as she was."

—Charles R. Swindoll, *Living on the Ragged Edge*

HENRI NOUWEN said he visited Mother Theresa of Calcutta a few years ago and asked her advice on how to live out his vocation as a priest. She simply said, "Spend one hour a day in adoration of your Lord and never do anything you know is wrong, and you'll be all right."

—*The Way of the Heart*

AGE

WHEN YOU GET TOO OLD for pimples, you go right into wrinkles.

—Lloyd Cory, *Quote Unquote*

YOU KNOW you're getting older when . . .

> your dreams are reruns;
> the stewardess offers coffee, tea, or Milk of Magnesia;
> you sit in a rocking chair and can't get it started;
> everything hurts, and what doesn't hurt doesn't work;
> a pretty girl prompts your pacemaker to lift the garage door;
> you sink your teeth into a juicy steak, and they stay there.

The Golden Age

I get up each morning, dust off my wits;
Pick up the paper and read the obits.

If my name is missing, I know I'm not dead;
So I eat a good breakfast, and go back to bed.

—Christine Taylor, quoted in J. Allan Petersen, The Marriage Affair

LORD, THOU KNOWEST BETTER than I know myself, that I am growing older, and
    will someday be old.
Keep me from getting talkative, and particularly from the fatal habit of
    thinking I must say something on every subject and on every occasion.
Release me from the craving to try and straighten out everybody's affairs.
Keep my mind free from the recital of endless details—give me
    wings to get to the point.
I ask for grace enough to listen to the tales of others' pains. Help me endure
    them with patience.
But seal my lips on my own aches and pains. They are increasing, and my
    love of rehearsing them is becoming sweeter as the years go by.
I dare not ask for improved memory, but for a growing humility and a
    lessening cocksureness when my memory seems to clash with the
    memories of others.
Teach me the glorious lesson that occasionally I may be mistaken.
Keep me reasonably sweet. I do not want to be a saint—some of them are
    so hard to live with—but a sour old woman (or man) is one of the
    crowning works of the devil.
Make me thoughtful, but not moody; helpful, but not bossy.
With my vast store of wisdom, it seems a pity not to use it;
    but Thou knowest, Lord, I want a few friends at the end.
Give me the ability to see good things in unexpected places, and talents in
    unexpected people. And give me, Lord, the grace to tell them so.

—Dale Evans Rogers, Time Out, Ladies

ZACHARIAS FELT LIMITED by the age issue when the angel announced that
he and Elizabeth would have a son to be named John. "How can I be certain of
this? I am an old man and my wife is well along in years." Now here is a man
well trained. He says, "I am an old man," but this seasoned, tactful husband
doesn't say, "She's an old lady."

A PRECOCIOUS little ten-year-old asked her grandmother, "Grandma, how old
are you?" "Well, honey, when you're my age, you don't share your age with just

anybody." "Please, I won't tell." "No, it's my secret." About twenty minutes passed and the little girl bounced in and said, "You're sixty-two and you weigh one-hundred forty pounds." The astonished grandmother said, "How in the world do you know that?" "Easy," she replied, "I looked at your driver's license on the table and did the math. I also saw you got an 'F' in sex."

—James Hewett, *Illustrations Unlimited*

MY WIFE, Cynthia, got a birthday card that said, "They don't make them any better than us . . . Younger yes, better no."

I LIKE THE QUESTION once asked by Satchel Paige, that venerable alumnus of baseball: "How old would you be if you didn't know how old you were?" An honest answer to that question depends on an honest admission of one's attitude. It has nothing to do with one's age. As someone young at heart has written:

I have become a little older since I saw you last, and a few changes have come into my life since then. Frankly, I have become quite a frivolous old gal. I am seeing five gentlemen every day.

As soon as I wake up, Will Power helps me get out of bed. Then I go to see John. Then Charlie Horse comes along, and when he is here he takes a lot of my time and attention. When he leaves Arthur Ritis shows up and stays the rest of the day. He doesn't like to stay in one place very long, so he takes me from joint to joint. After such a busy day I'm really tired and glad to go to bed with Ben Gay. What a life!

P.S. The preacher came to call the other day. He said at my age I should be thinking about the hereafter. I told him, "Oh, I do all the time. No matter where I am—in the parlor, upstairs, in the kitchen, or down in the basement—I ask myself what am I here after?"

—Charles R. Swindoll, *Laugh Again*

FIVE TIPS for staying young:
1. Your mind is not old, keep developing it.
2. Your humor is not over, keep enjoying it.
3. Your strength is not gone, keep using it.
4. Your opportunities have not vanished, keep pursuing them.
5. God is not dead, keep seeking Him.

REMEMBER, OLD FOLKS are worth a fortune—they have silver in their hair, gold in their teeth, stones in their kidneys, lead in their feet, and gas in their stomachs.

HAVE YOU SEEN THE POSTER "You're Over the Hill When . . ."

> Your friends wear black to your birthday party;
> You abandon stylish shoes for something comfortable;
> There's more hair stuck in the drain than on your head;
> You have too much skin for your face;
> The law of gravity takes on new meaning.

ERMA BOMBECK says, "I've got everything I had twenty-five years ago, but now it's all four inches lower."

—Charles R. Swindoll, *Strike the Original Match*

CANON C. H. NASH founded Melbourne Bible Institute and retired at age seventy. At eighty he began the most fruitful decade of his life. Nearing ninety he was reading Toynbee's six volumes of *Monumental History* as a mental exercise.

—J. Oswald Sanders, *Spiritual Manpower*

A WOMAN WAS FILLING OUT A JOB APPLICATION and came to the space asking the age of the applicant. She wrote "Nuclear."

—Bennett Cerf, quoted in Lloyd Cory, *Quote Unquote*

TED WILLIAMS, at age 42 slammed a home run in his last official time at bat.

Mickey Mantle, age 20, hit twenty-three home runs his first full year in the major leagues.

Golda Meir was 71 when she became prime minister of Israel.

William Pitt II was 24 when he became prime minister of Great Britain.

George Bernard Shaw was 94 when one of his plays was first produced.

Mozart was just 7 when his first composition was published.

Now, how about this? Benjamin Franklin was a newspaper columnist at 16, and a framer of the United States Constitution when he was 81. You're never too young or too old if you've got talent.

Let's recognize that age has little to do with ability.

—Charles R. Swindoll, *Living Above the Level of Mediocrity*

"It is too late!" Ah, nothing is too late—
Cato learned Greek at eighty; Sophocles
Wrote his grand "Oedipus," and Simonides
Bore off the prize of verse from his compeers
When each had numbered more than fourscore years;
And Theophrastus, at fourscore and ten,
Had begun his "Characters of Men."
Chaucer, at Woodstock, with his nightingales,
At sixty wrote the "Canterbury Tales."
Goethe, at Weimar, toiling to the last,
Completed "Faust" when eighty years were past.
What then? Shall we sit idly down and say,
"The night has come; it is no longer day?"
For age is opportunity no less
Than youth itself, though in another dress.
And as the evening twilight fades away,
The sky is filled with stars, invisible by day.

—Henry Wadsworth Longfellow

BY THE TIME OUR face clears up, our mind gets fuzzy.

—James Dobson

YOUTH IS A WONDERFUL THING. It's a shame to waste it on young people.

—George Bernard Shaw, quoted in Ray Stedman, *Solomon's Secret*

No matter how small a prune may be,
    he's always full of wrinkles.
A little prune is like his dad,
    but he ain't wrinkled half as bad.

—Charles R. Swindoll, *Strike the Original Match*

THE MONOTONOUS YEARS of middle-aged prosperity are excellent campaigning weather for the devil.

—C.S. Lewis, *Screwtape Letters*

CHARLES SCHULZ'S "Peanuts" cartoon has Lucy and Schroeder talking:

"Will you love me when I'm old and crabby?" asks Lucy.
Schroeder says, "You don't have to be crabby."
"I know but it's hard to change."
"Maybe you can be nice in the morning and crabby in the afternoon."
"Yes, but I'd still be old all day."

—Jeanne Hendricks, *Afternoon*

Middle-agers Are Beautiful

Middle-agers are beautiful!
Aren't we, Lord?
I feel for us
Too radical for our parents
Too reactionary for our kids
Supposedly in the prime of life
Like prime rib
Everyone eating off me
Devouring me
Nobody thanking me
Appreciating me
But still hanging in there
Communicating with my parents
In touch with my kids
And getting more in touch with myself
And that's all good
Thanks for making it good, Lord,
And could You make it a little better?

—Robert Raines, *Lord, Could You Make It Better?*

ON HIS SEVENTY-FIFTH BIRTHDAY Douglas MacArthur wrote, "In the heart is a recording chamber receiving messages of hope that keep you young; get pessimistic and you grow old."

—Adapted from Lloyd Cory, *Quote Unquote*

EVERYTHING IS FARTHER than it used to be. It's twice as far from my house to the station now, and they've added a hill which I've just noticed. The trains leave sooner, too, but I've given up running for them because they go faster than they used to. Seems to me they're making staircases steeper than in the old days. And have you noticed the small print they're using lately? Newspapers are getting farther and farther away when I hold them. I have to squint to make out the news. Now it's ridiculous to suggest that a person my age needs glasses, but it's the only way I can find out what's going on without someone reading aloud to me and that isn't much help because everybody seems to speak in such a low voice I can scarcely hear them.

Times are changing. The material in my clothes, I notice, shrinks in certain places. Shoelaces are so short they're next to impossible to reach. And even the weather's changing. It's getting colder in winter, and the summers are much hotter than they used to be. People are changing too. For one thing, they're younger than they used to be when I was their age. On the other hand, people my own age are so much older than I am.

I ran into my roommate the other night, and he had changed so much he didn't recognize me. "You've put on weight, Bob," I said. "It's this modern food," Bob replied, "it seems to be more fattening." I got to thinking about poor Bob this morning while I was shaving. Stopping for a moment, I looked at my own reflection in the mirror. You know, they don't use the same kind of glass in mirrors anymore.

—Ray Stedman, sermon *"Life Beyond Death,"* December 1, 1968

AMBITION

(Also see *Achievement, Finish Line, Motivation, Success*)

DO YOU EVER THINK about the direction of your life? Sometimes I like to ask students, "Where are you going?" Often the reply is, "Lunch."

A *SPORTS ILLUSTRATED* journalist was interviewing Ken Stabler, the former quarterback for the Oakland Raiders. The writer recited a quote from renowned author, Jack London, that went something like this: "I'd rather be ashes than dust. I'd rather my spark go out in a burning flame than it be stifled with dry rot. I'd rather be a splendid meteor blazing across the sky, every atom in me in magnificent glow, than to be a sleepy and permanent planet. Life is to be lived, not just to exist. I shall not waste my days trying to prolong them; I will use my time!"

The interviewer asked Stabler what that quote meant to him personally. The crusty, maverick veteran of the gridiron, standing with hands in his pockets and his usual slouched posture blinked and then responded with a shrug, "Throw deep?"

I asked of God that He should give success
To the high task I sought for Him to do;
I asked that every hindrance might grow less
And that my hours of weakness might be few;
I asked that far and lofty heights be scaled—
And now I humbly thank Him that I failed.

For with the pain and sorrow came to me
A dower of tenderness in act and thought;
And with the failure came a sympathy,
An insight which success had never brought.
Father, I had been foolish and unblest
If Thou hadst granted me my blind request.

—J. Oswald Sanders, *Robust in Faith*

POWER IS A POISON, well known for thousands of years. If only no one were ever able to acquire material power over others. But to the human being who has faith in some force that holds dominion over all of us and who is therefore conscious of his own limitations, power is not necessarily fatal. . . . But for those, however, who are unaware of any higher, power is a deadly poison. For them there is no antidote.

—Aleksandr Solzhenitsyn, *The Gulag Archipelago*

ANGER

(Also see *Revenge*)

WHEN I HAVE AN ARGUMENT with my wife, she doesn't get hysterical, she gets historical.

PEOPLE TODAY STILL HAVE murder (anger) in their heart. Take for example this classified ad:

Wedding dress for sale, never worn.
Will trade for .38 caliber pistol.

—*Preaching* magazine, March–April 1993

THOMAS JEFFERSON BELIEVED, "When angry count to ten, if very angry count to a hundred." Mark Twain said, "When angry count to four, if very angry swear."

—*Bartlett's Familiar Quotations*

ANGER WON'T FIX ITSELF . . . like a flat tire or a dirty diaper. I remember reading about an eagle that swooped to the ground one day, catching a weasel in its powerful talons. But when it flew away, its wings inexplicably went limp, and it dropped to the ground like a lifeless doll. As it turned out, the weasel had bitten its attacker in midflight, killing the proud eagle as it flew. If we cling to an attitude of anger or jealousy, it will, like the weasel, sink its teeth into us when we least expect it.

THE HEART OF FOOLS is in their mouth; but the mouth of the wise is in their heart. The heart in one's mouth means to speak without thinking as angry people usually do. The mouth in one's heart means to speak carefully. . . . I never work better than when I am inspired of anger; when I am angry, I can write, pray, and preach well, for then my whole temperament is quickened, my understanding sharpened, and my mundane vexations and temptations depart.

—Martin Luther

ANGER IS AN ERRONEOUS ZONE, a kind of psychological influenza that inca-pacitates you just as a physical disease would. . . . Anger is a choice, as well as a habit. It is a learned reaction to frustration, in which you behave in ways that you would rather not. In fact, severe anger is a form of insanity.

—Wayne W. Dyer, *Your Erroneous Zones*

THE MORE HEATED THE DISAGREEMENT, the more our inner steam tank builds to the breaking point; and it is all we can do to keep a level head through the whole explosive episode. This reminds me of the Quaker who owned an ornery cow. Every time he milked her, it was a clash of two wills. This particular morning she was unusually irritable, but he was determined to endure the session without so much as a cross word. As the farmer began to milk her, ol' Bossy stepped on his foot with all her weight. He struggled silently, groaned a little under his breath, pulled his foot free, then sat back down on the stool. She then swished her tail in his face like a long string whip. He merely leaned away so it wouldn't be able to reach him. Next she kicked over the bucket, by then half-full of warm milk. He started over, mumbling a few words to himself; but he never lost his cool. Once finished with the ordeal, he breathed a sign of relief, picked up the bucket and stool, and as he was leaving she hauled off and kicked him against the barn wall twelve to fifteen feet away. That did it. He stood to his feet, marched in front of his cow, stared into those big eyes, and as he shook a long bony finger in her face, he shouted, "Thou dost know that I am a Quaker. Thou dost know also that I cannot strike thee back . . . but I can sell thee to a Presbyterian!"

—Clyde Murdock, *A Treasury of Humor*

ANXIETY

(Also see *Fear, Stress, Worry*)

IN THE NORTHEASTERN United States, codfish are not only delectable, they are a big commercial business. There's a market for eastern cod all over, especially in sections farthest removed from the northeast coastline. But the public demand brought a problem to the shippers. At first they froze the cod, then shipped them elsewhere, but the freeze took away much of the flavor. So they experimented with shipping them alive, in tanks of seawater, but that proved even worse. Not only was it more expensive, but the cod still lost its flavor, and in addition, it became soft and mushy. The texture was seriously affected.

Finally, some creative soul solved the problem in a most innovative manner. The codfish were placed in the tank along with their natural enemy—the catfish. From the time the cod left the East Coast until it arrived in its westernmost destination, those ornery catfish chased the cod all over the tank! And you guessed it, when the cod arrived at the market, they were as fresh as when they were first caught. There was no loss of flavor nor was the texture affected. If anything, it was better than before.

—Charles R. Swindoll, *Come Before Winter*

WORRY AND FEAR are sort of Siamese twins. "Anxiety is a thin stream of fear, trickling through the mind. If encouraged, it cuts a channel into which all other thoughts are drained."

—Arthur Somers Roche, quoted in Bob Philips, *Philips' Book of Great Thoughts and Funny Sayings*

APPREHENSION IS A NOTCH or two above worry, but feels like its twin. It's the feeling you get when your mother-in-law goes over a cliff in your new Mercedes.

—Charles R. Swindoll, *Killing Giants, Pulling Thorns*

THE NATIONAL ANXIETY CENTER of Maplewood, New Jersey, gives a list of the top ten anxieties for the nineties: (1) AIDS, (2) drug abuse, (3) nuclear waste, (4) the ozone layer, (5) famine, (6) homelessness, (7) the deficit, (8) air pollution, (9) water pollution, and (10) garbage.

APATHY

(Also see *Complacency, Indifference*)

HATE IS NOT the opposite of love—apathy is.

—Rollo May

RECENTLY SOMEONE PAINTED this telling graffiti in bold, black letters on the wall of a university library: APATHY RULES.

—William MacDonald, *Chasing the Wind*

EVERY TIME I hear the word *apathy*, I remember the words of a friend of mine who taught high school just long enough to realize he shouldn't have been teaching high school. He was assigned to teach a course filled to the brim with students who did not want to learn. In fact, it was one of those classes where you had to arrive very early to get a back seat. A couple of the fellas got there so late, they were stuck on the front row. They couldn't care less what the subject was.

The teacher finally got fed up with their apathy. He grabbed a piece of chalk, whirled around to the chalkboard and began to slash away in big, foot-high letters, "A-P-A-T-H-Y!" He underlined it twice, then slammed an exclamation point on it that broke the chalk as he hammered it against the board.

One of the dull students up front frowned as he struggled to read the word. Unable to pronounce it, he tilted his head to one side as he started spelling it aloud then mispronounced it. Then he leaned over and muttered to his buddy, "What in the world is 'a-paythee'?" His friend yawned back with a sigh, "Who cares?"

—Charles R. Swindoll, *Living on the Ragged Edge*

APPEARANCE
(Also see *Health*)

HOWARD G. HENDRICKS stood up at a men's meeting at Forest Home, California, and said, "I feel very much at home with all of you who are here. I've never seen so many bald heads in my life." He is fast becoming bald. And he said, "I've learned that those who are bald in front are bald because they're thinkers." And all the guys bald on the front go, "Ah, that's right." And he said, "All of you who are bald on the back are bald there because you are lovers. Those of us who are bald all over think we are lovers."

—Robert Savage, *Pocket Smiles*

SOME CHRISTIANS are so long-faced they can eat corn out of a Coke bottle. Even if it isn't raining, they just spread gloom.

ATTITUDE
(Also see *Discouragement*)

IT'S BEEN SAID, "Cheer up, things could be worse." I cheered up and things got worse.

—David Roper, *The Law That Sets You Free*

A FEW YEARS AGO Lewis Timberlake was driving through North Carolina countryside on his way to a speaking engagement. As he neared the town where he was scheduled to speak there was a sign posted at the city limits which read, "We hear there's a recession coming and we've decided not to participate!" I like that positive attitude in a negative society.

—Lewis Timberlake, *Born to Win*

DO NOT PURSUE what is illusory, property, and position. All that is gained at the expense of your nerves decade after decade and is confiscated in the fell night. Live with steady superiority over life. Don't be afraid of misfortune. Do not yearn after happiness. The bitter doesn't last forever. And the sweet never fills the cup to overflowing. It is enough if you don't freeze in the cold and if thirst and hunger don't claw at your insides, if your back isn't broken, if your feet can walk, if both arms can bend, if both eyes can see, if both ears hear, then whom should you envy.

—Charles R. Swindoll, *Intimacy with the Almighty*

ORVILLE KELLY was informed two years ago that he had terminal cancer. He and his wife went home to cry—to die. Should they keep it a secret? They prayed. The answer was that they should *play* about it. So they decided to give a big party. They invited all their friends. During the festivities, Orville held up his hand to make an announcement: "You may have wondered why I called you all together. This is a cancer party. I have been told I have terminal cancer. Then my wife and I realized we are all terminal. We decided to start a new organization. It is called the M.T.C.—Make Today Count. You are all charter members." Since that time the organization has grown across the country. Orville has been too busy to die, pointing out the way we Christians are to play into the jaws of death—singing, loving, not losing a minute from "the joy the world cannot give nor take away."

—David Redding, *Jesus Makes Me Laugh with Him*

HAYDEN PLANETARIUM in New York City ran an advertisement in New York newspapers inviting those who would like to make the first journey to another planet to submit an application. Within a matter of days, over 18,000 people applied. These applications were then given to a panel of psychologists, who upon reviewing them concluded that the vast majority of those who had applied wanted to start a new life on another planet because they were so discouraged by life on this one.

VICTOR FRANKL, a Viennese Jew, was interned by the Germans for more than three years. He was moved from one concentration camp to another, even spending several months at Auschwitz. Later he wrote these words:

"The experiences of camp life show that man does have a choice of action. There were enough examples, often of a heroic nature, which proved that apathy could be overcome, irritability suppressed. Man can preserve a vestige of spiritual freedom, in independence of mind, even in such terrible conditions of psychic and physical distress.

"We who lived in concentration camps can remember the men who walked through the huts comforting others, giving away their last piece of bread. They may have been few in number, but they offer sufficient proof that everything can be taken from a man but one thing: the last of the human freedoms—to choose one's attitude in any given set of circumstances, to choose one's own way."

—Victor Frankl, *Man's Search for Meaning*

WORDS CAN NEVER adequately convey the incredible impact of our attitude toward life. The longer I live the more convinced I become that life is 10 percent what happens to us and 90 percent how we respond to it.

I believe the single most significant decision I can make on a day-to-day basis is my choice of attitude. It is more important than my past, my education, my bankroll, my successes or failures, fame or pain, what other people think of me or say about me, my circumstances, or my position. Attitude keeps me going or cripples my progress. . . . It alone fuels my fire or assaults my hope. When my attitude is right, there's no barrier too high, no valley too deep, no dream too extreme, no challenge too great for me.

—Charles R. Swindoll, *Strengthening Your Grip*

Present Tense

> It was spring
>> But it was summer I wanted,
> The warm days,
>> And the great outdoors.
> It was summer,
>> But it was fall I wanted,
> The colorful leaves,
>> And the cool, dry air.
> It was fall,
>> But it was winter I wanted,
> The beautiful snow,
>> And the joy of the holiday season.
> It was winter,
>> But it was spring I wanted,

The warmth
　　And the blossoming of nature.
I was a child,
　　But it was adulthood I wanted.
The freedom,
　　And the respect.
I was 20,
　　But it was 30 I wanted,
To be mature,
　　And sophisticated.
I was middle-aged,
　　But it was 20 I wanted,
The youth,
　　And the free spirit.
I was retired,
　　But it was middle age I wanted,
The presence of mind,
　　Without limitations.
My life was over.
　　But I never got what I wanted.

—Jason Lehman, *"Dear Abby"* column, February 14, 1989

DO YOU FATHERS ever teach your children how to get up in the morning? Not only to get up, but *how* to get up? There is a threefold technique in getting up: First, we stretch. That gets the body going. Then, smile. That puts the soul in the right attitude, so that we don't start the day grumbling. And then say, "God loves me." Because that sets the spirit right. You are reminding yourself of your identity in that way. And body, soul, and spirit, you are starting the day right. Stretch, smile, and say, "God loves me."

—Ray Stedman sermon, *"The Abiding Principles,"* August 12, 1973

FANNY CROSBY was blind since childhood and lived to be ninety-five. She wrote this poem at age eight:

Blind but Happy

O what a happy soul am I!
Although I cannot see,
I am resolved that in this world

Contented I will be;
How many blessings I enjoy
That other people don't!
To weep and sigh because I'm blind,
I cannot, and I won't.

—Donald Kauffman, *Baker's Pocket Treasury of Religious Verse*

AUTHENTICITY

(Also see *Hypocrisy*)

I REMEMBER HEARING Lorne Sanny of the Navigators, years ago, ministering on the campus of the Air Force Academy, where officers in the making are being trained—so much competition, so much peer pressure. One of the young men who got a Bible class going was very much involved in its success, and it seemed as though month after month the whole thing revolved around him. And he continued to keep it going by pushing and motivating others to be involved. Finally the group grew, and he was the acknowledged leader of the group.

On one occasion early one morning as Lorne was talking with the group about the importance of devotion and time with God, he said, "Young man (called the leader's name), tell us about your walk. Tell us what it is that keeps your heart warm." The young man blinked a few times through tears and looked around, and against the pressure of the moment he said, "Sir, I don't have any time with God." He said, "As a matter of fact, I'm a fake." And he admitted in front of the whole group that he was simply driven by this need to be known and viewed as the leader, when in reality there was no authenticity behind it.

I WAS ONLY NINE YEARS OLD when my dad broke the picket line in the machinist's union back in the days of the war when the union had the audacity to go on strike. My father's patriotism and love for his family was greater than his loyalty to the union. And I remember him driving our '41 Ford home with broken windshields and eggs running down the side of the car, now dried, because he was willing to be called a scab for his convictions. It left an impression on me and on my sister and older brother. We learned there are times it's important enough to stand alone even when friends don't understand, even when coworkers disagree.

Grant us the will to fashion as we feel,
Grant us the strength to labour as we know,
Grant us the purpose, ribbed and edged with steel,
To strike the blow.

Knowledge we ask not—knowledge Thou has lent,
But, Lord, the will—there lies our bitter need,
Give us to build above the deep intent
The deed, the deed.

—J. Drinkwater, *Poems of Men and Hours* as quoted in
James Hastings, *Greater Men and Women of the Bible*

CHARLES H. SPURGEON, Baptist minister of London, England, had a pastor-friend, Dr. Newman Hall, who wrote a book entitled *Come to Jesus*. Another preacher published an article in which he ridiculed Hall, who bore it patiently for a little while. But when the article gained popularity, Hall sat down and wrote a letter of protest. His answer was full of retaliatory invectives that out-did anything in the article which attacked him. Before mailing the letter, Hall took it to Spurgeon for his opinion.

Spurgeon read it carefully then, handing it back, asserted it was excellent and that the writer of the article deserved it all. "But," he added, "it just lacks one thing." After a pause Spurgeon continued, "Underneath your signature you ought to write the words, 'Author of *Come to Jesus.*'"

The two godly men looked at each other for a few moments. Then Hall tore the letter to shreds. —Leslie B. Flynn, *You Don't Have to Go It Alone*

ON ONE OF MY BIRTHDAYS my sister gave me a full-face rubber mask . . . one of those crazy things you slip over your entire head. She told me she'd give me ten dollars if I'd wear it into the pulpit one Sunday (my kids raised it to fifteen dollars), but I just couldn't do it! One night I wore it to a speaking engagement. Without any explanation, I just stood up and began to speak on being authentic. There I stood pressing on, making one statement after another as the place came apart at the seams. Why? Anybody knows why! My mask canceled out everything I had to say, especially on *that* subject. It's impossible to be very convincing while you wear a mask.

I finally pulled the thing off and the place settled down almost immediately. As soon as it did, everybody got the point. It's a funny thing, when we wear *literal* masks, nobody is fooled. But how easy it is to wear invisible ones and fake people out by the hundreds week after week. Did you know that the word *hypocrite* comes from the ancient Greek plays? An actor would place a large, grinning mask in front of his face and quote his comedy lines as the audience would roar with laughter. He would then slip backstage and grab a frowning, sad, oversized mask and come back quoting tragic lines as the audience would moan and weep. Guess what he was called. A *hypocritos,* one who wears a mask.

—Charles R. Swindoll, *Improving Your Serve*

GREAT IMPRESSIONS can be made from a distance, but reality can only be tested up close.

—Howard G. Hendricks

BE WHO YOU IS, cause if you ain't who you is, then you is who you ain't.

—Harry Hein

AUTHORITY

WE WANT HEROES! We want reassurance that someone knows what is going on in this mad world. We want a father or a mother to lean on. We want revolutionary folk heroes who will tell us what to do until the rapture. We massage the egos of these demagogues and canonize their every opinion.

—David Gill, *Radix* magazine

A POLICEMAN'S GLOVE has authority. Just try speeding by it. He will share a piece of paper with you, with your signature.

IN THE ABSENCE OF PARENTAL LEADERSHIP, some children become extremely obnoxious and defiant, especially in public places. Perhaps the best example was a ten-year-old boy named Robert, who was a patient of my good friend Dr. William Slonecker. Dr. Slonecker said his pediatric staff dreaded the days when Robert was scheduled for an office visit. He literally attacked the clinic, grabbing instruments and files and telephones. His passive mother could do little more than shake her head in bewilderment.

During one physical examination, Dr. Slonecker observed severe cavities in Robert's teeth and knew that the boy must be referred to a local dentist. But who would be given the honor? A referral like Robert could mean the end of a professional friendship. Dr. Slonecker eventually decided to send him to an older dentist who reportedly understood children. The confrontation that followed now stands as one of the classic moments in the history of human conflict.

Robert arrived in the dental office, prepared for battle.

"Get in the chair, young man," said the doctor.

"No chance!" replied the boy.

"Son, I told you to climb onto the chair, and that's what I intend for you to do," said the dentist.

Robert stared at his opponent for a moment and then replied, "If you make me get in that chair, I will take off all my clothes."

The dentist calmly said, "Son, take 'em off."

The boy forthwith removed his shirt, undershirt, shoes, and socks, and then looked up in defiance.

"All right, son," said the dentist. "Now get on the chair."

"You didn't hear me," sputtered Robert. "I said if you make me get on that chair, I will take off all my clothes."

"Son, take 'em off," replied the man.

Robert proceeded to remove his pants and shorts, finally standing totally naked before the dentist and his assistant.

"Now, son, get in the chair," said the doctor.

Robert did as he was told, and sat cooperatively through the entire procedure. When the cavities were drilled and filled, he was instructed to step down from the chair.

"Give me my clothes now," said the boy.

"I'm sorry," replied the dentist. "Tell your mother that we're going to keep your clothes tonight. She can pick them up tomorrow."

Can you comprehend the shock Robert's mother received when the door to the waiting room opened, and there stood her pink son, as naked as the day he was born? The room was filled with patients, but Robert and his mom walked past them and into the hall. They went down a public elevator and into the parking lot, ignoring the snickers of onlookers.

The next day, Robert's mother returned to retrieve his clothes, and asked to have a word with the dentist. However, she did not come to protest. These were her sentiments: "You don't know how much I appreciate what happened here yesterday. You see, Robert has been blackmailing me about his clothes for years. Whenever we are in a public place, such as a grocery store, he makes unreasonable demands of me. If I don't immediately buy him what he wants, he threatens to take off all his clothes. You are the first person who has called his bluff, doctor, and the impact on Robert has been incredible!"

—James Dobson, *Straight Talk to Men and Their Wives*

IT WAS SAID of William Carey, the missionary of India: "He has attained the happy art of ruling and overruling others without asserting his authority, or others feeling their subjection—all is done without the least appearance of design on his part."

—Charles R. Swindoll, *Living on the Ragged Edge*

Bb

BAPTISM

THE MINISTER OF A CHURCH of a different denomination contacted the pastor of a large downtown Baptist church and made an unusual request. He had several folks who had recently joined his church who preferred to be baptized by immersion rather than sprinkling, the church's normal mode of baptism. The minister requested not only the use of their baptistry but that the Baptist pastor himself baptize those who came. This posed a dilemma—what if those being baptized weren't born again? Since it was the pastor's conviction that only Christians should be baptized, he realized he couldn't with good conscience cooperate with the plan, but he wished to handle his answer with tact so as not to offend the other minister. I understand that he wrote a letter, a masterpiece of grace, in which he included this humorous statement: "We don't take in laundry, but we'll be happy to loan you our tub."

—Charles R. Swindoll, *The Grace Awakening*

WORDS THAT Philip Henry, father of Matthew Henry, wrote for his children became their baptismal statement:

> I take God to be my chief end and highest good.
> I take God the Son to be my prince and Savior.
> I take God the Holy Spirit to be my sanctifier,
>   teacher, guide, and comforter.
> I take the Word of God to be my rule in all my actions
>   and the people of God to be my people
>   under all conditions.
> I do hereby dedicate and devote to the Lord all that I am,
>   all that I have,
>   and all I can do.
> And this I do deliberately, freely, and forever.

—Charles R. Swindoll, *Growing Deep in the Christian Life*

BIBLE

(Also see *Books, Education, Knowledge, Wisdom*)

THE RUSSIAN DICTIONARY defines the Bible as a "collection of fantastic legends without scientific support. It is full of dark hints, historical mistakes, and contradictions. It serves as a factor for gaining power and subjugating unknowing nations."

—Glen Wheeler, *1010 Illustrations, Poems and Quotes*

Thy Word

Thy Word is like a garden, Lord,
    With flowers bright and fair;
And every one who seeks may pluck
    A lovely cluster there.
Thy Word is like a deep, deep mine;
    And jewels rich and rare
Are hidden in its mighty depths
    For every searcher there.

Thy Word is like a starry host
    A thousand rays of light
Are seen to guide the traveler,
    And make his pathway bright.
Thy Word is like an armory,
    Where soldiers may repair,
And find for life's long battle-day
    All needful weapons there.

Oh, may I love Thy precious Word;
    May I explore the mine;
May I its fragrant flowers glean;
    May light upon me shine.
Oh, may I find my armor there;
    Thy Word my trusty sword,
I'll learn to fight with every foe
    The battle of the Lord.

—Edwin Hodder, *Sourcebook of Poetry*

JOHN WYCLIFFE was banished as Oxford's Professor of Divinity and branded "an instrument of the Devil . . . the author of schism." But he was to win world acclaim for his masterful translation of the Scriptures into the English vernacular. That translation not only infused a new depth and beauty into the English language but imparted to all who read it, the good news of God's saving grace.

Having been driven into virtual exile by the hypocritical alliance of church and state authorities, he knew full well they would now unite to destroy his translation of the Bible. Therefore, with a bold defiance of all their threats and evil imaginings against him, Wycliffe wrote in the flyleaf of his Bible: "This Bible is translated and shall make possible a government of the people, by the people, and for the people."

Little did he know that five hundred years later his words would be immortalized by the president of a new government, founded on the shores of a new continent, as he arose to dedicate a blood-drenched battlefield.

—Stuart P. Garver, *Our Christian Heritage*

THE GOSPEL OF JOHN was written in the most basic Greek. Martin Luther said, "I never read a book written in simpler words, yet words that are inexpressible."

MARTIN LUTHER wished to make two contributions to Christendom: a Bible they could understand and a hymnal from which they could sing. He said, "Let them loose. The flame will spread on its own."

—Charles R. Swindoll, *Hand Me Another Brick*

BIBLE—APPLICATION

ONE WAG HAS WRITTEN, "We have 35 million laws on the books to enforce the Ten Commandments."

THE TEN COMMANDMENTS may seem narrow, but so does every runway on airports around the world. Yet no passenger wants his pilot to miss the narrow runway and land a few yards off the mark in some field or waterway or row of houses. The narrow ribbon of pavement is really the broad way that leads to a safe, comfortable landing. So the seemingly rigid Decalogue guides to happy, fulfilled living.

—Leslie Flynn, *Now a Word from Our Creator*

DR. RALPH KEIPER ASKED, "If you were wrecked at sea on an island and a single chapter of the Bible washed up from wreckage, which would you like it to be?" Five of twenty said Romans 8. Charles Hodge calls Romans 8 "a rhapsody on assurance."

GOD'S WORD IS LIKE A LOG sitting on top of the ice on a frozen lake. When the ice thaws and melts, the log penetrates into the water and becomes a part of the lake. The trials that come along in life are like that thawing process. They melt the heart and allow God's Word to penetrate and become a part of us.

BIBLE—IGNORANCE OF

ALBERT STAUDERMAN relates that he told in a sermon the old joke about Bible ignorance where someone asks, "What are the epistles?" And the answer received is, "They were the wives of the apostles." He relates, however, that after the sermon a woman asked, "Pastor, I didn't get the joke. If they weren't the wives of the apostles, whose wives were they?"

—Albert Stauderman, *Let Me Illustrate*

I HEARD ABOUT A MAN who was so ignorant of Scripture, when he read Psalm 105 written in Roman numerals, he called it "Pislemciv." Another man announced before he read from Scripture, "I'm reading from Isam 6."

I GOT SOME FUNNY ANSWERS when I took a poll regarding the Book of Habakkuk. Some of the answers were:
- a word spelled backwards,
- a Jewish holiday,
- a village in Vietnam,
- a new game,
- a disease of the lower back.

I HEARD ABOUT A BIBLE CLASS where a young Christian was just kind of stumbling his way along. He said to the teacher, "I'm having some struggles with Genesis." The teacher immediately began to dump the truck. You know, the authorship of Genesis and the JEDP theory and higher criticism that's come over from the Wellhausen theory, and on and on. And the guy, when he got through, said, "Well, I appreciate that. I'm having trouble *finding* Genesis."

BIBLE—INFALLIBILITY OF

THE DISTINCTIVE MARK of theology today is its dreadful ambiguity. The chaos of American theology today can be traced back to its roots in the rejection of biblical infallibility. Preaching is not the act of unfolding our personal convictions. It is the duty of informing men of all that God has spoken. To move off from the pages of Scripture is to enter into the wastelands of our own subjectivity. Scripture plays an important role in the salvation of men. The Bible is a divinely provided map of the spiritual order. It contains the directions and markings to guide a person into reconciliation with God.

—Clark Pinnock, *Bibliotheca Sacra*, October–December 1967

ONCE UPON A TIME there was a man who thought he was dead. His concerned wife and friends sent him to the friendly neighborhood psychiatrist. The psychiatrist determined to cure him by convincing him of one fact that contradicted his belief that he was dead. The psychiatrist decided to use the simple truth that dead men do not bleed. He put his patient to work reading medical texts, observing autopsies, etc. After weeks of effort, the patient finally said, "All right, all right! You've convinced me. Dead men do not bleed." Whereupon the psychiatrist stuck him in the arm with a needle, and the blood flowed. The man looked down with a contorted, ashen face and cried: "Good Lord! Dead men bleed after all!"

—Clark Pinnock, *Set Forth Your Case*

BIBLE—INFLUENCE OF

Last eve I paused beside the blacksmith's door
And heard the anvil ring the vesper chimes;
Then looking in, I saw upon the floor
Old hammers worn out with beating years of time.

"How many anvils have you had," said I,

"To wear and batter all these hammers so?"
"Just one," said he and then with twinkling eye,
"The anvil wears the hammers out, you know."
And so I thought, the anvil of God's Word
For ages skeptics' blows have beat upon.
Yet, though the noise of falling blows was heard,
The anvil is unharmed, the hammers are gone.

—John Clifford, quoted in W. A. Criswell, *Abiding Hope*

FOUND IN BILLY SUNDAY'S BIBLE:

Twenty-nine years ago, with the Holy Spirit as my Guide, I entered at the portico of Genesis, walked down the corridor of the Old Testament art galleries, where pictures of Noah, Abraham, Moses, Joseph, Isaac, Jacob, and Daniel hung on the wall. I passed into the music room of the Psalms where the Spirit sweeps the keyboard of nature until it seems that every reed and pipe in God's great organ responds to the harp of David, the sweet singer of Israel.

I entered the chamber of Ecclesiastes, where the voice of the preacher is heard, and into the conservatory of Sharon and the lily of the valley where sweet spices filled and perfumed my life.

I entered the business office of Proverbs and on into the observatory of the prophets where I saw telescopes of various sizes pointing to far off events, concentrating on the bright and morning Star which was to rise above the moonlit hills of Judea for our salvation and redemption.

I entered the audience room of the King of Kings, catching a vision written by Matthew, Mark, Luke, and John. Thence into the correspondence room with Paul, Peter, James, and John writing their Epistles.

I stepped into the throne room of Revelation where tower the glittering peaks, where sits the King of Kings upon His throne of glory with the healing of nations in His hand, and I cried out:

All hail the power of Jesus' name!
Let angels prostrate fall;
Bring forth the royal diadem
And crown Him Lord of all.

—W. A. Criswell, *Why I Preach That the Bible Is Literally True*

THE BIBLE CAN CHANGE NOT ONLY A LIFE but an entire lifestyle. Most of us have heard the story of the *Mutiny on the Bounty*, but few of us have heard how the Bible played a very vital part in that historical event. The *Bounty* was a British ship which set sail from England in 1787, bound for the South Seas. The idea was that those on board would spend some time among the islands, transplanting fruit-bearing and food-bearing trees, and doing other things to make some of the islands more habitable. After ten months of voyage, the *Bounty* arrived safely at its destination, and for six months the officers and the crew gave themselves to the duties placed upon them by their government.

When the special task was completed, however, and the order came to embark again, the sailors rebelled. They had formed strong attachments for the native girls, and the climate and the ease of the South Sea island life was much to their liking. The result was mutiny on the *Bounty*, and the sailors placed Captain Bligh and a few loyal men adrift in an open boat. Captain Bligh, in an almost miraculous fashion, survived the ordeal, was rescued, and eventually arrived home in London to tell his story. An expedition was launched to punish the mutineers, and in due time fourteen of them were captured and paid the penalty under British law.

But nine of the men had gone to another distant island. There they formed a colony. Perhaps there has never been a more degraded and debauched social life than that of that colony. They learned to distill whiskey from a native plant, and the whiskey, as usual, along with other habits, led to their ruin. Disease and murder took the lives of all the native men and all but one of the white men named Alexander Smith. He found himself the only man on an island, surrounded by a crowd of women and half-breed children. Alexander Smith found a Bible among the possessions of a dead sailor. The Book was new to him. He had never read it before. He sat down and read it through. He believed it and he began to appropriate it. He wanted others to share in the benefits of this book, so he taught classes to the women and the children, as he read to them and taught them the Scriptures.

It was twenty years before a ship ever found that island, and when it did, a miniature Utopia was discovered. The people were living in decency, prosperity, harmony, and peace. There was nothing of crime, disease, immorality, insanity, or illiteracy. How was it accomplished? By the reading, the believing, and the appropriating of the truth of God!

—Keith Miller, *Edge of Adventure*

BIBLE—KNOWLEDGE

ON OKINAWA, Chaplain George Vanderpoel challenged that he would give a twenty dollar bill to anyone who could quote the Ten Commandments word perfect. No one could. So I was determined to get them memorized in case I ever saw him again. And I did. George surprised me one day and showed up at the Fullerton church making the same offer. . . . Would you believe it? I couldn't remember them!

GOD'S WORD gives clear instruction in both precepts and principles. Examples of a precept would be no sexual immorality, do not repay evil for evil, pray without ceasing, in all things give thanks. Principles are judgment calls. The Bible doesn't mention cards, makeup, movies, or tobacco. The more you know about God's Word, the better judgment calls or decisions you can make. Another example of a precept is a sign that says "35 MPH." There's no give or take in that. "Drive carefully," however, is a principle since it can vary with road or traffic conditions.

DR. LOUIS EVANS, pastor of Hollywood Presbyterian Church, had a keen relationship with his college group. I had oversight of that group and used to take the group to talk with Dr. Evans because he had both the Old and New Testaments memorized. He would challenge them to memorize verses. They would discuss many of these verses. He would teach them how to study the Bible and how to teach and preach the Bible.

On one occasion he challenged them to memorize the entire chapter of 1 Corinthians 15, and then the following Sunday, when he preached for his son, Dr. Louis Evans, Jr., he started off by quoting the entire 58 verses. Then he preached on the subject.

Later, on another occasion, when he was preaching on the virgin birth, he decided that after preaching so long on the virgin birth if you weren't going to accept the Bible as the Word of God, then you should just go ahead and tear these sections right out of the Bible. As he stood there in the pulpit, he said, "So if you don't believe in the virgin birth, tear it out." With that statement he literally tore out the pages of his Bible and threw the pages over the pulpit. "If you don't believe He raised Lazarus from the dead, then tear that out." So he literally tore it out and threw it over the pulpit. "If you don't believe in the resurrection, tear it out." And he literally tore the pages right out and crumpled them and threw them over the pulpit. With those tattering pages floating down from the pulpit, he said, "What do you have left? All you have left is the Sermon on the Mount, and it's not worth anything unless a divine Christ preached it." And with that he said, "Let's bow for the benediction."

As soon as he bowed his head, in that sedate, vast congregation, a man stood up and said, "No! No! We want more! More!" Then another fellow said, "Yeah, we want more!" So Evans picked up his Bible and preached for another fifty minutes. And then gave the benediction.

—Henrietta Mears, *The Christian Circle*

BIBLE—STUDY

THE DELIGHTFUL STUDY of Psalms has yielded me boundless profit and ever-growing pleasure.

—Charles H. Spurgeon, *Treasury of David*

THE OLD COVENANT IS REVEALED in the New, and the New Covenant is veiled in the Old.

—Augustine

THE NEW IS IN THE OLD CONTAINED, and the Old is in the New explained.

—Graham Scroggie

ONE LADY SAID after studying the life of Moses: "I know Moses so well he doesn't even look like Charlton Heston."

I supposed I knew my Bible,
Reading piece-meal, hit or miss;
Now a bit of "John" or "Matthew,"
Next a snatch of "Genesis."
Certain chapters of "Isaiah,"
Certain "Psalms,"—the twenty-third,
Twelfth of "Romans," first of "Proverbs."
Yes, I thought I knew the Word.
But I found a thorough reading
Was a different thing to do,
And the way was unfamiliar
When I read the Bible through.
Ye who treat the Crown of Writings
As you treat no other book—
Just a paragraph disjointed,
Just a crude, impatient look—

Try a worthier procedure,
Try a broad and steady view;
You will kneel in very rapture
When you read the Bible through.

—Amos R. Wells, quoted in John R. Rice, *Poems That Preach*

Finding Christ in All the Bible

In Genesis	Seed of the woman
In Exodus	Passover Lamb
In Leviticus	Atoning Sacrifice
In Numbers	Bronze Serpent
In Deuteronomy	Promised Prophet
In Joshua	Unseen Captain
In Judges	My Deliverer
In Ruth	Kinsman Redeemer
In Samuel—Kings—Chronicles	Promised King
In Ezra—Nehemiah	Restorer of the nation
In Esther	My Advocate
In Job	My Redeemer
In Psalms	My All in All
In Proverbs	My Pattern
In Ecclesiastes	My Goal
In Song of Solomon	My Beloved
In all the Prophets	Coming Prince of Peace
In Matthew	Jesus King of Kings
In Mark	Jesus Servant of Man
In Luke	Jesus Son of Man
In John	Jesus Son of God
In Acts	Jesus Ascended—Sending
In Letters	Jesus Indwelling—Filling
In Revelation	Jesus Returning/Reigning

—J. B. Fowler, *Illustrating Great Words*

BOOKS

(Also see *Bible, Education, Knowledge, Wisdom*)

"SEND ME A MAN WHO READS" is no longer the clarion call of industry or management . . . or sales, for that matter. Nor is the professional person necessarily known today, as he once was, for his breadth of knowledge . . . and that includes (much to my disappointment) the clergy.

Few current tragedies pain me more. It is now a fact that one half of the students who graduate from college never read another book. Even though a Ph.D. is virtually obsolete in five years unless he or she continues to read, many of them opt for an easier out. It would shock us all if we knew how little the person reads who defends us in court or does surgery on our bodies or gives us financial counsel. Aside from daily doses of *TV Guide* (America's top-selling magazine), a chuckle at "Peanuts" on Sunday, and a quick skim over the sports section, many a man never cracks another magazine or book.

Reading sweeps the cobwebs away; it increases our power of concentration; it makes us more interesting to be around; and it strengthens our ability to glean truth from God's Word. Even in prison, Paul wanted his books, especially the parchments (2 Timothy 4:13) brought to him. He would have agreed with John Wesley who said, "Either read or get out of the ministry!"

—Charles R. Swindoll, *Come Before Winter*

SIR ROBERTSON NICOLL was undoubtedly the most prolific and respected religious journalist in the English-speaking world from 1886 to 1923. Listen to his resumé.

He was the "unofficial literary agent" of Marcus Dods, George Adam Smith, A. B. Bruce, and Alexander Maclaren. He persuaded Maclaren to publish all of his works. And those of us in ministry will be grateful for Nicoll the rest of our lives. Thanks to him, Maclaren put his stuff in print.

Nicoll himself wrote over 40 books. He himself compiled and edited or supervised the publication of over 250 more titles. He had a 25,000 volume personal library. He read on an average two books a day. He edited a weekly journal, three monthly magazines, and a steady stream of scholarly books, which included *The Expositor's Bible* (50 volumes) and *The Expositor's Greek Testament*. He was knighted in 1909 out of respect for distinguished service in his literary achievements.

When he died, Charles Haddon Spurgeon said, "He has fallen like a tower, and his removal means for many a change in the whole landscape of life."

—Warren W. Wiersbe, *Walking with the Giants*

BOOKS ARE LIKE FRIENDS . . . individual, unique, and inestimable. They each contribute something different yet valuable to our lives. They should be chosen carefully, enjoyed lovingly, and given time to grow on us. Reading brings us from darkness into light, from ignorance into knowledge, from imprisonment to freedom. By means of reading we are better able to ferret out the meanings and possibilities of life. The voices of Reason, Victory, Beauty, Faith, History, Poetry, Science . . . reach out to instruct and encourage us from the author's pen, and we are the better for it.

Books contain the power to lift us from the milieu in which we live and work. It is as though they have the capability of transporting us into another realm of being. Emily Dickinson captured that very thought.

> He ate and drank the precious words,
> His spirit grew robust;
> He knew no more that he was poor,
> Nor that his frame was dust.
> He danced along the dingy days,
> And this bequest of wings
> Was but a book. What liberty
> A loosened spirit brings.

—Luci Swindoll, *Wide My World, Narrow My Bed*

THE MAN WHO NEVER READS will never be read; he who never quotes will never be quoted. He who will not use thoughts of other men's brains proves he has no brain of his own. Brethren, what is true of ministers is true of all our people. You need to read.

—Charles H. Spurgeon, quoted in Bob L. Ross, *A Pictorial Biography of C. H. Spurgeon*

I HAD A SEMINARY PROFESSOR who used to encourage me to buy books. He would say, "Where else can you have two thousand professors if you have two thousand books?"

BUSINESS

(Also see *Jobs*)

A DECISION IS A JUDGMENT. It is a choice between alternatives. It is rarely a choice between right and wrong. It is at best a choice between "almost right" and "probably wrong"—but much more often a choice between two courses of action, neither of which is probably more nearly right than the other.

—Peter Drucker, *The Effective Executive*

I HEARD ABOUT A MAN who took a dinner flight. After the stewardess had served him his meal, he unwrapped the salad and noticed right on top a rather large roach. Infuriated, enraged, he couldn't wait to get home and write the president of the airline a letter—hot and to the point.

Within a matter of a very few days he received a special delivery letter in return, an answer signed by the president himself, typed beautifully on the letterhead of the airline. It was dripping with apologies. "I have taken immediate action," it said. "In fact, I have temporarily pulled that airplane off the line. We have stripped the seats. We have stripped the upholstery. It will not go back on line until everything is in shipshape condition. You have my word. The flight attendant who served you that meal, well, her job is in jeopardy. As a matter of fact, I promise you that will never occur again. Please, continue to fly on our airline."

Well, the man was remarkably impressed. However, he noticed something unusual. Quite by accident the president's secretary had somehow inadvertently allowed his original letter to be stuck to the back of this letter. And as he turned it over, a note at the bottom said, "Send this guy the standard roach letter."

Ten Commandments of Good Business

A Customer is the most important person
    in any business.
A Customer is not dependent upon us—
    we are dependent on him.
A Customer is not an interruption of our work—
    he is the purpose of it.
A Customer does us a favor when he calls—
    we are not doing him a favor by serving him.
A Customer is part of our business—
    not an outsider.
A Customer is not a cold statistic—
    he is a flesh-and-blood human being with feelings
    and emotions like our own.
A Customer is not someone to argue or match
    wits with.
A Customer is deserving of the most courteous
    and attentive treatment we can give him
A Customer is the life-blood of this and every
    other business.

ADVERTISING BOMBARDS ALL OF US. To wit:

TV Victim's Lament
(To the tune of "Blowin' in the Wind.")

How many times must a guy spray with Ban
    Before he doesn't offend?
How many times must he gargle each day
    Before he can talk to a friend?
How many tubes of shampoo must he buy
    Before his dandruff will end?
Ah, the sponsors, my friend, will sell you all they can.
    The sponsors will sell you all they can.

How many times must a man use Gillette
    Before shaving won't make him bleed?
How many cartons of Kent must he smoke
    Before the girls all pay him heed?
How many products must one person buy
    Before he has all that he'll need?
The sponsors, my friend, will sell you all they can.
    The sponsors will sell you all they can.

How many times must a girl clean her sink
    Before Ajax scours the stain?
How many times must she rub in Ben Gay
    Before she can rub out the pain?
How many ads on TV must we watch
    Before we are driven insane?
The sponsors, my friend, will broadcast all they can.
    The sponsors will broadcast all they can.

—Arthur Gish, *Beyond the Rat Race*

THE OLD ROMAN POLITICIAN, Publius, was right on when he wrote, "It is a bad plan that admits of no modification."

—Charles R. Swindoll, *Make Up Your Mind*

WILL CHRISTIANITY AND BUSINESS MIX? Is God interested in the way we do our work? Is He interested in a lathe operator and in the quantity and quality of his output? Is He interested in a watchman as he makes his rounds through the warehouse in the darkness and silence of the night? Is He interested in a stenographer, in the way she types her letters? Is He interested in a salesman and what he says to a prospect? Is God concerned about a businessman's business? Is God there when he makes out his income tax return or his expense account? Does He take an interest in the company's advertising campaign and the claims made for the company's product? Is He present at personal interviews, at conferences, director's meetings, labor union negotiations, trade conventions, business luncheons, and black-tie banquets? When a businessman succeeds or fails, is God interested?

To say No to these questions is to relegate God to a place of no importance in the very area of a person's life where he spends most of his waking hours. On the other hand, he who answers Yes to these questions, whether he be a supreme court justice or a garbage collector, transforms his career into a thing of dignity, high purpose, satisfaction, and excitement.

—John E. Mitchell, Jr., *The Christian in Business*

IN SPITE OF OUR HIGH-TECH WORLD and efficient procedures, people remain the essential ingredient of life. When we forget that, a strange thing happens: We start treating people like inconveniences instead of assets.

This is precisely what humorist Robert Henry, a professional speaker, encountered one evening when he went to a large discount department store in search of a pair of binoculars.

As he walked up to the appropriate counter he noticed that he was the only customer in the store. Behind the counter were two salespersons. One was so preoccupied talking to "Mama" on the telephone that she refused to acknowledge that Robert was there. At the other end of the counter, a second salesperson was unloading inventory from a box onto the shelves. Growing impatient, Robert walked down to her end of the counter and just stood there. Finally, she looked up at Robert and said, "You got a number?"

"I got a what?" asked Robert, trying to control his astonishment at such an absurdity.

"You got a number? You gotta have a number."

Robert replied, "Lady, I'm the only customer in the store! I don't need a number. Can't you see how ridiculous this is?" But she failed to see the absurdity and insisted that Robert take a number before agreeing to wait on him. By now, it was obvious to Robert that she was more interested in following procedures than helping the customer. So he went to the take-a-number machine, pulled number 37 and walked back to the salesperson.

With that, she promptly went to her number counter, which revealed that the last customer waited on had been holding number 34. So she screamed out, "35! ... 35! ... 36! ... 36! ... 37!"

"I'm number 37," said Robert.

"May I help you?" she asked, without cracking a smile.

"No," replied Robert, and he turned around and walked out.

—Michael Leboeuf, *How to Win Customers and Keep Them for Life*

A MAN SPEAKING ON INTEGRITY in the marketplace said Christians are often like the world in their lack of excellence. You need to:

- pay your bills,
- respect your boss,
- watch your mouth,
- value your people,
- know your limits,
- do your best.

EDWARD ROY HAD A PROBLEM that was earthy, but not earth-shattering. Not very enjoyable to talk about at dinner either, but big enough to make the man struggle through a few sleepless nights.

He ran a lowly business—*Jiffy Johns* of Pompano Beach, Florida. Five hundred portable toilets for rent. Band concerts, construction sites, church picnics, outdoor gatherings of any size could rent his product. But that wasn't Ed's problem. As expected, when he started his business in 1982, lots of folks in Florida needed a place to be alone when they were caught out in the open. Rentals were up. That was good and bad.

Now he had to figure out what to do with all that sewage . . . *that* was the problem.

Many a man would've thrown his hands in the air in exasperation and spent half his profit to have somebody haul off his product's product. Not Ed. There had to be a better way.

In his search for a solution, he found a solar-heating process that turned sewage into fertilizer. Then came a masterstroke of marketing: instead of trying to sell the technology directly to local Florida communities, his company expanded and began to operate three $3 million plants itself. Under this new arrangement, the company would treat sewage for a fee and convert it into fertilizer, which was, in turn, sold for a substantial profit. A limited partnership soon produced the cash—*Jiffy Industries, Inc.* (new name) provided a good tax shelter. I suppose we could say Edward Roy *literally* turned his problem into a project.

And what a project! Jiffy stock turned in the year's best performance on any American exchange, rising from 92 cents a share to a whopping $16.50—a spectacular 1,693 percent gain. *Newsweek* magazine recently reported that "with dozens of states suffering from a surfeit of sewage . . . Jiffy's 'Anaerobic Digester' is catching on everywhere."

Gross though it may seem, I doubt I'll ever forget the problem Edward Roy had with his johns. He simply refused to let all that stuff get the best of him. What a lesson for all of us!

—Charles R. Swindoll, *Growing Strong in the Seasons of Life*

THE STORY IS TOLD of two shopkeepers who were bitter rivals. Their stores were across the street from each other, and they would spend each day sitting in the doorway, keeping track of each other's business. If one got a customer, he would smile in triumph at his rival. One night, an angel appeared to one of the shopkeepers in a dream and said, "God has sent me to teach you a lesson. He will give you anything you ask for, but I want you to know that, whatever you get, your competitor across the street will get twice as much. Would you be wealthy? You can be very wealthy, but he will be twice as rich. Do you want to live a long and healthy life? You can, but his life will be longer and healthier. You can be famous, have children you will be proud of, whatever you desire. But whatever you get, he will get twice as much." The man frowned, thought for a moment and said, "All right, my request is: strike me blind in one eye."

—Harold S. Kushner, *When Bad Things Happen to Good People*

TOM FATJO IS INTO GARBAGE.

Oh, he hasn't always been. He used to be a quiet, efficient accounting executive. Another of those prim and proper Rice University grads who was going to play it straight, dodge all risk, and settle down easily into a life of the predictable. Boring but stable. Safe. Everything was running along as planned until that night Tom found himself surrounded by a roomful of angry homeowners. As he sat among all those irritated people at the Willowbrook Civic Club in the southwestern section of Houston, his internal wheels began to turn.

You see, the city had refused to pick up the garbage at the back door of their homes. They had hired a private company to do it, but now that company was having serious problems. So the garbage was starting to stack up. And flies were everywhere, which only added to the sticky misery of that hot south Texas summer. Heated words flashed across the room.

And that night Tom Fatjo couldn't sleep.

A crazy idea kept rolling around in his head. A dream too unreal to admit to anyone but himself. A dream that spawned a series of incredible thoughts. That resulted in the purchase of a garbage truck. That led to a ten-year adventure you'd have trouble believing. That evolved into the largest solid-waste disposal company in the world, Browning-Ferris Industries, Inc. With annual sales in excess of (are your ready for this?) $500 million. And that was only the beginning. Tom has also been instrumental in building over ten other companies—large companies—like the Criterion Capital Corporation, whose subsidiaries and affiliates manage well over $2 *billion*.

And to think it all started with a garbage truck.

No, a dream.

—Charles R. Swindoll, *Quest for Character*

Cc

CHARACTER

ALL CHILDREN MUST look after their own upbringing. Parents can only give good advice or put them on the right paths, but the final forming of a person's character lies in their own hands.

—John Bartlett, *Bartlett's Familiar Quotations*

NOTHING STANDS THE TEST like solid character. You can handle the blast (of adversity) like a steer in a blizzard. The ice may form on your horns, but you keep standing against the wind and the howling, raging storm because Christ is at work in your spirit. Character will always win the day. As Horace Greeley wrote: "Fame is a vapor, popularity an accident, riches take wing, and only character endures."

—Charles R. Swindoll, *Hope Again*

TO PARAPHRASE Ellen Wheeler Wilcox's "The Winds of Fate":

> One ship sails east
> One ship sails west
> Regardless of how the winds blow.
> It is the set of the sail
> And not the gale
> That determines the way we go.

—Charles R. Swindoll, *Laugh Again*

D. L. MOODY SAID, "Character is what you are in the dark." Another commented, "True character is what we are when nobody's looking, in the secret chambers of the heart."

—George Sweeting, *Great Quotes and Illustrations*

THE UNEXAMINED LIFE is not worth living.

—Socrates

NO CHARACTER IS SIMPLE unless it is based on truth, lived in harmony with one's own conscience and ideals. Simplicity is destroyed by any attempt to live in harmony with public opinion.

The Shaping of a Disciple

When God wants to drill a man,
And thrill a man, and skill a man,
When God wants to mold a man
To play for Him the noblest part,
When He yearns with all His heart
To build so great and bold a man
That all the world shall be amazed,
Then watch God's methods, watch His ways!
How He ruthlessly perfects
Whom He royally elects;
How He hammers him and hurts him
And with mighty blows converts him,
Making shapes and forms which only
God Himself can understand,
Even while His man is crying,
Lifting a beseeching hand . . .
Yet God bends but never breaks
When man's good He undertakes;
When He uses whom He chooses,
And with every purpose fuses
Man to act, and act to man,
As it was when He began,
When God tries His splendor out,
Man will know what He's about!

—Dale Martin Stone, *Sourcebook of Poetry*

THE PRIMARY DANGER of the television screen lies not so much in the behavior it produces as the behavior it prevents.

—*Christian Medical Society Journal,* 1978

IT'S IMAGE—that's what's important, not character.

A GENTLEMAN is one who considers the rights of others before his own feelings and the feelings of others before his own rights. . . . You should care more about your character than your reputation. Your character is what you really are. Your reputation is only what people think about you.

—John Wooten, *They Call Me Coach*

FOR SEVERAL YEARS I served on the board of Dallas Seminary with Tom Landry of the Dallas Cowboys. While the board was talking about the importance of character among the young men and women going into ministry, Mr. Landry leaned over and said to me, "You know, Chuck, for the Cowboys, when we draft men for our team, we look for five things, and the first is character." And I said, "Well, let me ask you something, a hard question. What if you find a terrific athlete who lacks character?" He said, "Chuck, that's easy. We don't draft him."

He also said something at lunch that I will never forget. When he talks, I listen. He said, "I've noticed that there's never been an exception. When any one of our men gets involved with drugs, their character leaves. They're finished. It's just a matter of time."

How come guys with all that talent and all that money and all that time would get involved with drugs? Why, that's what it takes. Money and talent and time.

And those people who are ready to get you into drugs are saying, "Look, this is like no high you've ever had. This'll turn your life around." And they make promises they can't keep. They ruin your character.

PROMISES MUST BE KEPT, deadlines met, commitments honored, not for the sake of morality, but because we become what we do or fail to do. Character is the sum of all that.

—Howard Sparks, quoted in Lloyd Cory, *Quote Unquote*

ROBERT E. LEE was a "foe without hate, a friend without treachery, a soldier without cruelty. . . . He was a public officer without vices, a neighbor without reproach, a Christian without hypocrisy, a man without guile. . . ."

—Benjamin Harvey Hill

CHARACTER IS THE DISTINCTIVE QUALITIES that reveal knowledge, wisdom, and understanding, which result in a worthy walk.

YOU CAN TELL A LOT ABOUT A MAN by the way he treats those who can do nothing for him.

HERBERT SPENCER, the English philosopher, wrote, "Not education but character is man's greatest need and man's greatest safeguard." My definition of character is not nearly as eloquent as Spencer's. Character is, in my opinion, the moral, ethical, and spiritual undergirding that rests on truth, that reinforces a life in stressful times, and resists all temptations to compromise.

ONE CAN ACQUIRE ANYTHING in solitude except character.

—Stendhal, French novelist

A MAN'S BEST COLLATERAL is his character.

—J. P. Morgan, quoted in Warren Wiersbe, *Making Sense of the Ministry*

PHIL DONAHUE, the television talk show host, has something of a reputation for giving clergy a hard time, and he has said the reason he's that way is that he has little respect for them. Most clergy will do anything for some media attention, he says.

In his autobiography, however, he tells about an encounter with a pastor who was different. It happened while Donahue was a young television reporter in Ohio, and one day he was sent to West Virginia in the bitter cold winter to cover a mine disaster. He went by himself in a battered little car, carrying a minicam to film the story.

It was so cold when he got there, however, that the camera wouldn't work. So he put it inside his coat to warm it up enough to run. In the meantime, the families of the trapped miners were gathered around. They were just simple mining people—women, old men, and children. Several of the trapped men were fathers.

Then the local pastor arrived. He was rough-hewn, and he didn't speak well at all. But he gathered all the families around in a circle, and they held one another in their arms while he prayed for them.

As this was going on, Donahue was still trying to get his camera to work, and he was incredibly frustrated because he couldn't film the poignant scene. Finally, after the prayer was over, Donahue managed to get his camera operating. So he told the pastor he had his camera working now and asked if the pastor would please do the prayer again so he could film it for the evening news.

Donahue says, by the way, that he's been with the world's best-known public figures, including preachers, and they're all willing to redo a scene in order to get on the news.

This simple West Virginia preacher, however, told Donahue, "Young man, we don't pray for the news. I'm sorry, but we've already prayed, and I will not pose."

To this day Donahue remembers that pastor with respect. You don't forget that kind of character, no matter who you are or what you believe.

—Jay Kesler, *Being Holy, Being Human*

LIFE IS A GRINDSTONE. Whether it grinds you down or polishes you up depends upon what you are made of.

—James S. Hewett, *Illustrations Unlimited*

CHARITY

(Also see *Giving, Money, Stewardship, Wealth*)

A TRAMP WAS LOOKING FOR A HANDOUT one day in a picturesque old English village. Hungry almost to the point of fainting, he stopped by a pub bearing the classic name, *Inn of St. George and the Dragon*.

"Please, ma'am, could you spare me a bite to eat?" he asked the lady who answered his knock at the kitchen door.

"A bite to eat?" she growled. "For a sorry, no-good bum—a foul-smelling beggar? No!" she snapped as she almost slammed the door on his hand.

Halfway down the lane the tramp stopped, turned around and eyed the words, *St. George and the Dragon*. He went back and knocked again on the kitchen door.

"Now what do you want?" the woman asked angrily.

"Well, ma'am, if St. George is in, may I speak with him this time?"

—David Augsburger, *The Freedom of Forgiveness*

Newsweek MAGAZINE HAD A CARTOON several years ago of a starving man in front of an empty bowl. A man with a big cigar was pouring out a sack of words to fill the bowl. We need more than just talk, we need to take action.

CHILD REARING

(Also see *Delinquency*)

PARENTS SHOULD SUSTAIN CONFRONTATION FAITHFULLY, diligently, habitually. I went to have my ear examined once and couldn't help overhear what was going on in the other room between the doctor and an emotional mother. She was saying, "You've got to do something about this boy of mine." And the doctor responded, "What do you want me to do, ma'am? You're the mother. Now if you don't keep him out of the swimming pool, he will have constant ear infections." She said, "He's too big for me to handle. I can't keep him out of the pool. You have to help me with medicine or something that will take away the problem and the infection."

And I thought as I listened, Man, it's obvious who's in charge in that home. And I expected when they walked out of that room that his boy would be about 6'2", you know, seventeen-year-old boy. But he was a kindergartner. He was! He was little. And I thought, confrontation is missing, and it has been missing too long. That boy is controlling the home.

ALAS, WE ARRIVE NOW AT THE DOOR OF ADOLESCENCE: that dynamic time of life which comes in with a pimple and goes out with a beard—those flirtatious years when girls begin to powder and boys begin to puff. It's an exciting phase of childhood, I suppose, but to be honest, I wouldn't want to stumble through it again. . . . (By the way, have you heard of the new wristwatch created exclusively for the anxious parents of teenagers? After 11 P.M. it wrings its hands every fifteen minutes.)

—James Dobson, *The Strong-Willed Child*

LEAVING A WARM BED when a voice in the night says, "I'm cold," is being a loving parent. Parents spend two years teaching children to walk and talk and eighteen years trying to teach them to sit down and be quiet.

—Ted Engstrom, *A Time for Commitment*

CARL SANDBURG ONCE RELATED THE STORY about a mother who brought her newborn son to General Robert E. Lee for a blessing. The southern gentleman tenderly cradled the lad in his arms then looked at the mother and said, "Ma'am, please teach him that he must deny himself."

—Jon Johnston, "Growing Me-ism and Materialism," *Christianity Today,* December 17, 1986

CHILD REARING IS LIKE BAKING A CAKE. You don't realize you have a disaster until it's too late.

—James Dobson, *The Strong-Willed Child*

Learning the Bicycle

The older children pedal past
Stable as little gyros, spinning hard
To supper, bath, and bed, until at last
We also quit, silent and tired
Beside the darkening yard where trees
Now shadow up instead of down.
Their predictable lengths can only tease
Her as, head lowered, she walks her bike alone
Somewhere between wanting to ride
And her certainty she will always fall.
Tomorrow, though I will run behind,
Arms out to catch her, she'll tilt then balance wide
Of my reach, till distance makes her small,
Smaller, beyond the place I stop and know
That to teach her I had to follow
And when she learned I had to let her go.

—Wyatt Prunty, *American Scholar* magazine

Children Learn What They Live

If a child lives with criticism,
He learns to condemn.
If a child lives with hostility,
He learns to fight.
If a child lives with ridicule,
He learns to be shy.
If a child lives with shame,
He learns to feel guilty.
If a child lives with tolerance,
He learns to be patient.
If a child lives with encouragement,
He learns confidence.
If a child lives with praise,
He learns to appreciate.

If a child lives with fairness,
He learns justice.
If a child lives with security,
He learns to have faith.
If a child lives with approval,
He learns to like himself.
If a child lives with acceptance and friendship,
He learns to find
love in the world.

—Dorothy Law Nolte, quoted in John W. Lawrence, *Life's Choices*

OURS MAY BE THE FIRST GENERATION in civilized times that has not raised its young on proverbs. From the beginning of recorded history . . . concise sayings which describe the benefit of good conduct or the harm of bad have been used to teach children how to behave.

—David Hubbard, *Beyond Futility*

Children's Ten Commandments for Parents

1. My hands are small; please don't expect perfection whenever I make a bed, draw a picture, or throw a ball. My legs are short; slow down so that I can keep up with you.

2. My eyes have not seen the world as yours have; let me explore it safely; don't restrict me unnecessarily.

3. Housework will always be there; I'm little only for a short time. Take time to explain things to me about this wonderful world, and do so willingly.

4. My feelings are tender; don't nag me all day long (you would not want to be nagged for your inquisitiveness). Treat me as you would like to be treated.

5. I am a special gift from God; treasure me as God intended you to do— holding me accountable for my actions, giving me guidelines to live by, and disciplining me in a loving manner.

6. I need your encouragement (but not your empty praise) to grow. Go easy on the criticism; remember, you can criticize the things I do without criticizing me.

7. Give me the freedom to make decisions concerning myself. Permit me to fail, so that I can learn from my mistakes. Then someday I'll be prepared to make the decisions life will require of me.

8. Don't do things over for me; that makes me feel my efforts didn't measure up to your expectations. I know it's hard, but don't compare me with my brother or my sister.

9. Don't be afraid to leave for a weekend together. Kids need vacations from parents, and parents need vacations from kids. Besides, it's a great way to show us kids that your marriage is something special.

10. Take me to Sunday school and church regularly, setting a good example for me to follow. I enjoy learning more about God.

—Kevin Lehman, quoted in "Dear Abby,"
Independent Press Telegram, January 12, 1981

A Parent's Prayer

O FATHER, help me to treat my children as You have treated me. Make me sensitive to their needs and frustrations. Help me to listen with attention, insight, and understanding to what they have to say. Help me to treat them as a person of Your design and therefore of real worth. Help me to respect . . . their times to talk without interrupting or contradicting them . . . their ideas . . . their need for freedom to make choices and to take responsibilities as they are able. O, give me the wisdom and understanding to teach my children as You have taught me.

Let me not forget they are children and not little adults, being patient and helpful as they are developing skills and mental abilities and to allow them mistakes and accidents without laughing at or belittling them.

Thank You for the provision of my need as a parent in charge of this flock of God. Thank You that in the Lord Jesus You have given all I need to be what I ought as a Christian parent.

—Anonymous

DURING MY DAYS IN SEMINARY there was a young man there with a very large birthmark across his face. It was crimson, or perhaps a bright, ruby red, that stretched from the eyelid on one side across part of the lips and mouth, down across the neck and into the chest area below the neck. We were fairly close friends. I asked him on one occasion how in the world he overcame that mark. I mean, he used to make his living in front of the public with that birthmark.

His response was unforgettable. He said, "Oh, it was my dad. You see my dad told me from my earliest days, 'Son, that's where an angel kissed you, and he marked you out just for me. You are very special, and whenever we are in a group, I'll know which one you are. You're mine.'" He said, "It got to where I felt sorry for people that didn't have red marks across the front of their face."

CHILDREN

(Also see *Family, Siblings*)

BRUCE LARSON TELLS about being at a family reunion and hearing a wonderful true story from his daughter. Her sister-in-law is a conservationist, and she and her husband and young son were driving up the coast of Florida on a vacation. They noticed a sign saying Naturist Camp and assumed that was the same as a naturalist camp. They drove in, parked their car, and headed toward the beach. They quickly realized that this naturist camp was actually a nudist camp when they came upon a group of people, all stark naked, cycling along the beach. Their five-year-old son stopped and stared in amazement. "Look, Mom and Dad," he said pointing, "they're not wearing safety helmets." Their obvious condition went unnoticed.

—Bruce Larson, *What God Wants to Know*

ONE OF THE BOOKS in my library is a little book of children's letters written to God. They have some interesting questions such as, "Dear God, who drew lines around the states?" Some are also thoughtful. "What does God do for fun?" And, "Is there a God for God?"

REMEMBER WAITING FOR THAT FIRST BABY—the anticipation of bringing home this soft, cuddly, wonderful, delightful infant? And finally the birth and everything's fine and a day or so later you come home. The first week you realize what you really have is a cross between "The Terminator" and "The Swamp Thing." I mean, this creature sleeps when you're awake and is wide awake when you're asleep, and has a set of lungs to drown out a Concord jet. My wife used to say, "Honey, I'm sort of forgetting what our baby's face looks like, I'm spending so much time at the other end."

What Is a Boy?

BETWEEN THE INNOCENCE OF BABYHOOD and the dignity of manhood we find a delightful creature called a boy. Boys come in assorted sizes, weights, and colors, but all boys have the same creed: to enjoy every second of every minute of every hour of every day, and to protest with noise (their only weapon) when their last minute is finished and the adult males pack them off to bed at night.

Boys are found everywhere—on top of, underneath, inside of, climbing on, swinging from, running around, or jumping to. Mothers love them, little girls hate them, older sisters and brothers tolerate them, adults ignore them, and Heaven protects them.

A boy is Truth with dirt on its face, Beauty with a cut on its finger, Wisdom with bubble gum in its hair, and the Hope of the future with a frog in its pocket.

When you are busy, a boy is an inconsiderate, bothersome, intruding jungle of noise. When you want him to make a good impression, his brain turns to jelly or else he becomes a savage, sadistic jungle creature bent on destroying the world, and himself with it.

A boy is a composite—he has the appetite of a horse, the digestion of a sword-swallower, the energy of a pocket-size atomic bomb, the curiosity of a cat, the lungs of a dictator, the imagination of a Paul Bunyan, the shyness of a violet, the audacity of a steel trap, the enthusiasm of a fire-cracker, and when he makes something he has five thumbs on each hand.

He likes ice cream, knives, saws, Christmas, comic books, the boy across the street, woods, water (in its native habitat), large animals, trains, Saturday mornings, and fire engines.

He is not much for Sunday school, company, schools, books without pictures, music lessons, neckties, barbers, girls, overcoats, adults, or bedtime.

Nobody else gets so much fun out of trees, dogs, and breezes. Nobody else can cram into one pocket a rusty knife, a half-eaten apple, three feet of string, two gumdrops, six cents, a slingshot, a chunk of unknown substance, and a genuine supersonic code ring with a secret compartment.

A boy is a magical creature—you can lock him out of your workshop, but you can't lock him out of your heart. You can get him out of your study, but you can't get him out of your mind.

You might as well give up. He is your captor, your jailer, your boss, and your master—a freckle-faced, pint-sized, cat-chasing bundle of noise. But when your dreams tumble down and the world is a mess, he can put together the broken pieces in just a twinkling, with a few magic words . . . "I love you."

—Dale Evans Rogers, *Time Out, Ladies!*

AN EPISCOPAL CHURCH, in one of its publications, revealed some answers given to church school questions by children. They're beautifully incorrect.

One answered, "Noah's wife was Joan of Arc."

The fifth commandment? "The fifth commandment is to humor your mother and father."

One of my favorites: Lot's wife?

"Lot's wife was a pillar of salt by day and a ball of fire by night."

They were studying church history, and one child said, "The Pope lives in a vacuum."

One little girl said, "A Christian can have only one wife. This is called monotony."

—*The Beacon,* St. Timothy's Episcopal Church

What Is a Girl?

LITTLE GIRLS ARE THE NICEST THINGS that happen to people. They are born with a little bit of angel-shine about them and though it wears thin sometimes, there is always enough left to lasso your heart—even when they are sitting in the mud, or crying temperamental tears, or parading up the street in Mother's best clothes.

A little girl can be sweeter (and badder) oftener than anyone else in the world. She can jitter around, and stomp, and make funny noises that frazzle your nerves, yet just when you open your mouth, she stands there, demure, and with that special look in her eyes.

A girl is Innocence playing in the mud, Beauty standing on its head, and Motherhood dragging a doll by the foot.

Girls are available in five colors—black, white, red, yellow or brown, yet Mother Nature always manages to select your favorite color when you place an order. They disprove the law of supply and demand—there are millions of little girls, but each is as precious as rubies.

God borrows from many creatures to make a girl. He uses the song of a bird, the squeal of a pig, the stubbornness of a mule, the antics of a monkey, the spryness of a grasshopper, the curiosity of a cat, the speed of a gazelle, the slyness of a fox, the softness of a kitten, and to top it all off He adds the mysterious mind of a woman.

A little girl likes new shoes, party dresses, small animals, first grade, noisemakers, the girl next door, dolls, make-believe, dancing lessons, ice cream, coloring books, makeup, cans of water, going visiting, tea parties, and one boy.

She doesn't care much for visitors, boys in general, large dogs, hand-me-downs, straight chairs, vegetables, snowsuits, or staying in the front yard. She is the loudest when you are thinking, the prettiest when she has provoked you, the busiest at bedtime, the quietest when you want to show her off, and the most flirtatious when she absolutely must not get the best of you again.

Who else can cause you more grief, joy, irritation, satisfaction, embarrassment, and genuine delight than this combination of Eve, Salome, and Florence Nightengale?

She can muss up your home, your hair, and your dignity—then, just when your patience is ready to crack, her sunshine peeks through and you're lost again.

Yes, she is a nerve-wracking nuisance, just a noisy bundle of mischief. But when your dreams tumble down and the world is a mess—when it seems you are pretty much of a fool after all—she can make you a king when she climbs on your knee and whispers, "I love you best of all!"

—Dale Evans Rogers, *Time Out, Ladies*

A MOTHER OF THREE unruly preschoolers was asked whether she would have children if she had to do it all over again. "Sure," she responded, "just not the same three."

—*Preaching* magazine, May–June 1990

RUNNING AWAY FROM HOME is nothing new. I remember reading a little quip not long ago of a young fellow who had his pack over his back and was walking hurriedly down the road. A policeman drove by and asked him, "Sonny, what are you doing?" The little boy said, "I'm running away from home." "Why are you doing that?" "Because Mother and Dad won't mind me anymore," was the young fellow's reply.

SOMETIMES MEMORIES with your young children are absolutely hilarious. I think back to an incident around the Swindoll supper table. Before supper began I suggested to Curtis (who was six) that he should serve Charissa (who was four) before he served himself. Naturally, he wondered why, since the platter of chicken sat directly in front of him . . . and he was hungry as a lion. I explained it is polite for fellas to serve girls before they serve themselves. The rule sounded weird, but he was willing . . . as long as she didn't take too long.

Well, you'd never guess what occurred. After prayer, he picked up the huge platter, held it for his sister, and asked which piece of chicken she wanted.

She relished all this attention. Being quite young, however, she had no idea which piece to take. So, very seriously, she replied, "I'd like the foot."

He glanced in my direction, frowned as the hunger pains shot through his stomach, then looked at her and said, "Uh . . . Charissa, Mother doesn't cook the foot!"

To which she replied, "Where is it?"

With increased anxiety he answered (a bit louder), "I don't know! The foot is somewhere else, not on this platter. Look, choose a piece. Hurry up."

She studied the platter and said, "OK, just give me the hand."

By now their mother and father were biting their lips to refrain from laughing out loud. We would have intervened, but decided to let them work it out alone. That's part of the training process.

"A chicken doesn't have a hand, it has a wing, Charissa."

"I hate the wing, Curtis . . . Oh, go ahead and give me the head."

By then I was headed for the bathroom. I couldn't hold my laughter any longer. Curtis was totally beside himself. His sister was totally frustrated, not being able to get the piece she wanted.

Realizing his irritation with her and the absence of a foot or hand or head, she finally said in an exasperated tone, "Oh, all right! I'll take the belly button!"

That did it. He reached in, grabbed a piece, and said, "That's the best I can do!" He gave her the breast, which was about as close to the belly button as he could get.

Fun. Just plain ol' nutty times when hearty laughs and silly remarks dull the edge of life's razor-sharp demands and intensity. Families and fun go together like whipped cream on a hot fudge sundae.

—Charles R. Swindoll, *Come Before Winter*

ONE OF THE REASONS I love to be around children is because they make me laugh. And I guess that's why I like certain people that interview children. Danny Kaye is one of the best. Bill Cosby is another great one. But the best is, no doubt, Art Linkletter. And Art Linkletter can get children to say, as he puts it, "the darndest things." He remembers a three-year-old girl with big, brown eyes whom he asked, "What do you do to help your mother?" "I help my mom cook brefas," she replied. "Well, how do you help your mom with brefas?" Art asked. She didn't hesitate: "I put the toast in the toaster, but she won't let me flush it!"

Art asked one grammar school youth what his father did for a living. The boy took the microphone as if it were an ice cream cone. "My dad's a cop! He catches crooks and burglars and spread-eagles 'em and puts cuffs on 'em and takes 'em down to the station and puts 'em in the slammer." "Wow," Art replied, "I bet your mother gets worried about his work, doesn't she?" "Heck no!" the youth assured Art. "He brings her lots of watches and rings and jewelry."

I really like the one where he interviewed the kid and said, "Now let me give you a situation. You're the pilot of a commercial airliner. And you've got 250 passengers. And you're flying to Hawaii. You're out over the ocean and all four engines go out. What would you do?" The little kid stood there and thought and he said, "I would press the fasten-seat-belt button and parachute!"

—Denis Waitley, *Seeds of Greatness*

CHRISTIANS

A REAL CHRISTIAN is an odd number anyway. He feels supreme love for One whom he has never seen, talks familiarly every day to Someone he cannot see, expects to go to heaven on the virtue of Another, empties himself in order to be full, admits he is wrong so he can be declared right, goes down in order to get up, is strongest when he is weakest, richest when he is poorest, and happiest when he feels worst. He dies so he can live, forsakes in order to have, gives away so he can keep, sees the invisible, hears the inaudible, and knows that which passeth knowledge.

—A. W. Tozer, *The Root of the Righteous*

> To dwell above with saints we love,
> That will be grace and glory.
> But to live below with saints we know,
> Well, that's another story!

—Henry R. Brandt, quoted in *Baker's Pocket Book of Religious Quotes*

THE STORY IS TOLD of Martin Luther one day answering a knock at his door. "Does Dr. Martin Luther live here?" the man asked. "No," Luther answered, "he died. Christ lives here now."

—Larry Christenson, *The Renewed Mind*

ONE WAG WROTE, "A Christian is a man who feels repentance on Sunday for what he did Saturday and is going to do again on Monday."

—Laurence J. Peter, *Peter's Quotations*

DONALD BARNHOUSE RELATES A STORY about Dr. H. A. Ironside in his earlier ministry.

He was on his way to the Pacific Coast at a time when it still took about four days to make the trip from Chicago. In his railway car was a party of nuns, and day by day he spoke to them and they spoke to him. He would sit reading his Bible, and at times the group of nuns talked with him about spiritual things. He read some of the stories from the Word, and they were delighted with the reading. About the third day, he asked them if any one of them had ever seen a saint. They all answered they never had. Then he asked them if they would like to see a saint. They all declared they would like to very much. Then he astonished them greatly by saying, "I am a saint. I'm Saint Harry." He then opened the New Testament and showed them the truth . . . that God Almighty does not make a saint by exalting an individual, but by exalting the Lord Jesus Christ.

—Donald Grey Barnhouse, *Romans,* Vol. 1

Am I a soldier of the cross? A foll'wer of the Lamb?
And shall I fear to own His cause Or blush to speak His name?
Must I be carried to the skies On flowery beds of ease,
While others fought to win the prize And sailed though bloody seas?
Are there no foes for me to face? Must I not stem the flood?
Is this vile world a friend to grace, To help me on to God?
Sure I must fight if I would reign—Increase my courage, Lord!
I'll bear the toil, endure the pain, Supported by Thy Word.

—Isaac Watts

You are writing a gospel, a chapter each day,
By deeds that you do, by words that you say.
Men read what you write, whether faithless or true.
Say, what is the gospel according to you?

—Quoted in John R. Rice, *Poems That Preach*

My Savior and My Friend

O Jesus, I have promised
    To serve thee to the end:
Be thou for ever near me,
    My Master and my Friend!
I shall not fear the battle,
    If thou art by my side,
Nor wander from the pathway,
    If thou wilt be my Guide. . . .
O let me see thy footmarks,
    And in them plant my own!
My hope to follow duly
    Is in thy strength alone.

O guide me, call me, draw me,
Uphold me to the end!
At last in heaven receive me,
My Savior and my Friend!

—John E. Bode, *The Best Loved Hymns and Prayers of the American People*

We Really Do Need Each Other

You know something—
we're all just people who need each other.
We're all learning
    and we've all got a long journey ahead of us.
       We've got to go together
       and if it takes us until Jesus comes
    we better stay together
    we better help each other.
And I dare say
    that by the time we get there
       all the sandwiches will be gone
    and all the chocolate will be gone
       and all the water will be gone
    and all the backpacks will be empty.
But no matter how long it take us
    we've got to go together.
    Because that's how it is
    in the body of Christ.
It's all of us
    in love
       in care
          in support
             in mutuality—
    we really do need each other.

—Reuben Welch, *We Really Do Need Each Other*

CHRISTIANITY HAS NOT been tried and found wanting; it's been found difficult and not tried.

—G. K. Chesterton, quoted in *Bartlett's Familiar Quotations*

CHRISTIAN GROWTH

A YOUNG MAN who works in an aquarium explained that the most popular fish is the shark. If you catch a small shark and confine it, it will stay a size proportionate to the aquarium. Sharks can be six inches long yet fully matured. But if you turn them loose in the ocean, they grow to their normal length of eight feet. That also happens to some Christians. I've seen some of the cutest little six-inch Christians who swim around in a little puddle. But if you put them into a larger arena—into the whole creation—only then can they become great.

—*Leadership* magazine, Winter 1986

MAY NOT THE INADEQUACY of much of our spiritual experience be traced back to our habit of skipping through the corridors of the Kingdom like children through the market place, chattering about everything, but pausing to learn the true value of nothing?

—A. W. Tozer, *The Divine Conquest*

I LOVE BABIES. I think others ought to have as many as they wish. I think it's a delightful, enjoyable experience to watch babies grow up and to become little people, little men and women, adolescents, and functioning persons. But you and I know that there are some things about little babies that are not very attractive. We humor them because they're babies.

Here's a list of things: They are dependent and demanding. They are unable to feed themselves. They are unable to stay out of messes. They love to be the center of attention. They are driven by impulses, such as hunger, pain, sleep. They're irritated when they're dirty, even though they made the mess, and you've gotta clean it up. They have no manners, no control. They have little attention span, no concern for others, no abilities or skills.

Now these are natural things that are a part of babyhood. But when you see adults with those characteristics, something tragic has happened, something terribly unfunny. The Christian who is not interested in growing wants to be entertained. He wants a diet of milk when he cries for it. He wants his way. And he's gonna get it, no matter how many he will have to disrupt to get it.

You see, in order for a Christian to handle solid food, he has to have a growing, mature digestive system. He needs teeth. He needs to have an appetite that is cultivated over a period of time for deep things, for the solid things of God. Spiritual babies must grow up. Some of the most difficult people to live with in the church of Jesus Christ are those who have grown old in the Lord but haven't grown up in Him.

WHENEVER YOU SEE Christians fussing, quarreling about their own rights, complaining because they are not properly recognized, because people do not greet them as they think they should, because they do not get enough applause for what they do, put it down as the "baby" spirit coming out . . . the mature man in Christ is indifferent to praise or to blame. May God deliver us from our baby-ishness. In some churches the minister spends half his time trying to keep weak Christians quiet over little slights. If you are living for God, people cannot slight you because you will not let them. It will not make any difference to you.

—H. A. Ironside, *Act like Men*

TOO MANY CHRISTIANS live on the right side of Easter, but the wrong side of Pentecost; the right side of pardon, but the wrong side of power; the right side of forgiveness, but the wrong side of fellowship. They are out of Egypt, but have not reached the land of promise and blessing. They are still wandering about in the wilderness of frustration and dissatisfaction.

—Graham Scroggie

CHRISTMAS

(Also see *Incarnation*)

A LADY HAD A CIRCLE OF FRIENDS for whom she really wanted to buy Christmas presents. Time slipped away and it was so busy at work for her she just wasn't able to get to the store to purchase those gifts. Time was running out. So not too many days before Christmas she decided to give up on the gift idea and just buy everybody the same beautiful Christmas card. She went to the local gift store and hurriedly went through the now picked over stack of cards and found a box of fifty, just exactly what she wanted. She didn't take time to read the message, she just noticed a beautiful cover on it and there was gold around it and a floral appearance on the front of the card and she thought, That's perfect. So she signed all of them, "With all my love."

As New Year's came and she had time to go back to two or three cards she didn't send from that stack, she was shocked to read the message inside. It said, in a little rhyme, "This Christmas card is just to say, a little gift is on its way."

I THINK IT WAS MY BARBER who told me several years ago what they used to do when their kids were small. He said, "We had the most curious kids in the world. And we knew no matter what we did, they would find the gifts. So we had a deal with our neighbors. We would keep all the neighbors' presents in our closet, and we would give all of our gifts to the neighbors. Naturally the kids would peek, but we acted like we didn't know about it. And then Christmas Eve, when all the kids were asleep, we would swap and wrap all the gifts." And he said, "You should have seen my kids when they looked out in the street and saw bicycles being ridden they thought they were gonna get for their Christmas!"

ACCORDING TO A LEGEND Satan and his demons were having a Christmas party. As the demonic guests were departing, one grinned and said to Satan, "Merry Christmas, your majesty." At that, Satan replied with a growl, "Yes, keep it merry. If they ever get serious about it, we'll all be in trouble." Well, get serious about it. It is the birth of the Baby. It is the coming of God. It is the intervention of God's presence among men.

CHRISTMAS won't be Christmas without any presents.

—Louisa May Alcott, *Little Women*

CAN YOU APPRECIATE THIS CARTOON of Dennis the Menace? He rushes into the room, with his mother standing there with her mouth open, and he says, holding a big box in his hand, "We'd better tell Santa Claus to forget about the train set I asked for. I just found one on the top shelf of Dad's closet."

THE LADY HAD TAKEN HER FIVE-YEAR-OLD SON shopping at a large department store during the Christmas season. She knew it would be fun for him to see all the decorations and window displays and toys and Santa Claus. As she dragged him by the hand, twice as fast as his little legs could move, he began to fuss and cry, clinging to his mother's coat. "Good heavens, what on earth is the matter with you?" she scolded, impatiently. "I brought you with me to get in the Christmas spirit. Santa doesn't bring toys to little crybabies!"

His fussing continued as she tried to find some bargains during the last-minute rush on December 23. "I'm not going to take you shopping with me, ever again, if you don't stop that whimpering! Oh well, maybe it's because your shoes are untied and you are tripping over your own laces," she said, kneeling down in the aisle to tie his shoes.

And as she knelt down beside him, she happened to look around. For the first time, she viewed the department store through the eyes of her five-year-old. From that position there were no baubles, no bangles, beads, presents, gaily decorated display tables, or animated toys. All that could be seen was a maze of corridors too high to see above, full of giant, stovepipe legs and huge posteriors. These mountainous strangers, with feet as big as skateboards, were pushing and shoving and bumping and thumping and rushing and crushing. Rather than fun, the scene looked absolutely terrifying! She elected to take her child home and vowed to herself never to impose her version of a good time on him again. On the way out of the store, the mother noticed Santa Claus seated in a pavilion decorated like the North Pole. She knew that letting her little boy meet Santa Claus in person would go a long way toward his remembering the Christmas shopping disaster as a pleasant, rather than unpleasant, experience.

"Honey, go stand in line with the other children, and then sit up on Santa's lap," she continued. "Tell him what you want for Christmas, and smile while you're talking so we can take your picture for the family album."

Even though a Santa Claus was standing outside the store entrance ringing a bell, and although they had seen another Santa at the previous shopping center, the little five-year-old was pushed forward to enjoy a personal chat with the "real Santa."

When the strange-looking man with the beard, glasses, and red suit stuffed with pillows hoisted the little boy onto his lap, he laughed loudly and tickled the little boy in the ribs.

"And what would you like for Christmas, son?" Santa boomed jovially.

"I'd like to get down," was the little boy's response.

—Denis Waitley, *Seeds of Greatness*

ONE OF OUR TALENTED FRIENDS at Insight for Living shared this Christmas thought:

> Another year of ministry ends,
>   Relieving so many of guilt and shame;
> A sinner believes—a new life begins,
>   Because in his heart, he whispers that Name.
> Another Christmas season dawns
>   Bringing its message, ever the same:
> A mother sighs, a Baby yawns,
>   And in His heart, He whispers your name.

Eternal Christmas

In the pure soul, although it sing or pray,
The Christ is born anew from day to day;
The life that knoweth Him shall bide apart
And keep eternal Christmas in the heart.

—Elizabeth Stuart Phelps, *Masterpieces of Religious Verse*

'Twas the Day after Christmas

'Twas the day after Christmas,
    When all through the place
There were arguments and depression—
    Even Mom had a long face.

The stockings hung empty,
    And the house was a mess;
The new clothes didn't fit . . .
    And Dad was under stress.

The family was irritable,
    And the children—no one could please;
Because the instructions for the swing set
    Were written in Chinese!

The bells no longer jingled,
    And no carolers came around;
The sink was stacked with dishes,
    And the tree was turning brown.

The stores were full of people
    Returning things that fizzled and failed,
And the shoppers were discouraged
    Because everything they'd bought was now on half-price sale!

'Twas the day AFTER Christmas—
    The spirit of joy had disappeared;
The only hope on the horizon
    Was twelve bowl games the first day of the New Year!

—Charles R. Swindoll, sermon, "Since Christ Has Come . . . What's Happening?" December 27, 1992

OF ALL THE BEAUTIFUL TRADITIONS of Christmas, few are so ancient in meaning and rich in symbolism as the simple candy cane.

Its shape is the crook of the Shepherd
One of the first who came;
The lively peppermint flavor is the regal gift of spice,
The white is Jesus' purity, the red His sacrifice;
The narrow stripes are friendship and the nearness of His love
Eternal sweet compassion, a gift from God above;
The candy cane reminds us all of just how much God cared
And like His Christmas gift to us, it's meant to be broken and shared.

Santa's Prayer on Christmas Eve

The sleigh was all packed, the reindeer were fed,
But Santa still knelt by the side of his bed.

Dear Father, he prayed, Be with me tonight,
There's much work to do and my schedule is tight.

I must jump in my sleigh and streak through the sky,
Knowing full well that a reindeer can't fly.

I will visit each household before the first light,
I'll cover the world and all in one night.

With sleighbells a-ringing, I'll land on each roof,
Amid the soft clatter of each little hoof.

To get in the house is the difficult part,
So I'll slide down the chimney of each child's heart.

My sack will hold toys to grant all their wishes,
The supply will be endless, like the loaves and the fishes.

I will fill all the stockings and not leave a track,
I'll eat every cookie that is left for my snack.

I can do all these things Lord, only through You,
I just need Your blessing, then it's easy to do.

All this to honor the birth of the One,
That was sent to redeem us, Your most Holy Son.

So to all of my friends, lest Your glory I rob,
Please Lord, remind them Who gave me this job. Amen.

—Warren D. Jennings

'Twas the Night before Jesus Came

'Twas the night before Jesus came and all through the house
   Not a creature was praying, not one in the house.
Their Bibles were lain on the shelf without care
   In hopes that Jesus would not come in there.
The children were dressing to crawl into bed,
   Not once ever kneeling or bowing a head,
And Mom in her rocker with baby on her lap
   Was watching the Late Show while I took a nap.
When out of the East there arose such a clatter,
   I sprang to my feet to see what was the matter.
Away to the window I flew like a flash
   Tore open the shutters and threw up the sash!
When what to my wondering eyes should appear
   But angels proclaiming that Jesus was here.
With a light like the sun sending forth a bright ray
   I knew in a moment that this must be THE DAY!
The light of His face made me cover my head
   It was Jesus! Returning just like He had said.
And though I possessed worldly wisdom and wealth,
   I cried when I saw Him in spite of myself.
In the Book of Life which He held in His hand
   Was written the name of every saved man.
He spoke not a word as He searched for my name;
   When He said, "It's not here," my head hung in shame.
The people whose names had been written with love
   He gathered to take to His Father above.
With those who were ready He rose without sound
   While all of the rest were left standing around.
I fell to my knees, but it was too late;
   I had waited too long and thus sealed my fate.
I stood and I cried as they rose out of sight.
   Oh, if only I had been ready tonight.
In the words of this poem the meaning is clear;

The coming of Jesus is soon drawing near.
There's only one life and when comes the last call—-
We'll find that the Bible was true after all!

—Anonymous

SOMETIME CHRISTMAS GIFTS are real surprises. Maybe you've had that experience. When I was a kid, I wanted a basketball so bad I could scream. I dropped all kinds of hints. I made false phone calls to my mother in another voice, telling her that her son really ought to have a basketball. I found the cheapest prices. I dropped those on the breakfast table. You know, all those things. And finally there appeared under the Christmas tree a box, looked just the size of a basketball. Whew! I could just feel myself making shots with it. Christmas Day came. I tore into that thing! And it was a world globe. Have you ever tried to dribble a world globe? I mean, you can't even inflate the dumb thing. Unbelievable surprise! Didn't look at all like what I expected!

CHURCH

(Also see *Worship*)

THE MINISTRY OF THE CHURCH is a ministry of people. When a church lives, it lives because the people within are vital and active. When a church dies, it withers and dies not because the brick and mortar and carpet and pews get old and begin to crack and rip and crumble. A church withers and dies because the people wither and die.

I think a vivid illustration of this comes from a true story of a young minister in Oklahoma who went to this little, though long-standing, church in hopes of really reviving the ministry of it. He had stars in his eyes and great hopes for the future. He thought he could turn it around. And he gave it his best effort and his best shot week after week, to no avail.

Finally, he had one last idea, and it seemed to work. He announced in the local newspaper on Saturday that the church had died, and on Sunday afternoon there would be a funeral service at the church itself, and all who wished could attend. For the first time in his years there the place was packed. In fact, people were standing outside on tiptoes looking through the window to see this most unusual funeral service for a church.

To their shock, because most of them got there twenty or thirty minutes early to get a seat, there was a casket down front. And it was smothered with flowers. He told the people as soon as the eulogy was finished they could pass by and view the remains of the dearly beloved that they were putting to rest that day. They could hardly wait until he finished the eulogy. He slowly opened the casket, pushed the flowers aside, and people walked by, filed by, one by one, to look in and leave sheepishly, feeling guilty as they walked out the door, because inside the casket he had placed a large mirror. As they walked by, they saw the church that had died.

—Lloyd Cory, *Quote Unquote*

LEADERSHIP MAGAZINE, known for its choice cartoons about the church, made all of us smile with understanding as one particular scene pictured a grim-faced preacher pausing during his sermon delivery and reading a note that said, "We interrupt this sermon to inform you that the fourth-grade boys are now in complete control of their Sunday school class and are holding Miss Moseby hostage."

—*Leadership* magazine, Summer 1981

THE CHURCH WORSHIP SERVICE is a huddle. We run the plays during the week. The game is not won in the huddle.

TOO OFTEN CHURCH SERVICES are the kind pictured in the story of the father who was showing his son through a church building. They came to a plaque on the wall and the little boy asked, "Daddy, what's this for?" His father said, "Oh, that's a memorial to those who died in the service." The little boy said, "Which service, Daddy, the morning service or the evening service?"

—Ray Stedman, *What More Can God Say?*

A city full of churches
Great preacher, lettered men,
Grand music, choirs and organs;
If these all fail, what then?
Good workers, eager, earnest,
Who labour hour by hour:
But where, oh where, my brother,
Is God's Almighty power?

Refinement: education!
They want the very best.
Their plans and schemes are perfect,
They give themselves no rest;
They get the best of talent,
They try their uttermost,
But what they need, my brother,
Is God the Holy Ghost!

—Samuel Stevenson, quoted in John R. Rice, *Poems That Preach*

A CHURCH WITHOUT LOVE is more tragic than a house without life. Alfred Joyce Kilmer wrote a poem. Here's a paraphrase of that poem.

Whenever I walk through Asia,
Along the harbor blue,
I go by a great big church house
With its people strong and true.
I suppose I've passed it a hundred times,
But today I stopped for a minute
And looked at that church—
That tragic church,
The church with no love for me in it.

Another variation/paraphrase was given:

Whenever I walk through the southland
Along the Fullerton track,
I go by a big congregation
With its cars parked in front and in back.
I suppose I've passed one hundred times,
But today I stopped for a minute
And I looked in that church with its thousands of folks—
That church needing my love within it.

ON A DANGEROUS SEACOAST notorious for shipwrecks, there was a crude little lifesaving station. Actually, the station was merely a hut with only one boat. But the few devoted members kept a constant watch over the turbulent sea. With little thought for themselves, they would go out day and night tirelessly searching for those in danger as well as the lost. Many, many lives were saved by this brave band of men who faithfully worked as a team in and out of the life-saving station. By and by, it became a famous place.

Some of those who had been saved as well as others along the seacoast wanted to become associated with this little station. They were willing to give their time and energy and money in support of its objectives. New boats were purchased. New crews were trained. The station that was once obscure and crude and virtually insignificant began to grow.

Some of its members were unhappy that the hut was so unattractive and poorly equipped. They felt a more comfortable place should be provided. Therefore emergency cots were replaced with lovely furniture. Rough, hand-made equipment was discarded, and sophisticated, classy systems were installed. The hut, of course, had to be torn down to make room for all the additional equipment, furniture, systems, and appointments.

By its completion, the lifesaving station had become a popular gathering place, and its objectives began to shift. It was now used as sort of a clubhouse, an attractive building for public gatherings. Saving lives and feeding the hungry and strengthening the fearful and calming the disturbed rarely occurred by now.

Fewer members were now interested in braving the sea on lifesaving mis-sions, so they hired professional lifeboat crews to do the work. The original goal of the station wasn't altogether forgotten, however. The lifesaving motifs still prevailed in the club's decorations. In fact, there was a liturgical lifeboat pre-served in the "Room of Sweet Memories" with soft, indirect lighting, which helped hide the layer of dust upon the once-used vessel.

About this time a large ship was wrecked off the coast and the boat crews brought in loads of cold, wet, and half-drowned people. They were dirty. Some were terribly sick and lonely. Others were black and they were "different" from the majority of the club members. The beautiful new club suddenly became messy and cluttered. A special committee saw to it that a shower house was immediately built "outside" and "away from" the club so victims of shipwreck could be cleaned up "before" coming inside the club.

At the next meeting there were strong words and angry feelings, which resulted in a division among the members. Most of the people wanted to stop the club's lifesaving activities altogether and place all involvements with ship-wreck victims somewhere else. "It's too unpleasant," they said. "It's a hindrance to our social life. It's opening the doors to folks who are not 'our kind.'"

Well, as you would expect, some still insisted upon saving lives, that this was their primary objective. Their only reason for existence was ministering to "anyone" needing help regardless of their club's beauty or size or decorations.

Well, they were voted down and they were told if they still wanted to be involved in saving lives of various kinds of people who were shipwrecked in those waters, they could begin their own lifesaving station down the coast! And so they did.

As years passed, the new station experienced the same old changes. It evolved into just another club. And yet another lifesaving station was begun. History continued to repeat itself. And if you visit that coast today, you'll find a large number of exclusive, impressive clubs along the shoreline owned and operated by slick professionals who have lost all involvement with the saving of lives.

Shipwrecks still occur in those waters, you understand, but now most of the victims are not saved. Every day they perish at sea, and so few seem to care . . . so very few.

—Charles R. Swindoll, *Growing Strong in the Seasons of Life*

THE GATES OF HELL will never prevail against the church . . . partly because it's so diversified you can't get a handle on it.

IT'S WONDERFUL TO BE IN A FOXHOLE with someone else. Mutual fellowship stirs others to good works. I was at a church in Reno that had a sign at the driveway as you exited from the church that said, "Now entering the mission field."

WHEN I WAS LITTLE we used to play church. We'd get chairs into rows, fight over who'd be preacher, vigorously lead the hymn singing, and generally have a great carnal time.

The aggressive kids naturally wanted to be up front, directing or preaching. The quieter ones were content to sit and be entertained by the up-fronters.

Occasionally we'd get mesmerized by a true sensationalistic crowd-swayer— like the girl who said, "Boo! I'm the Holy Ghost!" But in general, if the up-fronters were pretty good, they could hold their audience quite a while. If they weren't so good, eventually the kids would drift off to play something else—like jump rope or jacks.

Now that generation has grown up, but most of them haven't changed too much. Every Sunday they still play church. They line up in rows for the entertainment. If it's pretty good, their church may grow. If it's not too hot, eventually they'll drift off to play something else—like yachting or wife swapping.

—Anne Ortlund, *Up with Worship*

CHURCH—FELLOWSHIP

THE NEIGHBORHOOD BAR is possibly the best counterfeit there is to the fellowship Christ wants to give his church. It's an imitation, dispensing liquor instead of grace, escape rather than reality, but it is a permissive, accepting, and inclusive fellowship. It is unshockable. It is democratic. You can tell people secrets and they usually don't tell others or even want to. The bar flourishes not because most people are alcoholics, but because God has put into the human heart the desire to know and be known, to love and be loved, and so many seek a counterfeit at the price of a few beers.

With all my heart I believe that Christ wants his church to be unshockable, democratic, permissive—a fellowship where people can come in and say, "I'm sunk!" "I'm beat!" "I've had it!" Alcoholics Anonymous has this quality. Our churches too often miss it.

—Keith Miller and Bruce Larson, *Edge of Adventure*

CHURCH—GROWTH

DON'T BE AFRAID OF SIZE. I encourage pastors, when the Lord for some reason chooses you to be a part of a movement where growth, His kind of multiplying growth, occurs, don't fight it. Now, don't manipulate it. Don't act as though you're responsible for it. But you have to respond to it just like a family.

I mean, imagine your being a couple and you don't have children. And you try to have children. You go to the doctor and do what he advises. And you may pay sizable amounts of money to try to begin your family. And nothing works. You've been married eleven, twelve, maybe thirteen years, and you decide, "Look. We're gonna have to adopt if we're gonna have kids." So you go through that procedure. Takes another year or two.

Lo and behold, the Lord leads in a wonderful way. You don't just get one, you get twins. You bring them home and two months later, your wife is pregnant. It's happened before. You find out, to the surprise of you and your neighbors, that there are two heartbeats. She's carrying twins.

You've got this little apartment that you've been doing real well in, but now you need a condominium because you need more bedrooms. After the move and the birth of the new twins, maybe fifteen months later, you're gonna have triplets—three heartbeats. Now you're moving your family into a house. One day your wife says, "Honey, sit down. I've just found out something. We're gonna have twins." You have got a big family. And all the way along you've been adding bunk beds, room additions, another move. You've adjusted and adapted.

You've gotta do the same thing in a church. Adjust and adapt with growth.

OUR CHALLENGE is to stay up with the time, to serve our generation, yet in no way alter the truths of His Word. Styles and methods change and must be kept up to date. But truth? It is timeless. Not subject to change. . . . *We are to be willing to leave the familiar without disturbing the essentials.* To minister effectively the church must wake up to what changes . . . and what doesn't. . . . The church that sits around frowning at the future, doing little more than polishing yesterday's apples, will become a church lacking in relevance and excitement. At the same time, the church that softens its stand theologically and alters Scripture to fit the future's style, will lose its power.

—Charles R. Swindoll, *The Bride*

PETE: THIS MEETING has been called at the request of Matt, John, Tom, and Little Jim. Bart, will you please open with prayer?

Bart: Almighty God, we ask Your blessing on all we do and say and earnestly pray that You will see our side as Your side. Amen.

Pete: Jesus, we have been following you around for some time, and we are getting concerned about the attendance figures. Tom, how many were on the hill yesterday?

Tom: Thirty-seven.

Pete: It's getting to be ridiculous. You're going to have to pep things up. We expect things to happen.

John: I'd like to suggest you pull off more miracles. That walking on water bit was the most exciting thing I have ever seen, but only a few of us saw it. If a thousand or so had a chance to witness it, we would have more than we could handle on the hill.

Little Jim: I agree. The healing miracles are terrific, but only a limited number really get to see what has happened. Let's have more water to wine, more fish and chips (it never hurts to fill their stomachs), still more storms, give more signs. This is what the people need.

Pete: Right. And another thing, publicity is essential, and you tell half the people you cure to keep it quiet. Let the word get around.

Matt: I'm for miracles, but I want to hear a few stories I can understand. This "those who have ears to hear, let them hear" business just clouds the issue.

You have to make it clear or most of us aren't going to be able to take anything home.

Big Jim: I'd like to offer an order of service. First a story, then a big miracle followed by an offering, then maybe a saying or something, followed by a small miracle to bring them back next time. Oh yes, and a prayer if you'd like.

Tom: We have to do something.

Little Jim: That's for sure. Attendance has been awful.

Judas: I'd like to say if we are going to continue to meet in this upper room, we ought to do something about the carpet . . .

—Richard K. Wallarab, *Christianity Today,* January 17, 1979

CHURCH—PROBLEMS

IF YOU WANT TO JOIN a church with no problems . . . don't—you'll ruin it.

WHEN MY WIFE, CYNTHIA AND I RETURNED home from a combination of ministry and vacation in the summer of 1992, we opened the front door and were met with an awful stench. We hoped that it was bad food in the refrigerator. It wasn't. We thought it might be something left in one of the trash containers in the house, or maybe something had died in the garage. After a quick but thorough search, that wasn't it either. After spending a terrible night downstairs, she on the sofa and I in the rocker, because the upstairs was unbearable, we determined it had to be coming from the attic.

Well, I was led to call our oldest son, who came. It happened to be one of those 100-degree days in August. He was thumping around upstairs in the attic and to his shock, and to our amazement, he discovered the problem was a very large and very dead possum in the attic that had burst and was crawling with maggots.

"Dad!" he yelled from way across the attic. "Dad, it's like a Stephen King novel! It's so big it doesn't even fit between the rafters and it's just running all over!"

So we got a cardboard box and I held a plastic bag to put over it. Our son slid the box in my direction and I tied this plastic bag round it and took it down to the dumpster. What we didn't know was that when you get rid of the carcass, you don't get rid of the maggots and you don't get rid of the smell, because that stuff has soaked into the sheet rock and the wood up there.

I've been told that if you have a refrigerator that stinks, you get a big box of baking soda. I bought six big boxes of baking soda and my son went back up into the attic one more time. When he came down he said, "That's it, Dad. Whatever else needs doing, it's yours!"

Well, the six big containers of baking soda just became a white stink. Didn't do anything to the smell, just changed the color of the yuck.

All the while, you understand, this was right above our master bedroom closet where the doors have been closed all through these hot days. And naturally our clothes were kept in our closet. We took everything out and dumped it on the bed. . . . a mess, but I don't want to get sidetracked.

A month later the stench was still there. We had gotten rather comfortable on the sofa and the chair downstairs by now. But also by now, the maggots moved down through the wall and into our bedroom and then down into our kitchen and family room. And they snuggled into the fur of the carpet, like they thought it was the fur of an animal. So we tried to vacuum 'em up. This is the way we spent the last part of our vacation.

If you don't know, maggots turn into flies. And so the following week our home was swarming with thousands of filthy flies.

The final part of this story is that we located a chemical that would take care of the stink. It's called, Scout's honor, Anti-Icky-Poo. I promise you. I had a gallon of it inside the house and another gallon in the attic, poured all over the soda and all over the spot. It's supposed to take the smell away.

What does this story have to do with the subject of the church? Something tragic has happened in the last few years in the church that has caused the world to realize that their worst suspicions were true, that there is something dead in the attic of the church. There is a stench of compromised integrity, of scandal, of deception. We who live in the church need to address the problem, not ignore it, and set about to take every necessary action to keep our house clean.

I READ OF A FATHER who was in his study reading, and he heard a commotion outside the window. It was his daughter who was playing with her friends. And it got louder and it got louder and more heated and more argumentative, until finally he could restrain himself no longer. And he pushed the window open and said, "Stop it. Honey, what's wrong?" And after the reprimand she responded quickly, "But, Daddy, we were just playing church."

—Leslie Flynn, *Great Church Fights*

COMMITMENT

THE FOLLOWING LETTER was written by a young communist to his girl-friend, breaking off the relationship with her because of his devotion to the communist cause. The letter was given to her pastor who in turn sent it to Dr. Billy Graham. He published it.

We communists have a high casualty rate. We are the ones who get shot and hung and ridiculed and fired from our jobs and in every other way made as uncomfortable as possible. A certain percentage of us get killed or imprisoned. We live in virtual poverty. We turn back to the party every penny we make above what is absolutely necessary to keep us alive.

We communists do not have the time or the money for many movies or concerts or T-bone steaks or decent homes or new cars. We've been described as fanatics. We are fanatics. Our lives are dominated by one great, overshadowing factor: the struggle for world communism. We have a philosophy of life which no amount of money could buy. We have a cause to fight for, a definite purpose in life. We subordinate our petty personal selves into a great movement of humanity; and if our personal lives seem hard or our egos appear to suffer through subordination to the party, then we are adequately compensated by the thought that each of us, in his small way, is contributing to something new and true and better for mankind.

There is one thing in which I am in dead earnest about, and that is the communist cause. It is my life, my business, my religion, my hobby, my sweetheart, my wife, my mistress, my bread and meat. I work at it in the daytime and dream of it at night. Its hold on me grows, not lessens, as time goes on; therefore, I cannot carry on a friendship, a love affair, or even a conversation without relating it to this force which both drives and guides my life. I evaluate people, looks, ideas, and actions according to how they affect the communist cause, and by their attitude toward it. I've already been in jail because of my ideals, and if necessary, I'm ready to go before a firing squad.

—"Call to Commitment" by Billy Graham

WHEREVER YOU ARE, be all there. Live to the hilt every situation you believe to be the will of God.

—Jim Elliot, quoted in Elisabeth Elliot, *Through Gates of Splendor*

IT'S TOUGH TO LIVE A FOCUSED LIFE. From every direction, something or someone clamors for our attention. A distraction draws our eyes and the next thing we know, we've swerved off the road and headed down another detour.

One Chicago youth pastor came up with a clever way to keep his group on track. Concerned that the balmy beaches of Florida—the site of their upcoming evangelism trip—would lure the teens from their purpose, he fashioned a cross from two pieces of lumber. Just before they climbed on the bus, he showed it to the group.

"I want all of you to remember that the whole purpose of our going is to glorify the name of Christ, to lift up the Cross—the message of the Cross, the emphasis of the Cross, the Christ of the Cross," he announced. "So we're going to take this cross wherever we go."

The teenagers looked at one another, a little unsure of his plan. But they agreed to do it and dragged the cross on the bus. It banged back and forth in the aisle all the way to Florida. It went with them into restaurants. It stayed overnight where they stayed overnight. It stood in the sand while they ministered on the beach.

At first, lugging the cross around embarrassed the kids. But later, it became a point of identification. That cross was a constant, silent reminder of who they were and why they had come. They eventually regarded carrying it as an honor and privilege.

The night before they went home, the youth leader handed out two nails to each of the kids. He told them that if they wanted to commit themselves to what the cross stood for, they could hammer one nail into it and keep the other with them. One by one, the teens drove their nail into the cross.

About fifteen years later, one fellow—now a stockbroker—called the youth leader. He told him that he still keeps that nail with him in his desk drawer. Whenever he loses his sense of focus, he looks at the nail and remembers the cross on that beach in Florida. It reminds him of what is at the core of his life— his commitment to Jesus Christ.

ONCE WHEN I STOPPED by to pick up one of the children that was part of our church family for a skating trip, the folks were in the middle of hanging wallpaper together. After inquiring, "How are things going?" the husband and I chatted a little. I reminded him, "There are three stages couples go through that hang wallpaper together." First stage is: You talk about separation. The second stage: You separate. And if you keep hanging wallpaper, divorce proceedings are underway. He jokingly said, "I think we're in the third stage right now." We chuckled and then he commented, "You know what keeps our home together? Commitment. I am committed to her." All of a sudden things got really quiet. And I thought about that word. Commitment—you don't hear much about it today. Stay at it! Stay at it!

RAYMOND BROWN writes of David's followers: "Their duty at that moment was to obey the king's instructions and to trust his wisdom. It meant that they were going into a life of hardship, insecurity, privation, suffering, and possibly death, but they would be with the king, and that was enough."

—Raymond Brown, *Skillful Hands: Studies in the Life of David*

I HAD PREACHED a morning sermon that had a real appeal in it for us to get serious about this matter of committing ourselves to the ministry of this church. And I said to the congregation that making a vow to God is a serious thing, that we do not play games when it comes to giving God a promise.

Now unknown to most of the people in the congregation, there's a fellow in our church who had boat fever. He'd been down to the ocean and he'd picked out the boat that he felt God wanted him to have. His wife didn't have the same leading, but he felt that he had God's mind in it. And all through the morning message he was really wrestling with what he should do with this matter of making a vow and letting go of things that could really hold on to him. And he squirmed a little. Then after I finished the message and had talked about giving our possessions over to God, he came to me after the service. He said, "You know, I really believe that I know what God is saying now." And I was all ready for him to say that God had made it clear to him that in this case he shouldn't get the boat. You know what he said? He said, "It's clear to me now that I should get the boat and maybe start a Sunday school class on it."

FIRMNESS GIVES CREDIBILITY to the other attributes. The gentle heart leads across obstacles only if it is also the strong heart. Crossing snowcapped Rockies, parched plains, untamed rivers, scorching deserts means developing a strategy, suffering, and using defeats as course markers. No "wilting morning glories" need apply.

—Tom Haggai, *How the Best Is Won*

COMMUNICATION

(Also see *Advice, Speech, Tongue*)

PUNCTUATION IN COMMUNICATION is important. Think about the importance of a comma in this little note: A naval wife asked the church to pray, "John Anderson, having gone to sea, his wife desires the prayers of the congregation for his safety." When read without the first two commas: "John Anderson having gone to see his wife, desires the prayers of the congregation for his safety."

—Joe LoMusio, *If I Should Die Before I Live*

A WOMAN WHO TRAVELED ABROAD without her husband got to Paris and found this fabulous bracelet she'd been looking for. And so she sent a wire back home saying, "I have found this beautiful bracelet, one I've been looking for all my life. It only costs $7,500. Do you think I can buy it?" Her husband wired back a short but firm reply, "No, price too high!" And he signed his name. But in the transmission the comma was left out and the message read, "No price too high." Oh, she was thrilled! Omitting that comma almost put that guy in a coma.

—Joe LoMusio, *If I Should Die Before I Live*

IF ALL SPEAKERS could be lined up on their backs, head to foot, they ought to be left there.

WHEN CHUCK JR. was about twelve he had a couple of ingrown toenails that had to be cut out two days before Christmas. He had to lie on his back with his feet up in the air, two big toes wrapped up in gauze, eating his heart out about missing Christmas activities. I didn't think it would be too bad for us to build a little remote control car together. That would encourage him. So that's what I got him.

Inside the box was a brochure thicker than the New Testament and printed somewhere between Tokyo and Otsuki, Japan. The guy that sold it to me said, "Piece of cake." It would take three, oh, outside, four hours to build that thing. There were twenty-nine steps to assemble that little remote control car and after six hours, we were only on step thirteen. I knew we'd had a definite "failure to communicate." If frustration could kill a salesman, he'd never know what hit him.

BECAUSE JESUS used the word "kingdom," the Pharisees took it out of context and used it to accuse Him of trying to overthrow Rome. We should quote accurately or not at all.

———————

TACT IS ONE OF THE LOST ARTS of the twentieth century, isn't it? I heard about a man who lacked tact. He was the type of person who just couldn't say it graciously. He and his wife owned a poodle. They loved this dog. It was the object of their affection. The wife was to take a trip abroad and the first day away she made it to New York. She called home and asked her husband, "How are things?" He said, "The dog's dead!" She was devastated.

After collecting her thoughts, she asked, "Why do you do that? Why can't you be more tactful?" He said, "Well, what do you want me to say? The dog died." She said, "Well, you can give it to me in stages. For example, you could say when I call you from New York, 'The dog is on the roof.' And then when I travel to London the next day and call, you could tell me, 'Honey, the dog fell off the roof.' And when I call you from Paris, you could add, 'Honey, the dog had to be taken to the vet. In fact, he's in the hospital, not doing well.' And finally, when I call you from Rome, 'Honey, brace yourself. Our dog died.' I could handle that."

The husband paused and said, "Oh, I see." Then she asked, "By the way, how's mother?" And he said, "She's on the roof."

—Michael LeBoeuf, *How to Win Customers and Keep Them for Life*

———————

BRIEF MESSAGES can be emphatic. It happened in the Second World War. It was two days before Christmas, 1944. In a little place named Bastogne in southeastern Belgium, the 101st Airborne Division of the United States Army was trapped. It was encircled by Nazi troops. There was no escape. Seven days passed, and all supply routes had been cut off, and it was just a matter of time, it seemed, before they would fall. By and by, the Nazi commander in chief decided, "Press for an unconditional surrender." The appointment was given to the major who carried the message to the commanding officer, General McAuliffe, who, in good American fashion, snatched the paper from the German, looked it over, and wrote in one word the answer, "NUTS!" And they didn't surrender. And they did, in fact, get out of there, many of them, with their lives.

—Clifton Fadiman, quoted in *The Little, Brown Book of Anecdotes*

———————

JORGE RODRIGUEZ was the meanest, orneriest bandit on the Texas-Mexico border. The guy would often slip across the line, raid the banks of South Texas, and steal 'em blind. Before they could catch him, he would race back into Mexico and hide out. No matter how hard the law tried, they could never catch him.

Finally the Texans got fed up with this nonsense and decided to put the toughest Texas Ranger they had on the case. Sure enough, that got the job done. After only a few days of searching, the Ranger found the bandit in a dingy, dusty saloon south of the border. He bolted into the bar, pulled both guns, and yelled, "Okay, stick 'em up, Jorge; you're under arrest! I know you've got the money."

Suddenly a little guy over in the corner butted in. "Wait, wait . . . just a minute, señor," he said. "Jorge does not speak English. He's my amigo, so I'll translate for you."

The Ranger explained, "Look, we know he's the bandit we've been looking for. We know he's taken thousands and thousands of dollars—about a million bucks actually. We want it back NOW. Either he pays up or I'll fill him full of holes. You tell him that!"

"Okay, okay! I'll tell him . . . I'll tell him." So the little fellow turned to Jorge and repeated in Spanish everything the Ranger had said. The Texas Ranger, not knowing a word of the language, waited for the bandit's reply.

Jorge listened, frowned, then responded in Spanish, "Okay, they got me. Tell him to go down to the well just south of town, count four stones down from the top of the well, then pull out the one loose stone. All the money I have stolen I've hidden behind the stone."

Then the clever little translator turned to the Texas Ranger and translated with a shrug, "Jorge says, 'Go ahead, you big mouth; go ahead and shoot 'cause I'm not telling you where the money is.'"

—Charles R. Swindoll, *Simple Faith*

NINE-YEAR-OLD DANNY came bursting out of Sunday school like a wild stallion. His eyes were darting in every direction as he tried to locate either his mom or dad. Finally, after a quick search, he grabbed his daddy by the leg and yelled, "Man, that story of Moses and all those people crossing the Red Sea was great!" His father looked down, smiled, and asked the boy to tell him about it.

"Well, the Israelites got out of Egypt, but Pharaoh and his army chased after them. So the Jews ran as fast as they could until they got to the Red Sea. The Egyptian army was gettin' closer and closer. So Moses got on his walkie-talkie and told the Israeli Air Force to bomb the Egyptians. While that was happening, the Israeli Navy built a pontoon bridge so the people could cross over. They made it!"

By now old dad was shocked. "Is *that* the way they taught you the story?"

"Well, no, not exactly," Danny admitted, "but if I told it to you the way they told it to us, you'd *never* believe it, Dad."

—Harold S. Kushner, *When Bad Things Happen to Good People*

IT TAKES TWO to speak the truth. One to speak and another to listen.

—Henry Thoreau

THE FOLLOWING is a series of actual quotes taken from insurance or accident forms. They are the actual words of people who tried to summarize their encounters with trouble.

- "Coming home, I drove into the wrong house and collided with a tree I don't have."
- "The other car collided with mine without giving warning of its intentions."
- "I thought my window was down, but I found it was up when I put my hand through it."
- "I collided with a stationary truck coming the other way."
- "A truck backed through my windshield into my wife's face."
- "A pedestrian hit me and went under my car."
- "The guy was all over the road; I had to swerve a number of times before I hit him."
- "I pulled away from the side of the road, glanced at my mother-in-law, and headed over the embankment."
- "In my attempt to kill a fly, I drove into a telephone pole."
- "I had been shopping for plants all day and was on my way home. As I reached an intersection, a hedge sprang up obscuring my vision. I did not see the other car."
- "I had been driving for forty years when I fell asleep at the wheel and had an accident."
- "I was on the way to the doctor's with rear end trouble when my universal joint gave way, causing me to have an accident."
- "My car was legally parked as it backed into the other vehicle."
- "An invisible car came out of nowhere, struck my vehicle, and vanished."
- "I told the police that I was not injured, but removing my hat, I found a skull fracture."
- "The pedestrian had no idea which direction to go, so I ran over him."
- "I was sure the old fellow would never make it to the other side of the road when I struck him."

- "I saw the slow-moving, sad-faced old gentleman as he bounced off the hood of my car."
- "The indirect cause of this accident was a little guy in a small car with a big mouth."
- "I was thrown from my car as it left the road. I was later found in a ditch by some stray cows."
- "The telephone pole was approaching fast. I attempted to swerve out of its path when it struck my front end."
- "I was unable to stop in time and my car crashed into the other vehicle. The driver and passenger then left immediately for a vacation with injuries."

—Charles R. Swindoll, *Come Before Winter*

I SAT DOWN at McDonald's the other day. Kids were playing around there and they'd bought small french fries to feed the birds. And it was remarkable, there was not a bird in sight. They threw one fry. Whoosh! All of a sudden they were everywhere. And I thought, What are they saying? What are they talking about? Well, they're saying, "Hey, there's a fry down here. Let's get it," however birds say it. Completely unintelligible to me. I couldn't understand a bit of it.

What the bird squawk is to the human ear, the truth of God is to the ear of the unsaved person. He can't get it.

"DON'T GARBLE the message!"

If I heard that once during Marine boot camp, I must've heard it four dozen times. Again and again, our outfit was warned against hearing one thing, then passing on a slightly different version. You know, changing the message by altering the meaning a tad. It's so easy to do, isn't it? Especially when it's filtered through several minds, then pushed through each mouth. It is amazing how the original story, report, or command appears after it has gone through its verbal metamorphosis. Consider the following.

A colonel issued this directive to his executive officer:

"Tomorrow evening approximately 2000 hours, Halley's Comet will be visible in this area, an event which occurs only once every seventy-five years. Have the men fall out in the battalion area in fatigues, and I will explain this rare phenomenon to them. In case of rain we will not be able to see anything, so assemble the men in the theater and I will show them films of it."

Executive officer to company commander:

"By the order of the colonel, tomorrow at 2000 hours, Halley's Comet will appear above the battalion area. If it rains, fall the men out in fatigues; then march to the theater where the rare phenomenon will take place, something which occurs only once every seventy-five years."

Company commander to lieutenant:

"By order of the colonel in fatigues at 2000 hours tomorrow evening, the phenomenal Halley's Comet will appear in the theater. In case of rain in the battalion area, the colonel will give another order, something which occurs once every seventy-five years."

Lieutenant to sergeant:

"Tomorrow at 2000 hours, the colonel, in fatigues, will appear in the theater with Halley's Comet, something which happens every seventy-five years. If it rains, the colonel will order the comet into the battalion area."

Sergeant to squad:

"When it rains tomorrow at 2000 hours, the phenomenal seventy-five-year-old General Halley, accompanied by the colonel, will drive his Comet through the battalion area theater in fatigues."

Charles R. Swindoll, Come Before Winter

THE DIALOGUE in Luke 10 reminds me of a true story I heard theologian Carl F. H. Henry tell as he spoke to a group of radio broadcasters. The late Dr. Reinhold Niebuhr decided to write out his theological position, stating exactly where he stood philosophically—his credo. Being the profound thinker he was (and a bit verbose), it took him many sheets of paper to express himself. Upon completion of his masterwork, he realized it was in need of being read and evaluated by a mind much more practical than his own. He bundled up the material and sent it to a minister whom he knew had a practical mind and a pastoral "heart."

With great pains the clergyman sweated through this ream of paper, trying desperately to grasp the meaning. When he finally finished, he worked up the nerve to write a brief yet absolutely candid note in reply. It read:

My dear Dr. Niebuhr:
I understand every word you have written, but I do not understand one sentence.

—Charles R. Swindoll, Compassion

BLESSED IS THE MAN who having nothing to say, abstains from giving wordy evidence of the fact. —George Eliot, Popular Quotations for All Uses

LISTEN TO THE CONVERSATIONS of our world, between nations as well as those between couples. They are for the most part dialogues of the deaf.

—Paul Tournier, *To Understand Each Other*

COMPASSION

OTHERS WILL NOT CARE how much we know until they know how much we care. As one authority puts it:

> If I just do my thing and you do yours, we stand in danger of losing each other and ourselves. . . . We are fully ourselves only in relation to each other; the I detached from a Thou disintegrates. I do not find you by chance; I find you by an active life of reaching out.
>
> —Walter Tubbs, "Beyond Pearls," *Journal of Humanistic Psychology*

A GREEK CLASS was given an assignment to study the story of the Good Samaritan in Luke 10:25–37. These young theologs were to do an in-depth analysis of the biblical text, observing and commenting on all the major terms and syntactical factors worth mentioning. Each student was to write his own translation after having done the work on his commentary.

As is true in most language classes, a couple or three of the students cared more about the practical implications of the assignment than its intellectual stimulation. The morning the work was to be turned in, these three teamed up and carried out a plan to prove their point. One volunteered to play the part of an alleged victim. They tore his shirt and trousers, rubbed mud, catsup, and other realistic-looking ingredients across his "wounds," marked up his eyes and face so he hardly resembled himself, then placed him along the path that led from the dormitory to the Greek classroom. While the other two hid and watched, he groaned and writhed, simulating great pain.

Not one student stopped. They walked around him, stepped over him, and said different things to him. But nobody stooped over to help. What do you want to bet their academic work was flawless . . . and insightful . . . and handed in on time?

This incident always reminds me of a scripture that penetrates the surface of our intellectual concerns. "This is how we know what love is: Jesus Christ laid down his life for us. And we ought to lay down our lives for our brothers. If anyone has material possessions and sees his brother in need but has no pity on him, how can the love of God be in him?" (1 John 3:16–17, NIV).

—Charles R. Swindoll, *Compassion*

EVEN THOUGH the little creatures in *Winnie the Pooh* are imaginary, we can see ourselves in them. This particular scenario reveals how downright insensitive we often are.

Pooh Bear is walking along the river bank. Eeyore, his stuffed donkey friend, suddenly appears floating downstream . . . on his back of all things, obviously troubled about the possibility of drowning.

Pooh calmly asks if Eeyore had fallen in. Trying to appear in complete control, the anguished donkey answers, "Silly of me, wasn't it." Pooh overlooks his friend's pleading eyes and remarks that Eeyore really should have been more careful.

In greater need than ever, Eeyore politely thanks him for the advice (even though he needs action more than he needs advice). Almost with a yawn, Pooh Bear notices, "I think you are sinking." With that as his only hint of hope, drowning Eeyore asks Pooh if he would mind rescuing him. So, Pooh pulls him from the river. Eeyore apologizes for being such a bother, and Pooh, still unconcerned, yet ever so courteous, responds, "Don't be silly . . . you should have said something sooner."

—Charles R. Swindoll, *Compassion*

IT IS A FAIR RULE OF THUMB that only that love of neighbor which can also draw people to Christ is truly a reflection of that love for God which is its source.

—Jeremy C. Jackson, *No Other Foundation*

A FIRST-GRADER named Billy had a classmate Jim, who lost his father in a tractor accident. Billy prayed for Jim every day. One day as Billy was walking down the stairs at school, he saw Jim and decided to reach out to him.

"How are you getting along?"

"Oh, fine, jus' fine."

Billy continued, "Do you know, I've been praying for you ever since your daddy was killed."

The other little guy stopped and looked at Billy, grabbed his hand, then led him out back behind the school building. Then he opened up.

"You know, that was a lie when I said things were going fine; they aren't fine. We are having trouble with the cows and the machines. My mother doesn't know what to do. But I didn't know you were praying for me."

Just goes to show us, doesn't it, how many people are hurting, but don't feel free to say so until we voluntarily reach out to them.

—Marion Leach Jacobsen, *Crowded Pews and Lonely People*

IN 1945 MARTIN NIEMOELLER SAID, "The Nazis came first for the Communists, and I didn't speak up because I was not a Communist. Then they came for the Jews, and I did not speak up because I was not a Jew. Then they came for the Trade Unionists, and I didn't speak up because I wasn't a Trade Unionist. Then they came for the Catholics, and I was Protestant, so I didn't speak up. Then they came for me . . . by that time there was no one to speak up for anyone."

—Laurence J. Peter, *Peter's Quotations*

Lord, why did you tell me to love all
    men as my brothers?
I have tried, but I come back to you
    frightened.
Lord, I was so peaceful at home, so
    comfortably settled.
I was well furnished, and I felt so cozy.
I was alone—I was at peace.
Sheltered from wind and the rain,
    kept clean.

—Michael Quoist, quoted in William M. Fletcher, *The Second Greatest Commandment*

COMPASSION IS NOT A SNOB gone slumming. Anybody can salve his conscience by an occasional foray into knitting for the spastic home. Did you ever take a *real* trip down inside the broken heart of a friend? To feel the sob of the soul—the raw, red crucible of emotional agony? To have this become almost as much yours as that of your soul-crushed neighbor? Then, to sit down with him—and silently weep? This is the beginning of compassion.

—Jess Moody, quoted in Lloyd Cory, *Quote Unquote*

THE GREYHOUND BUS SLOWED—then stopped. It was just a wayside stop with a garage and a small store. A young Indian stepped aboard and after he had paid his fare he sat down behind me.

It was February. We were traveling from Flagstaff, Arizona, to Albuquerque, New Mexico. The night was cold. In the warm bus the tired youth was soon asleep. But after about 20 minutes he got up and walked to the front of the bus to ask if we were near his destination.

"We passed there a long time ago," the bus driver snapped. Acknowledging he had known the boy was riding beyond his stop, he ask angrily, "Why didn't you get off?"

The quiet passenger's shoulders drooped. He turned and came back to his seat. Barely had he sat down, when he rose again and went to the driver.

"Will you stop and let me off?" he asked. "I'll walk back."

"No! It's too far and too cold. You'd freeze to death. You'll have to go into Albuquerque and then take a bus back."

Disappointment showed in his walk as he came back to his seat.

"Were you asleep?" I asked him.

"Yes, and my sister was waiting for me there." He dropped into the seat behind me.

I was returning to Wisconsin after serving a quarter term as a volunteer teacher in an Indian mission school. This experience had taught me the hard living conditions of the Indians in the area. The small adobe houses with earth floors, the lack of privacy in those little one-or-two-room houses.

The role played by teenagers was very hard. There was no room for them at home, yet they were not really ready to go out on their own.

All the while we were nearing Albuquerque, a large and strange city. I thought he must be wondering what he would do after he got there. I turned to him and asked, "Are you afraid?"

"Yes," he said, in a "hate-to-admit" way.

"Stay with me," I said, "and I'll help you get on the right bus back."

I talked to the driver: "Will you please check with the return driver, so he need not pay return fare?"

"OK," the driver reluctantly agreed.

"Everything will be all right," I told the boy. "You need not worry about anything."

His eyes said, "Thank you!" .

We rode on for possibly ten more minutes. Then a hand tapped my shoulder. I turned to see my young friend leaning toward me. In a reverent voice he asked:

"Are you a Christian?"

—Olga Wetzel, *Eternity* magazine, February 1977

WHO BETTER TO MINISTER to those who are paralyzed and confined to wheelchairs than Joni Eareckson Tada? I've told Joni, "You don't even have to speak. All you've gotta do is roll your wheelchair up to that microphone and sit and smile and you minister." And everywhere she ministers, the place is full of people in wheelchairs. Why? Because she's in one. And no one is better able to help comfort those in wheelchairs than one who has been there and is there.

THE PHONE RANG in a high society Boston home. One the other end of the line was a son who had just returned from Viet Nam and was calling from California. His folks were the cocktail-circuit, party kind—drinking, wife-swapping, gambling, all the other things that go with it. The boy said to his mother, "I just called to tell you that I wanted to bring a buddy home with me." His mother said, "Sure, bring him along for a few days." "But, mother, there is something you need to know about this boy. One leg is gone, one arm's gone, one eye's gone, and his face is quite disfigured. Is it all right if I bring him home?"

His mother said, "Bring him home for a few days." The son said, "You didn't understand me, mother. I want to bring him home to live with us." The mother began to make all kinds of excuses about embarrassment and what people would think . . . and the phone clicked.

A few hours later the police called from California to Boston. The mother picked up the phone again. The police sergeant at the other end said, "We just found a boy with one arm, one leg, one eye and a mangled face, who has just killed himself with a shot in the head. The identification papers on the body say he is your son."

—Dale E. Galloway, *Rebuild Your Life*

WHEN MY WIFE, Cynthia, and I first were led by God to change careers and enter seminary and to begin ministry as our vocational service, which was something I had resisted for the longest time, we changed our whole life. In fact, we sold our house that we had bought in the outskirts of Houston, Texas, and moved to Dallas. And we knew, really, no one.

We set up housekeeping in a little, tiny apartment. It was really a dump. I mean, it was one of those places with hot and cold running rats. You know, those places they finally just condemned. I heard a friend say not long ago, "When we lived there, there wasn't a single roach in the place. They were all married and had a litter of roaches." I mean, there were roaches everywhere. I'm glad to say it's all been torn down. But we didn't know anybody. We didn't have any money. In fact, we had a little indebtedness we had to deal with.

But unknown to us when we came, there was a man in our home church who took an interest in our lives. And he's one of the great heroes of my past. You wouldn't know him if I called his name. He'd be embarrassed if I named him publicly, and so I won't. But year after year, he paid our tuition. Not only ours, but twelve or fourteen other fellas who were there from the same church. Regularly. In fact one year he bought us all new sports coats for Christmas. Never once did I have to write him and ask for help. He saw the need and filled it.

A LEADER MUST HAVE COMPASSION. Nehemiah was such a man. Alan Redpath writes this about Nehemiah: "You never lighten the load unless first you have felt the pressure in your own soul. You are never used of God to bring blessing until God has opened your eyes and made you see things as they are." Nehemiah was called to build the wall, but first he wept over ruins.

—Alan Redpath, *Victorious Christian Service: Studies in Nehemiah*

At the Winter Feeder

His feather flame doused dull
    by icy cold,
    the cardinal hunched
    into the rough, green feeder
    but ate no seed.
    Through binoculars I saw
    festered and useless
    his beak, broken
    at the root.
Then two: one blazing, one gray,
    rode the swirling weather
    into my vision
    and lighted at his side.
    Unhurried, as if possessing
    the patience of God,
    they cracked sunflowers
    and fed him
    beak to wounded beak
    choice meats.
    Each morning and afternoon
    the winter long,
    that odd triumvirate,
    that trinity of need,

returned and ate
their sacrament
of broken seed.

—John Leax, *The Sacrament of the Broken Seed*

WHEN NARCOTICS SQUAD DETECTIVES recently raided a loft apartment in a depressed area of New York City, they came on a scene straight out of "The Beggar's Opera." Every square foot of the long, dingy apartment was crowded with human derelicts who were sleeping on the floor, or sitting huddled in corners; dimly visible overhead were a number of gay paper ceiling ornaments, left over from the days when the loft had been a dance hall. After searching the crowd, the detectives arrested six men who were carrying hypodermic needles and packets of heroin; they also arrested the derelicts' host, a mild, weedy-looking man who was charged with harboring drug addicts in his apartment.

At police headquarters, the weedy-looking man claimed he was actually well-to-do, but that he had chosen to live among the homeless in order to provide them with food, shelter, and clothing. His door, he said, was open to all, including a small minority of narcotic addicts, since he had not known it was against the law to feed and clothe people with the drug habit. Checking his story, the police found that the man was indeed neither a vagrant nor a drug addict. He was John Sargent Cram, a millionaire who had been educated at Princeton and Oxford and whose family had long been noted for its philanthropies. Wishing to avoid the rigmarole of organized charity work, Cram had simply moved into the loft and set about helping the derelicts directly, at a cost of $100 or so a day. He made a point of not giving the men money, he told the police, because it only went for cheap wine.

At a later hearing, a variety of witnesses spoke of Cram's kindness and altruism, and it was brought out that the Spanish-speaking population of the area knew him as Papa Dio— "Father God." Amid cheers in the courtroom, the Prince Myshkin-like Mr. Cram was freed on his promise that he would bar drug addicts from his loft. He later told reporters, "I don't know that my work does much good, but I don't think it does any harm. I'm quite happy, you know. I'm anything but a despondent person. Call me eccentric. Call it my reason for being. I have no other."

—Robert Raines, *Creative Brooding*

A BUSINESSMAN AND HIS WIFE were busy to the point of exhaustion. They were committed to each other, their family, their church, their work, their friends.

Needing a break, they escaped for a few days of relaxation at an oceanfront hotel. One night a violent storm lashed the beach and sent massive breakers thundering against the shore. The man lay in his bed listening and thinking about his own stormy life of never-ending demands and pressures.

The wind finally died down and shortly before daybreak the man slipped out of bed and took a walk along the beach to see what damage had been done. As he strolled, he saw that the beach was covered with starfish that had been thrown ashore and helplessly stranded by the great waves. Once the morning sun burned through the clouds, the starfish would dry out and die.

Suddenly the man saw an interesting sight. A young boy who had also noticed the plight of the starfish was picking them up, one at a time, and flinging them back into the ocean.

"Why are you doing that?" the man asked the lad as he got close enough to be heard. "Can't you see that one person will never make a difference—you'll never be able to get all those starfish back into the water. There are just too many."

"Yes, that's true," the boy sighed as he bent over and picked up another and tossed it back into the water. Then as he watched it sink, he looked at the man, and smiled, and said, "But it sure made a difference to that one."

—Denis Waitley, *Seeds of Greatness*

_____

I was hungry
    and you formed a humanities club
    and you discussed my hunger.
    Thank you.
I was imprisoned
    and you crept off quietly
    to your chapel in the cellar
    to pray for my release.
I was naked
    and in your mind
    you debated the morality of my
    appearance.
I was sick
    and you knelt and thanked God
    for your health.
I was homeless
    and you preached to me
    of the spiritual shelter of the
    love of God.

I was lonely
    and you left me alone
    to pray for me.
You seem so holy;
    so close to God.
But I'm still very hungry
    and lonely
    and cold.
So where have your prayers gone?
    What have they done?
    What does it profit a man to page through his
    book of prayers when the rest of the world is
    crying for help?

—M. Lunn, *1,500 Inspirational Quotes and Illustrations*

PEGGY NOONAN, speechwriter for Ronald Reagan, relates a story about Frances Green, an eighty-three-year old woman who lived by herself on Social Security in a town just outside San Francisco. She had little money, but for eight years she'd been sending one dollar a year to the Republican National Convention.

Then one day Frances got an RNC fund-raising letter in the mail, a beautiful piece on thick, cream-colored paper with black-and-gold lettering. It invited the recipient to come to the White House to meet President Ronald Reagan. She never noticed the little RSVP card that suggested a positive reply needed to be accompanied by a generous donation. She thought she'd been invited because they appreciated her dollar-a-year support.

Frances scraped up every cent she had and took a four-day train ride across America. Unable to afford a sleeper, she slept sitting up in coach. Finally she arrived at the White House gate: a little elderly woman with white hair, white powder all over her face, white stockings, an old hat with white netting, and an all-white dress, now yellow with age. When she got up to the guard at the gate and gave her name, however, the man frowned, glanced over his official list, and told her that her name wasn't there. She couldn't go in. Frances Green was heartbroken.

A Ford Motor Company executive who was standing in line behind her watched and listened to the little scenario. Realizing something was wrong, he pulled Frances aside and got her story. Then he asked her to return at nine o'clock the next morning and meet him there. She agreed. In the meantime, he made contact with Anne Higgins, a presidential aide, and got a clearance to give her a tour of the White House and introduce her to the president. Reagan agreed to see her, "of course."

The next day was anything but calm and easy at the White House. Ed Meese had just resigned. There had been a military uprising abroad. Reagan was in and out of high-level secret sessions. But Frances Green showed up at nine o'clock, full of expectation and enthusiasm.

The executive met her, gave her a wonderful tour of the White House, then quietly led her by the Oval Office, thinking maybe, at best, she might get a quick glimpse of the president on her way out. Members of the National Security Council came out. High-ranking generals were coming and going. In the midst of all the hubbub, President Reagan glanced out and saw Frances Green. With a smile, he gestured her into his office.

As she entered, he rose from his desk and called out, "Frances! Those darn computers, they fouled up again! If I'd known you were coming I would have come out there to get you myself." He then invited her to sit down, and they talked leisurely about California, her town, her life and family.

The president of the United States gave Frances Green a lot of time that day—more time than he had. Some would say it was time wasted. But those who say that didn't know Ronald Reagan. He knew this woman had nothing to give him, but she needed something he could give her. And so he (as well as the Ford executive) took time to be kind and compassionate.

—Peggy Noonan, *Character Above All*

COMPLACENCY

(Also see *Apathy, Indifference*)

ONE OF THE BIG MILK COMPANIES makes capital of the fact that their cows are all satisfied with their lot in life. Their clever ads have made the term "contented cows" familiar to everyone. But what is virtue in a cow may be a vice in a man. And contentment, when it touches spiritual things, is surely a vice.

Contentment with earthly goods is the mark of a saint; contentment with our spiritual state is a mark of inward blindness. One of the greatest foes of the Christian is religious complacency. . . . Orthodox Christianity has fallen to its present low estate from lack of spiritual desire. Among the many who profess the Christian faith, scarcely one in a thousand reveals any passionate thirst for God.

—A. W. Tozer, *The Root of the Righteous*

MR. AVERAGE MAN is comfortable in his complacency and as unconcerned as a silverfish ensconced in a carton of discarded magazines on world affairs. Man is not asking any questions, because his social benefits from the government give him a false security. This is his trouble and his tragedy. Modern man has become a spectator of world events, observing on his television screen without becoming involved. He watches the ominous events of our times pass before his eyes, while he sips his beer in a comfortable chair. He does not seem to realize what is happening to him. He does not understand that his world is on fire and that he is about to be burned with it.

—Billy Graham, *World Aflame*

MY WIFE, Cynthia, and I were flying from Portland back to Los Angeles from a pastor's conference. We had reached cruising altitude, and they were just beginning to serve the meal when suddenly the plane banked rather sharply. We noticed that the flight attendants quickly put the food away and even took trays back from people and quietly whispered among themselves. I said to Cynthia, "We're in for trouble." I have a great grasp for the obvious at times like that.

As we banked, the pilot came on with that ice water flowing through his veins, "Good afternoon, ladies and gentlemen. We have a little mechanical difficulty. We're gonna have to drop back in on the Portland airport. We'll be there for a little while and then we'll be back on course."

So we reached Portland. And just as we touched down, immediately the flight attendant came. She hadn't answered any questions until the moment we touched down. She said, "Listen very carefully everyone. As soon as we come to a stop, you'll hear a sound, you'll hear a bell. At that moment, take the closest escape route you can. Some of you will go out the front. Some of you will go out the tail. We may even have to use the slide." And then as it pulled to a halt, she said, "There's a bomb threat. Take nothing with you. Get off."

Would you believe, people stopped and opened the overhead bin, "Is this your bag? Did you bring a briefcase?" We're supposed to get out! The attendant is saying, "It's a bomb threat, men and women! Get off the plane!" And even then they're grabbing under their seats for their belongings. And the guy doesn't want to leave his briefcase. It's funny, we don't take warnings seriously.

ALL THAT IS NECESSARY for the triumph of evil is for good men to do nothing.

—Edmund Burke, quoted in *Bartlett's Familiar Quotations*

THE DANISH PHILOSOPHER Kierkegaard is often very difficult to read. . . . But in Kierkegaard's parable of the wild duck there is a splendid illustration of how the soul declines from its ideals and becomes satisfied with lower standards. With his mates this duck was flying in the springtime northward across Europe. During the flight he came down in a Danish barnyard where there were tame ducks. He enjoyed some of their corn. He stayed for an hour, then for a day, then for a week, then for a month, and finally, because he relished the good fare and the safety of the barnyard, he stayed all summer. But one autumn day when the flock of wild ducks were winging their way southward again, they passed over the barnyard, and their mate heard their cries. He was stirred with a strange thrill of joy and delight, and with a great flapping of wings he rose in the air to join his old comrades in their flight.

But he found that his good fare had made him so soft and heavy that he could rise no higher than the eaves of the barn. So he dropped back again to the barnyard, and said to himself, "Oh well, my life is safe here and the food is good." Every spring and autumn when he heard the wild ducks honking, his eyes would gleam for a moment and he would begin to flap his wings. But finally the day came when the wild ducks flew over him and uttered their cry, but he paid not the slightest attention to them. What a parable that is of how the soul can forget its high ideals and standards and be content with lower things!

—Clarence Macartney, *Preaching without Notes*

CONSCIENCE

FORMER PRESIDENTIAL AIDE Jeb Stuart Magruder, commenting on the Watergate scandal, said, "We had conned ourselves into thinking we weren't doing anything really wrong, and by the time we were doing things that were illegal, we had lost control. We had gone from poor ethical behavior into illegal activities without even realizing it." . . . Our conscience will quickly be dulled if we must constantly try to justify our actions.

—Jerry White, *Honesty, Morality, and Conscience*

PRESENT-DAY RELIGION far too often soothes the conscience instead of awakening it; and produces a sense of self-satisfaction and eternal safety rather than a sense of our unworthiness.

—Martyn Lloyd Jones

MY DADDY USED TO READ the cartoon series "Moon Mullins" to me, him and Andy Gump. That was sort of our Sunday time together when my mother would leave me home with my dad to sort of shame him for not going to church. And we had a lot better time than she did going to church. But that's another subject.

One of the main characters in the comic strip was a guy named Willie. In one strip, he's slumped in front of the television set with a coffee cup resting on his pot belly as he flicks his cigar ashes into his cup. He says to his wife, "You're awful quiet this morning, Mamie." And she says in return, "Willie, I've decided to let your conscience be your guide on your day off."

Next scene, Willie is surrounded by a lawnmower and an edger and a hoe and a shovel and he's frantically washing the windows and muttering, "Every time I listen to that dumb thing I end up ruinin' my relaxin.'"

—Jerry White, *Honesty, Morality, and Conscience*

CONSCIENCE IS OUR MORAL INTUITION. It's that part of us that passes judgment on our own state. And it takes away our confidence when it is sour or when it is bad. It takes away our security when it is soiled. You have two very firm weapons for battle—faith and a good conscience. Without those weapons we crumble like a dry cookie that's been sitting on the shelf for three or four days. There's no tenacity. There's no resilience. We finally fall.

"LET YOUR CONSCIENCE BE YOUR GUIDE." Ever said that? Wait a minute. Sometimes that's reliable. But a great deal depends on the condition of your conscience. What if your conscience is seared?

Conscience is like a compass. If a compass is faulty, you'll quickly get off course. A conscience gets its signals from the heart, which can be dulled, hardened, calloused. Furthermore, a conscience can be overly sensitive or can even drive one mad.

Someone who has been reared by legalistic parents who used guilt and shame to manipulate their children often has a conscience that is overly sensitive. Some have consciences so twisted and confused, they need extensive help before they can start thinking correctly. Sometimes it takes the help of a good Christian therapist—someone who can help an individual with a shame-based conscience to understand how things got all fouled up. Sometimes a long-term friendship helps give grace to a conscience that has known only legalism. A conscience that is legalistic is not a good guide. A libertine conscience is not a good guide either, nor is a calloused conscience.

In order for one's conscience to be a good guide, one the Spirit can direct, it needs to be healthy, sensitive, and capable of getting God's message and truth.

—Charles R. Swindoll, *Flying Closer to the Flame*

CONSCIENCE IS NOT GIVEN to a man to instruct him in the right, but to prompt him to choose the right instead of the wrong when he has been instructed as to what is right. It tells a man what he ought to do right, but it does not tell him what is right. And if a man has made up his mind that a certain wrong course is the right one, the more he follows his conscience the more helpless he is as a wrongdoer.

—H. C. Trumbull, quoted in Ray Stedman, *The Birth of the Body*

REMEMBER Edgar Allan Poe's "The Telltale Heart?" The murderer, after retiring that evening, couldn't sleep, because he kept hearing the heart of the victim as it pounded in his chest. He didn't really hear the victim's heart. He heard his own heart. And it kept him awake. The guilt of his condition finally led to his revealing that he was the murderer. The power of a guilty conscience.

A. T. ROBERTSON, a fine, reliable Baptist scholar of years ago, taught for many years at the Southern Baptist Theological Seminary in Louisville. When he began to write on books of the Bible, he chose on one occasion the Book of 3 John, which talks about Diotrephes. Diotrephes was a man who became a self-appointed boss of a church. And over a period of time, he was the one that excommunicated certain people and he screened whatever was done in the church. As the self-appointed leader, he wouldn't even let John come to speak as a representative of Christ. So John wrote a letter and reproved him.

In writing about Diotrephes, A. T. Robertson said this: "Some forty years ago I wrote an article on Diotrephes for a denominational paper. The editor told me that twenty-five deacons stopped the paper to show their resentment against being personally attacked in the paper."

—A. T. Robertson, *Word Pictures in the New Testament*, Vol. 6

CONTENTMENT

CONTENTMENT IS A PERFECT CONDITION of life in which no aid or support is needed.

—Joseph Henry Thayer, *Greek-English Lexicon of the New Testament*

WE'LL MISS CONTENTMENT if keeping rather than releasing becomes our objective. We too often love things and use people, when we should be using things and loving people. We are most content when we're grateful for what we own, satisfied with what we make, and generous to those in need.

MY CROWN IS IN MY HEART not on my head; . . . my crown call'd content; a crown it is that seldom kings enjoy.

—William Shakespeare, *King Henry VI*

A QUAKER OFFERED PROPERTY to anyone who considered himself contented. When a man came to claim the lot, he was asked, "If you're contented, why do you want my lot?"

—H. A. Ironside, *Timothy, Titus, and Philemon*

THE GOOD LIFE EXISTS only when we stop wanting a better one. The itch for things is a virus draining the soul of contentment.

COURAGE

THE PARTY ABOARD SHIP was in full swing. Speeches were being made by the captain, the crew, and the guests enjoying the week-long voyage. Sitting at the head table was a seventy-year-old man who, somewhat embarrassed, was doing his best to accept the praise being poured on him.

Earlier that morning a young woman had apparently fallen overboard, and within seconds this elderly gentleman was in the cold, dark waters at her side. The woman was rescued and the elderly man became an instant hero.

When time finally came for the brave passenger to speak, the stateroom fell into a hush as he rose from his chair. He went to the microphone and, in what was probably the shortest "hero's" speech ever offered, spoke these stirring words: "I just want to know one thing—who pushed me?"

—Ted Engstrom, *Motivation to Last a Lifetime*

ONE OF THE GREAT American myths is that we are all a bunch of rugged individualists. We would like to think that, but it simply is not true. There are some exceptions, of course, but for the majority it is not that way at all.

Deep within, we imagine ourselves a mixture of Patrick Henry, Davy Crockett, John Wayne, and the prophet Daniel. But the truth of the matter is . . . rather than rugged individualists, we are more like Gulliver of old, tied down and immobilized by tiny strands of fear, real or imagined. The result is both predictable and tragic: loss of courage.

We can see these symptoms . . . throughout society, but the most visible one is loss of courage. People stand by and watch a fellow citizen being beaten or stabbed and they do not interfere. They are afraid. Our political leaders watch Communism gobble up other nations and they do nothing. They are afraid. People complain in private about the state of affairs but will not speak out in public. They are afraid.

—Robert Flood, *Rebirth of America*

MUST ONE POINT OUT that from ancient times a decline in courage has been considered the beginning of the end?

—Aleksandr Solzhenitsyn, Harvard Commencement address, June 8, 1978

God, Give Us Men!

God, give us men! A time like this demands
Strong minds, great hearts, true faith and ready hands;
    Men whom the lust of office does not kill;
Men whom the spoils of office cannot buy;
    Men who possess opinions and a will;
Men who have honor; men who will not lie;
Men who can stand before a demagogue
    And damn his treacherous flatteries without winking!
Tall men, sun-crowned, who live above the fog
    In public duty and in private thinking;
For while the rabble, with their thumb-worn creeds,
Their large professions and their little deeds,
Mingle in selfish strife, lo! Freedom weeps,
Wrong rules the land and waiting Justice sleeps.

—Josiah Gilbert Holland, quoted in Hazel Felleman, *The Best Loved Poems of the American People*

CHUCK MCILLHENNY, pastor of the Orthodox Presbyterian Church in the Sunset District of San Francisco for over twenty years, has written a book titled

When the Wicked Seize the City. When I first met him, I expected to find the man in a chrome helmet with loaded weapons all around him and double bars on the door. Here's a man whose home has been fire-bombed, whose bedroom for the children is built like a bunker (it's so fireproof) so his children can survive as he stands actively for Christ. He is now ministering a great deal in the hospitals to those dying of AIDS, but standing firm for the truth, that the only hope beyond this life is a faith in the Lord Jesus Christ.

He told a wonderful story of how he was sitting, reading the newspaper one day. And there was a council meeting being held the next day in San Francisco, and he thought he'd go to the city council and hear this particular issue. It was a homosexual rights issue. He thought, I can't just sit here and let that pass. He didn't take anyone with him. He didn't take any placards. He didn't march against them, like many of them march against him. It's not uncommon for his services to be interrupted by lesbians and homosexuals. He just went to the city-council meeting.

He sat there and heard the legislation. The council was about to take a vote. The chairman said, "Is there anyone who has anything to say?" No one moved. Then he stood up and said, "I would like to say something." He walked to the platform, stated his name, that he was a citizen residing in the Sunset District, San Francisco. "What would you like to say?" He replied, "Well, I would like to say nothing for myself, but I would like to quote three individuals that I've respected for years." And he read to them from Moses in Leviticus, from one of the psalms by David, and from Paul in Romans 1. Didn't preach, didn't scream, didn't sermonize—just closed it.

They said, "Wait. Before you sit down, who are those people—Moses and David and Paul?" And someone said, "You're reading from the Bible, aren't you?" "Yes," he said, "I am." And one of the council members then said, "I vote no," and another and another. And it didn't pass. He sat down. That is straight thinking and courage.

RAY STEDMAN told me he was sitting in his home one evening and he noticed there was a meeting of homosexuals in Palo Alto, California. He thought, *I'm gonna go to that meeting.* He went in, and everyone sat on the floor. I think he had an intern with him. Nobody knew who anybody else was. As a group they were railing on the church and railing on Christians and their attitude toward them—just that sense of militance and hatred and on and on.

Then the speaker asked, "Does anyone have anything else they want to say?" So Ray stood up (bless him). He stood up and said, "My name is Ray and I'm a citizen of this city. I'm one of the Christians you've been talking about. I'm sorry for the treatment you've received from many of my brothers and sisters. We meet down here at Peninsula Bible Church and all of you are invited, whoever would want to come." He went on, "I want all of you to know that there is one ray of hope, and it is *the* hope that will bring for you the relief and the life you need."

Of course there was disagreement and discussion back and forth. But I thought, *What a remarkable thing to do. Would you have done that? Would I?*

CREATION

THERE ARE TWO VERY PRACTICAL and human answers to the creation of man and woman. One is the man's view; the other is the woman's view. Are you ready? The woman's view of creation is this: God made the man and looked at him and said, "I can do better than that," and He made the woman. Now the man's view is: God made the beasts and man and then He rested. And then He created woman. And neither beast nor man nor God has rested since.

THE EXISTENCE OF OUR WORLD and mankind defies all mathematical calculations of chance! This was driven home to me many years ago when I came across an illustration from a noted scientist. As I recall, he was a former president of the New York Academy of Sciences. It went something like this: "Let's say I have ten pennies and I mark each one with a number (one to ten), then place all ten in your pocket. I would ask you to give your pocket a good shake so the pennies are no longer in any order in your pocket. What chance would I have to reach in and pull out penny number one? One in ten. Let's say I put the penny back. Then I reach again into your pocket and draw out penny number two. My chance of doing that would be one in a hundred. Putting the penny back, if I were to reach in and draw out penny number three, my chances would jump to one in a thousand. If I were to continue to do the same thing, in successive order, right up through number nine, do you know what my chance would be by the time I got to the number ten and pulled it out of your pocket? *One in ten billion.* If I pulled that off you would say, 'The game is fixed!' My answer: 'You're right . . . and so is creation.'"

—A. Cressy Morrison, *Man Does Not Stand Alone*

DURING ONE OF OUR VACATIONS with our family and our extended family, we rented a houseboat up at Lake Shasta. And while we were there, a couple of nights we decided we would sleep on top of the houseboat. So we dragged our sleeping bags up there. I mean, it fits me, but a classy lady like Cynthia—it just didn't seem to fit. So I reassured her we wouldn't roll off. And this was one place I could snore and not disturb anybody else. When we put our heads back on the pillow and we looked up and all the lights were off, of course, and the whole place was quiet, the stars by the thousands surrounded us. I mean, it was like you could reach out and touch the Milky Way. It was there and it has been there all the time, those same bodies that Abram looked at in the middle of the night. God loves visual aids.

NAPOLEON, the French military genius, was aboard ship in the Mediterranean one clear, starry night. He was on deck and was walking past a small group of officers who were mocking the idea of a Supreme Being. "God of creation, what a joke!" He stopped, stared at them, and then was sweeping his hands across the stars of the sky and said, "Gentlemen, you must get rid of those first!"

—Archibald Naismith, *2,400 Outlines, Notes, and Quotes*

THERE'S AN AGE-OLD AXIOM:

Wherever there is a thing, there must have been a preceding thought . . . and where there is a thought, there must have been a thinker.

Take a mental walk with me outside. I want us to look at some cars together. If possible, let's find a new one. While you're standing there admiring the beauty of that sparkling new automobile, let's imagine my saying to you rather quietly, "You know, there are folks who believe this car is a result of someone's design, but I know differently. Let me tell you what really happened."

Many, many centuries ago, all this iron, glass, rubber, plastic, fabric, leather, and wires came up out of the ground. Furthermore, each substance fashioned itself into various shapes and sizes, and holes evolved at just the right places, and the upholstery began to weave itself together. After a while threads appeared on bolts and nuts and—amazing as it may seem—each bolt found nuts with matching threads. And gradually everything sort of screwed up tightly in place. A little later correctly shaped glass glued itself in the right place. And you see these tires? They became round over the years. And they found themselves the right size metal wheels. And they sort of popped on. They also filled themselves with air somehow. And the thing began to roll down the street.

And one day, many, many years ago—centuries, really—some people were walking along and they found this vehicle sitting under a tree. And one of them looked at it and thought, "How amazing. I think we should call it 'automobile.'" But there's more! These little automobiles have an amazing way of multiplying themselves year after year, even changing ever so slightly to meet the demands of the public. Actually, that process is called "automutations."

TWO MEN WERE standing and looking over the Grand Canyon. Seeing the great depth of that world-famous canyon, one man said, "This is the hand of God. I'm amazed!" The man next to him looked over the edge and spit. He said, "That's the first time I ever spit a mile." I guess it's all how you look at things.

A JOURNALIST, LECTURER, and writer named Hendrick Van Loon, on his first visit to the Grand Canyon exclaimed, "I came an atheist; I leave a believer."

CRITICISM

A COUPLE OF MEN were serving on the same university campus. One was a professor of astronomy and the other one was the dean of students in the divinity school. Both of them were at a cocktail party conversing about their different fields of interest even though neither one had much respect for the other's area of study. In a rather sarcastic way, the astronomer said to the theologian, "I suppose everything about religion could sort of be boiled down to the Golden Rule; you know, love your neighbor as yourself. That's kinda it, isn't it?" The theologian looked at him and said, "Well, I suppose it could be put that way. Kind of like in astronomy, everything boils down to 'Twinkle, twinkle, little star.'"

—Charles Allen, *You Are Never Alone*

IT IS NOT THE CRITIC who counts; not the man who points out how the strong man stumbles or where the doer of deeds could have done them better. The credit belongs to the man who is actually in the arena, whose face is marred by dust and sweat and blood; who strives valiantly; who errs, and comes short again and again, because there is no effort without error and shortcoming; but who does actually try to do the deeds; who knows the great enthusiasms, the great devotions, who spends himself in a worthy cause; who at the best knows in the end the triumph of high achievement, and who at the worst, if he fails, at least fails while daring greatly, so that his place shall never be with those cold and timid souls who know neither victory nor defeat.

—Theodore Roosevelt, speech "Citizenship in a Republic," delivered in Paris, April 23, 1910

I REMEMBER while in the marines on Okinawa a group of us GIs decided to celebrate New Year's at a local club. We went down there and had the time of our lives. I mean, we acted like nuts. We were blowin' these crazy horns, wearin' silly hats, and havin' the neatest time with one another. When we returned to our van, which belonged to our friend who was our leader, he found a note written by some pharisaical Christian who left a comment, "What are Christians doing in a place like that?" He didn't even know what we were doing in there. If he had come in (which he would never do), he might have seen there was a lot of fun goin' on. There was not a thing wrong or vulgar about our evening. But it wasn't the normal place to find Christians. Normally on a New Year's Eve you're at a New Year's Eve service. But we were in there to have fun and we did! And the thing I loved about our friend is he took that note and he said, "Listen to this, guys." He read it and said, "Let me show you what I think of this." He rumpled the paper up into a ball and dumped it. And I learned a major lesson about unsigned notes.

A DOMINANT, AGGRESSIVE TYPE cartoon character is philosophizing along-side his friend, who happens to be quieter and more passive. With unhesitating boldness, the stronger one says to the weaker one, "If I were in charge of the world, I would change *everything!*" A bit intimidated, the friend who is forced to listen says rather meekly, "Uh, that wouldn't be easy. Like . . . where would you start?" Without hesitation he looks directly back and says, "I would start with *you!*"

—Charles R. Swindoll, *The Grace Awakening*

A MAN ONCE UNLOADED ON ME that I was a "wicked shepherd who was destroying and scattering the sheep." Those were his exact words. I asked him if he knew that he was quoting Scripture. He said he did. I asked him if he knew by whom it was said and about whom. He didn't. At that point I told him it was the prophet Jeremiah who first said it and that it was said about each of Judah's last four kings, four of the worst men who ever lived. I thought that would change his mind about me. It didn't.

The best of Christianity is sometimes swallowed up by the worst, and often I think the worst is mean-spirited attacks upon our brothers. It must make outsiders think that becoming a Christian turns someone into a swine. Something needs to be said to our critics.

Our Lord was very clear about what to do if you have something against another person. He said, "go and show him (your brother) his fault," and settle the matter "just between the two of you." The best way to handle a complaint against another is frontally. Though it may hurt initially, your loving concern can restore your relationship.

Critics need to lighten up, and the criticized need to toughen up. We mustn't let our detractors drive us to depression and despair. Every critique provides an opportunity to grow. Forget the critic; it's far more important to consider the criticism, especially if it comes from more than one source.

—David Roper, *The Strength of a Man*

A TYPICAL AMERICAN FAMILY was driving home from church. Dad was fussing about the sermon being too long and sort of boring. Mom said that she thought the organist played a little too loud during the second hymn we sang. Sis, who was a music major in college, said that the soloist sang about a half note off key during most of the song. Grandma said she couldn't hear very well—they were sitting in a bad place. Little Willie listened to all of this and started to fuss about the woman with this big hat who sat in front of him. He couldn't see around her. And then he nudged his dad and said, "But, Dad, you gotta admit, it was a pretty good show for a nickel."

—Walter Knight, *Knight's Master Book of New Illustrations*

CROSS

(Also see *Salvation*)

HOLMAN HUNT, a surrealistic artist, painted the interior of a carpenter's shop, with Joseph and the boy Jesus working. Mary was also present. As Jesus paused in His work and stopped to stretch Himself, the sun made a shadow of the Cross on the wall. Another of his pictures is a popular engraving which depicts the infant Jesus running with outstretched arms to His mother, the shadow of the Cross being cast by His form as He runs. Both pictures are fanciful in form, but their underlying idea is assuredly true. If we read the Gospels just as they stand, it is clear that the death of Jesus Christ was really in view from the outset of His earthly appearance.

—W. H. Griffith Thomas, *Christianity Is Christ*

_____

CENTURIES AGO on the South Coast of China, high up on a hill overlooking the harbor of Macao, Portuguese settlers built an enormous cathedral. They believed it would weather time, and they placed upon the front wall of this cathedral a massive bronze cross that stood high into the sky. Not too many years later, a typhoon came and God's fingerwork swept away man's handiwork, and all of that cathedral was pushed into the ocean and down the hill as debris, except the front wall and that bronze cross that stood high.

Centuries later, there was a shipwreck out a little beyond that harbor. And some died and a few lived. One of the men that was hanging onto wreckage from the ship, moving up and down in the crest of the ocean as the swells were moving, was disoriented, frightened, and he didn't know where land was. As he would come up on the swell, he'd spot that cross, tiny from that distance. His name was Sir John Bowring.

When he made it to land and lived to tell the story, he wrote,

> In the cross of Christ I glory,
> Towering o'er the wrecks of time;
> All the light of sacred story
> Gathers round its head sublime.

And the last stanza.

> When the woes of life o'er take me,
> Hopes deceive, and fears annoy,
> Never shall the cross forsake me:
> Lo! it glows with peace and joy.

John Bowring is just telling us that we have a cross, we have an altar. And when all of life seems to crush in on top of us, we just need to go back to the Cross and remember the empty tomb and call to mind the fact that a Man is neither on the cross nor in the tomb, but He lives and He stands ready and able to give us victory through whatever we are going through at the time. Come by grace to the Cross and say, "That is my sufficiency. That is my only hope."

—Kenneth Osbeck, *101 Hymn Stories*

_____

Return the Cross to Golgotha

I simply argue that the cross be raised again
  at the center of the market place
  as well as on the steeple of the church,

I am recovering the claim that
  Jesus was not crucified in a cathedral
  between two candles:

But on a cross between two thieves;
  on a town garbage heap;
  at a crossroad of politics so cosmopolitan
  that they had to write His title
  in Hebrew and in Latin and in Greek . . .

And at the kind of place where cynics talk smut,
  and thieves curse and soldiers gamble.

Because that is where He died,
  and that is what He died about.
  And that is where Christ's men ought to be,
  and what church people ought to be about.

—George MacLeod, *Focal Point,* January–March 1981

AS I WAS PREACHING a message titled "The Church: Who Needs It?" several years ago, I used George MacLeod's poem "Return the Cross to Golgotha" as an illustration and I closed with this personal paraphrase:

I simply argue that the church be raised again
  to its God-given place of significance.

I am recovering the claim that
  Jesus did not begin a project
  that was to be criticized and assaulted,
  destined for weakness, irrelevance, and decay.

But rather for strength, purity, and dignity
  in a world that has lost its way
  where cynics and thieves and gamblers
  have become its voices of authority
  rather than confident Christians
  who walk humbly and prayerfully with their God.

Because that is what the church was designed to be,
and that is why Christ predicted invincibility.
That is where Christ's people ought to be
and what church people ought to be about.

SHOULDERS HUNCHED, the man plods through life, straining with every step to carry the great burden to his back. It has been his night-and-day companion. Not once has he known relief from its merciless weight.

The man's name is Christian, the central character in John Bunyan's classic allegory *The Pilgrim's Progress*. In one moving scene from the book, Christian finds the path to salvation. Up the hill he staggers until he reaches the peak. There he sees a wooden cross and, just below it, an empty sepulcher. As he nears the cross, a miracle happens. The straps binding the massive weight to his shoulders loosen, and his load tumbles away into the sepulcher's waiting mouth, never to be seen again.

A delicious feeling of lightness buoys Christian's body, and joyous tears of relief stream down his face. Three Shining Ones then approach him. The first announces, "Thy sins be forgiven thee;" the second strips away his rags and dresses him in splendid clothes; the third hands him a sealed scroll, which he is to present upon entrance to the Celestial City.

Overwhelmed by his new freedom, Christian sings:
> Thus far did I come laden with my sin,
> Nor could aught ease the grief that I was in,
> Till I came hither. What a place is this!
> Must here be the beginning of my bliss?
> Must here the burden fall off from my back?
> Must here the strings that bound it to me crack?
> Blest Cross! blest Sepulchre! blest, rather, be
> The Man that there was put to shame for me!

In this brief scene, Bunyan has eloquently dramatized the message that we are all pilgrims, encumbered by a crushing load of sin. When we stumble to the cross, God releases our burdens, burying them forever in Christ's own grave.

—John Bunyan, *The Pilgrim's Progress*

CULTS

(Also see *Legalism, Religious People*)

CHRISTOPHER EDWARDS was graduated from Yale University in the early summer of 1975. He enrolled at Berkeley with plans to pursue a master's degree. While there he was approached by a stranger who offered him an alleged "fun" weekend at a local farm. What he didn't realize was that it was a front for the Sun Myung Moon's Unification Church in Berkeley. He went and that "fun" weekend turned into seven-and-a-half months of maddening brainwashing. Christopher was changed from a clear-thinking, brilliant, astute individual, into a completely subservient disciple of his new messiah, in his own words, "dependent on his leaders for every move, ready and willing to die or even kill to restore the world under the absolute rule of Reverend Moon."

He was kidnapped by his father and a team of trained professionals in January 1976, and not until he went through a full year of deprogramming and therapy under the direction of a specialist in cult-related problems, did Christopher Edwards gain mastery over what he called "months of madness." He wrote a book *Crazy for God* about his extraordinary experience.

OF ALL THE CONS we can fall prey to, one of the worst is being duped by a religious phony. Swindlers of this kind deal in counterfeit truth—something that looks and sounds right but is actually contrary to fact, an imitation meant to deceive the unsuspecting. These cons aren't always done for the benefit of some leader whose name you can't pronounce. No, every week, lies dressed up in their Sunday best receive nodding approval in mainline churches everywhere. Counterfeit truth is big business, and it's still owned and operated by the same insidious proprietor who began it all years ago.

Warren Wiersbe in commenting on the religious counterfeits in 2 Peter 2:3 says: "Plastic words! Words that can be twisted to mean anything you want them to mean! The false teachers use our vocabulary, but they do not use our dictionary. They talk about 'salvation,' 'inspiration,' and great words of the Christian faith, but they do not mean what we mean."

How can we avoid being hoodwinked by one of Satan's workers of deceit?

> *Stop:* Refuse to blindly accept someone else's teaching just because others have been "blessed" by it. Stop long enough to make a serious study, comparing what is being taught with what the Scriptures teach.

Look: Take a careful look at the life of the main spokesperson. Is the fruit of the Spirit evident? Don't be wowed because someone sounds intelligent or wooed because of someone's charisma.

Listen: Pay attention to the terms a person uses and how they're defined. Also listen to what's *not* being said. Don't judge truth just by how you feel; think, and make your judgments according to what the Scriptures teach.

—Warren W. Wiersbe, *Be Alert*

THE AMERICAN BANKING ASSOCIATION once sponsored a two-week training program to help tellers detect counterfeit bills. The program was unique—never during the two-week training did the tellers even look at a counterfeit bill, nor did they listen to any lectures concerning the characteristics of counterfeit bills. . . . All they did for two weeks was handle authentic currency, hour after hour and day after day, until they were so familiar with the true that they could not possibly be fooled by the false.

We need to study, meditate on, and apply God's Word until we are so familiar with it that we cannot be fooled by anything less than real truth.

—Ben Patterson, *Waiting*

Dd

DANGER

IN THE GREAT STATE of California there are many picturesque roads and highways through mountainous areas. Though some are narrow and a bit treacherous, all of them lead through sights that are breathtakingly beautiful. Those who have driven the Pacific Coast Highway, Highway 1, can never forget the incredible natural scenes that stretch along the craggy coastline from Los Angeles to San Francisco. A few of the curves are especially dangerous and must be driven slowly and with great care. There are treacherous drop-offs, which add both to the beauty and the danger of the journey.

It occurred to me that our state could offer two options to travelers along these dangerous mountain roads. First, the state could build very well-equipped clinics at the bottom of those high elevations where the narrow roads twist and turn. Every sharp curve could be provided with a clinic down below. When speeding drivers went over the side and tumbled down the cliff, those in the clinic would be there to rescue and treat them. Second, the state could erect very clear, well-placed signs before each sharp curve, reading *"Danger! Curve Ahead. Drive Slowly."* You are not surprised to know that the highway department chose the second option, not the first. Smart plan.

We should learn from that decision. First John 1:9 is the corrective clinic at the bottom of the hill. It rescues and treats us, which is wonderful, but it is not the best alternative. Romans 6, on the other hand, is preventive counsel, providing signs: "No need to crash . . . slow down . . . danger ahead." We must calculate the importance of these spiritual "signs" and reckon them as true.

—Charles R. Swindoll, *The Grace Awakening*

ON NOVEMBER 20, 1959, a small amount of solvent exploded and blew open the door of a processing cell at the Atomic Energy Commission Oak Ridge Laboratory. About 1/50th of an ounce of plutonium (a radioactive element) was scattered into the air . . . only 1/50th! The AEC later reported what it took to clean up this minor atomic mishap.

1. Everyone within a four-acre area turned in their clothing to be decontaminated.

2. Each person was thoroughly examined to ensure that they had not inhaled or ingested any plutonium.

3. The processing plant and nearby research reactor were completely shut down.

4. Buildings were washed with strong detergent—and all the buildings' roofs were resurfaced.

5. The surrounding lawn was dug up and the sod carried to a deep burial place a long distance away.

6. The surface was chiseled off one hundred yards of a nearby asphalt road.

7. To anchor the slightest speck of plutonium that might have remained, every building was totally repainted with heavy-duty substance.

The total cost of this renovation and cleaning process was $350,000!

I NEVER HAD THE RIGHT PERSPECTIVE on what Daniel must have faced until my family and I took a trip through Lion Country Safari several years ago. I'd been to zoos in several major cities, but I had never been through that tourist safari that was an attraction in Orange County. For some strange reason there was a rather sizable beast that took a liking to our kind of car, or something within the car. I remember there were not a lot of animals, but that one king of the jungle seemed to like us and he just sort of walked along with us. We were able to stop and study them, with a very thick car door between us and those creatures. But as I studied that particular regal lion, I got a whole new appreciation for what it must have been like for Daniel to have been in a den filled with several carnivorous beasts like that one.

I SAID TO MY WIFE, Cynthia, one afternoon, "I'm gonna take a drive. I need to think and pray about a situation." So while I was driving, I had my Bible open on my steering wheel, and I said, "Lord, I'm gonna read through the whole New Testament until I find Your mind on this situation."

OK, reading and driving are not naturally related activities. I mentioned this in a sermon and afterward a fellow walked up and just laid his card down. He said, "If you ever need me . . ." and walked away. It was a card for a body shop/towing service.

EVERYONE HAS ETERNAL LIFE. The question is where will we spend it? Picture a person helplessly trapped on the sixth floor of a burning hotel. The elevators no longer function, the stairways are flaming infernos. To live, the person must leap into a net which firemen down below are holding ready. Imagine the trapped man screaming from his broken window, "I will not jump until you give me a satisfactory explanation of several things: (1) How did the fire get started? (2) Why has it spread so quickly? (3) What happened to the sprinkler system? and (4) How do I know for sure that net will hold me? Until you guys can come up with some pretty substantial answers, I'm staying right here in room 612!"

Slice it up and analyze it any way you wish, when we reduce our response to God's offer of salvation, it comes down to faith: being willing to abandon oneself, without reservation, to the eternal net God has spread—leaping while believing with absolute confidence that He will do as He promised.

—Charles R. Swindoll, *Destiny*

SOMETIME AGO there appeared a cartoon in the *National Observer* that caught my eye, probably because the scene was very familiar. It was a busy intersection and cars were bumper to bumper in all four directions. Horns were honking and engines were steaming over and tempers were on edge. Impatience was written on the face of the drivers. And there was a pedestrian standing on the corner looking across the street in disbelief at the sign. Instead of its reading the normal "Walk" or "Don't Walk," it read, "Good Luck."

—*National Observer*, May 29, 1967

DEATH

(Also see *Grief*)

EPITAPH:
> Here lies the bones of Mary Jones
> For her life had no terrors;
> She lived an old maid
> She died an old maid
> No runs, no hits
> No errors.

EPITAPH:
> To follow you I'm not content
> Until I know which way you went.

AN OLD LADY went to a tombstone-cutter's office to order a stone for her husband's grave. After explaining that all she wanted was a small one with no frills, she told him to put the words, "To My Husband," in a suitable place. When the stone was delivered she saw, to her horror, this inscription:

> "To My Husband—
> In a Suitable Place."

—Lloyd Cory, *Quote Unquote*

MANY HANDLE DEATH through humor. A bumper sticker read, "Don't take life so seriously. You won't get out of it alive."

—Elbert Hubbard, *Dictionary of Humorous Quotations*

IT'S NOT THAT I'M AFRAID to die. I just don't want to be there when it happens.

—Woody Allen, quoted in Lloyd Cory, *Quote Unquote*

HARRY TRUMAN TOLD THE STORY of a man who was hit on the head and fell into a deep coma. He stayed there for a long time. People thought he was dead so they sent him to a funeral home and stuck him in a coffin. At two o'clock in the morning, all alone in this dimly lit room, he sat up and looked around. "Good night!" he said. "What's going on? If I'm alive, why am I in a casket? And, if I'm dead, why do I have to go to the bathroom?"

—James Hewett, *Illustrations Unlimited*

Death, Be Not Proud

> Death, be not proud, though some have called thee
> Mighty and dreadful, for thou are not so;
> For those whom thou think'st thou dost overthrow
> Die not, poor Death; nor yet canst thou kill me.
> From rest and sleep, which but thy pictures be,
> Much pleasure; then from thee much more must flow;
> And soonest our best men with thee do go—

Rest of their bones and souls' delivery!
Thou'rt slave to fate, chance, kings, and desperate men,
And dost with poison, war, and sickness dwell;
And poppy or charms can make us sleep as well
And better than thy stroke. Why swell'st thou then?
One short sleep past, we wake eternally,
And Death shall be no more: Death, thou shalt die.

—John Donne

A Psalm of Extremity

I cry tears
to you Lord
tears
because I cannot speak.
Words are lost
among my fears
pain
sorrows
losses
hurts
but tears
You understand
my wordless prayer
You hear.
Lord
wipe away my tears
all tears
not in distant day
but now
here.

—Joseph Bayly, *Psalms of My Life*

In Flanders Fields

In Flanders fields the poppies blow
Between the crosses, row on row,
   That mark our place; and in the sky
   The larks, still bravely singing, fly
Scarce heard amid the guns below.

We are the Dead. Short days ago
We lived, felt dawn, saw sunset glow,
    Loved and were loved, and now we lie
    In Flanders fields.

Take up our quarrel with the foe:
To you from failing hands we throw
    The torch; be yours to hold it high.
    If ye break faith with us who die
We shall not sleep, though poppies grow
In Flanders fields.

—John McCrae, quoted in Hazel Felleman, *The Best Loved Poems of the American People*

MAN ALONE . . . has foreknowledge of his coming death . . . and, possessing this foreknowledge, has a chance, if he chooses to take it, of pondering over the strangeness of his destiny. . . . [He] has at least a possibility of coping with it, since he is endowed with the capacity to think about it in advance and . . . to face it and to deal with it in some way that is worthy of human dignity.

—Arnold Toynbee, *Man's Concern with Death*

YOU AND I are going to die. There is no escaping it. Who hasn't heard of the two inescapable facts: death and taxes. I like the comment Joan Welsh made: "Maybe death and taxes are inevitable, but death doesn't get worse every time Congress meets."

—Lloyd Cory, *Quote Unquote*

THERE IS A LINE found in the Jewish Talmud that puts it well: "Man is born with his hands clenched; he dies with them wide open. Entering life, he desires to grasp everything; leaving the world, all he possessed has slipped away."

—Charles R. Swindoll, *Living Above the Level of Mediocrity*

THE FOLLOWING is a selection from the poem "Thanatopsis."

As the long train
Of ages glides away, the sons of men—
The youth in life's green spring, and he who goes
In the full strength of years, matron and maid,
And the sweet babe, and the gray-headed man—

Shall one by one be gathered to thy side,
By those, who in their turn shall follow them.

So live that when thy summons comes to join
The innumerable caravan that moves
To that mysterious realm, where each shall take
His chamber in the silent halls of death,
Thou go not, like the quarry-slave at night,
Scourged to his dungeon, but, sustained and soothed
By an unfaltering trust, approach thy grave,
Like one who wraps the drapery of his couch
About him, and lies down to pleasant dreams.

—James Gilchrist Lawson, *The World's Best Loved Poems*

THE STATISTICS ON DEATH are quite impressive—one out of one people die.

—George Bernard Shaw

AN OLD LEGEND TELLS of a merchant in Baghdad who one day sent his servant to the market. Before very long the servant came back, white and trembling, and in great agitation said to his master: "Down at the market place I was jostled by a woman in the crowd, and when I turned around I saw it was Death that jostled me. She looked at me and made a threatening gesture. Master, please lend me your horse, for I must hasten away to avoid her. I will ride to Samarra and there I will hide, and Death will not find me."

The merchant lent him his horse and the servant galloped away in great haste. Later the merchant went down to the market place and saw Death standing in the crowd. He went over to her and asked, "Why did you frighten my servant this morning? Why did you make a threatening gesture?"

"That was not a threatening gesture," Death said. "It was only a start of surprise. I was astonished to see him in Baghdad, for I have an appointment with him tonight in Samarra."

—Peter Marshall, *John Doe, Disciple: Sermons for the Young in Spirit*

THERE ARE TWO FIXED POINTS in our lives: birth and death. Death is especially unbendable. One astute writer used these words to describe what we've all felt.

This frustrates us, especially in a time of scientific breakthrough and exploding knowledge, that we should be able to break out of earth's environment and yet be stopped cold by death's unyielding mystery.

An electroencephalogram may replace a mirror held before the mouth, autopsies may become more sophisticated, cosmetic embalming may take the place of pennies on the eyelids and canvas shrouds, but death continues to confront us with its black wall. Everything changes; death is changeless.

We may postpone it, we may tame its violence, but death is still there waiting for us. Death always waits. The door of the hearse is never closed.

Dairy farmer and sales executive live in death's shadow, with Nobel prize winner and prostitute, mother, infant, teen, and old man. The hearse stands waiting for the surgeon who transplants a heart as well as the hopeful recipient, for the funeral director as well as the corpse he manipulates. Death spares none.

—Joseph Bayly, *The Last Thing We Talk About*

WHEN DAN RICHARDSON, an enthusiastic believer in Christ, lost his battle with cancer, the following piece was distributed at his memorial service.

> Cancer is limited . . .
> It cannot cripple love,
> It cannot corrode faith,
> It cannot eat away peace,
> It cannot destroy confidence,
> It cannot kill a friendship,
> It cannot shut out memories,
> It cannot silence courage,
> It cannot invade the soul,
> It cannot reduce eternal life,
> It cannot quench the spirit,
> It cannot lessen the power of the resurrection.
>
> —Charles R. Swindoll, *The Finishing Touch*

ASK MOST PEOPLE about dying or heaven and you get amazing answers, especially from children.
Alan, age 7,

"God doesn't tell you when you are going to die because He wants it to be a big surprise."

Aaron, age 8,

"The hospital is the place where people go on their way to heaven."

Raymond, age 10,

"A good doctor can help you so you won't die. A bad doctor sends you to heaven."

Stephanie, age 9,

"Doctors help you so you won't die until you pay all their bills."

Marsha, age 9,

"When you die, you don't have to do homework in heaven unless your teacher is there too."

Kevin, age 10, is very courageous.

"I'm not afraid to die because I'm a Boy Scout."

Ralph, age 8,

"When birds are ready to die they just fly to heaven."

—*Good Housekeeping,* March 1979

BILLY GRAHAM preached Dawson Trotman's funeral. Dawson had believed in Billy's ministry. He was an encourager. *Time* magazine said in reporting on his death: "Dawson Trotman was always holding somebody up." When he drowned in Schroon Lake after saving another's life, his wife, Lila said, "It was his time. Our God is in the heavens; He has done whatever He is pleased to do" (Ps. 115:3).

ON JANUARY 25, 1973, in Memorial Hospital, John Riso—red-haired, laughing, tall, eighteen, tractor-driving, cow-scratching, flirtatious, shy—died after two and a half years of leukemia. After six weeks of raging temperature, experimental drugs, bleeding, an abscess in his rectum that became gangrenous, he died softly and gently, finally, after six hours of violent death throes. His face was so thin, his hair only a memory, a soft red fuzz, arms blue and green from shots and intravenous feeding, he looked like an old picture of a saint after his torture was over.

His mother wrote, "Why would a kind God do what was done to John, or do such a thing to me? I am poor; I have only second-hand furniture and clothing. The things of value were my husband and son. All our lives we have struggled to make ends meet. How can I live with the memory of the agony he suffered. Part of the time he was in a coma, and he kept saying, 'Mama, help me. Mama, help me. Mama, help me.' And I couldn't; it's killing me. I whispered in his ear, 'John, John, I love you so much.' All of a sudden, his arm came up stiffly and fell across my back and very quietly he said from some vast depth, 'Me, too . . . me, too.'"

I would add this prayer, "Father, the view from the hearse is a grim one. It's one we don't like to think about. The tubes and pieces of equipment in hospitals and the smell of medicine, these things seem to repulse us. The white face of a dying child, the hollow eyes of a parent, a mate, the harsh blows of life—O God, there's a lot of it in this area. I pray for those who go through the valley and there are not many there to comfort. I pray that You would raise up merciful men and women who care enough to reach out and stand by, not with the heavy guns of doctrinal artillery, not at that time, but with the compassion of Jesus Christ, who gave Himself for us."

—Joseph Bayly, *A View from the Hearse*

A Psalm on the Death of an 18-Year-Old Son

What waste Lord
this ointment precious
here outpoured
is treasure great
beyond my mind to think.
For years
until this midnight
it was safe
contained
awaiting careful use
now broken
wasted
lost.
The world is poor
so poor it needs each drop
of such a store.
This treasure spent
might feed a multitude
for all their days
and then yield more.
This world is poor?
It's poorer now
the treasure's lost.
I breathe its lingering fragrance
soon even that
will cease.

What purpose served?
The act is void of reason
sense
Lord
madmen do such deeds
not sane.
The sane man hoards his treasure
spends with care
if good
to feed the poor
or else to feed himself.
Let me alone Lord
You've taken from me
what I'd give Your world.
I cannot see
such waste
that You should take
what poor men need.
You have a heaven
full of treasure
could You not wait
to exercise Your claim
on this?
O spare me Lord forgive
that I may see
beyond this world
beyond myself
Your sovereign plan
or seeing not
may trust You
Spoiler of my treasure
Have mercy Lord
here is my quitclaim.

—Joseph Bayly, *Psalms of My Life*

Before the winds that blow do cease,
Teach me to dwell within Thy calm;
Before the pain has passed in peace,
Give me, my God, to sing a psalm.

Let me not lose the chance to prove
The fullness of enabling love,
O love of God, do this for me:
Maintain a constant victory.
Before I leave the desert land
For meadow of immortal flower,
Lead me where streams at Thy command
Flow by the borders of the hours,
That when the thirsty come, I may
Shew them the fountains in the way.
O love of God, do this for me:
Maintain a constant victory.

—Amy Carmichael, quoted in V. Raymond Edman, *In Quiteness and Confidence*

REFLECT A FEW MOMENTS on this poignant analogy between birth and death:

Each of our individual deaths can be seen as a birth. Imagine what it would be like if you had had full consciousness as a fetus and could now remember those sensations.

Your world is dark, safe, secure. You are bathed in warm liquid, cushioned from shock. You do nothing for yourself; you are fed automatically, and a murmuring heartbeat assures you that someone larger than you fills all your needs. Your life consists of simple waiting—you're not sure what to wait for, but any change seems far away and scary. You meet no sharp objects, no pain, no threatening adventures. A fine existence.

One day you feel a tug. The walls are falling in on you. Those soft cushions are now pulsing and beating against you, crushing you downwards. Your body is bent double, your limbs twisted and wrenched. You're falling, upside down. For the first time in your life, you feel pain. You're in a sea of roiling matter. There is more pressure, almost too intense to bear. Your head is squeezed flat, and you are pushed harder, harder into a dark tunnel. Oh, the pain. Noise. More pressure.

You hurt all over. You hear a groaning sound and an awful sudden fear rushes in on you. It is happening—your world is collapsing. You're sure it's the end. You see a piercing, blinding light. Cold, rough hands pull at you. A painful slap. Waaaahhhhh!

Congratulations, you have just been born.

Death is like that. On this end of the birth canal, it seems fiercesome, portentous, and full of pain. Death is a scary tunnel and we are being sucked toward it by a powerful force.

—Philip Yancey, *Where Is God When It Hurts?*

There was a very cautious man
Who never laughed or played.
He never risked, he never tired
He never sang or prayed.
And when one day he passed away
His insurance was denied
For since he never really lived
They claimed he never died.

DECEIT

(Also see *Lies*)

MAYBE YOU HEARD about the guy who fell in love with an opera singer. He hardly knew her, since his only view of the singer was through binoculars from the third balcony. But he was convinced he could live "happily ever after" married to a voice like that. He scarcely noticed she was considerably older than he. Nor did he care that she walked with a limp. Her mezzo-soprano voice would take them through whatever might come. After a whirlwind romance and a hurry-up ceremony, they were off for their honeymoon together.

She began to prepare for their first night together. As he watched, his chin dropped to his chest. She plucked out her glass eye and plopped it into a container on the nightstand. She pulled off her wig, ripped off her false eyelashes, yanked out her dentures, unstrapped her artificial leg, and smiled at him as she slipped off her glasses that hid her hearing aid. Stunned and horrified, he gasped, "For goodness sake, woman, sing, sing, SING!"

—Charles R. Swindoll, *Strike the Original Match*

WHILE PARKING late at night, you slightly scrape the side of a Porsche. You are certain no one else is aware of what happened. The damage is minor and would be covered by insurance. Would you leave a note? I read not long ago about a fellow who really did that, except people were watching. And he took out a piece of paper and he wrote on it, "A number of people around me think I'm leaving you a note that includes my name and address, but I'm not."

—Sam Levenson, *You Don't Have to Be in Who's Who to Know What's What*

IN A SURVEY . . . it was found that 15 percent of the ladies tinted their hair, 38 percent wore a wig, 80 percent wore rouge, 98 percent wore eye shadow, 22 percent wore false eyelashes, 93 percent wore nail polish. And 100 percent voted in favor of a resolution condemning any kind of false packaging.

—Lloyd Cory, *Quote Unquote*

A SALESMAN was far away from home, driving down an unfamiliar country highway. All of a sudden he came upon a barn which had a huge bull's-eye painted in the middle of it. He could hardly believe his eyes. There in the middle of the bull's-eye were hundreds of arrows. Every arrow was inside the bull's-eye. As he drove on down the highway, his curiosity got the best of him. He turned his car around and drove back to where the barn was, to take another look. He spotted a farmhouse nearby, so he drove to where it was and met the farmer. After they got acquainted, he said, "Say, could you tell me who the excellent marksman is who shot all those arrows inside the bull's eye?" The farmer almost laughed out loud, then he explained, "That was the work of the village idiot. He had shot all those arrows at the side of the barn, then he climbed up there and painted a bull's-eye around all the arrows to create the false impression he was a great marksman."

—Dale Galloway, *Rebuild Your Life*

A MAN IN New York City met and married a wife who had a cat. Actually the cat had her. She loved the cat. She stroked it, combed its fur, fed it, and pampered it. The man detested the cat. He was allergic to cat hair; he hated the smell of the litter box; he couldn't stand the scratching on the furniture; and he couldn't get a good night's sleep because the cat kept jumping on the bed. When his wife was out of town for the weekend, he put the cat in a bag with some rocks, dumped it in the Hudson River, and uttered a joyful good-bye to the cat. When his wife returned and could not find her cat, she was overwhelmed with grief.

Her husband said, "Look, Honey, I know how much that cat meant to you. I'm going to put an ad in the paper and give a reward of five hundred dollars to anyone who finds the cat."

No cat showed up, so a few days later he said, "Honey, you mean more to me than anything else on earth. If that cat is precious to you, it is precious to me. I'll tell you what I'll do. I'll buy another ad and raise the ante. We'll increase the reward to one thousand dollars."

A friend saw the ad and exclaimed, "You must be nuts; there isn't a cat on earth that is worth a thousand dollars."

The man replied, "Well, when you know what I know, you can afford to be generous."

—Haddon Robinson, *What Jesus Said about Successful Living*

A FRIEND OF MINE ate dog food one evening. No, he wasn't at a fraternity initiation or a hobo party . . . he was actually at an elegant student reception in a physician's home near Miami. The dog food was served on delicate little crackers with a wedge of imported cheese, bacon chips, an olive, and a sliver of pimento on top. That's right, friends and neighbors, it was hors d'oeuvres *a la Alpo.*

The hostess is a first-class nut! You gotta know her to appreciate the story. She had just graduated from a gourmet cooking course, and so she decided it was time to put her skill to the ultimate test. Did she ever! After doctoring up those miserable morsels and putting them on a couple of silver trays, with a sly grin she watched them disappear. One guy (my friend) couldn't get enough. He kept coming back for more. I don't recall how they broke the news to him . . . but when he found out the truth, he probably barked and bit her on the leg! He certainly must have gagged a little.

AS SCREWTAPE once quoted to Wormwood their father's couplet,

Old error in new dress
is ever error nonetheless.

—Walter Martin, *Screwtape Writes Again*

DEGENERACY

(Also see *Depravity*)

GARY BAUER tells the shocking yet true story of a teacher who, twenty-five years ago, used to walk into her fourth-grade class and greet them. "Good morning, children," to which they would respond, "Good morning, Miss Jones." She left teaching for many years to have her own family and rear them. She returned recently to the classroom and began the day in her usual way, "Good morning, children." To which a young thug on the front row responded, "Shut up, b—!" That is the erosion of generations. If your youngster isn't alert, he or she will get swept up in it.

—Charles R. Swindoll, *The Finishing Touch*

FORMER SECRETARY OF EDUCATION, William Bennett, published *The Index of Leading Cultural Indicators* revealing how shockingly we have drifted as a nation. His book states, "In the past thirty years violent crime has increased 560 percent; illegitimate births 400 percent. There has been a tripling of the percentage of children living in single-parent homes. Teenage suicide increased more than 200 percent." Interesting also, in the past thirty years there has been "a drop in SAT scores of almost 80 percent."

—Steve Farrar, *Standing Tall*

I DON'T KNOW many people aged 35 to 50 who don't have a sense that they were born into a healthier country, and that they have seen the culture deteriorate before their eyes. . . .

You don't have to look far for the fraying of the social fabric. Crime, the schools, the courts. Watch Channel 35 in New York City and see your culture. See men and women, homo- and hetero-, dressed in black leather, masturbating each other and simulating sadomasochistic ritual. Realize this is pumped into everyone's living room, including your own, where your eight-year old is flipping through channels. Then talk to a pollster. You too will declare you are pessimistic about your country's future; you too will say we are on the wrong track.

—Peggy Noonon, "You'd Cry Too If It Happened to You," *Forbes*, September 1992

The thorns which I have reap'd are of the tree
I planted—they have torn me—and I bleed:
I should have known what fruit would spring from such a seed.

—Lord Byron, *Childe Harold's Pilgrimage*

LIKE MOST OF YOU in high school days, I took a class in chemistry. And like most of you, I don't remember a lot from the course, except one invaluable lesson that had very little to do with chemistry. My teacher's name was Mr. Williams, and one day we did an experiment that lives on in my mind to this day. We watched the killing of a frog in an oversized beaker. Water was placed in the beaker and the frog was put inside with no top on it. Then the beaker was set over a Bunsen burner. This Bunsen burner was on a very, very low flame. And it continued on for a period of about three hours. The water was heated at about .017 degrees Fahrenheit per second—very, very slight. As time passed, of course, the water became warmer and warmer. As we came back from class to class to check on it, that frog never gave a complaining kick, never jumped out of the water as it literally boiled to death in a period of about three hours.

The point is, little by little, degree by degree, hour by hour, day by day, death can be in the process of occurring and we don't even realize it.

—Paul Lee Tan, *Encyclopedia of 7,700 Illustrations*

THE IMMUTABLE LAW of sowing and reaping has held sway. We are now the hapless possessors of moral depravity, and we seek in vain for a cure. The tares of indulgence have overgrown the wheat of moral restraint. Our homes have suffered. Divorce has grown to epidemic proportion. When the morals of society are upset, the family is the first to suffer. The home is the basic unit of our society, and a nation is only as strong as her homes. The breaking up of a home does not often make headlines, but it eats like termites at the structure of the nation.

—Billy Graham, *World Aflame*

"MAN WAS MADE to dwell in a garden," says Dr. Harold C. Mason, "but through sin he has been forced to dwell in a field, a field which he has wrested from his enemies by sweat and tears, and which he preserves only at the price of constant watchfulness and endless toil. Let him but relax his efforts for a few years and the wilderness will claim his field again. The jungle and forest will swallow his labors and all his loving care will have been in vain."

Every farmer knows the hunger of the wilderness, that hunger which no modern farm machinery, no improved agricultural methods, can ever quite destroy. No matter how well prepared the soil, how well kept the fences, how carefully painted the buildings, let the owner neglect for a while his prized and valued acres and they will revert again to the wild and be swallowed up by the jungle or the wasteland. The bias of nature is toward the wilderness, never toward the fruitful field. That, we repeat, every farmer knows.

—A. W. Tozer, *The Root of the Righteous*

THROUGH THE PREACHING of George Whitefield in the eighteenth-century Robert Robinson was saved out of a background that was gross and godless. Robinson was in his young twenties. In fact, at the age of twenty-three, in 1758, he was led of God to put into print his testimony which we know today as the hymn words, "Come, Thou fount of every blessing, Tune my heart to sing Thy grace; Streams of mercy, never ceasing, Call for songs of loudest praise. Teach me some melodious sonnet, Sung by flaming tongues above; Praise His name—I'm fixed upon it—Name of God's redeeming love."

Robinson defected. He left the claims of Jesus Christ in the dust and he lived like a carnal, godless man, until one day he stepped into a stagecoach occupied by a woman whose face was buried in a book. It was a book of verse. She did not know him nor he her. But she began to read this particular poem, and said to him, the stranger, "Listen to this, 'Come, Thou fount of every blessing, Tune my heart to sing Thy grace; Streams of mercy, never ceasing, Call for songs of loudest praise.'" He sat quietly, surrounded by guilt.

And then she got to that stanza, "Prone to wander, Lord, I feel it, Prone to leave the God I love; Here's my heart, O take and seal it; Seal it for Thy courts above." He said, "Stop! Stop! I am the poor, unhappy man who composed that verse many years ago. I would give a thousand worlds to enjoy the feelings I then had."

—Kenneth W. Osbeck, *101 Hymn Stories*

_____

DELINQUENCY
(Also see *Child Rearing*)

DR. ALBERT SIEGEL wrote in the *Stanford Observer,* "When it comes to rearing children, every society is only twenty years away from barbarism. Twenty years is all we have to accomplish the task of civilizing the infants who are born into our midst each year. These savages know nothing of our language, our culture, our religion, our values, our customs of interpersonal relations. The infant is totally ignorant about communism, fascism, democracy, civil liberties, the rights of the minority as contrasted with the prerogatives of the majority, respect, decency, customs, conventions, and manners. The barbarian must be tamed if civilization is to survive."

—*Leadership* magazine, Winter 1987

_____

THE MINNESOTA CRIME COMMISSION reports, "Every baby starts life as a little savage. He is completely selfish and self-centered. He wants what he wants when he wants it—his bottle, his mother's attention, his playmate's toy, his uncle's watch. Deny him these wants, and he seethes with rage and aggressiveness, which would be murderous, were he not helpless. He is dirty. He has no morals, no knowledge, no skills. This means that all children, not just certain children, are born delinquent. If permitted to continue in the self-centered world of his infancy, given free reign to his impulsive actions to satisfy his wants, every child would grow up a criminal, a thief, a killer, a rapist."

—Ray Stedman, *From Guilt to Glory*

IN MY PARENTING and leadership seminars, I tell a true story about a young couple who invited me to their home for dinner some time ago after an all-day program at a university. This man and woman, both highly intelligent, with advanced degrees, had opted for a "child-centered" home so their five-year-old son Bradford would have everything at his disposal to become a winner out there in the competitive world.

When I arrived at their driveway in front of a fashionable two-story Tudor home at the end of a cul-de-sac, I should have known what was in store for me. I stepped on his E.T. doll getting out of the car and was greeted by, "Watch where you're going or you'll have to buy me a new one!"

Entering the front door, I instantly discovered that this was Bradford's place, not his parents'. The furnishings, it appeared, were originally of fine quality. I thought I recognized an Ethan Allen piece that had suffered "the wrath of Khan." We attempted to have a cup of hot cider in the family room, but Bradford was busy running his new Intellivision controls. Trying to find a place to sit down was like hopping on one foot through a mine field, blindfolded.

Bradford got to eat first, in the living room, so he wouldn't be lonely. I nearly dropped my hot cup in my lap in surprise when they brought out a high chair that was designed like an aircraft ejection seat with four legs and straps . . . He was five years old, and had to be strapped into a high chair to get through one meal!

As we started our salads in the dining room, which was an open alcove adjoining the living room, young Bradford dumped his dinner on the carpet and proceeded to pour his milk on top of it to ensure that the peas and carrots would go deep into the shag fibers. His mother entreated, "Brad, honey, don't do that. Mommy wants you to grow up strong and healthy like Daddy. I'll get you some more dinner while Daddy cleans it up."

While they were occupied with their chores, Bradford had unfastened his seat belts, scrambled down from his perch, and joined me in the dining room, helping himself to my olives. "I think you should wait for your own dinner," I said politely, removing his hand from my salad bowl. He swung his leg up, to kick me in the knee, but my old ex-pilot reflexes didn't fail me and I crossed my legs so quickly that he missed, came off his feet, and came down hard on the seat of his pants. You'd have thought he was at the dentist's office! He screamed and ran to his mother, sobbing, "He hit me!" When his parents asked what happened, I calmly informed them that he had fallen accidentally and that, besides, "I'd never hit the head of a household!"

I knew it was time to be on my way when they put Prince Valiant to bed by placing granola cookies on the stairs as enticers. He ate his way up to bed! "How are you ever going to motivate him to go to school?" I asked quietly. "Oh, I'm sure we'll come up with something," they laughed. "Yes, but what if the neighborhood dogs eat what you put out? He'll lose his way just like Hansel and Gretel!" (I asked the Lord for forgiveness for not remaining silent, as I drove back to the airport.)

—Denis Waitley, *Seeds of Greatness*

Who Is to Blame?

We read it in the papers and hear it on the air
    of killing and stealing and crime everywhere.
We sigh and we say as we notice the trend,
    "This young generation . . . where will it end?"
But can we be sure that it's their fault alone?

Are we less guilty, who place in their way
    too many things that lead them astray?
Too much money, too much idle time;
    Too many movies of passion and crime.
Too many books not fit to be read
    Too much evil in what they hear said.
Too many children encouraged to roam
    Too many parents who won't stay home.
Kids don't make the movies, they don't write the books
    They don't paint the pictures of gangsters and crooks.
They don't make the liquor, they don't run the bars,
    They don't change the laws, and they don't make the cars.
They don't peddle the drugs that muddle the brain;
    That's all done by older folks . . . eager for gain.
Delinquent teenagers; oh how we condemn
    The sins of the nation and blame it on them.
By the laws of the blameless, the Savior made known
    Who is there among us to cast the first stone?
For in so many cases—it's sad but it's true—
    The title "Delinquent" fits older folks too!

—Charles R. Swindoll, *Come Before Winter*

THE HOUSTON POLICE DEPARTMENT has Twelve Rules for Raising Delinquent Children:

1. Begin with infancy by giving the child everything he wants; in this way, he will believe the world owes him a living.
2. When he picks up that vulgar word, laugh at him; this will make him think he's cute.
3. Never give him spiritual training. Wait until he is twenty-one and then let him decide for himself.
4. Always avoid the use of the word "wrong." It may develop a guilt complex. This will condition him to believe later, when he's arrested, that society is against him and he's being persecuted.
5. Pick up everything he leaves around the house. Do everything for him so that he will be experienced in throwing all responsibility upon others.
6. Let him read any printed matter he gets his hands on. Be careful that the silverware and drinking glasses are sterilized, but let his mind feed on filth.
7. Quarrel frequently in the presence of your children; this way they won't be shocked when the home is broken up later on.
8. Give the child all the spending money he wants. Never make him earn his own.
9. Satisfy his every craving for food, drink, and comfort. See that every sensual desire is gratified; hold back nothing.
10. Take his part against neighbors and officers of the law and teachers. They're all prejudiced against your child.
11. When he gets into trouble, apologize for yourself by saying, "I never could do anything with that boy anyway."
12. Prepare yourself for a life of grief; you will likely have it!

—Paul Lee Tan, *Encyclopedia of 7,700 Illustrations*

DEMONIC ACTIVITY

THE UPSURGE in astrological interest is unmistakable evidence of moral and social decay. Occultism rises ominously in times of world turmoil, religious apostasy, and moral decline.

Carroll Righter is perhaps the best known and most successful of United States astrologers. Dubbed "the dean of America's public astrologers," he is one of about 10,000 full-time and 175,000 part-time practitioners in the U.S. alone. Astrology is booming and like almost everything else it is being computerized. A company called Time Pattern Research Institute, Incorporated, has programmed a computer to turn out a 10,000-word horoscope reading in two minutes. It set an early goal of 10,000 capacity in a month, with plans for continued expansion.

—Merrill Unger, *Demons in the World Today*

IN MY DAYS in Southeast Asia, I saw a woman who was so demonized she literally was held by a chain. She had a collar around her neck. Her nails had grown long and she howled at night like an animal. She had the wildest look in her eyes you can imagine. And incredible strength. On one occasion she got loose in the streets of Naha on the island of Okinawa. It took four policemen with all the strength they could muster to get her into the paddy wagon and back on her "leash."

I LIKE Gary Larsen's cartoons, "The Far Side." He had a cartoon once that shows a guy looking real slick, with his sleeves rolled up. He's got an incredible hairdo. His tie is pulled loose. He's holding a vacuum cleaner. In line are people with a television set, a toaster, and another appliance. And he says to the vacuum cleaner, with his hands on it, "I command the foul demons that have clogged this vacuum cleaner to come out." It struck me funny. But I'm not making light of demons; I'm making light of sensationalism.

THE DEVIL TAKES NO HOLIDAY; he never rests. If beaten, he rises again. If he cannot enter in front, he steals in the rear. If he cannot enter at the rear, he breaks through the roof or enters by tunneling under the threshold. He labors until he is in. He uses great cunning and many a plan. When one miscarries, he has another at hand and continues his attempts until he wins.

—Ewald M. Plass, *What Luther Says: An Anthology*, Vol. 1

DEPRAVITY

(Also see *Degeneracy*)

ONE EDUCATED INDIAN from Calcutta heard the first chapter of Romans read at a gathering and said, "The man who wrote that certainly knew India."

—Donald Barnhouse, *Romans*, Vol. 1

WE ARE ALL like the moon. We have a dark side we don't want anybody to see.

—Mark Twain

A JEWISH MAN stepped in and watched a part of Eichmann's trial and burst into tears. Someone next to him said, "Your anger must be unbearable." He said, "No, it isn't anger. The longer I sit here, the more I realize I have a heart like his."

—Charles Colson, 1993 Templeton Address, "The Enduring Revolution"

NO MAN suddenly becomes base.

—F. B. Meyer

ONCE, WHEN Thomas Carlyle was in London, he was the guest of a glittering socialite. She was light of mind, one of those butterflies that lives on the surface sipping here, sipping there. In the course of the conversation she began to speak of the guilt of the Jewish people in slaying the Son of God, the Savior of the world. She said that if Christ were to come today, we would open our homes to Him and welcome Him. Then she said, "Mr. Carlyle, do you agree?" The great Scot essayist replied, "No, I do not agree, madam. I think that had He come very fashionably dressed with plenty of money and preaching doctrines most palatable to the higher orders, I might have had the honor of receiving a card from you on the back of which would be written, 'To meet our Savior.' But if He came uttering His precepts and denouncing the Pharisees and associating with publicans as He did, you would have treated Him much as the Jews did, and cried out, 'Take Him to Newgate and hang Him.'"

—W. A. Criswell, *Expository Sermons on Galatians*

IF DEPRAVITY WERE BLUE, we'd be blue all over.

—Addison Laetsch

J. OSWALD SANDERS recounts a story about the great American preacher, Henry Ward Beecher, who was having constant trouble with the clock in his church. It was always either too fast or too slow. One day, in exasperation, he put a sign over it which read, "Don't blame my hands, the trouble lies deeper."

—J. Oswald Sanders, *For Believers Only*

STANLEY KRAMER'S FILM *Judgment at Nuremberg* is a cinematic masterpiece, intelligent and eloquent. Set in 1948, the film revolves around the trial of four German judges who have been indicted for their participation in Nazi atrocities. The crux of the film is the issue of moral responsibility, but it also paints a subtle yet penetrating contrast between the power of Hitler's followers and the helplessness of his victims.

After listening to the disquieting opening remarks of the prosecution and defense, the presiding judge, played by Spencer Tracy, goes for a walk around historic Nuremberg. He is taken by the city's charm—until he reaches the arena where so many Nazi rallies had been held. With his eyes on the vast stands and the platform where Hitler had screamed out his hateful messages, the judge hears the ghostly voices of that fateful place. The shouts and cheers of the tremendous throng rise and swell, finally giving way to the voice of Hitler himself. Tracy's character is struck by the ferocity of the pride, the immensity of the power.

Later, back in the courtroom, the prosecution shows films of concentration camps. Silently, image after image of starved men and babies, emaciated bodies of the nameless dead heaped in piles, and the charred remains in the crematoriums testify to the horror of the crimes and the depth of human depravity.

WEBSTER SAYS *depraved* means, "marked by corruption or evil, perverted, crooked." It's important that you understand this is an internal disease; you can't detect it from the outside. Most folks don't *look* depraved. Most of us do a masterful job of covering it up. But never doubt that underneath, deep down inside, there is this disease that eats away at us and pollutes our thoughts and our words (intellect), our relationships (emotions), and our actions (will).

THE AVERAGE PERSON would define depravity by saying that it means that man is as bad as he can be. However, if we adopt that as an acceptable definition, immediately our theology is brought into question because we know men who are not as bad as they can be. We know many men who are good men, kind men, generous men, moral men, men who contribute much in the home and in the community. Rather, the doctrine of depravity says that man is as bad *off* as he can be. There is a vast difference between being as *bad* as he can be and being as bad *off* as he can be.

The doctrine of depravity has to do, not with man's estimation of man, but rather with God's estimation of man. We are the heirs of generations of the teaching of evolution which sees man in an ever-ascending spiral, rising higher and higher from the depth from which he has sprung, until finally he will reach the stars. So widely accepted is that concept that we have come somehow to feel that there is so much good in the worst of us that man is not so bad off after all. When we measure men by man, we can always find someone who is lower than we are on the moral or ethical scale, and the comparison gives us a feeling of self-satisfaction. But the Scriptures do not measure men by man; they measure men by God who has created them. The creature is measured by the Creator and is found to be wanting.

—J. Dwight Pentecost, *Things Which Become Sound Doctrine*

THREE TORNADOES ripped through Omaha, Nebraska in 1975, destroying five hundred homes, damaging one thousand others, killing three people, and injuring one-hundred and thirty-two. National Guardsmen were called out, not to help in the calamity, but to patrol a 3,400-square-block area to prevent looting. The Nebraska governor surveyed the area and said it was the worst case of property damage in the history of Nebraska. It is a sad commentary on our modern society that men with guns had to prevent scavengers from helping themselves to things in devastated sections of the city.

DEPRESSION

A Psalm in a Hotel Room

I'm alone Lord
alone
a thousand miles from home.
There's no one here who knows my name
except the clerk
and he spelled it wrong
no one to eat dinner with
laugh at my jokes
listen to my gripes
be happy with me about what happened today
and say that's great.
No one cares.

There's just this lousy bed
and slush in the street outside
between the buildings.
I feel sorry for myself
and I've plenty of reason
to. Maybe I ought to say
I'm on top of it
praise the Lord
things are great
but they're not.
Tonight
it's all
gray slush.

—Joseph Bayly, *Psalms of My Life*

MANY YEARS AGO when I was living in Dallas, I received a phone call which led me to a tiny and dirty garage apartment. I was met at the screen door by a man with a twelve-gauge shotgun. He invited me in. We sat for over an hour at a tiny kitchen table with a naked light bulb hanging above it. He poured out a heartbreaking story. He had just been released from the hospital, recovering from back surgery. He was alone, having lost contact with his wife (and their only son) when his marriage failed many years before. As we talked of the man's intense struggles, I noticed that his apartment was full of pictures—all of them of his son at various stages of growth.

There were photos taken of the boy when he was still in diapers. Others were with his dad when the lad was graduating from kindergarten. Still others showed him in his Little League uniform with a bat over his shoulder— on and on, right up through high school. The man's entire focus centered upon a marriage that had failed and especially a boy he no longer was able to enjoy. Those nostalgic "misty, water-colored memories of the way we were" held him captive in a prison-house of despondency. Unfortunately, my attempts to help him see beyond the walls of his anguish proved futile. In less than a week, he shot himself to death in his car which he had driven deep into the woods in East Texas. To him, life was no longer worth the fight.

CANDIDLY, of all the groups I minister to, few are more depressed and exhausted than a group of pastors. They are overworked, usually underpaid, and almost without exception underappreciated, though most of them are doing a remarkable piece of work. Mild depressions can come on us unexpectedly and erode our willingness. Often we can't explain such depression at the time.

Though writing more than a hundred years ago, Charles Spurgeon described in a chapter of his book, *Lectures to My Students,* exactly some of the reasons we suffer from burnout in ministry today. He even admitted to depression in his own life, often before a great success, sometimes after a great success, and usually because of something he couldn't explain. He called this chapter "The Minister's Fainting Fits." Listen to his candid remarks.

> Fits of depression come over most of us. Usually cheerful as we may be, we must at intervals be cast down. The strong are not always vigorous, the wise not always ready, the brave not always courageous, and the joyous not always happy. There may be here and there men of iron . . . but surely the rust frets even these.

> Spring is past,
> Summer is gone,
> Winter is here,
> And my song that I was meant to sing
> Is still unsung.
> I have spent my days
> Stringing and unstringing my instrument.
>
> —Robert Schuller, *Self-Love*

JOHN BUNYAN'S CLASSIC ALLEGORY of the Christian Life, *The Pilgrim's Progress,* follows the hero, Christian, on his treacherous journey from the City of Destruction to his heavenly destination, the Celestial City. Along the way, Christian and a companion approach "a very miry slough, that was in the midst of the plain; and they being heedless, did both fall suddenly into the bog. The name of the slough was Despond. Here, therefore, they wallowed for a time, being grievously bedaubed with dirt; and Christian, because of the burden that was on his back, began to sink in the mire."

His traveling companion manages to get out, but rather than giving Christian a hand up, he turns away from the path of life and flees home. Christian, then, is left struggling alone in the boggy, muddy hole until a man named Help—the Holy Spirit—kindly pulls him free from despondency's pit and sets him on solid ground.

Christian asks Help why this dangerous plot of land has not been "mended, that poor travellers might go" on heaven's journey "with more security?" And Help tellingly replies; "This miry slough is such a place as cannot be mended."

How true this is in real life! No matter how hard we try or how spiritually mature we are, miry sloughs are inevitable. Not because we have failed somehow, but because no one is immune to despondency; it is "such a place as cannot be mended"—only traveled through.

—John Bunyan, *The Pilgrim's Progress*

"I AM NOW the most miserable man living," wrote a famous American leader. "If what I feel were equally distributed to the whole human family, there would not be one cheerful face on earth. To remain as I am is impossible. I must die or be better." You may be surprised to know that the man who wrote that was Abraham Lincoln.

Years later, in the darkest days of the Civil War, Lincoln wrestled constantly with the specter of unrelenting depression. It can strike anyone. No one is immune. Not even a nation's president. Here is this marvelous man with magnificent character, feeling absolutely alone. . . . Surely, the president ought to sleep well because of his protection, because of his wise counsel, to say nothing of his financial security. Yet there he was, tossing and turning through the night, haunted by dark and debilitating thoughts.

Roy P. Basler, *The Collected Works of Abraham Lincoln*

DISCIPLESHIP

I Met the Master

I had walked life's path with an easy tread,
I had followed where comfort and pleasure led;
And then by chance in a quiet place—
I met my Master face to face.

With station and rank and wealth for goal,
Much thought for body but none for soul,
I had entered to win this life's mad race—
When I met my Master face to face.

I met Him and knew Him, and blushed to see
That His eyes full of sorrow were fixed on me;

And I faltered, and fell at His feet that day
While my castles vanished and melted away.

Melted and vanished; and in their place
I saw naught else but my Master's face;
And I cried aloud: "Oh, make me meet
To follow the marks of Thy wounded feet."

My thought is now for the souls of men;
I have lost my life to find it again,
Ever since alone in that holy place
My Master and I stood face to face.

—John R. Rice, *Poems That Preach*

Hast Thou No Scar?

Hast thou no scar?
No hidden scar on foot, or side, or hand?
I hear Thee sung as mighty in the land,
I hear them hail thy bright ascendant star,
Hast thou no scar?

Hast thou no wound?
Yet I was wounded by the archers, spent,
Leaned Me against a tree to die; and rent
By ravening beasts that compassed Me, I swooned:
Hast *thou* no wound?

No wound? no scar?
Yet, as the Master shall the servant be,
And pierced are the feet that follow Me;
But thine are whole: can he have followed far
Who has nor wound nor scar?

—Amy Carmichael, *Toward Jerusalem*

Make Me Thy Fuel

FROM prayer that asks that I may be
Sheltered from winds that beat on Thee,
From fearing when I should aspire,
From faltering when I should climb higher,

From silken self, O Captain, free
Thy soldier who would follow Thee.

From subtle love of softening things,
From easy choices, weakenings,
Not thus are spirits fortified,
Not this way went the Crucified,
From all that dims Thy Calvary,
O Lamb of God, deliver me.

Give me the love that leads the way,
The faith that nothing can dismay,
The hope no disappointments tire,
The passion that will burn like fire,
Let me not sink to be a clod:
Make me Thy fuel, Flame of God.

—Amy Carmichael, *Toward Jerusalem*

IT IS POSSIBLE to be a follower of Jesus without being a disciple; to be a camp follower without being a soldier of the king; to be a hanger-on in some great work without pulling one's weight. Once someone was talking to a great scholar about a younger man. He said, "So and so tells me that he was one of your students." The teacher answered devastatingly, "He may have attended my lectures, but he was not one of my students." There is a world of difference between attending lectures and being a student. It is one of the supreme handicaps of the Church that in the Church there are so many distant followers of Jesus and so few real disciples.

—William Barclay, *The Gospel of Luke*

ROBERT FROST'S POEM "The Road Not Taken" describes two roads discovered during a walk in the woods. Frost knows he can only explore one, and he tells himself that someday he will travel the other. But, realistically, he knows he will never return. And by the time we reach the end of the poem, we realize the poet is talking about something infinitely more important than a simple choice of paths.

I shall be telling this with a sigh
Somewhere ages and ages hence:
Two roads diverged in a wood, and I—
I took the one less traveled by,
And that has made all the difference.

No, Frost is not talking about the choice of paths in a wood, but the choice of paths in a person's life. Choosing a road symbolizes any choice we must make between alternatives that appear equally attractive but lead to entirely different destinations.

—Robert Frost, *Complete Poems of Robert Frost*

_____

DISCIPLESHIP IS anything that causes what is believed in the heart to have demonstrable consequences in our daily life.

—Eugene Peterson

_____

DISCOURAGEMENT
(Also see *Attitude*)

I ENJOYED a Charles Schulz cartoon that showed Snoopy sliding along the frozen pond on his little bare paws. He's havin' a great time. He's smiling and he has a little skullcap on. Lucy walks up and slides out onto the pond with her skates on, and Snoopy doing a little twirl, slides up right in front of her. She says to him, "That's not skating, that sliding." And he just stands there and looks up at her as she goes on with her lecture, "You don't have any skates on. Skating is when you have skates on. You're not skating at all. YOU'RE JUST SLIDING!"

Snoopy finally walks off with his little feet to the side and says, "How could I have been so stupid. And I thought I was having fun."

_____

AS A RECENTLY RETIRED MAN was sitting on his porch down in Kentucky, his Social Security check was delivered. He went to the mailbox to retrieve it and thought to himself, *Is this all my life is going to be from this time on? Just sitting on the porch waiting for my next Social Security check to arrive?* It was a discouraging thought.

So he took a legal pad and began to write down all the gifts, all the blessings, all the talents, and everything that he had going for him. He listed them all, even small things. For example, he included the fact that he was the only one in the world who knew his mother's recipe for fried chicken in which she used eleven different herbs and spices.

He went down to the local restaurant, asked if he could get a job cooking their chicken. Very soon the chicken became the most popular item on the menu. He opened his own restaurant in Kentucky. Then he opened a string of restaurants and eventually sold the Kentucky Fried Chicken franchise to a national organization for millions of dollars. He became their public representative and continued in that role until his death.

LARRY OLSEN describes a man lost in the desert: "He has been out of food and water for days. His lips are swollen, his tongue is swollen, he's all beat up and bloody. Some of his bones are almost peeking through. He has been scraped and beat up by the cactus and sand and sun. He's blistered. As he's crawling over this little hill he comes across this little plant and props himself up on one bloody elbow, looks down at this plant and says, 'You know, if things keep going like this I might get discouraged!'"

—Larry Olsen, *Outdoor Survival Skills*

IT WAS ADVERTISED that the devil was going to put his tools up for sale. On the date of the sale the tools were placed for public inspection, each being marked with its sale price. There were a treacherous lot of implements. Hatred, Envy, Jealousy, Doubt, Lying, Pride, and so on. Laid apart from the rest of the pile was a harmless-looking tool, well-worn and priced very high.

"The name of the tool?" asked one of the purchasers.

"Oh," said the adversary, "that's Discouragement."

"Why have you priced it so high?"

"Because it's more useful to me than the others. I can pry open and get inside a person's heart with that one, when I cannot get near him with other tools. Now once I get inside, I can make him do what I choose. It's a badly worn tool, because I use it on almost everyone since few people know it belongs to me."

The devil's price for Discouragement was so high, he never sold it. It's still his major tool, and he still uses it on God's people today.

—John Lawrence, *Down to Earth*

DISOBEDIENCE
(Also see *Rebellion*)

ADAM'S DISOBEDIENCE severed him from God, the source of power, and gradually, as time passed, nullified the development of the faculties with which God had originally endowed him.

—Merrill Tenney, *The Reality of the Resurrection*

Grumbler's Song

In country, town, or city, some people can be found
Who found their lives in grumbling at everything around;
O yes, they always grumble, no matter what we say,
For these are chronic grumblers and they grumble night and day.
They grumble in the city, they grumble on the farm;
They grumble at their neighbors, they think it is no harm;
They grumble at their husbands, they grumble at their wives;
They grumble at their children, but the grumbler never thrives.
They grumble when it's raining, they grumble when it's dry;
And if the crops are failing, they grumble and they sigh.
They grumble at low prices and grumble when they're high;
They grumble all the year 'round, they grumble till they die.
They grumble on Monday, Tuesday, Wednesday,
Grumble on Thursday too,
Grumble on Friday, Saturday, Sunday,
They grumble the whole week through.

—Thoro Harris, quoted by Leslie Flynn, *Did I Say That?*

I REMEMBER BACK WHEN I was in my early teens, one of my earliest jobs was throwing a paper route. I threw the *Houston Press* for a couple of years during junior high school. It was a good job and kept me out of mischief, but it got tiring.

After a long afternoon of folding about two hundred papers, throwing my route, and turning toward home on my bike, I remember coming to the backyard of a large home at the corner across the street from our house. I thought to myself, *I'm tired . . . no need to go all the way down to the end of the street and around this big yard. I'll just cut across and be home in a jiffy.* It was a quick and easy shortcut. The first time I did that I entertained a little twinge of guilt as I rode my bike across that nice, plush grass. You need to understand, this was a beautiful yard. To make matters worse, our neighbor was very particular about it. I had watched him manicure it week after week. Still, I figured it wouldn't hurt just this once. Late the next afternoon I came tooling down the same street, thinking, *I wonder if I ought to use that same shortcut?* I did . . . with less guilt than the first time. Theoretically, something told me I shouldn't; but practically, I rationalized around the wrong.

In less than two weeks my bicycle tires had begun to wear a narrow path across the yard. By then, I knew in my heart I really should be going down and around the corner, but I didn't. I just shoved all those guilt feelings down out of sight.

By the end of the third week, a small but very obvious sign appeared near the sidewalk, blocking the path I had made. It read: "Keep Off the Grass—No Bikes." Everything but my name was on the sign! I confess, I ignored it; I went around the sign and rode right on over my path, glancing at the sign as I rode by. Admittedly, I felt worse! Why? The sign identified my sin which, in turn, intensified my guilt. But what is most interesting, the sign didn't stop me from going across the yard. As a matter of fact, it held a strange fascination. It somehow prodded me on to further wrong.

DO YOU REMEMBER the last time you got a spanking? I remember the last time I got one. I had reached the ripe old and wise age of thirteen. That's the age where you are amazed that your father has been able to make it as far in life, being so ignorant without your counsel. As a matter of fact, the spanking was on my thirteenth birthday. And in our home, since this fell on a Saturday, when you had a birthday you were sort of "king for a day." I remember lying around in the bed and on the sofa, barking orders here and there, demanding response.

And so my father, from the flower bed outside, sensing the need for some correction, called me, "Charles." And I said, "Yeah," which was mistake number one, because in our home you didn't say "Yeah"; you said, "Yes sir." And then he called my name again and said, "Come out and help me weed the flower bed." And I said, "No," which was mistake number two. He graciously continued his pleading by saying, "Now don't lie there and act like a three-year-old. Come out and help me weed this flower bed." I said, "Daddy, I'm not three, I'm thirteen." Now that's the last thing I remember on that day, because with both hands and both feet he landed on my body. And he did not let go until I was very vigorously weeding the flower bed.

I still remember it even though it was years ago. As we worked together through most of that day, he said to me at a time that was well chosen, "Son, I would be less than a good dad if I did not correct you when you disobey."

DIVORCE

(Also see *Marriage*)

A WOMAN, married thirty years, was asked, "In your many years of marriage did you ever consider divorce?" She said, "No, I never considered divorce . . . murder, maybe."

—Ray Stedman, sermon "How to Repent," January 13, 1980

BILLY ROSE told a story about a man who, after twenty years of marriage, decided to divorce his wife. In preparing for the financial settlement, he began to rummage through his old checks. One canceled check after another stirred up memories of a long-forgotten past: the check to the hotel where he and his wife had spent their honeymoon, the check for their first car, the check for the hospital bill for their daughter's birth, the check for the $2,000 down payment on their first home.

Finally, he could stand it no longer. He pushed the checks aside, reached for the telephone, and called his wife. Telling her they had invested too much in each other to throw it all away, he asked her to start over with him in a fresh beginning. Checkbooks often reveal where our treasure is.

A FEW YEARS AGO a divorce lawyer submitted the opinion that most divorces result from romanticized expectations. Jack thinks that being married to Jill will be utter bliss. He calls her "Angel" and "Sweetie." Then, shortly after the wedding bells have become an echo, the truth sets in: There are unpleasant moods, weight gains, burned dinners, hair curlers. He silently wonders how he ever got into this. He secretly thinks that she has deceived him.

On the other side, before marriage Jill's heart beats a little faster when she thinks of Jack. It will be such heaven to be married to him. Then there are cigarette ashes, his addiction to sports events on television, minor but painful insensitivities. . . . The doorknob he promised to fix still comes off in her hand. Jill cries a lot and starts looking up "marriage counselors" in the yellow pages.

Disillusionment always seems to follow when we expect someone else to make us happy. Such expectations are a parade that always gets rained on. The place called "Camelot" and the person call "Right" just don't exist. . . . I once saw a cartoon of a huge woman standing over her diminutive, seated husband, demanding "Make me happy."

—John Powell, *Happiness Is an Inside Job*

GETTING MARRIED is like buying a phonograph record: you buy it for what's on one side, but you have to take the flip side too. Getting divorced is like getting the hole in the record.

—Jim Smoke, *Growing through Divorce*

RABBI EARL GROLLMAN, a professional divorce lecturer and author who believes divorce can be more traumatic than death, says, "The big difference is, death has closure, it's over. With divorce, it's never over."

—Charles R. Swindoll, *Strike the Original Match*

SURRENDERING IS NOT AN OPTION if you plan to win a war . . . or succeed in a marriage. I firmly agree with a San Francisco attorney whom I heard say, "There are two processes that must never be started prematurely: embalming and divorce."

—Charles R. Swindoll, *Strike the Original Match*

DUTY

IN A SPEECH before the House of Commons in 1940 Winston Churchill said, "Let us . . . brace ourselves to do our duties, and so bear ourselves that if the British Empire and its Commonwealth last for a thousand years, men will still say: 'This was their finest hour.'"

—John Bartlett, *Bartlett's Familiar Quotations*

> Theirs is not to make reply,
> Theirs is not to reason why,
> Theirs but to do or die.
> Into the valley of Death
> Rode the six hundred.

—Alfred Lord Tennyson from "The Charge of the Light Brigade"

I DON'T REMEMBER MANY of the speakers who spoke in chapel during my four student years at Dallas Seminary, but I'll never forget one soft-spoken man, who addressed our temptation simply to carry out a profession. And as he looked across this audience of three hundred young theologs he said, "Men, we don't have a profession to practice, we have a debt to discharge." The realization of a debt owed to God for His mercy and the gift of His Son should motivate us in our duty.

STEVE BROWN relates the story of a soldier in World War I who was so distraught with the war that he deserted. He tried to find his way to the coast so he could catch a boat and make his way back incognito to his homeland in England.

In the darkness of the night he stumbled on a road sign. It was so pitch black and he was so lost. He had no idea where he was or what the sign said. He decided to climb the pole. When he got to the crossbeam, he held on to read the sign. Taking out a match, he lit it, and looked directly in the face of Jesus Christ. He had climbed an outdoor crucifix!

Stunned by what he saw, he realized the shame of his life. He was looking into the face of the One who had endured it all and had never turned back. The next morning the soldier was back in the trenches.

—*Preaching* magazine, 1989

$\mathcal{E}e$

EASTER

(Also see *Resurrection*)

DR. GORDON one Easter brought an old beat-up rusty bird cage and sat it next to the pulpit. As he gave his sermon that Easter morning he held up the cage and said, "You might be wondering why this is here. As a matter of fact, that's not the normal part of an Easter service, having a bird cage here."

He said, "Let me tell you the story of it. Several days ago I was noticing a little boy in tattered and torn blue jeans and a dirty T-shirt, cap off to the side, whistling, walking down an alley, swinging this bird cage. Clinging to the bottom of the cage were little field sparrows he had caught. So I stopped him and asked, 'Say, sonny, what do you have there?' He said, 'Oh, I've got some birds.' 'What are you gonna do with 'em?' I asked. 'Oh, mess around with them, tease 'em, something like that.' 'Well,' I asked, 'when you get tired of 'em, what are you gonna do?' He thought a moment and said, 'Well, I got a couple of cats at home and they like birds. I think I'll just let them have at 'em.'"

Dr. Gordon said his heart went out to the little birds so he made the little lad an offer. "How much do you want for the birds?" Surprised, the boy, said, "Mister, these birds ain't no good." "Well," Dr. Gordon said, "regardless, how much would you like for 'em?" The little fellow said, "How about two bucks?" He said, "Sold." So he reached in his pocket and peeled off two dollar bills. The little boy shoved the bird cage forward pleased with his stroke of good fortune.

When the boy left, the pastor walked a good distance away, lifted open the little cage door and said, "Shoo, shoo." And he shoved them out of the door and they flew free.

The empty bird cage was the perfect illustration of how Satan had the human race trapped and frightened. Jesus Christ not only paid the price for our freedom; He has set us free.

—Paul Lee Tan, *Encyclopedia of 7,700 Illustrations*

IF I WERE TO ASK YOU to describe Easter without using any words, you could only use punctuation marks, which punctuation mark would you choose to describe this Easter for yourself? Maybe this Easter is a comma for you. It makes you stop, pause, think, and listen, but that's about it. Perhaps today is a downer—a big bold period. You thought you'd feel excited, but instead it seems to be more like empty ritual. You feel like you're not on the inside, but on the outside . . . an onlooker.

It was a day when life felt like a period for Jesus' disciples. He was dead. He was buried. An end to expectations. But wait—news of an empty tomb . . . the period is no longer a period, it's a question mark. That's worse than a period. Now they're beginning to doubt. Where is He? They're perplexed. The guards are gone, the stone is rolled away. He is not there. And if not there, where?

An angel speaks, "Why do you seek the living One among the dead? He is not here, but He has risen. Remember how He spoke to you while He was in Galilee, saying that the Son of Man must be delivered into the hands of sinful men, and how He must be crucified, and the third day He must rise again." Of course they remembered! The periods are gone. The question marks are removed. There is one massive exclamation point!

That's what Easter is all about . . . an exclamation of gratitude and of praise for the resurrection of Jesus Christ and for the salvation His victory over death brought to us.

—Joe LoMusio, *If I Should Die Before I Live*

EDUCATION

(Also see *Bible, Books, Knowledge, Wisdom*)

EVER NOTICE HOW some just seem to be professional students? I heard one say, "College? The best twelve years of my life."

SOME PEOPLE STRUGGLE for answers. One student told the medical school professor that in some points his lectures disagreed with the textbook. When shown where in the textbook, the professor tore those pages out of it . . . "Now it agrees with me."

I LAUGHED at the little elementary school child who took a test on human anatomy and failed it. She was the only one in the class who failed that particular examination. This is how her test read: "The human body is composed of three parts: the branium, the borax, and the abominable cavity. The branium contains the brain. The borax contains the lungs, the liver, and the living things. The abominable cavity contains the bowels, of which there are five: *a, e, i, o,* and *u.*"

—Anne Ortlund, *Disciplines of a Beautiful Woman*

A STUDENT ONCE ASKED the president of his school if there was a course he could take that was shorter than the one prescribed. "Oh yes," replied the president, "but it depends on what you want to be. When God wants to make an oak, He takes a hundred years, but when He wants to make a squash, it only takes six months."

—Miles J. Stanford, *Principles of Spiritual Growth*

A SCHOOLBOY SAID, "The pilgrims came here seeking freedom from you know what; landed and gave thanks to you know who; now we can worship on Sundays you know where."

EDUCATION—the great mumbo jumbo and fraud of the ages—purports to equip us to live and is prescribed as a universal remedy for everything from juvenile delinquency to premature senility. For the most part it serves to enlarge stupidity, inflate conceit, enhance credulity, and put those subjected to it at the mercy of brainwashers with printing presses, radio, and television at their disposal.

—Malcolm Muggeridge, *Jesus Rediscovered*

READING MAKETH a full man; speaking, a ready man; writing, an exact man.

—Francis Bacon

EGO
(Also see *Pride*)

THERE WAS A young, gifted minister whose preaching was a cut above the ordinary. As the ranks of his congregation began to swell, his head followed suit. After he had delivered his latest barnburner one morning, one of his loyal parishioners earnestly shook his hand and said, "You're becoming one of the greatest expositors of this generation, pastor."

As he squeezed his head into the car and slid behind the steering wheel, his weary wife alongside him and all the kids stuffed into the back seat, he could not resist sharing the story.

"Mrs. Franklin told me she thought I was one of the greatest expositors of this generation," he said proudly, caught up in the heady swirl of the woman's exaggerated compliment.

No response.

Fishing for affirmation, he glanced at his silent wife with a weak smile and prodded, "I wonder just how many 'great expositors' there are in this generation?"

Unable to resist the opportunity to set the record straight, she said quietly, "One less than you think, my dear."

—Al Bryant, *1,000 New Illustrations*

AT THE CLOSE OF the European phase of World War II, General George Patton was having a conversation with General Omar Bradley. Patton was concerned that now that the battle in Europe was ending, there would be no more need for his services. Bradley assured Patton that that was not so. There was still a battle to be fought in the Pacific, and General Douglas MacArthur would be glad to have his help. Patton replied, "No, MacArthur wouldn't have me. You see, we fought in the same company in World War I; MacArthur was a captain, and I was his lieutenant. One day our company was commanded to take a hill, but our troops were pinned down by enemy artillery. When MacArthur got the order, he jumped to his feet and charged up that hill urging his men to follow him. I advanced with him step by step all the way to the top." Then Patton added, "MacArthur never forgave me for that."

—Haddon Robinson, "Responsible and Dynamic Leadership: A Challenge"

EDITH LIVED in a little world bounded on the north, south, east, and west by Edith.

—Martha Ostenso, *Dictionary of Humorous Quotations*

WHENEVER I'M TEMPTED to become self-important and authoritative, I'm reminded of what the mother whale said to her baby: "When you get to the top and start to 'blow,' that's when you get harpooned!"

—James Dobson, *The Strong-Willed Child*

A GOOD TEST OF EGOTISM is to notice how you listen to others being praised. Until you can do it without indulging in distraction, you still need that impulse to be brought under the grace of God.

—Robert Louis Stevenson, *The Reaper*

BOB ZUPPKE, a famous football coach, once asked the question, "What makes a man fight?" He answered his own question by saying, "Two forces are at war in every fighter, the ego and a goal. An overdose of self-love, coddling of the ego, makes bums of men who ought to be champions. Forgetfulness of self, complete absorption in the goal, often makes champions out of bums."

—Charles Allen, *Joyful Living in the Fourth Dimension*

EGOTISM IS one of the repulsive manifestations of pride. It is the practice of thinking and speaking much of oneself, the habit of magnifying one's attainments or importance. It leads one to consider everything in its relation to himself rather than in relation to God and the welfare of His people.

—J. Oswald Sanders, *Spiritual Leadership*

EMOTIONS

I wish that there were some wonderful place
 Called the land of Beginning Again,
Where all our mistakes and all our heartaches
 And all our poor selfish grief
Could be dropped like a shabby old coat at the door
 And never put on again.
I wish we could come on it all unaware,
 Like the hunter who finds a lost trail;
I wish that the one who our blindness had done
 The greatest injustice of all
Could be at the gates, like an old friend who waits
 For the comrade he's gladdest to hail.

—Hazel Felleman, *Best Loved Poems of the American People*

Feeling blue?

Buy some clothes.

Feeling lonely?

Turn on the radio.

Feeling despondent?

Read a funny book.

Feeling bored?

Watch TV.

Feeling empty?

Eat a sundae.

Feeling worthless?

Clean the house.

Feeling sad?

Tell a joke.

Ain't this modern age wonderful?

You don't gotta feel nothin',

There's a substitute for everythin'!

God have mercy on us!

—Lois Cheney, *God Is No Fool*

A YOUNG BOY lived with his grandfather on the top of a mountain in the Swiss Alps. Often, just to hear the sound of his own voice echoing back to him, he would go outside, cup his hands around his mouth and shout, "HELLO!" Up from the canyons the reply reverberated, "HELLO . . . HELLO . . . hello . . . hello. . . ." Then he would call out, "I LOVE YOU . . . I LOVE YOU . . . I love you . . . love you . . . love you. . . ."

One day the boy seriously misbehaved and his grandfather disciplined him severely. Reacting violently, the child shook his fist and screamed, "I HATE YOU!" To his surprise, the rocks and boulders across the mountainside responded in kind: "I HATE YOU . . . I HATE YOU . . . I hate you . . . hate you . . . hate you . . . ."

And so it is in a family. We could call it one of the immutable laws of physical nature. More particularly, *human nature*. We get in return exactly what we give. It all comes back. Incredible echoes mirror our actions to an emphatic degree, sometimes in greater measure than we give. The results are often embarrassing . . . or tragic.

Tennyson said: "Our echoes roll from soul to soul and grow forever and forever."

—Charles R. Swindoll, *Standing Out*

A PASTOR I KNOW told me about a lady who came to see him about joining the church. She said her doctor had sent her. Recently she had a facelift and when her doctor dismissed her he gave her this advice: "My dear, I have done an extraordinary job on your face, as you can see in the mirror. I have charged you a great deal of money and you were happy to pay it. But I want to give you some free advice. Find a group of people who love God and who will love you enough to help you deal with all the negative emotions inside of you. If you don't, you'll be back in my office in a very short time with your face in far worse shape than before."

—Bruce Larson, *There's A Lot More to Health Than Not Being Sick*

"I can't see, I can't see,"
    says the man who won't look.
Are there colors in the rainbow?
    Are the meadows still green?
Are flowers still blooming,
    and the butterflies seen?

"I can't hear, I can't hear,"
    says the man who won't listen.
Have birds stopped their singing?
    the brooks lost their song?
Has music stopped playing,
    the symphonies gone?

"I don't feel, I don't feel,"
    says the man who won't care.
Aren't feelings but knowing
    of good things and bad?
Of caring for others
    of gladness and sad?

"There's no life, there's no life,"
    says the man who won't live.
Life is naught but what is sought;
    yes, life is simply living.
And life is not collecting things,
    life is really giving.

"I'm not loved, I'm not loved,"
    says the man filled with rage.

Isn't love just reflections
    of what you first give
For all of the others
    with whom you must live?

"There's no God, there's no God,"
    says the man with no faith.
See God's hand in the stars
    in the skies.
In the prayers of a child,
    in your silent sighs.

—Anonymous

ENCOURAGEMENT

I THINK MANY Christians are "dying on the vine" for lack of encouragement from other believers. Proverbs 15:23 says, "A man has joy in an apt answer, And how delightful is a timely word." Isn't that true? It's a delightful thing to receive a timely word. Proverbs 15:30 says, "Bright eyes gladden the heart; Good news puts fat on the bones." Now don't take "fat" literally. It means it will give you emotional prosperity, make your heart lighter, make the day seem more bearable.

A LITTLE NINE-YEAR-OLD boy got tired of practicing the piano. His mother heard the great Paderewski was coming into town to do a concert. She bought two tickets, one for herself and one for her boy. And she dragged him along, sat him down by her in his little tuxedo, and she began visiting with her friends. He looked up on the platform and there was this giant, ebony black, Steinway concert grand piano. The lid on the keyboard was lifted and the leather bench was there. He looked at this piano, popped his knuckles, and said to himself, "Oh, man, I'd like to play that."

So he slipped down the aisle, walked across the front, up the steps, sat down, and started playing "Chopsticks."

Well, the people down front said, "Who . . . who is . . .?" "Quit!" "Hey, kid, stop!" "Where's his mother?" Of course she was embarrassed beyond words.

The great Paderewski, who was back fixing his tie, heard what was going on. So without the boy seeing him, he slipped out on the stage and came in behind the little boy, reached around him and improvised a beautiful melody to go with "Chopsticks." Then he said to the boy, "Keep playing. Don't quit. Don't stop."

—D. H. DeHaan, *Windows on the Word*

ONE OF THE HIGHEST of human duties is the duty of encouragement. . . . It is easy to laugh at men's ideals; it is easy to pour cold water on their enthusiasm; it is easy to discourage others. The world is full of discouragers. We have a Christian duty to encourage one another. Many a time a word of praise or thanks or appreciation or cheer has kept a man on his feet. Blessed is the man who speaks such a word.

—William Barclay, *The Letter to the Hebrews*

IN A CARTOON some years ago a little guy was taking heat from his sister and friends for a newly found "calling"—patting little birds on the head. The distressed birds would approach, lower their little feathered pates to be patted, sigh deeply, and walk away satisfied. It brought him no end of fulfillment—in spite of the teasing he took from others. "What's wrong with patting birds on the head?" he wanted to know. "What's *wrong* with it?" his embarrassed friends replied. "No one else does it!"

If your niche is encouraging, please don't stop. If it is embracing, demonstrating warmth, compassion, and mercy to feathers that have been ruffled by offense and bruised by adversity, for goodness' sake, keep stroking. Don't quit, whatever you do. If God made you a "patter," then keep on patting to the glory of God.

THE LACK OF ENCOURAGEMENT is almost an epidemic. To illustrate this point, when did you last encourage someone else? I firmly believe that an individual is never more Christlike than when full of compassion for those who are down, needy, discouraged, or forgotten. How terribly essential is our commitment to encouragement!

Is there some soul known to you in need of encouragement? A student off at school . . . a young couple up against it . . . a divorcée struggling to gain back self-acceptance . . . a forgotten servant of God laboring in an obscure and difficult ministry . . . a widow who needs your companionship . . . someone who tried something new and failed? Encourage generously!

ENCOURAGEMENT! A new watchword for our times. Shout it out. Pass it around.

ENEMIES

May those that love us, love us;
and those that don't love us,
may God turn their hearts;
and if He doesn't turn their hearts,
may He turn their ankles
so we'll know them by their limping.

—Irish prayer

WE CAN'T IGNORE ENEMIES. When I was a little kid, my dad and I went down to a bay cottage in southern Texas. When we got there, we discovered that the cottage was filled with wasps. I've never seen anything like it in my life. There were absolutely millions of wasps. When we opened the door they just flooded out on us. They were even in the roll in the shade. You pulled the window shade down and out would come the wasps. They were all over the place. Well, we went to work and we cleaned out all the wasps. Then we laid down that evening to go to sleep and I heard something go buzz, buzz, buzz underneath me. I lifted my pillow and wasps were still everywhere between the two mattresses on my bunk. Again, we cleaned them out. Why? Well, with a family reunion beginning in a day or two, we wanted it clean for them. It was essential for the health and happiness of all the family that we deal with this problem.

ENEMIES COME IN ALL SIZES. I read sometime ago about a man who backed his bright, shiny new Cadillac out of the driveway and headed for the freeway on his daily commute to work downtown. He was busily shaving himself as he drove—a normal operation for him. I suppose he had his radio on, and he was listening to the news and traffic reports as he made his way to his office. Witnesses say that suddenly he reached up behind his neck and slumped over the wheel. The car swerved and went into a culvert, and he was killed. His car was completely demolished.

An autopsy was ordered. As they began to put together the details, a keen-thinking physician noticed a small pinprick behind the man's ear where a wasp had probably flown from behind the seat, or some part of the car, and had stung him, temporarily paralyzing a particular area of the nerve and blinding him with pain. He slumped over the wheel, lost control of the car, and died. Normally a grown man with normal strength can just swat away a little wasp with no problem. But when that wasp struck its mark, it led to a fatal crash.

ENTHUSIASM

WHEN GEORGE WHITEFIELD was getting the people of Edinburgh out of their beds at five o'clock in the morning to hear his preaching, a man on his way to the tabernacle met David Hume, the Scottish philosopher and skeptic. Surprised at seeing him on his way to hear Whitefield, the man said, "I thought you did not believe in the gospel." Hume replied, "I don't, but he does!"

—Clarence E. Macartney, *Preaching without Notes*

NOTHING GREAT was ever achieved without enthusiasm.

—Ralph Waldo Emerson

YEARS AGO someone asked Charles Haddon Spurgeon, "How can I communicate like you do?" "It's very simple," he answered. "All you've got to do is pour a bucket of kerosene over yourself and set yourself on fire, and people will come to watch you burn."

—Howard G. Hendricks, *Say It with Love*

ENVIRONMENT

ONE TIME I did a little experiment with something that turned out exactly as I expected. I snipped a piece off the pretty vine that grew outside my window. I purposely selected a piece that was extremely healthy looking to begin with. It was growing. It had little shoots on it reaching upward. It was a deep green, a luxurious color. I put it in my study in a great environment—right between two books, *Robust in Faith* and *All the Prayers of the Bible*. And you know what? Those books didn't do a bit of good for that vine. It just began to wilt even though it was surrounded by good books, a good environment, quietness, and ease. As soon as it was snipped, it lost all its value.

ENVY

(Also see *Jealousy*)

SHAKESPEARE CALLED ENVY "the green sickness." Bacon admitted "it has no holidays." Horace declared that "tyrants never invented a greater torment." Barrie said it "is the most corroding of the vices." Sheridan referred to it in his play *The Critic* when he wrote, "There is not a passion so strongly rooted in the human heart as this." Philip Bailey, the eloquent English poet of yesteryear, vividly described it as "a coat [that] comes hissing hot from hell."

And speaking of hell, no one has done a better job of portraying envy than Dante. In his *Purgatory* . . . the envious sit like blind beggars by a wall. Their eyelids are sewn shut. The symbolism is apt, showing the reader that it is one of the blindest sins—partly because it is unreasonable, partly because the envious person is sewed up in himself and swollen with poisonous thoughts in a dark, constricting world of almost unendurable self-imposed anguish.

Envy Went to Church

Envy went to church this morning.
Being Legion, he sat in every other pew.
Envy fingered wool and silk fabrics,
Hung price tags on suits and neckties.
Envy paced through the parking lot
Scrutinizing chrome and paint.
Envy marched to the chancel with the choir
During the processional. . . .
Envy prodded plain-jane wives
And bright wives married to milquetoast dullards,
Any kind men married to knife-tongued shrews.
Envy thumped at widows and widowers,
Jabbed and kicked college girls without escorts,
Lighted invisible fires inside khaki jackets.
Envy conferred often this morning
With all of his brothers;
He liked his Sunday scores today
But not enough:
Some of his intended clients
Had sipped an antidote marked Grace,
And wore a holy flower named Love.

—Elva McAllaster, *Christian Life*, January 1970

WHAT EXACTLY IS ENVY? How does it differ from its twin, jealousy? Envy (the more sophisticated of the two) is a painful and resentful awareness of an advantage enjoyed by another . . . accompanied by a strong desire to possess the same advantage. Envy wants to have what someone else possesses. Jealousy wants to possess what it already has. Jealousy is coarse and cruel. Envy is sneaky and subtle. Jealousy clutches and smothers. Envy is forever reaching, longing, squinting, thinking (and saying) sinister insinuations.

ETERNITY

(Also see *Heaven*)

A PASTOR WAS PREACHING on going to heaven. He said, "How many of you would like to go to heaven tonight?" And everybody raised their hands but a little boy in the balcony. He tried again, "How many of you would like to go to heaven?" Everybody but that one little fellow in the balcony. So he said to him, "Son, don't you want to go to heaven?" The little boy said, "Yeah, someday, but I thought you were gettin' up a load right now."

—James Hewett, *Illustrations Unlimited*

IF YOU HAVE A STEEL BALL, solid steel, the size of this earth, 25,000 miles in circumference, and every one million years a little sparrow would be released to land on that ball to sharpen his beak and fly away only to come back another million years later and begin again, by the time he would have worn that ball down to the size of a BB, eternity would have just begun.

EVANGELISM

(Also see *Witnessing*)

THE EVANGELISTIC HARVEST is always urgent. The destiny of men and of nations is always being decided. Every generation is strategic. We are not responsible for the past generation, and we cannot bear the full responsibility for the next one; but we do have our generation. God will hold us responsible as to how well we fulfill our responsibilities to this age and take advantage of our opportunities.

—Billy Graham, quoted in Lloyd Cory, *Quote Unquote*

IT IS MY OPINION that the best evangelistic center in the greater metropolitan Boston area is not a church. It is a filling station in Arlington. It was owned and operated by a man named Bob who caught the vision early in his life that his vocation and his calling were to be welded together. As time passed, his station became known as the place to go for gas, new tires, or other car service. I have seen a half-dozen cars lined up bumper to bumper near two pumps in front of that little station just waiting to be served by that man. He has no banners out, no "Jesus Saves" flags, no signs, no "ichthuses," nothing plastered all over the station or in the windows, no sign, "Bring your car to Bob and take your soul to Jesus." He simply *did his job!* He did it well and people knew he was in partnership with the Lord. He led dozens of people to faith in Jesus Christ.

I HAVE PLAYED ENOUGH SPORTS, been in touch with enough coaches, watched enough games, and read closely enough to know that there's one strategy that's deadly. And it's so subtle. You think you can win by doing it, but you lose. It's called sitting on the lead. If you're an athlete or a sportsman, you know what I'm talking about.

When I was in high school, our basketball team went to state finals in Texas. In one state final game we were ahead at halftime 26 to 18. The coach said, "Now we got 'em. We got 'em. Just take it easy." You know what? We lost, 41 to 40. Why? Because we tried to sit on our lead. We thought we had them beat, so we played with a maintenance mentality.

A growing church never gets so far ahead that it can afford to "sit on the lead." Complacency is a major peril to evangelism.

ECCLESIASTICAL CORPSES lie all about us. The caskets in which they repose are lined with satin, and are decorated with flowers. Like the other caskets, they are just large enough for their own occupants with no room for converts. These churches have died of respectability and have been embalmed in self-complacency. If, by the grace of God, our church is alive, be warned of our opportunity or the feet of them that buried thy sisters will be at the door to carry thee out.

—A. J. Gordon

MY MOTHER LOVED the woman who lived across the street from our home who had married late in life. She really had found her security in her husband. He was a wonderful man, and one day, he had a sudden heart attack and died within seconds. After his funeral, she began to visit the gravesite. My mother became very concerned over her friend Thelma.

She said to me one hot summer afternoon, "Charles, I want you to pray. I'm gonna take these cookies and this lemonade across the street and I'm gonna try to encourage Thelma. Just pray that her heart will be open to what I have to say. I'm gonna talk to her about Jesus."

And so I did. My mother, wonderfully, very graciously, led her to Christ. She said to Thelma, "You know, Thelma, there's something I need to mention to you. You really don't need to keep going back to the cemetery." "Oh," she said, "Lovell, I just have to do that." So my mother said, "Well, let me suggest you do it for another reason." She said, "Why don't you go back, not to try to make a 'connection' with your husband, but to minister to other people who are trying to do that."

Thelma took my mother's advice. As a matter of fact, she's the only cemetery evangelist I ever knew. There at the memorial park in Houston she has led a number of people to Jesus Christ.

EXAMPLE

(See *Influence*)

EXCELLENCE

IN HIS BOOK *Lyrics,* Oscar Hammerstein tells of the time he saw a picture of the top of the head of the Statue of Liberty, taken from a helicopter. He was amazed at the detail and painstaking work that was done on the lady's coiffure. Hammerstein reflected that the sculptor could not have imagined, even in his wildest dreams, that one day there would be a device that could look on top of the head of his creation. Yet he gave as much care to that part of the statue as he did to the face, arms, and legs. He wrote, "When you are creating a work of art, or any other kind of work, finish the job off perfectly. You never know when a helicopter, or some other instrument not at the moment invented, may come along and find you out."

—Ben Patterson, *The Grand Essentials*

WHEN I MISS A WEEK in practice, my audience knows it. When I miss a day, I know it.

—Paderewski, quoted in Jacob Braude, *Braude's Handbook of Stories for Toastmasters and Speakers*

A RECORD WAS SET in the summer of 1995 that literally brought the sports world to its feet. Strangely, it was not some incredible record-setting blazing speed or absolute accuracy or some great display of muscular power. As a matter of fact, it was simply an honor given to someone who showed up more than anybody else in that particular sport. His name is Cal Ripkin Jr., a shortstop for the Baltimore Orioles for years. He broke a record that many people thought would never be broken. It had been set by the legendary Lou Gehrig, New York Yankees' first baseman—2,130 games before he hung up his glove and called it quits because of a disease that finally took his life.

When Ripkin walked on the field to begin game 2,131, the crowd exploded. Of course, they were there that night for that purpose. For twenty-two uninterrupted minutes they stood and applauded. And a lot of us made it a point to be by the television that particular day so that we could watch history being made.

He stood there, in Ripkin style, and just looked. Eyes became misty as he looked all around the stadium, a stadium where he has played ball throughout his professional career. And then he did a wonderful thing. He walked over to his family and embraced each one of them and gave something to one and a cap to another. It was just one of those great moments. It was a gracious, public declaration in honor of a man who showed up for 2,131 games, and still went on without missing.

I SMILE thinking of what happened when I had my oil changed recently. I knelt down and watched as the mechanic took a section off underneath my truck that I'd never seen taken off before, though I had had the oil changed by other mechanics.

I asked, "Hey, what are you doin' down there?" He looked at me and said, "You the owner?" I said, "Yup!" He said, "Well, this ought to be taken off and cleaned every eight to ten thousand miles." When he finally got it off, it was gunky-looking underneath. He took a rag and he wiped it all off. Then he put this shield back on underneath where nobody would ever see what he had done. And I said, "You always wipe all that off underneath there?" He said, "Yup!" I said, "Nobody'll ever see it." "I do." Excellence in his work. And guess where I'm going next time to have my oil changed and a lube job done?

LEONARDO DA VINCI was once at work for a long period of time on a great masterpiece. He had labored long to create this work of art and it was near completion. Standing near him was a young student who spent much of his time with his mouth open, amazed at the master with the brush. Just before finishing the painting, da Vinci turned to the young student and gave him the brush and said, "Now, you finish it." The student protested and backed away, but da Vinci said, "Will not what I have done inspire you to do your best?"

A SOCIETY THAT SCORNS excellence in plumbing because it's a humble occupation and promotes shoddy philosophy because it's exalted, has neither good plumbing nor good philosophy. Neither pipes nor theories will hold water.

—John Gardner, quoted in *Leadership* magazine, Summer 1983

GOOD, better, best, never let it rest—until your good is better and your better is your best!

—Daisy Hepburn, *Lead, Follow, or Get Out of the Way*

Anyway

People are unreasonable, illogical, and self-centered.
    LOVE THEM ANYWAY!
If you do good, people will accuse you of selfish ulterior motives.
    DO GOOD ANYWAY!
If you are successful you win false friends and true enemies.
    SUCCEED ANYWAY!
The good you do today will be forgotten tomorrow.
    DO GOOD ANYWAY!
Honesty and frankness make you vulnerable.
    BE HONEST AND FRANK ANYWAY!
People favor underdogs but follow only the top dogs.
    FIGHT FOR SOME UNDERDOGS ANYWAY!
What you spend years building may be destroyed overnight.
    BUILD ANYWAY!
People really need help but may attack you if you help them.
    HELP PEOPLE ANYWAY!
Give the world the best you have and you'll get kicked in the teeth.
    GIVE THE WORLD THE BEST YOU'VE GOT ANYWAY!

—Robert Schuller, *Tough Times Never Last but Tough People Do*

EXCUSES

AN EXCUSE HAS BEEN DEFINED as the skin of reason stuffed with a lie.

—Michael Green, *Illustrations for Biblical Preaching*

CAN'T AND WON'T. Christians need to be very careful which one they choose. It seems that we prefer to use *can't*.

"I just *can't* get along with my wife."

"My husband and I *can't* communicate."

"I *can't* discipline the kids like I should."

"I just *can't* give up the affair I'm having."

"I *can't* stop overeating."

"I *can't* find the time to pray."

"I *can't* quit gossiping."

No, any Christian who takes the Scriptures seriously will have to confess the word really should be *won't*. Why? Because we have been given the power, the ability to overcome. Literally!

One of the best books you can read on overcoming depression is a splendid work by two psychiatrists, Frank Minirth and Paul Meier. The volume is appropriately entitled *Happiness Is a Choice*. "As psychiatrists we cringe whenever [Christian] patients use the word can't. . . . Any good psychiatrist knows that 'I can't' and 'I've tried' are merely lame excuses. We insist that our patients be honest with themselves and use language that expresses the reality of the situation. So we have our patients change their *can'ts* to *won'ts*. . . . If an individual changes all his *can'ts* to *won'ts*, he stops avoiding the truth, quits deceiving himself, and starts living in reality. . . ."

"I just *won't* get along with my wife."

"My husband and I *won't* communicate."

"I *won't* discipline the kids like I should."

"I just *won't* give up the affair I'm having."

"I *won't* stop overeating."

"I *won't* find the time to pray."

"I *won't* quit gossiping."

Non-Christians have every right and reason to use *can't*, because they really can't! They are victims, trapped and bound like slaves in a fierce and endless struggle. Without Christ and His power, they lack what it takes to change permanently. They don't because they can't! It is a fact . . . a valid excuse.

But people like us? Hey, let's face it, we don't because we won't . . . we disobey because we want to, not because we have to . . . because we choose to, not because we're forced to. The sooner we are willing to own up realistically to our responsibility and stop playing the blame game at pity parties for ourselves, the more we'll learn and change and the less we'll burn and blame.

—Charles R. Swindoll, *Come Before Winter*

TRUE SPORTS FANS have an amazing ability to remember details, statistics, a little technicality of a rule . . . you know, stuff nobody really cares to hear about except another sports fan. Another characteristic of a fan is an indomitable sense of commitment or determination. Against incredible odds, sound logic, and even medical advice, sports fans will persevere to the dying end!

I've often wondered what would happen if people were as intense and committed and determined about church as they are about sports—or a number of other pastimes. This was reinforced some years back in a *Moody Monthly* piece which illustrated twelve excuses a fella might use for "quitting sports." The analogy isn't hard to figure out.

Every time I went, they asked me for money.

The people with whom I had to sit didn't seem very friendly.

The seats were too hard and uncomfortable.

The coach never came to see me.

The referee made a decision with which I could not agree.

I was sitting with some hypocrites—they only came to see what others were wearing.

Some games went into overtime, and I was late getting home.

The band played numbers I had never heard before.

The games are scheduled when I want to do other things.

My parents took me to too many games when I was growing up.

Since I read a book on sports, I feel that I know more than the coaches anyhow.

I don't want to take my children, because I want them to choose for themselves what sport they like best.

FAILURE

THE PRIZE for the most useless weapon of all times goes to the Russians. They invented the "dog mine." The plan was to train the dogs to associate food with the undersides of tanks, in the hope that they would run hungrily beneath advancing Panzer divisions. Bombs were then strapped to the dogs' backs, which endangered the dogs to the point where no insurance company would look at them.

Unfortunately, the dogs associated food solely with Russian tanks. The plan was begun the first day of the Russian involvement in World War II . . . and abandoned on day two. The dogs with bombs on their backs forced an entire Soviet division to retreat.

—Charles R. Swindoll, *Growing Strong in the Seasons of Life*

STEPHEN PILE has written a book titled *The Book of Failures*. It's got unbelievable stuff in it. Like that time back in 1978 during the firemen's strike in England. It made possible one of the greatest animal rescue attempts of all time. Valiantly, the British Army had taken over emergency firefighting. On January 14 they were called out by an elderly lady in South London to rescue her cat. They arrived with impressive haste, very cleverly and carefully rescued the cat, and started to drive away. But the lady was so grateful she invited the squad of heroes in for tea. Driving off later with fond farewells and warm waving of arms, they ran over her cat and killed it.

—Charles R. Swindoll, *Growing Strong in the Seasons of Life*

WHEN WEST GERMAN INDUSTRIALIST Herr Friedrich Flick died, he left a personal fortune estimated at $1.5 billion, a business empire that embraced all or part of some three hundred firms and a reputation as perhaps the crustiest and craftiest magnate ever to operate on the German business scene. Flick was dedicated wholly to his work (he buried his wife at 3 P.M. one day in 1966 and was back at his desk two hours later), but unlike [other] German industrialists . . . he never really made anything; he simply put companies together. "He always made the right moves," summed up one awed observer. "He was the Bobby Fischer of the industrialist world."

At his death, the Flick empire generated annual sales in excess of $3 billion. But for all his enormous power and wealth, *the old man had one very human shortcoming: He could not control his family.* Said one observer, "Herr Flick's dilemma is dramatic. He could 'put companies together,' but he couldn't mold his family together. Like the powerless horses and men of Humpty Dumpty's poem, all the experts were having a struggle coping with the broken pieces left behind by Flick's failure as a father. What a human shortcoming!"

—*Newsweek,* September 25, 1972

I WOULD RATHER FAIL in a cause that will ultimately succeed than to succeed in a cause that will ultimately fail.

—Woodrow Wilson, quoted in Lloyd Cory, *Quote Unquote*

SNAKE RIVER CANYON coiled up, rattled its tail, and sank its fangs into its would-be captor. On a sultry Sunday afternoon its 1,700-foot jaws yawned wide as it swallowed a strange tasting capsule prescribed for it by Dr. Robert C. Truax, the scientist-designer of *Sky Cycle X-2.* Starring in the show was a guy some people tagged Captain Marvel, who looked more like Billy Batson unable to remember the magic word. But before we label him a showman—or a show-off—I suggest we consider the outcome of this showdown.

Any third grader could have told you the vaunted skycycle leap across the canyon was a triple-A flop—a classic fizzle. The skycycle gave up in midair; the driver floated to safety beneath a nylon cloud. But you won't find him sitting long-faced in a dark corner today. Most people send an ambulance and a wrecker to mop up their mistakes. He could have sent a Brink's armored car. As bystanders shouted "Rip off!" he was thinking about write-offs. Anyone who can walk away from a failure with a smile, a bulging rear pocket, and his pride still intact has to have *something* going for him. The real six-million dollar man, if you can believe it, is a two-wheeled wonder named Evel Knievel. Nobody— but nobody in the long history of sports ever came off a more abysmal failure better than he. The remains of Dr. Truax's flopcycle littered the canyon, but the man who took off like a bird made out like a banker.

When you stop and think it over, there's an abiding truth in that Idaho extravaganza all of us ought to capture and cultivate. It's much greater than money and far deeper than a canyon jump. There's a philosophy of life here I'm now convinced is worth one's pursuit. Here it is:

The person who succeeds is not the one who holds back, fearing failure, nor the one who never fails, but rather the one who moves on in spite of failure.

As Lowell wrote:

Not failure, but low aim, is crime.

—Charles R. Swindoll, *Growing Strong in the Seasons of Life*

ON THE ONCE BLOODY BATTLEFIELD at Saratoga there stands a towering obelisk. A one-hundred-and-fifty-five-foot high monument commemorative of that decisive struggle where the British made their last stand over two centuries ago. It is a solemn and sober moment as visitors stand on that windswept hill, savoring that slice of national history. In the distance are the stately Adirondacks and the Taconics. The monument gives mute testimony to those heroes of yesteryear who refused to bow the knee to England.

About its base are four deep niches, and in each niche appears the name of one of the American generals who commanded there. Above the names stand giant bronze figures on horseback, as famous today as in the day they shouted their commands. You can almost hear their voices. In the first stands Horatio Gates; in the second, Philip John Schuyler; and in the third, Daniel Morgan.

But the niche on the fourth side is strangely vacant. The name appears, but the soldier is absent. Conspicuously absent. As one reads the name, the mind rushes on to the foggy banks of the Hudson where the man sold his soul and forfeited the right to be remembered. How the mighty are fallen! The brigadier general who once commanded West Point, the major general who distinguished himself at battles along Lake Champlain, Mohawk Valley, Quebec, and Saratoga, committed treason and died a synonym of disgrace—the infamous Benedict Arnold. As Clarence Macartney once put it so eloquently, "The empty niche in that monument shall ever stand for fallen manhood, power prostituted, for genius soiled, for faithlessness to a sacred trust."

—Charles R. Swindoll, *Come Before Winter*

WHATEVER FAILURES I HAVE KNOWN, whatever errors I have committed, whatever follies I have witnessed in private and public life, have been the consequence of action without thought.

—Bernard Baruch

ROBERT WISE MENTIONS an experience that encouraged him to be real. "I had a friend who used to call me on the phone on Monday mornings. I'd pick up the phone and this minister would say, 'Hello, this is God. I have a gift for you today. I want to give you the gift of failing. Today you do not have to succeed. I grant that to you.' Then he would hang up. I would sit there for ten minutes, staring at the wall.

"The first time I couldn't believe it. It was really the gospel. God's love means it's even OK to fail. You don't have to be the greatest thing in the world. You can just be you."

—Robert Wise, *Your Churning Place*

BEFORE BECOMING A SCREEN STAR, young Burt Lancaster was a circus performer—a job he was fortunate to land, considering his less-than-flawless audition. He was asked to perform on the parallel bars, so he leaped on the bars and began his routine. Because he was nervous, his timing was off, and he spun over the bar, falling flat on his face some ten feet below. He was so humiliated that he immediately leaped back on the bar. As he spun again at the same point, he flipped off and smashed to the ground once more!

Burt's tights were torn, he was cut and bleeding, and he was fiercely upset! He leaped back again, but the third time was even worse, for this time he fell on his back. The agent came over, picked him up, and said, "Son, if you won't do that again, you've got the job!"

—Robert Wise, *Your Churning Place*

AN ASSISTANT of Thomas A. Edison once tried to console the inventor over the failure to achieve in a series of experiments what he had set out to find: "It's too bad," he said, "to do all that work without results." "Oh," said Mr. Edison, "we have lots of results. We know seven hundred things that won't work."

—Peter Marshall, *John Doe, Disciple*

C. S. LEWIS, in *The Screwtape Letters,* vividly describes Satan's strategy: He gets Christians to become preoccupied with their failures; from then on, the battle is won.

—Erwin Lutzer, *Failure: The Back Door to Success*

FAITH

YOUR FAITH ought to get you in trouble at times. If everybody thinks you are nuts, you may be. It's OK if some think you are. You're probably in trouble if no one thinks you are.

A UNIVERSITY PROFESSOR once boasted, "One of my callings in life is to shatter the faith of naive fundamentalists as they come to my class. Just give me a room of young, naive evangelicals and let me at 'em. You can just watch them drop like flies hit with Raid when I challenge their faith in a deliberate, consistent manner."

WE WERE IN SEMINARY at Dallas in 1959. And, boy, it was hot. Cynthia and I said, "We really need an air conditioner," since we didn't have one in this little apartment.

So I said to Cynthia, "I'll tell you what let's do. Let's not tell anybody about our need; let's just pray." You do a lot of strange things like that in seminary, you know. You just trust God and you don't say anything to anybody. And so we did that.

Winter passed. Spring came. Still praying. We went home for a quick visit in Houston. We were staying with her folks. And out of the clear blue a phone call came from a guy who lived across town who had known us years before. He said, "Chuck, we've got an air conditioner. It's almost new. Could you use it?" I thought, Walk around a wall six times and then seven times. Is it really impossible? That's the way God operates.

He brought it over, put it in our car trunk, and we took it back to Dallas, stuck it in the window and it worked all through those four years there. It was fantastic. Impossible situation which we didn't announce and God met it in an impossible way. Just like God told Joshua to take Jericho. Faith would win the victory.

FAITH IS RESTING in the fact that God has an objective in leaving me on the scene when I feel useless to Him and a burden to others.

—Pamela Reeve, *Faith Is*

What you gonna do when the river overflows?
Faith answers,
I'm gonna sit on the porch and watch her go.
What you gonna do when the hogs all drown?
I'm gonna wish I lived on higher ground.
What you gonna do when the cow floats away?
I'm gonna throw in after her a bale of hay.
What you gonna do with the water in the room?
I'm gonna sweep her out with a sedge-straw broom.
What you gonna do when the cabin leaves?
I'm gonna climb on the roof and straddle the eaves.
What you gonna do when your hold gives way?
I'm gonna say, "Howdy, Lord! It's judgment day."

—Ben Patterson, *Waiting*

If I Had Only Known You

Lord,
   I crawled
    across the barrenness
      to You
      with my empty cup
uncertain
   in asking
      any small drop
      of refreshment.
   If only
    I had known You
    better
   I'd have come
   Running
   With a bucket.

—Nancy Spiegelberg and Dorothy Purdy, *Fanfare: A Celebration of Belief*

TRADITION IS the living faith of those now dead. Traditionalism is the dead faith of those still living.

—Jaroslav Pelikan, *The Vindication of Tradition*

LEGEND HAS IT that a man was lost in the desert, just dying for a drink of water. He stumbled upon an old shack—a ramshackled, windowless, roofless, weatherbeaten old shack. He looked about this place and found a little shade from the heat of the desert sun. As he glanced around he saw a pump about fifteen feet away—an old, rusty water pump. He stumbled over to it, grabbed the handle, and began to pump up and down, up and down. Nothing came out.

Disappointed, he staggered back. He noticed off to the side an old jug. He looked at it, wiped away the dirt and dust, and read a message that said, "You have to prime the pump with all the water in this jug, my friend. P.S.: Be sure you fill the jug again before you leave."

He popped the cork out of the jug and sure enough, it was almost full of water! Suddenly, he was faced with a decision. If he drank the water, he could live. Ah, but if he poured all the water in the old rusty pump, maybe it would yield fresh, cool water from down deep in the well, all the water he wanted.

He studied the possibility of both options. What should he do, pour it into the old pump and take a chance on fresh, cool water or drink what was in the old jug and ignore its message? Should he waste all the water on the hopes of those flimsy instructions written, no telling how long ago?

Reluctantly he poured all the water into the pump. Then he grabbed the handle and began to pump, squeak, squeak, squeak. Still nothing came out! Squeak, squeak, squeak. A little bit began to dribble out, then a small stream, and finally it gushed! To his relief fresh, cool water poured out of the rusty pump. Eagerly, he filled the jug and drank from it. He filled it another time and once again drank its refreshing contents.

Then he filled the jug for the next traveler. He filled it to the top, popped the cork back on, and added this little note: "Believe me, it really works. You have to give it all away before you can get anything back."

—Charles R. Swindoll, *Living Above the Level of Mediocrity*

FAITH IS engaging in the deepest joy of heaven, knowing His unfathomable love for me as I walk through the thorny desolate now.

—Pamela Reeve, *Faith Is*

DURING Aleksandr Solzhenitsyn's eight years in Russian camps, his parents died and his wife divorced him. Upon his release from prison he was dying of a cancer that was growing in him so rapidly that he could feel the difference in a span of twelve hours. It was at that point that he abandoned himself to God, so beautifully illustrated in three lines of the incredible prayer that came in that dark hour: "Oh God, how easy it is for me to believe in You. You created a path for me through despair. . . . O God, You have used me, and where You cannot use me, You have appointed others. Thank You."

—Aleksandr Solzhenitsyn, *One Day in the Life of Ivan Denisovich*

FAITH IS speaking truth in love even at the cost of position of relationship.

—Pamela Reeve, *Faith Is*

FAMILY
(Also see *Children, Siblings*)

TWO FAMILIES from the state of New York were studied very carefully. One was the Max Jukes family and the other was the Jonathan Edwards family. The thing that they discovered in this study is remarkable: like begets like.

Max Jukes was an unbelieving man and he married a woman of like character who lacked principle. And among the known descendants, over 1,200 were studied. Three hundred and ten became professional vagrants; 440 physically wrecked their lives by a debauched lifestyle; 130 were sent to the pen for an average of thirteen years each, 7 of them for murder. There were over 100 who became alcoholics; 60 became habitual thieves; 190 public prostitutes. Of the 20 who learned a trade, 10 of them learned the trade in a state prison. It cost the state about $1,500,000 and they made no contribution whatever to society.

In about the same era the family of Jonathan Edwards came on the scene. And Jonathan Edwards, a man of God, married a woman of like character. And their family began and they became a part of this study that was made. Three hundred became clergymen, missionaries, and theological professors; over 100 became college profs; over 100 became attorneys, 30 of them judges; 60 of them became physicians; over 60 became authors of good classics, good books; 14 became presidents of universities. There were numerous giants in American industry that emerged from this family. Three became United States congressmen and one became the vice president of the United States.

—J. Oswald Sanders, *A Spiritual Clinic*

THIRTY-EIGHT PERCENT of all first marriages fail, 79 percent of those will remarry, and 44 percent of those will divorce again. As many as four out of ten children born in the 1970s will spend part of their childhood in a single-parent family, usually with the mother as head of the household. Seventeen percent of all children under 18 are now living in single-parent families.

One of the most distressing developments in the family structure is the high tide of illegitimacy. Fifteen percent of all births are illegitimate, and more than half of all out-of-wedlock babies are born to teenagers. Illegitimacy was particularly high among black women in 1976—50.3 percent bore illegitimate children. These illegitimate children, both black and white, are the most likely to be impoverished, dependent on welfare, deprived of educational opportunities, and destined to repeat the cycle with illegitimate children of their own.

—"Saving the Family," *Newsweek,* May 15, 1978

A STUDY BY the University of Rhode Island described the American home as the most dangerous place to be, outside of riots and war! Although exact statistics are difficult to obtain, all the other available studies had echoed the same sad story. The Plan A home is filled with anger and violence. Thirty percent of all American couples experience some form of domestic violence in their lifetime, and two million couples have used a gun, knife, or other lethal weapon on each other during their marriage. Twenty percent of all police officers killed in the line of duty are killed while answering calls involving family fights, and it's estimated that anywhere from six to fifteen million women are battered in the United States each year! As one law officer expressed it: "This is probably the highest unreported crime in the country."

—"The Battered Wife: What's Being Done?" *Los Angeles Times,* April 27, 1978

NO PURSUIT IS MORE IMPORTANT than the cultivation of a godly family. Christiaan Barnard tells his sad story in his book *One Life.*

It was a bright April morning when I drove out of Minneapolis. It seemed a century since I had first arrived there, a time longer than all the years before it. In New York I put the car in a boat and caught a plane for Cape Town. A northwest wind was blowing when we came over the sea with the waves close below.

My wife was there with the children. I had not written much in the last two months, yet I was unprepared for her greeting. "Why did you come back?" There was no longer a smile in her eyes. *Oh God,* I thought, *I've made the most terrible mistake of my life.* "Don't look so surprised," she said. "We gave you up. We decided you were never coming back." I responded, "It was only a little delay. I wrote you about it." "No, you wrote once to say you weren't coming home." "We were building valves, aortic valves," he answered. "No, you were building a family. That is, you were until you dumped it into my lap," she said bitterly. "We have ceased to exist for you." I wanted to say I'd come home because I love my children and I believed I loved her. I wanted to because I felt it, but what could I say now that would not sound meaningless.

—Christiaan Barnard, *One Life*

FAMILY INSTABILITY AFFECTS EVERYONE—especially the children.

...the most vulnerable victims of family instability are the children who are too young to understand what has happened to their parents.

That tragic impact on the next generation was graphically illustrated to me in a recent conversation with a sixth-grade teacher in an upper middle-class California city. She was shocked to see the results of a creative writing task assigned to her students. They were asked to complete a sentence that began with the words "I wish." The teacher expected the boys and girls to express wishes for bicycles, dogs, television sets, and trips to Hawaii. Instead, twenty of the thirty children made reference in their responses to their own disintegrating families. A few of their actual sentences were as follows:

"I wish my parents wouldn't fight and I wish my father would come back."

"I wish my mother didn't have a boyfriend."

"I wish I could get straight A's so my father would love me."

"I wish I had one mom and one dad so the kids wouldn't make fun of me. I have three moms and three dads and they botch up my life."

"I wish I had an M-1 rifle so I could shoot those who make fun of me."

—James Dobson, *Love Must Be Tough*

Laughter in the Walls

I pass a lot of houses on my way home—
   some pretty,
      some expensive,
         some inviting—
but my heart always skips a beat
   when I turn down the road
and see my house nestled against the hill.

I guess I'm especially proud
of the house and the way it looks because
    I drew the plans myself.
It started out large enough for us—
    I even had a study—
two teenaged boys now reside in there.
    And it had a guest room—
my girls and nine dolls are permanent guests.
    It had a small room Peg
had hoped would be her sewing room—
    the two boys swinging on the dutch door
have claimed this room as their own.
    So it really doesn't look right now
as if I'm much of an architect.
    But it will get larger again—
one by one they will go away
    to work,
        to college,
    to service,
   to their own houses,
and then there will be room—
    a guest room,
    a study,
   and a sewing room
   for just the two of us.
But it won't be empty—
    every corner
        every room
    every nick
        in the coffee table
will be crowded with memories.
Memories of picnics,
    parties, Christmases,
   bedside vigils, summers,
    fires, winters, going barefoot,
   leaving for vacation, cats,
    conversations, black eyes,
   graduations, first dates,
    ball games, arguments,

washing dishes, bicycles,
   dogs, boat rides,
getting home from vacation,
   meals, rabbits, and
a thousand other things
   that fill the lives
of those who would raise five.
   And Peg and I will sit
quietly by the fire
   and listen to the
     laughter in the walls.

—Bob Benson, *Laughter in the Walls*

AN ANONYMOUS PIECE portrays the family as a garden. It suggests various things we can plant in our family relationships that will result in great benefits.

A family is like many things, perhaps most like a garden. It needs time, attention, and cultivation. The sunshine of laughter and affirmation. It also needs the rains of difficulties, tense moments, serious discussions about issues that matter. And there must be spade work, where hardness is broken loose and planting of fresh seeds is accomplished with lots of TLC. Here are some suggestions for fifteen rows worth planting:

Four rows of peas:	Preparedness
	Perseverance
	Promptness
	Politeness
Then three rows of squash:	Squash gossip
	Squash criticism
	Squash indifference
Along with five rows of lettuce:	Let us be faithful
	Let us be unselfish
	Let us be loyal
	Let us love one another
	Let us be truthful
And three rows of turnips:	Turn up with a smile
	Turn up with a new idea
	Turn up with determination

And then? Well, from then on it's pretty simple. Water, weed, tend with care, and patiently watch the garden grow. Someday you'll look back and realize it was worth all the years of all the work and effort and prayer. Like a lovely garden, your family will be a thing of grateful pride, of seasonal beauty, of daily sustenance.

—Charles R. Swindoll, *Living beyond the Daily Grind*

FATHERHOOD

To Any Daddy

There are little eyes upon you, and
    they're watching night and day,
There are little ears that quickly take in
    every word you say;
There are little hands all eager to do
    everything you do,
And a little boy who's dreaming of the
    day he'll be like you.

You're the little fellow's idol, you're the
    wisest of the wise;
In his little mind about you no suspicions
    ever rise;
He believes in you devoutly, holds that
    all you say and do
He will say and do in your way when
    he's grown up like you.

There's a wide–eyed little fellow who
    believes you're always right,
And his ears are always open and he
    watches day and night,
You are setting an example every day in
    all you do,
For the little boy who's waiting to grow
    up to be like you.

—Croft M. Pentz, *The Speaker's Treasury of 400 Quotable Poems*

WILLIAM FRANKLIN WRITES, "If he's wealthy and prominent, and you stand in awe of him, call him 'father.' If he sits in shirt sleeves and suspenders at a ballgame and picnic, call him 'Pop.' If he wheels the baby carriage and carries bundles meekly, call him 'Papa' (with the accent on the first syllable). If he belongs to a literary circle and writes cultured papers, call him 'Papa' (with the accent on the last syllable). If, however, he makes a pal of you when you're good, and is too wise to let you pull the wool over his loving eyes when you're not; if, moreover, you're quite sure no other fellow you know has quite so fine a father, you may call him 'Dad.'"

—Peter S. Seymour, "A Father's Love," Hallmark card

A FATHER is a creature that is forced to endure childbirth without an anesthetic. A father growls when he feels good and laughs when scared half to death.

A father never feels worthy of the worship in a child's eyes. He's never quite the hero his daughter thinks; never quite the man his son believes him to be, and this worries him—sometimes. So he works too hard to try to smooth the rough places in the road for those of his own who will follow him.

A father gets very angry when the school grades aren't as good as he thinks they should be. So he scolds his son—though he knows it's the teacher's fault. A father gives his daughter away to another man who is not nearly good enough—so he can have grandchildren who are smarter than anybody's. A father makes bets with insurance companies about who will live the longest. One day, he loses—and the bet is paid off to those he leaves behind.

—Paul Harvey, quoted in Lloyd Cory, *Quote Unquote*

WHEN I WAS JUST ELEVEN YEARS OLD, our family drove from Toronto to Eastern Ontario, to the region north of the St. Lawrence River, where my father had been born. We reached the little villages of Ventnor and Spencerville just before midnight; the residents had long since gone to bed. But Dad needed directions to find the old homestead, where we were to spend the night. Reluctantly he stopped at a darkened house and knocked on the door. After several minutes of waiting, the yard light came on, and an older man opened the door. I could hear my father apologizing for the inconvenience; and then he identified himself as the son of Pearson Lockerbie—my grandfather dead for more than a score of years.

"Oh, come in, come in," said the old man. "No trouble at all. We knew your father."

. . . That's the greatest legacy a man can leave his son.

—Bruce Lockerbie, *Fatherlove*

I REMEMBER STEALING six softballs when I was working as a stock boy in a five-and-dime store in my early years in high school. And I remember trying to find a place to hide them when I got home. I don't know what in the world I planned to do with six softballs. To this day it just baffles me, the logic of it. But I stuck them in the back of my drawer and my mother found them. My father presented himself to me and told me that we were going to make a trip back to the store where I was going to talk to the owner and I was going to confess.

I will never forget his instruction on the way. I mean, I was sitting there just dying thinking about it. It was just like passing razor blades to think about standing in front of my employer. Well, I stood there and told him what I had done. My dad was waiting in the car. He didn't go in with me. And I heard my boss say, "You're fired."

I stumbled back out to the car and sat down. I was as low as I could remember ever being. On the way, I remember my dad beginning to rebuild my emotions. I had done wrong, and I had learned an incredible lesson. He didn't overdo it, but he drilled into me that when you steal, you get fired. And if you don't get fired at the moment, you lose something that can't be bought with any price, and that's your self–respect. I remember, too, we got on the subject of what in the world I was gonna do with those six softballs.

But there was something about the ornament of grace that came around my neck from my father who before we went in the house took the time to put his arms around me and to understand. This teenage kid was most concerned about my father's not telling my friends. And as far as I know, he took that story to his grave and never told on me.

FEAR

(Also see *Anxiety, Stress, Worry*)

YOU CAN SEE the face of panic in a car with the sign "Student Driver"—not on the driver, but on the face in the passenger seat.

DEAN MARTIN comments, "Show me a man who doesn't know the meaning of fear and I'll show you a dummy who gets beat up a lot."

—Alan Loy McGinnis, *The Friendship Factor*

EVERY TIME I think about driving across a desert I remember one particular time I did it. Cynthia was carrying our first child and we had just finished our internship with Ray Stedman in Palo Alto. Since she was pregnant, they flew her back and I drove. I pulled a little trailer that had a washing machine given us by the folks in the church.

It was about 1:00 when I came to a place called Desert Center. And I knew in order for me to make it all the way to Needles, I needed some coffee. So I bought the biggest cup of coffee you could imagine. And as I began to drink this, I tasted something in it. I thought, "Boy, they must have given me the bottom of the pot when they poured that cup of coffee." I was about fifty or sixty miles along the way when I got to the bottom, and right in the bottom was a cigarette butt. It was terrible!!

I have to tell you one more thing that happened on that trip because it was unforgettable. When I got to the edge of California, I stopped about daybreak and went into the washroom at a service station to freshen up for the rest of the trip across Arizona. There was a fellow in there washing his hands. And he said, "Hey, where are you going?" And I, of course, had never seen him before, and I said, "I'm traveling across country." He said, "Good. I'll go with you."

I said, "No. I'm traveling alone." He says, "Hey, you look tired. You look like you could use someone to help you make the trip, so why don't I just travel with you?" And I said, "No. I'm traveling alone." He frowned and said, "Look, I'll drive. You sleep. It's no problem." I said, "I'M TRAVELING ALONE!" just like that. And he left.

I was a little uneasy when he left because I wasn't sure what that meant. He looked like a guy you couldn't trust, and I was afraid that maybe he might follow me.

In the back of our car I had fixed an ironing board so that I could sleep back there. It was between the back of the front seat and the front of the back seat.

So when I got in the car, I noticed that some of the covers that we had put over the ironing board were moved. And I began to drive off thinking to myself, "He's in there." Why I drove off I'll never know, but I did, and I thought, "Well, I might as well deal with it now."

I had a big crescent wrench underneath the front seat so I just reached down and got it, like a good marine. I was really scared to death, as a matter of fact, but there was a streetlight up ahead and I thought, "I'll pull in here and I'll hit him right there. So I stopped, opened the car back door, pulled up the covers— and nobody was there! I felt so dumb. I had this crescent wrench in my hand and the first thing I did was look around to see if anybody saw me.

THERE'S NO GUARANTEE that bad things won't happen, even if we try with all our might to keep them from happening. That reminds me of a humorous story I heard about a man on the streets of Belfast. Obviously, he was afraid, as are many in Belfast today. He hoped to get home safely without being attacked. Suddenly, a dark figure jumped out of the shadows and grabbed him around the neck. He stuck the point of a knife against his throat and asked, in a gruff voice, "Catholic or Protestant?" Seized with panic the man reasoned to himself, "If I say Catholic and he's a Protestant—whoosh! If I say Protestant and he's a Catholic, I'm a goner." Then he thought of a way out. He said, "I'm a Jew!" The assailant chuckled, "Ha, I'm the luckiest Arab terrorist in Belfast!"

—Charles R. Swindoll, *Living on the Ragged Edge*

MANY YEARS AGO my brother worked at the old Houston Public Library in downtown Houston. Among the crew that worked at the library it was always a toss-up as to who would turn off the lights in the upstairs stacks. You had to walk along the stacks and when you got to the final switch you were in darkness. And there were busts of Sidney Lanai, Andrew Jackson, and others. It was very musty and very few, except real bookworms would go to the third or fourth floor of that library. So the crew hated to turn the lights off.

One night it fell the lot of one of the younger fellows on the crew to have to do that. Well, my brother Orville, knowing that the young guy was already jumpy, slipped up the back stairway and hid behind the stacks. This little guy was walking along turning off lights and humming to himself. You know how you do when you are scared. You bump things. And you sing, "Jesus loves me, this I know." So this kid's walking along. Hum, hum, click, hum, click, hum, click, click. He gets to the last switch and as he turns off the light, my brother says, "What are you doing up here?"

Orville says that's the last they ever saw of that young man. He ran down those stairs and out into the street. He never came back even to get his check.

MRS. MONROE lives in Darlington, Maryland. She's the mother of eight children. And except for a few interesting experiences, she's just like any other mother across America.

She came home one afternoon from the grocery store and walked into her home. Everything looked pretty much the same, though it was a bit quieter than usual. She looked into the middle of the living room and five of her darlings were sitting around in a circle, exceedingly quiet, doing something in the middle of the circle. She put down the sacks of groceries and walked over closely and saw that they were playing with five of the cutest skunks you can imagine.

She was instantly terrified and yelled, "Run, children, run!" Each child grabbed a skunk and ran in five different directions. She was beside herself and screamed louder. It so scared the children that each one squeezed his skunk. And as we all know, skunks don't like to be squeezed.

—John Haggai, *How to Win over Worry*

IT HAPPENED OVER FIFTY YEARS AGO. The irony of it, however, amazes me to this day.

A mural artist named J. H. Zorthian read about a tiny boy who had been killed in traffic. His stomach churned as he thought of that ever happening to one of his three children. His worry became an inescapable anxiety. The more he imagined such a tragedy, the more fearful he became. His effectiveness as an artist was put on hold once he began running scared.

At last he surrendered to his obsession. Canceling his negotiations to purchase a large house in busy Pasadena, California, he began to seek a place where his children would be safe. His pursuit became so intense that he set aside all his work while scheming and planning every possible means to protect his children from harm. He tried to imagine the presence of danger in everything. The location of the residence was critical. It must be sizable and remote, so he bought twelve acres perched on a mountain at the end of a long, winding, narrow road. At the turn along the road he posted signs, "Children at Play." Before starting construction on the house itself, Zorthian personally built and fenced a playground for his three children. He built it in such a way that it was impossible for a car to get within fifty feet of it.

Next, the house. With meticulous care he blended beauty and safety into the place. He put into it various shades of the designs he had concentrated in the murals he had hanging in forty-two public buildings in eastern cities. Only this time his objective was more than colorful art—most of all, it had to be safe and secure. He made sure of that. Finally, the garage was to be built. Only one automobile ever drove into that garage—Zorthian's.

He stood back and surveyed every possibility of danger to his children. He could only think of one remaining hazard. He had to back out of the garage. He might, in some hurried moment, back over one of the children. He immediately made plans for a protected turnaround. The contractor returned and set the forms for that additional area, but before the cement could be poured, a downpour stopped the project. It was the first rainfall in many weeks of a long West Coast drought.

If it had not rained that week, the concrete turnaround would have been completed and been in use by Sunday. That was February 9, 1947—the day his eighteen-month old son, Tiran, squirmed away from his sister's grasp and ran behind the car as Zorthian drove it from the garage. *The child was killed instantly.*

—Charles R. Swindoll, *Quest for Character*

I REMEMBER ONE NIGHT when I was taking care of a couple of our grandchildren. It was late in the evening, but since grandfathers usually let their grandchildren stay up longer than they should, they were still awake. We were laughing, messing around, and having a great time together when we suddenly heard a knock on the door. Not the doorbell, but a mysterious knocking. Immediately one of my grandsons grabbed hold of my arm. "It's OK," I said. The knock came again, and I started to the door. My grandson followed me, but he hung on to my left leg and hid behind me as I opened the door. It was one of my son's friends who had dropped by unexpectedly. After the person had left and I'd closed the door, my grandson, still holding on to my leg, said in a strong voice, "Bubba, we don't have anything to worry about, do we?" And I said, "No, we don't have anything to worry about. Everything's fine." You know why he was strong? Because he was hanging on to protection. As long as he was clinging to grandfather's leg, he didn't have to worry about a thing.

—Charles R. Swindoll, *Hope Again*

ONE FALL Cynthia and I had the scare of our lives—literally. I was ministering at a hotel in Cancun—a nice, safe, well-equipped hotel. We turned in for the night around 11:30 or so and were soon in Dreamland. Shortly before 1:00 A.M. Cynthia's loud, shrill scream startled me awake. "There's a man in our room!"

I looked toward the sliding-glass door that opened onto the patio, and there he stood, silent and staring into our room. A chill raced down my spine. The door had been slid open, and the curtains were blowing like sails into the room from the wind off the Gulf waters. In fact, it was the surge of the surf that had awakened Cynthia, not the intruder. He had not made a sound, nor was he easily visible, since he was dressed in dark clothing.

I jumped out of bed and stood nose-to-nose with him—and yelled at the top of my lungs, hoping to frighten him away. For all I knew he had a gun or a knife, but this was no time to close my eyes and pray and lie there like a wimp. Slowly, he backed out of the room, jumped the seawall, and quickly escaped.

Hotel security never found a trace of him, except for a few footprints in the sand. He was a prowler who came, most likely, to steal from our room. Talk about a lasting memory!

—Charles R. Swindoll, *Hope Again*

FINISH LINE
(Also see *Achievement, Ambition, Motivation, Success*)

A MINNESOTA TOWN with a volunteer fire department has this slogan, "We'll know where we're going when we get there."

IN THE 1988 SUMMER OLYMPICS in Seoul, South Korea, Ben Johnson of Canada won the 100-meter dash, setting a new Olympic record and a new world record. Our American contender, Carl Lewis, came in second, and most were shocked that he hadn't won the gold. After the race, the judges learned that Johnson had had an illegal substance in his body. He ran the race illegally, so the judges took away his medal. Though he ran faster and made an unforgettable impression, he did not deserve the reward.

—Charles R. Swindoll, *Hope Again*

HOURS BEHIND the runner in front of him, the last marathoner finally entered the Olympic stadium. By that time, the drama of the day's events was almost over and most of the spectators had gone home. This athlete's story, however, was still being played out.

Limping into the arena, the Tanzanian runner grimaced with every step, his knee bleeding and bandaged from an earlier fall. His ragged appearance immediately caught the attention of the remaining crowd, who cheered him on to the finish line.

Why did he stay in the race? What made him endure his injuries to the end? When asked these questions later, he replied, "My country did not send me 7,000 miles away to start the race. They sent me 7,000 miles to finish it."

—*Quote* magazine, July 1991

FRED DIXON ran the decathlon back in the '70s. He was excellent. He came to the 1976 decathlon in Montreal. If you know anything about the particular endurance of it, you have a respect for whoever is in the finals. There are five events, two days in a row, making a decathlon. Dixon had high hopes, running alongside Bruce Jenner.

Fred ran but he didn't do well. He ran the next one and didn't do well then either. He competed in the next event and did even more poorly. When he finally finished the fifth run, he realized he was hopelessly unable to win, so he quit. Alone with his thoughts, and struggling with what that meant, and knowing that it went against the grain of his inner fiber, he realized, "Someday I am going to have children, and they are going to read about the events in Montreal. And they're going to read that their daddy quit." And so, with some strong, firm, consistent talking, he talked the officials into letting him finish the decathlon.

The next day he finished all ten events. Dixon became number one in the decathlon in '77, our American hopeful. In 1980 he made the team and was expected to win it, but the '80 Olympics were called off. Though Dixon never won it, he endured.

AT A PASTORS' CONFERENCE several years ago there was a man who had returned from a tour of duty in the Vietnam War. He served both as an infantryman in a mortar platoon and then as a chaplain. He said things were harder as a chaplain than they were in that mortar platoon because he was constantly on the front line. He just breathed the vapors of death continually for about a six or seven months. I asked him, "How long were you over there?" He said, "Three-hundred sixty-six days." I think he could have even told me the hours and seconds if I had pressed him on it. I said, "Toward the end, how was it?" He responded, "I longed for home like no one can imagine."

IN 1952, a very brave and strong young lady waded into the Pacific Ocean. Florence Chadwick was determined to break another record. To date, no woman had ever crossed the channel between Catalina Island and the California coast.

Long-distance swimming wasn't new to Florence. She was a seasoned long-distance competitor. In fact, she was the first woman to swim the English Channel in both directions.

But this was a twenty-six-mile stretch. And the conditions that July morning were not optimal. Not only was the water incredibly cold, but a thick blanket of fog had settled in. And to make matters worse, there were sharks who trailed her course and had to be driven off several times!

Florence's coach and family followed along in a small boat, cheering her on. "Go for it, Florence! You can do it!"

But it was foggy. Real foggy. And even when she'd been swimming for fifteen hours, Florence still couldn't see the shoreline.

A bit discouraged and very tired, she finally took her last stroke, telling her family she just couldn't go on.

She quit.

They all consoled Florence as they pulled her aboard, and she collapsed with exhaustion.

Well, as it turned out, Florence quit much too soon that cold July morning. She swam twenty-five and a half miles, but because she couldn't see the end—couldn't see the coast—Florence fell short of her goal by just half-a-mile. Had she only known! One half mile!

By the way, Florence didn't give up. She gave it another try. Just two months after her first attempt, she became the first woman in history to swim the twenty-six-mile channel. She set a new speed record, as well.

—*Leadership Journal*

FOCUS

THE OUTER DISTRACTIONS of our interests reflects an inner lack of integration in our own selves. We are trying to be several selves at once without all our selves being organized by a single, mastering Life within us.

—Thomas Kelly, *A Testament of Devotion*

HOW CAN I GET THE MOST for the least? Most of us are notorious bargain-hunting people. Whether it's those annual or semiannual clothing sales or searching through the newspaper for those little cents off coupons. It's also true of the cars we drive. We want to get the most car for the least amount of money. That's the way we think. When it comes to buying, that's our philosophy. We like to bargain.

Reminds me of the story of a tourist group that was going through the ancient city of Rome. The Italian guide was having the time of his life as he had this international group with him. And they were just "ooing" and "aahing" over all sorts of things. He got a little carried away when he came to a pen full of chickens. And he stepped back and he said, "Ladies and gentlemen, these are very unusual and distinctive chickens. They happen to be descendants of that rooster that crowed the night Peter denied his Master, Jesus of Nazareth."

Well, everyone pushed his nose up against the chicken wire and stared at these chickens. And then there was an Englishman in the group who said, "My word! What a remarkable pedigree!" And typically, an American in the group immediately reached for his checkbook and asked the guide, "How much do they cost?" In the group was a Scottish fellow who had watched it all happen. He quietly asked the guide, "Do they lay any eggs?"

—Ray Stedman, *What More Can God Say?*

BEFORE ANDREW JACKSON became the seventh president of the United States, he served as a major general in the Tennessee militia. During the War of 1812 his troops reached an all-time low in morale. As a result they began arguing, bickering, and fighting among themselves. It is reported that Old Hickory called them all together on one occasion when tensions were at their worst and said, "Gentlemen! Let's remember, the enemy is over *there!*"

—Charles R. Swindoll, *Hope Again*

THOMAS HENRY HUXLEY was a devoted disciple of Darwin. Famous biologist, teacher, and author. Defender of the theory of evolution. Bold, convincing, self-avowed humanist. Traveling lecturer.

Having finished another series of pubic assaults against several truths Christians held sacred, Huxley was in a hurry the following morning to catch his train to the next city. He took one of Dublin's famous horse-drawn taxis and settled back with his eyes closed to rest himself for a few minutes. He assumed the driver had been told the destination by the hotel doorman, so all he had said as he got in was, "Hurry, I'm almost late. *Drive fast!*" The horses lurched forward and galloped across Dublin at a vigorous pace. Before long Huxley glanced out the window and frowned as he realized they were going west, away from the sun, not toward it.

Leaning forward, the scholar shouted, "Do you know where you are going?" Without looking back, the driver yelled a classic line, not meant to be humorous. "No, your honor! But I am driving *very* fast!"

—Charles R. Swindoll, *Growing Strong in the Seasons of Life*

OBJECTIVES CAN BE EASILY LOST. They slowly erode rather than suddenly explode, have you noticed? To illustrate how this can happen, consider this actual experience one man had in the Deep South.

When I lived in Atlanta, several years ago, I noticed in the Yellow Pages, in the listing of restaurants, an entry for a place called Church of God Grill. The peculiar name aroused my curiosity and I dialed the number. A man answered with a cheery, "Hello! Church of God Grill!" I asked how his restaurant had been given such an unusual name, and he told me: "Well, we had a little mission down here, and we started selling chicken dinners after church on Sunday to help pay the bills. Well, people liked the chicken, and we did such a good business, that eventually we cut back on the church service. After a while we just closed down the church altogether and kept on serving the chicken dinners. We kept the name that we started with, and that's Church of God Grill."

—Charles Paul Conn, *Making It Happen*

IT IS AN OLD AND IRONIC HABIT of human beings to run faster when we have lost our way.

—Rollo May

FORGIVENESS
(Also see *Acceptance, Self-esteem*)

A CARTOON in the *New Yorker* magazine showed an exasperated father saying to his prodigal son, "This is the fourth time we've killed the fatted calf." God does that over and over in our lifetime.

—Bruce Larson, *Setting Men Free*

A SUCCESSFUL IRISH BOXER was converted and became a preacher. He happened to be in a new town setting up his evangelistic tent when a couple of tough thugs noticed what he was doing. Knowing nothing of his background, they made a few insulting remarks. The Irishman merely turned and looked at them. Pressing his luck, one of the bullies took a swing and struck a glancing blow on one side of the ex-boxer's face. He shook it off and said nothing as he stuck out his jaw. The fellow took another glancing blow on the other side. At that point the preacher swiftly took off his coat, rolled up his sleeves, and announced, "The Lord gave me no further instructions." Whop!

—J. Vernon McGee, *Matthew*

Beginning Anew
(Also titled in some poetry books "A New Leaf")

He came to my desk with quivering lip;
    The lesson was done . . .
"Have you a new leaf for me, dear Teacher?
    I have spoiled this one!"
I took his leaf, all soiled and blotted,
And gave him a new one, all unspotted;
    Then into his tired heart I smiled:
"Do better now, my child!"

I went to the throne with trembling heart;
    The day was done.
"Have you a new day for me, dear Master?
    I have spoiled this one!"
He took my day, all soiled and blotted,
And gave me a new one, all unspotted;
    Then into my tired heart He smiled:
"Do better now, my child!"

—Kathleen Wheeler, quoted in John R. Rice, *Poems That Preach*

JOHN D. ROCKEFELLER built the great Standard Oil empire. Not surprisingly, Rockefeller was a man who demanded high performance from his company executives. One day, one of those executives made a two million dollar mistake.

Word of the man's enormous error quickly spread throughout the executive offices, and the other men began to make themselves scarce. Afraid of Rockefeller's reaction, they didn't even want to cross his path.

One man didn't have any choice, however, since he had an appointment with the boss. So he straightened his shoulders and tightened his belt and walked into Rockefeller's office.

As he approached the oil monarch's desk, Rockefeller looked up from the piece of paper on which he was writing.

"I guess you've heard about the two million dollar mistake our friend made," he said abruptly.

"Yes," the executive said, expecting Rockefeller to explode.

"Well, I've been sitting here listing all of our friend's good qualities on this sheet of paper, and I've discovered that in the past he has made us many more times the amount he lost for us today by his one mistake. His good points far outweigh this one human error. So I think we ought to forgive him, don't you?"

—Dale Galloway, *You Can Win with Love*

WE ARE MOST LIKE BEASTS when we kill. We are most like men when we judge. We are most like God when we forgive.

—William Arthur Ward, *Thoughts of a Christian Optimist*

FORGIVENESS IS surrendering my right to hurt you for hurting me.

—Archibald Hart, quoted in James Dobson, *Love Must Be Tough*

THERE'S A GREAT MINISTRY in our generation. It's called Prison Fellowship, directed by Chuck Colson. After his time behind bars, he realized the awful lifestyle that's facing the criminal who now is out, pardoned, and trying to get his or her life back together. I found these words in one of Colson's pieces of literature: "Nothing is more Christian than forgiveness . . . demonstrating trust in one who has fallen."

IT IS A WONDERFUL THING to see a prodigal return and to applaud it. I know a pastor who went through the horrors of public discipline of a brother in their church and it was dreadful. In fact, it made the news. Many of us heard about the discipline of this well-known Christian who had shipwrecked. And that brother walked away from God for several years. Finally he turned around and came back. He wrote a letter of apology ultimately. He said, "You were right. I was in sin. You put your finger on it. I rebelled and I rejected. But I want you to know, I see the wrong of my actions and I've come back."

You know what the church did? They had a party—this same church that had disciplined him. They bought him a sport coat and a new pair of shoes. They put a gold ring on his finger. And they served him prime rib. It was an evening of praise as this brother was brought back into fellowship. And that also made the news. There's not enough of that kind of news.

ONCE PRESIDENT LINCOLN was asked how he was going to treat the rebellious Southerners when they had finally been defeated and returned to the Union of the United States. The questioner expected that Lincoln would take a dire vengeance, but he answered, "I will treat them as if they had never been away."

—William Barclay, *The Gospel of Luke*

FREEDOM

ETERNAL VIGILANCE is the price of liberty.

—William Barclay, *The Revelation of John*

HAVING BEEN RAISED in the South for most of my younger years, it was a long time, believe it or not, before I really believed the South had lost the war. I know that seems unbelievable to people from the North or from the West, but it's true. I remember distinctly the day it dawned on me. It was in an American History class my junior year in high school that I finally had to face the fact we had lost. Under the prejudice of the way I was raised, I had always felt that we just ran out of time or supplies or something. But the truth was, we lost the battle.

Now as a result of this kind of prejudiced training, I had in my mind the feeling that those Union troops had to be some of the worst kind of rascals on earth, until I began to discover through fact and literature that such was not the case. They hated war like everybody else.

As a matter of fact, it was General William Sherman who, shortly after the invasion of Atlanta, and faced with the assault of the city government, wrote these words, "War is cruel and you cannot refine it. I'm tired and sick of this war. It is only those who have neither fired a shot nor heard the shrieks and groans of the wounded who cry aloud for more blood, more vengeance, more desolation. War? War is hell."

That statement made in 1864 is true both on or off the military battlefield. However, sometimes fighting can be necessary for survival. The reason you're able to sit here today without the interference of government or the enemy off our shores is because somebody fought and won. Some were willing to fight and die for freedom.

SOME MAY HAVE LIVED in the realm of freedom so long they've forgotten what it was like to be enslaved in the lost estate Paul describes in Romans 6:2 when he says, "How shall we who died to sin still live in it?" If so, the following words will help:

It is my earnest conviction that everyone should be in jail at least once in his life and that imprisonment should be on suspicion rather than proof; it should last for four months; it should seem hopeless; and preferably the prisoner should be sick half the time. . . . Only by such imprisonment does he learn what real freedom is worth.

—Gordon S. Seagrave, quoted in Lloyd Cory, *Quote Unquote*

A WAR HAD BEEN FOUGHT—the bloodiest in our history. A president had been assassinated. An amendment to the Constitution had been signed into law. Once-enslaved men, women, and children were now legally emancipated. Yet amazingly, many continued living in fear and squalor as though it had never happened. In a context of hard-earned freedom, slaves chose to remain as slaves.

—Charles R. Swindoll, *The Grace Awakening*

AN UNEXPECTED SHIFT of attention occurred during the presidential campaign in the fall of 1988. Instead of the evening news focusing on the Democratic and Republican candidates, all eyes were on two California whales up in Alaska, trapped in a breathing hole many miles from the ocean.

Strange as it may seem, Bush and Dukakis were upstaged by "Bonnett" and "Crossbeak," the names biologists gave the whales.

It all started when the gentle giants of the sea overlooked the fact that winter arrived early that year in northern Alaska. This mistake left them trapped, stranded inland by the ever-increasing covering of solid ice that prevented them from swimming to freedom.

At first few bothered to notice—only a few compassionate Eskimos who decided the creatures needed help. In a rather primitive fashion they hauled their chain saws and dragged long poles to the site and began to gouge out ice holes, enabling the whales to breathe en route to open water. Crude, rugged, and tiresome though the work was, they were determined to work their way toward the open ocean.

The weather wasn't cooperating. During some of the days, the temperature dropped below zero. That meant the small band of rescuers had to add some water-churning devices to keep the surface of the water from freezing over, especially during the screaming winds of the night. Interest in the project intensified once it caught the attention of the media. Other volunteers joined in the rescue efforts. Because the original plan wasn't moving along fast enough, in rolled an "Archimedean Screw Tractor," an enormous eleven-ton vehicle that rode on two screw-shaped pontoons, resembling something taken from a sci-fi movie set. That clumsy behemoth would clear away the ice after it was broken up and push it aside inch by inch, slowly grinding out a pathway to the sea. But that was also too slow and tedious. Next came the National Guard, who brought in two CH–54 Skycrane helicopters that systematically dropped five-ton concrete bashers onto the ice, mile after mile, so the journey to freedom could be accelerated.

If you can believe it, the Soviets arrived next, having dispatched two of their ships to the scene. One was a mammoth twenty-ton, eleven-story-tall icebreaker, and the other a smaller vessel with similar equipment. Interestingly, two flags flew on the stern of the Russian ships. Perhaps for the first and only time, the United States' stars and stripes flew alongside the familiar hammer and sickle. All political contrasts, economic differences, and military conflicts were set aside for this unusual mission—so a couple of whales could be free. Eureka! It finally happened at Point Barrow, Alaska. The world cheered as the exhausted creatures silently slipped out to sea.

—*Leadership* magazine, Spring 1990

THE SIXTEENTH PRESIDENT made an interesting comment shortly after the Emancipation Proclamation was passed by Congress early in 1863. Sounding more like Captain Ahab in Melville's novel *Moby Dick* than Abraham Lincoln delivering a speech, he warned, "We are like whalers who have been on a long chase. We have at last got the harpoon into the monster, but we must now look how we steer, or with one flop of his tail he will send us into eternity."

—Abraham Lincoln, August 26, 1863

THE KILLING FIELDS is quite a movie. It is the true story of a *New York Times* reporter who was working in Cambodia during a time of awful bloodshed. His closest assistant was a Cambodian who was later captured by the Marxist regime, the Khmer Rouge, a totalitarian group known for its torturous cruelty. What the Cambodian assistant endured while trying to find freedom is beyond belief.

The plot of the story revolves around the assistant's escape from the bondage of that terrible regime. It isn't a movie for the squeamish. There are things he sees and endures that defy the imagination. He is brutally beaten, imprisoned, and mistreated. Starving, he survived by sucking the blood from a beast in the field. He lives in the worst possible conditions. Finally, he plans his escape. He runs from one tragic scene to another. On one occasion, while fleeing, he sinks into a bog only to discover it is a watery hellhole full of rotting flesh and human bones and skulls that foam to the top as he scrambles to climb out. Fleeing from one horror to another, he is surprised as he stumbles into a clearing.

Having endured the rigors of the jungle while being chased by his captors, he finally steps out into a clearing and looks down. To his utter amazement, he sees the Cambodian border. Down below him is a small refugee camp. His eyes catch sight of a hospital and a flag. And on that flag, a cross. There, at long last, hope is awakened! At that point the music builds to a climax. Light returns to his weary face, which says in a dozen different ways, "I'm free. I'm free!" The joys and delights of his long-awaited freedom are his once again. Ultimately, he makes it to America and enjoys a tearful reunion with his friend—all because he is free. Free at last!

—Stuart Briscoe, *Spiritual Stamina*

FRIENDSHIP

ONE OF MY GOALS in life is to wind up with eight men who are willing to carry one of my handles.

—Jay Kesler, *Being Holy, Being Human*

SOON AFTER Jack Benny died, George Burns was interviewed on TV. "Jack and I had a wonderful friendship for nearly 55 years," Burns said. "Jack never walked out on me when I sang a song, and I never walked out on him when he played the violin. We laughed together, we played together, we worked together, we ate together. I suppose that for many of those years we talked every single day."

—Alan Loy McGinnis, *The Friendship Factor*

IN A MAGAZINE CARTOON: A thief was wearing one of those "Lone Ranger" masks. His gun was pointed toward his frightened victim as he yelled: "Okay, gimme all your valuables!"

The victim began stuffing into the sack all his *friends.*

THE WORD *philadelphia* means "human affection, brotherly love." It means being an affectionate friend. Samuel Coleridge wrote a poem titled "Youth and Age" with the line, "Friendship is a sheltering tree." That is a wonderful word picture. Friends are those whose lives are like branches. They provide shade, they provide refuge from the demanding, irritating, and searing rays of the hot sun. You can find comfort by them. You can find strength near them. They are tree-like in that they bear fruit that provides nourishment and encouragement. Isn't it interesting that when something occurs in your life and you are alone, you pick up the phone and call a friend? You want to connect with someone else. Few things are more lonely than going through a sudden test or joy and having no friend to call.

WHEN YOU REALLY HAVE A FRIEND, you will disregard personal sacrifice. If you have ever read Charles Dickens's *A Tale of Two Cities,* there is a classic illustration of John 15:13. In fact, Dickens quotes it in the book.

The two people who become friends are Charles Darnay and Sydney Carton. Darnay is a young Frenchman who is thrown in a dungeon and faces the guillotine the next morning. Carton is a wasted lawyer who has finished his life, as it were, as a loose-living individual there in England. Carton hears of Darnay's imprisonment and through a chain of events he gets into the dungeon and he changes garments with Darnay who escapes. The next morning Sydney Carton makes his way up the steps that lead to the guillotine. And Dickens says, as he writes of this, "Greater love has no one than this, than one lay down his life for his friend." And that's a classic example of the ultimate in friendship.

—Paul Lee Tan, *Encyclopedia of 7,700 Illustrations*

Oh, the comfort—the inexpressible comfort of feeling safe with a person,
Having neither to weigh thoughts,
Nor measure words—but pouring them
All right out—just as they are—
Chaff and grain together—
Certain that a faithful hand will
Take them and sift them—
Keeping what is worth keeping—
And with the breath of kindness
Blow the rest away.

—Dinah Maria Mulock Craik, quoted in *Handbook of Preaching Resources from Literature*

HENRY LUCE, founder of Time-Life, Inc., probably influenced world opinion more than any other publisher in history. . . . Luce frequently reminisced about his boyhood years as a missionary's son in Shantung, China. In the evenings he and his father had gone for long walks outside the compound, and his father had talked to him as if he were an adult. The problems of administering a school and the philosophical questions occupying him were all grist for their conversational mill. "He treated me as if I were his equal," said Luce. Their bond was tight because they were friends, and both father and son were nourished by the relationship.

—Alan Loy McGinnis, *The Friendship Factor*

OUT OF THE FURNACES OF WAR come many true stories of sacrificial friendship. One such story tells of two friends in World War I, who were inseparable. They had enlisted together, trained together, were shipped overseas together, and fought side-by-side in the trenches. During an attack, one of the men was critically wounded in a field filled with barbed wire obstacles, and he was unable to crawl back to his foxhole. The entire area was under a withering enemy crossfire, and it was suicidal to try to reach him. Yet his friend decided to try. Before he could get out of his own trench, his sergeant yanked him back inside and ordered him not to go. "It's too late. You can't do him any good, and you'll only get yourself killed."

A few minutes later, the officer turned his back, and instantly the man was gone after his friend. A few minutes later, he staggered back, mortally wounded, with his friend, now dead, in his arms. The sergeant was both angry and deeply moved. "What a waste," he blurted out. "He's dead and you're dying. It just wasn't worth it."

With almost his last breath, the dying man replied, "Oh, yes, it was, Sarge. When I got to him, the only thing he said was, 'I knew you'd come, Jim!'"

One of the true marks of friend is that he is there when there is every reason for him not to be, when to be there is sacrificially costly. As Proverbs 17:17 puts it, "A friend loves at all times, and a brother is born for adversity."

—Gary Inrig, *Quality Friendship*

FUTILITY

(Also see *Mistakes*)

I HEARD ABOUT A CARTOON not too long ago of Martians who were observing Earthlings scurrying about, busily engaging in nothing. And one Martian said, "What are they doing?" The other one answered, "They're going." The first

one said, "Going where?" The second one answered, "Oh, they're not going anywhere; they're just going."

—William Barclay, *Letters to the Corinthians*

Richard Cory

Whenever Richard Cory went downtown,
We people on the pavement looked at him:
He was a gentleman from sole to crown,
Clean favored, and imperially slim.

And he was always quietly arrayed,
And he was always human when he talked;
But still he fluttered pulses when he said,
"Good morning," and he glittered when he walked.

And he was rich—yes, richer than a king—
And admirably schooled in every grace:
In fine, we thought that he was everything
To make us wish that we were in his place.

So on we worked, and waited for the light,
And went without the meat, and cursed the bread;
And Richard Cory, one calm summer night,
Went home and put a bullet through his head.

—Edwin Arlington Robinson, quoted in Hazel Felleman, *Poems That Live Forever*

Tell me not, in mournful numbers,
Life is but an empty dream!
For the soul is dead that slumbers,
And things are not what they seem.

—Henry Wadsworth Longfellow, "A Psalm of Life"

OUR GREATEST PROBLEM is not the mistakes we make in life, but that we fail
to learn from them. If you can come up with creative new mistakes, that's
something else, but if you're making the same ones over and over, you're not
learning. A feeling of futility may set in. You may start to identify with that line

from Lewis Carroll's *Alice in Wonderland* that says, "I have to run real fast just to stay in place." Maybe it's time to stop running. Stop and learn.

IF I HAD MY ENTIRE LIFE to live over again, I don't think I'd have the strength.

—Flip Wilson, quoted in James Dobson, *What Wives Wish Their Husbands Knew about Women*

FUTILE DAYS WE CAN expect from time to time. Some of what we plan will miscarry. Paths that look promising will peter out and force us to backtrack. Pillars that we lean on will collapse and send our hopes tumbling down on us.

When sickness strikes or financial reverses hit, futile days stretch into empty weeks or months. There have been times when we heaved huge sighs as we ripped December's page from the calendar and welcomed a new year that offered better days than the old.

This futility is akin to irony, because it is full of surprises. We find it where we least expect it. Values that we treasure prove false; efforts that should succeed come to failure; pleasures that should satisfy increase our thirst. Ironic futility, futile irony—that is the color of life. . . .

—David Allan Hubbard, *Beyond Futility*

NEVER TRY TO TEACH a pig to sing. It wastes your time and it annoys the pig.

—Van Crouch, *Stay in the Game*

FUTURE
(Also see *Second Coming*)

J. DWIGHT PENTECOST, long-time Dallas Seminary faculty member, accepted an invitation to speak at a rather small church. They asked him to speak on prophecy. He said he would. But along with five sermons on prophecy, he planned specifically in the middle of the series to give a message which he entitled "The Loveliness of Christ," on the historical events that led up to the death of Christ. It was a message not at all on prophecy.

The five nights he spoke on prophecy, the place was packed. They even had loud speakers outside, so people could sit in the cool of the evening and at least hear what was said. The night he spoke on, "The Loveliness of Christ" the church wasn't quite half full. All the meetings were equally publicized, and the same kind of encouragement to attend was given. There is an incredible, inquisitive nature within us that has an itch to know what tomorrow will bring, but there's sort of a ho-hum feeling when we look back into history and see what yesterday left.

DUE TO UNFORESEEN CIRCUMSTANCES, no clairvoyant meeting wil be held tonight until further notice.

—*Union-Sun and Journal*, quoted in Lloyd Cory, *Quote Unquote*

WE SHOULD ALL BE CONCERNED about the future; because we will have to spend the rest of our lives there.

—Charles Kettering, quoted in Lloyd Cory, *Quote Unquote*

IN THE EARLY PART of the twelfth century, in the Dark Ages, a haggard old sorceress went to the papacy with six envelopes that she claimed had within them God's revelation for the Roman Catholic Church. She appeared before the pope and said, "I will sell this revelation from God to the church for $500,000." Well, they groaned, like you would, on the inside. And the prelates, along with the pope, decided no, they wouldn't buy. And so in front of them she burnt the first envelope to ashes.

With a measure of excitement and anxiety the pope watched it burn up and began to rethink his answer as she said, "Now I have five envelopes. And I will sell you the five remaining envelopes which contain the future for the church of Rome for $500,000. My price has not gone down." They murmured and talked among themselves and decided no. And so she burnt the second envelope, leaving four.

With an increased sense of anxiety there was a sort of low roar up among the clergy. And she said, "Now I have four envelopes left and for $500,000 I'll sell 'em to you." And again, the answer was no. In predictable fashion she burned up the third envelope, leaving three. And then she did the same with the fourth, leaving two.

And finally she said, "Now, for $500,000 I'll let you see the last two envelopes which contain the revelation of God." Well, by that time, they couldn't hold back. So they agreed.

And wouldn't you know it. The contents of the envelope were written in Latin, and I can't read Latin. So I can't tell you what it said. I'm still wondering.

—Abel Ahlquist, *Light on the Gospels*

YOU REMEMBER COMING HOME in the afternoon after school feeling very hungry and your mother had supper on the stove? And you remember at times she would have a cake in the oven? I don't know why mothers put children through such torture. When you were so hungry, the aroma of the cake filled the house, and you wanted a piece of that cake. "Not until after supper." Every mother I've ever met says that. Being the model child I was, I would wait patiently, except on a few occasions when I would badger her for a slice of that cake. And then she would take an exceedingly sharp knife with an exceedingly thin blade and slice off the smallest slice of cake one can imagine and give me a little taste of first fruit of the cake. It was only a sample of what was to come later.

Our Lord's Resurrection was a slice off of much more of the same to come later on.

YEARS AGO, during the presidential term of office of Dwight Eisenhower, the president was vacationing in Denver. It came to his attention that a six-year-old boy named Paul Haley was dying of an incurable cancer. And he had one great dream—that was to someday see the president.

Dwight Eisenhower made an act that will long outlive his great speeches when he said to one of his aides, "Let's go see young Paul Haley." They got in the presidential limousine and they drove over one August Sunday morning to the home of Paul Haley who didn't know he was coming. Flags on the fenders were flying as this black limousine drove up. Doors flew open, and out walked the President, who knocked on the door.

Mr. Donald Haley, the father, wearing blue jeans, an old dirty shirt, and one day's growth of beard, opened the door. He said, "Yes, can I help ya?" And the president responded, "Is Paul here? Tell him the president would like to see him."

And little Paul, to his amazement, walked around his father's legs and stood and looked up into the face of the man he admired most. Dwight Eisenhower kneeled down, shook his hand, took him out to see the presidential limousine, and before he said good-bye, he hugged little Paul Haley. They shook hands again, and he left.

The neighbors, I'm sure, are still talking about the visit from the president. Only one man was not entirely happy about it, and that was Donald Haley, who said, "How can I ever forget standing there dressed like I was in those jeans and an old, dirty shirt and an unshaven face to meet the president of the United States?" He just wasn't prepared.

—Billy Graham, *World Aflame*

A SHORT TIME AGO, I took occasion to go through the New Testament to mark each reference to the coming of the Lord Jesus Christ and to observe the use made of that teaching about His coming. I was struck anew with the fact that almost without exception, when the coming of Christ is mentioned in the New Testament, it is followed by an exhortation to godliness and holy living. While the study of prophecy will give us proof of the authority of the Word of God, it will also reveal the purpose of God and the power of God, and will give us the peace and assurance of God. We have missed the whole purpose of the study of prophecy if it does not conform us to the Lord Jesus Christ in our daily living.

—J. Dwight Pentecost, *Prophecy for Today*

THE STORY IS TOLD of the man who, while walking on the beach, found washed up on the sand a used magic lamp. When the genie answered his rub, he told him that the lamp contained but one remaining wish. The man pondered for a moment, and then requested a copy of the stock page from the local newspaper, dated exactly one year later. In a puff of smoke, the genie was gone, and in his place was the financial news. Gleefully, the man sat down to peruse his trophy; he could invest with certainty, knowing the winners one year in advance. As the paper fell to his lap, it turned over to the obituary column found on the reverse of the page, and the name on the top of the listing caught his attention—it was his!

—Robert R. Shank, *Winning over Uncertainty*

THE POPULATION BOOM is not stopping. In January 1982 the *Reader's Digest* quoted an article from the *New York Times* called "Off the Chart—The People Boom."

There's a chart that looks like the toe of a boot to the top of a boot (it's about the best way I know to describe it), as it illustrates the growing population. It is estimated that in the dawn of agriculture there were 5 million people. By the birth of Christ there were 200 million. When the literate age began, in 1650, there were 500 million. And it gets to the edge of the boot and it shoots up about six inches, so that in our space age in 1982 the world population about 4.4 billion. Now we can't imagine that many, but I want you to get a picture of the growth. It went on to say if the human population continued to explode at the present rates through A.D. 3000, the line would soar upward 74 million feet! That kind of growth will create enormous complications for the future.

𝒢g

GIFTS

I RECENTLY HEARD ABOUT a guy who gave his girlfriend his lottery ticket, and to their surprise, it won $3 million! But the government taxed him for the cash. And then, if that wasn't bad enough, when his ex-wife heard that he was now worth a lot of money, she upped the ante on the alimony payments.

"IT'S NOT THE GIFT, it's the thought behind it." You've heard that before. Well, these two brothers put a lot of thought in the giving of a pair of pants that they gave back and forth to each other every Christmas.

First, the pants were tied to a car wheel and run over snow and ice, then removed from the wheel, wrapped in a lovely box, and presented at Christmas-time.

When the other brother got them the next Christmas, he placed those same pants in a form where wet cement was poured and allowed to dry. They were presented that year along with a sledge hammer.

So the next year they were placed in the framing of a small tool shed, and the entire shed had to be ripped apart in order to get to the pants.

Now the next year, the same old sorry, miserable pair of pants sat in the front seat of a car which was demolished, compressed into a flattened piece of metal. It took a tractor and crowbars to get to that same pair of pants.

Again, it wasn't the gift—it was the fun and joy in giving it.

A GIFT IS A DEMONSTRATION of love from one heart to another. Calvin Miller once sent me an acrostic poem that spelled out my name. You cherish those special, personal gifts.

Late afternoon on Christmas Eve, when I was about seven years old, my mother was making something special. Instead of the traditional Jell-O, whipped cream, and bananas, she was baking a towering pie!

"I stood at her elbow, as small boys always will, as she peeked for a moment through the partly open oven door. "Perfect," she said. Carefully, so cautiously, she drew it out, when suddenly there was a slip of those sure hands, and a cap-sized tower slithered across the floor, never to be pie again.

And Mother, not a weeper, covered her face with her apron and cried. I was outraged that God would let it happen because no one—but no one—cries on Christmas Eve!

"Why did she do it, prepare this gift for hungry little gluttons when Jell-O was enough? I know: it was her language for telling us that we were special. More than sixty years have come and gone, sixty Christmases, and I remember that one the best—and its gift of tears."

—Gerhard Frost, *Blessed Is the Ordinary*

GIVING

(Also see *Charity, Money, Stewardship, Wealth*)

IF YOU HAVE LITTLE CHILDREN or if you have been around little children, you've seen this scene a dozen times. The older child gets a toy, perhaps a spe-cial little truck he loves to play with. In fact, he plays with it 'till he about wears all the paint off it. And one day it's sitting on the coffee table and nobody's touching it. Along comes little sister, who toddles up to the table and reaches her little hand over to the well-worn truck, only to have it snatched away by the gorilla in the family. "It's my truck!" He doesn't want to part with something that important.

How many of us parents have looked at the older child saying, "Let her play with it," and had the child say, "Oh, of course. Here, sis"? Are you kidding? "MINE! MINE!" And you just about have to break his arm to get the truck out of his hand. He doesn't want to give it up. And your compulsion makes him grip it tighter.

That's an illustration of giving "grudgingly." And yet the remarkable thing is that the standard approach in fund-raising is causing people to feel forced. You see, compulsion results in reluctance. When you are compelled to do something, you are all the more reluctant to give it up.

Somehow, not only for Christmas
But all the long year through,
The joy that you give to others

Is the joy that comes back to you.
And the more you spend in blessing
The poor and the lonely and sad,
The more of your heart's possessions
Return to make you glad.

—John Greenleaf Whittier

JESUS TALKED ABOUT MONEY. One-sixth of the Gospels, and one-third of the parables address the subject of stewardship. Jesus was no fund-raiser. He dealt with money matters, however, because money matters. It's a surprise to many people, Christians included, that the Bible has so much to say about this subject.

God has given us three ways on this earth to invest in eternity. Two of them are up for discussion and we approach them with open-mindedness, we can never seem to hear enough about them, but the third seems to be nobody else's business.

The preacher who fails to address *time* and how we spend it is considered derelict in his duty. For time is one of those irretrievable values in life you can only spend once and never capture again.

The pastor who overlooks teaching on *talents* and gifts that help the church body function smoothly and well and even efficiently is not doing his job. The congregation has a right to feel slighted because that subject is not mentioned.

But let the man address the subject of *treasure* and he's back on that age-old subject and just trying to get our money. I find that not only amazing but ridiculous.

GOD

A KINDERGARTEN TEACHER told everyone to draw a picture of what was important to them. In the back of the room Johnny began to labor over his drawing. Everybody else finished and handed in their picture but he didn't. He was still drawing. The teacher graciously walked back and put her arm around Johnny's shoulder and said, "Johnny, what are you drawing?" He didn't look up; he just kept on working feverishly at his picture. He said, "God." "But Johnny," she said gently, "no one knows what God looks like." He answered, "They will when I'm through."

—Em Griffin, *The Mind Changers*

DO YOU REMEMBER when the cosmonauts made that primitive little journey around the earth the first time? They came back with their thumbs under their suspenders bragging, "We have been in the air. We have been around the earth. And we did not see God!" The following Sunday W. A. Criswell, pastor of the First Baptist Church in Dallas, made a classic statement. He said, "Ah, if those cosmonauts had stepped out of their spacesuit, they would have seen God!"

MISS THOMPSON had a tough task. Her Sunday school lesson plan called for teaching her primary class about the Trinity. It was difficult enough to hold their attention with stories and creative object lessons, but when it came to keeping them interested in the identity, attributes, and purpose of the Father, Son, and Spirit . . . well, that was next to impossible.

While thinking through her lesson, she had a creative thought: She would use a big, thick pretzel, with its three holes in the middle. Perfect!

When Sunday morning came she stood before her class, holding the pretzel high in the air, explaining how it was made up of one strand of dough but was so intricately interwoven that there were three distinct holes, each one having its own special shape.

She pointed first to the hole at the top, "Children, this is like God the Father. Think of this first hole as your heavenly Father." She then pointed to the second, explaining slowly and carefully, "This is like God the Son. Think of the hole here on the right as Jesus, your Savior." The class of fresh little faces seemed to be following her with keen interest, so she continued, "And this third hole is God the Holy Ghost. Just as this is one pretzel made up of three separate holes, so the Trinity is one unit made up of three distinct Persons: Father, Son, and Holy Ghost."

Miss Thompson had the children repeat those names aloud: "Father . . . Son . . . and Holy Ghost." Again and again she had the class say the names.

Hoping to cement this concept in their minds, she singled out little Jimmy, sitting close to the front, and asked him if he could repeat the names of the "holey" members of the Trinity for the rest of the class. Though reluctant, he slowly stood to his feet and took the pretzel she held out to him.

"This here is God . . . God the Father," he said, pointing to the first hole. (Miss Thompson smiled with delight.) "And this one is Jesus." (Again she beamed over his excellent memory.) "And this third one is . . . uh . . . the Holy Smoke."

—Charles R. Swindoll, *Flying Closer to the Flame*

ROBERT DICK WILSON taught Hebrew at Princeton Theological Seminary and one of his students was Donald Barnhouse. Barnhouse tells of his going back to the seminary to preach after having graduated from there twelve years earlier. Dr. Wilson came into Miller Chapel and sat down near the front. There is something rather intimidating about going back to the school where you were trained and you teach the Scriptures to those who taught you.

At the close of the meeting Dr. Wilson came up to Donald Barnhouse and said, "If you come back again, I will not come to hear you preach. I only come once. I am glad that you are a big-godder. When my boys come back, I come to see if they are big-godders or little-godders, and then I know what their ministry will be." Barnhouse asked him to explain.

"Well, some men have a little God and they are always in trouble with Him. He can't do any miracles. He can't take care of the inspiration and transmission of the Scripture to us. He doesn't intervene on behalf of His people. They have a little God and I call them little-godders. Then there are those who have a great God. He speaks and it is done. He commands and it stands fast. He knows how to show Himself strong on behalf of them that fear Him. You, Donald, have a great God; and he will bless your ministry." He paused a moment, smiled, said, "God bless you," and walked out.

—Donald Barnhouse, *Romans*

WE WANT, in fact, not so much a Father in heaven as a grandfather in heaven—a senile benevolence who, as they say, "likes to see young people enjoying themselves" and whose plan for the universe was simply that it might be truly said at the end of each day, "a good time was had by all."

—C. S. Lewis, *The Problem of Pain*

HAVE YOU SERVED IN THE MILITARY? Remember how wonderful it was to go into the office of the company commander? I remember doing that one time. He did not say, "Oh, Chuck, how nice of you to drop by. Come in, son. Have a seat. What's on your heart?" First words I heard that I can repeat here were "What do you want?" Now that's a wonderful greeting for a guy who's standing there with his knees knocking against each other. You know what? I couldn't even remember, which made it worse.

When I was a little boy, I had that feeling about God. I'd got it from a Lil Abner cartoon. This little guy is walking around with a club. Had a nail in it, more like a spike. He was lookin' for people. And when I was a little kid I used to think, "That's God! Just lookin' for folks and saying, 'There he is!'" Then *whomp.*

The Eternal Goodness

I see the wrong that round me lies,
I feel the guilt within;
I hear, with groan and travail-cries,
The world confess its sin.

Yet in the maddening maze of things,
And tossed by storm and flood,
To one fixed trust my spirit clings:
I know that God is good!

—John Greenleaf Whittier

I Am

I was regretting the past
And fearing the future . . .
Suddenly my Lord was speaking:
"MY NAME IS I AM." He paused.
I waited. He continued,

"WHEN YOU LIVE IN THE PAST,
  WITH ITS MISTAKES AND REGRETS,
  IT IS HARD. I AM NOT THERE.
    MY NAME IS NOT *I WAS*.

"WHEN YOU LIVE IN THE FUTURE,
  WITH ITS PROBLEMS AND FEARS,
  IT IS HARD. I AM NOT THERE.
    MY NAME IS NOT *I WILL BE*.

"WHEN YOU LIVE IN THE MOMENT,
  IT'S NOT HARD.
  I AM HERE.
    MY NAME IS *I AM*."

—Helen Mallicoat, quoted in Tim Hansel, *Holy Sweat*

High Flight

Oh! I have slipped the surly bonds of Earth
And danced the skies on laughter-silvered wings;
Sunward I've climbed, and joined the tumbling mirth

Of sun-split clouds, and done a hundred things
You have not dreamed of—wheeled and soared and swung
High in the sunlit silence. Hov'ring there,
I've chased the shouting wind along, and flung
My eager craft through footless halls of air.

Up, up the long, delirious, burning blue
I've topped the wind-swept heights with easy grace
Where never lark nor ever eagle flew—
And, while with silent lifting mind I've trod
The high untrespassed sanctity of space,
Put out my hand, and touched the face of God.

John Gillespie Magee Jr., quoted in Donald T. Kauffman, *Baker's Pocket Treasury of Religious Verse*

GOD'S LOVE

What God Hath Promised

God hath not promised
  Skies always blue,
Flower-strewn pathways
  All our lives through;
God hath not promised
  Sun without rain,
Joy without sorrow,
  Peace without pain.

But God hath promised
  Strength for the day,
Rest for the labor,
  Light for the way,
Grace for the trials,
  Help from above,
Unfailing sympathy,
  Undying love.

—Annie Johnson Flint, quoted in Donald Kauffman, *Baker's Pocket Treasury of Religious Verse*

KARL BARTH, famed theologian, was once asked, "What is the greatest thought you ever had?" His answer: "Jesus loves me this I know, for the Bible tells me so."

—Dale Galloway, *Rebuild Your Life*

WHAT MATTERS SUPREMELY, therefore, is not, in the last analysis, the fact that I know God, but the larger fact which underlies it—that He knows me. I am graven on the palms of His hands. I am never out of His mind. All my knowledge of Him depends on His sustained initiative in knowing me. I know Him because He first knew me, and continues to know me. He knows me as a friend, one who loves me; and there is no moment when His eye is off me, or His attention distracted from me, and no moment, therefore, when His care falters. This is momentous knowledge. There is unspeakable comfort . . . in knowing that God is constantly taking knowledge of me in love and watching over me for my good. There is tremendous relief in knowing that His love is utterly realistic, based at every point on prior knowledge of the worst about me, so that no discovery now can disillusion Him about me, in the way I am so often disillusioned about myself, and quench His determination to bless me.

—J. I. Packer, *Knowing God*

ONE NIGHT I HAD A DREAM. I was walking along the beach with the Lord, and across the skies flashed scenes from my life. In each scene, I noticed two sets of footprints in the sand. One was mine, and one was the Lord's. When the last scene of my life appeared before me, I looked back at the footprints in the sand, and to my surprise, I noticed that many times along the path of my life there was only one set of footprints. And I noticed that it was at the lowest and saddest times in my life. I asked the Lord about it, "Lord, You said that once I decided to follow You, You would walk with me all the way. But I notice that during the most troublesome times in my life, there is only one set of foot-prints. I do not understand why You left my side when I needed You the most." The Lord said, "My precious child, I never left you during your time of trial. Where you see only one set of footprints, I was carrying you."

—Margaret Rose Powers, *Guideposts* magazine, July 1992

WHEN I WAS IN THE MARINE CORPS in the Orient I became serious about the ministry. It was amazing to me that God was changing my heart at that time. My sister, Luci, who knew of my interest through a letter I had written her, sent me a book I still have in my library. I treasure it. I opened the book the afternoon I received it and saw she had written in the front part of the book this inscription, "Whom have we, Lord, but Thee, soul thirst to satisfy. Exhaustless spring, the water is free, all other streams are dry." (This is from the hymn "Whom Have We, Lord, but Thee" by Mary Bowley Peters.) God's love is an exhaustless spring.

THERE IS NO OTHER BLESSING I can give you, no gift so precious no treasure so refreshing, nothing that can provision you for the journey we are all making, than to tell you that Someone is searching diligently for you. He is not a stationary God. He is crazy about you. The expense to which He has gone isn't reasonable, is it? The Cross was not a very dignified ransom. To say the least, it was a splurge of love and glory lavishly spent on you and me: "While we were yet sinners, Christ died for the ungodly." "A shepherd having a hundred sheep, if he loses one, leaves the ninety-nine to go after the one and searches diligently until he finds it."

God is like that shepherd. That is enough to make me laugh and cry.

—David A. Redding, *Jesus Makes Me Laugh with Him*

GOD'S MERCY

J. DWIGHT PENTECOST used to say, "Mercy is God's ministry to the miserable." It is both intensely personal and immensely practical. For when I am treated unfairly, God's mercy relieves my bitterness. When I grieve over loss, it relieves my pain and anger and denial. When I struggle with disability, it relieves my self-pity. When I endure physical pain, it relieves my hopelessness. When I deal with being sinful, it relieves my guilt.

THE FILM *Tender Mercies* is about two opposites who marry. He is a man battling with alcohol, bitter over a lost career as a country-western musician. She is a widow whose husband was killed in Vietnam. She never makes enormous demands on her alcoholic husband, never threatens him, never expects too much. Quietly, graciously, patiently, with tender mercy, she trusts God to deal with her husband.

The story comes to a climax when the husband, in the throes of depression, buys a bottle and peels out in his pickup. Meanwhile, his wife waits in bed, quoting Scripture to encourage herself while he's gone. Finally, he returns, telling her, "I bought a bottle, but I poured it out. I didn't drink anything." His life turns a corner at this point. And he goes back to the work he once loved—songwriting.

Tender mercies—that's what God uses to change lives.

WE COUNT ON God's mercy for our past mistakes, on God's love for our present needs, on God's sovereignty for our future.

Augustine

_____

NOTHING ELSE in the circumference of his [Abraham's] life could have been such a test as anything connected with the heir of promise, the child of his old age, the laughter of his life. . . . So He put him to a supreme test, that all men might henceforth know that a mortal man could love God so much as to put Him first, though his dearest lay in the opposite scale of the balance of the heart.

—F. B. Meyer, *Abraham*

_____

STAY FERVENT IN LOVE. *Fervent* is a word that speaks of intensity and determination. It is an athletic term for stretching to reach the tape. Have you watched the fellows and gals who run the dash? When they come around that last turn and they're pressing for the tape, they'll get right to the end and then they'll lunge forward. I've even seen them fall right there on the track, because they're pushing to reach the tape ahead of the one they're competing against. It's the idea of intensity at the tape, stretching yourself. Those who do the long jump leap into the air and throw their feet forward and they, with intensity, stretch every muscle of their body to reach as far as they can. The same with the high jumpers or with the pole vaulters. They stretch to the uttermost to reach the limit. That's the word *fervent*.

_____

God the Source of All Good

O Lord God, Who inhabitest eternity,
The heavens declare thy glory,
The earth thy riches,
The universe is thy temple;
Thy presence fills immensity,
Yet thou hast of thy pleasure created life,
    and communicated happiness;
Thou hast made me what I am,
and given me what I have;
In thee I live and move and have my being;
Thy providence has set the bounds of my habitation,
    and wisely administers all my affairs.

I thank thee for thy riches to me in Jesus,
    for the unclouded revelation of him in thy Word,
        where I behold his person, character, grace, glory,
        humiliation, sufferings, death and resurrection;
Give me to feel a need of His continual saviourhood,
    and cry with Job, 'I am vile,'
        with Peter, 'I perish,'
        with the publican, 'Be merciful to me, a sinner.'
Subdue in me the love of sin,
Let me know the need of renovation as well as of forgiveness
    in order to serve and enjoy thee for ever.
I come to thee in the all-prevailing name of Jesus,
    with nothing of my own to plead,
    no works, no worthiness, no promises.
I am often straying,
    often knowingly opposing thy authority,
    often abusing thy goodness;
Much of my guilt arises from my religious privileges,
    my low estimation of them,
    my failure to use them to my advantage,
But I am not careless of thy favor regardless of thy glory;
Impress me deeply with a sense of thine omnipresence,
    that thou art about my path, my ways, my lying down, my end.

—Arthur Bennett, *The Valley of Vison*

GOD'S SOVEREIGNTY

Hearts that are great are always lone
They never will manifest their best
Their greatest greatness is unknown
Earth knows a little
God the rest.

—Abram Joseph Ryan

THERE WAS A MAN who gave his business to God. He had hassled over it for years. He had wrestled with it and fought it for two decades. One day he decided, "I've had it; that's enough!" He had heard from his pastor that Sunday morning about the value of turning his entire business over to God. It was when he drove away from church that he decided he had worried enough. By the time he got home, he had totally and unequivocally committed his business to God.

That very night his place of business caught on fire. He got an emergency call. He rather calmly drove down to the commercial residence and was standing on the street, watching the place go up in flames. He was sort of smiling to himself. One of his colleagues raced to his side and questioned his relaxed attitude about what was happening. "Man! Don't you know what's happening to you? . . . It's . . . it's burning up!"

He replied, "I know it. I know it. No problem, Fred. This morning I gave this company to God, and if He wants to burn it up, that's His business."

—Charles R. Swindoll, *Living on the Ragged Edge*

MAN'S WILL IS FREE because God is sovereign. . . . Perhaps a homely illustration might help us to understand.

An ocean liner leaves New York bound for Liverpool. Its destination has been determined by proper authorities. Nothing can change it. This is at least a faint picture of sovereignty.

On board the liner are several scores of passengers. These are not in chains, neither are their activities determined for them by decree. They are completely free to move about as they will. They eat, sleep, play, lounge about on the deck, read, talk, altogether as they please; but all the while the great liner is carrying them steadily onward toward a predetermined port.

Both freedom and sovereignty are present here and they do not contradict each other. So it is, I believe, with man's freedom and the sovereignty of God. The mighty liner of God's sovereign design keeps its steady course over the sea of history. God moves undisturbed and unhindered toward the fulfillment of those eternal purposes which He purposed in Christ Jesus before the world began. We do not know all that is included in those purposes, but enough has been disclosed to furnish us with a broad outline of things to come and to give us good hope and firm assurance of future well-being.

—A. W. Tozer, *The Knowledge of the Holy*

God's Handwriting

He writes with characters too grand
For our short sight to understand;
We catch but broken strokes, and try
To fathom all the mystery

Of withered hopes, of death, of life,
The endless war, the useless strife—
But there, with larger, clearer sight,
We shall see this—His way was right.

—John Oxenham, quoted by V. Raymond Edman, *Disciplines of Life*

The Loom of Time

Man's life is laid in the loom of time
To pattern he does not see,
While the weavers work and the shuttles fly
Till the dawn of eternity.

Some shuttles are filled with silver threads
And some with threads of gold,
While often but the darker hues
Are all that they may hold.

But the weaver watches with skillful eye
Each shuttle fly to and fro,
And sees the pattern so deftly wrought
As the loom moves sure and slow.

God surely planned the pattern:
Each thread, the dark and fair,
Is chosen by His master skill
And placed in the web with care.
    He knows only its beauty,
    And guides the shuttles which hold
    The threads so unattractive,
    As well as the threads of gold.

    Not till each loom is silent,
    And the shuttles cease to fly,
    Shall God reveal the pattern
    And explain the reason why.

    The dark threads were as needful
    In the weaver's skillful hand
    As the threads of gold and silver
    For the pattern which He planned.

—Author Unknown, quoted in Hazel Felleman, *Best Loved Poems of the American People*

THERE WAS A MAN in Kansas whose house was blown away in a cyclone. The local preacher, seeing this as an opportunity, told the man, "Punishment for sin is inevitable." "Oh, really," said the man, "and did you know your house was blown away too?" "Well," responded the preacher, "the Lord's ways are beyond understanding."

—Oren Arnold, *Snappy Steeple Stories*

God's Sovereignty

With thoughtless and
Impatient hands
We tangle up
The plans
The Lord has wrought.

And when we cry
In pain, He saith,
"Be quiet, dear,
While I untie the knot."

—V. Raymond Edman, *The Disciplines of Life*

A Prayer to the God of Ebb and Flow

Dear Lord,

Today I thought of the words of Vincent Van Gogh. It is true that there is an ebb and flow but the sea remains the sea. You, oh God, are the sea. Although I experience many ups and downs in my emotions and often feel great shifts and changes in my inner life, You remain the same. Your sameness is not the sameness of a rock, but the sameness of a faithful lover. I am sustained and to Your love I am always called back. My only real temptation is to doubt Your love, to think of myself as beyond Your love, to remove myself from the healing radiance of Your love. To do these things is to move into the darkness of despair.

Oh, Lord, sea of love and goodness, let me not fear too much the storms or winds of my daily life. And, let me know that there is ebb and flow, but that the sea remains the sea. Amen.

Light Shining Out of Darkness

God moves in a mysterious way,
His wonders to perform;
He plants His footsteps in the sea,
And rides upon the storm.

Deep in unfathomable mines
Of never failing skill,
He treasures up his bright designs,
And works his sovereign will.
Ye fearful saints, fresh courage take;
The clouds ye so much dread
Are big with mercy, and shall break
In blessings on your head.

—William Cowper

Things Don't Just Happen

Things don't just happen to us who love God,
        They're planned by His own dear hand,
Then molded and shaped, and timed by His clock,
        Things don't just happen—they're planned.
We don't just guess on the issues of life;
        We Christians just rest in our Lord,
We are directed by His sovereign will,
        In the light of His holy Word.
We who love Jesus are walking by faith,
        Not seeing one step that's ahead,
Not doubting one moment what our lot might be,
        But looking to Jesus, instead.
We praise our dear Saviour for loving us so,
        For planning each care of our life;
Then giving us faith to trust Him for all
        The blessings as well as the strife.
Things don't just happen to us who love God,
        To us who have taken our stand;
No matter the lot, the course, or the price,
        Things don't just happen—they're planned.

—Esther Fields, quoted in Barbara Johnson, *Fresh Elastic for Stretched Out Moms*

First, He brought me here, it is by His will I am in this strait place: in that fact I will rest.

Next, He will keep me here in His love, and give me the grace to behave as His child.

Then, He will make the trial a blessing, teaching me lessons He intends for me to learn, and

working in me the grace He means to bestow.

Last, in His good time He can bring me out again—how and when He knows.

Let me say I am here,

(1) By God's appointment

(2) In His keeping

(3) Under His training

(4) For His time.

—V. Raymond Edman, *In Quietness and Confidence*

The Present Crisis

Truth forever on the scaffold,
Wrong forever on the throne—
Yet that scaffold sways the future, and,
Behind the dim unknown,
Standeth God within the shadow,
Keeping watch above His Own.

—James Russell Lowell

WE, AS AMERICANS, are a people uniquely blessed. We even had a most unique origin. Christopher Columbus, in an unusual book, his *Book of Prophecies,* includes these words:

It was the Lord who put into my mind (I could feel his hand upon me) the fact that it would be possible to sail from here to the Indies. All who heard of my project rejected it with laughter, ridiculing me. There is no question that the inspiration was from the Holy Spirit, because He comforted me with rays of marvelous inspiration from the Holy Scriptures. . . .

I am a most unworthy sinner, but I have cried out to the Lord for grace and mercy and they have covered me completely. I have found the sweetest consolation since I made it my whole purpose to enjoy His marvelous presence. For the execution of the journey to the Indies, I did not make use of intelligence, mathematics or maps. It is simply the fulfillment of what Isaiah had prophesied. . . .

No one should fear to undertake any task in the name of our Savior, if it is just and if the intention is purely for His holy service. The working out of all things has been assigned to each person by our Lord, but it all happens according to His sovereign will, even though He gives advice. He lacks nothing that it is in the power of men to give Him. Oh, what a gracious Lord, who desires that people should perform for Him those things for which He holds Himself responsible! Day and night, moment by moment, everyone should express their most devoted gratitude to Him.

—Peter Marshall, *The Light and the Glory*

HELEN ROSEVEARE, British medical missionary in the Congo uprising when the Mau-Mau revolutionaries invaded, was attacked. This pure, godly, gracious, innocent woman of God, was raped, assaulted, humiliated, hanging on with her life to a faith that would not be shaken. While recovering from that horrible event, Helen and the Lord grew closer together than they had ever been before. And she wrote a statement in the form of a question that every person needs to ask himself or herself: "Can you thank Me for trusting you with this experience, even if I never tell you why?"

THE SOUND WAS DEAFENING.

Although no one was near enough to hear it, it ultimately echoed around the world. None of the passengers in the DC-4 ever knew what happened; they died instantly. That was February 15, 1947. The *Avianca Airline* flight bound for Quito, Equador, crashed clumsily into the 14,000 foot-high towering peak of El Tablazo not far from Bogota. Then it dropped, a flaming mass of metal, into a ravine far below. A young New Yorker, Glenn Chambers, was one of its victims. He planned to begin a ministry with the *Voice of the Andes,* a lifelong dream that suddenly aborted into a nightmare.

Before leaving the Miami Airport earlier that day, Chambers hurriedly dashed off a note to his mom on a piece of paper he found on the floor of the terminal. That scrap of paper was once a printed piece of advertisement with the single word WHY sprawled across the center. But between the mailing and the delivery of that note, Chambers was killed. When the letter did arrive, there staring up at his mom was the haunting question—*WHY?* Of all the questions it is the most searching, the most tormenting. No single truth removes the need to ask Why? like this one. Here it is:

GOD IS TOO KIND TO DO ANYTHING CRUEL . . .

TOO WISE TO MAKE A MISTAKE . . .
TOO DEEP TO EXPLAIN HIMSELF.

Mrs. Chambers stopped asking Why? when she saw the Who behind the scene. All other sounds are muffled when we claim His absolute sovereignty. Even the deafening sound of a crashing DC-4.

—William Petersen, *How to Be a Saint While Lying Flat on Your Back*

ACCEPTANCE IS taking from God's hand absolutely anything He chooses to give us, looking up into His face in love and trust—even in thanksgiving—and knowing that the confines of the hedge within which He has placed us are good, even perfect, however painful they may be, simply because He Himself has given them.

GOD'S WILL

THE WAY SOME PEOPLE attempt to know the will of God would make a great television series entitled *That's Unbelievable.* I read this last week of a lady who had a lifetime ambition of going to the Holy Land. She got a pamphlet on the Holy Land tour and read it over carefully. She had the time and the money to make the trip, but she wasn't certain if it was God's will. So before going to bed that night, she read again the pamphlet and noticed in the details of the plan that they would be traveling on a 747 jumbo jet, there and back. She wrestled through the night, tossed back and forth, wondering what God's will might be. And she woke up the next morning, looked at her digital clock, and it read 7:47. It convinced her it was God's will for her to make the trip. That's unbelievable.

—Leslie and Bernice Flynn, *God's Will: You Can Know It*

A PASTOR FOR MANY YEARS was a deacon in several churches before God called him into vocational Christian service as a minister before he was ever ordained. And then while a minister he was tempted to buy a doctor's degree from a degree mill. He read in his King James Bible the words of 1 Timothy 3:13 and he got his answer from God: "For they that have used the office of deacon well, purchase to themselves a high degree. . . ."

—Leslie and Bernice Flynn, *God's Will: You Can Know It*

WHO HASN'T HEARD OF holding out a fleece before God? A man who was wrestling with knowing God's will, prayed as he was driving, "If it is Your will for me to do this, then may the light at the next corner stay green until I get there." Another one wrestling with God's will said, "Lord, may my phone ring at 9:21 tonight if Your answer to me is yes."

—Leslie and Bernice Flynn, *God's Will: You Can Know It*

THEN THERE'S THE EXAMPLE of Christians who use the open window method in seeking God's will. You put your Bible by a window and (whew!) the pages blow and you put your finger on a verse. One man did that and pointed to the verse, "Judas went and hanged himself." Not a very good life verse, and he did it again. This time he put his finger on the verse that said, "Go and do thou likewise." The third verse he found said, "Whatsoever thou doest, do quickly."

—Leslie and Bernice Flynn, *God's Will: You Can Know It*

AS A MAN WAS DRIVING in Washington, D.C., he was searching for God's will for his future. His car ran out of gas in front of the Philippines embassy. He took it as a sign of God's will he should go to the Philippines as a missionary. I wonder what he would do if he were single and stuck on an elevator with a single young lady named Mary.

—Leslie and Bernice Flynn, *God's Will: You Can Know It*

A GROUP OF THEOLOGIANS were discussing predestination and free will. When the argument became heated, the dissidents split into two groups. One man, unable to make up his mind which group to join, slipped into the pre-destination crowd. Challenged as to why he was there, he said, "Hey, I came of my own free will." The group reported, "Free will? You can't join us!" He retreated to the opposite group and met the same challenge. "I was sent here," he said honestly. "Get out!" they stormed. "You can't join us unless you come of your own free will."

Which is right? I heard of a man who stumbled and fell down the steps of a large church. One Arminian watched and said, "I wonder why he did that? I wonder how that happened?" A Calvinist watched and said, "I'll bet he's glad it's over."

—Leslie Flynn, *Great Church Fights*

A COLLEGE SOPHOMORE was in need of a car and had a series of dreams one night and everything was in yellow, everything! Early the next morning he began to hit the used car lots, looking at one car after another. Finally he found

God's will for him: a yellow car, yellow inside and out. He didn't even ask to drive it. He just bought it. Turned out to be a lemon.

—Leslie and Bernice Flynn, *God's Will: You Can Know It*

_____

Thy Way, Not Mine

Thy way, not mine, O Lord,
However dark it be!
Lead me by Thine own hand,
Choose out the path for me.

Smooth let it be or rough,
It will be still the best;
Winding or straight, it leads
Right onward to Thy rest.

I dare not choose my lot;
I would not, if I might;
Choose Thou for me, my God;
So shall I walk aright.

The kingdom that I seek
Is Thine; so let the way
That leads to it be Thine;
Else I must surely stray.

Take Thou my cup, and it
With joy or sorrow fill,
As best to Thee may seem;
Choose Thou my good and ill.

Choose Thou for me my friends,
My sickness or my health;
Choose Thou my cares for me,
My poverty or wealth.

Not mine, not mine the choice,
In things or great or small;
Be Thou my guide, my strength,
My wisdom, and my all!

—Horatius Bonar, quoted in Donald T. Kauffman, *Baker's Pocket Treasury of Religious Verse*

GOD'S WORD

(See *Bible*)

GOVERNMENT

(Also see *Politics*)

IT COULD PROBABLY BE SHOWN by facts and figures that there is no distinctly native American criminal class except Congress.

—Mark Twain, quoted in James Patterson and Peter Kim, *The Day America Told the Truth*

WE HAVE STAKED THE WHOLE FUTURE of American civilization not upon the power of government, far from it. We have staked the future of all of our political institutions upon the capacity of each and all of us to govern ourselves according to the Ten Commandments of God.

—President James Madison

GRACE

CYNTHIA AND I were on vacation at Sea World with some of our children and grandchildren. It is always amazing to watch those brave men and women who dive in the tank with Shamu the whale and other big creatures. I thought, "That whale is so gracious not to put them into eternity with just a nudge of her nose." In fact, you get the feeling at times that they are fed handfuls of fish just to placate them, just to keep them in a real good mood so that when the trainers get in the tank they'll be able to get out of the tank a little later on. And I watched as they hung on to their fins and tried to get their arms around those big bodies.

The subject of grace is like that—a big subject to try and get your arms around or to get a hold on.

TO SEEK TO EARN, merit, or purchase salvation is to insult the Giver. Imagine yourself invited to a banquet in the White House by the president of the United States. You are seated at a table that is filled with the choicest foods. Every effort is made to give you a most enjoyable evening. At the end of a lovely visit, the president stands at the front door to bid you good-bye.

What do you do? As you leave, do you press a dime into his hand and say, "Thank you very much for your kindness. I have enjoyed the evening very much. I realize it has cost you a lot of money, and I want to help you pay for the meal"?

Is that the proper response to his kindness? On the contrary, it is a rude and insulting gesture. So it would be with God's grace.

—William MacDonald, *The Grace of God*

———————————

THE BIBLE IS A PHOTO ALBUM filled with pictures of God's grace. One striking image is found in the pages of 2 Samuel. The setting is the palace of King David. Gold and bronze fixtures gleam from the walls. Lofty, wooden ceilings crown each spacious room. In the banquet room, David and his children gather for an evening meal. Absalom, tanned and handsome, is there, as is David's beautiful daughter Tamar. The call to dinner is given, and the king scans the room to see if all are present. One figure, though, is absent.

Clump, scraaape, clump, scraaape. The sound coming down the hall echoes into the chamber. *Clump, scraaape, clump, scraaape.* Finally, the person appears at the door and slowly shuffles to his seat. It is the lame Mephibosheth seated in grace at David's table. And the tablecloth covers his feet. Now the feast can begin.

———————————

Grace in a Barren Place

I was that Mephibosheth
Crippled by my twisted pride and
   hiding from you in a barren place
      where You could not find me
      where You would not give me what I
      deserved.
But somehow You found me and
I don't understand why but You
   give me what I do not deserve.
You not only spared my desolate life but
   You made it bountiful
And here at Your table
I will thank You, my
   King.

—Julie Martin

ONE SATURDAY AFTERNOON I was too lazy to wash my little red Volkswagen convertible. Now you really have to be lazy not to wash half a car on an entire afternoon. So I said to my two younger children, "I'll give you 75 cents to wash the car." (I'm known as the last of the big-time spenders.) And so my younger son, Chuck, walked inside and turned up his nose as if to say, "Who in the world wants to wash a car for 75 cents?" So I turned to Colleen, our younger daughter, and I said, "Honey, I'll give you $1.50 if you wash it." Well, she quickly took out the bucket and the brush and the hose and started in. Worked on it for an hour or so. Did a terrific job. Then she called me out front for two reasons. One was to see how clean it was, and the other was to pick up her paycheck.

Chuck came along. Since it was time to dole out the money, he told me he had encouraged his sister. If I had given him even a dime, that would have been a grace gift. For me to pay her $1.50 was a wage. She earned it.

HUMPTY DUMPTY had an unsolvable problem. We have a problem too, but ours has a solution.

Jesus Christ came to our wall,

Jesus Christ died for our fall;

So that regardless of death and in spite of sin,

Through grace, He might put us together again.

SEVERAL YEARS AGO my family and I were enjoying an evening at a restaurant. We looked over in the corner and saw a couple from our church. We waved at 'em and they winked back in our direction. And just before they left they came by our table, shook hands and said "Hi." When our meal was over, I got up and walked to the cash register and said, "I didn't get a check for our meal." They said, "Oh, well, you don't have to worry about it because someone else paid for it." I asked, "Who paid for it?" They said, "Well, we don't know who they are, but they were the couple that walked over and said 'Hello' to you." I was astonished, but said, "Well, why don't I take care of the tip?" "No, that was all taken care of too." It was paid in full. I had the hardest time accepting that. I wanted to go home and call them up and say, "Hey, why don't I split it halfway with you?"

There was another fellow who that year wanted to give us a Christmas present of washing all the windows in the house—inside and out. I had the hardest time saying, "Fine, do it all." I was pacing up and down, wondering what I could do to pay him back. It's difficult to accept something absolutely free. We think there's a gimmick or we think there's something we must do to pay our way.

God's grace says, "I've picked up the tab. I'll take care of everything inside and out. Accept it. Believe it. It's a declared fact."

> "Do this and live!" the Law demands,
> But gives me neither feet nor hands.
> A better word God's grace does bring,
> It bids me fly and gives me wings.
>
> —Kenneth Wuest, *Romans in the Greek New Testament*

He Giveth More

> He giveth more grace when the burdens grow greater,
>   He sendeth more strength when the labors increase;
> To added affliction He addeth His mercy,
>   To multiplied trials, His multiplied peace.
>
> When we have exhausted our store of endurance,
>   When our strength has failed ere the day is half done,
> When we reach the end of our hoarded resources,
>   Our Father's full giving is only begun.
>
> His love has no limit, His grace has no measure;
>   His power no boundary known unto men;
> For out of His infinite riches in Jesus
>   He giveth and giveth and giveth again.
>
> —Annie Johnson Flint, quoted in John R. Rice, *Poems That Preach*

IT WOULD SEEM ... that grace is what happens between two persons. It is one giving himself to the other. It is responsibility to another. It is a distinctive kind of relating. In a world of men turning their backs on one another, exploiting one another, killing one another, gossiping about one another, trying to possess one another, and controlling one another, grace is one person accepting and confronting another in freedom and responsibility.

—R. Lofton Hudson, *Grace Is Not a Blue–Eyed Blond*

BENJAMIN WARFIELD said, "Grace is free sovereign favor to the ill-deserving."

—George Sweeting, *Great Quotes and Illustrations*

GRIEF
(Also see *Death*)

DR. R. A. TORREY, founder of the Bible Institute of Los Angeles, lost his twelve-year-old daughter in an accident. The funeral was on a rainy day. They stood there beside that hole in the ground, surrounded by loved ones. It was dark and dismal. Mrs. Torrey said to her husband, "I'm so glad Elizabeth is not in that box." Their grief went home with them that night as they tried to sleep.

Dr. Torrey got up in the morning and went for a walk. A wave of grief broke over him anew, the loneliness of her absence, the terrible feeling knowing they would never hear her laughter again, never see her face, never witness her growth. He couldn't take it. And he leaned against the street light and he looked up and he began to pray. This is what he experienced: "And just then the fountain, the Holy Spirit, whom I had in my heart, broke forth with such power as I think I had never experienced before. And it was the most joyful moment I had ever known in my life! It is an unspeakably glorious thing to have within you a fountain ever springing up, springing up, springing up, ever springing up 365 days in every year, springing up under all circumstances."

—Michael Green, *Illustrations for Biblical Preaching*

I WAS SITTING, torn by grief. Someone came and talked to me of God's dealings, of why it happened, of hope beyond the grave. He talked constantly, he said things I knew were true.

I was unmoved, except to wish he'd go away. He finally did.

Another came and sat beside me. He didn't talk. He didn't ask leading questions. He just sat beside me for an hour and more, listened when I said something, answered briefly, prayed simply, left.

I was moved. I was comforted. I hated to see him go.

—Joseph Bayly, *The Last Thing We Talk About*

SCRIPTURE NEVER CONDEMNS GRIEF. Tears are valuable. They are God-given relief mechanisms.

There are some who chide tears as unmanly, unsubmissive, unchristian. They would comfort us with a chill and pious stoicism, bidding us meet the most agitating passages of our history with rigid and tearless countenance. With such the spirit of the Gospel, and of the Bible, has little sympathy. We have no sympathy with a morbid sentimentality; but we may well question whether the man who cannot weep can really love; for sorrow is love, widowed and bereaved—and where that is present, its most natural expression is in tears. Religion does not come to make us unnatural and inhuman; but to purify and ennoble all those natural emotions with which our manifold nature is endowed. Jesus wept. Peter wept. The Ephesian converts wept on the neck of the Apostle whose face they were never to see again. Christ stands by each mourner, saying, "Weep, my child; weep, for I have wept."

Tears relieve the burning brain, as a shower the electric clouds. Tears discharge the insupportable agony of the heart, as an overflow lessens the pressure of the flood against the dam. Tears are the material out of which heaven weaves its brightest rainbow.

—F. B. Meyer, *Abraham*

GUIDANCE

WHEN I WAS in the Marine Corps our ship one time was at the northeastern corner of Formosa (now called Taiwan) near Taipei. We stopped there at the mouth of the harbor and awaited the arrival of the harbor pilot, who came out and took the wheel of the ship and began to weave us through the pathless waters that led to the dock itself. At first glance that semed like an unnecessary thing to do. We could see the dock less than a mile ahead. But the closer we looked and the longer we looked over the side of the ship into the crystal clear waters, we could tell why. There were mines located randomly beneath the surface of the water. If the hull of our ship had nudged a mine just enough, disaster would have occurred. But the pilot of the harbor knew where every mine was located.

SUPPOSE YOU AND I wanted to go to Africa on a big-game hunt. Now I don't know the first thing about Africa. All I know is that it's a great big continent, that you have to get there by boat or air, and that once landed, you've lost me. So what do we do? We hire a guide, a fellow who is a specialist at finding big game. So off we go on safari with the guide. Sure enough, he does his job, and we come eyeball-to-eyeball with the target. Do we say to the guide, "Shoot him; shoot him"? No. We say, "Get out of the way." And then we load up and we aim and shoot.

You never take the guide to the taxidermist to have him stuffed. And nobody comes back from a safari with a huge picture of their guide to line the den walls. What does the guide become? Insignificant. You can't even remember his name. Whether you're fishing for bass in the lake or big game in Africa, the guide is a part of the trip, but only a transitory part. He works himself out of a job. He carries you from the unknown to the known and then backs off and says, "Now it's your turn."

Hh

HABIT

I USED TO BITE MY FINGERNAILS right down to the quick. I'd bite them off just as soon as the first signs of new growth would appear. Research has shown that it takes only about three or four weeks for an activity to become a habit. That is wonderfully comforting if it's a good habit we're trying to promote, like more prayer or Bible study. But for most of us it's the destructive habits, like my nail-biting, that get a hold on us until we are enslaved—mastered and manipulated by the beast of habit. We become a living contradiction of the liberating truth of 1 Corinthians 6:12: "All things are lawful for me, but not all things are profitable. All things are lawful for me, but I will not be mastered by anything."

You can't believe the fire of conviction this verse once set ablaze within me. A close look reveals that this isn't a verse talking about something lawless or wicked, but something that is actually lawful, but not profitable. My first encounter with this verse was not my final encounter with this painful habit. But it was certainly a turning point toward change, thank God.

The backwash of this nail-biting testimony has far-reaching effects. Not a person who reads this is completely free from bad habits, whether lawless or lawful. It's the price we pay for being human. Habits are as numerous as every detail of life; the list is endless. But let's focus on five suggestions that will help us blend 1 Corinthians 6:12 into our lives.

Stop rationalizing. Refuse to make comments like: "Oh, that's just me. I'm just like that—always have been, always will be. After all, nobody's perfect." Such excuses take the edge off disobedience and encourage you to diminish or completely ignore the Spirit's work of conviction.

Apply strategy. Approach your target with a rifle, not a shotgun. Take on each habit one at a time, not all at once.

Be realistic. It won't happen fast. It won't be easy. Nor will your resolve be permanent overnight. Periodic failures, however, are still better than habitual slavery.

Be encouraged. Realize you're on the road to ultimate triumph, for the first time in years! Enthusiasm strengthens self-discipline and prompts an attitude of stick-to-it-iveness.

Start today. This is the best moment thus far in your life. To put it off is an admission of defeat and will only intensify and prolong the self-confidence battle.

Extracting the hurtful thorns of habit enables the pilgrim to focus less attention on himself and more attention on the One who is worthy. And the most exciting thought of all is that He will be right there in the morning ready to help you through the day with all the power you will need, one moment at a time.

Need proof? How about ten fingernails and an emery board?

—Charles R. Swindoll, *Growing Strong in the Seasons of Life*

MRS. SMITH WAS SO HAPPY. "I've cured my husband of biting his nails." I said, "After all these years? Tell me how." "I hide his teeth," was her reply.

BAD HABITS can bring personal embarrassment and physical limitations. American educator, Horace Mann, once described the predicament this way: "Habit is a cable; we weave a thread of it every day, and at last we cannot break it."

—Charles R. Swindoll, *Growing Strong in the Seasons of Life*

THE CHAINS OF HABIT are too weak to be felt until they are too strong to be broken.

—Lloyd Cory, *Quote Unquote*

HANDICAPS

I SMILED WITH DELIGHT when I read Art Linkletter's story of Wendy Stoker, age 19, freshman at the University of Florida. Young athlete. She placed third, just 2.5 points from first place, in the Iowa girls' state diving championship. She worked two hours a day for four years to get there. "Now she's at the University of Florida," he says. "She's working twice as hard and has earned the number two position on the varsity diving squad. She's aiming for the national finals. Wendy carries a full academic load, finds time for bowling, and is an accomplished water skier. But perhaps the most remarkable thing about Wendy Stoker is her typing. She bangs out 45 words a minute on her typewriter with her toes!" And then he says, "Oh, did I fail to mention? Wendy was born without arms!"

—Ted Engstrom, *A Time for Commitment*

IT'S SATURDAY AFTERNOON. Late. You have fifteen minutes to run into the store, bag a few items, and hurry home before your company arrives. You pull into the parking lot, crossing your fingers for a spot close to the front. The place is packed with cars, not an empty space anywhere except three open slots right by the door entrance. Each of them is marked with a wheelchair painted in a blue circle.

As you drive by, you grumble, "These handicapped spaces are always empty. What a waste of good parking."

Finally, way out in the cracked and weedy part of the lot, you find a spot. It only takes a moment to hike to the entrance, but it's enough to raise beads of sweat on your forehead—and a flush of embarrassment when you see who has parked in one of the handicapped spaces. A man with braces on his legs struggles to lift himself out of his car. Adjusting his crutches, he slowly plants one foot in front of the other and hobbles into the store. A thought crosses your mind: "Imagine how hard it would have been for him to walk to the entrance from the back of the parking lot."

Handicap parking spaces are one of the few places of honor that disabled people are given in our society. Yet, to our shame, we sometimes resent those and other allowances our government makes for the disabled. Jesus never grumbled about the lame or the blind. He gave them a special invitation to His kingdom party and encourages us to make a place for them too.

A CEREBRAL PALSY VICTIM, Shirley has little control of her muscles. When someone stops to say hello, her face will brighten, but all she can manage is a nod and a wide, welcoming smile. Behind that silent smile, though, is an intelligent, charming person few people take the time to see. One avenue to her inner spirit is the worn book of original poems she always keeps by her side. Peek into the book, and you'll discover Shirley's heart:

Inside My Heart

Inside my heart, there are feelings that few know about.
When people see my wheelchair,
They don't see me as a person,
That I have a mind and a heart.
Once they get to know me,
They see me as a person,
My face shows feeling,
And my eyes tell it all.

My feelings are like a sea—
The water goes up and down,
My life goes up and down, too.
I'm always giving and never taking;
That is the way God wants me to be.
He gave me a heart full of love
For all.

Like Shirley, many disabled people are beautiful displays of God's love. So look past the wheelchairs and braces—get to know the people inside.

—Shirley Fields, "Inside My Heart"

CATHY WARD was born blind, or so they told her. Three weeks after birth they informed her parents, who immediately changed in their feelings toward Cathy. She felt her father never really cared for her; perhaps her mother loved her. But at the age of sixteen there was a parting of the ways. Cathy went in one direction and her parents in another. And through a wonderful chain of events she came to know real light—Jesus Christ.

As we visited, she once said to me, "The hardest thing in the world to accept is being blind in a society that is oriented to sight. At times I feel like a monkey in a cage. I feel eyes staring at me. People don't know how to treat a blind person." She has a wonderful job. She works for Biola University keeping the greenhouse green. Her companion who drives her commented, "You know, it's an interesting, curious humor that Cathy has. Someone will ask her how that plant is doing. And she'll say, 'I don't know. I'll have to look and see how it's doing.'"

Isn't that a beautiful attitude?

WATCHING THE HANDICAPPED LIVE with their disability can be very inspiring. Take the time the fellow and his mother walked into the doctor of optometry's office. They didn't have an appointment, but they certainly had a sweet spirit. They asked the doctor if he could give them a little bit of help. And he said, "Sure, what can I do?" The mother answered, "Well, my son's plastic eye needs to be polished. There's a scratch on it. Could you take care of that?" The doctor said, "Certainly." He took it to the wheel and cleaned it up, honed it, brought it back. And she said, "Could I trouble you with just one more request?" "Sure." "Could you do the other eye as well? It's also scratched." And the doctor said, when he went to the back room, he uttered, "Lord, I'll never complain again." He took the polished eye back to the boy, fit it into the eye, and the pair walked away with a cheerful spirit.

—Jack Cooper, *Light for the Blind*

ONE OF THE GREATEST EVANGELISTIC HYMNS of all time was written by a woman who knew well the release and peace that come from confessing one's sins and failures to God. "Just As I Am," a hymn frequently sung at the close of evangelistic meetings, was written by Charlotte Elliott, who at one time had been very bitter with God about the circumstances in her life.

Charlotte was an invalid from her youth and deeply resented the constraints her handicap placed on her activities. In an emotional outburst on one occasion, she expressed those feelings to Dr. Cesar Malan, a minister visiting her home. He listened and was touched by her distress, but he insisted that her problems should not divert her attention from what she most needed to hear. He challenged her to turn her life over to God, to come to Him just as she was, with all her bitterness and anger.

She resented what seemed to be an almost callous attitude on his part, but God spoke to her through him, and she committed her life to the Lord. Each year on the anniversary of that decision, Dr. Malan wrote Charlotte a letter, encouraging her to continue to be strong in the faith. But even as a Christian she had doubts and struggles.

One particularly sore point was her inability to effectively get out and serve the Lord. At times she almost resented her brother's successful preaching and evangelistic ministry. She longed to be used of God herself, but she felt that her health and physical condition prevented it. Then in 1836, on the fourteenth anniversary of her conversion, while she was alone in the evening, the forty-seven-year-old Charlotte Elliott wrote her spiritual autobiography in verse. Here, in the prayer of confession, she poured out her feelings to God—feelings that countless individuals have identified with in the generations that followed. The third stanza, perhaps more than the others, described her own pilgrimage.

> Just as I am, tho tossed about
> With many a conflict, many a doubt,
> Fightings and fears within, without,
> O Lamb of God, I come! I come!

Many years later, when reflecting on the impact his sister made in penning this one hymn, the Reverend Henry Venn Elliott said, "In the course of a long ministry I hope I have been permitted to see some fruit of my labors, but I feel far more has been done by a single hymn of my sister's, "Just As I Am.'"

—Ruth A. Tucker, *Sacred Stories*

I SAT WAITING in a white hospital gown—terrified. I was in the infirmary of Morristown School, a boys' private school. A group of boys from my grade were waiting our turns for a physical examination.

Some of the boys were making small, unfunny jokes about what the examination would be like, but I could not join in their laughing and kidding. I was too conscious of what an ordeal the examination was going to be for me. I was fully aware that of all the boys there I was the only one who was very different physically. To put it bluntly, in an ugly way, I knew I was deformed.

Though this could be concealed for the most part with my clothes on, when I was undressed it was all too clear to see. I lived with a feeling of shame—and I hated it. I wished more than anything else I would be like those other boys with their fine, straight bodies. Soon the doctor would be saying, "Now, Joe, take off that robe and let's have a look at you," and I dreaded it. I never, never, never undressed in front of anyone. . . .

An accident and tuberculosis of the spine had left me with a hump in the middle of my back which I could conceal fairly well when I had all my clothes on, but I could never conceal this defect from myself, and living with this constant feeling of physical inferiority hurt me greatly.

At last it was my turn, and I walked into the examining room. Behind the desk sat a tall, gray-haired man, reading the chart in his hand.

"Umm, Joseph," he said, "you're in the fourth grade. . . . All right, let's get on with it. Hop up on the scale first." He came over and balanced the weights and then lowered the stick over my head to measure my height. He carefully marked these statistics on my chart, and then, without looking up, said, "Now, take that robe off."

I fumbled with the string, my hands shaking, but I finally got the cord at the neck untied and slipped out of the robe. It was an awful feeling standing there.

Suddenly the doctor put down the chart and came forward and gently put his hands on either side of my face, looking deep into my eyes.

"Do you believe in God?" he asked.

I was astonished, but I told the truth. "Yes, sir," I said.

"That's good," he said, "because there's nothing we can do in this world alone. The more faith we have in Him, the greater the faith we have in ourselves."

"Yes, sir," I said again. There was something about the touch of this man's hands on my face and the intensity of his belief in man's dependency on God that went right into me and made me shiver. Then, just as suddenly as he had shown that side of his character, he became once again the businesslike doctor. He left me standing there while he went back to the desk and wrote something on my chart. The he stood up and said, "Excuse me for just a minute—I'll be right back."

I stood there for a moment, feeling chilly and hoping that he would soon be back and the whole ordeal over. Then my eyes traveled to the chart he had left lying on the desk. "I wonder what it really says about me," I said to myself. "I wonder what he has written about my deformity." My throat was tight, I was steeling myself for the worst. But there on the paper, beside the words "Physical Characteristics," I saw clearly written just five words: "Has an unusually well-shaped head."

For a moment I just stared at the words in confusion—they were so unexpected, so completely different from the thoughts that had been obsessing me. . . . "Has an unusually well-shaped head." I read those words again. No, there was no mistake, that was what he had actually written—and, most important, nothing else. Nothing else at all!

Almost before I knew it, he came back in the room, smiling at me with those blue eyes so full of insight and compassion.

"All right, Joseph, get your robe on and tell the next boy to come in now," he said.

I stood there a moment, half-dazed, but at last I fumbled my robe back on and said, "Thank you, sir, thank you," and let myself out of the room.

It is years since that brief incident—and I know that my head is no better shaped than anyone else's. But I got the message that this great man had to give: To focus on the best, not the worst, in any situation, to believe that with God's help a person can learn to live with any handicap or any difficulty.

I got the message, and I'll treasure it as long as I live.

—Joseph Lahey, *Guideposts* magazine, 1976

HEALING

YOUR ADVERSARY would love for you to assume the worst about your situation. He would enjoy seeing you heave a sigh and resign yourself to feelings of depression. However, it's been my experience that when God is involved, anything can happen. The One who directed that stone in between Goliath's eyes and split the Red Sea down the middle and leveled that wall around Jericho and brought His Son back from beyond takes delight in mixing up the odds as He alters the inevitable and bypasses the impossible.

The blind songwriter, Fanny Crosby, put it another way: "Chords that were broken will vibrate once more."

—Charles R. Swindoll, *Encourage Me*

A MAN HAD A TERRIBLY LENGTHY SURGERY. It was expensive and the results weren't very promising. He went to his doctor for the post-op visit, and the doc said, "Well, I have some sad news for you. You're not going to live more than six months." And the man says, "Good night, doc. It's gonna take me, you know, a year just to pay you back what I owe you." And the doc said, "Well, I'll give you a year then."

—*Preaching* magazine, July–August 1989

JAMES PACKER tells about a patient who had an acute abdominal pain. The doctor was called in and quickly gave him a pill. A friend standing nearby said, "Oh, doctor, will it make him better?" The doctor responded, "No, but it's gonna give him a fit, and I can cure fits."

HEALTH

(Also see *Appearance*)

MY CHILDREN pulled a fast one on me one Christmas. They teamed up, pooled their vast financial resources, and bought me a small, framed motto to put on my desk. It read:

> DIETS ARE FOR PEOPLE
> WHO ARE THICK—AND TIRED OF IT

At first it made me thmile. Then I got thad. Especially when I realized I wasn't thick of being thick!

WHEN YOU STEP ON THE SCALES, you don't yell out to the neighborhood what you weigh. Maybe you step on the scales and a little tag comes out that says, "One at a time, please." People don't announce their weight for the world to hear. It's a private matter, but it may be saying, "Do something about that."

A HEAVY MAN weighing on the scales once remarked, "I'm not overweight, I just need to be six inches taller."

DO YOU THINK Weight Watcher's favorite hymn is "And Can It Be That I Should Gain?"

MOST PEOPLE, when they have a heart attack, begin with denial. "This isn't happening to me. This is a bad dream. That was just a bad taco I had a few moments ago. I must have misunderstood the doctor." Denial. Not many people are like Field Marshall Montgomery. After the Second World War he was sitting at the House of Lords in session and he calmly turned to the man next to him and said, "Excuse me, but I'm having a coronary thrombosis," as he quietly walked out to find medical help. Most continue what they're doing until they collapse.

—Daniel George, *Book of Anecdotes*

HEAVEN

(Also see *Eternity*)

> Think of—
> Stepping on shore, and finding it Heaven!
> Of taking hold of a hand, and finding it God's hand.
> Of breathing a new air, and finding it celestial air.
> Of feeling invigorated, and finding it immortality.
> Of passing from storm to tempest to an unknown calm.
> Of waking up, and finding it Home.
>
> —Hazel Felleman, *Poems That Live Forever*

HELL

THE SAFEST ROAD TO HELL is the gradual one—the gentle slope, soft underfoot, without sudden turnings, without milestones, without signposts. . . . The long, dull, monotonous years of middle-aged prosperity or middle-aged adversity are excellent campaigning weather [for the devil].

—Charles R. Swindoll, *Living Above the Level of Mediocrity*

E. STANLEY JONES wrote about a fictional person (one of his characters) who lived out a fantasy life. All he had to do was think of it and (poof!) it happened.

And so this man in a moment of time stuck his hands in his pocket and leaned back and imagined a mansion and (poof!) he had a fifteen-bedroom mansion, three stories, with soft-footed servants to wait upon his every need.

A place like that needs several fine cars, so he again closed his eyes, and he imagined the driveway full of the finest that money could buy. He drove them where he wished, or he sat in the back of the car that's got Mafia glass on it, as the chauffeur drove him wherever he wished.

There's no other place to travel so he returned home and wished for a sumptuous meal and (poof!) there's a meal in front of him in all its fragrance and beauty—which he ate alone. But there's still something needed more than that.

Finally he grew bored and unchallenged, and he whispered to one of the attendants, "I want to get out of this. I want to create something. I want to earn something. I even want to suffer some things again. I'd rather be in hell than be here." To which the servant replied quietly, "Where do you think you are?"

—E. Stanley Jones, Growing Spiritually

SOMETIME AGO A TRAFFIC OFFICER gave a citation to a woman in Brooklyn. And when the officer handed it through the window to her, she snapped it out of his hands and said, "You can go straight to hell!" So the officer took her to court. A few days later they appeared before the judge, and he dismissed the officer's complaint about the woman's language, because he said, and I quote, "It wasn't a command, or a wish, but a statement of fact, for going to hell is a possibility."

—Spiros Zodhiates, Behavior of Belief

HERE ARE SOME THOUGHTS from "hell-fire and damnation preachers" who told it like it is:

Unconverted men walk over the pit of hell on a rotten covering, and there are innumerable places in this covering so weak that they will not bear their weight, and these places are not seen. The wrath of God burns against them

—Jonathan Edwards

Conceive this much, if all the diseases in the world did seize on one man, and if all the torment that all the tyrants of the would could devise, were cast against him; and if all the creatures in heaven and earth did conspire the destruction of this man; and if all the devils in hell did labor to inflict punishment upon him, you would think this man to be in a miserable condition. And yet all this is but a beam of God's indignation. If the beams of God's indignation be so hot, what is the full sum of His wrath when it shall seize upon the soul of a sinful creature in full measure?

—Thomas Hooker

There is a real fire in hell, as truly as you have a real body—a fire exactly like that which we have on this earth, except this: it will not consume you though it will torture you. You have seen asbestos lying amid red hot coals, but not consumed. So your body will be prepared by God in such a way that it will burn forever without being consumed. With your nerves laid raw by searing flame, yet never desensitized for all its raging fury, and the acrid smoke of the sulfurous fumes searing your lungs and choking your breath, you will cry out for the mercy of death, but it shall never, never, no never come.

—Charles H. Spurgeon

THESE WORDS ARE INSCRIBED over the gates of hell:

Only those elements time cannot wear
Were made before me, and beyond time I stand.
Abandon all hope, ye who enter here.

—Dante, *The Inferno*

IN 1741, Jonathan Edwards, a brilliant student of Scripture, preached the never-to-be-forgotten sermon, "Sinners in the Hands of an Angry God." People who were there to hear that sermon testified that they could feel the flames of hell licking about them in the pews where they sat.

HERITAGE

WHEN I MINISTERED in New England, I took the time to visit Harvard University campus on a number of occasions. I could look across through the wrought iron that was now rusted with time and see the pale green statue of John Harvard. One snowy afternoon I stood there knee-deep in the snow and wiped snow and ice from the school cornerstone and read these words: "After God had carried us safe to New England and we had builded our houses, provided necessaries for our livelihood, reared convenient places for God's worship and settled the civil government, one of the next things we longed for and looked after was to advance learning and perpetuate to posterity, dreading to leave an illiterate ministry to the churches when our present ministers shall lie in the dust."

IN ADDITION TO THE SAINTS in Scripture, we have nearly 2,000 years of history that can and should be used as challenges to piety and faith. We Protestants have been so concerned about avoiding the veneration of the saints that we often have bypassed a rich heritage, a rich heritage of faith. Just as the book of Hebrews gives a roll call of believers, so we can look to countless examples of equally courageous lovers of God.

—Harold Myra, *Christianity Today,* October 22, 1982

HOLINESS
(Also see *Morality, Righteousness*)

HOLINESS DOES NOT CONSIST in mystic speculations, enthusiastic fervors, or uncommanded austerities; *it consists in thinking as God thinks and willing as God wills.*

—John Brown, *Expository Discourses on 1 Peter*

IN OUR KIND OF CULTURE anything, even news about God, can be sold if it is packaged freshly; but when it loses its novelty, it goes on the garbage heap. There is a great market for religious experience in our world; there is little enthusiasm for the patient acquisition of virtue, little inclination to sign up for a long apprenticeship in what earlier generations of Christians called holiness.

—Eugene Peterson, *A Long Obedience in the Same Direction*

HOLINESS SOUNDS SCARY. It need not be, but to the average American it is. Our tendency is to say that holiness is something for the cloistered halls of a monastery. It needs organ music, long prayers, and religious-sounding chants. It hardly seems appropriate for those in the real world of the twentieth century. Author John White seems to agree with that as he wrote in *The Fight* the images that came to his mind when he thought about holiness:

thinness
hollow-eyed gauntness
beards
sandals
long robes
stone cells
no sex
no jokes
hair shirts
frequent cold baths
fasting
hours of prayer
wild rocky deserts
getting up at 4 A.M.
clean fingernails
stained glass
self-humiliation

Is that the mental picture you have when you think of holiness? Most do. It's almost as though holiness is the private preserve of an austere group of monks, missionaries, mystics, and martyrs. But nothing could be further from the truth

I couldn't be in greater agreement with Chuck Colson's statement in *Loving God:* "Holiness is the everyday business of every Christian. It evidences itself in the decisions we make and things we do, hour by hour, day by day."

RESOLVED, never to do anything which I would be afraid to do if it were the last hour of my life.

—Jonathan Edwards, quoted in Jerry Bridges, *Pursuit of Holiness*

HOLY SPIRIT

A NUMBER OF MILES from the Los Angeles basin there is a river. The river has been damned up by man, and through the genius and innovation of engineers, they have put together a dam that has, in its process of working, housed electricity—hundreds of thousands of volts that are fed into the Los Angeles basin. And if you were to go the plant, the source, and follow the lines that come into the city, you would come to various transmission plants along the way that would be marked "Danger. High Voltage." "No trespassing. Danger." Hundreds of thousands of volts are available in energy for your home, but who needs a hundred thousand volts, unless he wants to burn up his home? Knowing that, the engineers have built transformers into the system—not transmitters, but transformers. And the transformer does nothing more than break down into meaningful units just the electricity you need.

I have in my home, for example, another transformer. One Christmas I gave myself an HO gauge train. I put my son's name on it, but it was really for me. So we had a great time putting it all together. And there's a little tiny unit called a transformer on the train set, and it breaks down the 110 volts from the wall to even less. Why, if you plugged into a straight 110 outlet, that thing would go (pzzzttt!) for one second and be burned to a crisp. But that transformer breaks it down to where a little tiny train, whose engine can be held in your fist, can just putt putt putt all around the track and entertain me for hours on end—all because there's a little transformer that dispenses it in the needed level.

When the Holy Spirit (the Transformer) comes, He will take the majestic truth of God and will dispense it just the way you need it, give it to you with handles that you can take and use. It is the Spirit's delight to take the full truth of God and make one thing meaningful to that woman, something altogether different to that man, and something different again to that fellow down there. That's the work of the Spirit, and He never makes a mistake. He gives you just what you can handle.

Where Is God's Power?

A city full of churches
Great preacher, lettered men,
Grand music, choirs and organs;
If all these fail, what then?
Good workers, eager, earnest,
Who labour hour by hour:
But where, oh where, my brother,
Is God's Almighty power?

It is the Holy Spirit,
That quickeneth the soul.
God will not take man-worship,
Nor bow to man's control.
No human innovation,

No skill, or worldly art,
Can give a true repentance,
Or break the sinner's heart.

Great God, revive us truly!
And keep us every day;
That men may all acknowledge,
We live just as we pray.
The Lord's hand is not shortened,
He still delights to bless,
If we depart from evil
And all our sins confess.

—Samuel Stevenson, quoted in John R. Rice, *Poems That Preach*

HAVE YOU EVER LIVED with a roommate that puts you down? Let's say you're a crummy student and you get a Phi Beta Kappa as a roommate. Now that's rather threatening, isn't it? And let's say you're not disciplined, but your roommate has discipline as his middle name. Let's say you're sloppy and leave things laying around. Of course, your roommate is just so—it's like living with Mr. Prim. Well, after a while, what happens? If you're controlled by the flesh, you get mad, you get competitive.

That's what happened when the new nature and the Holy Spirit move in at salvation into your body. The new nature shares his room with the old nature, and a constant civil war is waging.

No Distant Lord

No distant Lord have I,
Loving afar to be.
Made flesh for me He cannot rest
Until He rests in me. . . .

Ascended now to God
My witness there to be,
His witness here am I because
His Spirit dwells in me.

—Maltbie D. Babcock, quoted in James Dalton Morrison, *Masterpieces of Religious Verse*

I REMEMBER QUOTING years ago in school, "How much wood does a woodchuck chuck if a woodchuck could chuck wood? He would chuck you wood as much as he could and chuck as much wood as a woodchuck would if a woodchuck could chuck wood." Doesn't that change your life? It's called a tongue twister designed to display the use of the same words over and over and over again.

Sounds like 2 Corinthians 1:3–4: "Blessed be the God and Father of our Lord Jesus Christ, the Father of mercies and the God of all comfort; who comforts us in all our affliction so that we may be able to comfort those who are in any affliction with the comfort with which we ourselves are comforted by God."

The same thought over and over: comfort, comfort, comfort. To comfort is to bring someone alongside. *Parakletos. Para* ("alongside") and *kaleō* ("to call"). It describes the Holy Spirit. And it always has in mind the idea of helping.

When my car won't run any longer, I call a guy who drives a big truck to pull my car into the place where it can be repaired. That's because when I lift the hood, all I can do is pray. I call someone alongside to help. That's the word used in John 16:7 when Jesus said, "But I tell you the truth, it is to your advantage that I go away; for if I do not go away, the Helper [*paraklētos*] shall not come to you; but if I go, I will send Him to you." The Holy Spirit is a *parakletos* for Christians.

HONESTY

(Also see *Integrity*)

A PREACHER was to preach on honesty and he told everyone to read Joshua 25. The next Sunday he came and said, "How many read it?" Half the hands in church were raised. He said, "Great. Now you're the ones I want to talk to. Joshua has only twenty-four chapters, and I am especially concerned about you tonight."

—Bob Phillips, *The World's Greatest Collection of Heavenly Humor*

A FELLOW in Long Beach went into a fried chicken franchise to get some chicken for himself and the young lady with him. She waited in the car while he went in to pick up the chicken. Inadvertently the manager of the store handed the guy the box in which he had placed the financial proceeds of the day instead of the box of chicken. You see, he was going to make a deposit and had camouflaged it by putting the money in a fried chicken box.

The fellow took his box, went back to the car, and the two of them drove away. When they got to the park and opened the box, they discovered they had a box full of money. Now that was a very vulnerable moment for the average individual. However, realizing the mistake, he got back in his car and returned to the place and gave the money back to the manager. Well, the manager was elated! He was so pleased that he told the young man, "Stick around, I want to call the newspaper and have them take your picture. You're the most honest guy in town."

"Oh, no, don't do that!" said the fellow.

"Why not?" asked the manager.

"Well," he said, "you see, I'm married, and the woman I'm with is not my wife!"

—*Dallas Times Herald*, September 23, 1966

_____

ONE MAN WRITES a moving account of his attempt to get a group of fourteen men and women in the church to communicate with one another at more than a superficial level. As he surveyed the group, he was dismayed that many of the people had been attending the same church for years without knowing anyone else's personal feelings about anything. No hurt was ever admitted.

In an effort to help the people learn how to communicate with each other at a deeper level, this man suggested that each person simply relate incidents from their past which had helped form their personalities. Much to his disappointment, every one of the fourteen seemed to be faking it by relating basically positive experiences and feelings. We really do that, don't we?

Near the end of the session, as he was about to conclude the experiment had been a failure, one young woman poured out her feelings of insecurity, inferiority, and despair. She finished the confession by stating that all she wanted was what other people in the group already had.

Then the man made this closing comment. "We sat there stunned by the reality which had drawn us irresistibly toward this thin, totally unprotected young woman. And I realized that it was we who needed what she had: the ability to be open, personal, honest in a vulnerable way. As I looked around the group, I knew that somehow because this theologically unsophisticated, honest woman had turned loose her silence and her pride and had reached out in total honesty that it was safe for us to start becoming one in Jesus Christ."

DOUGLAS AIRCRAFT was competing with Boeing Aircraft Company to sell Eastern Airlines its first big jets years ago. Eddie Rickenbacker, then head of Eastern Airlines, reportedly told Donald Douglas that the specifications and the claims made by Douglas Company for the DC-8s were close to Boeing's on everything except the noise suppression. Rickenbacker then gave Douglas one last chance to outpromise Boeing on this feature. After consulting with his engineers, Mr. Douglas reported back to Rickenbacker that he did not feel he could make that promise. Rickenbacker smilingly replied, "Oh, I know you can't; I just wanted to see if you were still honest. You've just got yourself an order for $135 million. Now go home and silence those jets!"

—Jerry White, *Honesty, Morality, and Conscience*

HOPE

A MISSIONARY was sitting at her second-story window when she was handed a letter from home. As she opened the letter, a crisp, new, ten-dollar bill fell out. She was pleasantly surprised, but as she read the letter her eyes were distracted by the movement of a shabbily dressed stranger down below, leaning against a post in front of the building. She couldn't get him off her mind. Thinking that he might be in greater financial stress than she, she slipped the bill into an envelope on which she quickly penned "Don't despair." She threw it out the window. The stranger below picked it up, read it, looked up, and smiled as he tipped his hat and went his way.

The next day she was about to leave the house when a knock came at the door. She found the same shabbily dressed man smiling as he handed her a roll of bills. When she asked what they were for, he replied:

"That's the sixty bucks you won, lady. *Don't Despair* paid five to one."

—Charles R. Swindoll, *Growing Strong in the Seasons of Life*

WHILE I WAS ON VACATION I finished a book called *Adrift*. It's a story of a man who built a vessel that was to sail him through the whole of the Atlantic, sort of a large loop. He hit bad weather and his vessel went down. He existed on a raft for almost eighty days. The thing that kept the man alive was hope. His lowest days were the days when he could see no hope and he could not see the possibility of being rescued or making it to the islands or coming into the shipping lanes and being found by one of those vast vessels on its way on the trade routes. His hope kept him alive.

Someone has said, "We can live forty days without food, eight days without water, four minutes without air, but only a few seconds without hope."

We did not dare to breathe a prayer,
Or give our anguish scope.
Something was dead within each of us,
And what was dead was Hope.

—Oscar Wilde, *The Ballad of Reading Gaol*

YEARS AGO an S-4 submarine was rammed by a ship off the coast of Massachusetts. It sank immediately. The entire crew was trapped in a prison house of death. Every effort was made to rescue the crew, but all ultimately failed. Near the end of the ordeal, a deep-sea diver, who was doing everything in his power to find a way for the crew's release, thought he heard a tapping on the steel wall of the sunken sub. He placed his helmet up against the side of the vessel and he realized it was the Morse Code. He attached himself to the side and he spelled out in his mind the message being tapped from within. It was repeating the same question. The question was, from within: "Is . . . there . . . any . . . hope?"

—Ben Patterson, *The Grand Essentials*

HOPE DELIVERS US from the despair that nothing we do matters, and enables us to tackle even the most menial job with vigor. Elmer Bendiner tells the remarkable story of a B-17 bomber that flew a bombing mission over Germany in the latter days of World War II. The plane was hit several times by shells and flak, with some of the hits directly in the fuel tank. Miraculously, the bomber did not explode. When it landed, eleven unexploded twenty-millimeter shells were taken out of the fuel tank! The shells were dismantled, and to the amazement of everyone, all were empty of explosives. Inside of one shell was a note written in Czech. Translated, it read, "This is all we can do for you now." A member of the Czech underground, working in a German munitions factory, had omitted the explosives in at least eleven of the twenty-millimeter shells on his assembly line.

That worker must have wondered often if the quiet work he was doing to subvert the Nazi war effort was going to make any difference whatsoever to the outcome of the war.

—Ben Patterson, *The Grand Essentials*

HOPE IS A PROJECTION of the imagination; so is despair. Despair all too readily embraces the ills it foresees; hope is an energy that arouses the mind to explore every possibility to combat them. In response to hope the imagination is aroused to picture every possible issue, to try every door, to fit together even the most heterogeneous pieces in the puzzle. After the solution has been found it is difficult to recall the steps taken—so many of them are just below the level of consciousness.

—Thornton Wilde, quoted in Ben Patterson, *The Grand Essentials*

HUMANISM

MY DAUGHTER LORI, who is eight, told me that she wants to grow up to sing like either Judy Garland or Michael Jackson. "Try for Judy Garland," I said. "A girl needs a great soprano voice to be Michael Jackson."

These two singers have become Lori's first hero and heroine. They are hardly figures for commemorative stamps, but many children have no heroes or heroines anymore, no noble achievers they yearn to emulate. . . . One day last spring I stood before 20 children of eight and nine in Lori's third-grade class to see if any heroes or heroines were inspiring them. I asked each child to give me the names of the three greatest people he had ever heard about.

"Michael Jackson, Brooke Shields, and Boy George," said a small blond girl, giving me one from all three sexes.

"Michael Jackson, Spider-Man, and God," a boy then said, . . .

When the other children recited, Michael Jackson's name was spoken again and again, but Andrew Jackson never, nor Washington, Lincoln, or any other presidential immortal. Just Ronald Reagan, who made it twice, once behind Batman and once behind Mr. T, a hero who likes to move people by saying, "Sucker, I'll break your face." . . . And I heard no modern equivalent of Charles A. Lindbergh, America's beloved "Lone Eagle."

In answer to my request for heroes, I had expected to hear such names as Michael Jackson, Mr. T, Brooke Shields, and Spider-Man from the kids, but I had not expected the replies of the eight who answered "Me." Their heroes were themselves.

It is sad enough to see the faces on Mount Rushmore replaced by rock stars, brawlers, and cartoons, but it is sadder still to see Mount Rushmore replaced by a mirror.

—Ralph Schoenstein, "The Modern Mount Rushmore"

THERE IS A SHOCKING AGENDA in our narcissistic twentieth century. I realized how radical and severe it was when I read the words from a *Washington Post* interview with the New Age prophetess, Shirley MacLaine.

The most pleasurable journey you take is through yourself. The only sustaining love involvement is with yourself. When you look back on your life and try to figure out where you've been and where you're going, when you look at your work, your love affairs, your marriages, your children, your pain, your happiness—when you examine all that closely, what you really find out is that the only person you really go to bed with is yourself. The only thing you have is working to the consummation of your own identity. And that's what I've been trying to do all my life.

And that is the opposite, the antithesis, of what Jesus demands of His followers.

—Charles Colson, *Loving God*

HUMANISM HAS no way to find the universal in the areas of meaning and values. . . . Humanism has changed the Twenty-third Psalm:

> They began—I am my shepherd
> Then—Sheep are my shepherd
> Then—Everything is my shepherd
> Finally—Nothing is my shepherd.

There is a death wish inherent in humanism.

—Francis Schaeffer, *How Should We Then Live?*

AN EDITORIAL CARTOON pictured a rock monument where words had been chiseled out of stone. It was a pyramid form:

I

ME

MINE

MYSELF

Surrounding this monument were people with their hands raised as if in worship of this shrine. And surrounding this, in the borders, were words like, "Do yourself a favor," "You owe it to yourself," "You deserve a break today," and all the slogans that revolve around us. And at the bottom were those penetrating words, "Speaking of American cults. . . ."

—Visual Products Division/3M

Invictus

Out of the night that covers me,
Black as the Pit from pole to pole,

I thank whatever gods may be
For my unconquerable soul.

In the fell clutch of circumstance
I have not winced nor cried aloud.
Under the bludgeonings of chance
My head is bloody, but unbowed.

Beyond this place of wrath and tears
Looms but the Horror of the shade,
And yet the menace of the years
Finds and shall find me unafraid.

It matters not how strait the gate
How charged with punishment the scroll,
I am the master of my fate;
I am the captain of my soul.

—William Ernest Henley

IF YOU AND I have souls that are unconquerable, the sky's the limit. If we really are our own master and captain, watch out, world!

What seems so right is, in fact, heresy—the one I consider the most dangerous heresy on earth. What is it? *The emphasis on what we do for God, instead of what God does for us....*

Most people see themselves as "masters" of their own fate, "captains" of their own souls. It's an age-old philosophy deeply ingrained in the human heart. And why not? It supports humanity's all-time favorite subject: self.

—Charles R. Swindoll, *The Grace Awakening*

HUMILITY

I HEARD ABOUT the pastor who was voted the most humble pastor in America. And the congregation gave him a medal that said, "To the most humble pastor in America." Then they took it away from him on Sunday because he wore it.

THE ONLY HOPE of a decreasing self is an increasing Christ.

—F. B. Meyer, *John the Baptist*

THE DIMITRI VAIL GALLERY is an interesting gallery in Dallas. Dimitri Vail is an artist. He's one of these individuals who can paint so delicately and perfectly that you would swear it is a photograph, until you come up close to it. His paintings include Jack Benny with his notorious violin, Sophie Tucker, Bill Cosby, Rowan and Martin, Ed Sullivan, Red Buttons, Frank Sinatra, John Wayne, James Dean.

And while walking through the gallery, I saw paintings of a couple of presidents. Then I came to a small-framed picture that hung there that was absolutely unfamiliar. It was drab, done in browns and grays. At first I thought how inappropriate. In the midst of these dazzling entertainers and famous people hangs this unknown. I asked someone on duty, "Who's that?" He smiled and he said, "I'm asked that a lot. It's a self-portrait of the artist. It's Dimitri Vail. He painted it during one of the darkest periods of his life. It's a very recent work."

SO LONG, THEN, as I am not united to God, I am divided within myself and at perpetual strife within myself. Now this union with God can only be secured by love. And the subjection to him can only be grounded in humility. And the humility can only be the result of knowing and believing the truth, that is to say, having the right notions of God and of myself.

—Bernard of Clairvaux

OUT OF HIS WISDOM Robert Morrison of China wrote, "The great fault, I think, in our mission is that no one likes to be second." The world has yet to see what could happen if everyone lost the desire to get the glory. Wouldn't it be a marvelous place if nobody cared who got the credit?

—J. Oswald Sanders, *Spiritual Leadership*

A GROUP OF ENGLISH TOURISTS were visiting the house where Beethoven, the great composer, spent his last years. And they came to the special room, the conservatory, where his piano sat. The guide said rather quietly to the group, "And here is the master's piano." One thoughtless young woman pushed her way from the back of the room all the way up, sat down at the bench, and began to play one of Beethoven's sonatas, and then paused and said to the guide and the others in the group, "I suppose a lot of people enjoy playing this piano." "Well, Miss," the guide said, "Ignacy Paderewski was here last summer with a group and some wanted him to play. And his answer was, "'No, I cannot. I am not worthy.'"

The greatest expression of humility on occasion is simply to remain silent and let the applause go to the other person, the person of greatness.

—G. B. F. Hallock, *2,500 Best Modern Illustrations*

IF I APPEAR TO BE GREAT in their eyes, the Lord is most graciously helping me to see how absolutely nothing I am without Him and helping me to keep little in my own eyes. He does use me. But I'm so concerned that HE uses me and that it is not of me the work is done. The ax cannot boast of the trees it has cut down. It could do nothing but for the woodsman. He made it, he sharpened it, he used it. The moment he throws it aside it becomes only old iron. Oh, that I may never lose sight of this. The spiritual leader of today is in all probability one who yesterday expressed his humility by working gladly and faithfully in second place.

—Samuel Logan Brengle, quoted in C. W. Hall, *Samuel Logan Brengle*

IF YOU'RE HUMBLE, you don't write the book on how humble you are, with twelve life-sized pictures in it.

—Leslie Flynn, *Humorous Incidents and Quips*

THE BEST PROTECTION one can have from the devil and his schemes is a humble heart.

—Jonathan Edwards quoted in Frank S. Mead, *12,000 Religious Quotations*

ISN'T IT WONDERFUL to meet up with significant, truly famous people who don't read their own clippings? John Wooden, the most famous basketball coach I've ever heard of, led his UCLA Bruins to a national championship ten out of twelve years. One time when he called on an acquaintance Wooden said, "Hello. My name is John Wooden." He said, "I understand your little school needs a coach, and I have a man in mind I would like to recommend." He said, "I've had a couple of years coaching basketball and I thought you might like to take a recommendation I have."

A couple of years coaching basketball! The guy writes the book on it. But isn't it refreshing that he doesn't assume the man will know his voice or be impressed with his name?

I READ ABOUT a Britisher named Thomas Hardy, who around the turn of the century became so famous that as a novelist and a poet he could have commanded whatever figure any newspaper would have been willing to pay if he would just submit anything for them to print. But every time he submitted a poem or some literary piece he always included a self-addressed, stamped envelope for the return of his manuscript should it be rejected. He remained humble enough to think that his work could be turned down by an editor who would never be as famous as he.

—William Barclay, *The Gospel of Luke*

THE HUMILITY OF Principal Cairns was phenomenal, so well-known in the educational world. He would never enter a room first. He would always step back and say, "No, here, you go and I'll follow," though he was so well known and respected by the public.

On one occasion, as he stepped up to climb the steps to go to one of the seats on the platform, the public noticed who he was and immediately burst into applause. Shocked, he turned and looked and stepped back and had the man behind him go ahead. And he applauded the man who had walked up behind him, thinking the applause was for him. That isn't phony humility; that's true humility. It never dawned on him that the public would applaud for him.

—William Barclay, *The Gospel of Luke*

I BELIEVE that the first test of a truly great man is his humility. I do not mean by humility, doubt of his own power. But really great people have a curious feeling that the greatness is not in them, but through them. And they see something divine in others and are endlessly, foolishly, incredibly merciful.

—John Ruskin, quoted in Lloyd Cory, *Quote Unquote*

HUMOR

IT IS BAD to suppress your laughter because when you do, it goes back down and spreads to your hips.

—Fred Allen, quoted in Lloyd Cory, *Quote Unquote*

HOW IS YOUR SENSE OF HUMOR? Are the times in which we live beginning to be reflected in your attitude, your face, your outlook? Solomon talks straight, friend. He (under the Holy Spirit's direction) says three things will occur when we have lost our sense of humor: a broken spirit, a lack of inner healing, and dried-up bones (Prov. 15:13, 15; 17:22). What a barren portrait!

Have you begun to shrivel into a bitter, impatient, critical Christian? The Lord tells us that the solution is simple: "A joyful heart" is what we need . . . and if ever we needed it, it is now.

By a sense of humor I am not referring to distasteful or vulgar jesting, nor to foolish and silly talk that is ill-timed, offensive, and tactless. I mean that necessary ingredient of wit: those humorous, enjoyable, and delightful expressions or thoughts that lift our spirits and lighten our day. When we lose our ability to laugh—I mean *really* laugh—life's oppressive assaults confine us to the dark dungeon of defeat.

Humor is not a sin. It is a God-given escape hatch, a safety valve. Being able to see the lighter side of life is a rare, vital virtue. Personally, I think a healthy sense of humor is determined by at least four abilities:

The ability to laugh at our own mistakes.

The ability to accept justified criticism—and get over it!

The ability to interject (or at least enjoy) wholesome humor when surrounded by a tense, heated situation.

The ability to control those statements that would be unfit— even though they may be funny.

James M. Gray and William Houghton were two great, godly men of the Word. Dr. Houghton writes of an occasion when he and Dr. Gray were praying together. Dr. Gray, though getting up in years, was still interested in being an effective witness and expositor. He concluded his prayer by saying: "And, Lord, keep me cheerful. Keep me from becoming a cranky, old man!"

You and I should pray the same prayer.

—Charles R. Swindoll, *The Finishing Touch*

HUMOR IS A GREAT ASSET in missionary life, believe it or not. Indeed, if a missionary lacks a good sense of humor, it is a serious deficiency.

I read recently of a missionary from Sweden who was urged by friends to give up the idea of returning to India because it was so hot there. "Man," he was urged, "it's 120 degrees in the shade!" "Vell," said the Swede in noble contempt, "ve don't always have to stay in the shade, do ve?"

—J. Oswald Sanders, *Spiritual Leadership*

CHARLES HADDON SPURGEON was criticized by the press constantly because of his humor. Do you know at times in the middle of his sermon he would lean back and laugh to the top of that great London Tabernacle? Shocked those people to death. The press would write it out, "Look at that. Irreverent." I think the best answer he ever gave was this, "If my critics only knew how much I held back, they would commend me."

—J. Oswald Sanders, *Spiritual Leadership*

SHOULD WE NOT SEE that lines of laughter about the eyes are just as much marks of faith as are the lines of care and seriousness? Is it only earnestness that is baptized? Is laughter pagan? We have already allowed too much that is good to be lost to the church and cast many pearls before swine. A church is in a bad way when it banishes laughter from the sanctuary and leaves it to the cabaret, the nightclub, and the toastmasters.

—Helmut Thielecke

THERE ARE THREE THINGS that are real—God, human folly, and laughter. Since the first two are beyond our comprehension, we must do what we can with the third. This is a philosophy I live by.

—Jerry Lewis

ROBERT HALL GLOVER, a missionary statesman of the last generation, brought an address to a group of dignified people in New York City. His address was entitled, "Things I Would Pack in My Missionary Trunk if I Were Returning to the Field Today." You know the first thing he mentioned? A sense of humor.

THREE TESTS of good humor: Can you laugh at your own mistakes? Can you restrain when it isn't fitting? Can you enjoy it all alone?

ELEVATORS ARE WEIRD PLACES, aren't they? Especially crowded ones.

You're crammed in close with folks you've never met, so you try really hard not to touch them. And nobody talks, either. The one thing you may hear is an occasional "Out, please" or "Oh, I'm sorry" as somebody clumsily steps on someone's toes. You don't look at anyone; in fact, you don't look anywhere but up, watching those dumb numbers go on and off. Strange. People who are all about the same height and speak the same language are suddenly as silent as a roomful of nuns when they occupy common space.

It's almost as if there's an official sign that reads: *"No talking, no smiling, no touching, and no contact allowed without written consent of the management. No exceptions!!"*

Years ago I was speaking on the campus of the University of Oklahoma. After the meeting, a crazy group of three or four guys invited me to have a Coke with them. Since we were several floors up in the student center, we decided to take the elevator down. As the door slid open, the thing was full of people who gave us that hey-you-guys-aren't-gonna-try-to-get-in-are-you? look. But we did, naturally. I was last. There wasn't even room to turn around. I felt the door close against my back as everyone stared in my direction. I smiled big and said loudly, "You might have wondered why we called this meeting today!" The place broke open with laughter. It was the most amazing thing to watch—people actually *talking,* actually relating to each other—*on an elevator.*

—Charles R. Swindoll, *Growing Strong in the Seasons of Life*

THE FIRST TIME I ever heard the name Nehemiah or anything about the Book of Nehemiah it was sort of a joke told by a youth pastor who had come to the church I attended as a little boy. I had spent many boring hours in this church, as I recall. Forgive me, but it's true. But I thought the fellow was terrific. He said, "The Bible includes the names of the two shortest people who have ever lived." And he got my attention. I sat up as a little boy waiting for this great revelation. "First," he said, "Bildad the Shoe-height, mentioned over in the Book of Job. And second, Knee-high Miah." Well, I thought that was terrific, which shows you how bored I really was in that church.

He was the same fellow who said, "The Bible includes a tennis game: Joseph served in Pharaoh's court." I thought, "Boy, this guy is really something."

And then he said, "There's smoking in the Bible." My mother sort of frowned and my father cleared his throat and I was on the edge of my seat. And I thought, "Where is he is going with that one?" And this youth pastor said, "You remember that story where Rebekah saw Isaac, her husband-to-be? It says in the Scriptures, "'She lit off her camel.'" Well, I thought my mother was gonna get up and leave. But I thought it was terrific.

SOMETIME AFTER I went to California, I was invited to go to the Southwest District Conference at the Evangelical Free Church in Los Angeles. The pastor of the church, and a committee had planned the conference right to the last detail.

On Friday night as the conference began all the pastors sat up in the choir loft on folding chairs. As I started to get up to read Scripture, my coat got caught in the seat that folded down, and I heard something rip. I thought, "What shall I do right now?" As the others waited for me to get up, I finally took my coat off and left it there and went and read Scripture.

After the Scripture reading, a fellow was to play a baritone solo. As he got up to play, he dropped his mouthpiece. When he reached over to pick it up, his horn hit the music stand, and music sheets scattered.

Nothing went the way it had been planned. Before long, everyone was laughing. To make matters worse, the next thing on the program was one of the church members to tell about his new work, but his foot had gone to sleep, so as he got up he stumbled and fell down. Then the soloist forgot his words!

To top it all off, in the background jazz music was playing through the P.A. system. It had picked up the bar music about four or five doors down.

The committee didn't get their way, but I'll tell you, we had the time of our lives because we turned it into something we could laugh over. When we don't get our way, we should handle it with humor.

———————————————

HYPOCRISY
(Also see *Authenticity*)

HYPOCRISY IS HIDEOUS. What cancer is to the body, hypocrisy is to the church. It is a killing agent. Unfortunately, hypocrisy is also addictive. And even though Jesus reserved His most severe words of condemnation for the hypocrite, we still seem to prefer that lifestyle to truth and authenticity.

—John R. W. Stott, *Sermon on the Mount*

———————————————

A MAN SAT THROUGH a church service and then on the way home he fussed about the sermon, he fussed about the traffic, he fussed about the heat, and he fussed about the lateness of the meal being served. Then he bowed and prayed. His son was watching him all the way through this post-church experience. Just as they were beginning to pass the food he said, "Daddy, did God hear you when we left the church and you started fussin' about the sermon and about the traffic and about the heat?" The father sort of blushed and said, "Well, yes, son, He heard me." "Well, Daddy, did God hear you when you just prayed for this food right now?" And he says, "Well, yes, son, He . . . He . . . He heard me." "So, well, Daddy, which one did God believe?"

—Spiros Zodhiates, *Behavior of Belief*

IN *The Pilgrim's Progress* John Bunyan talked about "the parson of our parish, Mr. Two-Tongues." In that same congregation was Mr. Smooth-Man, Mr. Anything, and Mr. Facing-Two-Ways. These are all people of duplicity.

Hypocrisy

> It is all in vain to preach the truth,
> To the eager ears of a trusting youth,
> If, whenever the lad is standing by,
> He sees you cheat and he hears you lie.
>
> —Edgar A. Guest, quoted in Jacob M. Braude, *Speaker's Encyclopedia*

JESUS WARNED His disciples, we must beware of hypocrisy—pretending to be something we aren't, acting with a mask covering our face. Hypocrisy is a terrible sign of trouble in our hearts—it waits only for the day of exposure. For as John Milton put it in *Paradise Lost*, "Neither men nor angels can discern hypocrisy, the only evil that walks invisible—except to God."

> —Joseph Bayly, quoted in Charles R. Swindoll, *The Quest for Character*

> I am like James and John.
> Lord, I size up other people
>   in terms of what they can do for me;
>   how they can further my program,
>   feed my ego,
>   satisfy my needs,
>   give me strategic advantage.
>
> I exploit people,
>   ostensibly for your sake,
>   but really for my own sake.
>
> Lord, I turn to you
>   to get the inside track
>   and obtain special favors;
>   your direction for my schemes;
>   your power for my projects;
>   your sanction for my ambitions;
>   your blank check for whatever I want.
> I am like James and John.

Change me, Lord.
Make me a man who asks of you and of others,
    what can I do for you?

—Robert Raines, *Creative Brooding*

DOUBLE-MINDEDNESS is a common disease that leaves its victims paralyzed by doubt.

How much better to be single-minded! No mumbo-jumbo. No religious phony-baloney. No say-one-thing-but-mean-something-else jive. No Pharisaic hypocrisy where words come cheap and externals are sickeningly pious. The single-minded are short on creeds and long on deeds.

They care . . . really care. They are humble . . . truly humble. They love . . . genuinely love. They have character . . . authentic character.

A Psalm of Single-Mindedness

Lord of reality
make me real
not plastic
synthetic
pretend phony
an actor playing out his part
hypocrite.
I don't want
to keep a prayer list
but to pray
nor agonize to find Your will
but to obey
what I already know
to argue
theories of inspiration
but submit to Your Word.
I don't want
to explain the difference
between eros and philos
and agape
but to love.
I don't want

to sing as if I mean it
I want to mean it.
I don't want
to tell it like it is
but to be it
like you want it.
I don't want
to think another needs me
but I need him
else I'm not complete.
I don't want
to tell others how to do it
but to do it
to have to be always right
but to admit it when I'm wrong.
I don't want to be a census taker
but an obstetrician
nor an involved person, a professional
but a friend.
I don't want to be insensitive
but to hurt where other people hurt
nor to say I know how you feel
but to say God knows
and I'll try
if you'll be patient with me
and meanwhile I'll be quiet.
I don't want to scorn the clichés of others
but to mean everything I say
including this.

—Joseph Bayly, *Psalms of My Life*

I CHUCKLED when I read veteran Bible teacher Ralph L. Keiper's paraphrase of Paul's confrontation with Peter's hypocrisy in Galatians 2:11–13. "Peter, I smell ham on your breath. You forgot your Certs. There was a time when you wouldn't eat ham as part of your hope of salvation. Then after you trusted Christ it didn't matter if you ate ham. But now when the no-ham eaters have come from Jerusalem you've gone back to your kosher ways. But the smell of ham still lingers on your breath. You're most inconsistent. You're compelling Gentile believers to observe Jewish law, which can never justify anyone."

That's a strong confrontation. And lest any of us think it was done in the shadows or the secret chamber of Peter's study, let's notice, "I said to Cephas in the presence of all." (Whew!) That's tough stuff.

—Leslie Flynn, *Great Church Fights*

Ti

ILLUSTRATIONS

SOMETIMES WE COME TO some knotty problems in Scripture. It's like buying a little can of Minute Maid orange juice that's concentrated. No one drinks out of that little can, that is, no one who can read and follow instructions. You mix that with a lot more water to dilute it so that it becomes delectable and tasty to your palate. It's too concentrated for you to take it all in. You have to mix it with a lot of water. Knotty texts need the mixture of other Scriptures to make their full flavor come into balance.

___

THE MIND OF MAN delights in a stirring scene or spectacle, whether it is a battlefield of temptation or an imaginary scene of triumph and glory in the heavenly places. Let the preacher remember this, and throw open as wide as he can the golden gates of imagination. Napoleon said, "Men of imagination rule the world." The preacher of imagination is the prince of the pulpit.

—Clarence Macartney, *Preaching without Notes*

___

GOLIATH WAS A CHAMPION of the Philistines "whose height was six cubits and a span." Let me tell you a story of what happened when I tried to illustrate him to my congregation.

Realizing our inability to understand that distance since we don't measure things by a cubit or a span but in feet and inches, I brought a cardboard visual aid to the pulpit one Sunday to show how tall Goliath was. Goliath was nine feet and nine inches tall. He could have jumped center for Abominable State. Let's face it, he was an enormous man.

Of course, it was interesting just getting this thing to the church in the first place. I was driving a little bug—a Volkswagen—and I couldn't get this thing inside. I was in a little bit of a hurry and had forgotten to plan ahead. So about 7:20 in the morning I hopped in the car and leaned this against the side of the car. After closing the door, I reached out through the window and held Goliath outside the car.

As I was driving to the church the wind began to sort of shake the poster around. I went around the corner, slinging this thing around, and there was an officer on the corner, who motioned for me to pull over.

Now I had written on this little board, "Do not remove. This is Goliath." I'd planned to set this board down by the pulpit, and I didn't want the custodian to run off with it.

So when the officer walked up, he said to me, "What are you doing?" I said, "I'm taking this to church." And he said, "What in the world is it?" And I said, "It is Goliath." He asked, "Who are you?" I said, "I am a minister and I'm on my way to church." He said, "Is that the church that you go to down there?" I said, "Yes sir, that's the church." He said, "Go on." I've always wanted to thank him for his graciousness.

I think the congregation was impressed with nine feet and nine inches. Add to that the height of his arms when he would lift them up over his head and you see what an imposing creature he was.

IMMORALITY

(Also see *Adultery, Sin*)

SENECA ONCE SAID, "Women were married to be divorced and divorced to be married." In Rome the years were identified by the names of the consuls; but it was said that fashionable ladies identified the years by the names of their husbands. Juvenal quotes an instance of a woman who had eight husbands in five years. Morality was dead in the first century.

In Greece immorality had always been quite blatant. Demosthenes long ago wrote, "We keep prostitutes for pleasure; we keep mistresses for the day to day needs of the body; we keep wives for the begetting of children and for the faithful guardianship of our homes."

—William Barclay, *The Letters to the Thessalonians*

YEARS AGO John Steinbeck wrote a letter to Adlai Stevenson. In it he said, "There is a creeping all-pervading gas of immorality which starts in the nursery and does not stop until it reaches the highest offices both corporate and governmental."

—Billy Graham, *World Aflame*

WHEN I DID MY DUTY overseas in the Marine Corps, I was in a hut of forty-eight fellows. Over ninety percent of them then or in the past had venereal disease. The whole unit was shot through with an illicit lifestyle.

One young man, from Idaho, lived in open sin. He had never known what it was like to be free of parental guidance. One night he went into the town and he shacked up with a woman. He came back terribly afraid he had a disease. He stumbled half-drunk down to the bunk where I was. He was talking with another guy and then grabbed hold of me and said, "Hey, I want you to talk to me. I'm scared to death." We took a walk that night out by the chow hall and then down toward the only place that was lighted—by the chapel. That night Frank got down on his knees and he said, "I ask Jesus Christ to come into my life." And he also said, "Lord, I've got a habit that You've got to break for me." For the next seven months I discipled him in the things of Christ. But when I left the island, he was right back in the village. You see, this enslavement won another victory.

FIRST CORINTHIANS 5:6 says, "a little leaven leavens the whole lump of dough." I remember hearing an interesting story one of my Greek professors told on one of his students. He taught a class at eight o'clock in the morning. Now at that hour, some people just don't function well, especially in Greek. One student was struggling to translate 1 Corinthians 5:6. He knew how the King James Version read, but knew he could not quote that because the professor would know he was not translating the Greek. So he came out with the familiar "a little dab'll do you." That was the best he could do.

That's true! A little dab will affect the whole bunch. You put a little, rotten, insignificant apple in a bucket of good apples, and the good apples will never make that rotten apple good. What will happen? Just the opposite. First, those around that rotten apple will begin to become rotten and decayed. And leave them there long enough and you've got a bucket of waste, ruined by that little dab of rottenness.

HOMOSEXUALITY SWEPT LIKE A CANCER through Greece and from Greece invaded Rome. We can scarcely realize how riddled the ancient world was with it. Even so great a man as Socrates practiced it; Plato's dialogue *The Symposium* is said to be one of the greatest works on love in the world, but its subject is unnatural love. Fourteen out of the first fifteen Roman emperors practiced this unnatural vice. During this time Nero was emperor. He had taken a boy called Sporus and had him castrated. He then married him with a full marriage ceremony and took him home in procession to his palace and lived with him. . . . When Nero was eliminated and Otho came to the throne, one of the first things he did was take possession of Sporus. Much later than this the Emperor Hadrian's name is forever associated with a Bithynian youth called Antinous. He lived with him inseparably, and when he died he deified him and covered the world with statues that immortalized his sin by calling a star after him.

—William Barclay, *The Letters to the Corinthians*

INCARNATION

(Also see *Christmas, Jesus*)

A baby's hands in Bethlehem
Were small and softly curled.
But held within their dimpled grasp
The hope of all the world.

—Leslie Savage, quoted in Charles R. Swindoll, *Growing Deep in the Christian Life*

They were all looking for a King
To slay their foes and lift them high;
Thou cam'st a little baby thing
That made a woman cry.

—George MacDonald, quoted in Charles R. Swindoll, *Growing Deep in the Christian Life*

ONE RAW WINTER NIGHT a man heard an irregular thumping sound against the kitchen storm door. He went to a window and watched as tiny, shivering sparrows, attracted to the evident warmth inside, beat in vain against the glass.

Touched, the farmer bundled up and trudged through fresh snow to open the barn for the struggling birds. He turned on the lights, tossed some hay in a corner, and sprinkled a trail of saltine crackers to direct them to the barn. But the sparrows, which had scattered in all directions when he emerged from the house, still hid in the darkness, afraid of him.

He tried various tactics: circling behind the birds to drive them toward the barn, tossing cracker crumbs in the air toward them, retreating to his house to see if they'd flutter into the barn on their own. Nothing worked. He, a huge alien creature, had terrified them; the birds could not understand that he actually desired to help.

He withdrew to his house and watched the doomed sparrows through a window. As he stared, a thought hit him like lightning from a clear blue sky: *If only I could become a bird—one of them—just for a moment. Then I wouldn't* frighten them so. I could show them the way to warmth and safety. At the same moment, another thought dawned on him. He had grasped the whole principle of the Incarnation.

A man's becoming a bird is nothing compared to God's becoming a man. The concept of a sovereign being as big as the universe He created, confining Himself to a human body was—and is—too much for some people to believe.

—Paul Harvey

A bald red head,
   A puckered face,
Hands blindly wand'ring
   Into space;
A wee faint smile,
   A stalwart squall,
And yards of clothes
   To hide it all;
Yes, that's a baby.
A bunch of sweetness
   Full of bliss,
A thing to cry
   About and kiss;
A blessing sent
   Straight from above,
A pound of care,
   A ton of love;
Now that's a baby!

—G. B. F. Hallock, *2500 Best Modern Illustrations*

WINSTON CHURCHILL described Russia as "A riddle, wrapped in a mystery, inside an enigma." That's appropriate to describe the Incarnation also.

—John Bartlett, *Bartlett's Familiar Quotations*

Made Flesh
After the bright beam of hot annunciation
   fused heaven with earth, His searing,
   sharply focused light went out for a while,
   eclipsed in amniotic gloom.

His cool immensity of splendor, His universal grace,
    small folded in a warm, dim, female space,
    the Word stern sentenced to be nine months dumb.
Infinity walled in a womb until the next enormity,
    the mighty.
After submission to a woman's pains,
    helpless in a barn bare floor,
    first tasting bitter earth.
But now I in Him surrender
    to the crush and cry of birth.
Because eternity was closeted in time,
    He is my open door to forever.
    From His imprisonment my freedoms grow, find wings.
Part of His body, I transcend this flesh.
    From His sweet silence my mouth sings.
Out of His dark I glow. My life,
    as His, slips through death's mesh times bar,
    joins hands with heaven, speaks with stars.
Immanuel.

—Luci Shaw, *Listen to the Green*

INDIFFERENCE

(Also see *Apathy, Complacency*)

THE WORST SIN is not to hate a fellow creature but to be indifferent toward him. That's the essence of humanity.

—George Bernard Shaw, quoted in John Bartlett, *Bartlett's Familiar Quotations*

ON THE SUBJECT OF INDIFFERENCE, an old saint said, "I want deliberately to encourage this mighty longing after God. The lack of it has brought us to our present low estate. The stiff and wooden quality about our religious lives is a result of our lack of holy waiting. Complacency is a deadly foe of all spiritual growth. Acute desire must be present or there will be no manifestation of Christ to His people. He waits to be wanted. Too bad that with many of us He waits so long, so very long, in vain."

INFLUENCE
(Also see *Leadership*)

In 1645, one vote gave Oliver Cromwell control of England.
In 1649, one vote caused Charles I of England to be executed.
In 1845, one vote brought Texas into the Union.
In 1868, one vote saved President Andrew Johnson from impeachment.
In 1875, one vote changed France from a monarchy into a republic.
In 1876, one vote gave Rutherford B. Hayes the United States presidency.
In 1923, one vote gave Adolf Hitler control of the Nazi party.

—Paul Lee Tan, *Encyclopedia of 7,700 Illustrations*

Tell me not, in mournful numbers,
Life is but an empty dream!

. . . .

Lives of great men all remind us
We can make our lives sublime,
And, departing, leave behind us
Footprints on the sands of time.

—Henry Wadsworth Longfellow

IN 1809, the evening news broadcasts would have concentrated on Austria—not Britain or America. The attention of the entire world was on Napoleon as he swept across helpless hamlets like a fire across a Kansas wheat field. Nothing else was half as significant on the international scene. The broad brush strokes on the historian's canvas give singular emphasis to the bloody scenes of tyranny created by the diminutive dictator of France. From Trafalgar to Waterloo his name was a synonym for superiority.

During that time of invasions and battles, babies were being born in Britain and America. But who was interested in babies and bottles, cradles and cribs while history was being made? What could possibly be more important in 1809 than the fall of Austria? Who cared about English-born infants that year when Europe was in the limelight?

Somebody should have. A veritable host of thinkers and statesmen drew their first breath in 1809.

- William Gladstone was born in Liverpool.
- Alfred Tennyson began his life in Lincolnshire.
- Oliver Wendell Holmes cried out in Cambridge, Massachusetts.

- Edgar Alan Poe, a few miles away in Boston, started his brief and tragic life.
- A physician named Darwin and his wife called their infant son Charles Robert.
- Robert Charles Winthrop wore his first diapers.
- A rugged cabin in Hardin County, Kentucky, owned by an illiterate wandering laborer, was filled with the infant screams of a newborn boy named Abraham Lincoln.

Only a handful of history buffs today could name even one Austrian campaign—but who can measure the impact of those other lives? What appeared to be super-significant to the world has proven to be no more exciting than a Sunday afternoon yawn. What seemed to be totally insignificant was, in fact, the genesis of an era.

—Charles R. Swindoll, *Growing Strong in the Seasons of Life*

WHEN I WAS A SMALL BOY, I attended church every Sunday at a big Gothic Presbyterian bastion in Chicago. The preaching was powerful and the music was great. But for me, the most awesome moment in the morning service was the offertory, when twelve solemn, frock-coated ushers marched in lock-step down the main aisle to receive the brass plates for collecting the offering. These men, so serious about their business of serving the Lord in this magnificent house of worship, were the business and professional leaders of Chicago.

One of the twelve ushers was a man named Frank Loesch. He was not a very imposing-looking man, but in Chicago he was a living legend, for he was the man who had stood up to Al Capone. In the prohibition years, Capone's rule was absolute. The local and state police and even the Federal Bureau of Investigation were afraid to oppose him. But single-handedly, Frank Loesch, as a Christian layman and without any government support, organized the Chicago Crime Commission, a group of citizens that was determined to take Mr. Capone to court and put him away. During the months that the Crime Commission met, Frank Loesch's life was in constant danger. There were threats on the lives of his family and friends. But he never wavered. Ultimately he won the case against Capone and was the instrument for removing this blight from the city of Chicago. Frank Loesch had risked his life to live out his faith.

Each Sunday at this point of the service, my father, a Chicago businessman himself, never failed to poke me and silently point to Frank Loesch with pride. Sometimes I'd catch a tear in my father's eye. For my dad and for all of us this was and is what authentic living is all about.

—Bruce Larson, *There's a Lot More to Health Than Not Being Sick*

IN THE SUMMER OF 1805, a number of Indian chiefs and warriors met in council at Buffalo Creek, New York, to hear a presentation of the Christian message by a Mr. Cram from the Boston Missionary Society. After the sermon, a response was given by Red Jacket, one of the leading chiefs. Among other things, the chief said:

> Brother, you say that there is but one way to worship and serve the Great Spirit. If there is but one religion, why do you white people differ so much about it? Why not all agree, as you can all read the same Book?
>
> Brother, we are told that you have been preaching to the white people in this place. These people are our neighbors. We are acquainted with them. We will wait a little while and see what effect your preaching has upon them. If we find it does them good, makes them honest and less disposed to cheat Indians, we will then consider again what you have said.
>
> —Warren W. Wiersbe, *Be Hopeful*

THE FAMOUS New York diamond dealer Harry Winston heard about a wealthy Dutch merchant who was looking for a certain kind of diamond to add to his collection. Winston called the merchant, told him that he thought he had the perfect stone, and invited the collector to come to New York and examine it.

The collector flew to New York and Winston assigned a salesman to meet him and show the diamond. When the salesman presented the diamond to the merchant he described the expensive stone by pointing out all its fine technical features. The merchant listened and praised the stone but turned away and said, "It's a wonderful stone but not exactly what I wanted."

Winston, who had been watching the presentation from a distance, stopped the merchant and asked, "Do you mind if I show you that diamond once again?" The merchant agreed and Winston presented the same stone. But instead of talking about the technical features of the stone, Winston spoke spontaneously about his own genuine admiration of the diamond and what a rare thing of beauty it was. Abruptly, the customer changed his mind and bought the diamond.

While he was waiting for the diamond to be packaged and brought to him, the merchant turned to Winston and asked, "Why did I buy it from you when I had no difficulty saying no to your salesman?"

Winston replied, "The salesman is one of the best men in the business and he knows more about diamonds than I do. I pay him a good salary for what he knows. But I would gladly pay him twice as much if I could put into him something that I have and he lacks. You see, he *knows* diamonds, but I *love* them."

That story illustrates one of the single greatest principles of persuasion: People are far more persuaded by the depths of your beliefs and emotions than any amount of logic or knowledge you possess.

—Michael LeBoeuf, *How to Win Customers and Keep Them for Life*

POSSESSIONS OF THE POWERFUL, or famous, no matter how common, can become extremely valuable, even priceless. Napoleon's toothbrush sold for $21,000. Can you imagine paying thousands of dollars for someone's cruddy old toothbrush? Hitler's car sold for over $150,000. Winston Churchill's desk, a pipe owned by C. S. Lewis, sheet music handwritten by Beethoven, a house once owned by Ernest Hemmingway—all were sold at many times their intrinsic value. At Sotheby's auction of Jackie Kennedy Onassis's personal belongings, her fake pearls sold for $211,500, and JFK's wood golf clubs went for $772,500. Not because the items themselves are worthy but because they once belonged to someone significant.

—Charles R. Swindoll, *Hope Again*

AFTER SERVING the Lord for some fifteen years in Pakistan, missionary Warren Webster was invited to speak at the now famous Urbana Missionary Conference. Part of his message are these words:

If I had my life to live over again, I would live it to change the lives of people, because you have not changed anything until you've changed the lives of people.

Changing the world required changing the lives of people.

—Charles R. Swindoll, *Growing Deep in the Christian Life*

ONE MORNING IN 1888, Alfred Nobel, inventor of dynamite, the man who had spent his life amassing a fortune from the manufacture and sale of weapons, awoke to read his own obituary. The obituary was printed as a result of a simple journalistic error. Alfred's brother had died, and a French reporter carelessly reported the death of the wrong brother. Any man would be disturbed under the circumstances, but to Alfred the shock was overwhelming because he saw himself as the world saw him—"the dynamite King (the weapon maker)," the great industrialist who had made an immense fortune from explosives. This—as far as the general public was concerned—was the entire purpose of his life (so said the obituary). None of his true intentions—

to break down the barriers that separated men and ideas—were recognized or given serious consideration. He was quite simply in the eyes of the public a merchant of death, and for that alone he would be remembered. . . . As he read his obituary with shocking horror, he resolved to make clear to the world the true meaning and purpose of his life. This could be done through the final disposition of his fortune. His last will and testament would be the expression of his life's ideals. . . . And the result was the most valued of prizes given to this day to those who have done most for the cause of world peace—the Nobel Peace Prize.

That caught my eye because I at times wonder how it would read if my obituary suddenly appeared. And I ask you to entertain that frightful thought for a moment. What is your life known for? What will you be remembered for?

—Nicholas Halasz, quoted by Robert Raines, *Creative Brooding*

I LOVE FOOTBALL. And in the '60s the Green Bay Packers were unbelievable. But do you know, I tried to remember the simple starting lineup of either their offense or defense and I batted zero. I could remember only three or four on each team. And I thought I would never forget them. Famous people back then, but forgotten today.

Bobby Richardson talks about this in a poem at the end of his book on his life. As long as you've got your batting average up there, everybody knows about Bobby Richardson, everybody knows who plays second base for the Yankees, but three, four, five years later, "Who was the fellow?" Famous then, but forgotten now. Or some great basketball team in the days of the Celtics when they just swept it year after year in the NBA.

And I'm just using sports as an example. The same could be said of stardom. The same could be said for great scientists. They've come and gone. They've left their works, but their names are forgotten. Men honor and highlight the famous and then they forget them. God, however, remembers the unknowns and never forgets us. That is a very encouraging thought.

"DO NOT BE DECEIVED: Bad company corrupts good morals"(1 Cor. 15:33). All things being equal, if you run with bad company, it will corrupt you. It's like putting on a pair of white gloves, picking up mud and mixing it around in your hand. The mud never gets glovey. Never saw glovey mud in my life. But invariably, the gloves get muddy.

TEDDY STALLARD certainly qualified as "one of the least." Disinterested in school, musty, wrinkled clothes, hair never combed. One of those kids in school with a deadpan face, expressionless—sort of a glassy, unfocused stare. When Miss Thompson spoke to Teddy he always answered in monosyllables. Unattractive, unmotivated, and distant, he was just plain hard to like. Even though his teacher said she loved all in her class the same, down inside she wasn't being completely truthful.

Whenever she marked Teddy's papers, she got a certain perverse pleasure out of putting Xs next to the wrong answers and when she put the Fs at the top of the papers, she always did it with a flair. She should have known better; she had Teddy's records and she knew more about him than she wanted to admit. The records read:

1st Grade: Teddy shows promise with his work and attitude, but poor home situation.

2nd Grade: Teddy could do better. Mother is seriously ill. He receives little help at home.

3rd Grade: Teddy is a good boy but too serious. He is a slow learner. His mother died this year.

4th Grade: Teddy is very slow, but well behaved. His father shows no interest.

Christmas came and the boys and girls in Miss Thompson's class brought her Christmas presents. They piled their presents on her desk and crowded around to watch her open them. Among the presents was one from Teddy Stallard. She was surprised that he had brought her a gift, but he had. Teddy's gift was wrapped in brown paper and was held together with Scotch tape. On the paper were written the simple words, "For Miss Thompson from Teddy." When she opened Teddy's present, out fell a gaudy rhinestone bracelet, with half the stones missing, and a bottle of cheap perfume.

The other boys and girls began to giggle and smirk over Teddy's gift, but Miss Thompson at least had enough sense to silence them by immediately putting on the bracelet and putting some of the perfume on her wrist. Holding her wrist up for the other children to smell, she said, "Doesn't it smell lovely?" And the other children, taking their cues from the teacher, readily agreed with oohs and aahs.

At the end of the day, when school was over and the other children had left, Teddy lingered behind. He slowly came over to her desk and said softly, "Miss Thompson . . . Miss Thompson, you smell just like my mother . . . and her bracelet looks real pretty on you, too. I'm glad you like my presents." When

Teddy left, Miss Thompson got down on her knees and asked God to forgive her.

The next day when the children came to school, they were welcomed by a new teacher. Miss Thompson had become a different person. She was no longer just a teacher; she had become an agent of God. She was now a person committed to loving her children and doing things for them that would live on after her. She helped all the children, but especially the slow ones, and especially Teddy Stallard. By the end of that school year, Teddy showed dramatic improvement. He had caught up with most of the students and was even ahead of some.

She didn't hear from Teddy for a long time. Then one day, she received a note that read:

> *Dear Miss Thompson:*
> *I wanted you to be the first to know.*
> *I will be graduating second in my class.*
> *Love,*
> *Teddy Stallard*

Four years later, another note came:

> *Dear Miss Thompson:*
> *They just told me I will be graduating first in my class. I wanted you to be the first to know. The university has not been easy, but I liked it.*
> *Love,*
> *Teddy Stallard*

And four years later:

> *Dear Miss Thompson:*
> *As of today, I am Theodore Stallard, MD. How about that? I wanted you to be the first to know. I am getting married next month, the 27th to be exact. I want you to come and sit where my mother would sit if she were alive. You are the only family I have now; Dad died last year.*
> *Love,*
> *Teddy Stallard*

Miss Thompson went to that wedding and sat where Teddy's mother would have sat. She deserved to sit there; she had done something for Teddy that he could never forget.

—Anthony Campolo, *Who Switched the Price Tags?*

INTEGRITY

(Also see *Honesty*)

THERE WAS A YOUNG CHRISTIAN MAN in a southern university. He made the football team as the starting split end. And he continually was before God saying, "Help me in the climax of moments to be absolutely honest. I pray for honesty—that one mark of integrity. I want to be that, Lord, and I'll work on it through the season."

The rival team came that night, homecoming. He ran his route and went into the end zone. The quarterback shot him the pass and he got it low. He landed on it, and the referee shouted, "Touchdown!" But that boy knew he had trapped that ball. (For you who aren't into that, it means that he didn't really catch it. He landed on it while it was on the ground and it looked like he caught it.) The stands were just cheering, you know, sending him on his way, the hero of the game. He said, "Wait a minute." Can you imagine this? Walked up to the referee and shook his head. He said, "I trapped it." The referee canceled the touchdown and they lost the game.

Now you may not understand much about football, but you know what it is to be a fan. And that boy stood all alone, not only against a team that said, "What does it matter, man?" but against the stands full of people. He said, "I can't take the credit. I did not catch it."

—James K. Krames, "Tender Loving Heart," *Living Free*

AFTER HIS SUNDAY MESSAGES, the pastor of a church in London got on the trolley Monday morning to go back to his study downtown. He paid his fare, and the trolley driver gave him too much change. The pastor sat down and fumbled the change and looked it over, counted it eight or ten times. And, you know the rationalization, "It's wonderful how God provides." He realized he was tight that week and this was just about what he would need to break even, or at least enough for his lunch. He wrestled with himself all the way down that old trolley trail that led to his office. And finally he came to the stop and he got up, couldn't live with himself, walked up to the trolley driver, and said, "Here, you gave me too much change. You made a mistake." The driver said, "No, it was no mistake. You see, I was in your church last night when you spoke on honesty, and I thought I would put you to the test."

—Paul Lee Tan, *Encyclopedia of 7,700 Illustrations*

The World Needs Men ... [and I might add *women*]
who cannot be bought;

whose word is their bond;
who put character above wealth;
who possess opinions and a will;
who are larger than their vocations;
who do not hesitate to take chances;
who will not lose their individuality in a crowd;
who will be as honest in small things as in great things;
who will make no compromise with wrong;
whose ambitions are not confined to their own selfish desires.
who will not say they do it "because everybody else does it";
who are true to their friends through good report and evil report,
in adversity as well as in prosperity;
who do not believe that shrewdness, cunning and hardheadedness
are the best qualities for winning success;
who are not ashamed or afraid to stand for the truth when it is unpopular;
who say "no" with emphasis, although the rest of the world says "yes."

—Ted Engstrom, *The Making of a Christian Leader*

BACK IN 1958 a small community in northeastern Pennsylvania built a little, red brick building that was to be their police department, their fire department, and their city hall. They were proud of that building; it was the result of sacrificial giving and careful planning. When the building was completed, they had a ribbon-cutting ceremony, and more than six thousand people were there—nearly all the town's residents. It was the biggest event of the year!

Within less than two months, however, they began to notice some ominous cracks on the side of this red brick building. Sometime later, it was noticed that the windows wouldn't shut all the way. Then it was discovered that the doors wouldn't close correctly. Eventually, the floor shifted and left ugly gaps in the floor covering and corners. The roof began to leak. Within a few more months, it had to be evacuated, to the embarrassment of the builder and the disgust of the taxpayers.

A firm did an analysis shortly thereafter and found that the blasts from a nearby mining area were slowly but effectively destroying the building. Imperceptibly, down beneath the foundation, there were small shifts and changes taking place that caused the whole foundation to crack. You couldn't feel it or even see it from the surface, but quietly and down deep there was a weakening. A city official finally had to write across the door of that building, "Condemned. Not fit for public use." Ultimately, the building had to be demolished.

—Charles R. Swindoll, *Hand Me Another Brick*

THE BETTER THE MAN, the better the preacher. When he kneels by the bed of the dying or when he mounts the pulpit stairs, then every self-denial he has made, every Christian forbearance he has shown, every resistance to sin and temptation, will come back to him to strengthen his arm and give conviction to his voice. Likewise every evasion of duty, every indulgence of self, every compromise with evil, every unworthy thought, word, or deed, will be there at the head of the pulpit stairs to meet the minister on Sunday morning, to take the light from his eye, the power from his blow, the ring from his voice, and the joy from his heart.

—Clarence Macartney, *Preaching without Notes*

INTEGRITY IS NOT ONLY THE WAY ONE THINKS but even more the way one acts. Simply put, integrity is doing what you said you would do. It is as basic as keeping your word, fulfilling your promise.

—Ted Engstrom, *Integrity*

MY MARINE COMMANDING OFFICER called me in and asked me why I had not participated in a particular event that was, in his terms, "required" of the entire company. As far as I can remember, it was the only time I had directly disobeyed a command. And Captain Burch said to me, "Who do you think you are?" I answered at that moment, "Not very much, right now. But I want you to know, Captain, why I said I could not participate." He said, "Talk fast." And I did. And I declared my allegiance to Jesus Christ. His mouth literally dropped open. And his final words to me were, "I admire you. Get out!"

THE STRONGEST MAN ON EARTH is the one who stands most alone.

—Henrik Ibsen

WHEN TED WILLIAMS WAS FORTY YEARS OLD and closing out his career with the Boston Red Sox, he was suffering from a pinched nerve in his neck. "The thing was so bad," he later explained, "that I could hardly turn my head to look at the pitcher." . . . For the first time in his career he batted under .300, hitting just .254 with ten home runs. He was the highest salaried player in sports that year, making $125,000. The next year the Red Sox sent him the same contract.

"When I got it, I sent it back with a note. I told them I wouldn't sign it until they gave me the full pay cut allowed. I think it was twenty-five percent. My feeling was that I was always treated fairly by the Red Sox when it came to contracts.

"I never had any problem with them about money. Now they were offering me a contract I didn't deserve. And I only wanted what I deserved."

Williams cut his own salary by $31,250!

—Jerry White, *Honesty, Morality, and Conscience*

INTIMACY

A COUPLE WAS DRIVING HOME from a lovely evening out to celebrate their twenty-fifth anniversary. She was sitting way over there and he was sitting right here behind the steering wheel. She said, with a little bit of ache, "Honey, remember when we used to sit really close together in the car?" And without a hesitation, he replied, "Well, honey, I never moved. I've been right here all this time."

—Leslie Flynn, *Humorous Incidents and Quips*

MATTHEW 9:36–37 has a change in metaphor showing an intimacy of partnership. "In the sheep and the shepherd we see man's need met by God. But in the harvest and the workers we see God's need met by man."

—G. Campbell Morgan, *The Gospel of Matthew*

Good-bye

O, when I am safe in my sylvan home,
I tread on the pride of Greece and Rome;
And when I am stretched beneath the pines,
Where the evening star so holy shines,
I laugh at the lore and the pride of man
As the sophist schools, and the learned clan;
For what are they all, in high conceit,
When man in the bush with God may meet?

—Ralph Waldo Emerson

THE EASE WITH WHICH we once approached God can be seen in the letters written to Him by children. See if the ones below don't take you back to a time of innocence and openness in your own relationship with Him.

Dear Lord,

Thank you for the nice day today. You even fooled the TV weatherman.

Hank (age 7)

Dear Lord,

Do you ever get mad?

My mother gets mad all the time but she is only human.

Yours truly,

David (age 8)

Dear Lord,

I need a raise in my allowance. Could you have one of your angels tell my father?

Thank you.

David (age 7)

—Bill Adler, Dear Lord

Dear God,

Charles, my cat, got run over. And if you made it happen you have to tell me why.

Harvey

Dear God,

Can you guess what is the biggest river of all of them? The Amazon.

You ought to be able to because you made it. Ha, ha.

Guess who

—Eric Marshall and Stuart Hample, More Children's Letters to God

---

FATHER, I WANT TO KNOW THEE, but my coward heart fears to give up its toys. I cannot part with them without inward bleeding, and I do not try to hide from Thee the terror of the parting. I come trembling, but I do come. Please root from my heart all those things which I have cherished so long and which have become a very part of my living self, so that Thou mayest enter and dwell there without a rival. Then shalt Thou make the place of Thy feet glorious. Then shall my heart have no need of the sun to shine in it, for Thyself wilt be the light of it, and there shall be no night there. In Jesus'name, Amen.

—A. W. Tozer, The Pursuit of God

TELL GOD ALL THAT IS IN YOUR HEART, as one unloads one's heart, its pleasures and its pains, to a dear friend. Tell Him your troubles, that He may comfort you; tell Him your joys, that He may sober them; tell Him your longings, that He may purify them; tell Him your dislikes, that He may help you to conquer them; talk to Him of your temptations, that He may shield you from them; show Him the wounds of your heart, that He may heal them; lay bare your indifference to good, your depraved tastes for evil, your instability. Tell Him how self-love makes you unjust to others, how vanity tempts you to be insincere, how pride disguises you to yourself and others.

If you thus pour out all your weaknesses, needs, troubles, there will be no lack of what to say. You will never exhaust the subject. It is continually being renewed. People who have no secrets from each other never want for subject of conversation. They do not weigh their words, for there is nothing to be held back; neither do they seek for something to say. They talk out of the abundance of the heart, without consideration they say just what they think. Blessed are they who attain to such familiar, unreserved intercourse with God.

—François Fénelon

<hr />

THERE IS SOMETHING EXTREMELY EXCITING about a little potluck breakfast down on the shore, isn't there? When is the last time you did that? Well, that's been too long. We need to get away. Just get a little time by the sea. The sea has a language all its own, doesn't it? It is almost as though the fingers of God are rolling in those great, great waves. And in some mysterious tie between the moon and the tide, and in the swamping awesomeness of that walk on the beach, you somehow come back together with God. Somehow there's a place where the child of God's heart is just washed, made fresh. We spend too long in the sidewalk jungles of our habitat. Thank God He has preserved some places for us to be near Him.

Jj

JEALOUSY

(Also see *Envy*)

I MARRIED A COUPLE several years ago whom I shall not soon forget. During the premarital counseling sessions, I detected a strong jealous streak in the young man. I mentioned this to both of them, but they passed it off as not that important. He assured me he "used to struggle a little with it," but no more. Following their honeymoon and the first few months of marriage, they returned for some follow-up time—and what a change! Brimming with anger, she blurted out, "This man is so jealous of me, before he leaves for work in the morning he checks the odometer on my car. Then when he comes home, sometimes even before he comes into the house, he checks it again. If I have driven a few extra miles, he quizzes me during supper." Lacking trust and encouragement, she was dying slowly, sadly, angrily.

I USED TO BE TERRIBLY JEALOUS. I remember an occasion when I was dating my wife. She had promised a fellow that she would go with him to a Texas A & M Aggies football game. I didn't want her to go—sort of felt I had all the rights. But she went to the game. It was common practice at each Aggie touchdown for the fellow to kiss his date. I listened on the radio, fervently praying that they wouldn't score. I recall the first touchdown that took place. Then they made another one a little later on. I don't think A&M ever made as many touchdowns in one game as they made in that one. The score was 48–0, and I just seethed on the inside.

Little did I realize how destructive that would have been to my relationship if that had continued. Through the patience of a wife with one given to jealousy, that's been overcome. I dealt with it and got rid of it.

THERE WERE ONCE TWO MEN, both seriously ill, in the same small room of a great hospital. Quite a small room, just large enough for the pair of them—

two beds, two bedside lockers, a door opening on the hall, and one window looking out on the world.

One of the men, as part of his treatment, was allowed to sit up in bed for an hour in the afternoon, (something that had to do with draining the fluid from his lungs) and his bed was next to the window.

But the other man had to spend all his time flat on his back—and both of them had to be kept quiet and still. Which was the reason they were in the small room by themselves, and they were grateful for peace and privacy—none of the bustle and clatter and prying eyes of the general ward for them.

Of course, one of the disadvantages of their condition was that they weren't allowed much to do: no reading, no radio, certainly no television—they just had to keep quiet and still, just the two of them.

They used to talk for hours and hours—about their wives, their children, their homes, their former jobs, their hobbies, their childhood, what they did during the war, where they had been on vacations, all that sort of thing. Every afternoon, when the man in the bed next to the window was propped up for his hour, he would pass the time by describing what he could see outside. And the other man began to live for those hours.

The window apparently overlooked a park with a lake where there were ducks and swans, children throwing them bread and sailing model boats, and young lovers walking hand in hand beneath the trees. And there were flowers and stretches of grass and games of softball, people taking their ease in the sunshine, and right at the back, behind the fringe of the trees, a fine view of the city skyline.

The man on his back would listen to all of this, enjoying every minute—how a child nearly fell into the lake, how beautiful girls were in their summer dresses, and then an exciting ball game, or a boy playing with his puppy. It got to the place that he could almost see what was happening outside.

Then one fine afternoon, when there was some sort of parade, the thought struck him: Why should that man next to the window have all the pleasure of seeing what's going on? Why shouldn't I get the chance?

He felt ashamed and tried not to think like that, but the more he tried, the worse he wanted to change. He'd do anything!

In a few days he had turned sour. He should be by the window. And he brooded and couldn't even sleep, and grew even more seriously ill—which none of the doctors understood.

One night, as he stared at the ceiling, the man by the window suddenly woke up coughing and choking, the fluid congesting in his lungs, his hands groping for the button that would bring the night nurse running. But the other man watched without moving.

The coughing racked the darkness—on and on—choked off—then stopped—and the man continued to stare at the ceiling.

In the morning, the day nurse came in with water for their baths and found the other man dead. They took away his body, quietly, with no fuss.

As soon as it seemed decent, the man asked if he could be moved to the bed next to the window. They moved him, tucked him in, made him quite comfortable, and left him alone to be quiet and still.

The minute they'd gone, he propped himself up on one elbow, painfully and laboriously, and looked out the window. It faced a blank wall.

—G. W. Target, "The Window," in *The Window and Other Essays*

JESUS

(Also see *Incarnation, Resurrection*)

LIKE A JEWEL'S BRILLIANCE is displayed on a black cloth, Jesus' love is displayed against the blackness of sin, and the filth of the flesh.

The Touch of the Master's Hand

'Twas battered and scarred and the auctioneer
Thought it scarcely worth his while
To waste much time on the old violin,
But he held it up with a smile:
"What am I bidden, good folks," he cried,
"Who'll start the bidding for me?"
"A dollar, a dollar; then Two! Only two?
Two dollars, and who'll make it three?
Three dollars once; three dollars, twice;
Going for three—" but no,
From the room, far back, a gray-haired man
Came forward and picked up the bow;
Then, wiping the dust from the old violin,
And tightening up the loose strings,
He played a melody pure and sweet
As a caroling angel sings.

The music ceased, and the auctioneer,
With a voice that was quiet and low,
Said: "What am I bid for the old violin?"

And he held it up with the bow.
"A thousand dollars, and who'll make it two?
Two thousand! And who'll make it three?
Three thousand, once, three thousand, twice,
And going, and gone," said he.
The people cheered, but some of them cried,
"We do not quite understand
What changed its worth." Swift came the reply:
"The touch of a master's hand."

And many a man with life out of tune,
And battered and scarred with sin,
Is auctioned cheap to the thoughtless crowd,
Much like the old violin.
A "mess of pottage," a glass of wine;
A game—and he travels on.
He is "going once," and "going" twice,
He's "going" and almost "gone."
But the Master comes, and the foolish crowd
Never can quite understand
The worth of a soul and the change that's wrought
By the touch of the Master's hand.

—Myra Brooks Welch, quoted in John R. Rice, *Poems That Preach*

IN A DREAM I saw the Savior. His back was bare and there was a soldier lifting up his hand and bringing down that awful cat-o'-nine-tails. In a dream I rose and grasped his arm to hold it back. When I did, the soldier turned in astonishment and looked at me. And when I looked at him, I recognized myself.

—W. A. Criswell, *Expository Sermons on Galatians*

WE ARE REPRESENTATIVES of the Lord Jesus Christ . . . like hands fitting into a glove. We are the glove. He is the hand. People see us. They see our movement. They see our impact. They feel the squeeze of our life, the warmth of the hand. They can't see Him but through the glove. And so the glove appears regularly on the surface of life. And people spot it when there is peace in our lives, because there isn't peace in our world.

—Ian Thomas, *The Saving Life of Christ*

I AM TRYING HERE to prevent anyone saying the really foolish thing that people often say about Him: "I'm ready to accept Jesus as a great moral teacher, but I don't accept His claim to be God." That is the one thing we must not say. A man who was merely a man and said the sort of things Jesus said would not be a great moral teacher. He would be either a lunatic—on a level with the man who says he is a poached egg—or else he would be the Devil of Hell. You must make your choice. Either this man was, and is, the Son of God: or else a madman or something worse.

—C. S. Lewis, *Mere Christianity*

If our greatest need had been information,
  God would have sent us an educator.
If our greatest need had been technology,
  God would have sent us a scientist.
If our greatest need had been money,
  God would have sent us an economist.
If our greatest need had been pleasure,
  God would have sent us an entertainer.
But our greatest need was forgiveness,
  so God sent us a Savior!

—Charles R. Swindoll, *The Grace Awakening*

HE WAS THE GOD-MAN. Not God indwelling a man. Of such there have been many. Not a man deified. Of such there have been none save in the myths of pagan systems of thought; but God and man, combining in one personality the two natures, a perpetual enigma and mystery, baffling the possibility of explanation.

—G. Campbell Morgan, *The Crises of the Christ*

The Maker of the Universe

His holy fingers formed the bough
  Where grew the thorns that crowned His brow;
The nails that pierced the hands were mined
  In secret places He designed.

He made the forests whence there sprung
  The tree on which His holy body hung;

He died upon a cross of wood,
Yet made the hill upon which it stood.

The sun which hid from Him its face
By His decree was poised in space!
The sky which darkened o'er His head
By Him above the earth was spread.

The spear that spilt His precious blood
Was tempered in the fires of God.
The grave in which His form was laid
Was hewn in rocks His hands had made.

—F. W. Pitt, quoted in Henry Gariepy, *100 Portraits of Christ*

There was a Knight of Bethlehem,
Whose wealth was tears and sorrows,
His men-at-arms were little lambs,
His trumpeters were sparrows.
His castle was a wooden cross
On which He hung so high;
His helmet was a crown of thorns,
Whose crest did touch the sky.

—William Barclay, *The Gospel of Luke*

One Solitary Life

Here is a man who was born in an obscure village, the Child of a peasant woman. He worked in a carpenter shop until He was thirty, and then for three years He was an itinerant preacher. He never wrote a book. He never held an office. He never owned a home. He never had a family. He never went to college. He never put His foot inside a big city. He never traveled two hundred miles from the place where He was born. He never did one of the things that usually accompany greatness. He had no credentials but Himself. He had nothing to do with this world except the naked power of His Divine manhood. While still a young man, the tide of popular opinion turned against Him. He was turned over to His enemies. He went through the mockery of a trial. He was nailed to a Cross between two thieves. His executioners gambled for the only piece of property He had on earth while He was dying—and that was His coat. When He was dead He was taken down and laid in a borrowed grave through the pity of a friend. Such was His human life—He rises from the dead. Nineteen wide centuries have come and gone and today He is the Centerpiece of the human race and the Leader of the column of progress. I am within the mark when I say that all the armies that ever marched, and all the navies that ever were built, and all the parliaments that ever sat, and all the kings that ever reigned, put together, have not affected the life of man upon this earth as powerfully as has that One Solitary Life.

—James C. Hefley, quoted in J. B. Fowler Jr., *Great Words of the New Testament*

Face to Face

Face to face with Christ my Savior,
Face to face—what will it be—
When with rapture I behold Him,
Jesus Christ who died for me?

Only faintly now I see Him,
With the darkling veil between;
But a blessed day is coming
When His glory shall be seen.

Face to face! O blissful moment!
Face to face—to see and know;
Face to face with my Redeemer,
Jesus Christ who loves me so.

—Carrie Breck

What Would He Say?

If He should come today and find my hand so full
Of future plans, however fair,
In which my Savior has no share,
What would He say?

If He should come today and find my love so cold,
My faith so very weak and dim
I had not even looked for Him,
What would He say?

If He should come today and find that I had not told
One soul about my heavenly Friend

Whose blessings all my way attend,
What would He say?

If He should come today, I would be glad,
Remembering that He died for all
And none through me had heard His call,
What would He say?

—Grace Troy

"I like to think of our Lord's ascension in this simple but sublime manner. I might have been terrified if I had been Elisha walking with Elijah when the horses of fire and the chariots of fire came to take him away, but there was nothing terrible about this ascension of Christ. He was not a prophet of fire; He was gentle, meek, and lowly, and there was nothing to inspire terror in the way He ascended to heaven. It is, to my mind, very beautiful to think of there being no medium employed in connection with His ascension, no angels' wings to bear Him upward, no visible arm of omnipresence to lift Him gently from the earth,—no eagle of Jupiter to steal away this choice and chosen One. No; but He rises by His own power and majesty; He needs no one to help. Glad would the angels have been to come once more to the earth as they had come at His birth, as they had come to the wilderness, as they had come to the tomb—gladly would they have come and ministered to Him; but He needed not their ministry. He proved the innate power of His Deity, by which He could depart out of the world just when He willed, breaking the law of gravitation. And "A cloud received Him out of their sight," for I suppose they had then seen all that they ought to see; and, perhaps, behind that cloud there were scenes of glory which it was not possible for human eyes to gaze upon, and words which it was not lawful for human beings to hear. I do not know about that. But I like the thought of our hymn-writer concerning the angels, after the cloud had hidden Him from mortal view:

They brought His chariot from above,
To bear Him to His throne.
Clapp'd their triumphant wings and cried,
The glorious work is done.

—Charles H. Spurgeon, *The Treasury of the Bible*

FIND THE BODY of that Jew, and Christianity crumbles into ruins.

—Arnold Toynbee, *Man's Concern with Death*

JOBS

(Also see *Business*)

THE AVERAGE PERSON puts only 25 percent of his energy and ability into his work. The world takes off its hat to those who put in more than 50 percent of their capacity, and stands on its head for those few and far between souls who devote 100 percent.

—Andrew Carnegie, quoted in Lloyd Cory, *Quote Unquote*

_____

YES, I'M TIRED. For several years I've been blaming it on middle age, iron poor blood, lack of vitamins, air pollution, water pollution, saccharin, obesity, dieting, underarm odor, yellow wax buildup, and a dozen other maladies that make you wonder if life is really worth living.

But now I find out, tain't that.

I'm tired because I'm overworked.

The population of this country is over 200 million. Eighty-four million are retired. That leaves 116 million to do the work. There are 75 million in school, which leaves 41 million to do the work. Of this total, there are 22 million employed by the government.

That leaves 19 million to do the work. Four million are in the armed forces, which leaves 15 million to do the work. Take from that total the 14,800,000 people who work for the state and city governments and that leaves 200,000 to do the work. There are 188,000 in hospitals, so that leaves 12,000 to do the work. Now there are 11,998 people in prisons. That leaves just 2 people to do the work. You and me. And you're standing there reading this. No wonder I'm tired.

—Anonymous

_____

THERE ARE ONLY TWO KINDS OF COACHES: those who have been fired and those who are gonna be.

—Bum Phillips

_____

WHEN DR. CLYDE COOK was at Sea World he noticed there were some trained parrots who had been taught to roller skate. Little roller skates were strapped to their claws and they were skating on the sidewalk in different places throughout Sea World. He said, "You know, Chuck, as I watched those little parrots, I could tell that they could do it, but they just didn't have their heart in it."

YEARS AGO Walt Kelly, the originator of the lovable comic-strip character Pogo, pictured his little friend fishing in a swamp. By and by a duck comes along and sits down beside Pogo. The duck opens the conversation, "Has you seen my cousin?" Pogo answers, "Your cousin?" "Yes, my cousin. He's migrating north by kiddy car." Pogo asks, "By kiddy car?" "Yep. He's afraid to fly. He's afraid he's gonna fall off." "Then why don't he swim?" Pogo responds. "Well, he don't like to swim 'cause he gets seasick." With a measure of insight, Pogo states, "When your cousin decided to be a duck, he chose the wrong business."

That little comic strip is a "beatitude of life." "Blessed is the duck who, when he decides to be a duck, does what a duck is supposed to do!"

—Haddon Robinson sermon, Ontario Bible College, September 12, 1983

THE LATE PETER MARSHALL, an eloquent speaker and for several years the chaplain of the United States Senate, used to love to tell the story of "the Keeper of the Spring," a quiet forest dweller who lived high above an Austrian village along the eastern slopes of the Alps. The old gentleman had been hired by a young town council to clear away the debris from the pools of water up in the mountain crevices that fed the lovely spring flowing through their town. With faithful, silent regularity, he patrolled the hills, removing the leaves and branches, and wiped away the silt that would otherwise choke and contaminate the fresh flow of water. By and by, the village became a popular attraction for vacationers. Graceful swans floated along the crystal clear spring, the mill-wheels of various businesses located near the water turned day and night, farm-lands were naturally irrigated, and the view from restaurants was picturesque beyond description.

Years passed. One evening the town council met for its semi-annual meeting. As they reviewed the budget, one man's eye caught the salary figure being paid the obscure keeper of the spring. Said the keeper of the purse, "Who is the old man? Why do we keep him year after year? No one ever sees him. For all we know the strange ranger of the hills is doing us no good. He isn't necessary any longer!" By a unanimous vote, they dispensed with the old man's services.

For several weeks nothing changed. By early autumn the trees began to shed their leaves. Small branches snapped off and fell into the pools, hindering the rushing flow of sparkling water. One afternoon someone noticed a slight yellowish-brown tint in the spring. A couple days later the water was much darker. Within another week, a slimy film covered sections of the water along the banks and a foul odor was soon detected. The millwheels moved slower, some finally ground to a halt. Swans left as did the tourists. Clammy fingers of disease and sickness reached deeply into the village.

Quickly, the embarrassed council called a special meeting. Realizing their gross error in judgment, they hired back the old keeper of the spring . . . and within a few weeks the veritable river of life began to clear up. The wheels started to turn, and new life returned to the hamlet in the Alps once again.

—Catherine Marshall, *Mr. Jones, Meet the Master*

DONALD BARNHOUSE tells a terrific story of a young man who went to the employment office of Western Union looking for a job delivering telegrams. The manager said he needed someone to start at once and asked if the young man would be willing to begin right then.

"Well," said the boy, "there's one thing I must warn you about before I get started. I am psychologically so constituted that I cannot stand any scene of unhappiness. I'm only willing to deliver good news. Birth announcements, that's fine. Congratulations for success, fortunes that have been received, promotions, acceptance of marriages—all the joys and bliss news, that I'll deliver. But sickness and death and failure and all of that, that's alien to my nature. I just won't deliver them."

It didn't take the manager very long to say, "I guess I'm still looking for the one that's gonna fill this job, because this responsibility requires that you also announce bad news."

That's the job of one who delivers the gospel. It is wonderful Good News, but it isn't complete until the bad news is also delivered.

—Donald Barnhouse, *Man's Ruin, Romans*, Vol. 1

CHARLIE STEINMETZ was a dwarf and terribly deformed, but what he lacked physically he made up for mentally. Few people knew more about electricity than Mr. Steinmetz. Henry Ford realized this and hired him to build those vast generators that would run their first plant in Dearborn, Michigan. Along came Steinmetz, who, with remarkable genius, put together those vast, wonderful pieces of machinery that make great profit for the Ford Motor Company.

One day, suddenly, without announcement, the place ground to a stop. Ford hired a few ordinary mechanics and a number of hard-working helpers, but no one seemed to be able to find the problem. He finally pressed his friendship with Mr. Steinmetz and asked him to come and do a little repair work. Steinmetz fiddled around with this gauge, tinkered with that motor, tried this button, did a little wiring, tinkered with this switch, and threw the master switch. In a matter of a few hours everything was fixed and the motors were running again.

Within a few days, Steinmetz mailed Ford a bill for $10,000. Henry Ford, though emminently wealthy, balked at paying such an exorbitant amount of money for what appeared to be a little bit of work. And so he wrote a letter to his friend and he included the bill. "Charlie: It seems awfully steep, this $10,000, for a man who for just a little while tinkered around with a few motors." Steinmetz wrote a new bill and sent it back to Mr. Ford, "Henry: For tinkering around with motors, $10; for knowing where to tinker, $9,990."

JOY

THE HABIT of always putting off an experience until you can afford it, or until the time is right, or until you know how to do it is one of the greatest burglars of joy. Be deliberate, but once you've made up your mind—jump in.

—Charles R. Swindoll, *Living on the Ragged Edge*

PIERRE TEILHARD DE CHARDIN, a pivotal Christian thinker of our time, said, "Joy is the surest sign of the presence of God." This Jesuit priest-theologian-anthropologist had a good deal in common with the Presbyterian sages who penned the Westminster Confession of Faith. The bottom line for you and me is simply this: grimness is not a Christian virtue. There are no sad saints. If God really is the center of one's life and being, joy is inevitable. If we have no joy, we have missed the heart of the Good News and our bodies as much as our souls will suffer the consequences.

—Bruce Larson, *There's a Lot More to Health Than Not Being Sick*

JOY IS THE FLAG that flies over the castle of our hearts announcing that the king is in residence today.

—Walter B. Knight, *Knight's Master Book of New Illustrations*

C.S. LEWIS TOLD ME, there is too much solemnity and intensity in dealing with sacred matters, too much speaking in holy tones. The tragic loss in all this pious gamesmanship is to the individual in the pew, who begins to feel that in the midst of the religious razzle-dazzle he cannot get through to the Lord Himself.

We have learned that joy is more than a sense of the comic, more than earthly pleasure, and to a believer even more than what we call happiness. Joy is the enjoyment of God and the good things that come from the hand of God. If our new freedom in Christ is a piece of angel food cake, joy is the frosting. If the Bible gives us the wonderful words of life, joy supplies the music. If the way to heaven turns out to be an arduous steep climb, joy sets up the chair lift.

—Sherwood Wirt, *Jesus, Man of Joy*

JOY IS A WINSOME MAGNET that draws people in because it is one thing they do not have.

WE ARE CHOSEN FOR JOY. However hard the Christian way, it is both in the travelling and in the goal, the way of joy. There is always a joy in doing the right thing. When we evade some duty or some task, when at last we set our hand to it, joy comes to us. The Christian is the man of joy. The Christian is the laughing cavalier of Christ. A gloomy Christian is a contradiction in terms, and nothing in all religious history has done Christianity more harm than its connection with black clothes and long faces.

—William Barclay, *The Gospel of John*, Vol. 2

JUDGMENT

ONE OF THE MOST FREQUENT Bible illustrations of judgment has to do with Sodom and Gomorrah. Twenty-two times it is used in the Bible.

A POET, Friedrich Von Logau, said, "Though the mills of God grind slowly, yet they grind exceedingly small." William Wadsworth Longfellow elaborated and said, "Though the mills of God grind slowly, yet they grind exceedingly small. Though with patience He stands waiting, with exactness He grinds all."

—John Bartlett, *Bartlett's Familiar Quotations*

HE WHO DOES NOT PUNISH EVIL, commands it to be done.

—Leonardo da Vinci

SURELY THIS PHRASE "the wrath of God" is greatly misunderstood. Many think, invariably, of some sort of peeved deity, a kind of cosmic, terrible-tempered Mr. Bang, who indulges in violent, uncontrolled displays of temper when human beings do not do what they ought to do. But such a concept only reveals the limitations of our understanding. The Bible never deals with the wrath of God that way. According to Scriptures, the wrath of God is God's moral integrity. When man refuses to yield himself to God, he creates certain conditions, not only for himself but for others as well, which God has ordained for harm. It is God who makes evil result in sorrow, heartache, injustice, and despair. It is God's way of saying to man, "Now look, you must face the truth. You were made for Me. If you decide that you don't want Me, then you will have to bear the consequences." The absence of God is destructive to human life. That absence is God's wrath. And God cannot withhold it. In His moral integrity, He insists that these things should occur as a result of our disobedience. He sets man's sin and His wrath in the same frame.

—Charles R. Swindoll, *Living Above the Level of Mediocrity*

MY SISTER brought a record home from college many years ago, when I was just an adolescent at home. It was called "God's Trombones." I think the narration was done by Harry Belafonte. "God's Trombones," by James Johnson, originally published in 1927, is seven sermons from the black culture of the twenties. If you have ever heard black preachers, you have heard vivid terms about whatever the subject may be—creation, life, death, or in this case, the judgment day.

The Judgment Day

In that great day,
People, in that great day,
God's a-going to rain down fire.
God's a-going to sit in the middle of the air
To judge the quick and the dead.

Early one of these mornings,
God's a-going to call for Gabriel,
That tall, bright angel, Gabriel;
And God's a-going to say to him: Gabriel,
Blow your silver trumpet,
And wake the living nations.

And Gabriel's going to ask him: Lord,
How loud must I blow it?
And God's a-going to tell him: Gabriel,
Blow it calm and easy.

Then putting one foot on the mountain top,
And the other in the middle of the sea,
Gabriel's going to stand and blow his horn,
And wake the living nations.

Oh-o-oh, sinner,
Where will you stand,
In that great day when God's a-going to rain down fire?
Oh, you gambling man—where will you stand?
You whore-mongering man—where will you stand?
Liars and backsliders—where will you stand,
In that great day when God's a-going to rain down fire?

And God will divide the sheep from the goats,
The one on the right, the other on the left.
And to them on the right God's a-going to say:
Enter into my kingdom.
And those who've come through great tribulations,
And washed their robes in the blood of the Lamb,
They will enter in—
Clothed in spotless white,

And to them on the left God's a-going to say:
Depart from me into everlasting darkness,
Down into the bottomless pit.
And the wicked like lumps of lead will start to fall,
Headlong for seven days and nights they'll fall,
Plumb into the big, black, red-hot mouth of hell,

Too late, sinner! Too late!
Good-bye, sinner! Good-bye!
In hell, sinner! In hell!
Beyond the reach of the love of God.

And I hear a voice, crying, crying:
Time shall be no more!
Time shall be no more!
Time shall be no more!
And the sun will go out like a candle in the wind,

The moon will turn to dripping blood,
The stars will fall like cinders,
And the sea will burn like tar;
And the earth shall melt away and be dissolved,
And the sky will roll up like a scroll.
With the wave of his hand God will blot out time,
And start the wheel of eternity.

Sinner, oh. sinner,
Where will you stand
In that great day when God's a-going to rain down fire?

—James Weldon Johnson, *God's Trombones*

JUSTIFICATION

SOMEONE ONCE TOLD ME, "Justification is the sovereign act of God whereby He declares righteous the believing sinner while he is still in his sinning state." It means that while we were still prone to sin, God saw us in Christ and said, "You're righteous! I declare you to be right in My eyes. You don't have to work to find favor with Me." Grace says, God reached down in Christ, captured us, declared us righteous and said, "You're right from now on in My eyes."

Some people have misused this word and taught that it means "just as if I'd never sinned," taking the little syllables "just-if-ied." That's too shallow. That doesn't say enough. It is, "Although I am terribly sinful, He declared me righteous," not just as if I'd never been sinful.

Let me illustrate it. A couple of friends of mine from the church and I rented a rototiller to replant the backyard for the fourth time. Out there in that dirt, we began to run that rototiller. Dust and dirt and junk went everywhere, and all of it settled on our bodies, so that from head to foot we were really dirty.

We finished up and I walked into the shower and turned on that fresh water. I got all cleaned up and toweled off. I could have walked in front of the mirror and said, "Ah, it's just as if I'd never been dirty." But that wouldn't have adequately conveyed the power and the value of the water and soap. I could otherwise look in the mirror and say, "I was filthy and now I'm clean." That's the difference.

SOMEONE HAS PASSED ALONG THE LEGEND (whether it is fanciful or true, I don't know) that Martin Luther, when he came to see the truth that a person is justified by faith apart from works, was literally staggered under the blow of it. He stepped out of his cell and made his way through the cloistered halls of the monastery and he saw a rope. He was about to fall and he grabbed the rope to support himself. And when he did, of course his weight pulled it, and it was a rope that led to the belfry and rang the chimes in the middle of the night, as if to say to the world, "The just shall live by faith! The just shall live by faith!"

Kk

KINDNESS

SOMETIME WE REAP KINDNESS because we sowed a little of it. I like the way one poet put it.

> I have wept in the night
> For the shortness of sight,
> That to somebody's need made me blind:
> But I never have yet
> Felt a twinge of regret,
> For being a little too kind.
>
> —Anonymous, quoted in John Lawrence, *Down to Earth*

HAVE YOU EVER OFFERED an act of kindness and had it backfire on you? I did that once in one of my rare kind moments. I was on the little jitney that takes you from the car rental to the airport. It was a very crowded little shuttle bus.

I'd gotten on early, and I had a seat right behind the driver. I noticed that among those having to stand with their bags, one or two of these were women. I thought, "That's a shame. I'll offer them a seat." So I stood up and said, "Would you li—" She said, "What's wrong?" I said, "Nothing. Would you like.—" "No, I can stand!" Fine, I'll be glad to let you stand was sort of my feeling.

Now I don't know what it was. Maybe I'd said it the wrong way or perhaps she was of the persuasion that women aren't weak and that they can stand like anybody else. I looked toward the back and saw another woman who looked at me. The fella next to me said, "You can't win." Sometimes trying to show a little kindness backfires.

I LIKE MY SISTER's simple, yet practical interpretation of kindness: Be nice to one another, just be nice. Say nice things to one another.

That best portion of a good man's life,
His little, nameless, unremembered acts
Of kindness and love.

—William Wordsworth

THE ANCIENT PROPHET Micah isn't exactly a household word. Too bad. Though obscure, the man had his stuff together. Eclipsed by the much more famous Isaiah, who ministered among the elite, Micah took God's message to the streets. . . .

Micah states exactly what many, to this day, wonder about pleasing God. Teachers and preachers have made it so sacrificial, so complicated, so extremely difficult. To them, God is virtually impossible to please. Therefore, religion has become a series of long, drawn-out, deeply painful acts designed to appease this peeved Deity in the sky who takes delight in watching us squirm.

Micah erases the things on the entire list, replacing the complicated possibilities with one of the finest definitions of simple faith:

He has told you, O man, what is good;
And what does the LORD require of you
But to do justice, to love kindness,
And to walk humbly with your God? (Mic. 6:8)

God does not look for big-time, external displays. . . . What is required? Slow down and read the list aloud: To do justice. . . . to love kindness. . . . and to walk humbly with your God. Period.

—Charles R. Swindoll, *The Finishing Touch*

DR. HARRY EVANS of Trinity College, Deerfield, Illinois, has a sign in his office that reads, "Kindness Spoken Here."

AS GANDHI STEPPED ABOARD A TRAIN one day, one of his shoes slipped off and landed on the track. He was unable to retrieve it as the train was moving. To the amazement of his companions, Gandhi calmly took off his other shoe and threw it back along the track to land close to the first. Asked by a fellow passenger why he did so, Gandhi smiled. "The poor man who finds the shoe lying on the track," he replied, "will now have a pair he can use."

—*The Little, Brown Book of Anecdotes*

KNOWLEDGE

(Also see *Bible, Books, Education, Wisdom*)

THERE'S A STORY OF A TEACHER teaching a group of fifth graders. He looked around the room, and said, "Does anybody here understand electricity?" One rather anxious little boy named Jimmy, half way down the middle aisle, pushed his hand up in the air and said, "I understand electricity." The teacher looked at him and said, "Jimmy, would you explain electricity to the class?" And he suddenly put his hand over his face and he said, "Oh, last night I knew, but this morning I've forgotten." The teacher, with tongue in cheek, said, "Now this is a tragedy. The only person in all history who ever understood electricity and this morning he forgot it."

—Billy Graham, *The Holy Spirit*

SOME COLLEGIANS THINK manual labor is the president of Mexico—until they graduate. Suddenly the light dawns. Reality frowns. And that sheltered, brainy, fair-skinned, squint-eyed scholar who has majored in medieval literature and minored in Latin comes of age. He experiences a strange sensation deep within his abdomen two weeks after framing his diploma. Hunger. Remarkable motivation accompanies this feeling.

His attempts at finding employment prove futile. Those places that have an opening don't really need a guy with a master's in medieval lit. They can't even spell it. Who cares if a truck driver understands European poetry from the twelfth century? Or what does it matter if the fella stocking the shelves at Safeway can give you the ninth letter in the Latin alphabet? When it comes to landing a job, most employers are notoriously pragmatic and unsophisticated. They are looking for people who have more than academic, gray wrinkles between their ears. They really couldn't care less about how much a guy or gal knows. What they want is someone who can put to use the knowledge that's been gained, whether the field is geology or accounting, engineering or plumbing, physics or barbering, journalism or welding.

Just now finishing school? Looking for a job?. . . . Remember this—dreams are great and visions are fun. But in the final analysis, when the bills come due, they'll be paid by manual labor. Labor. . . . hard work forged in the furnace of practicality.

A SCIENTIST WAS USING THE INDUCTIVE METHOD to observe the characteristics of a flea. Plucking a leg off the flea, he ordered, "Jump!"

The flea promptly jumped.

Taking another leg off, the scientist again commanded, "Jump!"

The flea jumped again.

The scientist continued this process until he came to the sixth and final leg. By now the flea was having a little more difficulty jumping, but it was still trying.

The scientist pulled the final leg off and again ordered the flea to jump. But the flea didn't respond.

The scientist raised his voice and demanded, "Jump!" Again the flea failed to respond.

For a third time the scientist shouted at the top of his lungs, "Jump!" But the hapless flea lay motionless.

The scientist then made the following observation in his notebook: "When you remove the legs from a flea, it loses its sense of hearing."

—Howard G. Hendricks, *Living by the Book*

THE HUMAN MIND is a fabulous computer. As a matter of fact, no one has ever been able to design a computer as intricate and efficient as the human mind. Consider this: your brain is capable of recording 800 memories per second for seventy-five years without ever getting tired. . . .

I have heard some persons complain that their brain is too tired to get involved in a program of Scripture memorization. I have news for them—the body can get tired, but the brain never does. A human being doesn't use more than two percent of his brain power, scientists tell us. And, of course, some demonstrate this fact more obviously than others. The point is, the brain is capable of an incredible amount of work and it retains everything it takes in. You never really forget anything: you just don't recall it. Everything is on permanent file in your brain.

—Earl D. Radmacher, *You and Your Thoughts*

LV

LEADERSHIP
(Also see *Influence*)

LEADERSHIP IS NECESSARY. Leaders are the ones who dream the dreams. Leaders are the ones who are the visionaries. They are the ones that have to answer the hardest questions within the outfit. They deal with the most complicated of issues. There is both risk and exhilaration in the full view that they have in mind, for they are the ones that are out front and continually address the perspective, where we are going.

Even a pack of Eskimo dogs, when hitched to a sled, needs a leader. The main difference between the dog that leads and those who follow is the scenery. The one out front has a much better view.

_____

THE LEADER'S TRUE WORTH may sometimes be measured by the amount of time he could remain dead in his office without anyone noticing it.

—W. J. Redden

_____

WE CANNOT THINK RIGHTLY of God until we begin to think of Him as always being there, and there first. Joshua had this to learn. He had been so long the servant of God's servant Moses, and had with such assurance received God's word at his mouth, that Moses and the God of Moses had become blended in his thinking, so blended that he could hardly separate the two thoughts; by association they always appeared together in Joshua's mind. Now Moses is dead, and lest the young Joshua be struck down with despair God spoke to him with assurance, "As I was with Moses, so I will be with you." Moses was dead, but the God of Moses still lived. Nothing had changed; nothing had been lost. Nothing of God dies when a man of God dies.

—A. W. Tozer, *The Divine Conquest*

GOD DID NOT RAISE ME UP to lead the liquidation of an empire. I promise blood, sweat, toil and tears but we will never give in.

—Winston Churchill

SIR WINSTON CHURCHILL at a cabinet meeting during World War II was encouraging no surrender. He said, "I find it rather inspiring [to stand alone]. Nothing in life is so exhilarating as to be shot at without result."

— *Bartlett's Familiar Quotations*

WHEN I WAS SERVING A CHURCH in Waltham, Massachusetts, there was a neighboring church with an amazing history. It had done a job for Christ that was virtually unparalleled in that area. It had been pastored by a unique fella who is now the president of a school on the East Coast. But when he became the pastor, the church was a terrible mess. People sat in the last three rows of the church, and it's a *long* building. First thing he did was pick up the pulpit and carry it down the aisle and put it down in front of the first pew where they were sitting.

Historians tell me, as they made a study of that interesting work, he kept having to move the pulpit back, Sunday after Sunday, until finally he was almost in the choir loft, with people everywhere. And he preached the Word, and he faithfully labored under tremendous opposition. He was bruised and bloody. But God graciously lifted him from that situation and took him to a fantastic school that has just gone right on under his guidance.

He was followed by a retaliatory man, a fighter—a brilliant man with two doctor's degrees. He had experience, he had traveled, he had been an officer in the military. But as someone put it, he could have begun to move his pulpit back, until finally, do you know what that led to? He hired police and guards to guard who would play the instruments and who would be allowed entrance and exit from the church. And one by one, through one public debate and argument and retaliatory action after another, the church emptied. And I thought as I drove by and would see six, eight, at the most ten cars, I thought God could write "Ichabod" across the door of that church. Sure, the pastor won the arguments, but he lost the battle.

A QUALITY WHICH IS PROMINENT IN EVERY LEADER is a strongly developed sense of dominant purpose and direction in life. He is one who knows with greater than average strength of conviction what he wants to get done and where he wants to go. The world stands aside to let pass the man who knows where he is going.

—Ordway Tead, *The Art of Leadership*

ON FEBRUARY 12, 1959, the one-hundred-fiftieth anniversary of the birthday of Abraham Lincoln, the distinguished poet and historian Carl Sandburg was invited to Washington, D.C. to speak. Before a joint session of congress and assembled diplomatic corps, the astute, eloquent student of Lincoln held the attention of everyone as he portrayed a very great leader with very human characteristics. Calling his speech, appropriately, "Man of Steel and Velvet," Sandburg helped everyone see that a respected leader can be both capable and vulnerable. The mixture may be rare, but when it is there it is truly effective.

Not often in the story of mankind does a man arrive on earth who is both steel and velvet, who is as hard as rock and soft as drifting fog, who holds in his heart and mind the paradox of terrible storm and peace unspeakable and perfect. . . .

While the war winds howled, he insisted that the Mississippi was one river meant to belong to one country. . . .

While the luck of war wavered and broke and came again, as generals failed and campaigns were lost, he held enough forces . . . together to raise new armies and supply them, until generals were found who made war as victorious war has always been made, with terror, frightfulness, destruction . . . valor and sacrifice past words of man to tell.

In the mixed shame and blame of the immense wrongs of two crashing civilizations, often with nothing to say, he said nothing, slept not at all, and on occasions he was seen to weep in a way that made weeping appropriate, decent, majestic.

—Charles R. Swindoll, *Leadership*

THE GREAT DANGER of the Christian leader is intellectual sloth and the shut mind. The Christian must be a thinker or he fails in his task. And to be a Christian thinker is to be an adventurous thinker so long as life lasts. It is all too true that most of us have the same things conquer us year in and year out, that we are the victims of the same faults, the same character failures. We fail for the same reasons that, as year succeeds year, we are no further on.

—William Barclay, *The Letters to Timothy, Titus, and Philemon*

THE MAN WHO IS IMPATIENT with weakness will be defective in his leadership. The evidence of our strength lies not in streaking ahead but in a willingness to adapt our stride to the slower pace of our weaker brethren, while not forfeiting our lead. If we run too far ahead, we lose our power to influence.

—J. Oswald Sanders, *Spiritual Leadership*

AS FAR AS LEADERSHIP TRAITS are concerned, Nehemiah was not that different from outstanding people whose names are far more familiar to us. Our nation's twenty-sixth president, for example, was a hard-charging leader. Throughout his days in office Theodore Roosevelt was either hated or admired. An ardent admirer once exclaimed to him, "Mr. Roosevelt, you are a great man!" In characteristic honesty he replied, "No, Teddy Roosevelt is simply a plain, ordinary man—highly motivated." It's safe to say that his answer describes most great leaders.

—Charles R. Swindoll, *Hand Me Another Brick*

WHAT DO WE MEAN when we use the word *leadership?* If I were asked to define it in one single word, the word would be *influence.*

The late President Harry Truman often referred to leaders as people who can get others to do what they don't want to do—and make them like doing it.

—J. Oswald Sanders, *Spiritual Leadership*

I WILL PAY MORE for the ability to deal with people than any other ability under the sun.

—John D. Rockefeller, quoted in Ted Engstrom, *The Making of a Christian Leader*

LEADERSHIP IS THE CAPACITY and will to rally men and women to a common purpose, and having the character which inspires confidence.

—Bernard L. Montgomery, *Memoirs of Field Marshal Montgomery*

IF I CAN'T PUT MY FEET ON THE DESK and look out the window and think without an agenda, I may be managing Yale, but I won't be leading it.

—Benno Schmidt Jr., *New York Times*, December 11, 1985

DR. NICHOLAS MURRAY BUTLER, president of Columbia University, divides the world into three parts: Those who make things happen, those who watch what's happening and those who don't know what's happening.

—Bill Bright, *Revolution Now*

LEGALISM

(Also see *Cults, Religious People*)

ONE OF THE MOST SERIOUS PROBLEMS facing the orthodox Christian church today is the problem of legalism. One of the most serious problems facing the church in Paul's day was the problem of legalism. In every day it is the same. Legalism wrenches the joy of the Lord from the Christian believer, and with the joy of the Lord goes his power for vital worship and vibrant service. Nothing is left but cramped, somber, dull, and listless profession. The truth is betrayed, and the glorious name of the Lord becomes a synonym for a gloomy kill-joy. The Christian under law is a miserable parody of the real thing.

—S. Lewis Johnson, "The Paralysis of Legalism," *Bibliotheca Sacra*, April–June 1963

SEVERAL MONTHS AGO I was conversing with a man I greatly admire. He is a Christian leader in a position that carries with it heavy and extensive responsibility. He said he was grieved on behalf of a missionary family he and his wife had known for years. The legalism they had encountered again and again on the mission field from fellow missionaries was so petty, so unbelievably small-minded, they had returned to the States and no longer planned to remain career missionaries. He said it was over a jar of peanut butter. I thought he was joking, to which he responded, "No, it's no joke at all." I could hardly believe the story.

The particular place they were sent to serve the Lord did not have access to peanut butter. This particular family happened to enjoy peanut butter a great deal. Rather creatively, they made arrangements with some of their friends in the States to send them peanut butter every now and then so they could enjoy it with their meals. The problem is they didn't know until they started receiving their supply of peanut butter that the other missionaries considered it a mark of spirituality that you not have peanut butter with your meals. I suppose the line went something like this: "We believe since we can't get peanut butter here, we should give it up for the cause of Christ," or some such nonsense. A basis of spirituality was "bearing the cross" of living without peanut butter.

The young family didn't buy into that line of thinking. Their family kept getting regular shipments of peanut butter. They didn't flaunt it, they just enjoyed it in the privacy of their own home. Pressure began to intensify. You would expect adult missionaries to be big enough to let others eat what they pleased, right? Wrong. The legalism was so petty, the pressure got so intense and the exclusive treatment so unfair, it finished them off spiritually. They finally had enough. Unable to continue against the mounting pressure, they packed it in and were soon homeward bound, disillusioned and probably a bit cynical. What we have here is a classic modern-day example of a group of squint-eyed legalists spying out and attacking another's liberty. Not even missionaries are exempted.

—Charles R. Swindoll, *The Grace Awakening*

I HEARD ABOUT A FELLOW who attended a legalistic college where students were to live according to very strict rules. They weren't supposed to do any work on Sundays. None! Guess what? He spied on his wife and caught her hanging out a few articles of clothing she washed on Sunday afternoon. Are you ready? The guy turned in his wife to the authorities! I'll bet she was fun to live with the next day or two.

—Charles R. Swindoll, *The Grace Awakening*

I KNOW A MAN approaching sixty years of age today who is still haunted by the memory of being raised by hypocritical parents. It has taken him most of his adult life to face the full truth that he was emotionally and spiritually abused by their deception. Throughout his childhood his family attended a church where they were taught you shouldn't go to the movies. This was so firmly enforced that in Sunday church services people would be called to come forward to an altar and confess that they had done that or some other "sins." The problem is, his family went to movies on Friday or Saturday night, always in secret. But they made it very clear that he shouldn't say anything about it. They drilled it into him, "Keep your mouth shut." Here he is, a little boy, being lectured on the way home from the theater, "Don't tell anybody on Sunday that we did this." Of course, they went to see the film miles away from the church so church folks wouldn't know. Not until recently has the man come to realize how damaging that hypocrisy was to his walk with Christ.

LEGALISM HAS NO PITY on people. Legalism makes my opinion your burden, makes my opinion your boundary, makes my opinion your obligation.

—Max Lucado, *Up Words,* May 1993

NOTHING WILL KEEP a Christian more immature than trying to keep a list.

———————————

IN A CHURCH a woman was knitting, waiting for the service to start. She had been there forty-five minutes. Some other dear woman said, "Oh, honey, we don't do that in the house of God." Well, what in the world do you do for an hour if you come waiting for a church service to start? Another was boning up for a test in college, and somebody said, "You know, here we read the Bible."

———————————

AROUND 1928, I led a Bible conference at Montrose, Pennsylvania, for about two hundred young people and a few older people. One day two old ladies complained that some of the girls were not wearing stockings. These ladies wanted me to rebuke them. Looking them straight in the eye, I said, "The Virgin Mary never wore stockings." They gasped and said, "She didn't?" I answered, "In Mary's time, stockings were unknown. So far as we know, they were first worn by prostitutes in Italy in the fifteenth century, when the Renaissance began. Later, a lady of the nobility scandalized the people by wearing stockings at a court ball. Before long everyone in the upper classes was wearing stockings, and by Queen Victoria's time stockings had become the badge of the prude." These ladies, who were hold-overs from the Victorian epoch, had no more to say. I did not rebuke the girls for not wearing stockings. A year or two afterward, most girls in the United States were going without stockings in summer and nobody thought anything about it.

Nor do I believe that this led toward disintegration of moral standards in the United States. Times were changing, and the step away from Victorian legalism was all for the better.

—Donald Barnhouse, *Let Me Illustrate*

———————————

WHEN I WAS A BOY, I grew up in a small congregation in a little town. There was a somewhat affluent man who belonged to the church. All the rest of us were poor as turkeys, but he was just one notch above the poverty of the rest of us, so he shined. He was the president of our little state bank in the town, a bank that later went bankrupt and defunct. He dressed nattily and spoke like a cultured man.

One day they hailed him before the church and accused him of dancing. The church was called into council. You never saw such a dogfight in your life.

This man went up to the preacher and slapped him in the face. There I was, a little boy sitting in the church and looking at all that going on, all that acrimonious castigation. They turned the banker out of the church. It tore the little church to shreds.

Now, I'm not saying here whether they should have turned him out or not, but I can tell you how I felt about it as a little boy. As I sat there in the church and listened to the people of the church bring charges against the banker for dancing and all the things that they said to him about him, and all that went on in that session, then they finally voted him out, I saw the sad repercussion in the hearts of angry people. The tragedy made an indelible impression upon me. When I looked at it as a little boy I wondered about those that turned him out, if they were any better than the one they turned out. Maybe he should have turned them out!

—W. A. Criswell, *Expository Sermons on Galatians*

SUPPOSE WE BEGAN A FAMILY VACATION in a new car. We filled it with gas, put our family in it, and took off. The car operated beautifully; the engine purred, and we zipped along at 55, maybe 60 miles an hour down the highway.

However, the further we got along the way, long before the need to fill up with gas again, we noticed more and more people were pushing their cars. They'd wave at us as we'd go by and we would wave at them and keep driving.

Finally we came to a rest stop 250 miles from L.A., out of the smog, out in the clear country. While we were stopped to relax a little, somebody who had been pushing his car comes in the same rest stop and asks, "Hi, how are you doin'?" We reply, "Fine." The car-pusher asks, "Where are you goin'?" "Well, we're takin' a trip up north. We're gonna get up into Oregon and enjoy the beautiful country." He then asks us, "Well, why are you driving? We're all pushing."

"Yes, we noticed that, but we don't understand why," we remarked back to him. "Oh, if you push your car the air stays clean. It makes a lot of sense to push your car. We used to rely on gasoline a lot, but no longer. Now that we really understand what it's all about, we're pushers. We're not drivers," was his explanation.

And so you let your car run out of gas. All the family gets out and we begin to push this beautiful, lovely, comfortable car to our vacation site and back.

That's what Paul is writing about in Galatians 3:2–3. In essence, he says, "You're telling me that you who began with a full tank of the Spirit are now pushing your way through life? You're telling me that that's an advantageous message? I'm telling you, it's a degenerating message. That means that Christ, the miracle-working One, now He lays back and He watches you as you (so-called) 'pull off' a spiritual life that you never had before. Whom are you kidding? Cars are made to drive, not push."

THE ISSUE OF LEGALISM can be illustrated by a person who questions another guy's spending of his money. Here is the legalist: "Stop me if I'm wrong, George, but haven't you—uh, been spending a lot of money on a car?" George, the strong, answers, "Nope (sounds like a guy that has liberty doesn't it?), nope." "No? You don't think the money could be better used, say in the leprosy fund?"

—Fritz Ridenour, *How to Be a Christian without Being Religious*

LEISURE

I've wasted an hour one morning beside a mountain stream.
I seized a cloud from the sky above and fashioned myself a dream.
In the hush of the early twilight, far from the haunts of men,
I wasted a summer evening and fashioned my dream again.
Wasted? Perhaps. Folks say so who never have walked with God.
When lanes are purple with lilacs or yellow with goldenrod.
But I have found strength for my labors in that one short evening hour.
I have found joy and contentment, I have found peace and power.
My dreaming has left me a treasure, a hope that is strong and true.
From wasted hours I have built my life and found my faith anew.

—Tim Hansel, *When I Relax I Feel Guilty*

LEISURE IS AN ATTITUDE OF MIND and a condition of the soul that fosters the capacity to perceive the reality of the world. . . . In our Western world, total labor has vanquished leisure. Unless we regain the art of silence and insight, the ability for nonactivity, unless we substitute true leisure for our hectic amusements, we will destroy our culture and ourselves. Culture depends for its very existence on leisure. And leisure, in its turn, is not possible unless it has a durable, living link with divine worship.

—Josef Pieper, *Leisure: The Basis of Culture*

THOSE OF US WHO ENJOY riding on two-wheel vehicles will tell you that the reason there is such a thrill in it is that you feel so free.

"GRAB HERE, AMIGO." I grabbed.

"Hold tight, *por favor.*" I held on.

"When you come back toward shore and I blow whistle, you pull cord *pronto!*"

Within seconds I was airborne. A loud "whoosh," a long, strong jerk, and I was 300 feet or so above the picturesque beach at Puerto Vallarta. You guessed it . . . my first try at parasailing. Four-and-a-half minutes of indescribable ecstasy sandwiched between a few seconds of sheer panic. Talk about fun!

Above me was the bluest, clearest sky you could imagine. Behind me was a full-blown, dazzling red and white parachute. Down in front, attached to my harness and a long yellow rope, was a speed boat at full throttle. Below, the turquoise sea, various sailing vessels, a long row of hotels, sunbathers the size of ants, and one beautiful lady wondering if she would soon be a widow.

The wind whipped through my hair and tore at my swimsuit. But the sensation of flying in silence with nothing surrounding me besides a few nylon straps was absolutely breathtaking. The spectacular view plus the enjoyable feelings of soaring like a seagull introduced me to an adventurous freedom rarely encountered by earth dwellers.

I must confess, for those few minutes I lost all concern for things that otherwise occupy my attention. Self-consciousness vanished. Worries fled away. Demands and deadlines were forgotten, strangely erased by the swishing sound of the wind. *It was glorious!* I don't believe that as an adult I've ever felt quite so free, so unencumbered, so completely removed from others' expectations and my own responsibilities.

Such are the benefits of leisure. True, authentic, carefree relaxation. The kind Jesus had in mind when He encouraged His twelve to come apart and rest awhile. How easy to forget the necessity of recreation; how quick we are to discount its value! In our neurotic drive for more, more, more, we ignore how uncreative and boring we become. All roots and no wings has the makings of Dullsville, U.S.A. Life closes in and takes the shape of a chore instead of a challenge. Fun and laughter, originally designed by God to remove the friction of monotony from the machinery of existence, begin to be viewed as enemies instead of friends. Intensity, that ugly yet persuasive twin of hurry, convinces us we haven't the right to relax. We must not take time for leisure, we can't afford such rootless, risky luxury. Its message is loud, logical, sensible, strong, *and wrong.*

We *do* need relief. We *must* discover ways to loosen the strings periodically and fly. To quote the venerable prophet, Vance Havner, "If we don't come apart, we *will* come apart."

Take it from a rookie parasailer—go for it! Stop thinking *"mañana."* Grab here. Hold on tight, *amigo.*

—Charles R. Swindoll, *Growing Strong in the Seasons of Life*

ARNOLD TOYNBEE was interviewed and asked, "Would the abolition of poverty ensure that America's civilization would continue to grow and be dynamic?" "No," he replied. "There is more to it than that in the age of automation. I think the essential question is what Americans do with their leisure."

—Billy Graham, *World Aflame*

IF I HAD MY LIFE TO LIVE OVER again I'd try to make more mistakes next time.

I would relax, I would limber up, I would be sillier than I have been this trip.

I know of very few things I would take seriously. I would take more trips.

I would be crazier. I would climb more mountains, swim more rivers, and watch more sunsets.

I would do more walking and looking. I would eat more ice cream and less beans.

I would have more actual troubles, and fewer imaginary ones.

You see, I'm one of those people who live life prophylactically and sensibly hour after hour, day after day. Oh, I've had my moments, and if I had to do it over again I'd have more of them.

In fact, I'd try to have nothing else, just moments, one after another, instead of living so many years ahead each day.

I've been one of those people who never go anywhere without a thermometer, a hot-water bottle, a gargle, a raincoat, aspirin, and a parachute.

If I had to do it over again I would go places, do things, and travel lighter than I have.

If I had my life to live over I would start barefooted earlier in the spring and stay that way later in the fall.

I would play hooky more. I wouldn't make such good grades, except by accident.

I would ride on more merry-go-rounds. I'd pick more daisies.

—Tim Hansel, *When I Relax I Feel Guilty*

LIES

(Also see *Deceit*)

I LOVE THE ANSWER the little boy gave to his mother when she asked, "What is a lie, honey?" He said, "Mother, a lie is an abomination to the Lord, but a very present help in time of need." At times it seems like it's a very present help, but it'll backfire on you and it'll turn blessing into cursing and you'll live to hate it.

—Paul E. Holdcraft, *Snappy Stories That Preachers Tell*

THE DIFFERENCE BETWEEN A PERSON WHO TELLS THE TRUTH and tells
a lie is that the liar's gotta have a better memory.

—Mark Twain, quoted in Burton Stevenson, *The Home Book of Proverbs, Maxims, and Familiar Phrases*

A SALESMAN KNOCKED on the door of a rundown apartment house in a low-
rent district. The mother didn't want to talk to the guy, so she told her little boy
to tell him she couldn't come to the door because she was in the bathtub. Her
son answered the door this way: "We ain't got no bathtub, but Mom told me to
tell you she's in it."

—Jerry White, *Honesty, Morality, and Conscience*

BACK IN THE DAYS when kids traveled on trains to get somewhere with their
parents, they didn't charge for kids that were five or under. And so this six-year-
old fellow was told by his mother, as they were carrying their bags to the train,
"Tell 'em you're five." The little boy frowned and he got on the train and sat
down. And the conductor came by and said, "How old are you, son?" And he
says, "Ah, five." So he didn't pay anything. His mother paid her fare and the conductor left.

The conductor came back a couple of hours later just to talk to him—
rubbed his hand in the little fellow's hair and said, "Well, how are you gettin'
along?" The boy answered, "Really good." The conductor continued their chat
and said, "Let's see, when you gonna be six?" And the little boy said, "About the
time I get off this train I'm gonna be six."

The Everlasting Gospel

This Life's dim Windows of the Soul
Distort the Heavens from Pole to Pole.
And lead you to Believe a Lie
When you see with not thro the Eye.

—William Blake, *The Poetry and Prose of William Blake*

LIVING

YOU CAN LIVE ON BLAND FOOD so as to avoid an ulcer, drink no tea or coffee or other stimulants in the name of health, go to bed early and stay away
from night life, avoid all controversial subjects so as never to give offense, mind

your own business and avoid involvement in other people's problems, spend money only on necessities and save all you can. You can still break your neck in the bathtub, and it will serve you right.

—Eileen Guder, *God, But I'm Bored*

LIFE IS EITHER a daring experience or nothing at all.

—Helen Keller

A YOUNG BUSINESS WOMAN was approached by a real estate agent who wanted to sell her a home. "A home? I was born in a hospital, educated in a boarding school, courted in a car, married in church. We eat in restaurants, spend our mornings playing golf, and spend our afternoons playing bridge at the club. Evenings we go to the movies, and when I die I'm going to be buried from a funeral home. I don't need a home; all I need is a garage!"

—Albert Stauderman, *Let Me Illustrate*

Life passes like a flash of lightning
Whose blaze barely lasts long enough to see.
While the earth and the sky stand still forever
How swiftly changing time flies across man's face.
O you who sit over your full cup and do not drink,
Tell me, for whom are you still waiting?

—Hermann Hesse, *Klingsor's Last Summer*

MOST MEN IN THIS WORLD live out their lives in quiet desperation.

—Henry David Thoreau

IN ONE OF Charles Schulz's famous "Peanuts" cartoons, Lucy is philosophizing and Charlie is listening.

"Charlie Brown," she begins, "life is a lot like a deck chair. Some place it to see where they've been. And some so they can see where they are at the present."

Charlie sighs, "I can't even get mine unfolded."

—Michael Green, *Illustrations for Biblical Preaching*

ARE YOU ENJOYING LIFE NOW, or have you put all that on "hold"? For most people, life has become a grim marathon of misery, an endurance test full of frowns, whines, groans, and sighs. And perhaps that explains why so many who were once close to them have a tendency to drift away. Can you think of anyone who would rather spend a lot of time with those who have stopped enjoying life? They'd probably rather invest their hours in a pet, an animal that can't even talk, than in someone who resembles a depressing, dark rain cloud.

In his work *Leaves of Grass,* poet Walt Whitman confessed that was true of him:

> I think I could turn and live with animals, they are so
>   placid and self-contained.
> I stand and look at them long and long.
> They do not sweat and whine about their condition.
> They do not lie awake in the dark and weep for their sins,
> They do not make me sick discussing their duty to God,
> Not one is dissatisfied, not one is demented with the
>   mania of owning things,
> Not one kneels to another, nor to his kind that lived
>   thousands of years ago,
> Not one is respectable or unhappy over the whole earth.

Maybe that explains the little bumper sticker, "Have you hugged your horse today?" That used to make me smile; now I understand. Sometimes it's easier to hug a horse than it is to stay close to another person. When you get next to a horse, it never says, "Man, have I had a rotten day!" or, "I'm depressed today." So if we don't want to drive others away with our groans and moans, we need to learn how to enjoy life.

—Charles R. Swindoll, *Living on the Ragged Edge*

ONE OF MY MENTORS once declared, "Much of our activity these days is nothing more than a cheap anesthetic to deaden the pain of an empty life."

WHEN I WAS A CHILD, a black fellow served my granddad all through his life. His name was Coats. He passed much of his wisdom on to this little cotton-headed kid when I was standing out there by the barbecue pit which he maintained. He put his leathery hand on my head and shook it. I remember that like it was yesterday. And he said, "Little Charles, brother, the trouble with life is that it's so daily."

Festus

We live in deeds, not in years, in thoughts, not breaths;
In feelings, not in figures on a dial.
We should count time by heart-throbs. He most lives
Who thinks most, feels the noblest, acts the best.
And he whose heart beats quickest lives the longest.
Life's but a means unto an end; that end—God.

—Philip Bailey, quoted in *Handbook of Preaching Resources from Literature*

EVERY MAN OUGHT TO BE INQUISITIVE through every hour of his great adventure down to the day when he shall no longer cast a shadow in the sun.

—Frank Colby

COUNTRY-WESTERN SINGER Glen Campbell cut a hit record several years ago entitled "Gentle on My Mind." Like all ballads it tells a story. This one is about a man who longs to be free. He wants a life that is uncluttered with irritating things like binding contracts and lifelong commitments. He's satisfied to stop off for a night or two, but he doesn't want anyone to hassle him with talk of a permanent relationship. As in another popular song, he's "gotta be free"; it's enough for him just knowing that the "door is always open" and the "path is free to walk." That's sufficient.

Woven through the lyrics of that same piece is an interesting expression most of us can remember. He mentions again and again "the back roads of my memory" that keep things "gentle on my mind." Looking back over his shoulder with a superficial shrug, the playboy-cowboy refuses all attempts others make to tie him down. Not even a wife and a houseful of kids—*his* kids—can anchor him down—that wouldn't be "gentle." He's on a search for another path, another pleasure, another back road that will somehow satisfy. You get the distinct impression he will never find what he's looking for.

Whether it's in a song we like to sing or in a book we like to read, most of us have entertained thoughts of pursuing a few of those back roads, especially when we feel like we're just grinding out an existence today.

James Dobson colors "the straight life" as relentlessly drab.

The straight life for a homemaker is washing dishes three hours a day; it is cleaning sinks and scouring toilets and waxing floors; it is chasing toddlers and mediating fights between preschool siblings. (One mother said she had raised three "tricycle motors" and they had worn her out.) The straight life is driving your station wagon to school and back twenty-three times per week; it is grocery shopping and baking cupcakes for the class Halloween party. The straight life eventually means becoming the parent of an ungrateful teenager, which I assure you is no job for sissies. (It's difficult to let your adolescent find himself—especially when you know he isn't even looking!) Certainly, the straight life for the homemaker can be an exhausting experience at times.

The straight life for a man is not much simpler. It is pulling your tired frame out of bed, five days a week, fifty weeks out of the year. It is earning a two-week vacation in August, and choosing a trip that will please the kids. The straight life is spending your money wisely when you'd rather indulge in a new whatever; it is taking your son bike riding on Saturday when you want so badly to watch the ball game; it is cleaning out the garage on your day off after working sixty hours the prior week. The straight life is coping with head colds and engine tune-ups and crab grass and income-tax forms; it is taking your family to church on Sunday, when you've heard every idea the minister has to offer; it is giving a portion of your income to God's work when you already wonder how ends will meet. The straight life for the ordinary, garden-variety husband and father is everything I have listed and more . . . much more.

The good life—the one that truly satisfies—exists only when we stop wanting a better one. It is the condition of savoring what is rather than longing for what might be. The itch for things, the lust for more—so brilliantly injected by those who peddle them—is a virus draining our souls of contentment. Have you noticed? A man never earns enough. A woman is never beautiful enough. Clothes are never fashionable enough. Cars are never nice enough. Gadgets are never modern enough. Houses are never furnished enough. Food is never fancy enough. Relationships are never romantic enough. Life is never full enough.

Satisfaction comes when we step off the escalator of desire and say, "This is enough. What I have will do. What I make of it is up to me and my vital union with the living Lord."

That, in essence, is the message Solomon announced in Ecclesiastes. Honestly now, do you believe it?

—James Dobson, *Straight Talk to Men and Their Wives*

WE HUMANS CANNOT BEAR very much reality.

—T. S. Eliot

The Rock

The endless cycle of idea and action,
Endless invention, endless experiment,
Brings knowledge of motion, but not of stillness;
Knowledge of speech, but not of silence;
Knowledge of words, and ignorance of the Word.
All our knowledge brings us nearer to our ignorance,
All our ignorance brings us nearer to death,
But nearness to death no nearer to GOD.
Where is the Life we have lost in living?
Where is the wisdom we have lost in knowledge?
Where is the knowledge we have lost in information?
The cycles of Heaven in twenty centuries
Bring us farther from GOD and nearer to the Dust.

—T. S. Eliot, quoted in Donald Kauffman, *Baker's Pocket Treasury of Verse*

THE BASIC FACT ABOUT HUMAN EXPERIENCE is not that it is a tragedy, but that it is a bore. It is not that it is so predominantly painful, but that it is lacking in any sense.

—H. L. Mencken, quoted in Charles R. Swindoll, *Living on the Ragged Edge*

Lord of all pots and pans and things,
        Since I've no time to be
A saint by doing lovely things,
        Or watching late with Thee,
Or dreaming in the dawnlight,
        Or storming heaven's gates,
Make me a saint by getting meals
        And washing up the plates.

—William Barclay, *The Gospel of Luke*

LONELINESS

AFTER MORE THAN FORTY YEARS OF MARRIAGE, a woman's husband suddenly died. For several months she sat alone in her house with the shades pulled and the doors locked. Finally she decided she needed to do something about her situation. The loneliness was killing her.

She remembered that her husband had a friend who owned a nice pet store—a pet might be good company. So she dropped in one afternoon to look over the selection. She looked at dogs, cats, goldfish—even snakes! Nothing seemed quite right. She told the store owner she wanted a pet that could be a real companion—"almost like another human being in the house."

Suddenly he thought of one of his prized parrots. He showed her the colorful bird.

"Does it talk?"

"Absolutely—a real chatterbox. Everybody who comes in the store is astounded by this parrot's friendly disposition and wide vocabulary. That's why it's so expensive."

"Sold!" She bought the expensive parrot and hauled it home in a large, elegant cage. At last she had a companion she could talk to, who could answer back. Perfect!

But there was a problem. A full week passed without the bird's saying one word. Beginning to worry, she dropped by the pet shop.

"How's the parrot doing? Quite a talker, huh?"

"Not one word. I haven't been able to get a sound out of that bird. I'm worried!"

"Well, did you buy a *mirror* when you got the parrot and the cage last week?"

"Mirror? No. There's no mirror in the cage."

"That's your problem. A parrot needs a mirror. It's funny, but while looking at itself, a parrot starts to feel comfortable. In no time it will begin to talk." So she bought the mirror and put it into the cage.

Time passed, still nothing. Each day the woman talked to the bird, but not a peep came out of its beak. For hours on end she would talk as the parrot stared in silence. Another week passed without a word. By now she was really getting worried.

"The parrot isn't talking," she told the pet store owner. "I'm worried. All that money, the mirror—and still nothing."

"Say, did you buy a *ladder* when you got the cage?"

"A ladder? No. I didn't know it needed a ladder. Will that make it talk?"

"Works like a charm. The parrot will look in the mirror and get a little exercise, climbing up and down this ladder several times. Before long you won't believe what you hear. Trust me, you need a ladder."

She bought the ladder and put it into the cage next to the mirror . . . and waited. And waited. Another seven, eight days, still nothing. By now her worry was beginning to approach the panic stage. "Why doesn't it talk?" That was all she could think about. She returned to the store in tears with the same complaint.

"Did you buy a *swing?*"

"A swing! No. I have a cage, a mirror, and a ladder—I thought I had everything. I had no idea I needed a swing."

"Ya gotta have a swing. A parrot needs to feel completely at home. It glances in the mirror, takes a stroll up and down the ladder, and before long it's on the swing enjoying itself—and bingo! I've found that parrots usually talk when they are perched on a swing."

The woman bought the swing. She attached it to the top of the cage near the ladder and coaxed the parrot up the ladder and onto the swing. Still, absolute silence. For another ten days not one sound came from the cage.

Suddenly she came bursting into the pet store, really steaming. The owner met her at the counter.

"Hey, how's my parrot? I'll bet—"

"It died! My expensive bird is dead in the bottom of the cage."

"Well, I can't believe that. I'm just shocked. Did it ever say anything at all?"

"Yes, as a matter of fact, it did. As it lay there taking its last few breaths, it said very faintly, 'Don't they have any *food* down at that store?'"

—*Preaching* magazine, March–April 1991

No Lover

No lover makes my kiss his daily quest.
No hand across the table reaches mine.
No precious baby nestles at my breast.
No one to need my love. Where is the sign
That God, my Father, loves me? Surely He
Created this wealth of love to overflow.
How can it be that none who wanted me
Has become mine? Why did I tell them,
    "No?"

But do they really matter, all the Why's?
Could all the answers take away the pain,
Or all the reasons really dry my eyes,
Though from Heaven's court? No, I
    would weep again.
My God, You have saved me from
    Hell's black abyss;
Oh, save from the tyranny of bitterness!

—Natalie Ray, *Eternity* magazine, 1975

I KNOW OF NO MORE POTENT KILLER than isolation. There is no more destructive influence on physical and mental health than the isolation of you from me and of us from them. It has been shown to be a central agent in the etiology of depression, paranoia, schizophrenia, rape, suicide, mass murder, and a wide variety of disease states.

— Philip Zimbardo, "The Age of Indifference," *Psychology Today*, August 30, 1980

The days are long, but the nights longer—and lonelier
I wait for the daylight—
    but darkness holds me in her grip.

Sleep escapes me as memories of the good times—
    and the bad—
Crowd out the vestiges of euphoria and leave me restless—
    hurting—
Filling my mind with thoughts of love—
    and hostility,
Of thoughtfulness—
    and remorse,
Of guilt—
    and despair.
O God, I cry, is there no end to the hurt?
Must shame plague my steps forever?
Is there not another who will walk with me—
    accepting
        loving
            caring
                forgiving—
Willing to build with me a new life on foundations more sure—
To whom I will pledge, as will she, faithfulness forever?

Others have cried with me in the darkness—
    they have cared—
But in the confinements of our own humanness,
The demands of their lives must take precedence.
And in the end I shall stand alone—
    apart from Thee.
I have attempted to build again—
    on my own—
Too soon, unwise and unstable.

New hurts have come to tear open the wounds not yet healed.
The struggle is not ended.

And so I crawl—
    uneasy, yet unyielding to defeat and sure despair—
Toward better days,
    Toward light that is unending,
        Toward God who keeps me in His care.

—Charles R. Swindoll, *Strengthening Your Grip*

The House with Nobody in It

Whenever I walk to Suffern, along the Erie track
I go by a poor old farmhouse with its shingles broken and black.
I suppose I've passed it a hundred times
But I always stop for a minute
And look at that house, the tragic house,
The house with nobody in it.

    I've never seen a haunted house,
    But I hear there are such things;
    They hold the talk of spirits,
    Their mirth and sorrowings.
    I know this house isn't haunted,
    But I wish it were, I do;
    For it wouldn't be so lonely
    If it had a spirit or two.

    If I had a lot of money
    And all my debts were paid,
    I'd put a gang of men to work,
    With brush and saw and spade.
    I'd buy that place
    And I'd fix it up the way it used to be
    And I'd find some people who wanted a home
    And I'd give it to them, free.

    So whenever I go to Suffern,
    Along the Erie track,
    I never go by that empty house
    Without stopping and looking back.
    It hurts me to look at the crumbling roof

And the shutters falling apart,
For I can't help thinking the poor old house
Is a house with a broken heart.

—Alfred Joyce Kilmer

MOST OF THE WORLD'S GREAT SOULS have been lonely.

—A. W. Tozer, *Man, the Dwelling Place of God*

NOVEMBER SKY is chill and drear; November's leaf is red and searing.

—Sir Walter Scott

WHEN I WAS IN THE MARINE CORPS we were seventeen days at sea. About the tenth day out, we were far removed from any body of land in the Pacific. Swells were sometime thirty or forty feet high. The ship that looked *enormous* in that dock as we boarded now felt like a toothpick in the middle of this circle of the horizon.

I remembered Samuel Taylor Coleridge's words in "Rime of the Ancient Mariner":

Alone, alone, all, all alone,
Alone on a wide, wide sea!
Not a saint took pity on
My soul in agony.

LONELINESS IS . . . SPENDING YOUR DAYS ALONE with your thoughts, your discouragements, and having no one to share them with.

—Neil Strait, quoted in Lloyd Cory, *Quote Unquote*

LOVE

I READ ABOUT A YOUNG MAN who was determined to win the affection of a lady who refused to even talk to him anymore. He decided that the way to her heart was through the mail, so he began writing her love letters. He wrote a love letter every day to this lady. Six, seven times a week she got a love letter from him. When she didn't respond, he increased his output to three notes every twenty-four hours. In all, he wrote her more than seven hundred letters. And she wound up marrying the postman.

Everywhere I look I see
Fact or fiction, life or play
Still the little game of three,
B and C in love with A.

—Jeanne Hendricks, *A Woman for All Seasons*

To "Let Go" Takes Love

To "let go" does not mean to stop caring, it means that I can't do it for someone else.

To "let go" is not to cut myself off, it is the realization that I can't control another.

To "let go" is not to enable, but to allow learning from natural consequences.

To "let go" is to admit powerlessness, which means the outcome is not in my hands.

To "let go" is not to try to change or blame another, it is to make the most of myself.

To "let go" is not to care for, but to care about.

To "let go" is not to fix, but to be supportive.

To "let go" is not to judge, but to allow another to be a human being.

To "let go" is not to be in the middle arranging all the outcomes, but to allow others to effect their own destinies.

To "let go" is not to be protective, it is to permit another to face reality.

To "let go" is not to deny, but to accept.

To "let go" is not to nag, scold, or argue, but instead to search out my own shortcomings and correct them.

To "let go" is not to adjust everything to my desires, but to take each day as it comes, and cherish myself in it.

To "let go" is not to criticize and regulate anybody, but to try to become what I dream I can be.

To "let go" is not to regret the past, but to grow and to live for the future.

To "let go" is to fear less and to love more.

—Margaret J. Rinck, *Can Christians Love Too Much?*

If

IF I belittle those whom I am called to serve, talk of their weak points in contrast perhaps with what I think of as my strong points; if I adopt a superior attitude, forgetting "Who made thee to differ? and what hast thou that thou has not received?" then I know nothing of Calvary love.

IF I take offense easily, if I am content to continue in a cool unfriendliness, though friendship be possible, then I know nothing of Calvary love.

IF I feel bitterly towards those who condemn me, as it seems to me, unjustly, forgetting that if they knew me as I know myself they would condemn me much more, then I know nothing of Calvary love.

—Amy Carmichael, *If*

WE MUST KEEP REACHING OUT to people . . . After all, that is what love is all about.

> Love has a hem to her garment
> That trails in the very dust;
> It can reach the stains of the streets and the lanes . . .
> And because it can, it must.

—G. Frederick Owen, *Abraham to the Middle East Crisis*

Paul's Girl

> Paul's girl is rich and haughty;
> My girl is poor as clay.
> Paul's girl is young and pretty;
> My girl looks like a bale of hay.
>
> Paul's girl is smart and clever;
> My girl is dumb but good
> But would I trade my girl for Paul's?
> You bet your life I would!

—David Roper, *The Law That Sets You Free*

'TIS BETTER TO HAVE LOVED AND LOST, than never to have loved at all.

—Alfred Lord Tennyson

Constancy

You gave me the key to your heart, my love;
Then why do you make me knock?
Oh, that was yesterday, Saints above!
And last night—I changed the lock!

—John Boyle O'Reilly, quoted in Kathleen Hoagland, *1,000 Years of Irish Poetry*

ONE EVENING just before the great Broadway musical star, Mary Martin, was to go on stage in *South Pacific,* a note was handed to her. It was from Oscar Hammerstein, who at that moment was on his deathbed. The short note simply said:

"Dear Mary, A bell's not a bell till you ring it. A song's not a song till you sing it. Love in your heart is not put there to stay. Love isn't love till you give it away."

—James Hewett, *Illustrations Unlimited*

Love

I love you,
Not only for what you are,
But for what I am
When I am with you.

I love you,
Not only for what
You have made of yourself,
But for what
You are making of me.

I love you
For the part of me
That you bring out;
I love you
For putting your hand
Into my heaped-up heart
And passing over
All the foolish, weak things
That you can't help

Dimly seeing there,
And for drawing out
Into the light
All the beautiful belongings
That no one else had looked
Quite far enough to find.

I love you because you
Are helping me to make
Of the lumber of my life
Not a tavern
But a temple;
Out of the works
Of my every day
Not a reproach
But a song.

—Roy Croft, quoted in Hazel Felleman, *The Best Loved Poems of the American People*

LITTLE CHAD was a shy, quiet young fella. One day he came home and told his mother, he'd like to make a valentine for everyone in his class. Her heart sank. She thought, "I wish he wouldn't do that!" because she had watched the children when they walked home from school. Her Chad was always behind them. They laughed and hung on to each other and talked to each other. But Chad was never included. Nevertheless, she decided she would go along with her son. So she purchased the paper and glue and crayons. For three whole weeks, night after night, Chad painstakingly made thirty-five valentines.

Valentines Day dawned and Chad was beside himself with excitement! He carefully stacked them up, put them in a bag, and bolted out the door. His mom decided to bake him his favorite cookies and serve them up warm and nice with a cool glass of milk when he came home from school. She just knew he'd be disappointed; maybe that would ease the pain a little. It hurt her to think that he wouldn't get many valentines—maybe none at all.

That afternoon she had the cookies and milk out on the table. When she heard the children outside she looked out the window. Sure enough here they came, laughing and having the best time. And, as always, there was Chad in the rear. He walked a little faster than usual. She fully expected him to burst into tears as soon as he got inside. His arms were empty, she noticed, and when the door opened she choked back the tears.

"Mommy has some warm cookies and milk for you."

But he hardly heard her words. He just marched right on by, his face aglow, and all he could say was:

"Not a one . . . not a one."

Her heart sank.

And then he added, "I didn't forget a one, not a single one!"

—Dale Galloway, *Rebuild Your Life*

TRUE LOVE is a splendid host.

There is love whose measure is that of an umbrella. There is love whose inclusiveness is that of a great marquee. And there is love whose comprehension is that of the immeasurable sky. The aim of the New Testament is the conversion of the umbrella into a tent and the merging of the tent into the glorious canopy of the all-enfolding heavens . . . Push back the walls of family love until they include the neighbor; again push back the walls until they include the stranger; again push back the walls until they comprehend the foe.

—John Henry Jowett, *The Epistles of St. Peter*

L—listening when another is speaking,

0—overlooking petty faults and forgiving all failures;

V—valuing other people for who they are;

E—expressing love in a practical way.

—Denis Waitley, *Seeds of Greatness*

STAY FERVENT IN LOVE. *Fervent* is a word that speaks of intensity and determination. It is an athletic term for stretching to reach the tape. Have you watched the fellows and gals who run the dash? When they come around that last turn and they're pressing for the tape, they'll get right to the end and then they'll lunge forward. I've even seen them fall right there on the track, because they're pushing to reach the tape ahead of the one they're competing against. It's the idea of intensity at the tape, stretching yourself. Those who do the long jump leap into the air and throw their feet forward and they, with intensity, stretch every muscle of their body to reach as far as they can. The same with the high jumpers, or with the pole vaulters. They stretch to the uttermost to reach the limit. That's the word *fervent*.

WHAT DOES IT LOOK LIKE? It has hands to help others, feet to hasten to the poor and needy, eyes to see misery and want, ears to hear the sighs and sorrows of men. That is what love looks like.

—Augustine

HEAT MAKES ALL THINGS EXPAND. And the warmth of love will always expand a person's heart.

—Chrysostom

Love is not love
Which alters when it alteration finds,
Or bends with the remover to remove.
O, no it is an ever-fixed mark,
That looks on tempests and is never shaken;

It is the star to every wandering bark,
Whose worth's unknown, although his height be taken.

Love alters not with his brief hours and weeks,
But bears it out even to the edge of doom.

—William Shakespeare, "Sonnet 116"

LOVE OF GOD
(See *God's Love*)

Mm

MARRIAGE
(Also see *Divorce*)

SOMEONE TOLD ME about a fiftieth anniversary their grandparents had cele-brated together. They were by then, I'm sure, great-grandparents, because they were in their 70s. Ted had lost much of his hearing during this time. And yet they were still getting along together and celebrating this great anniversary. Their family came from all over and enjoyed celebrating together through the midmorning into the afternoon. Finally, toward sundown, all the family went home.

Bessie and Ted decided to walk out on the front porch and sit down on the swing and watch the sunset. The old gentleman pulled his tie loose and leaned back and didn't say much. Bessie looked at him somewhat in wonder and said to him, "You know, Ted, I'm real proud of you." The old gentleman turned and looked at her rather quizzically and after a moment said, with a puzzled look on his face, "Well, Bessie, I'm real tired of you too!"

IF YOU LIKE STORIES THAT END WELL, you'll love Christianity. It is tri-umph, victory, unity, harmony, joy, praise, delight with Jesus. In one sermon I also said there would be no more arguments with your wife and four men said, "Amen." And when I added, "or with your husband," hundreds of women said, "Amen."

FOUR WORDS SAID IT ALL. They appeared printed in bold type inside the store window of a Hollywood jewelry store. It read, "We Rent Wedding Rings." If there is anything on the critic's list today that would run a close second to motherhood, it is marriage. You talk about bad press. You talk about a conver-sational football to kick across the television talk-show platforms. You talk about a joke in the office.

You doubt that? Listen the next time someone in your office announces their future plans for matrimony. Just listen. Don't say anything. Listen for words of affirmation and then compare those with the snide remarks and the sarcastic jabs. You would think the person had just announced plans to buy a pet twenty-foot python when they tell you their plans are to get married this summer.

FOUR-YEAR-OLD Suzie had just been told the story of "Snow White" for the first time in her life. She could hardly wait to get home from nursery school to tell her mommy. With wide-eyed excitement, she retold the fairy tale to her mother that afternoon. After relating how Prince Charming had arrived on his beautiful white horse and kissed Snow White back to life, Suzie asked loudly:

"And do you know what happened then?"

"Yes," said her mom, "they lived happily ever after."

"No," responded Suzie, with a frown, " . . . they got married."

—Cecil Osborne, *The Art of Understanding Your Mate*

MARRIAGES BEGIN WARM AND INTIMATE but over time they can become cold and businesslike. Consider the seven ages of a marriage cold.

The first year the husband says, "Sugar, I'm worried about my little baby girl. You've got a bad sniffle. I want to put you in the hospital for a complete checkup. I know the food is lousy, but I've arranged for your meals to be sent up from Rossini's. It's all arranged."

The second year: "Listen, honey, I don't like the sound of that cough. I've called Dr. Miller and he's going to rush right over. Now will you go to bed like a good girl just for me, please?"

The third year: "Maybe you'd better lie down, honey. Nothing like a little rest if you're feeling bad. I'll bring you something to eat. Have we got any soup in the house?"

The fourth year: "Look, dear. Be sensible. After you've fed the kids and washed the dishes you'd better hit the sack."

The fifth year: "Why don't you take a couple of aspirin?"

The sixth year: "If you'd just gargle or something, instead of sitting around barking like a seal."

The seventh year: "For heaven's sake, stop sneezing. What are you trying to do, give me pneumonia?"

—Bruce Larson, *The One and Only You*

SEVERAL YEARS AGO when I was speaking at Moody Bible Institute, a lady wrote me a note saying, "I didn't worry about getting married. I did leave my future to God's will. But every night I hung a pair of men's pants on the bed and knelt down and prayed this prayer, 'Father in heaven, hear my prayer. And grant it if You can. I've hung a pair of trousers here. Please fill them with a man.'" Isn't that a great letter?

Well, I read that the next week when I got back to the church I pastored in Fullerton, California. It didn't fit my sermon; I just rammed it in because I thought it was such a great letter. The father and the older son of a family I knew were in the church, but the mother was home with a sick daughter. When I read the woman's note I watched them. The father just cracked up laughing, but the boy was rather serious. Interestingly, several weeks later I got a letter from the mother who hadn't been in that service. She wrote, "Dear Chuck, I'm wondering if I have something to worry about. I've noticed that our son, when he goes to bed at night, has this bikini hanging over the foot of his bed."

SVEN AND HULDA, a Scandinavian couple, were Christians. They sang in the choir, they were at Sunday school every Sunday, they had prayer at every meal, they went to all the church functions. But they could not get along. A home, it was terrible: bickering, complaining, fussing. After both of them had devotions one morning, separately, of course, Hulda said to Sven, "You know, Sven, I been tinking. I got de answer to dis hopeless problem we're livin wit. I tink ve should pray for de Lord to take vun of us home to be with Him. And then, Sven, I could go live wit my sister."

—Bruce Larson, *Believe and Belong*

HEAR ABOUT THE FELLOW who had a nagging wife? "Talk, talk, talk, talk," he said to his friend. "That's all my wife ever does is talk, talk, talk." His friend responded, "Well, what does she talk about?" "I don't know," he said, "she don't say."

—Ray Stedman, *Solomon's Secret*

A CHIEF IN AFRICA called all his men to come to his hut in the center of the village. It was his fear, he said to them, that there were no longer any real men in the village. He had the impression the men were being ruled too much by their wives.

To find out if this were true, he asked all the men who felt their wives bossed them around to leave the hut through the door on the right. Those who felt they were in charge at home should leave through the door on the left. Lo and behold, all of the chief's men left through the door on the right, except one who stood all alone.

He finally left through the door on the left. So the chief called the men together again and gave a speech of praise to the lone wolf. "At least we have one real man in our village," he said. "Could you please share with us your secret?" The man looked rather sheepish and at last he muttered, "Chief, when I left home this morning, my wife said to me, 'Husband, never follow the crowd!'"

—Walter Trobisch, *The Misunderstood Man*

A LADY WANTED TO MARRY FOUR DIFFERENT MEN in her lifetime. She said each one would help her with the four things she needed most. First, she wanted to marry a banker. Second, a movie star. Next, a clergyman. And finally, a funeral director. When asked why, she answered, "One for the money, two for the show, three to get ready, and four to go!"

—Charles R. Swindoll, *Growing Deep in the Christian Life*

DR. DAN AMSLER told me about Marriage Anonymous. He read about it in the writing of one of his friends. And it's this: When a guy who is single really gets the urge to get married, he sits down and dials this telephone number. And the people in Marriage Anonymous send an old hag over in an ugly nightgown and old tattered robe. Her hair is rolled up, her hose are rolled down, she's got cold cream all over her face, and she nags him until he loses the desire to get married.

—Ray Stedman, "Alone but Not Lonely" sermon, October 15, 1978

IT DOESN'T TAKE LONG for the newlyweds to discover that "everything in one person nobody's got." They soon learn that a marriage license is just a learner's permit, and ask with agony, "Is there life after marriage?"

An old Arab proverb states that marriage begins with a prince kissing an angel and ends with a bald-headed man looking across the table at a fat lady. Socrates once told his students, "By all means marry. If you get a good wife, twice blessed you will be. If you get a bad wife, you'll become a philosopher." Count Herman Keyserling said it well when he stated that "the essential difficulties of life do not end, but rather begin with marriage."

—Joe Aldrich, *Secrets to Inner Beauty*

SUCCESS IS NOT SO MUCH marrying one who makes you happy as escaping the many who could make you miserable.

—Clyde Narramore

_____

Marriage!

It's rough. It's tough. It's work.
Anybody who says it isn't
Has never been married.
Marriage has far bigger problems
Than toothpaste squeezed
From the middle of the tube.

Marriage means . . .
Grappling, aching, struggling.
It means putting up
With personality weaknesses
Accepting criticism
And giving each other freedom to fail.
It means sharing deep feelings
About fear and rejection.
It means turning self-pity into laughter
And taking a walk to gain control.

Marriage means . . .
Gentleness and joy
Toughness and fortitude
Fairness and forgiveness
And a walloping amount of sacrifice.

Marriage means . . .
Learning when to say nothing
When to keep talking
When to push a little
When to back off.
It means acknowledging
"I can't be God to you—
I need Him, too."

Marriage means . . .
You are the other part of me

I am the other part of you.
We'll work through
With never a thought of walking out.

Marriage means . . .
Two imperfect mates
Building permanently
Giving totally
In partnership with a perfect God.
Marriage, my love, means us!

—Ruth Harms Calkin, *Love Is So Much More, Lord*

In those days
the words, "I love you, honey,"
were said with five different inflections
and meant fifty different things.
   They could have meant
thank you for opening the catsup bottle,
even though you said that I had loosened it first.
   Or I enjoy our talks
when you come home from work
and there's just the two of us to share and dream.
   Or simply that I appreciate all those things
that make up you:
your sensitive strength,
the way you smile me off my soapbox,
or the way that you pretend you are listening
when you read the paper.
   But somewhere along the way we turned
and instead of floating with the current,
we now struggle against it.
   It wasn't one action, or one word,
but a series of little unresolved spats and quarrels
that now make the TV the solution
to the problems of a hard day
and silences us when we should say
"Thank you" or "You really look nice today."
   Today, I no longer tell you that I love you
because the sound of those words

mocks the special meaning that they carried
when we were first wed,
and it is too painful to remember
that those feelings we said we would never lose
were, tear by tear, left in the past.

—Deborah Jean Morris Swindoll, March 2, 1980

A WOMAN WAS NOT MADE out of his head to top him, nor out of his feet to be trampled upon by him; but out of his side, to be equal to him; under his arm to be protected; and near his heart to be loved.

—Matthew Henry, quoted in Benjamin P. Browne, *Illustrations for Preaching*

A WIFE WAS SITTING at the breakfast table and asked her husband, "What if something happened to me and I died first? Would you marry again?" He thought for a while then responded, "Yes, I probably would." Then she asked, "Well, would you bring your new wife to live in this house and have her sleep in our bed?" "Well, I hadn't thought about it, but I probably would," he said. She probed further, "Would you let her use my golf clubs?" To which he replied, "No, because she's left-handed."

ON A TELEVISION TALK SHOW some time ago the guest was an actor, well-known for his romantic roles on film. Predictably, he was asked, "What makes a great lover?" I am confident everyone watching the show (myself included) expected the standard macho-playboy response. To the surprise of the host and the audience, his answer must have raised eyebrows all across America. It went something like this:

> "A great lover is someone who can satisfy one woman all her life long, and who can be satisfied by one woman all his life long. A great lover is not someone who goes from woman to woman to woman. Any dog can do that."

Wow! May his tribe increase.

—Charles R. Swindoll, *Strike the Original Match*

MARRIAGE IS NOT SO MUCH FINDING THE RIGHT PERSON as it is being the right person.

—Charles W. Shedd, *Letters to Karen*

_____

MATURITY

UNDER ROMAN LAW there was a time for the coming of age of a son. But the age when this took place was not fixed as one might assume. Rather, the father had the discretion in setting the time of his son's maturity. A Roman child became an adult at the sacred family festival known as the *Liberalia* held annually on the seventeenth of March. At this time, the child was formally acknowledged as the son and heir by his father, and he received the plain toga adults wore in place of the toga with a narrow purple band at the foot of it which children wore. He was then conducted by his friends and relations down to the forum and formally introduced to public life. Lloyd Douglas gave us a glimpse of the moving nature of this moment as he described the coming of age of Marcellus in the opening pages of his book *The Robe*.

_____

HOW FAR YOU GO IN LIFE depends on your being tender with the young, patient with the old, sympathetic with the striving, tolerant with the weak and the strong, because someday in life you will have been all of these.

—George Washington Carver

_____

If

If you can keep your head when all about you
    Are losing theirs and blaming it on you;
If you can trust yourself when all men doubt you,
    But make allowance for their doubting too;
If you can wait and not be tired by waiting,
    Or, being lied about, don't deal in lies,
    Or, being hated, don't give way to hating,
And yet don't look too good, nor talk too wise;

If you can dream—and not make dreams your master;
    If you can think—and not make thoughts your aim;
If you can meet with triumph and disaster
    And treat those two impostors just the same;

If you can bear to hear the truth you've spoken
    Twisted by knaves to make a trap for fools,
Or watch the things you gave your life to broken,
    And stoop and build 'em up with wornout tools;

If you can make one heap of all your winnings,
    And risk it on one turn of pitch-and-toss,
And lose, and start again at your beginnings
    And never breathe a word about your loss;
If you can force your heart and nerve and sinew
    To serve your turn long after they are gone,
And so hold on when there is nothing in you
    Except the Will which says to them: "Hold on";

If you can talk with crowds and keep your virtue,
    Or walk with kings—nor lose the common touch;
If neither foes nor loving friends can hurt you;
    If all men count with you, but none too much;
If you can fill the unforgiving minute
    With sixty seconds' worth of distance run—
Yours is the Earth and everything that's in it,
    And—which is more—you'll be a Man, my son!

—Rudyard Kipling, quoted in Hazel Felleman, *The Best Loved Poems of the American People*

After a While

After a while you learn the subtle difference between
    holding a hand and chaining a soul,
    and you learn that love doesn't mean leaning
    and company doesn't mean security.
After a while you begin to learn that kisses aren't contracts
    and presents aren't promises,
    and you begin to accept your defeats
    with your head up and your eyes open,
    with the grace of an adult, not the grief of a child.
After a while you learn to build your roads on today because
    tomorrow's grounds are too uncertain for plans.
After a while you learn that even sunshine burns
    if you get too much. So plant your own garden
    and decorate your own soil instead of waiting

for someone to bring you flowers.
And you learn that you really can endure,
. . . that you really are strong,
. . . and you really do have worth.

—Anonymous

MATURITY BEGINS TO GROW when you can sense your concern for others outweighing your concern for yourself.

—John McNaughton, quoted in Lloyd Cory, *Quote Unquote*

ONE OF THE MARKS OF MATURITY is the ability to disagree without becoming disagreeable.

—Charles R. Swindoll, *The Grace Awakening*

MATURITY IS THE ABILITY TO DO A JOB whether supervised or not; finish it once started; carry money without spending it; and . . . bear an injustice without wanting to get even.

—Fred Cook, quoted in Lloyd Cory, *Quote Unquote*

MATURITY PROCEEDS THROUGH FOUR STAGES: help me, tell me, show me, follow me.

WHAT DOES IT MEAN TO BE GROWN UP? It means such things as being fully developed, having marks of wisdom, not just knowledge; the self-discipline and commitment of an authentic walk with Christ seven days a week; the determination to obey God and to submit to the truth of His Word at any cost; the ability to nourish myself as an individual believer in God's Word; the compassion to reach out and care for other people whose needs are different from my own; the willingness to share in the responsibilities of the household—all of the above with an attitude of a contagious, positive spirit.

We're not unlike the thirteen-year-old kid that's six feet, ten inches in junior high school, whose dad says to him one day, "Son, I think you maybe ought to think about basketball." He has the height for it, but there's not a person who would question his lack of maturity for it. Put him on the same court with Moses Malone and he'd get his lunch eaten. Malone loves that kind of person on the court with him. Why? Not because the kid can't match him in height, but he hasn't the resiliency. He hasn't the maturity. He needs to do what? He needs to grow up. Even if he never grows another inch he has plenty of height to play in any pro basketball team. What he needs is to grow up.

MATURITY IS MOVING from soft skin-tough heart to tough skin-soft heart.

MEDIOCRITY

SEVERAL DECADES HAVE PASSED since my unforgettable days in boot camp. But some of the lessons learned back then are still with me—lessons like listening to the right voice, like ignoring the movements of the majority, and like being disciplined enough to filter the essential from the incidental. The ramifications of this kind of discipline have been life-changing. They include, for example, committing myself to excellence while many are comfortable with the mediocre, aiming high though most seem to prefer the boredom of aiming low, and marching to the distinct beat of another drummer while surrounded by a cacophony of persuasive sounds pleading for me to join their ranks. Remember the way James Russell Lowell put it:

> Life is a leaf of paper white
> Whereon each one of us may write
> His word or two, and then comes night.
> Greatly begin! though thou have time
> But for a line, be that sublime—
> Not failure, but low aim, is crime.

> —Charles R. Swindoll, *Living Above the Level of Mediocrity*

Mediocrity

I'm a small and lonely man, my friend,
The world will not build a monument to me,
Somehow I've become sunken
In the mire of mediocrity.
Alone along life's torturous trail
Repeating my meaningless deeds,
Early errors now haunt me

And like a tumor on me feeds.
Great things left to other men,
Great decisions not my care,
Noble steps and moments
Not my privilege to share.
Each life has its crossroads,
Be careful which you choose,
A life of greatness and happiness
Is all too easy to lose.

It is my firm conviction that those who impact and reshape the world are the ones committed to living above the level of mediocrity. There are still too many opportunities for excellence, too much demand for distinctiveness, to be satisfied with just getting by. As Isaac D'Israeli once wrote, " . . . it is a wretched taste to be gratified with mediocrity when the excellent lies before us."

—Charles R. Swindoll, *Living Above the Level of Mediocrity*

COMPETITIVE EXCELLENCE requires one hundred percent all of the time. If you doubt that, try maintaining excellence by setting your standards at 92 percent. Or even 95 percent. People figure they're doing fine so long as they get somewhat near it. Excellence gets reduced to acceptable, and before long, acceptable doesn't seem worth the sweat if you can get by with adequate. After that mediocrity is just a breath away.

Ever tracked the consequences of "almost but not quite"? Thanks to some fine research by Natalie Gabal, I awoke to a whole new awareness of what would happen if 99.9 percent were considered good enough. If that were true, then this year alone . . . 2,000,000 documents would be lost by the IRS; 12 babies would be given to the wrong parents each day; 291 pacemaker operations would be performed incorrectly; 20,000 incorrect drug prescriptions would be written; 114,500 mismatched pairs of shoes would be shipped (to cite just a few examples).

—Charles R. Swindoll, *The Finishing Touch*

MINISTERS
(See *Pastors*)

MINISTRY
(Also see *Pastors, Preaching*)

A STRANGE SIGN appeared on the desk of a Pentagon official. In bold black letters it read:

> THE SECRECY OF MY JOB DOES NOT PERMIT ME
> TO KNOW WHAT I AM DOING.

That reminds me of a similar sign that could be placed on many a young minister's desk:

> THE SACREDNESS OF MY JOB DOES NOT PERMIT ME
> TO KNOW WHAT I AM DOING.

—Charles R. Swindoll, *The Bride*

IF YOU'VE EVER TRAVELED up Highway 1 along the coast of California on your way to San Francisco, you have come to the little town of Castroville. And there's one thing that Castroville is noted for, and that's artichokes. If you like artichokes, you like Castroville. And if you don't like artichokes, there's nothing else to like in Castroville.

And as you drive through, you think things like, "Oh, I'm so grateful God has not called me to Castroville." And if you're in the ministry, you always add, "But I'm available. I'll go if that's what You'd like me to do." You learn to say that.

I have a physician friend, David Onstad, who left Fort Lauderdale and moved to Tyler, Texas, to practice academic medicine. It was great. They lived in an old house and put down deep roots and enjoyed things like backyard barbecues, sandlot baseball, and all that. One day we got a letter from Lil, his wife, from Fort Lauderdale, saying they had moved back. And she said, "Do you know why we now live in Fort Lauderdale? Because I said when we were in Tyler, 'We will never move back to Fort Lauderdale.' And here we are."

So take it from me, God may call you to Castroville. You go. Eat a lot of artichokes while you're there, by the way.

I REMEMBER THE WORDS of Sonny Jurgensen when he was quarterback of the Washington Redskins football team. He was being attacked by fans and sportswriters alike as his team was in a slump. Somebody asked him if all that flack was getting to him. He flashed a big toothless grim and replied, "Naw, not me. I've be in this game long enough to know that every week the quarterback is either in the penthouse or the outhouse."

That can apply to ministry too.

—Charles R. Swindoll, *Dropping Your Guard*

SOME TIME AGO I read an article in which the pastor of a church described his activities during a certain day, supposedly typical of his usual routine. It went something like this: Arriving in the church office at eight o'clock in the morning, he had intended to spend at least two hours in preparation for his Sunday sermon, a noonday talk at a local service club, and five radio talks during the coming week. However, he was reminded by his secretary that he had agreed to write an article for the church bulletin, scheduled to go to press at noon. He was also obligated to make three phone calls, one of them to the Chairman of the Church Finance Committee. After finishing with these duties, only thirty minutes were left for the preparation of his messages, since at ten o'clock he was to meet with the Program Committee of the Ministerial Association. Just as he began to study again he received word that the mother of the president of one of the women's societies in the church had passed away, and his presence was wanted at their home at once. This, of course, caused him to miss his meeting with the Ministerial; but he was able to attend the 12:30 luncheon of the Women's Auxiliary. Following this he spoke at a study class. At two o'clock he officiated at a wedding ceremony. At three o'clock he began his visiting in the city hospitals, and finished just in time to make the Men's Supper, where he gave the invocation. The supper lasted until 7:30, allowing the pastor to get away just in time to attend a meeting of the Every Member Canvas Committee. He was on hand simply to make suggestions and to boost the Committee's morale. Having done that, his day of service was finally ended and he arrived home exhausted 9:30 that evening.

This was the pastor's own account of the way in which he spent an entire day. Now, without any reflection upon, or criticism of, this man, since I don't know all of the circumstances which may have demanded him to keep such a schedule, I would ask: Was he fulfilling his God-given obligation as pastor of the church? Is this the way in which God intended him to spend his day? When a man assumes a pastorate is he justified in spending most of his time in administrative meetings, board meetings, committee meetings, budget-planning meetings, building-program meetings, luncheons, dinners, and banquets?

—Richard DeHaan, *Men Sent from God*

A BACKWOODS PREACHER was not very eloquent but was often right on the mark. God definitely stepped into his life and called him and changed him. And though he was not very educated, he was deeply devoted to his calling. He listened on one occasion to a proud, young preacher—well educated but very impressed with his own background and skills, evidencing little power of God at work in his life. When the sermon was over and most people had left, the old preacher walked up to him and said, "Young man, was you sent or did you just went?"

—Donald Barnhouse, *Romans*, Vol. 1

TEN REASONS WHY pastors should stay at their churches for the long haul and not resign too quickly:

1. I need to grow in the new demands I am facing rather than find an excuse to cop out.
2. I refuse to be guided by my emotions.
3. My family needs love and stability.
4. Building people takes time.
5. I want our missionaries to have a sense of permanence in their home church.
6. A longer ministry better serves the church and the community.
7. The support of elders comes gradually.
8. Our people have been generous with me.
9. I must not avoid confession and forgiveness.
10. I can trust God and not panic.

—Don Bubna, "Ten Reasons Not to Resign," *Leadership*, Fall 1983

THE NATURE OF MINISTRY is service. You may be surprised to know that the word "minister" or "ministry" has in its root form in Greek the term for "service" or "to serve." Remember our Lord Himself "did not come to be served, but to serve," Mark 10:45.

In a day of upholding a big image, it is easy to miss the value of service. We indeed suffer. As John R. W. Stott has written, we suffer "the shameful cult of human personalities."

—Warren W. Wiersbe, *Making Sense of the Ministry*

MIRACLES

GARY RICHMOND SAID, "If they were happening every day, they wouldn't be called miracles, they'd be called regulars." I think that's a great statement. Miracles aren't regulars. They're every once in a while, maybe once in a lifetime, maybe twice.

A parking place at Christmas time in Nordstroms' parking lot isn't a miracle. (I know it seems like a minor miracle, but it isn't a miracle, you know.) The fact that your toothache stops hurting isn't a miracle . . . or that your appendectomy scar isn't large. That isn't a miracle; that's a very good surgeon.

———————————

JONAH SWALLOWED BY A FISH? I'd believe it if Scripture said Jonah swallowed the fish! It's not difficult to believe if you believe in a God of miracles.

—Billy Graham

———————————

MISSIONS

A CHURCH gave its members a self-evaluation questionnaire to see how concerned they were about missions. Compare for yourself where you might be, considering these examples of the "High" and "Low" criteria:

When it comes to a biblical understanding of missions, I . . .

can explain how every book of the Bible relates to world evangelism.

do not own a Bible.

When it comes to missions education, I . . .

assist others in understanding what God is doing in missions.

conscientiously avoid any missions emphasis or any missions information.

When it comes to prayer, I . . .

regularly fast and pray for specific requests from missionaries.

do not believe in prayer.

When it comes to encouraging missionaries, I . . .

visit them at their assignments.

don't do anything with missionaries.

When it comes to giving, I . . .

encourage others and sacrifice myself to give to missions.

take money from missionaries.

When it comes to missionary recruitment, I . . .

actively educate others to the need for more missionaries around the world.

feel they should stay home and earn a living.

———————————

A FEW YEARS AGO I stood on the banks of a river in South America and watched a young man in western clothes climb out of a primitive canoe. The veteran missionary with whom I was traveling beamed at the young man and he whispered to me, "The first time I saw him he was a naked Indian kid standing right on this bank, and he pulled in my canoe for me. God gave me a real concern for him, and eventually he came to Christ, committed himself to the Lord's work and is just returning home after graduating from seminary in Costa Rica." I could understand the beam on the missionary's face, and I think Paul beamed when he talked of his men. And he had good cause to be thrilled with them.

—Stuart Briscoe, *Bound for Joy*

A MISSIONARY COUPLE came home aboard a ship after many years of faithful service in Africa. It so happened that there was a very important diplomat also on the same ship who got special treatment and special attention. When the ship arrived, this couple stood back and watched from the deck as the band played and the people had gathered and there was great applause. As the diplomat walked down the gangplank and was whisked off in a lovely limousine to the sounds of music and applause, this dear fellow put his arm around his wife and he walked off with her and got into the streets of New York. "Honey," he said, "it just doesn't seem right after all of these years that we would have this kind of treatment and here this fellow gets that kind of special treatment." And she put her arms around her husband and said to him, "But, honey, we're not home yet."

—Al Bryant, *1,000 New Illustrations*

A COUPLE OF YEARS after Cynthia and I were married, I had an obligation to fulfill in the military. I joined the Marine Corps, did my boot camp and infantry training, and got orders for my tour of duty to be in San Francisco.

Then I got a letter in the mail from President Dwight Eisenhower. And it was a speed letter for me to change from San Francisco to Okinawa. I did just what you would have done. I looked on the envelope to make sure it went to the right person. And yes, it was addressed to me. My whole frame of reference changed. We wept ourselves to sleep that night. That tour of duty would take me sixteen months or more away from her, early in our marriage. Little did I realize that would be a whole change in my entire career. What I considered to be the most God-awful letter became the most God-ordained statement for me.

As I left, my brother shoved a book in my hand called *Through Gates of Splendor,* a story of five missionaries who lost their lives, and whose widows went on with their lives, ultimately evangelizing the Auca Indians in Ecuador. On the troop ship, going from San Diego to Japan, and then later down to Okinawa, I got a whole new frame of reference. My mind stopped resisting for the first time since I'd gotten that letter. For the first time I began to think, maybe there's a plan here.

A special relationship was cultivated with a man named Bob Newkirk while I was on the island of Okinawa. One of the first things Bob gave me was the Amplified New Testament. I read that little book of the Scriptures about three times before I left the island. He had marked one verse for me. It was Philippians 3:10. [For my determined purpose is] that I may know Him—that I may progressively become more deeply and intimately acquainted with Him, perceiving and recognizing and understanding [the wonders of His Person] more strongly and more clearly.

That's it! That's why I went! Humanly speaking, I would never have met a Bob Newkirk in Houston or San Francisco. But over there, away from all the crutches, all those things that make us comfortable, all the familiarity, I got a chance to see missions for the first time. And the government paid my way. For the first time I would be in a missionary home. For the first time I would be in another culture surrounded by another language. For the first time in my life I would be the foreigner. And I would find myself again and again having to look up and to learn a whole new way of walking. And my love for Christ really began to bloom.

A FAMOUS ARTIST once was asked to paint a picture of a dying church. It was expected that he would paint a small and humble congregation in a dilapidated building. Instead, he painted a stately edifice with a rich pulpit and magnificent windows—and near the door, an offering box, marked "Missions," with the contribution slot blocked by cobwebs.

WILLIAM CAREY, the great missionary of India, said to a body of people, "I will go down if you will hold the ropes." It's a great idea. It's a great mental picture. "I'll go into the caves, I'll go into the places where you will never go, but you must hold the ropes. I'll go down if you'll hold on. I'll go if you are here holding fast, holding tight."

—Basil Miller, *William Carey: The Father of Modern Missions*

MISTAKES
(Also see *Futility*)

EVANGELIST JACK VAN IMPE was closing a citywide crusade in Green Bay, Wisconsin. It was to end on Sunday afternoon. The very same public arena also featured wrestling on Sunday night. Interestingly, on Monday evening (the following day) Rex Humbard was scheduled to begin a new series of evangelistic meetings. One wonders if the man who set up the sign didn't have his tongue in his cheek when he arranged the letters on the marquee,

JACK VAN IMPE
WRESTLING
REX HUMBARD

—Leslie Flynn, *When Saints Come Storming In*

A WRONG FORMULA CAN BE LETHAL. It reminds me of a little jingle I picked up in high school chemistry class. "Say a prayer for Jimmy Brown, for Jimmy is no more; what he thought was H_2O was really H_2SO4!"

I THINK THE WORST TYPEWRITTEN MISTAKE I've ever heard of came from a friend of mine who was ministering during a summer internship in a Lutheran church. In the bulletin the typist left out the little letter "g." "There will be a sin-in at the Smith home this evening following the pastor's message on intimate fellowship."

WHEN A FELLOW was getting ready to travel abroad, several people warned him to watch out for pickpockets when he got to a particular busy city. If he went down to the crowded subway, a pickpocket could grab his wallet and get on the train, the doors would shut, and the pickpocket would be gone. So he determined to be very careful.

One evening after arriving in the city he was dressed casually in a sport coat, and he came to the crush of people down in the subway. Sure enough, just about the time the door opened and some people were pouring on, a fellow bumped up against him and he thought, "That was strange." So he reached into his pocket and he didn't find his wallet! Well, he grabbed this fellow's coat just as the door began to close and began to pull. Finally he got the coat all the way out even though the guy was struggling, and the door closed and the fellow inside looked bewildered as the subway train took off. Proud of himself, the guy thought, *Well, that showed him.* But when he looked in the fellow's coat, he didn't find his wallet. All that for nothing. But the story has a happy ending— he found his wallet on the bureau at the hotel.

A NEWSPAPER IN SAN DIEGO printed the story of a woman who had a little canary whom she affectionately named Chirpy. The little bird brought all kinds of song and beauty into their home.

One day while vacuuming, she thought, "My, the bottom of Chirpy's cage is dirty. I'll just vacuum the bottom of his cage." While she was vacuuming, the phone rang. So when she reached over for the phone, she lifted up the vacuum cleaner and it sucked in Chirpy, all the way down the tube, down to the little bag. Of course, she opened the vacuum cleaner and cut the bag open and there was Chirpy inside trying to survive. She breathed a sigh of relief. But she thought, "Oh, he's so dirty." So she put him under a faucet and ran water all over him. And then when she finished with him under the faucet, where he was about to drown, she dried him with a blow dryer. A newspaper reporter asked, "Well, what's he like now?" She replied, "Well, he doesn't sing very much anymore."

—Max Lucado, *In the Eye of the Storm*

A BIOLOGY PROFESSOR took a small group of young biologists into the desert for intensive study. Miles from civilization, the vehicle in which they were traveling broke down. The group set out on foot on an estimated three-day trek back to their campus. After two days of hard travel, they reached the summit of a huge sand dune. Thirsty and sunburned, they looked around them. Far off to their right was what appeared to be a lake with small trees surrounding it. The students jumped and screamed for joy. But the teacher, who had often been in the area before, knew they were seeing a mirage. He presented the bad news to them, sharing the facts as best he could. But insisting their eyes could not deceive them, the students rebelled. Unable to convince them of their error, the professor permitted them to head off in the direction of the alleged "lake," while he would take another course. He made them promise that after they discovered it was a mirage, they would sit down and wait for him to return with help. Three hours later the students arrived at a plush new desert resort which had four swimming pools and six restaurants. Two hours after that they set out in a Land Rover with rangers to search for their teacher. And he was never found.

—Charles Sell, *The House on the Rock*

A FELLOW HAD FINISHED LAYING CARPETING in a home. He was so pleased to have it done, because he finished a little early. But he noticed, as he looked over the carpet, that there was a little lump in the corner. He didn't want to rip the carpeting all up. Then he noticed that his package of cigarettes was gone. And he thought, "That's what the lump is". So he hit it with a hammer and mashed it down nice and flat so the carpet was nice and flat. Satisfied, he walked out, got in his pickup, and noticed his cigarettes were on the dashboard of his truck. Then he heard the woman of the house holler out the door, "Have you seen my parakeet?"

FOR WANT OF A NAIL the shoe was lost, for want of a shoe the horse was lost, for want of a horse the rider is lost.

—Benjamin Franklin

A WOMAN IN HER EIGHTIES was determined she would keep driving. Naturally her family was concerned about her slower reflexes. She would go out at night alone, so they were disturbed about her safety. They told her about muggings, kidnappings, carjackings. They thought that it would keep her at home. But it didn't.

Instead, she went out and bought a gun—a .38 special. She didn't know a thing about handling a gun, but she loaded it up and shoved it in her purse. She decided she would use it if someone gave her problems.

Well, she was walking out of this store during the Christmas season with her packages. She looks over and sees these three guys in the car and they're slammin' the door. She thinks, "This is my moment." So she reaches in her purse, pulls out her gun, walks right up to the car window and says, "Get out of my car! Get away from behind that steering wheel! You guys, move!" Three guys got out and ran in three different directions.

By now a crowd had gathered and they were staring at her and smiling. She was feeling pretty proud of herself. So she put her gun in her purse and got her keys out and the keys didn't fit. It wasn't her car.

A MAN WHO HAD NEVER BEEN ICE FISHING got the paraphernalia together to fish on the ice. And late one evening he slipped onto the ice and put the tent up and he began to chop through the ice. Then he heard a voice that said, "There are no fish there!"

So he slid the tent over maybe fifteen or twenty feet and sat back down on the stool and began chopping again. Again a voice said, "There are no fish there either!"

Feeling fearful, he said, "Who are you? God?" The voice answered, "No. I'm the manager of the skating rink."

A LARGE COMMERCIAL JET was flying from Chicago to Los Angeles. About an hour after takeoff, the passengers on board, heard a voice over the loud-speaker. It began, "This is a recording. You have the privilege of being on the first wholly electronically controlled jet. This plane took off electronically. It is now flying at 40,000 feet electronically. And it will land in Los Angeles electronically.

"This plane has no pilot, it has no copilot, and no flight engineer, because they are no longer needed. But do not worry, nothing can possibly go wrong . . . go wrong . . . go wrong . . . go wrong . . . go wrong . . . go wrong."

—James C. Humes, *Podium Humor*

A WOMAN WAS IN BETWEEN FLIGHTS at an airport. She had about an hour and a half wait and decided that she would spend the time looking over the newspaper. She had a little twinge of hunger, so she dropped by the lounge and picked up a small package of cookies and sat down at a table to look over her paper.

While she was reading, she began to detect a small rustling sound, almost like cellophane being crinkled and torn. She looked over the top of the newsprint and, to her amazement, a well-dressed man, sitting at the same table, a total stranger to her, was opening her cookies and helping himself.

Flabbergasted, she didn't want to make a scene, and so she just kept the paper up in front of her face and reached around and deliberately took the package of cookies and slid them toward her and took out one and began to eat it.

About a minute passed and, to her amazement, she heard more crinkling of the cellophane. She looked around the paper and the man, not looking at her, was simply eating another of her cookies.

Before she could reach over (by now they were at the bottom of the stack), he looked at the last cookie and broke it in two and with a frown slid it across to her side. He finished his half cookie, picked up his briefcase, and made his way down the terminal.

She was fuming as she munched on her last half of cookie. Then she heard the call for her flight and began to make her way to the gate where she would get on the plane. She needed her ticket, and so she opened her purse and, to her shock, she saw her package of unopened cookies still in her purse.

Somewhere in that same airport was a man still shaking his head, wondering how this strange lady had the nerve to eat part of his cookies!

—James Hewett, *Illustrations Unlimited*

ROY REIGALS was a member of a team that played in the Rose Bowl years ago. In the middle of a rather complicated play, he wound up with the ball. He streaked for the goal line, made a sensational run, zigzagging here and there, outrunning everyone on the field. The fans came unglued. He crossed the goal line. But there was one problem. It was the wrong goal line. The wrong fans cheered. It was a demoralizing effect. He has never lived it down. He is known today as Wrong-way Reigals.

—James Hewett, *Illustrations Unlimited*

_____

FOR OF ALL SAD WORDS of tongue or pen, the saddest are these: "It might have been!"

—John Greenleaf Whittier

_____

TWO YOUNG WOMEN from Southern California spent the day doing some last-minute Christmas shopping in Tijuana, a Mexican border town several miles below San Diego. After a successful day of bargain hunting, they returned to their hotel. One of the ladies glanced down in the gutter and noticed something moving, sort of squirming, as if in pain. As they bent down and looked closer, the two women saw what appeared to be a dog—a tiny Chihuahua—struggling for its life. It was breathing heavily, shivering, and barely able to move. Their hearts went out to the pathetic little animal. Their compassion wouldn't let them drive off and leave it there to die.

They decided to take it home with them and do their best to nurse it back to health. Afraid of being stopped and having the little creature detected by the border patrol officers, they carefully placed it on some papers among their packages in the trunk of the car. No problem. Within minutes they were back in California and only a couple of hours from home. One of the women held the sick little Chihuahua the rest of the way home.

As they pulled up in front of one gal's home, they decided she would be the one to keep the little orphan through the night and do everything she could to help it regain strength. She tried feeding it some of her food, but it wouldn't eat. She patted it, talked to it, cuddled it, and finally wrapped it in a small blanket and placed it beneath the covers on her bed to sleep beside her all through the night. She kept feeling it to make sure it was OK.

By early the next morning she could see it was not doing at all well. Before dawn she decided to take it to an emergency animal clinic nearby. Handing the weak animal to the doctor on duty, she began to describe all the things she had done to help the tiny creature.

He quickly interrupted her and asked, "Where did you get this animal?"

For fear of being reprimanded for bringing an animal across the border, she told him she was keeping it for a friend who had found it.

"I'm not letting you leave," he insisted sternly, "until you tell me where you got this thing."

She said, "We were shopping in Tijuana and found this little Chihuahua in the gutter near our car. Our hearts went out to it when . . ."

"This is no Chihuahua, young lady. What you brought home with you is a rabid Mexican river rat!"

—Charles R. Swindoll, Living Above the Level of Mediocrity

JOE GIBBS, former head coach of the Washington Redskins, told me a funny story that had to do with one of his friends.

Joe's friend, whom I will call Frank, owns a fine Labrador retriever. Frank looked out his window one morning and saw his faithful, obedient dog sitting on his haunches near the front porch. Frank thought he saw something hanging from the dog's jaws. Sure enough, a closer look revealed it was his neighbor's pet rabbit—now dead. Frank was stunned. Not exactly sure what to do, his brain clicked through several options until he landed on one that seemed best, though it would require a rather tedious process.

He gingerly pulled the rabbit from the Lab's mouth, took the thing to the sink, and washed off all the dirt and gunk. He then took it into the bathroom, pulled out a hair dryer, and spent several minutes blow-drying the dead creature until it was nice and fluffy. That night, after it was dark and quiet in the neighborhood, Frank crawled over the back fence, slipped across the neighbor's backyard, opened the door on the rabbit hutch, placed the dead rabbit in the cage, and snapped the door shut. He then slithered back through the darkness, hopped the fence, and breathed a big sigh of relief.

Next morning there was a loud knocking at his front door. Frank opened it and, to his surprise, found his neighbor clutching the dead rabbit. He was steaming.

"Frank, we have a real sickie in our neighborhood."

"Really? Why do you say that?"

"Well, see . . . my rabbit here died three days ago and I buried it. Some guy just dug it up, cleaned it off nice 'n' neat, and *stuck it back in the hutch.* We're talkin' a *real sickie,* Frank!"

—Charles R. Swindoll, Simple Faith

I READ OF THE CRASH of an Eastern Airlines jumbo jet in the Florida Everglades. The plane was the now-famous flight 401, bound for Miami from New York City, with a heavy load of holiday passengers. As the huge aircraft approached Miami Airport for its landing, a light that indicates proper deployment of the landing gear failed to come on. The plane flew in a large, looping circle over the swamps of the Everglades while the cockpit crew checked out the light failure. Their question was this: Had the landing gear actually not deployed or was it just the light bulb that was defective?

To begin with, the flight engineer fiddled with the bulb. He tried to remove it, but it wouldn't budge. Another member of the crew became curious and tried to help him out . . . and then another. By and by, if you can believe it, all eyes were on the little light bulb that refused to be dislodged from its socket. No one noticed that the plane was losing altitude. Finally, it flew right into the swamp. Many were killed in that plane crash. While an experienced crew of high-priced and seasoned pilots messed around with a seventy-five-cent light bulb, an entire airplane and many of its passengers were lost The crew momentarily forgot the most basic of all rules in the air—"Don't forget to fly the airplane."

—Charles Paul Conn, *Making It Happen*

OUR OLDEST SON was getting ready to go on a Christian Service Brigade overnight. We had all the supplies ready for it, except that he needed a little canteen. So I raced down to a local discount house and quickly looked through the shelves to find a canteen. I found one in a bin by itself—the only one left. The problem with it, however, was that it had no price tag on it. So I picked it up and I thought, "That's just what I need. I wonder how much it costs?" I looked all around. And right in the bin was a price tag, separate from the canteen. I picked up the tag and I put it on the canteen. Mistake number one.

Not knowing it, I was being photographed by a surveillance camera. I went to the checkout stand, paid for the canteen, and walked out. Just as I got out the door, two enormous gorillas walked up and said, "Just a minute." I knew right away that I should not have picked up that price tag and put it on this canteen because that was the wrong price tag. The police took me downtown and I was dropped in jail.

I was so embarrassed I didn't know what to do. And I was kept in custody until my gracious wife bailed me out of jail.

That is one of my most embarrassing moments in all of life. When that jail door closes, it is real. Thankfully I was there only minutes. But some are there for years for the mistakes they made.

WE ALL MAKE MISTAKES. Blunders are a sign of our humanity. Scripture records man's mistakes to teach us. I think they fall into five categories:

1. Panic-prompted mistakes usually involve fear, hurry, or worry.
2. Good-intention mistakes come from wrong timing or wrong methods.
3. Passive-negligence mistakes result from laziness, lack of discipline, or inconsistency.
4. Unrestrained-curiosity mistakes relate to the demonic or sensational.
5. Blind-spots mistakes usually come from ignorance, habit, or influences.

A MAN OPENED A NEW BUSINESS and his best friend sent him a floral arrangement. The friend dropped in a few days later to visit his buddy and was pained to see that the flowers had a sign that read, "Rest in Peace." He called the florist to complain. The florist said, "It could be worse. Somewhere in this city is an arrangement in a cemetery that reads, 'Congratulations on your new location.'"

A CLOSE FRIEND OF MINE has a friend in Texas who is a young attorney. He is a member of a sizable law firm run by a rather traditional kind of boss who enjoys a special kind of ritual at Thanksgiving time. Every year this young attorney participates in the ritual because it means so much to his employer.

On the large walnut table in the board room of the office suite sits a row of turkeys, one for each member in the firm. It isn't just a matter of "if you want it, you can have it; if you don't, you can leave it." The members go through some rather involved protocol.

Each man stands back from the table and looks at his turkey. When his turn comes, he steps forward and picks up the bird, announcing how grateful he is for the turkey this Thanksgiving.

This young attorney was single, lives alone, and has absolutely no use for a huge turkey. He has no idea how to fix it, and even if it were properly prepared he has no way to use all its meat. But because it was expected of him, he takes a turkey every year.

One year his close friends in the law office replaced his turkey with one made of papier-mâché. They weighted it with lead to make it feel genuine, and attached a real turkey neck and tail to make it look just like a real turkey. But it was a bogus bird through and through.

On the Wednesday before Thanksgiving, everyone gathered in the board room. When it came his turn, this young man stepped up, picked up the large bird, and announced his gratitude for the job and for the turkey.

Later that afternoon, he got on the bus to go home. With the big turkey in his lap, he wondered what in the world he would do with it. A little farther down the bus line, a rather run-down, discouraged-looking man got on. The only vacant seat on the bus was the one next to our young attorney friend.

He sat down and they began to talk about the holiday. The lawyer learned that the stranger had spent the entire day job-hunting with no luck, that he had a large family, and that he was wondering what he would do about Thanksgiving tomorrow.

The attorney was struck with a brilliant idea: *This is my day for the good turn. I'll give him my turkey!*

Then he had a second thought. "This man is not a freeloader. He's no bum. It would probably injure his pride for me to *give* it to him. I'll *sell* it to him."

He asked the man, "How much money do you have?"

"Oh, a couple of dollars and a few cents," the man answered.

The attorney said, "I would like to sell you this turkey." And he placed it on the man's lap.

"Sold!" The stranger handed over the two dollars and whatever coins he had. He was moved to tears, thrilled to death that his family would have a turkey for Thanksgiving. He got off the bus and he waved good-bye to the attorney. "God bless you. Have a wonderful Thanksgiving. I'll never forget you." The bus pulled away from the curb, as both men smiled.

The next Monday, the attorney went to work. His friends were dying to know about the turkey. You cannot imagine their chagrin when they heard the story of what happened. I understand, through my friend, that they all got on the bus every day that week, looking in vain for a man who, as far as I know, to this day still entertains a misunderstanding about a guy who innocently sold him a fake turkey for a couple of bucks and a few cents.

—David Roper, *The Law That Sets You Free*

STOP AND THINK OF WAYS certain people can keep from coming out and confessing they blew it. Doctors can bury their mistakes. Lawyers' mistakes get shut up in prison—literally. Dentists' mistakes are pulled. Plumbers' mistakes are stopped. Carpenters turn theirs into sawdust. I like what I read in a magazine recently.

Just in case you find any mistakes in this magazine, please remember they were put there for a purpose. We try to offer something for everyone. Some people are always looking for mistakes and we didn't want to disappoint you!

HEY, THERE HAVE BEEN SOME REAL WINNERS! Back in 1957, Ford bragged about "the car of the decade." The Edsel. Unless you lucked out, the Edsel you bought had a door that wouldn't close, a horn that kept getting stuck, paint that peeled, and a transmission that wouldn't fulfill its mission. One business writer likened the Edsel's sales graph to an extremely dangerous ski slope. He added that as far as he knew, there was only one case on record of an Edsel ever being stolen. . . .

A friend of mine, realizing how adept I am in this business of blowing it, passed on to me an amazing book (accurate, but funny) entitled *The Incomplete Book of Failures,* by Stephen Pile. Appropriately, the book itself had two missing pages when it was printed, so the first thing you read is an apology for the omisssions—and an erratum slip that provides the two pages.

MONEY
(Also see *Charity, Giving, Stewardship, Wealth*)

SAID OF MONEY: "I don't necessarily like it, but it quiets my nerves."

—Joe Louis, quoted in Lloyd Cory, *Quote Unquote*

A CHURCH BOARD DECIDED that people in the congregation were embarrassed when the offering plates were passed. So they thought they ought to have a new system that wouldn't embarrass anybody, especially those who couldn't give. They asked the pastor to design a way of handling it so people could give as they came in or went out. So he built several interesting boxes and put them at each door. But these boxes were different. If you dropped in a dollar or more, it made no noise, it was silent. If you gave a half dollar, a little bell tingled. If you gave a quarter, it blew a whistle. If you gave a dime, a siren went off. If you gave a nickel, a shot sounded. If you gave nothing, it took your picture!

—Clyde Murdock, *A Treasury of Humor*

IN A CHURCH BULLETIN these words appeared: "The Lord loveth a cheerful giver. He also accepteth from a grouch."

—Lloyd Cory, *Quote Unquote*

DO YOUR GIVIN' while you're livin', then you're knowin' where it's goin'.

WHILE ON VACATION in Dublin, Ireland, Henry Ford visited an orphanage where a building project was being planned. The director of the fund-raising committee decided to make a call on the famous and rich man, Henry Ford. After their discussion, Ford judged the cause a worthy one, and so he wrote out a check then and there for 2,000 pounds, which was quite a gift. His generosity was so incredible it made the headlines of the local newspaper. The problem was, they misquoted the figure and reported, "Ford gave 20,000 pounds." The director of the orphanage called Henry Ford to apologize. In fact, he said, "I'll be happy to phone the editor right away and correct the mistake." But, feeling a little guilty, Ford said that there was no need for that. With a sigh, he took out his pen and checkbook and said, "I'll give you a check for the remaining 18,000 pounds." But he made only one request. He said, "When the new building opens, I want this inscription put on it, 'I was a stranger and you took me in.'"

—*The Little, Brown Book of Anecdotes*

AN OLD, RICH MAN with a cranky, miserable attitude visited a rabbi who lived a simple life. They weren't together very long before the rabbi got a wonderful idea on how to illustrate to the man that his cranky attitude was wrong. He took him by the hand and led him over to his window and he said, "Now look out the window and tell me what you see." As the man stood there, he said, "Well, I see some men and some women and I see a few children." "Fine." The rabbi then took him by the hand and led him across the room to a mirror. "Now, look and tell me what you see." The man frowned and said, "Well, obviously I see myself."

"Interesting," the rabbi replied. "In the window there is glass, in the mirror there is glass, but the glass of the mirror is covered with a little bit of silver. And no sooner is the silver added than you cease to see others, only yourself."

IN A CHURCH in the Deep South the preacher was moving toward the end of his sermon, and with growing crescendo he said, "This church, like the crippled man, has got to get up and walk." And the congregation responded, "That's right, reverend, let it walk." And he added, "This church, like Elijah on Mount Carmel, has got to run." "Run, let it run, preacher. Let it run." "This church has got to mount up on wings like eagles and fly." "Let it fly, preacher. Let it fly." Then he added, "Now if this church is gonna fly, it's gonna take money." "Let it walk, preacher. Let it walk. Let it walk."

—Clyde Murdock, *A Treasury of Humor*

SIGN IN A FT. LAUDERDALE restaurant: "If you are 80 years old and accompanied by your parents we will cash your check."

—Lloyd Cory, *Quote Unquote*

A YOUNG MAN was prompted by his father's example of giving at church—an area in which he had been negligent—to do the same. So the next Sunday he gave a dollar. He told me about it Sunday night and commented, "And would you believe I found a dollar in the parking lot! Next Sunday I plan to give twenty!"

IN JESUS' PARABLE of the rich fool that Jesus told, recorded in Luke 12:16–21, the man had amassed so much material wealth that he needed to tear down his existing barns and build bigger ones. Then he told himself, "Soul, you have many goods laid up for many years to come; take your ease, eat, drink, and be merry."

In the *Cotton Patch Gospel,* by Clarence Jordan, the rich man decides to, "Recline, dine, wine, and shine, fool!"

Borneaux, a French painter, musing about this parable, was so moved over it, he took out a canvas, a pallet, paint and brush, and began to paint the scene. He painted a man sitting behind a desk, rather portly in size, several bags of money on the front of his desk. Behind him was a shelf, on which was a small bag, as if for a very special purpose. Outside the window of that man's home was a bumper crop blowing in the afternoon breeze and a warm sunshine beating down on it.

Then Borneaux painted the opposite side of the canvas. Same man, same desk, same bags of money, same little treasured bag behind him on the shelf, same crops, same window, but now everything was covered with dust. The death angel had his hand on the man's shoulder. And the angel's lips were pursed, as if to say, "Fool . . . fool."

DID YOU HEAR ABOUT THE DRUNK who was down on all fours late one night under a streetlight? He was groping around on the ground, feeling the cement, peering intently at the little cracks. A friend drove up and asked, "Sam, what are you doing there?" Sam answered, "I lost my wallet." So the friend got out of his car, walked over, got down on his hands and knees with him, and they both started looking. Neither of them could find it. Finally the friend said to his drunk buddy: "Are you sure you lost the wallet here?"

"Of course not! I dropped it a half a block over there."

"Then why are we looking here?"

"Because there's no *streetlight* over there."

—Billy Graham, *How to Be Born Again*

THE FOLLOWING SIGN was being carried by an employee who was on strike: "Time heals all wounds. Time and a half heals them faster!"

—Earl Wilson, quoted in Lloyd Cory, *Quote Unquote*

RAY STEDMAN once traveled across the country for a week of meetings. The only problem was, that his baggage didn't make it. As I recall, the bags went on to Berlin! He needed a couple of suits so he went down to the local thrift shop and was pleased to find a row of suits. When he told the salesman, "I'd like to get a couple of suits," the man smiled and said, "Good, we've got several. But you need to know they came from the local mortuary. They've all been cleaned and pressed, but they were used on stiffs. Not a thing wrong with 'em; I just didn't want that to bother you." Ray said, "No, that's fine." So he hurriedly tried some on and bought a couple for about twenty-five dollars each.

When he got back to his room, he began to get dressed for the evening's meetings. As he put one on, to his surprise there were no pockets. Both sides were all sewn up! Though surprised, he thought, "Why, of course! Stiffs don't carry stuff with 'em when they depart!" The suits looked as if they had pockets, but they were just flaps on the coat. He told me later, "I spent all week trying to stick my hands in my pockets. I had to hang my keys on my belt!"

—Charles R. Swindoll, *Living Above the Level of Mediocrity*

THERE ARE MANY THINGS THAT MONEY CANNOT BUY. Money can buy: A bed but not sleep. Books but not brains. Food but not an appetite. Finery but not beauty. A house but not a home. Medicine but not health. Pleasures but not peace. Luxuries but not culture. Amusements but not joy. A crucifix but not a Savior. A church building but not heaven.

—Paul Lee Tan, *Encyclopedia of 7,700 Illustrations*

I WAS IN A CHURCH a number of years ago where just before the offering the pastor said, "There'll be no tips to God. No coins. Only bills." I wanted to give him my electric bill so bad I could hardly stand it.

I SAW A FUNNY 1040 FORM in a cartoon. It had two things listed on the new form. Number one said, "List all the money you made." Number two says, "Send it all in."

—Ben Patterson, *The Grand Essentials*

HAPPINESS IS NOT BASED ON MONEY. And the best proof of that is our family.

—Christina Onassis

THE LACK OF MONEY IS THE ROOT OF ALL EVIL, not the love of it.

—George Bernard Shaw

DR. KARL MENNINGER once asked a very wealthy patient, "What on earth are you going to do with all of that money?" The patient replied, a bit reluctantly, "Just worry about it, I suppose." Well, Menninger went on, "Do you get that much pleasure out of worrying about it?" "No," replied the patient, "but I get such terror when I think of giving some of it to somebody else."

—Richard Foster, *Money, Sex, and Power*

WHEN I WAS YOUNG, I used to think that money was the most important thing in life; now that I am older I *know* that it is!

—Oscar Wilde

WHEN YOU FIX YOUR EYES ON THINGS, invariably it leads to materialism. You fix your eyes on things and you will continually be attracted to gadgets, money, an abundance of the plastic, chrome, metal, wood, all the elements about us. You will continually be dissatisfied. The millionaire, John D. Rockefeller, was asked one time, "How much does it take to satisfy a man completely?" He said, "It takes a little bit more than he has."

—Spiros Zodhiates, *Behavior of Belief*

I OFTEN ENJOY THE COMMENTS made by sportsmen and women who still have a sense of humor. Lee Trevino is one of those people. He is a rather intense golfer, but he never has lost his sense of humor. He said when he was little his family was so poor that when his mother tossed the dog a bone, the dog had to call for a "fair catch" or the kids would get it.

—Denis Waitley, *Seeds of Greatness*

A MAN EXPLAINED why he bought his new car: "I was faced with the choice of buying a $32 battery for my old car or an $8,000 car—and they wanted cash for the battery."

AFTER BEING FIRED by Ford Company, Lee Iacocca was forced to rethink his motives and answer some gut-level questions regarding his reasons for hanging on so tenaciously to his job at Ford. His confession of greed is not hidden. Face it, it's tough for anyone to turn his back on almost a million a year, plus perks! A guy who has white-coated waiters available at the snap of his fingers and a chauffeur to and from work finds it extremely difficult to put on the brakes. In a moment of vulnerable honesty Iacocca admitted that of the seven deadly sins, greed is by far the worst. Hear him as he quotes his Italian-born father: "My father always said, 'Be careful about money. When you have five thousand, you'll want ten. When you have ten, you'll want twenty.' He was right. No matter what you have, it's never enough."

—*Iacocca: An Autobiography*

YOU SPEND A BILLION HERE and a billion there. Sooner or later it adds up to real money.

—Senator Everett Dirkson

THE GOVERNMENT'S VIEW of the economy could be summed up in a few short phrases: If it moves tax it. If it keeps moving, regulate it. And if it stops moving, subsidize it.

—Ronald Reagan

THE LOCAL BAR PATRONS were so sure that their bartender was the strongest man around that they offered a standing $1000 bet. The bartender would squeeze a lemon until all the juice ran into a glass and hand the lemon to a contender. Anyone who could squeeze just one more drop of juice out of the lemon would win the money. Many people had tried over time (weightlifters, longshoremen, etc.) but nobody could do it. One day a short, thin, balding, little man came into the bar, wearing thick, black-rimmed glasses and a double knit polyester leisure suit. He announced to the bartender in a faint, tiny squeaky voice, "I'd like to try the bet."

After the laughter had died down, the bartender said, "OK," grabbed a lemon, and squeezed away. Then he handed the dry, wrinkled remains of the lemon rind to the little man. The man clenched his fist around the lemon and the crowd's laughter turned to total silence as one drop fell into the glass—then another and another. Six drops, in all, were squeezed from the emaciated lemon rind.

As the crowd cheered, the bartender paid the $1000, and asked the little man, "What do you do for a living? You're obviously not a lumberjack or a weightlifter."

An almost imperceptible smile came across the little man's lips as he replied in a quiet, but satisfied voice, "I work for the IRS."

MORALITY

(Also see *Holiness, Righteousness*)

YOU CANNOT PLAY WITH THE ANIMAL in you without becoming wholly animal. He who wants to keep his garden tidy doesn't reserve a plot for weeds.

—Dag Hammarskjold, *Markings*

ON TYPICAL NIGHTS, television networks run show after show of police activities, social problems, sexual problems, perversion.

For example, on a Christmas Eve, a married couple separates after a fight; there's a drunk in a bar menacing people with a broken bottle; a priest is killed viciously in a church; a drunken driver is there; there's a stripper; a Peeping Tom; six other killings; and more than a half-dozen woundings.

Researchers have found that by the time an American child reaches the age of eighteen, he has spent more than 20,000 hours before the television set, much more than he does in any of the classrooms.

Last season, television showed the rape of a housewife, the story of a prostitute's life and emotions, and a homosexual couple living together—topics that were unmentionable on the air not long ago.

The morning and afternoon "soap operas" of the '70s continue to mirror a version of the "typical" American life that includes abortion, premarital sex, extramarital relationships, blackmail, murder, drugs, wiretapping, and embezzlement.

Violence is so much a part of television's simulated "real life," that studies have shown that it may occur five to nine times in one hour in "prime-time" television, as often as thirty times an hour during Saturday morning and after-school cartoons. In studying the responses of 120 boys from the ages of five to fourteen, researchers found clear evidence that "heavy TV watchers" were no longer shocked or horrified by violence. . . .

It will be difficult for the children who are raised in this era when they reach adult life to be decision-makers about right and wrong, because they have been without guidelines. They will have no idea what moral concepts are all about.

—*U. S. News and World Report,* October 13, 1975

MOTHERHOOD

What Is a Mother?

SOMEWHERE BETWEEN THE YOUTHFUL ENERGY of a teenager and the golden years of a woman's life, there lives a marvelous and loving person known as "Mother."

A mother is a curious mixture of patience, kindness, understanding, discipline, industriousness, purity and love.

A mother can be at one and the same time, both "lovelorn counselor" to a heartsick daughter, and "head football coach" to an athletic son.

A mother can sew the tiniest stitch in the material for that dainty prom dress and she is equally experienced in threading through the heaviest traffic with a station wagon.

A mother is the only creature on earth who can cry when she's happy, laugh when she's heartbroken, and work when she's feeling ill.

A mother is as gentle as a lamb and as strong as a giant. Only a mother can appear so weak and helpless and yet be the same one who puts the fruit jar cover on so tightly even Dad can't get it off.

A mother is a picture of helplessness when Dad is near, and a marvel of resourcefulness when she's all alone.

A mother has the angelic voice of a member in the celestial choir as she sings Brahms lullaby to a babe held tight in her arms; yet this same voice can dwarf the sound of an amplifier when she calls her boys in for supper.

A mother has the fascinating ability to be almost everywhere at once and she alone can somehow squeeze an enormous amount of living into an average day.

A mother is "old-fashioned" to her teenager; just "Mom" to her third-grader; and simply "Mama" to little two-year old sister.

But there is no greater thrill in life, than to point to that wonderful woman and be able to say to all the world, "That's my mother!"

—Fred Kruse

Mother O' Mine

If I were hanged on the highest hill,
    Mother o' mine, O mother o' mine!
I know whose love would follow me still,
    Mother o' mine, O mother o' mine!
If I were drowned in the deepest sea,
    Mother o' mine, O mother o' mine!
I know whose tears would come down to me,
    Mother o' mine, O mother o' mine!
If I were damned by body and soul,
    Mother o' mine, O mother o' mine!
I know whose prayers would make me whole,
    Mother o' mine, O mother o' mine!

—Rudyard Kipling, quoted in John R. Rice, *Poems That Preach*

THE FOLLOWING IS A LIST of "I owe you's" which apply to mothers all over the country, all of which are long overdue. Stop after each one and consider the priceless value of the one who made your life possible—your mother. Dear Mom:

As I walk through my museum of memories,
I owe you—for your *time.* Day and night.
I owe you—for your *example.* Consistent and dependable.
I owe you—for your *support.* Stimulating and challenging.
I owe you—for your *humor.* Sparky and quick.
I owe you—for your *counsel.* Wise and quiet.
I owe you—for your *humility.* Genuine and gracious.
I owe you—for your *hospitality.* Smiling and warm.
I owe you—for your *insight.* Keen and honest.
I owe you—for your *flexibility.* Patient and joyful.
I owe you—for your *sacrifices.* Numerous and quickly forgotten.
I owe you—for your *faith.* Solid and sure.
I owe you—for your *hope.* Ceaseless and indestructible.
I owe you—for your *love.* Devoted and deep.

—Charles R. Swindoll, *Strong Family*

Housewife's Lament

Make the beds, bandage heads,
Straighten up the room;
Wash the windows, cut the grass,
See the tulips bloom.

Drive the children to school,
Drive them back again.
Have the Cubs to meeting
Then I clean the den.

Serve on my committee,
Attend the P.T.A.
Forgot to buy the children shoes . . .
Can't do it today.

Pay the bills, write a note,
Fill the cookie jar.
Oh dear, I forgot to go
And have them grease the car.

Catch up on the ironing,
Scrub the kitchen floor.
Answer phone and doorbell,
Need I list some more?

My pet peeve I must admit,
You surely will agree,
When someone asks, "Are you employed?"
I answer, "No, not me."

—Caryl M. Kerber

A CARTOON shows a three-year-old, freckle-faced boy in a hallway. His pajamas are unsnapped, his diaper's bagging, and he's got a little teddy bear, dangling in his hand. He's standing in front of his mother and father's bedroom door, which is shut. On the door is a little sign written by a weary mother: "Closed for Business. Motherhood Out of Order."

—Charles R. Swindoll, *Laugh Again*

What Is a Grandmother?
By a third-grader

A GRANDMOTHER IS A LADY who has no children of her own. She likes other people's little girls and boys. A grandfather is a man grandmother. He goes for walks with boys, and they talk about fishing and stuff like that.

Grandmothers don't have to do anything except be there. They're old so they shouldn't play hard or run. It is enough if they drive us to the market where the pretend horse is, and have a lot of dimes ready. Or if they take us for walks, they should slow down past things like pretty leaves and caterpillars. They should never say, "Hurry up."

Usually grandmothers are fat, but not too fat to tie your shoes. They wear glasses and funny underwear. They can take their teeth and gums out.

Grandmothers don't have to be smart, only answer questions like, "Why isn't God married?" and "How come dogs chase cats?"

Grandmothers don't talk baby talk like visitors do, because it is hard to understand. When they read to us they don't skip or mind if it is the same story over again.

Everybody should try to have a grandmother, especially if you don't have television, because they are the only grown-ups who have time.

—James Dobson, *What Wives Wish Their Husbands Knew about Women*

I SMILE as I remember the Mother's Day card I saw that was really cute. It was a great big card written in little child's printing—little first-grade printing. On the front was a little boy with untied sneakers. He had a wagon, and toys were everywhere. He had a little cut on his face and there were smudges all over this card. It read, "Mom, I remember that little prayer you used to say for me every day," Inside, "God help you if you ever do that again."

A GOOD FRIEND OF MINE, who was raised by a godly pastor's wife, tells me that when he was rocked to sleep at night by his mother, she didn't sing to him just little ditties and lullabies, she sang him the hymns of the faith. When he was in the crib, he remembers her leaning over and singing to him "A Mighty Fortress Is Our God"; "And Can It Be?"; "More Love to Thee, O Christ"; "My Jesus, I Love Thee"; "Come, Thou Fount of Every Blessing." She sang the deep songs. And he says, "I remember. I remember those hymns. In fact," he says, "when I got into church, I had heard and learned most of the hymns," a contribution in that young man's life that he'll never forget.

NO ONE IS POOR who had a godly mother.

—Abraham Lincoln

Not for the star-crowned heroes,
    the men that conquer and slay,
But a song for those that bore them,
    the mothers braver than they.
With never a blare of trumpets,
    with never a surge of cheers,
They march to the unseen hazard—
    pale, patient volunteers.

—Mark De Wolfe Howe, "The Valiant"

Mothers, it's worth it. It's worth it. It's worth every hour of it. It's worth every sleepless night of it. It's worth every moment of counsel.

MOTIVATION

(Also see *Achievement, Ambition, Finish Line, Success*)

A PROVEN MOTIVATOR will make it to the top before a proven genius. When Andrew Carnegie hired Charles Schwab to administer his far-flung steel empire, Schwab became the first man in history to earn $1 million a year while in someone else's employ. Schwab was asked once what equipped him to earn $3,000 a day. Was it his knowledge of steel manufacturing? "Nonsense," snorted Schwab. "I have lots of men working for me who know more about steel than I do." Schwab was paid such a handsome amount largely because of his ability to inspire other people. "I consider my ability to arouse enthusiasm, the greatest asset I possess," he said, "and any leader who can do that can go almost anywhere and name almost any price."

—Alan Loy McGinnis, *Bringing Out the Best in People*

OPTIMISM, COURAGE, AND FAITHFULNESS feed on high morale. The ability to push on, alone if necessary, requires clear vision. In order for goals to be reached, there has to be a stirring up from within, a spark that lights the fire of hope, telling us to "Get at it" when our minds are just about to convince us with "Aw, what's the use?" It's called motivation.

Coaches are good at this. (They better be. There's a name for those who aren't—unemployed.) We've all seen it happen. The team is getting stomped. They can't get anything going during the entire first half. It's like they're playing with boxing gloves on. Rather than taking charge, they're being charged.

But then—magic!

Back in the locker room, away from the fans, the coach and team meet head-on. What results is nothing short of phenomenal. You'd swear that another bunch of athletes put on the same uniforms and played the victorious second half as they took charge and blew away their opponents. But these really are the same guys—or are they? They were transformed through the inspiration of a few minutes with one who is a master at building morale and clearing vision.

—Charles R. Swindoll, *The Finishing Touch*

A TRUE EVENT happened in the football season in the Southeast Conference between that great rivalry of Alabama and Auburn back in the days when Bear Bryant was still living and Pat Dye was the coach for the Auburn team.

The first-string quarterback for the Alabama team had been injured, so they were left with the second-string quarterback. They were on the opposing team's twenty-yard line. They were ahead by five points, leading Auburn. There were two minutes left in the game and it was first down for Alabama. Bear Bryant yelled into the ear hole in the helmet of the second-string quarterback, "Whatever you do, do not pass! Run the ball all four plays. And then if we have to hold them, our defense will get us through and we will win."

Second-string quarterback ran in full of zeal, determination. First down, they were smeared. Second down, Auburn held 'em. Third down, they gained a yard. Fourth down came. The hand-off was somehow muffled and the quarterback wound up with the ball. Running around the backfield, he looked in the end zone and he saw his split end ready to catch the ball, and he passed it. What he failed to see was the fastest man on the field, the safety for the Auburn team, also saw the pass coming. He came in front of the receiver, intercepted the ball, and started racing down the field. The quarterback, not very fast himself normally, raced down the field, caught the man, tackled him, and Alabama won the game.

Coach Dye said later to Bear Bryant, "I read the scouting reports, and that second-string quarterback is supposed to be slow. How is it he caught up with the fastest man on the field?" Bear Bryant replied, "It's very simple. Your man was running for the goal line and a touchdown. My man was running for his life!"

—*Preaching* magazine, July-August 1988

THE MOST MOTIVATED PERSON ON EARTH is a five-foot, ten-inch non-swimmer in six feet of water.

DURING THE HEIGHT of the Civil War, Abraham Lincoln often found refuge at a Presbyterian church in Washington, D.C. He would go with an aide, sit with his stovepipe hat in his lap, and never interrupt the meeting because the congregation would all be in a dither if they knew the president had come to sit in that midweek meeting. He sat off to the side, near the pastor's study, as the minister would open the Scriptures and teach God's Word and would lead the congregation in worship. The war was tearing the nation apart and tearing his soul. Having just lost his own son, Lincoln was on the bottom, and he needed solace and sustenance.

As the pastor finished his message and the people began to leave, the president stood quietly and straightened his coat and took his hat in hand and began to leave. The aide stopped him and said, "What did you think of the sermon, Mr. President?" He said, "I thought the sermon was carefully thought through, eloquently delivered." The aide said, "You thought it was a great sermon?" He said, "No, I thought he failed." "He failed? Well, how? Why?" "Because he did not ask of us something great."

—Bruce Larson, *What God Wants to Know*

JAKE, A GAME WARDEN, was always amazed that Sam, a fisherman, showed up at the end of the day with a couple or three stringers full of fish. This happened even when all the other fishermen came back with only two or three fish. Now this particular lake was loaded with fish, but they seemed to elude the average fisherman, so there was no limit on number, only on size. And all of Sam's fish were big enough to bring home.

The curiosity of the game warden finally got the best of him. So on one occasion he said to Sam, "I'd like to know your secret." Sam, a man of not too many words, said, "Show up tomorrow morning."

The next morning, long before dawn, the game warden was there. Sam showed up and met him, started the motor, and thirty or forty minutes later they were out in some secluded part of the lake. It was important to Sam that no one else be around. When they stopped the motor, everything was as still as it could be. Jake decided to sit back, fold his arms, and watch Sam do his thing. Sam reached down in his tackle box, pulled out a slender stick of dynamite, lit it, tossed it in the air. When it hit the level of the lake, there was an enormous explosion. In a matter of seconds, fish of all sizes began to float up to the top of the lake. Without a word Sam just began to row his way over and with his net pick up the largest fish and string them.

Jake screamed. "Wait! You break every rule in the book. I'm gonna throw the book at you. You'll be paying fines. I'm gonna stick you in jail."

About that time Sam reached in his box and pulled out another stick of dynamite. He lit it and tossed it in Jake's lap and said, "Are you gonna sit there watchin' all day or are you gonna fish?"

—Max Lucado, *No Wonder They Call Him Savior*

SOMETIME AGO I stayed a couple of nights in the Peabody Hotel in Orlando, Florida. One of the things that makes that hotel famous is that twice a day they have the one-and-only parade of the ducks. While John Phillip Sousa's march, "Stars and Stripes Forever," plays in the background, ducks come from everywhere and muster at the fountain on the main floor and a red carpet is unrolled. They march, without a quack as they go from the fountain back to the curtain. I couldn't believe it. And I thought as I watched it, there has to be a reason. These little things waddle on the carpet and then leave while everybody around is applauding this nonsense.

So I decided one afternoon I would do what no one else in the big group that had gathered was doing. I would follow them behind the curtain. So I did, not on the carpet, obviously, but off to the side. I walked all the way to the curtain and while the march dwindled down to silence and the crowd began to leave, I looked behind the curtain. Now I know why those ducks do that. Back behind the curtain there is no order at all. There is duck food everywhere. There are quacks and sounds and all kinds of other things back there behind the curtain. That's why they do it! I could tell by looking at them when they were marching that they were doing it, but they didn't have their heart in it at the time. Their heart, their mind (you could see it in their eyes), was on the food at the end of the parade.

TEN ACTION REMINDERS FOR STAYING MOTIVATED:

One: Wake up happy. Optimism and pessimism are behavioral attitudes. Listen to a motivational tape on your way to work. Read educational and inspirational books and articles that will give you a lift in the morning, first thing. Begin your day with prayer and the reading of God's Word.

Two: Use positive self-talk from morning to bedtime. "Things usually work out." "I expect a great year this year." "Next time I'll do better." "We'll make it."

Three: Look at problems as opportunities. Make a list of your most pressing problems, the ones that block your professional and personal fulfillment. Write a one or two sentence definition of each problem. Now rewrite the definition, only this time view it as an opportunity or exercise to challenge your creativity and ingenuity.

Four: Concentrate your energy and intensity without distraction on the successful completion of your current, most important project. Forget about the consequences of failure. Failure is only a temporary change in direction to set you straight for your next step.

Five: Find something good in all your personal relationships and accentuate the blessings.

Six: Learn to stay relaxed and friendly no matter how much tension you're under.

Seven: Think and speak well of your health.

Eight: Expect the best from others too. Remember that encouragement and praise are contagious.

Nine: This week seek and talk in person to someone currently doing what you want to do most and doing it well.

Ten: The best way to remain optimistic is to associate with optimists.

—Denis Waitley, *The Winner's Edge*

WHEN THE HEART IS RIGHT, the feet are swift.

—Thomas Jefferson

MUSIC

MARTIN LUTHER was a lover of song. By age fourteen his parents required that he earn his own way and he did that by singing in the streets. He must have sung well or he would have starved to death. So he knew something of song. And it became his passion, ultimately, to have Christianity expressed in the language of his people, the Germans, so that they could sing.

Someone wrote, "The evangelical church substituted the worship of Christ, as our only Mediator, for the worship of the virgin-mother. It reproduced and improved the old Latin and vernacular hymns and tunes, and produced a larger number of original ones. It introduced congregational singing." The German Reformation introduced to the people a hymnal by which they could sing their faith. "This singing was in the place of the chanting of priests and choirs. The hymn became, next to the German Bible and the German sermon, the most powerful missionary of the evangelical doctrines of sin and redemption, and they accompanied the Reformation in its triumphal march. They were first printed as tracts. These hymns were scattered wide and far, and they were sung in the house, and in the school, and in the church, and on the street."

Another person said of the reformation time, "One cannot go into the fields without finding the plower at his hallelujahs and the mower at his hymns." Isn't that great? Do you sing your faith as you drive along, or as you walk, or as you motivate yourself for some difficult task? What a treasure to have in our possession a Bible in one hand and a hymn book in another.

WILLIAM CONGREVE, an eighteenth-century English dramatist, was the first one to use these familiar words, "Music hath charms to soothe the savage beast, to soften rocks, to bend a knotted oak."

I was interested in reading in *Sports Illustrated* about the leisure activities of many professional football players. To my surprise, over half of them spend their leisure time listening to music. So do a lot of us.

I came from a musical family. My fondest memories, aside from summers spent down at a little bay cottage with a grandfather whom I dearly idolized, are the memories of singing with a family that gathered around a piano with a brother who could play like crazy, a mother who sang soprano, and a sister who could handle a little alto. I would bring up the rear in whatever was left and we would just sing through the evening.

The Bloodworth family lived next door. They were very affluent. The parents often left their kids at home for a weekend as they had their fun, which ended tragically in the mother's suicide and the father's departure. The kids were left to raise themselves.

At Christmastime one season we were singing through the hours of the evening. As it got late we decided we wouldn't bother the neighbors anymore and we pulled a window down. Our phone rang in less than a minute. It was the oldest of the four children who asked, "Would you please pull the window back up? We haven't heard singing like that and we . . ." I remember lifting the window up and looking out across the little area between our homes and there they were sitting like little ducks in the window, alone that evening, finding music to soothe their hearts. That is the ministry of music. Nothing can duplicate it.

Without a song the day would never end;
Without a song the road would never bend;
When things go wrong a man ain't got a friend,
Without a song.

. . . .

I got my trouble and woe,
but sure as I know the Jordan will roll,
I'll get along as long as a song is strong
In my soul. . . .

EVEN THOUGH THIS SONG was composed before I was born, I often find myself returning to the tune. It slips out in places like my shower at the beginning of a busy day, between appointments and assignments in the middle of a hectic day, and on the road home at the end of a tiring day. Somehow it adds a touch of oil to the grind, smoothing things up a bit. Willie Nelson recently blew the dust off the old lyrics. I still sing them to myself. . .

True, isn't it? The right combination of words, melody, and rhythm seldom fails to work like magic. And given the pressures and demands folks like us are forced to cope with on a daily basis, we could use a little magic. Most of the people I know are never totally free of a relentless daily grind. Fact is, the grind is not going away! The salesperson has to live with a quota. The performer must constantly rehearse. The therapist can't escape one depressed soul after another. The pilot has to stay strapped in for hours. The preacher is never free of sermon preparation. The broadcaster cannot get away from the clock any more than the bureaucrat can escape the hassle of red tape. Days don't end, roads don't bend. Help!

Instead of belaboring the point, since we cannot escape the grind, we must find a way to live beyond it. The question is, how? The answer is, a song. Remember? "Without a song the day would never end." But not just any song! Certainly not some mindless, earsplitting tune yelled at us by a bunch of weird-looking jerks with blue and orange hair, dressed in black leather and spikes, and microphones stuffed halfway down their throats. No, not that. I have in mind some songs that are really old. We're talking ancient. In fact, they are the ones inspired and composed by our Creator—God—the original Rock music with a capital R. They're called psalms.

These are timeless songs—that have yielded delicious fruit in every generation. They're not silly ditties, but strong, melodious messages written with life's daily grind in mind and specially designed to help us live beyond it. That's right, beyond it. To borrow again from the songwriter, "We'll get along as long as a psalm is strong in our souls." I really do believe that. Why else would God have inspired those age-old compositions? Surely, He realized the lasting value of each musical masterpiece and therefore preserved them to help us persevere. They drip with the oil of glory that enables us to live beyond the grind.

—Charles R. Swindoll, *Living beyond the Daily Grind*

MYSTERY

A FELLOW WAS RAISED in the back hills of West Virginia—I mean, so far out in the sticks, never in his life had he seen a big city, to say nothing of modern inventions and neon lights. He married a girl just like himself and they spent all their married years in the backwoods. They had one son, whom they creatively named Junior. Around the time Junior reached his sixteenth birthday, his dad began to realize it wouldn't be too many years before their son would become a man and would strike out on his own. It troubled him that his boy could reach manhood and wind up getting a job in the city, not prepared to face the real world. He felt responsible and decided to do something about it.

He and his wife started saving for a trip the three of them would take to the city. About three years later the big day arrived. They tossed their belongings in the ol' pickup and started the long journey over winding, rough roads to the city. Their plan was to spend several days at a swanky hotel and take in all the sights. As they approached the outskirts of the metropolis, Papa began to get a little jumpy: "Mama, when we pull up at th' hotel, you stay in th' truck while Junior an' I go in an' look around. We'll come back and git ya, OK?" She agreed.

Flashing neon lights and uniformed doormen greeted them as they pulled up. Mama stayed put as Papa and Junior walked wide-eyed into the lobby. Neither could believe his eyes! When they stepped on a mat, the doors opened automatically. Inside, they stood like statues, staring at the first chandelier either of them had ever seen. It hung from a ceiling three stories high. Off to the left was an enormous waterfall, rippling over inlaid stones and rocks. "Junior, look!" Papa was pointing toward a long mall where busy shoppers were going in and out of beautiful stores. "Papa, looka there!" Down below was an ice-skating rink—*inside.*

While both stood silent, watching one breathtaking sight after another, they kept hearing a clicking sound behind them. Finally, Papa turned around and saw this amazing little room with doors that slid open from the center. "What in the world?" People would walk up, push a button and wait. Lights would flicker above the doors and then, "click," the doors would slide open from the middle. Some people would walk out of the little room and others would walk inside and turn around as, "click," the doors slid shut. By now, dad and son stood *totally* transfixed.

At that moment a wrinkled old lady shuffled up to the doors all by herself. She pushed the button and waited only a few seconds. "Click," the doors opened with a swish and she hobbled into the little room. No one else stepped in with her, so "click," the doors slid shut. Not more than twenty seconds later the doors opened again—and there stood this fabulously attractive blond, a young woman in her twenties—high heels, shapely body, beautiful face—a real knockout! As she stepped out, smiled, and turned to walk away, Papa nudged his boy and mumbled, "Hey, Junior…*go git Mama!*"

—Michael Green, *Illustrations for Biblical Preaching*

A LOT OF THINGS ABOUT LIFE are mysteries. Death is like that. No one has ever come back and told us what it's about, so it remains a distinct enigma, a riddle, a mystery. So is the sea. It's strange marriage to the moon that controls its tide continues to be in the poet's mind a great, constant, moving mystery.

So are the spaces above us. Who can fathom the mysterious movement of that masterful piece of time that stays on track continually, twenty-four hours a day, 365 days a year. If we look long enough through a telescope, our eyes bug out against the lens and our mouths drop open as we try to fathom the mystery of the spaces above us.

Consider also the invisible world around us that can be seen only through the lens of a microscope. Whether it's telescopic or microscopic, life seems to be shrouded in mystery. Did you realize that if an electron could be increased in size until it became as large as an apple, and if a human being could be increased by the same proportion, that person could hold the entire solar system in the palm of his hand and would have to use a magnifying glass in order to see it?

Not all mysteries are as profound as that. Many are somewhere between just baffling and humorous. Every home has the mystery of a washing machine. My home is the worst. You can put in twelve perfectly matched pairs of socks and in some phenomenal, mysterious manner, you can pull out eight socks, none of which match anything. And don't send me the little things that stick them together, because we have lost even those. I'm waiting someday to pull the socks out unmatched *and* stuck together.

Add to that the mystery of traffic lanes. The mystery is that every lane you get into slows down. Who can ever explain it? There's the mystery of peanut butter and jelly and the slice of bread. It never falls in the kitchen. It always falls in the living room. One wag has said that whether your sandwich falls face down or face up is in direct proportion to the cost of the carpet.

Then there's the mystery of the auto repairman. Your car gives you trouble for three weeks. You finally hurry up before work one morning to get it to him. It runs perfectly as the repairman scratches his head, wondering why you even brought the car in. You drive it to work and it stalls one block from work and you have to be towed back to the repairman.

_____

Nn

NAMES

ALL THOSE FAMILIAR with *Pilgrim's Progress* have no trouble remembering that the pilgrim's name throughout the book is Christian. To my surprise few remember his original name, even though it is plainly stated in the allegory. In the scene where it first appears, the pilgrim is conversing with a porter:

> Porter: What is your name?
> Pilgrim: My name is now *Christian,* but my name at the first was *Graceless.*

The same could be said for all of us today who claim the glorious name of Jesus Christ as our Lord and Savior. Our name is now Christian, but it has not always been so. That title was given to us the moment we believed, the day we took God at His word and accepted the gift of eternal life He offered us. Prior to the name change, we were Graceless, indeed.

—Charles R. Swindoll, *The Grace Awakening*

IN CHRYSOSTOM'S SERMON on how to bring up children he advised parents to "give their boys some great scriptural name, to teach them repeatedly the story of the original bearer of that name, and thus to give them a standard to live up to and an inspiration for living when they grow to manhood." Isn't that great? You know what your name is? Child of God. Work on that. Child of Light. In a sinful, lawless society a clean Christian is a silent rebuke.

—William Barclay, *The Letters of John and Jude*

NEATNESS

I WAS PREACHING through a series on spiritual gifts and a father told me, "We're kinda messy as a family except for one of our kids—the oldest, Bill." He said, "The other day Bill got behind the steering wheel of the car to drive the family home after hearing you talk about the gift of administering, which is his gift. He sat there pensive after starting the motor while we were all waiting for him to back out of the parking lot, and he said, 'How can this be? To have this neat gift of administration in a family of messy pigs.'"

_____

BENJAMIN WEST, a British artist, tells how he became an artist. One day his mother went out, leaving him in charge of his little sister Sally. In his mother's absence, he discovered some bottles of colored ink and began to paint Sally's portrait. In doing so, he made a very considerable mess of things about him, with ink blots all over.

His mother came back. She saw the mess but she said nothing. She picked up the piece of paper and she saw the drawing. "Why," she said, "it's Sally!" And she stooped and kissed Benjamin. Ever after, Benjamin West used to say, "My mother's kiss made me a painter."

—William Barclay, *The Letters to the Galatians and Ephesians*

_____

I HEARD ABOUT A WOMAN who was such a lousy housekeeper that *Good Housekeeping* canceled her subscription.

—Charles R. Swindoll, *The Finishing Touch*

_____

SOMEDAY WHEN THE KIDS ARE GROWN, things are going to be a lot different. The garage won't be full of bikes, electric train tracks on plywood, sawhorses surrounded by chunks of two-by-fours, nails, a hammer and a saw, unfinished "experimental projects," and the rabbit cage. I'll be able to park both cars neatly in just the right places, and never again stumble over skateboards, a pile of papers (saved for the school fund drive), or the bag of rabbit food—now spilled. Ugh!

Someday when the kids are grown, the kitchen will be incredibly neat. The sink will be free of sticky dishes, the garbage disposal won't get choked on rubber bands or paper cups, the refrigerator won't be clogged with nine bottles of milk, and we won't lose the tops to jelly jars, catsup bottles, the peanut butter, the margarine, or the mustard. The water jar won't be put back empty, the ice trays won't be left out overnight, the blender won't stand for six hours coated with the remains of a midnight malt, and the honey will stay inside the container. . . .

Yes, someday when the kids are grown, things are going to be a lot different. One by one they'll leave our nest, and the place will begin to resemble order and maybe even a touch of elegance. The clink of china and silver will be heard on occasion. The crackling of the fireplace will echo through the hallway. The phone will be strangely silent. The house will be quiet, and calm, and always clean, and empty, and filled with memories, and lonely, and we won't like it at all. And we'll spend our time not looking forward to Someday but looking back to Yesterday. And thinking, "Maybe we can baby-sit the grandkids and get some life back in this place for a change!"

—Charles R. Swindoll, *Come Before Winter*

NOISE

AN INDIAN was walking in downtown New York City alongside a friend who was a resident of the city. Right in the center of Manhattan, the Indian seized his friend's arm and whispered, "Wait! I hear a cricket."

His friend said, "Come on! Cricket? Man, this is downtown New York."

He persisted, "No, seriously, I really do."

"It's impossible!" was the response. "You can't hear a cricket! Taxis going by. Horns honkin'. People screamin' at each other. Brakes screeching. Both sides of the street filled with people. Cash registers clanging away. Subways roaring beneath us. You can't possibly hear a cricket!"

The Indian insisted. "Wait a minute!" He led his friend along, slowly. They stopped, and the Indian walked down to the end of the block, went across the street, looked around, cocked his head to one side but couldn't find it. He went across another street, and there, in a large cement planter where a tree was growing, he dug down into the mulch and found the cricket. "See!" he yelled, as he held the insect high above his head.

His friend walked across the street, marveling, "How in the world could it be that you heard a cricket in the middle of downtown, busy Manhattan?"

The Indian said, "Well, my ears are different from yours. It simply depends on what you're listening to. Here let me show you." And he reached in his pocket and pulled out a handful of change—a couple of quarters, three or four nickels, and dimes and pennies. Then he said, "Now watch." He held the coins waist high and dropped them to the sidewalk. Every head within a block turned around and looked in the direction of the Indian.

—Robert G. Lee, *Sourcebook of 500 Illustrations*

MOST NOISES IN CHURCH don't bug me. I've heard 'em all.

People snoring. Babies crying. Rain falling. Crickets chirping. Sound systems popping. Toilets flushing. Offering and communion plates dropping.

Sirens screaming and cars speeding outside. Kids yelling and phones ringing inside. Hymnals hitting a bunch of piano keys. Organists standing up on a foot full of bass notes. Coughing. Sneezing. Blowing. Laughing. Crying. Shouting. Whispering. Gasping. Yawning. Clapping.

You don't spend most of your life in church without encountering the full spectrum.

It's no big deal. Noises really come with the territory. Even some "joyful noises"are part of the package. I've heard some guys sing so badly they sounded like a bull moose with its hind legs caught in a trap as they bellow the baritone part to "Wonderful Grace of Jesus." And I've heard a few sopranos who really needed to be put out of their misery. (I've often been thankful that stained glass doesn't shatter.) But their motives were right, so they will receive their reward. (I hope it includes heavenly voice lessons or we're all in for an awfully long eternity.)

There is one shrill noise, however, unique to this electronic age, that I find both irritating and irresponsible. It's those plagued digital watches! It's bad enough to have 'em chime and dong and zip and blip and bzzt and ting every hour on the hour, but since they're not synchronized to go off exactly at the same time, it's fifteen to twenty seconds of every conceivable tone. It's enough to make a hound lift his head and holler. . . .

Somehow worship and watches seem to be strange bedfellows. Surely, time and eternity weren't made to mix. Or, as one creative friend wrote:

> In this world of noise and bustle
> Could we not escape this
> High-tech age for one hour
> In Your house?

I think I'll make this suggestion to pastors everywhere: Tell your congregation that if they promise to be more thoughtful with their hourly chimes, you'll be more punctual with your closing time. But warn them that for every weird blip, blip, blip you hear, you'll add another ten minutes to the sermon. Won't it be fun watching everybody glare at the guys who turn the meeting into a marathon? Come to think of it, while I've heard lots of sounds and seen lots of sights in churches, I've never seen a Sunday morning congregational mutiny. We could make history!

—Charles R. Swindoll, *The Finishing Touch*

Oo

OBEDIENCE

AT A CERTAIN CHILDREN'S HOSPITAL, a boy gained a reputation for wreaking havoc with the nurses and staff. One day a visitor who knew about his terrorizing nature made him a deal: "If you are good for a week," she said, "I'll give you a dime when I come again." A week later she stood before his bed. "I'll tell you what," she said, "I won't ask the nurses if you behaved. You must tell me yourself. Do you deserve the dime?"

After a moment's pause, a small voice from among the sheets said: "Gimme a penny."

—Lewis and Faye Copeland, *10,000 Jokes, Toasts, and Stories*

MARK TWAIN encountered a ruthless businessman from Boston during his travels who boasted that nobody ever got in his way once he determined to do something. He said, "Before I die I mean to make a pilgrimage to the Holy Land. I'm gonna climb Mount Sinai. And when I'm up there I'm gonna read the Ten Commandments aloud at the top of my voice!" Unimpressed, Twain responded, "I got a better idea. Stay in Boston and keep 'em."

—*The Little, Brown Book of Anecdotes*

A GOOD CHRISTIAN is a good citizen. You keep the law of the land. You don't run red lights. You don't purposely overpark. And you don't evade your income tax. You maintain the speed limit. Someone has said, "The last thing to get saved on a Christian is his right foot."

A. J. FOYT is a remarkable race-car driver. When you put that guy in a racing car on the Indianapolis 500, get out of the way. But, you know, most of A. J. Foyt's life is not spent at the 500. He has to drive a car on city streets and highways just like the rest of us, paying attention to speed limits just like we do.

Now let's say Foyt pulls up to a stop sign in Houston one day, and some kid with peach fuzz on his cheeks and a grin on his face pulls up next to him, not knowing who he is. He thinks his car is cool. It has wide tires and lots of chrome stuff underneath it and a really loud exhaust. Foyt is just sitting in his passenger car, but the kid says, "Hey, wanna race?" He doesn't know he is talking to A. J. Foyt. Of course Foyt could easily beat the boy in the drag race. But when the light turns green, Foyt has to apply a whole lot of restraint. There are speed limits on the highway, so he has to sit on his pride as this other kid peels off in the distance.

> Grant us the will to fashion as we feel,
> Grant us the strength to labor as we know,
> Grant us the purpose, ribbed and edged with steel
>   To strike the blow.
> Knowledge we ask not–knowledge Thou has lent,
> But, Lord, the will–there lies our bitter need
> Give us to build above the deep intent
>   The deed, the deed.
>
> —J. Drinkwater, quoted in James Hastings, *Esther*

MY WIFE AND I had the pleasure of spending an evening with former astronaut, General Charles M. Duke. All of us in the room sat in rapt fascination as the man told of the *Apollo 16* mission to the moon, including some interesting tidbits related to driving "Rover," the lunar vehicle, and his actually walking on the surface. We were full of questions which General Duke patiently and carefully answered one after another.

I asked, "Once you were there, weren't you free to make your own decisions and carry out some of your own experiments . . . you know, sort of do as you pleased—maybe stay a little longer if you liked?" He smiled back, "Sure, Chuck, if we didn't want to return to earth!"

He then described the intricate plan, the exact and precise instructions, the essential discipline, the instant obedience that was needed right down to the split second. By the way, he said they had landed somewhat "heavy" when they touched down on the moon. He was referring to their fuel supply. They had plenty left. Guess how much. *One minute.* They landed with sixty seconds of fuel remaining. Talk about being exact! I got the distinct impression that a rebel doesn't fit inside a spacesuit. Whoever represents the United States in the space program must have an unconditional respect for authority.

—Charles R. Swindoll, *Strengthening Your Grip*

OPPORTUNITY

WE ARE ALL FACED with a series of great opportunities brilliantly disguised as unsolvable problems.

—Howard G. Hendricks, *Taking a Stand*

ONE OF MY FAVORITE PHILOSOPHERS writes rather regularly. His name is Pogo. Pogo put his finger on one of the greatest challenges of our life when he said, "Gentlemen, we are surrounded by insurmountable opportunities."

—Tim Hansel, *When I Relax I Feel Guilty*

TIME IS SHORT. Opportunity is knocking. Please answer it. The age-old aphorism remains true: "Four things come not back: the spoken word; the spent arrow; time past; the neglected opportunity."

—Charles R. Swindoll, *The Finishing Touch*

OPTIMISM

ZIG ZIGLAR says he is such an optimist he would go after Moby Dick in a rowboat and take the tartar sauce with him.

—James S. Hewett, *Illustrations Unlimited*

MARINE CORPS GENERAL Chesty Puller made a landing at Inchon. There were Koreans in front of them, there were North Koreans to the flank, there were North Koreans to the other flank, there was the ocean behind them, and he said, "That's great! They'll never get away this time."

Pp

PAIN
(Also see *Adversity, Suffering, Trials*)

I HAVE NEVER READ a poem extolling the virtues of pain, nor seen a statue erected in its honor, nor heard a hymn dedicated to it. Pain is usually defined as "unpleasantness." Christians don't really know how to interpret pain. If you pinned them against the wall, in a dark, secret moment, many Christians would probably admit that pain was God's one mistake. He really should have worked a little harder and invented a better way of coping with the world's dangers. I am convinced that pain gets a bad press. Perhaps we should see statues, hymns, and poems to pain. Why do I think that? Because up close, under a microscope, the pain network is seen in an entirely different light. It is perhaps the paragon of creative genius.

—Philip Yancey, *Where Is God When It Hurts?*

SOMEONE ELSE SAID, "Pain plants the flag of reality in the fortress of a rebel heart." C. S. Lewis said, "God whispers to us in our pleasures, speaks in our conscience, but shouts in our pains: it is His megaphone to rouse a deaf world."

—C. S. Lewis, *The Problem of Pain*

PLEASURE IS NOTHING ELSE but the intermission of pain.

—John Selden, quoted in John Bartlett, *Bartlett's Familiar Quotations*

PASTORS
(Also see *Ministry*)

ONE OF THE REASONS I held back from entering the ministry is that I met so many who look like ministers. Could I be a minister and not look like it? Well, yes, that's possible. Ever once in a while I slip and I look ministerial, kind of slumped over, sad, down in the mouth, judgmental, you know, that look. A girl saw a fellow in line. He was rather straightfaced and serious, and she said,

"Excuse me, are you a minister?" He said, "No ma'am, but I've been sick for about three weeks."

—John Haggai, *How to Win over Worry*

MY WORD to those of us engaged in ministry is, keep a healthy balance. If you teach, also remain a good student. Be teachable. Read. Listen. Learn. Observe. Be ready to change. And change! Admit wrong where you are wrong. Stand firm where you know you are right. Since you are called to be a leader, follow well. You cannot do it all, so delegate. You have a big job to do, let others help you do it. And when they do it well, give them credit. You have a serious work, so keep a good sense of humor.

I often say, take God seriously but don't take yourself too seriously. Laugh often. And don't be afraid even to laugh at things you've once said. I do that once a year. You see, tapes are made of all my messages, which is sort of a frightening thought to begin with. And at the end of the year those who produce our tapes and do the work of putting them on the radio give me a cassette tape of all the things they took out during the year. It's sort of a Christmas gift. Some have even had the audacity to play this tape at a Christmas party for hundreds to hear and enjoy. I cannot believe some of the dumb things I have said. It is enough to reduce one to the size of an ant.

THERE'S THIS NEW CHAIN LETTER going around among churches. No cost is involved. You send a copy of the letter to six other churches that are tired of their ministers too. Then you bundle up your pastor and send him to the church at the bottom of the list. In one week you will receive 16,436 ministers, one of whom should be a dandy! But beware, one church broke the chain and got their old minister back.

—Paul Lee Tan, *Encyclopedia of 7,700 Illustrations*

BACK IN THE OLD TESTAMENT, we have a wonderful portrait of a man I'm going to call the senior pastor of the Wilderness Bible Church. His name is Moses. What an unusual minister! You would never have chosen him had you sat in on the candidating committee looking for the pastor of this unusual "church." For starters, the place he will minister is an unusual church because of its size—about two million, give or take a few thousand. Furthermore, his background is questionable. He killed a man. Nor has this gentleman set many impressive records in the last forty years of his life—which bring us to his age. He's now *eighty*, not the ideal age for a man who must shepherd so many people with no staff. And no building! . . . And did I mention his speech impediment? Along with old age, and a bad resumé working against him, the man *stutters*. Dear Moses . . . what a challenge!

—Charles R. Swindoll, *The Bride*

A MOTHER HAD WATCHED HER SON through the week begin to drain in energy. And by the end of the week he had simply lost the desire to get up and get with the day. She heard the alarm go off through the door. She listened as nine minutes passed and the alarm went off again. Apparently he just kept punching the little snooze button on top of the alarm. Finally, after three or four extra rings, she decided to take charge so she walked in and said, "Son, it's time to get up. You've got to get up." He peeked out from under the covers and said, "Can you give me three good reasons I have to get up?" She said, "Well, yes. First of all, it's Sunday, and you need to get dressed for church. Second, you're forty-three years old and you know better than to lie there. Third, you're the pastor of the church and they expect you to be there!"

—James Hewett, *Illustrations Unlimited*

AFTER HUNDREDS OF YEARS, a model preacher has been found to suit everyone. He preaches exactly twenty minutes and then sits down. He condemns sin, but never hurts anyone's feelings. He works from 8 A.M. to 10 P.M. in every type of work from preaching to custodial service. He tithes weekly to the church and stands ready to contribute to every good work that comes along.

He is twenty-six years old and has been preaching thirty years. He is tall and short, thin and heavyset, and handsome. He has one brown eye and one blue, hair parted down the middle, left side dark and straight, the right brown and wavy.

He has a burning desire to work with teenagers, and spends all his time with older folks. He smiles all the time with a straight face because he has a sense of humor that keeps him seriously dedicated to his work. He makes fifteen calls a day on church members, spends all his time evangelizing the unchurched, and is never out of the office.

—*Christian Beacon*, quoted in Paul Lee Tan, *Encyclopedia of 7,700 Illustrations*

MY MINISTER is a lot like God—I don't see him all week, and I don't understand him on Sunday.

—Haddon Robinson, *Biblical Preaching*

HERE ARE SOME RATHER INTERESTING and creative ways a church could get rid of their pastor. First, you could look him straight in the eye while he's preaching and say "Amen" once in a while and he would preach himself to death in a few weeks. Or you could build him up and encourage him on his good points and he would probably work himself to death by the end of the year. Another way to do it would be to dedicate your life to Christ and ask the preacher to give you a job to do, preferably some lost person you could win to Christ, and the pastor would die immediately of heart failure. Or, you could get the church to unite in prayer for the pastor . . . he'll soon become so effective some larger church will come and take him off your hands and you won't have to worry about it.

—Richard DeHaan, *Men Sent from God*

I HEARD ABOUT A PASTOR who left the pastorate after twenty years. He decided to become a funeral director. Somebody asked, "Why did you do that?"

He answered: "Well, I spent about twelve years trying to straighten out John. He never did straighten out. I spent fourteen months trying to straighten out the marriage of the Smiths, and it never did get straightened out. I spent three years trying to straighten out Susan, and she never did get straightened out. Now when I straighten them out, they stay straight."

GENTLEMEN, understanding your pulpit is vacant, I should like to apply for the position. I have many qualifications: I've been a preacher with much success and also had some success as a writer. Some say I'm a good organizer. I've been a leader most places I've been.

I'm over 50 years of age. I have never preached in one place for more than three years. In some places I have left town after my work has caused riots and disturbances. I must admit I have been in jail three or four times, but not because of any real wrongdoing. My health is not good, though I still get a great deal done. The churches I have preached in have been small, though located in several large cities. I've not got along well with religious leaders in towns where I have preached. In fact, some have threatened me and even attacked me physically. I am not too good at keeping records. I have been known to forget whom I have baptized.

However, if you can use me, I shall do my best for you.

Paul

—Paul Lee Tan, *Encyclopedia of 7,700 Illustrations*

A FRIEND GAVE ME SOME HELPFUL ADVICE. "There are four S's you have to wrestle with as a spiritual leader: self, sex, sloth, and silver."

A good pastor must have:
The strength of an ox,
The tenacity of a bulldog,
The daring of a lion,
The wisdom of an owl,
The harmlessness of a dove,
The industry of a beaver,
The gentleness of a sheep,
The versatility of a chameleon,
The vision of an eagle,
The hide of a rhinoceros,
The perspective of a giraffe,
The disposition of an angel,
The endurance of a camel,
The bounce of a kangaroo,
The stomach of a horse,
The loyalty of an apostle,
The faithfulness of a prophet,
The tenderness of a shepherd,
The fervency of an evangelist,
The devotion of a mother.
And then, he would not please everybody!
—Richard DeHaan, *Men Sent from God*

YOU CANNOT SEPARATE TRUTH from the one who preaches it to you.
—Merrill Tenney

SOMETIME AGO at a seminary graduation: "I'm afraid for this class—that we are turning out too many graduates who have a great number of beliefs but not enough conviction."
—John Walvoord

WANTED: MINISTER FOR GROWING CHURCH. A real challenge for the right man! Opportunity to become better acquainted with people!

Applicant must offer experience as a shop worker, office worker, educator (all levels, including college), artist, salesman, diplomat, writer, theologian, politician, Boy Scout leader, children's worker, minor league athlete, psychologist, vocational counselor, psychiatrist, funeral director, wedding consultant, master of ceremonies, circus clown, missionary, social worker. Helpful, but not essential: experience as a butcher, baker, cowboy, Western Union messenger.

Must know all about problems of birth, marriage, and death; also conversant with latest theories and practices in areas like pediatrics, economics, and nuclear science.

Right man will hold firm views on every topic, but is careful not to upset people who disagree. Must be forthright but flexible; returns criticism and backbiting with Christian love and forgiveness.

Should have an outgoing, friendly disposition at all times. Should be captivating speaker and intent listener.

Education must be beyond Ph.D. requirements, but always concealed in homespun modesty and folksy talk. Able to sound learned at times but most of the time talks and acts like good-ol'-Joe. Familiar with literature read by average congregation.

Must be willing to work long hours, subject to call any time day or night; adaptable to sudden interruption. Will spend at least twenty-five hours preparing sermon. Additional ten hours reading books and magazines.

Applicant's wife must be both stunning and plain, smartly attired but conservative in appearance, gracious and able to get along with everyone. Must be willing to work in church kitchen, teach Sunday school, baby-sit, run multilith machine, wait tables, never listen to gossip, never become discouraged.

Applicant's children must be exemplary in conduct and character; well behaved, yet basically no different from other children; decently dressed.

Opportunity for applicant to live close to work. Furnished home provided; open door hospitality enforced. Must be ever mindful the house does not belong to him.

Directly responsible for views and conduct of all church members and visitors, not confined to direction or support from any one person. Salary not commensurate with experience or need; no overtime pay. All replies kept confidential. Anyone applying will undergo full investigation to determine sanity.

—*Kethiv Qere,* Dallas Theological Seminary student newsletter, March 26, 1975

MINISTERS OUT THERE are dying because the congregation expects them to walk on water. "I feel like a cow that's been milked too many times."

—Jay Kesler, *Being Holy, Being Human*

What Is a Pastor?

If the pastor is young, they say he lacks experience. If his hair is gray, he's getting too old for the young people. If he has five children, he has too many. If he has no children, he's setting a bad example. If he preaches from his notes, he has canned sermons and he's dry. And if his messages are extemporaneous, he isn't deep. If he's attentive to the poor people of the church, they claim he's playing to the grandstand. If he pays attention to the wealthy, he's trying to be an aristocrat. If he uses too many illustrations, he neglects the text. If he doesn't use enough stories, he isn't clear. If he condemns wrong, he's cranky. If he doesn't preach against sin, he's a compromiser. If he preaches the truth, he's offensive. If he doesn't preach the truth, he's a hypocrite. If he fails to please everybody, he's hurting the church and ought to leave. If he does please everybody, he has no convictions. If he drives an old car, he shames his congregation. If he drives a new car, he's setting his affection on earthly things. If he preaches all the time, then the people get tired of hearing one man. If he invites guest preachers, he's shirking his responsibility. If he receives a large salary, he's a mercenary. If he receives a small salary, well, they say he isn't worth much anyway.

—Richard DeHaan, *Men Sent from God*

Who Changed?

There was a preacher whom I used to like. I thought that he was great.
His sermons were wonderful—as long as I liked him.
His speech was passing fair—as long as I liked him.
He lived a clean life—as long as I liked him.
He was a hard worker—as long as I liked him.
He was the man for the job—as long as I liked him.
In fact, I was strong for him—as long as I liked him.

But, he offended me one day. Whether he knew it or not, I do not know.
Since that day, he has ceased to be a good preacher.
His sermons are not so wonderful—since he offended me.
His speech is of no account—since he offended me.
His faults are more prominent—since he offended me.
He is not a hard worker—since he offended me.
He's not the man for the job—since he offended me.
In fact, I am trying to turn everybody against him and get rid of him—since he offended me.
It's really a shame he's changed so much.

—Glen Wheeler, *1010 Illustrations, Poems, and Quotes*

THE MINISTRY is one of the most perilous of professions....

Satan knows that the downfall of a prophet of God is a strategic victory for him, so he rests not day or night devising hidden snares and deadfalls for the ministry. Perhaps a better figure would be the poison dart that only paralyzes its victim, for I think that Satan has little interest in killing the preacher outright. An ineffective, half-alive minister is a better advertisement for hell than a good man dead. . . .

There are indeed some very real dangers of the grosser sort which the minister must guard against, such as love of money and women; but the deadliest perils are far more subtle than these. . . .

There is, for one, the danger that the minister shall come to think of himself as belonging to a privileged class. Our "Christian" society tends to increase this danger by granting the clergy discounts and other courtesies. . . .

Another danger is that he may develop a perfunctory spirit in the performance of the work of the Lord. Familiarity may breed contempt even at the altar of God. How frightful a thing it is for the preacher when he becomes accustomed to his work, when his sense of wonder departs, when he gets used to the unusual, when he loses his solemn fear in the presence of the High and Holy One; when, to put it bluntly, he gets a little bored with God and heavenly things. . . .

Another peril that confronts the minister is that he may come unconsciously to love religious and philosophic ideas rather than saints and sinners. It's altogether possible to feel for the world of lost men the same kind of detached affection that the naturalist Fabre felt for a hive of bees or a hill of blank ants. They are something to study, to learn from, possibly even to help, but no longer to weep over or die for. . . .

Another trap into which the preacher is in danger of falling is that he may just do what comes naturally and just take it easy. . . .It is easy for the minister to be turned into a privileged idler, a social parasite with an open palm and an expectant look. He has no boss within sight; he's not often required to keep regular hours, so he can work at a comfortable pattern of life that permits him to loaf, putter, play, doze, and run about at his pleasure. And many do just that.

To avoid this danger the minister should voluntarily work hard.

—A. W. Tozer, *God Tells the Man Who Cares*

DO I ADDRESS any servant of God here who is afraid of losing his reputation? This is not a reason which will stand examination. My brother, that is a fear which does not trouble me. I have lost my reputation several times, and I would not go across the street to pick it up. It is often seemed to me to be a thing that I should like to lose, that I might no longer be pressed with this huge throng, but might preach to two or three hundred people in a country village, and look after their souls, and stand clear at last to God about each one of them; whereas, here I am tied to a work I cannot accomplish—pastor to more than five thousand people! A sheer impossibility! How can I watch over all your souls? I should have an easy conscience if I had a church of moderate size, which I could efficiently look after. If a reputation gets one into the position I now occupy, it certainly is not a blessing to be coveted. But if you have to do anything for Christ which will lose you the respect of good people, and yet you feel bound to do it, never give two thoughts to your reputation; for, if you do, it is already gone into that secret place where you should most of all cherish it. The highest reputation in the world is to be faithful—faithful to your God and your own conscience. As to the approbation of the unconverted multitude, or of worldly professors, do not care the turn of a button for it; it may be a deadly heritage. Many a man is more a slave to his admirers than he dreams of: the love of approbation is more a bondage than an inner dungeon would be. If you have done the right thing before God, and are not afraid of His great Judgment Seat, fear nothing, go forward.

—Charles H. Spurgeon, *Metropolitan Tabernacle Pulpit*

PATIENCE

In every life
There's a pause that is better than onward rush,
Better than hewing or mightiest doing;
'Tis the standing still at Sovereign will.
There's a hush that is better than ardent speech,
Better than sighing or wilderness crying;
'Tis the being still at Sovereign will.
The pause and the hush sing a double song
In unison low and for all time long.
O human soul, God's working plan
Goes on, nor needs the aid of man!
Stand still, and see!
Be still, and know!

—V. Raymond Edman, *The Disciplines of Life*

THERE WAS ONCE A FELLOW who, with his dad, farmed a little piece of land. Several times a year they would load up the old ox-drawn cart with vegetables and go into the nearest city to sell their produce. Except for their name and the patch of ground, father and son had little in common. The old man believed in taking it easy. The boy was usually in a hurry—the go-getter type.

One morning, bright and early, they hitched up the ox to the loaded cart and started on the long journey. The son figured that if they walked faster, kept going all day and night, they'd make market by early the next morning. So he kept prodding the ox with a stick, urging the beast to get a move on.

"Take it easy, son," said the old man. "You'll last longer."

"But if we get to market ahead of the others, we'll have a better chance of getting good prices," argued the son.

No reply. Dad just pulled his hat down over his eyes and fell asleep on the seat. Itchy and irritated, the young man kept goading the ox to walk faster. His stubborn pace refused to change.

Four hours and four miles later down the road, they came to a little house. The father woke up, smiled, and said, "Here's your uncle's place. Let's stop in and say hello."

"But we've lost an hour already," complained the hot shot.

"Then a few more minutes won't matter. My brother and I live so close, yet we see each other so seldom," the father answered slowly.

The boy fidgeted and fumed while the two old men laughed and talked away almost an hour. On the move again, the man took his turn leading the ox. As they approached a fork in the road, the father led the ox to the right.

"The left is the shorter way," said the son.

"I know it," replied the old man, "but this way is much prettier."

"Have you no respect for time?" the young man asked impatiently.

"Oh, I respect it very much! That's why I like to use it to look at beauty and enjoy each moment to the fullest."

The winding path led through graceful meadows, wildflowers, and along a rippling stream—all of which the young man missed as he churned within, preoccupied and boiling with anxiety. He didn't even notice how lovely the sunset was that day.

Twilight found them in what looked like a huge, colorful garden. The old man breathed in the aroma, listened to the bubbling brook, and pulled the ox to a halt. "Let's sleep here," he sighed.

"This is the last trip I'm taking with you," snapped the son. "You're more interested in watching sunsets and smelling flowers than in making money!"

"Why, that's the nicest thing you've said in a long time," smiled the dad. A couple of minutes later he was snoring—as his boy glared back at the stars. The night dragged slowly, the son was restless.

Before sunrise the young man hurriedly shook his father awake. They hitched up and went on. About a mile down the road they happened upon another farmer—a total stranger—trying to pull his cart out of a ditch.

"Let's give him a hand," whispered the old men.

"And lose more time?" the boy exploded.

"Relax son. You might be in a ditch sometime yourself. We need to help others in need—don't forget that." The boy looked away in anger.

It was almost eight o'clock that morning by the time the other cart was back on the road. Suddenly, a great flash split the sky. What sounded like thunder followed. Beyond the hills, the sky grew dark.

"Looks like a big rain in the city," said the old man.

"If we had hurried, we'd be almost sold out by now," grumbled his son.

"Take it easy, you'll last longer. And you'll enjoy life so much more," counseled the kind old gentleman.

It was late afternoon by the time they got to the hill overlooking the city. They stopped and stared down at it for a long, long time. Neither of them said a word. Finally, the young man put his hand on his father's shoulder and said, "I see what you mean, Dad."

They turned their cart around and began to roll slowly away from what had once been the city of Hiroshima.

—Charles R. Swindoll, *Come Before Winter*

Could You Hurry a Little?

Lord, I know there are countless times
When I must wait patiently for You.
Waiting develops endurance.
It strengthens my faith
And deepens my dependence upon You.
I know You are Sovereign God—
Not an errand boy
Responding to the snap of my finger.
I know Your timing is neatly wrapped
In Your incomparable wisdom.
But, Lord
You have appointed prayer
To obtain answers!
Even David the Psalmist cried
With confident boldness:
"It is time, O Lord, for you to act."
God, on this silent sunless morning
When I am hedged in on every side
I too cry boldly.

You are my Father, and I am Your child.
So, Lord, could You hurry a little?

—Ruth Harms Calkin, *Lord, Could You Hurry a Little?*

GOD HAS HIS SET TIMES. It is not for us to know them. Indeed, we cannot know them. We must wait for them. If God had told Abraham in Haran that he must wait all those years until he pressed the promised child to his bosom, his heart would have failed him. So in gracious love, the length of the weary years was hidden. And only as they were nearly spent and there were only a few more months to wait, God told him, according to the time of life, "Sarah shall have a son."

If God told you on the front end how long you would wait to find the fulfillment of your desire or pleasure or dream, you'd lose heart. You'd grow weary in well doing. So would I. But He doesn't. He just says, "Wait. I keep My word. I'm in no hurry. In the process of time I'm developing you to be ready for the promise."

—F. B. Meyer, *Abraham*

A YOUNG MAN desired to go to India as a missionary with the London Missionary Society. Mr. Wilks was appointed to consider the young man's fitness for such a post. He wrote to the young man, and told him to call on him at six o'clock the next morning.

Although the applicant lived many miles off, he was at the house punctually at six o'clock and was ushered into the drawing room. He waited—and waited—and waited wonderingly, but patiently. Finally Mr. Wilks entered the room about mid-morning.

Without apology, Mr. Wilks began, "Well, young man, so you want to be a missionary?"

"Yes, sir, I do."

"Do you love the Lord Jesus Christ?"

"Yes, sir, I certainly do."

"And have you any education?"

"Yes, sir, a little."

"Well, now, we'll try you; can you spell 'cat'?"

The young man looked confused, and hardly knew how to answer so preposterous a question. His mind evidently halted between indignation and submission, but in a moment he replied steadily, "C, a, t, cat."

"Very good," said Mr. Wilks. "Now can you spell 'dog'?"

The youthful Job was stunned but replied, "D, o, g, dog."

"Well, that is right; I see you will do in your spelling, and now for your arithmetic; how much is two times two?"

The patient youth gave the right reply and was dismissed.

Mr. Wilks gave his report at the committee meeting. He said, "I cordially recommend that young man; his testimony and character I have duly examined. I tried his self-denial, he was up in the morning early; I tried his patience by keeping him waiting; I tried his humility and temper by insulting his intelligence. He will do just fine."

—Charles H. Spurgeon, *Lectures to My Students*

PEACE

In Acceptance Lieth Peace

He said, "I will forget the dying faces;
The empty places,
They shall be filled again.
O voices moaning deep within me, cease."
But vain the word; vain, vain:
Not in forgetting lieth peace.

He said, "I will crowd action upon action,
The strife of faction
Shall stir me and sustain;
O tears that drown the fire of manhood cease."
But vain the word; vain, vain:
Not in endeavor lieth peace.

He said, "I will withdraw me and be quiet,
Why meddle in life's riot?
Shut be my door to pain.
Desire, thou dost befool me, thou shalt cease."
But vain the word; vain, vain:"
Not in aloofness lieth peace.

He said, "I will submit; I am defeated.
God hath depleted
My life of its rich gain.
O futile murmurings, why will ye not cease?"
But vain the word; vain, vain:"
 Not in submission lieth peace.

He said, "I will accept the breaking sorrow
Which God to-morrow
Will to His son explain."
Then did the turmoil deep within him cease.
Not vain the word, not vain;
For in Acceptance lieth peace.

—Amy Carmichael, *Toward Jerusalem*

Spiritual Retreat

This was my calculated plan:
I would set aside my usual schedule —
The menial tasks that wedge in routinely.
In the peace and quiet of my living room
I would relax in Your glorious presence.
How joyfully I envisioned the hours —
My personal spiritual retreat!
With Bible and notebook beside me
I would study and meditate —
I would intercede for the needy world.

But how differently it happened, Lord:
Never has the phone rung so persistently.
Sudden emergencies kept pouring in
Like summer cloudbursts.
My husband came home ill.
There were appointments to cancel
Plans to rearrange.
The mailman brought two disturbing letters
A cousin whose name I couldn't remember
Stopped by on her way through town.
My morning elation became drooping deflation.

And yet, dear Lord,
You were with me in it all!
I sense Your vital presence—
Your sure and steady guidance.
Not once did you leave me stranded.
Perhaps, in Your great wisdom
You longed to teach me a practical truth:

When *You* are my Spiritual Retreat
I need not be a spiritual recluse.

—Ruth Harms Calkin, *Lord, You Love to Say Yes*

PEACE IS THE BRIEF GLORIOUS MOMENT in history when everybody stands around reloading.

—Lloyd Cory, *Quote Unquote*

Lord, keep me still,
Though stormy waves may blow
And waves my little bark may overflow,
Or even if in darkness I must go;
Lord, keep me still.

The waves are in Thy hand,
The roughest seas subside at Thy command.
Steer Thou my bark in safety to the land
And keep me still,
Keep me still.

—Author unknown, quoted in Al Bryant, *Sourcebook of Poetry*

PEACE IS that calm of mind that is not ruffled by adversity, overclouded by a remorseful conscience, or disturbed by fear.

HORATIO SPAFFORD, a businessman in Chicago, sent his wife and three daughters to Europe by ship while he remained back in the States, intending to join them later. En route there was a terrible storm and a shipwreck during which their three daughters drowned. Mrs. Spafford made it to safety and wired back saying, "All of our daughters have been lost. Only I have been saved."

He took the next vessel. As they came near the place where his daughters drowned, the skipper of the ship pointed to the place where the other ship had gone down. It was there on the deck of the ship he wrote these stirring words:

When peace like a river attendeth my way,
When sorrows like sea billows roll;

Whatever my lot, Thou hast taught me to say,
"It is well, it is well with my soul."

—John Haggai, *How to Win over Worry*

Lord, make me an instrument of Your peace!
Where there is hatred, let me sow love;
Where there is injury, pardon;
Where there is doubt, faith;
Where there is despair, hope;
Where there is darkness, light;
Where there is sadness, joy.
Oh, Divine Master, grant that I may not so much seek
To be consoled, as to console;
To be understood, as to understand;
To be loved, as to love.
For it is in giving that we receive;
It is in pardoning that we are pardoned;
It is in dying that we are born to eternal life!

—Francis of Assisi

THE TIME HAS COME for me to reorganize my life, my peace—I cry out. I cannot adjust my life to secure any fruitful peace. Here I am at sixty-four, still seeking peace. It is a hopeless dream.

—H. G. Wells, quoted in Leroy Brownlow, *Better Than Medicine*

WASHINGTON has a large assortment of peace monuments. We build one after every war.

—Don MacLean quoted in Lloyd Cory, *Quote Unquote*

I WANT FIRST OF ALL—in fact, as an end to these other desires—to be at peace with myself. I want a singleness of eye, a purity of intention, a central core to my life that will enable me to carry out these obligations and activities as well as I can. I want, in fact—to borrow from the language of the saints—to live "in grace" as much of the time as possible. I'm not using this term in a strictly theological sense. By grace I mean inner harmony, essentially spiritual, which can be translated into outward harmony. I'm seeking perhaps what

Socrates asked for in the prayer from the Phaedrus when he said, "May the outward and inward man be as one." I would like to achieve a state of inner spiritual grace from which I could function and give as I was meant to in the eye of God.

—Anne Morrow Lindbergh, *Gift from the Sea*

PEER PRESSURE

ONCE A SPIDER built a beautiful web in an old house. He kept it clean and shiny so that flies would patronize it. The minute he got a "customer" he would clean up after him so the other flies would not get suspicious.

Then one day this fairly intelligent fly came buzzing by the clean spiderweb. Old man spider called out, "Come in and sit." But the fairly intelligent fly said, "No, sir. I don't see other flies in your house, and I am not going in alone!"

But presently he saw on the floor below a large crowd of flies dancing around on a piece of brown paper. He was delighted! He was not afraid if lots of flies were doing it. So he came in for a landing.

Just before he landed, a bee zoomed by, saying, "Don't land there, stupid! That's flypaper!" But the fairly intelligent fly shouted back, "Don't be silly. Those flies are dancing. There's a big crowd there. Everybody's doing it. That many flies can't be wrong!" Well, you know what happened. He died on the spot.

Some of us want to be with the crowd so badly that we end up in a mess. What does it profit a fly (or a person) if he escapes the web only to end up in the glue?

—Charles R. Swindoll, *Living Above the Level of Mediocrity*

IF A MAN DOES NOT KEEP PACE with his companions, perhaps it is because he hears a different drummer. Let him step to the music which he hears, however measured or far away.

—Henry David Thoreau, *Thoreau: Walden and Other Writings*

I KNEW A BLIND fifteen-year-old girl who refused to admit she had a handicap. She would not accept the help of a special teacher provided by the school. And her parents could not even get her to use a white cane. To thump along the corridor of the school marked her as different from her peers and she couldn't tolerate that distinction. I watched one day as she walked to her next class with her head erect as though she knew where she was going. Before I could stop her, she walked straight into a post. Even this experience was insufficient to make her use the device which other teenagers did not need. . . .

I worked with the parents of a second grade boy having a hearing problem. He simply would not let them put a hearing aid in his ear. He would rather be deaf than different. Truly, conformity is a powerful drive in children of all ages. . . .

In summary, it is important for your pre-teenager to know about group pressure before it reaches its peak. Someday he may be sitting in a car with four friends who decide to shoot some heroin. Your preparation is no guarantee that he will have the courage to stand alone at that critical moment, but his knowledge of peer influence could provide the independence to do what is right.

—James Dobson, *Hide or Seek*

A FEW YEARS AGO psychologist Ruth W. Berenda and her associates carried out an interesting experiment with teenagers designed to show how a person handled group pressure. The plan was simple. They brought groups of ten adolescents into a room for a test. Subsequently each group of ten was instructed to raise their hands when the teacher pointed to the longest line on three separate charts. What one person in the group did not know was that nine of the others in the room had been instructed ahead of time to vote for the second-longest line.

Regardless of the instructions they heard, once they were all together in the group, the nine were not to vote for the longest line, but rather vote for the next-to-the-longest line.

The desire of the psychologists was to determine how one person reacted when completely surrounded by a large number of people who obviously stood against what was true.

The experiment began with nine teen-agers voting for the wrong line. The stooge would typically glance around, frown in confusion, and slip his hand up with the group. The instructions were repeated and the next card was raised. Time after time, the self-conscious stooge would sit there saying a short line is longer than a long line, simply because he lacked the courage to challenge the group. This remarkable conformity occurred in about seventy-five percent of the cases, and was true of small children and high-school students as well. Berenda concluded that, "Some people had rather be president than right," which is certainly an accurate assessment.

—James Dobson, *Hide or Seek*

IT IS DOUBTFUL if the majority has ever been right.

—Arnold Toynbee, quoted in Charles R. Swindoll, *Living Above the Level of Mediocrity*

PEOPLE

EVERY TIME I read the names of Isaiah's two sons—Maher-shalal-hash-baz and Shear-jashub—I chuckle to myself that dinner would be over before they could get called in to supper.

A HASSLED SHOPPER approached the perfume counter and asked the busy clerk, "Do you still have Elizabeth Taylor's *Passion?*" To which she replied, "If I did, honey, would I be working here?"

THERE ARE NO ORDINARY PEOPLE. You have never talked to a mere mortal. Nations, cultures, arts, civilizations—these are mortal, and their life is to ours as the life of a gnat. But it is immortals whom we joke with, work with, marry, snub, exploit—immortal horrors of everlasting splendours.

—C. S. Lewis, *The Weight of Glory*

GARY SMALLEY and John Trent put on a delightful seminar in which they discuss temperaments in a family. They have linked these temperaments with the animal kingdom.

The *Lion* temperament is the strong-hearted, determined, resilient individual. Decisive, opinionated, usually loud.

Then there's the *Golden Retriever,* care-giving, and compassionate. Doesn't make any demands. You can unload on the Golden Retriever. He lies right down there and understands.

Next is the Otter. Fun-loving, kick-back Otter. Usually it's the youngest in the family. You know the Otter. "Man, it doesn't make a lot of difference, you know? My older brother, he'll handle it. Just go see him. I'm kickin' back, baby. This is no big deal."

Fourth, is the hard-working, diligent *Beaver.* Responsible, organizing. Beavers don't have one briefcase, they have two. And they're not those little tiny, thin, slim-line Samsonites. They're expandable and look like small luggage.

They need dollies to carry them in the airport. And they know exactly where they're going. You get a Lion/Beaver combination, whoa! It is really something.

A FRUSTRATED PIANIST shouted to the soloist, "I'm playing on white keys and I'm playing on black keys, so why must you sing in the cracks?"

A FOOLISH SCIENTIST made plans to send a rocket to the sun. Someone said, "You're gonna burn up." "No," he answered, "we're going at night."

SUFFERING FROM COMPARISONS? Someone once told me, "There's no one quite like a former pastor or a first husband."

IT'S A SCIENTIFIC FACT that people who are right-handed use the left side of their brain. So left-handed people are the only ones in their right mind.

A MAN PAID A VISIT to a local psychologist. When the doctor asked him what had prompted the visit, the man said, "I'm suffering from an inferiority complex."

In the ensuing weeks, the psychologist put his new patient through an intensive battery of tests. Next came the long wait while the test results were tabulated and appropriate correlations were made.

Finally, the doctor called the man and asked him to return to the clinic. "I have some interesting news for you," the doctor began.

"What's that?" asked the man.

"It's no complex," the psychologist retorted. "You are inferior."

—Charles R. Swindoll, *Three Steps Forward, Two Steps Back*

A PHRASE I STILL HEAR occasionally is "all shook up," a phrase made popular by the late Elvis Presley. Several years ago an issue of *Newsweek* magazine had an interesting article about this man. It was titled, "All Shook-Up." Elvis

Presley was born dirt-poor in a little town in Mississippi, the only child. At the young age of eighteen, while making fourteen dollars a week as a truck driver, he, just on a lark, decided to make a recording. And he became the best paid male entertainer in the history of America. At age twenty-three he lost his mother.

Just before his death at age forty-two, he wished he could find one week when he could just live a normal life, going up and down the streets of his city without being harassed. He would pay a million dollars, for one week of peace.

Pat Boone said of Elvis, "I cared a lot for Elvis." He said, "He went in the wrong direction. Ironically, we met for the last time when I was going toward the East and he was on his way to Las Vegas. He said to me, 'Say, Pat, where you going?' And I told him I was going to be involved in some kind of ministry. And he says, 'Hey, I'm going to Vegas. Pat, as long as I've known you, you've been going in the wrong direction.' Pat Boone answered, 'Elvis, that just depends on where you're coming from and where you're going.'"

—*Newsweek*, August 29, 1977

PERFECTIONISM

A MAN WAS SUCH A PERFECTIONIST he kept a newspaper under the cuckoo clock.

—Tom Eisenman, *Temptations Men Face*

ONE OF THE MOST CLEVER Volkswagen ads shows an impeccable little car— with a flat tire. And the caption reads, "Nobody's Perfect."

A PERFECTIONIST IS a person who takes pains and gives them to others.

—*Education Digest*, quoted in Lloyd Cory, *Quote Unquote*

PERSEVERANCE

REMEMBER THE CHILD'S TOY that's a big vinyl doll with a heavy round weight of sand in the bottom? You punch it, it bounces right up again. Punch it again and it comes back to the upright position. Similarly those Christians in the early church kept bouncing back.

—Donald Barnhouse, *Romans*

Keeping On

I've dreamed many dreams that never came true,
I've seen them vanish at dawn;
But I've realized enough of my dreams, thank God,
To make me want to dream on.

I've prayed many prayers when no answer came,
I've waited patient and long;
But answers have come to enough of my prayers
To make me keep praying on.

I've trusted many a friend who failed
And left me to weep alone;
But I've found enough of my friends true-blue
To make me keep trusting on.

I've sown many seeds that fell by the way
For the birds to feed upon;
But I've held enough golden sheaves in my hand,
To make me keep sowing on.

I've drained the cup of disappointment and pain,
I've gone many days without song,
But I've sipped enough nectar from the rose of life
To make me want to live on.

—Charles Allen, *The Secret of Abundant Living*

AN ADDRESS at Harrow School, October 29, 1941: "Never give in, never give in, never, never, never, never—in nothing, great or small, large or petty—never give in except to convictions of honor and good sense. Never give in." Then he sat down.

—Winston Churchill

WILLIAM CAREY said of his biographer, "If he gives me credit for being a plodder, he will describe me justly. Anything beyond that will be too much. I can plod. I can persevere in any definite pursuit. To this I owe everything."

—John Woodbridge, *Great Leaders of the Christian Church*

THE LIFE OF FRANCIS THOMPSON was a downward spiral that landed him on the streets of nineteenth-century London—a useless vagabond, an opium addict, a starving derelict. There, God caught him. Finally.

The son of a doctor, Thompson started out with great potential. His father sent him to study for the priesthood, and then to another school to become a doctor. But he failed at both professions and became a wastrel instead, running from responsibility, family, and God.

Eventually, this prodigal hit bottom. Wandering the back alleys of London, he was hungry, friendless, and addicted to drugs. With tattered clothes and broken shoes, he barely survived by selling matches and newspapers. Still, God did not relent in His dogged chase to capture the young man's soul.

A ray of hope came when Thompson began to write poetry. Wilfred Meynell, an editor, immediately saw Thompson's genius. He published his works, encouraged him to enter a hospital, and personally nursed him through his convalescence. This marked a spiritual turnaround in Thompson's life. In the poem "The Hound of Heaven," he writes of his flight from God and God's pursuit of him.

> I fled Him, down the nights and down the days;
> I fled Him, down the arches of the years;
> I fled Him, down the labyrinthine ways
> Of my own mind; and in the mist of tears
> I hid from Him, and under running laughter. . . .
> Still with unhurrying chase,
> And unperturbed pace,
> Deliberate speed, majestic instancy,
> Came on the following Feet,
> And a Voice above their beat—
> "Naught shelters thee, who wilt not shelter Me."

With this same breathless pursuit, the Hound of Heaven once chased another running man. This person was not a vagrant; he was a well-educated Pharisee. Nonetheless, he stubbornly fled from Christ until, one day, the Hound caught him on the dusty road to Damascus.

—Frank N. Magill, *Cyclopedia of World Authors*

I ONCE HEARD W. A. CRISWELL, long-time beloved pastor of the First Baptist Church in Dallas, Texas, tell a story about an evangelist who loved to hunt. As best I can recall, the man bought two setter pups that were topnotch bird dogs.

He kept them in his backyard, where he trained them. One morning, an ornery, little, vicious looking bulldog came shuffling and snorting down the alley. He crawled under the fence into the backyard where the setters spent their days. It was easy to see he meant business. The evangelist's first impulse was to take his setters and lock them in the basement so they wouldn't tear up that little bulldog. But he decided he would just let the creature learn a lesson he would never forget. Naturally, they got into a scuffle in the backyard, and those two setters and that bulldog went round and round and round! The little critter finally had enough, so he squeezed under the fence and took off. All the rest of that day he whined and licked his sores. Interestingly, the next day at about the same time, here came that same ornery little bulldog—back under the fence and after those setters. Once again those two bird dogs beat the stuffing out of that little bowlegged animal and would have chewed him up if he hadn't retreated down the alley. Would you believe, the very next day he was back! Same time, same station, same results. Once again after the bulldog had had all he could take, he crawled back under the fence and found his way home to lick his wounds.

"Well," the evangelist said, "I had to leave for a revival meeting. I was gone several weeks. And when I came back, I asked my wife what had happened. She said, 'Honey, you just won't believe what's happened. Every day, at the same time every morning, that little bulldog came back in the backyard and fought with our two setters. He didn't miss a day! And I want you to know it has come to the point that when our setters simply hear that bulldog snorting down the alley and spot him squeezing under the fence, they immediately start whining and run down into our basement. That little, old bulldog struts around our backyard now just like he owns it."

—Charles R. Swindoll, *Living Above the Level of Mediocrity*

Two frogs fell into a deep cream bowl,
One was an optimistic soul;
But the other took the gloomy view,
"We shall drown," he cried, without more ado.
So with a last despairing cry,
He flung up his legs and said, "Good-bye."
Quoth the other frog with a merry grim,
"I can't get out, but I won't give in.
I'll just swim round till my strength is spent,
Then will I die the more content."
Bravely he swam till it would seem
His struggles began to churn the cream.

On the top of the butter at last he stopped,
And out of the bowl he gaily hopped.
What of the moral? 'Tis easily found:
If you can't hop out, keep swimming round.

—Walter Knight, *Knight's Master Book of New Illustrations*

PRESS ON. Nothing in the world can take the place of persistence. Talent will not; nothing is more common than unsuccessful individuals with talent. Genius will not; unrewarded genius is almost a proverb. Education will not; the world is full of educated derelicts. Persistence and determination alone are omnipotent.

—Calvin Coolidge

SOMETIMES IT IS VERY HARD TO KEEP ON when we do not seem to be getting anywhere. When Thomas Carlyle had finished the first volume of his book, *The French Revolution,* he gave the finished manuscript to his friend John Stuart Mill and asked him to read it. It took Mr. Mill several days to read it and as he read, he realized that it was truly a great literary achievement. Late one night as he finished the last page he laid the manuscript aside by his chair in the den of his home. The next morning the maid came; seeing those papers on the floor, she thought they were simply discarded. She threw them into the fire, and they were burned.

On March 6, 1835—he never forgot the date—Mill called on Carlyle in deep agony and told him that his work has been destroyed. Carlyle replied, "It's all right. I'm sure I can start over in the morning and do it again."

Finally, after great apologies, John Mill left and started back home. Carlyle watched his friend walking away and said to his wife, "Poor Mill. I feel so sorry for him. I did not want him to see how crushed I really am."

Then heaving a sigh, he said, "Well, the manuscript is gone, so I had better start writing again."

It was a long, hard process especially because the inspiration was gone. It is always hard to recapture the verve and the vigor if a man has to do a thing like that twice. But he set out to do it again and finally completed the work.

Thomas Carlyle walked away from disappointment. He could do nothing about a manuscript that was burned up. So it is with us: There are times to get up and get going and let what happened happen.

—William Barclay, *The King and the Kingdom*

PERSPECTIVE

FROM BIRTH TO EIGHTEEN a girl needs good parents; from eighteen to thirty-five she needs good looks; from thirty-five to fifty-five she needs a good personality, and from fifty-five on she needs cash.

—Sophie Tucker, quoted in Rosalind Russell, *Life Is a Banquet*

The Blind Man and the Elephant

It was six men of Indostan
To learning much inclined,
Who went to see the elephant
   (Though all of them were blind),
That each by observation
   Might satisfy his mind.

The first approached the elephant,
   And, happening to fall
Against his broad and sturdy side,
   At once began to bawl,
"God bless me! but the elephant
   Is very like a wall!"

The second, feeling of the tusk
   Cried, "Ho! What have we here
So very round and smooth and sharp?
   To me 'tis mighty clear
This wonder of an elephant
   Is very like a spear!"

The third approached the animal,
   And, happening to take
The squirming trunk within his hands,
   Thus boldly up and spake:
"I see," quoth he, "the elephant,
   Is very like a snake!"

The fourth reached out his eager hand,
   And felt about the knee;
"What most this wondrous beast is like
   Is mighty plain," quoth he;
"'Tis clear enough the elephant
   Is very like a tree."

The fifth, who chanced to touch the ear,
    Said, "E'en the blindest man
Can tell what this resembles most.
    Deny the fact, who can,
This marvel of an elephant
    Is very like a fan!"

The sixth no sooner had begun
    About the beast to grope,
Than, seizing on the swinging tail
    That fell within his scope,
"I see," quoth he, "the elephant
    Is very like a rope!"
And so these men of Indostan
    Disputed loud and long,
Each in his own opinion
    Exceeding stiff and strong,
Though each was partly in the right,
    And all were in the wrong.

So, oft in theologic wars
    The disputants, I ween,
Rail on in utter ignorance
    Of what each other mean,
And prate about an elephant
    Not one of them has seen!

—John Godfrey Saxe, quoted in James Gilchrist Lawson, *The World's Best-Loved Poems*

A NEW MEMBER of British parliament took his eight-year-old daughter on a brief tour of his beloved London. They came to Westminster Abbey and the awesomeness of it struck that little girl. She stood looking way up at those columns, and studying the beauty and grandeur of the Gothic church building. Her father was intrigued at her concentration. He looked down and said, "Sweetheart, what are you thinking about?" She said, "Daddy, I was thinking how big you seem at home and how small you look in here."

CONSIDERING THE ALTERNATIVE often helps one's perspective. A fellow who had a heavy, heavy pack of worries, cares, and responsibilities of life on his back, trudged along. The road seemed rougher and rougher and the pack got heavier and heavier. Finally, he just dropped down and said, "I'm ready to die!" Suddenly, the death angel appeared and said, "Did you call for me?" Rising quickly, he said, "Yeah, would you help me get this pack back up on my back?"

A MAN LOOKED LIKE he lived life on top of all circumstances. Never had a down day. Came to work happy. Went home cheery. People around him wondered what his secret was.

One day a friend discovered that he was faking it. He said, "Now I know why you're always so cheery. You've really got it made! Just yesterday afternoon I was riding in a taxi when I passed you. You were sitting there listening intently to this beautiful young woman whose back was to the street and you were enjoying a snack in a lovely sidewalk cafe."

"Well," he whispered, "let me tell you the truth. That lovely young woman is my wife who was telling me she was leaving me—and that was our furniture on the sidewalk." Things aren't always as they seem. Sometimes they're worse.

—Lloyd Cory, *Quote Unquote*

THERE ARE FEW THINGS WORSE than living in a city and not knowing your way around. This happened to us when we lived in San Francisco for a few months the latter part of 1957. It is easy to get lost. All the streets on one side of Mission run in one direction—on the diagonal. And all the streets on the other side of Mission run in the perpendicular. Then you add those incredible hills and the winding streets and the little tiny signs that should have been repainted years ago, all the buildings, many of which look alike, and the fog and the hills and the fog and the trolleys, and you're apt to get lost.

Cynthia and I were with some friends atop the new San Francisco Hilton one year and things changed. The Hilton has over twenty stories. For the first time the layout of that city fell into place for me. I can't really explain why, but it didn't until then. Off in this direction was the Golden Gate. Over here was the Bay Bridge. Down here was Fisherman's Wharf, and then Nob Hill and then Chinatown, and back down south were Daly City and points down the peninsula. From that perspective, we could see everything at once.

A MAN WHO WAS LOSING HIS MEMORY went to his doctor for advice. He received this diagnosis from the doctor, "We cannot help your memory with out impairing your eyesight. Now the choice is yours. Would you rather be able to see or to remember?" The man thoughtfully replied, "Frankly, I'd rather have my eyesight than my memory. You see, I'd rather see where I'm going than remember where I've been."

—Erwin Lutzer, *Failure: the Back Door to Success*

A CO-ED WROTE THE FOLLOWING LETTER to her parents:

> Dear Mom and Dad:
>
> Just thought I'd drop you a note to clue you in on my plans. I've fallen in love with a guy called Jim. He quit high school after grade eleven to get married. About a year ago he got a divorce.
>
> We've been going steady for two months and we plan to get married in the fall. Until then, I've decided to move into his apartment (I think I might be pregnant).
>
> At any rate, I dropped out of school last week, although I'd like to finish college sometime in the future.

On the next page, the letter continued,

> Mom and Dad,
>
> I just want you to know that everything I've written so far in this letter is false. NONE of it is true.
>
> But, Mom and Dad, it IS true that I got a C- in French and flunked my Math. . . . It IS true that I'm going to need a lot more money for my tuition payments.

This girl made her point! Even bad news can sound good if it is seen from a different perspective.

—Erwin Lutzer, *Failure: the Backdoor to Success*

A FARMER HAD A COW that gave birth to twin calves. That afternoon at the supper table he was just delighted when he was able to tell his wife, "Ol' bossy had twins today. You know, honey, we're gonna give one of those calves to the Lord and we're gonna keep one for ourselves. That's the way it oughta be." A couple of days later he was rather quiet and solemn and she asked what was wrong. He said, "Well, honey, I was in the barn today and I noticed the Lord's calf had died."

—D. Martyn Lloyd-Jones

PESSIMIST

A PESSIMIST IS a person who is seasick during the entire voyage of life.

—*Grit,* quoted in Lloyd Cory, *Quote Unquote*

TWO PESSIMISTS met at a party. Instead of shaking hands, they shook heads.

—*Chicago Tribune,* quoted in Lloyd Cory, *Quote Unquote*

I'VE GOT A PASTOR FRIEND who has been in a church now about forty years. Some of the board members were there when his predecessor was there, and they're still on the board. When I saw him last he said to me, "I ran into one of those old guys the other day. He told me he was sorry to have missed the board meeting the other evening. He said, 'I was looking forward to voting no.'"

I ONCE HEARD ABOUT A FARMER who was continually optimistic, seldom discouraged or blue. He had a neighbor who was just the opposite. Grim and gloomy, he faced each new morning with a heavy sigh.

The happy, optimistic farmer would see the sun coming up and shout over the roar of the tractor, "Look at the beautiful sun and clear sky!" And with a frown, the negative neighbor would reply, "Yeah—it'll probably scorch the crops!"

When clouds would gather and much-needed rain would start to fall, our positive friend would smile across the fence, "Ain't this great—God is giving our corn a drink today!" Again, the same negative response, "Uh huh, but if it doesn't stop 'fore long it'll flood and wash everything away."

One day the optimist decided to put his pessimistic neighbor to the maximum test. He bought the smartest, most expensive bird dog he could find. He trained him to do things no other dog on earth could do—impossible feats that would surely astonish anyone.

He invited the pessimist to go duck hunting with him. They sat in the boat, hidden in the duck blind. In came the ducks. Both men fired and several ducks fell into the water. "Go get 'em!" ordered the owner with a gleam in his eye. The dog leaped out of the boat, walked on the water, and picked up the birds one by one.

"Well, what do you think of that?"

Unsmiling, the pessimist answered, "He can't swim, can he?"

—John Haggai, *How to Win over Worry*

PHILOSOPHERS

PHILOSOPHERS ARE PEOPLE who write about things they don't understand, and make it sound like it's your fault.

—S. Lewis Johnson, *Bibliotheca Sacra*, October–December 1962

PHILOSOPHY

GOOD PHILOSOPHY MUST EXIST if for no other reason than because bad philosophy needs to be answered. The learned life then, is, for some, a duty.

—C. S. Lewis, *The Weight of Glory*

THERE IS THAT GLORIOUS EPICUREAN PHILOSOPHY uttered by my friend, the historian, in one of his flashing moments: "Give us the luxuries of life, and we will dispense with its necessities." Just bring me what is fun and we'll get away from the things that hurt.

—John Bartlett, *Bartlett's Familiar Quotations*

WORLD PHILOSOPHIES HAVE BEEN SUMMARIZED in this manner: Greece said, "Be wise, know yourself." Rome said, "Be strong, discipline yourself." Religion says, "Be holy, conform yourself." Epicureanism says, "Be sensuous, enjoy yourself." Education says, "Be resourceful, expand yourself." Materialism says, "Be satisfied, please yourself." Psychology says, "Be confident, fulfill yourself." Pride says, "Be superior, promote yourself." Asceticism says, "Be inferior, suppress yourself." Humanism says, "Be capable, believe in yourself." Philanthropy says, "Be generous, give yourself." Legalism says, "Be pious, limit yourself."

Isn't it interesting how all of the philosophies end with the same word, and how each one seems to differ from the philosophy of Jesus Christ: "Be a servant, think of others."

IN 1845, Henry David Thoreau built a tiny cabin beside Walden Pond in Concord, Massachusetts. Thoreau lived in utter simplicity during the two years in which he called that cabin home. His book, *Walden*, stands as a classic in American literature as it presents Thoreau's philosophy of simplifying our environment, needs, and ambitions by redefining pleasure and success.

—Jean Fleming, *Between Walden and the Whirlwind*

IT IS SAID that the great French philosopher, Sartre, summed up all of life with the statement, "To do is to be." Camus, his contemporary, summed up all of life with a conflicting statement, "To be is to do!" Then Frank Sinatra came along and put them both together in a song— "Do-be-do-be-do!"

—Tim Timmons, *Maximum Living in a Pressure Cooker World*

POLITICS

(Also see *Government*)

A SIGN ON THE DESK of a Pentagon official read, "The secrecy of my job does not permit me to know what I'm doing."

—Charles R. Swindoll, *The Bride*

PRESIDENT GEORGE BUSH died and went to heaven. When he entered, he was met by Saint Peter, who asked him if he had any requests. "Yes, I do," he said. "I've studied the leadership of Moses and I would love to talk to Moses." And when Saint Peter found Moses, he told him President Bush wanted to talk with him. Moses said, "No way. Last time I talked to a bush, I got forty years."

RONALD REAGAN kept his mouth shut today. Tomorrow he'll explain what he meant by that.

—Johnny Carson

TEDDY ROOSEVELT was interrupted during a campaign speech by a man in the audience who kept yelling out, "I'm a Democrat." Roosevelt stopped his speech and addressed the heckler, "Why are you a Democrat?" The man proudly replied, "My grandfather was a Democrat and my father was a Democrat. That's why I am a Democrat!" Roosevelt shook his head and replied, "And suppose your grandfather was a jackass and your father was a jackass. What would you be?" "A Republican," answered the heckler.

—Tim Timmons, *Maximum Living in a Pressure Cooker World*

MORE IMPORTANT THAN WINNING THE ELECTION is governing the nation. That is the test of political party—the acid, final test.

—Adlai Stevenson, quoted in John Bartlett, *Bartlett's Familiar Quotations*

WE NEGOTIATE with the Russians eyeball to eyeball and both sides are afraid to blink.

—Dean Rusk, quoted in John Bartlett, *Bartlett's Familiar Quotations*

TO BE PRESIDENT of the United States is to be lonely, very lonely, at times of great decisions. Having to make decisions creates loneliness because of the consequences that are involved. You make a decision, you sign a paper, you issue an order, and many people are involved in the consequences.

I think, too, that leaders are lonely because of the great demand on their time and their energy. President Woodrow Wilson said this: "It's an awful thing to be President of the United States. It means giving up nearly everything one holds dear. The presidency becomes a barrier between a man and his wife, between a man and his children."

—Warren W. Wiersbe, *Lonely People*

JOHN WYCLIFFE could be called the genesis of an era. Although the man has been virtually forgotten in our world today, this fourteenth-century saint was a stern and determined individual. He could not bear the thought that the Bible should remain chained to a pulpit in the dead language of the clergy and the prelates of the church. And so he set out as an English speaker to put into the English vernacular both the Old and the New Testament.

It was a mammoth undertaking and it was done against all kinds of verbal and physical assault upon him. Nevertheless this faithful scholar, this preacher of righteousness stayed at the task until it was virtually completed. And then in bold defiance against the enemies of his day, he wrote these words in the flyleaf of that first English translation: "This Bible is translated and shall make possible a government of the people, by the people, and for the people."

Little did Wycliffe realize that five hundred years later a lean and broken president of a new government that had established itself on a new continent would borrow from the flyleaf of his Bible the very same words he would use on a bleak November day in a place called Gettysburg. In that blood-drenched battlefield Lincoln said, "We here highly resolve that these dead shall not have died in vain, that this nation under God shall have a new birth of freedom, and that government of the people, by the people, for the people shall not perish from the earth."

It was less than a year and half later that President Lincoln was assassinated. And among the hundreds of men and women who reported his death, one very keen reporter was right on target when he said: "This is not a death. Lincoln's assassination is the end of an era."

—Stuart P. Garver, *Our Christian Heritage*

ABOUT TWO HUNDRED YEARS AGO, while the thirteen colonies were still part of Great Britain, Professor Alexander Tyler addressed himself to the fall of the Athenian Republic. He declared:

> A democracy cannot exist as a permanent form of government. It can only exist until the voters discover they can vote themselves excessive gratuities from the public treasury. From that moment on the majority always votes for the candidates promising the most benefits from the treasury, with the result that democracy collapses over loose fiscal policy, always followed by a dictatorship.

—Charles R. Swindoll, *Come Before Winter*

PRAISE
(See *Worship*)

PRAYER

PRAYER IS A TIME OF REFRESHMENT. Howard Taylor says of his father, Hudson Taylor, "For forty years the sun never rose on China that God didn't find him on his knees."

—Howard Taylor, *Hudson Taylor and the China Inland Mission*

FRANÇOIS FÉNELON, a seventeenth-century Roman Catholic Frenchman, said this about prayer:

> Tell God all that is in your heart, as one unloads one's heart, its pleasures and its pains, to a dear friend. Tell Him your troubles, that He may comfort you; tell Him your joys, that He may sober them; tell Him your longings, that He may purify them; tell Him your dislikes, that He may help you to conquer them; talk to Him of your temptations, that He may shield you from them; show Him the wounds of your heart, that He may heal them; lay bare your indifference to good, your depraved tastes for evil, your instability. Tell Him how self-love makes you unjust to others, how vanity tempts you to be insincere, how pride disguises you to yourself and others.
>
> If you thus pour out all your weaknesses, needs, troubles, there will be no lack of what to say. You will never exhaust the subject. It is continually being renewed. People who have no secrets from each other never want

for subject of conversation. They do not weigh their words, for there is nothing to be held back; neither do they seek for something to say. They talk out of the abundance of the heart, without consideration they say just what they think. Blessed are they who attain to such familiar, unreserved intercourse with God.

—Charles R. Swindoll, *Strengthening Your Grip*

ON ONE OCCASION, evangelist Dwight L. Moody had been the recipient of numerous benefits from the Lord. In his abundance, he was suddenly seized with the realization that his heavenly Father was showering on him almost more than he could take. Encouraged and overwhelmed, he paused to pray. With great volume he simply stated, "Stop, God!" Now that's *spontaneous*. It is also a beautiful change from, "Eternal, almighty, gracious Father of all good things, Thy hand hath abundantly and gloriously supplied our deepest needs. How blessed and thankful we are to come to Thee and declare unto Thee . . ." and on and on and on, grinding into snore city.

After I had told that story in one service, a fellow said to me, "I've got another one for God. God, start! I mean, He can stop on Moody, but I want Him to start with me, I need some of that."

—Charles R. Swindoll, *Strengthening Your Grip*

THE LATE DR. DONALD BARNHOUSE, greatly admired American pastor and author, once came to the pulpit and made a statement that stunned his congregation: "Prayer changes nothing!" You could have heard a pin drop in that packed Sunday worship service in Philadelphia. His comment, of course, was designed to make Christians realize that God is sovereignly in charge of everything. Our times are literally in His hands. No puny human being by uttering a few words in prayer takes charge of events and changes them. God does the shaping, the changing; it is He who is in control. Barnhouse was correct, except in one minor detail. Prayer changes me. When you and I pray, we change, and that is one of the major reasons prayer is such a therapy that counteracts anxiety.

—Charles R. Swindoll, *Strengthening Your Grip*

Thank You for Saying No

Lord, day after day I've thanked You
For saying yes.

But when have I genuinely thanked You
For saying no?

Yet I shudder to think
Of the possible smears
The cumulative blots on my life
Had You not been sufficiently wise
To say an *unalterable* no.

So thank You for saying no
When my want list for things
Far exceeded my longing for You.
When I asked for a stone
Foolishly certain I asked for bread
Thank You for saying no

To my petulant "Just this time, Lord?"
Thank You for saying no
To senseless excuses
Selfish motives
Dangerous diversions.

Thank You for saying no
When the temptation that enticed me
Would have bound me beyond escape.

Thank You for saying no
When I asked You to leave me alone.

Above all
Thank You for saying no
When in anguish I asked
"If I give You all else
May I keep *this?*"

Lord, my awe increases
When I see the wisdom
Of Your divine no.

—Ruth Harms Calkin, *Tell Me Again Lord, I Forget*

YOU CAN DO MORE THAN PRAY after you have prayed, but you cannot do more than pray until you have prayed.

—John Bunyan

PRAYER IS SURRENDER—surrender to the will of God and cooperation with that will. If I throw out a boat hook from a boat and catch hold of the shore and pull, do I pull the shore to me, or do I pull myself to the shore? Prayer is not pulling God to my will, but the aligning of my will to the will of God.

—E. Stanley Jones, *A Song of Ascents*

WILLIAM R. NEWELL says kneeling is a good way to pray because it is uncomfortable. Daniel prayed on his knees. Jim Elliot said, "God is still on His throne, we're still His footstool, and there's only a knee's distance between!" He also said, "That saint who advances on his knees never retreats."

—Elisabeth Elliot, *Shadow of the Almighty*

DURING OUR SEMINARY DAYS, Cynthia and I had a dear lady in our home church by the name of Aunt Mae. She was in touch with us regularly to ask us what our needs were. And she would say, "Now you're accountable to me. I'm praying for you. And I need to know how you're doing." Later she would say, "Now the last time we were together, you mentioned _____. How did that work out?" "Well, it's pretty good." "OK." She would take her pen and scratch that off her list. Then she would say, "I want to know what else I need to pray for."

THERE'S SOMETHING EXQUISITELY LUXURIOUS about room service in a hotel. All you have to do is pick up the phone and somebody is ready and waiting to bring you breakfast, lunch, dinner, a chocolate milkshake, whatever your heart desires and your stomach will tolerate. Or by another languid motion of the wrist, you can telephone for someone who will get a soiled shirt quickly transformed into a clean one or a rumpled suit into a pressed one. That's the concept that some of us have of prayer. We have created God in the image of a divine bellhop. Prayer, for us, is the ultimate in room service, wrought by direct dialing. Furthermore, no tipping, and everything is charged to that great credit card in the sky. Now prayer is many things, but I'm pretty sure this is not one of the things it is.

—Kenneth Wilson, quoted in Lloyd Cory, *Quote Unquote*

HEAVEN IS FILLED with a room that will surprise all of us when we see it. The room has within it large boxes neatly packaged with a lovely ribbon on top with your name on it, "Never delivered to Earth because never requested from Earth."

PRAYER IS NOT A SUBSTITUTE for work, thinking, watching, suffering, or giving; prayer is a support for all other efforts.

—George Buttrick, quoted in Lloyd Cory, *Quote Unquote*

> I asked God for strength, that I might achieve;
> I was made weak, that I may learn humbly to obey.
> I asked God for health, that I may do greater things;
> I was given infirmity, that I might do better things.
> I asked for riches, that I may be happy;
> I was given poverty, that I might be wise.
> I asked for power, that I might have the praise of men;
> I was given weakness, that I might feel the need of God.
> I asked for all things, that I might enjoy life;
> I was given life, that I might enjoy all things.
> I got nothing I asked for but everything I hoped for.
> I am, among all men, most richly blessed.
>
> —*A Confederate Soldier*
>
> —Croft M. Pentz, *Speaker's Treasury of 400 Quotable Poems*

DONALD BARNHOUSE often closed his church services with the prayer, "Lord, dismiss us with Your peace, except for those who don't know You; keep them miserable until they come to know the Prince of Peace."

DEPTH, not length, is important. . . . When the Gettysburg battleground became a national cemetery, Edward Everett was to give the dedication speech and Abraham Lincoln was asked to say "a few appropriate words." Everett spoke eloquently for one hour and fifty-seven minutes then took his seat as the crowd roared its enthusiastic approval. Then Lincoln stood to his feet, slipped on his steel spectacles, and began what we know today as the "Gettysburg Address." Poignant words ". . . The world will little note nor long remember . . ." —suddenly, he was finished. No more than two minutes after he had begun he stopped. His talk had been so prayerlike it seemed almost inappropriate to applaud. As Lincoln sank into his settee, John Young of the *Philadelphia Press* whispered, "Is that all?" The President answered, "Yes, that's all."

Don't underestimate two minutes with God in prayer.

—Charles R. Swindoll, *Quest for Character*

IF I COULD HEAR Christ praying for me in the next room, I would not fear a million enemies. Yet distance makes no difference. He is praying for me.

—Robert Murray McCheyne, quoted in Lloyd John Ogilvie, *Drumbeat of Love*

GOD ANSWERS SHARP and sudden on some prayers, / and thrusts the thing we have prayed for in our face. / A gauntlet with a gift in 't.

—Elizabeth Barrett Browning, "Aurora Leigh"

IT IS POSSIBLE to move men through God by prayer alone.

—J. Oswald Sanders, *Spiritual Leadership*

BROOM HILDA, a cartoon character, is a little three-foot-high witch who is all hair and face. In one amusing comic strip she approaches a wishing well and, standing next to it, puts her hands on the edge of the well and says loudly, "I don't want anything!" And the next panel is quiet. Then she steps back and says, "I just thought you'd enjoy knowing there was one satisfied person around."

THE CARTOON CHARACTER Ziggy is standing, looking up on a mountain. The sky is dark and there's one cloud up there. Ziggy says, "Have I been put on hold for the rest of my life?"

Sometimes prayer feels like that, doesn't it? "Will You ever answer?" As one man put it, "The heavens are brass and nothing comes back."

—Tom Wilson cartoon, Universal Press Syndicate, July 18, 1980

DR. LEWIS SPERRY CHAFER told a story on the subject. It seems that a certain minister was in the habit of profound prayers, oftentimes resorting to words beyond the ken of his simple flock. This went on week after week, to the dismay and frustration of the congregation. At last, a wee Scottish woman in the choir ventured to take the matter in hand. On a given Sunday, as the minister was waxing his most eloquently verbose, the little woman reached across the curtain separating the choir from the pulpit. Taking a firm grasp on the frock tail of the minister, she gave it a yank, and was heard to whisper, "Jes' call Him Fether, and ask 'im for somethin'."

—Richard Seume, *Shoes for the Road*

TWO IRISHMEN, Pat and Mike, had narrowly escaped death on a sinking ship. They were floundering around in icy ocean waters on a couple of planks. Pat was addicted to the grossest profanity and he thought he ought to repent of it and then the Lord would come to his rescue. Mike thought his theology was sound. Pat began to pray, but just before arriving at the main thesis of his repentant prayer, Mike spotted a ship coming toward them. As delighted as Columbus when he first spotted the North American shore, Mike hollered, "Hold it, Pat. Don't commit yourself. Here's a ship." Pat immediately stopped praying! Isn't that the way many of us are? The only time we pray is when we are "in a jam." As soon as things improve we forget God.

—John Haggai, *How to Win over Worry*

O THOU WHO HAS GIVEN US SO MUCH, mercifully grant us one thing more— a grateful heart.

—George Herbert

MINISTER: "So your mother says your prayers for you each night. What does she say?" The youngster replied, "Thank God he's in bed."

A MAN WAS BEING PURSUED by a roaring, hungry lion. Feeling the beast's hot breath on his neck and knowing his time was short, he prayed as he ran. He cried out in desperation, "O Lord, please make this lion a Christian." Within seconds, the frightened man became aware the lion had stopped the chase. When he looked behind him, he found the lion kneeling, lips moving in obvious prayer. Greatly relieved at this turn of events—and desirous of joining the lion in meditation, he approached the king of the jungle. When he was near enough, he heard the lion praying, "And bless, O Lord, this food for which I'm exceedingly grateful!"

PREACHING

(Also see *Ministry, Pastors*)

C. S. LEWIS went to visit one of his young preacher friends and listen to him preach. Everything was fine until the man reached the climax of his message. And he said, in so many words, "If you will not believe in Jesus Christ, if you refuse to take Him as your Lord, you will suffer grave eschatological ramifications." And then he went on and ended his message. Lewis frowned. When he had occasion to talk with the young man about the conclusion of his message, he said, "Did you mean that those who refuse to receive the gospel message would go to hell?" "Well, yes," said the young man. "Yes, that's what I meant." Lewis's response was beautiful, "Then say that!"

—Michael Green, *Illustrations for Biblical Preaching*

SOME BIBLE TEXTS are more difficult to preach on than others. I've often said if you give a preacher five minutes, he can complicate or confuse any passage of Scripture in the whole Bible.

A PREACHER WAS GIVING A LECTURE on the Minor Prophets one after another. He came finally to the Book of Amos. "We have now come to Amos," he said, "and what shall we do with Amos?" A man sitting in the rear of the house said, loud enough to be heard by everyone, "He can have my seat, I'm going home."

—F. B. Meyer, *Expository Preaching*

IN THE LATE 1960S, I did a wedding in a small Mennonite church in Iowa. I remember looking over at the pulpit that had been placed to the side for the wedding ceremony and on this old pulpit I read the etched words, "Stand up, speak truth, sit down." This reminds me of the story of the preacher who did fairly well in his sermon. He preached a little long, but he did a good job. Fishing for a compliment from his wife over lunch, he said, "Well, what did you think of the sermon?" She responded, "It wasn't bad," she said, "but you did miss several opportunities to sit down."

—Asburg Lenox, quoted in Lloyd Cory, *Quote Unquote*

I READ OF A YOUNG MINISTER whose besetting sin was not laziness, but conceit. He frequently boasted in public that all the time he needed to prepare his

Sunday sermon was the few moments it took to walk to the church from the parsonage next door. You could probably guess what the congregation voted to do: They bought a new parsonage eight miles away.

A YOUNG PASTOR with a small flock had been at his church only a few monhs. One week he was preparing a message on the love of family members, but he couldn't find the introduction he wanted. He had read in the local newspaper that a well known, experienced minister would be preaching in a nearby town that week. So on Thursday he decided to slip in the back of the church and listen to that pulpiteer. He thought for sure he might find inspiration for the introduction he needed.

Amazingly, when the minister came to the pulpit he said he wanted to speak on love. "As a matter of fact," he said, "the sweetest, most wonderful, loving woman I ever held in my arms was another man's wife. And she was my mother."

Oh, he heard very little else. He thought, "What a great introduction for my talk. I'll use that one." And, of course, he was a little troubled, because it was risky to use an introduction like that, especially since he had been at his church only a few months.

Well, even though he was nervous, he stood up to preach and his opening line was, "The sweetest, most wonderful, loving woman I ever held in my arms was another man's wife." And the shock that came over the congregation caused him to have a mental block. And he added, "For the life of me I can't remember who she was."

—Dudley Dennison Jr., *Windows, Ladders, and Bridges*

A PASTOR WAS TRYING TO REMEMBER the names of Shadrach, Meshach, and Abednego whom he wanted to refer to in his Sunday sermon. So he wrote them down on a card and stuck it inside his coat. That way, when the time came to refer to the trio, he could just look inside. Unfortunately, when he came to that particular part of his sermon, he peeked inside and read "Hart, Schaffner, and Marx."

—Clyde Murdock, *A Treasury of Humor*

BRUCE WALTKE tells of his wife's days in home economics in college. They did a test on two white mice. They fed them completely different diets. They fed the first mouse whole milk, wheat bread, oatmeal, carrots, fruit juices. And they fed the second mouse coffee and doughnuts for breakfast, white bread and jelly for lunch, candy, potato chips, and Coke for supper.

In less than ten days there were marked differences in the two mice. One was healthy and robust, dancing around in the cage, and the other one was already showing signs of ill health, losing its hair, becoming irritable, becoming a loner, removed. As the diet continued, that mouse lay down and was completely listless and soon died. Why? Wrong diet.

You feed your congregation spiritually the wrong diet and they will wind up listless, irritable, aggravating, lacking in peace. You feed them the right diet of the "whole wheat" of God's Word and the living water of life and the difference in their spiritual health will be remarkable.

JOSEPH PARKER'S COMMENT to a young minister is always timely for pastors to remember. "In every pew there is a broken heart. Speak often on suffering and you will never lack for a congregation."

—*Leadership* magazine, Fall 1982

A YOUNG MAN, upon graduation, became a pastor of a small church in a rather small town we'll call Centerville. One week a cyclone hit Centerville. This young man decided to preach the following Sunday on "Why God Sent the Cyclone to Centerville." The place was packed.

That next week he made a trip back to seminary to talk to his professor friend. The old man said to the young theolog, "Now if you preach the Word, you will always have a text. But if you wait for cyclones you'll not have enough to go around."

—A. W. Tozer, *God Tells the Man Who Cares*

MOST STIRRING SPEECHES or sermons have two critical phases: an introduction, which is memorable, and a conclusion, which seems to drive the point home. I've often compared speaking in public to an airplane flight. You need a good, safe, strong takeoff, and then you need a comfortable and, if possible, smooth landing. You don't have a complete flight without both a takeoff and a landing. Anyone who speaks before the public very much knows the exasperating experience of trying to find just the right words to grab the attention of the listener and to shake them loose from the ho-hum attitude that many of us have when we settle in for a thirty- or forty-five-minute talk. I had a mentor in seminary who used to give us the old Russian proverb, "It is the same with people as it is with donkeys: whoever would hold them fast must get a very good grip on their ears."

—Haddon Robinson, *Biblical Preaching*

SERMON ILLUSTRATIONS are "windows of light that bring clarity and allow something that is a bit abstruse and abstract to come to an understanding, to clear up."

—Charles H. Spurgeon, *Lectures to My Students*

> I always came to his church before my Sally was dead,
> I heard him a bumming away like a buzzard clock over my head;
> I never knew what he meant, but I thought he had something to say,
> And I thought he said what he ought to have said and I went away.

—William Hendriksen, *Exposition of the Gospel according to Luke*

IF WORDS ARE TO ENTER PEOPLE'S HEARTS and bear fruit, they must be the right words shaped so as to pass men's defenses and explode silently and effectually within their minds.

—J. B. Phillips, *Making Men Whole*

THERE ARE TIMES when the pastor's task is not enviable. I suppose that's what Vance Havner had in mind when he was the first to say that our job is to comfort the afflicted and on occasion afflict the comfortable. I would a lot rather do the first, though there are times that I have to do both.

—Bruce Larson, *Setting Men Free*

GOD TOLD ME TO FEED MY SHEEP, not my giraffes.

—H. A. Ironside, quoted in Clarence Roddy, *We Prepare and Preach*

MOST OF US WERE BORN HEARING WELL, but all of us must learn to *listen* well. Listening is a skill, an art that is in need of being cultivated.

Ralph Nichols, an authority on the subject of listening, says we think four or five times faster than we talk. This means that if a speaker utters one hundred twenty words a minute, the audience thinks at about five hundred words a minute. That difference offers a strong temptation to listeners to take mental excursions, to think about last night's bridge game or tomorrow's sales report or the need to get that engine tuneup before next weekend's trip to the mountains, then phase back into the speaker's talk.

Research at the University of Minnesota reveals that in listening to a ten-minute talk, hearers operate at only a 28 percent efficiency. And the longer the talk, the less we understand, the less we track with our ears what somebody else's mouth is saying. That could be downright frightening to guys like me who preach from forty to forty-five minutes at a crack! That also explains why some wag has described preaching as "the fine art of talking in someone else's sleep."

—Charles R. Swindoll, *Come Before Winter*

EVERY WORKMAN KNOWS the necessity of keeping his tools in a good state of repair.... If the workman loses the edge ... he knows that there will be a greater draught upon his energies, or his work will be badly done. Michelangelo, the elect of the fine arts, understood so well the importance of his tools, that he always made his own brushes with his own hands. And in this he gives us an illustration of the God of grace, who with special care fashions for Himself all true ministers.

We are, in a certain sense, our own tools, and therefore must keep ourselves in order. If I want to preach the gospel, I can only use my own voice; therefore I must train my vocal powers. I can only think with my own brains, and feel with my own heart, and therefore I must educate my intellectual and emotional faculties. I can only weep and agonize for souls with my own renewed nature, therefore must I watchfully maintain the tenderness which was in Christ Jesus. It will be in vain for me to stock my library, or organize societies, or project schemes, if I neglect the culture of myself; for books, and agencies, and systems, are only remotely the instruments of my holy calling; my own spirit, soul, and body are my nearest machinery for sacred service; my spiritual faculties, and my inner life, are my battle axe and weapons for war. . . .

Then, quoting from a letter of the great Scottish minister, Robert Murray McCheyne, he concludes, "Remember, you are God's sword, His instrument— I trust a chosen vessel unto Him to bear His name. In great measure, according to the purity and perfection of the instrument, will be the success. It is not great talent God blesses so much as likeness to Jesus. A holy minister is an awful weapon in the hand of God."

—Charles H. Spurgeon, *Lectures to My Students*

HAROLD OCKENGA AND DONALD BARNHOUSE traveled together for thirty days on a speaking circuit. Each night they switched off who went first. Ockenga preached a different sermon nightly, while Barnhouse preached the same, identical sermon night after night.

Ockenga, being a man of brilliance, sat through that same sermon night after night and decided to memorize Barnhouse's sermon. They concluded the circuit at the First Presbyterian Church, Richmond, Virginia.

That night Ockenga went first. He stood and preached word-for-word Barnhouse's sermon. Barnhouse sat and listened with rapt attention and never flinched. When his turn came, Barnhouse stood and preached another sermon without hesitation.

Unable to contain himself, Ockenga said to Barnhouse as they left the congregation that night, "The congregation seemed to have enjoyed your sermon this evening," he said with a wry smile. To which Barnhouse responded, "Yes, but not nearly as much as when I preached it here three months ago!"

IT IS BLESSED to eat into the very soul of the Bible until you come to talk in scriptural language and your spirit is flavored with the words of the Lord, so that your blood is bibline and the very essence of the Bible flows through you.

—Charles H. Spurgeon, quoted in John R. W. Stott, *Preacher's Portrait*

PREDICAMENT

A PREDICAMENT occurs when an attorney who specializes in medical malpractice suits finds himself in need of major surgery.

—Clyde Moore, *Columbus Dispatch*

WE HAVE A NUMBER OF American idioms for being in a predicament: a fine kettle of fish, in a pinch, in a jam, in a pickle, between a rock and a hard place, up a tree, up a wall, in a corner, hard-pressed.

PREPAREDNESS

WHAT IF YOU READ IN A NEWSPAPER about a new airline. The "Old World Airline" let's call it. They've been in business eight days. You pick up the phone and call. The girl answers is in a hurry because she's also the stewardess on the next flight. She says, "If you want to know about us, come on over. Our fares are half-price, you know." So you go over. And out on the runway is a 1944 B-17. A nineteen-year-old pilot is getting on, and you ask him, "What are you doing?" "Well, we're sort of in a hurry. We're running behind." "How is it that you're able to provide half-rate fares?" "Well, we don't worry about unnecessary things like maintenance and checking gasoline. And, we serve leftovers on the flight over." Then you notice he's got on a parachute. No person in his right mind would get on that airplane! At least not without his own parachute. Why? Insufficient preparation!

———————————————

WHEN I WAS A LITTLE BOY, I knew nothing about the politics of war. I did not understand why wars started or how they ended. The big question in my formative years during World War II was, how come the attack on Pearl Harbor happened that lazy, hazy, laid-back Hawaiian Sunday morning, the seventh of December, sometime before dawn? I didn't understand. As I read the records now, I do hear admissions like, "We weren't ready. We never expected it. It was a genius plan."

George Washington wrote decades ago, "To be prepared for war is one of the most effectual means of preserving peace."

———————————————

TO BE A PERSON OF FAITH does not mean you are not a person who plans. We need to remember the Revolutionary War saying, "Trust in God, but keep your powder dry."

—William Barclay, *The Letters of James and Peter*

———————————————

IN THE EARLY 50S, I was an apprentice in a machine shop. My father felt it would be wise for me not only to get book learning but also to get a practical taste of life.

On one occasion I was working in the machine shop with the tracer lathe. It was an intricate piece of equipment. I spent months on it. I was always told, "Before you change the tool that cuts the aluminum, turn the machine off. Otherwise you could hurt yourself or maybe even kill yourself." Once I was fighting against time to make the production that day and I did not turn off the machine. The wrench I was using to loosen the tool on the lathe slipped and my hand went into the chuck and out again. The bone that led to my little finger was now in a place it shouldn't be—outside my skin.

I went down to see the industrial nurse and showed her the finger and said, "I think I might need a shot." She said, "I think I might need one too. Why don't you sit down?" Then she called the paramedics who hauled me off to a hospital where a surgeon put a long stainless steel pin in my hand.

Week after week I would go back for checkups. Finally he said to me, "Come back in three or four days and we'll pull the pin out. But actually I won't be here to do it. My assistant will do it." I was curious and asked, "Why won't you be here?" And he explained that he had a little black mole on his stomach that he was going to have removed. In fact, he opened his white top and pulled open his shirt and showed me a place about the size of half of his small fingernail.

When I went back, to have the pin pulled out, I asked when my surgeon was coming back for my final checkup. The assistant became very grim and said, "Oh, he's dead." I'll never forget the feeling of emptiness and unbelief.

When they'd cut him open, the saw that his abdomen was covered with cancer. Two days after surgery he died. Just enough time to write his will.

WHILE I SERVED MY APPRENTICESHIP as a machinist in Houston years ago, I worked just behind a man named Tex on a row of turret lathes. Tex chewed tobacco. He'd stick the pouch in his back pocket and leave the pouch open. We were working second shift one night and a little cricket hopped in the door of the shop. I watched the cricket since my lathe was running and I didn't have to give attention to it for the next five or six minutes. I thought, "That cricket is the same color as Tex's tobacco—I wonder if he would ever know?"

So I grabbed this cricket, pulled its head off, and dropped it in the top of his tobacco pouch and waited. After a while, he shoved a couple callused fingers back into the pouch and jammed a big wad of tobacco into his mouth. He spit wings and body parts throughout the evening. It was a delight to watch him. I don't think Tex ever knew that he chewed up a cricket—which proves, if you chew tobacco, you don't know what you've got in your mouth.

Anyway, Tex had a saying I'll never forget. He was always washed up when it was time for the final whistle. When you work in a machine shop, a whistle blows at the beginning of your day shift, then you punch the clock, and then there's another whistle for lunch , and then the day stops with a whistle and you punch out. Tex was always washed up, ready to go. And, you know, he was every employer's nightmare, ready to leave before time was up. One day I said, "Tex, how do you do it?" I'll never forget what he said: "Let me tell you something, Sonny. I just stay ready to keep from gittin' ready."

PRIDE
(Also see *Ego*)

I GOT NAUSEATED LAST WEEK. It wasn't from something I ate, but from *someone* I met. My out-of-town travels resulted in a short-term liberal arts education of self-praise to teach me some things I hope I never fully forget. This individual was a widely traveled, well-educated, much-experienced Christian in his fifties. He is engaged in ministry that touches many lives. He is fundamental in faith, biblical in belief, and evangelical in emphasis. For a number of years he has held a respected position that carries with it a good deal of responsibility and a great deal of time logged in the limelight. Such credentials deserve a measure of respect like the rank on the shoulders of a military officer or the rows of medals on his chest. Both merit a salute in spite of the man inside the uniform. In no way do I wish to diminish the significance of his position nor his record of achievement. But my point here is this. He knew better. He had the ability to correct himself, but he chose to be, quite frankly, a pompous preacher!

You got the distinct impression that when the two of you were together, the more important one was not you. Little mistakes irked him. Slight omissions irritated him. The attitude of a servant was conspicuous by its absence. It was highly important to him that everyone knew who he was, where he'd been, how he'd done, and what he thought. While everyone else much preferred to be on a first-name basis (rather than "Reverend" or "Mister") he demanded, "Call *me* Doctor." His voice had a professional tone. As humorous things occurred, he found no reason to smile, and as the group got closer and closer in spirit, he became increasingly more threatened. I confess that I was tempted to short-sheet him one night—or to order a Schlitz in his name and have it brought up to his room—or to ask the desk clerk to give him a call about 2:30 A.M. and yell, "OK, buddy, out of the sack, rise and shine!" But I didn't. Now I almost wish I had. Just for the fun of watching the guy squirm!

—Charles R. Swindoll, *Growing Strong in the Seasons of Life*

PRIDE IS THE ONLY DISEASE known to man that makes everyone sick except the person who has it.

—Buddy Robinson, quoted in Lloyd Cory, *Quote Unquote*

A GUY NAMED UNCLE ZEKE who lived in Muleshoe, Texas, could not admit when he was wrong, no matter what!

One day Uncle Zeke was walking along the street and he happened to shuffle into the blacksmith shop, sawdust all over the floor. What he didn't know was, just before he got there, the blacksmith had been working with an uncooperative horseshoe and beat on it till it was black. It was still hot, but it wouldn't cooperate, so he tossed it over in the sawdust. Zeke walked in, looked down and saw that black horseshoe. He picked it up, not knowing it was still hot. Naturally he dropped it very fast. The old blacksmith looked over his glasses and said, "Kinda hot, ain't it, Zeke?" You know what Zeke said? "Nope, just doesn't take me long to look at a horseshoe."

—Jess Moody, *A Drink at Joel's Place*

CARL REINER, as an airport reporter, is interviewing Sid Caesar as Professor Von Houdinoff, an expert on magicians.

> REINER (confused): As I understand what you're trying to explain, your book is saying that there's a connection between the illusions of magicians and what happens to people in real life.
>
> CAESAR: You got it, fella.
>
> REINER: Can you give me an example?
>
> CAESAR: You vant an example of great illusionary power? Hans Schnorkel, a Frenchman. He vas working on a trick mit a shark. So he got this shark—a two-thousand pound tiger shark—und he put that shark in a tank mit over a million gallons of sea vater. Und then he stood on the side of the tank und he had himself handcuffed, behind his back. There he vas, handcuffed mit just a bathing suit. Und then, Hans threw himself into the tank mit the shark. And soon as Hans hit the water, the shark spun around und started svimming slowly, slowly towards Hans. Und Hans, he just stood there in the tank and looked the shark right in the eye. Und the shark just slowly stopped and looked Hans right back in the eye. Und then, all of a sudden, the shark just rolled right over on his belly—und ate 'im.
>
> REINER (incredulous): He ate him? What kind of illusion is that?
>
> CAESAR: It's a very good illusion. But you gotta do it right. You see, don't start off rehearsing mit a shark. You start with a guppy, a goldfish, a nice herring, a piece of salmon is not bad—don't get crazy mit a shark right away.

REINER: That's an interesting story, Professor, but how does it apply to real life?

CAESAR: How? You can't see? You don't make the connection?

REINER: Sorry, Professor. I don't.

CAESAR: If you start out too big, you could let yourself be eaten up.

—Charles R. Swindoll, *Come Before Winter*

A PASTOR FRIEND said to me on one occasion, "You know, I preached this terrific message one Sunday, and afterward, boy the comments were terrific. One great comment after another. I was so glad to see the people realized it was an outstanding message."

Then he went home. His wife was busy trying to get lunch on the table and the five kids seemed to be everywhere at once. Rather than "Welcome home, O great orator (or whatever else she might want to say)," he heard from the kitchen, "Honey, the baby's dirty. Would you change him?" That's the first comment he got when he got home. So he thought, "That's an awfully lowly task for someone who just preached such a fantastic message." But he got the baby cleaned up. Then she said, "The garbage needs to be dumped too. It's been here for a couple of days." He thought, "This is terrible." But he did it.

Finally lunch was ready and they came to the table, and sat down, ready to eat. He said, "Well, what did you think of the message?" He was all ready for her to just go wild over it. She said, "Honey, I heard them at the door today and they said enough to last for two weeks."

Sometime when you're feeling important,
Sometime when your ego's way up;
Sometime when you take it for granted
That you are the prize winning "pup";
Sometime when you feel that your absence
Would leave an unfillable hole,
Just follow these simple instructions,
And see how it humbles your soul.
Take a bucket and fill it with water,
Put your hand in it up to your wrist.
Now pull it out fast and the hole that remains
Is the measure of how you'll be missed.

> You may splash all you please as you enter,
> And stir up the water galore,
> But STOP and you'll find in a minute,
> It's back where it was before.
>
> —A. Dudley Dennison Jr., *Windows, Ladders, and Bridges*

NOTHING IS MORE DISTASTEFUL to God than self-conceit. This first and fundamental sin in essence aims at enthroning self at the expense of God. . . . Pride is a sin of whose presence its victim is least conscious. . . . If we are honest, when we measure ourselves by the life of our Lord who humbled Himself even to death on a cross, we cannot but be overwhelmed with the tawdriness and shabbiness, and even the vileness, of our hearts.

—J. Oswald Sanders, *Spiritual Leadership*

PRIORITIES

PUT FIRST THINGS FIRST and we get second things thrown in: Put second things first and we lose both first and second things.

—Wayne Martindale, *The Quotable Lewis*

ARE YOUR PRIORITIES STRAIGHT? A couple I heard about in Atlanta read that *My Fair Lady* was still playing on Broadway in New York City. They wanted to go so badly, so they bought their tickets months ahead of time and planned their vacation.

The long-awaited day came and they flew to New York City. They presented their tickets, walked in, and sat down in wonderful seats, seven rows from the front, near the orchestra.

To the man's amazement, the entire place filled up except the seat right next to him. He was curious about that. At the intermission, he leaned over in conversation with the lady in the second seat away from him and commented how they had to wait so many months to get tickets to a performance. When there was such a demand for seats, why would someone not come. Did she have any idea? She said, "Yes, as a matter of fact, these two seats are mine. This one and that one." She explained further, "You see, that seat belonged to my husband, and he died." The man said, "I'm . . . I'm terribly sorry. But couldn't you have invited a friend to come with you?" Her answer was classic. She said, "No, they're all at the funeral home right now."

—B. Clayton Bell, *Preaching* magazine, May–June 1989

A FRIGHTENED WOMAN on the *Titanic* found her place in the lifeboat that was about to be dropped into the raging North Atlantic. She thought suddenly of something she needed in light of death that was breathing down her neck. She asked for permission to go to her state room. She was granted just a moment or so, or they would have to leave without her.

She ran across a deck that was already slanted at a dangerous angle. She ran through the gambling room that had money pushed aside in one corner ankle deep. She came to her stateroom and pushed aside her jewelry and reached above her bed and got three small oranges and found her way back to the lifeboat and got in.

Death had boarded the *Titanic*. One blast of its awful breath had transformed all values. Instantaneously, priceless things had become worthless. Worthless things had become priceless. And in that moment she preferred three small oranges to a crate of diamonds.

—W. E. Sangster, *The Craft of Sermon Illustration*

A CALIFORNIA INDUSTRIALIST addressed a group of executives at a leadership seminar some time ago. His topic concerned employee motivation—how to get the job done while maintaining the enthusiasm and commitment of your personnel. He offered a lot of helpful advice, but one concept in particular has stuck in my head: "There are two things that are the most difficult to get people to do: to think, and do things in the order of their importance."

—Charles R. Swindoll, *Hand Me Another Brick*

PRIVACY

A BEWILDERED FOREIGN-EXCHANGE STUDENT once blurted out in my presence: "Americans are loners." I was, at first, defensive. His evaluation seemed unduly harsh. But since the time I heard that young man make that statement, I have come to the conclusion that he is correct. There are some wonderful exceptions, but they are only that—exceptions rather than the rule.

WE AMERICANS value mobility, convenience and privacy. Of these, privacy is our most cherished value.

—Ralph Keys, *We the Lonely People*

PROCRASTINATION

> Procrastination is my sin,
> It brings me naught but sorrow.
> I know that I should stop it,
> In fact I will—tomorrow.
>
> —Gloria Pitzer, quoted in Lloyd Cory, *Quote Unquote*

ONE WIFE SAID, "When a man needs to do a household job, he goes through three periods: contemplating *how* it will be done, contemplating *when* it will be done, contemplating."

—Marcelene Cox, quoted in Lloyd Cory, *Quote Unquote*

Around the Corner

> Around the corner I have a friend,
> In this great city that has no end;
> Yet days go by, and weeks rush on,
> And before I know it, a year is gone,
> And I never see my old friend's face,
> For Life is a swift and terrible race.
> He knows I like him just as well
> As in the days when I rang his bell
> And he rang mine.
> We were younger then,
> And now we are busy, tired men:
> Tired with playing a foolish game,
> Tired with trying to make a name.
> "To-morrow," I say, "I will call on Jim,
> Just to show that I'm thinking of him."
> But to-morrow comes—and to-morrow goes,
> And the distance between us grows and grows.
>
> Around the corner! yet miles away …
> "Here's a telegram, sir,"
> *"Jim died today."*
>
> And that's what we get, and deserve in the end:
> Around the corner, a vanished friend.

—Charles Hanson Towne, quoted in Hazel Felleman, *Poems That Live Forever*

A GERMAN FARMER settled in Guatemala and became prosperous. After a while he decided he would go back to visit his family in Germany. And so he saved up his money and got on the ship.

After a few days at sea he noticed he had an infection in his toe and realized that a small tropical flea, a *nigua* was under the toenail and had laid its eggs, causing a terrible itching and inflammation. "Now the way you relieve the problem," says Townsend, "is to get a needle, go under the nail, and dig it out." Sounds terrible, but it relieves the problem.

Well, this German farmer decided to do that. So he got a needle and sat down. Then he thought, "My uncle and his family in Hamburg have never seen a *nigua*." So he thought, "I'll leave it here, preserve it, and then when I get there and they see it, we'll take care of it."

By the time he reached Hamburg his toe was swollen and his foot was hurting terribly. But he showed it to Uncle Otto who looked at it and said, "Aw, the whole family would love to see this." And so he left it in until all the family could see the toe. And you know what happened? Blood poisoning set in and he died.

If you want to commit spiritual suicide, that might even lead to physical death, let something smolder in your heart against someone else. Nurse it. Let others know about it. Let others know how mean that person was to you. And if you keep it up, a root of bitterness will form, and you are in trouble.

—Cameron Townsend, cofounder of Wycliffe Bible Translators

PRODIGAL

MARIA AND HER DAUGHTER, Christina, lived in a poor neighborhood on the outskirts of a Brazilian village. Maria's husband had died when Christina was an infant and she never remarried. Times were tough but at last Christina was old enough to get a job to help out.

Christina spoke often of going to the city. She dreamed of trading her dusty neighborhood for exciting avenues and the city life. Just the thought of that horrified her mother, who knew exactly what Christina would have to do for a living. That's why her heart broke. That's why she couldn't believe it when she awoke one morning to find her daughter's bed empty. Knowing where her daughter was headed, she quickly threw some clothes in a bag, gathered up all of her money, and ran out of the house.

On her way to the bus stop she entered a drugstore and got one last thing. Photos. She sat in the photograph booth, closed the curtain, and spent all the time she could on making photos of herself. With her purse full of small black-and-white photos, she boarded the next bus to Rio de Janeiro.

Maria knew Christina had no way of earning money. She also knew that her daughter was too stubborn to give up. When pride meets hunger, a human being will do things that were before unthinkable. Knowing this, Maria began her search. Bars, hotels, nightclubs, any place with the reputation for street walkers or prostitutes. She went to them all. And at each place Maria left her photo—taped to a bathroom mirror, tacked to a hotel bulletin board, fastened to a corner telephone booth. And on the back of each photo she wrote a note. Then her money and the pictures ran out, Maria went home.

A few weeks later young Christina descended the hotel stairs. Her young face was tired. Her dreams had become a nightmare. But as she reached the bottom of the stairs, her eyes noticed a familiar face. She looked again, and there on a lobby mirror was a small picture of her mother. Christina's eyes burned and her throat tightened as she walked across the room and removed the small photo. Written on the back was a compelling invitation, "Whatever you've done, whatever you have become, it doesn't matter. Please come home." And she did.

—Adapted from Max Lucado, *No Wonder They Call Him Savior*

A PRODIGAL SON named Robert left home for Paris. Robert awoke one morning to the bitter realization that his money was gone. All his creditors were hounding him. Hurriedly he left Paris for a small town in Normandy. But his past caught up with him. Everything was repossessed. There was nothing to do but to seek work with one of the local farmers. In that environment something—the wooing of God's spirit in his heart—brought him back to himself.

He thought of "Twin Oaks" and the gracious, orderly life he had left behind. Wistfully he compared his days with those of the workers on his father's plantation. Nostalgically he remembered Christmas back home. The roast turkey with chestnut stuffing, the platters of fried chicken, the beaten biscuits, watermelon-rind preserves, pecan pies, spoon bread, and cold floating island.

He remembered the look in his father's eyes as he had stood at the head of the table carving the turkey, the look of tender pride as he had surveyed his family.

Once again he could feel his father's strong arms around him . . . a big hand laid tenderly on a little boy's head that day his puppy had been killed.

Dimly he recalled certain moments of growing up when he had thought his father stuffy, old-fashioned. Now everything in him cried out for some of that old-fashioned love.

That night he crept away from the farm, and on foot made his way to Cherbourg, where he worked his way back across the Atlantic on a freighter.

He was going home.

What drew the boy back? The love of a father. The love of a home. Never once did the prodigal son in Luke 15 say, "I will arise and go back to my *house*." There is little in a house to draw someone back to it. It's love that draws us home.

—Peter Marshall, *John Doe, Disciple*

PROPITIATION

(See *Substitution*)

PSYCHIATRISTS

TWO PSYCHIATRISTS passed a lady in the hall. She said, "Good morning." They looked at each other and said, "I wonder what she meant by that?"

—Paul Lee Tan, *Encyclopedia of 7,700 Illustrations*

WOODY ALLEN has a monologue about how a man thought he was a chicken. Since he was convinced he was a chicken, he tried to look like a chicken. He did the things of a chicken. And he was married to a wife who was terribly frustrated—terribly.

So she finally hauled him to a psychiatrist. When they got to the doctor's office, she told the doctor, "He thinks he's a chicken. He acts like a chicken. Sometimes he sounds like a chicken. It's driving me crazy." And the physician, as he sat there, looked at the man and he looked at the woman and he said, "This is ridiculous! Just simply tell him he's not a chicken!" And she said, "But I need the eggs."

—Tim Timmons, *Maximum Living in a Pressure Cooker World*

I went to my psychiatrist to be psychoanalyzed
To find out why I killed the cat and blacked my husband's eyes.
He laid me on a downy couch to see what he could find,
And here is what he dredged up from my subconscious mind:
When I was one, my mommie hid my dolly in a trunk,
And so it follows naturally that I am always drunk.

When I was two, I saw my father kiss the maid one day,
And that is why I suffer from kleptomania.
At three, I had the feeling of ambivalence toward my brothers,
And so it follows naturally I poison all my lovers.
But I am happy now. I've learned the lesson this has taught;
That everything I do that's wrong is someone else's fault.

—Anna Russell, quoted in Billy Graham, *How to Be Born Again*

WELCOME TO THE PSYCHIATRIC HOTLINE!

If you are obsessive-compulsive: Please press 1 repeatedly.

If you are codependent: Please ask someone to press 2.

If you have multiple personalities: Please press 3, 4, 5, and 6.

If your are paranoid-delusional: We know who you are and what you want. Just stay on the line so we can trace the call.

If you are schizophrenic: Listen carefully—a little voice will tell you which number to press.

If you are manic-depressive: It doesn't matter which number you press. No one will answer.

—Charles R. Swindoll, *Hope Again*

ANYONE WHO GOES to a psychiatrist should have his head examined.

—Samuel Goldwyn, quoted in Lloyd Cory, *Quote Unquote*

CHARLES SCHULZ has endeared himself to the American public with his famous and humorous comic strip "Peanuts." When we think of psychiatrists we can't help but remember the most famous of them all—Lucy. She sits behind the very familiar booth and usually Charlie Brown is in front pouring out his troubles. The sign reads, "The Psychiatrist Is In—5 Cents Please!"

—Robert L. Short, *The Parables of Peanuts*

Rr

REBELLION
(Also see *Disobedience*)

A FATHER had a rather strong-willed son. On the way to the store he kept telling the child, "Sit down and buckle the seat belt." But the little kid just kept standing in the seat. Again he said, "Sit down and buckle the seat belt." And after a time or two more the boy was convinced he had better sit down or disaster would strike. So he slipped down onto the seat, snapped the seat belt closed, and said, "Daddy, I'm sitting down on the outside, but I'm still standing up on the inside."

—Vance Havner, *The Best of Vance Havner*

ALL OF US sometimes act out of sheer cussedness, even while justifying our actions to ourselves.

A FINE CHRISTIAN DOCTOR I know had a boy named Keith. He was an intellectual and graduated at the top of his class in high school. But the father began to sense some real seeds of rebellion that did not respond to his father's counsel. Keith wanted his first year of college to be at Stanford. Since they lived in the southwest and it meant a significant outlay of money, Keith was told it would mean that he'd have to work to help with the expenses. He reluctantly said he would, and off he went.

While at Stanford, he never got a job, but he did get fed all the gunk from the secular world about parents and how terrible it is to be in submission and all that rot. So he went back home in the summer after his first year and announced to his dad that he was taking off.

Big mistake. His dad said, "Okay, son, tell you what. Everything you have, I bought for you." He played violin beautifully. So he said, "That Stradivarius violin, you leave in my home." The boy kind of gulped and blinked and, "Okay." Then he said, "By the way, that new Chevelle that you drove to school is mine, so leave that in the garage." "Okay." "And the clothes hanging in your closet? I bought them for you. Leave them there." "The clothes?" "Yeah, all the clothes. You may leave with the clothes that you've got on and you may have the shoes you're wearing. Also, the money in your pocket is mine. Leave it there on the counter before you leave. And let's see if there's anything else." Keith was shaken and said, "Dad, I think you've picked everything that there is." He said, "Okay, then you can leave."

That evening they sat down and had a long talk. Eyeball-to-eyeball that very wise father leveled that young rebel. Today they have a relationship that's something to behold.

RELATIONSHIPS

SOME JOKESTERS tell about the three churches situated at the same downtown intersection. One congregation could be heard singing, "Will There Be Any Stars in My Crown?" followed by the second's, "No, Not One,"and the third's triumphant, "Oh, That Will Be Glory for Me."

—Leslie Flynn, *When the Saints Come Storming In*

A STORY IS TOLD of two unmarried sisters who had so bitter a ruckus they stopped speaking to each other. Unable or unwilling to separate, the pair lived in a large single room with two beds. A chalk line divided the sleeping area into two halves, separating doorway and fireplace, so that each could come and go and get her own meals without trespassing on her sister's domain. In the black of night each could hear the breathing of the foe. For years they coexisted in spiteful silence. Neither was willing to take the first step to reconciliation.

—Leslie Flynn, *When the Saints Come Storming In*

TWO PORCUPINES in Northern Canada huddled together to get warm, according to a forest folktale. But their quills pricked each other, so they moved apart. Before long they were shivering, so they sidled close again. Soon both were getting jabbed again. Same story; same ending. They needed each other, but they kept needling each other.

—Leslie Flynn, *When the Saints Come Storming In*

TWO LITTLE TEARDROPS were floating down the river. One teardrop asked the other, "Who are you?" The second teardrop replied, "I'm from a woman who lost her lover. And you?" The first teardrop said, "I'm from the woman who got him."

—Michael Green, *Illustrations for Biblical Preaching*

FOR WOLVES TO WORRY lambs is no wonder, but for lambs to worry one another, this is unnatural and monstrous.

—Thomas Brookes, *The Golden Treasure of Puritan Quotations*

UNTHINKABLE AND UNNATURAL though it may seem, the bride has been brawling for centuries. We get along for a little while and then we are back at each other's throats. After a bit we make up, walk in wonderful harmony for a few days, then we turn on one another. We can switch from friend to fiend in a matter of moments.

In a "Peanuts" cartoon, Lucy says to Snoopy: "There are times when you really bug me, but I must admit there are also times when I feel like giving you a big hug."

Snoopy replies: "That's the way I am . . . huggable and buggable."

—Robert L. Short, *Parables of Peanuts*

> It was hard to let you go:
> To watch womanhood reach out and snatch you
> Long before the mothering was done.
> But if God listened to mothers and gave in,
> Would the time for turning loose of daughters ever come?
>
> It was hard when you went away—
> For how was I to know
> The serendipity of letting go
> Would be seeing you come home again
> And meeting in a new way
> Woman to woman—
> Friend to friend.

—Marilee Zdenek, quoted in Charles R. Swindoll, *Make Up Your Mind*

BEFORE I BUILT A WALL, I'd ask to know what I was walling in or walling out.

—Robert Frost, "Mending Wall"

THE PURE RELATIONSHIP, how beautiful it is! How easily it is damaged, or weighed down with irrelevancies—not even irrelevancies, just life itself, the accumulations of life and of time. For the first part of every relationship is pure, whether it be with friend or lover, husband or child. It is pure, simple, unencumbered . . .

And then how swiftly, how inevitably the perfect unity is invaded; the relationship changes; it comes complicated, encumbered by its contact with the world.

The original relationship is very beautiful. Its self-enclosed perfection wears the freshness of a spring morning. . . . It moves to another phase of growth which one should not dread, but welcome as one welcomes summer after spring. But there is also a deadweight accumulation, a coating of false values, habits, and burdens which blights life. It is this smothering coat that needs constantly to be stripped off, in life as well as in relationships.

—Ann Morrow Lindbergh, quoted in Charles R. Swindoll, *Come Before Winter*

THOMAS CARLYLE had married his secretary, whom he dearly loved, but he was thoughtless and absorbed in his own interests and activities, treating his wife as if she were still his employee.

Stricken with cancer, she was confined to bed for a long time before she died. After her funeral, Carlyle went back to his empty house. Disconsolate and grieving, he wandered around downstairs thinking about the woman he had loved. After a while he went upstairs to her room and sat down in the chair beside the bed on which she had been lying for months. He realized with painful regret that he had not sat there very often during her long illness. He noticed her diary. While she was alive, he never would have read it, but now that she was gone he felt free to pick it up and thumb through its pages. One entry caught his eye: "Yesterday he spent an hour with me. And it was like being in heaven. I love him so much." He turned a few more pages and read, "I listened all day to hear his steps in the hallway. And now it's late. I guess he won't come to see me." Carlyle read a few more entries and then threw the book on the floor and rushed out through the rain back to the cemetery. He fell on his wife's grave in the mud, sobbing, "If only I had known . . . if only I had known."

—Clarence Macartney, *Macartney's Illustrations*

NOT LONG AGO I walked by a wall poster that brought me back for a second look. I can't remember the artwork, but I've never forgotten the pithy, pointed message: "Involvement with people is always a very delicate thing. . . . It requires real maturity to become involved and not get all messed up."

—Pamela Reeve, *Relationships*

RELIGIOUS PEOPLE

(Also see *Cults, Legalism*)

OLD PHARISEES never die; they just multiply.

OLD PHARISEES never die, you just wish they would.

HAVING SPENT CONSIDERABLE TIME with good people, I can understand why Jesus liked to be with tax-collectors and sinners.

—Mark Twain

IT IS OFTEN DIFFICULT to preach to a "religious" audience. To paraphrase Matthew 22:14, "Many are cold and a few are frozen."

WE'RE ALL MOLDED by God . . . some are just moldier than others.

—Ray Stedman, "Pots, Pressures, and Power," sermon, September 8, 1968

CARTOON OF A PHARISEE WITNESSING: "Have you heard of the 4,973 spiritual laws?"

—*Leadership* magazine

I WOULD LIKE TO BUY $3.00 worth of God, please. Not enough to explode my soul or disturb my sleep, but just enough to equal a cup of warm milk or a snooze in the sunshine.

I don't want enough of Him to make me love a black man or pick beets with a migrant. I want ecstasy, not transformation; I want the warmth of the womb, not a new birth. I want a pound of the Eternal in a paper sack.

I would like to buy $3.00 worth of God, please. No, no, not the flesh and blood one . . . He will keep me from my appointment with the hair dresser and make me late for the cocktail party. He will soil my linen and break my strand of matched pearls. I can't put up with pundits from Persia or sweaty shepherds trampling over my nylon carpet with their muddy feet. My name isn't Mary, you know!

I want no living, breathing Christ—but one I can keep in its crib with a rubber band. That plastic one will do just fine.

—Wilbur Rees, quoted in Charles R. Swindoll, *Improving Your Serve*

AN ARTICLE ENTITLED "The Startling Beliefs of our Future Ministers," included the results of a survey taken among several major denominational seminaries. These questions were asked and answered as follows:

"Do you believe in a physical resurrection?" Fifty-four percent said, "No."

"Do you believe in the virgin birth of Christ?" Fifty-six percent answered, "No."

"Do you believe in a literal heaven and hell?" Seventy-one percent said, "No."

"Do you believe in the deity of Christ?" Eighty-nine percent said, "No."

"Do you believe that man is separated from God by birth (the doctrine of depravity)?" Ninety-eight percent responded either "No" or they weren't concerned about this.

"Do you believe in the Second Coming of Jesus Christ?" Ninety-nine percent said, "No."

—*Redbook,* August 1961

IN OLIVER CROMWELL'S DAY the British government ran out of silver for coins. Cromwell sent his men to the cathedral to see if they could find any there. They reported, "The only silver we can find is in the statues of the saints standing in the corners." To which the great soldier and statesman of England replied, "Good. We'll melt down the saints and put them in circulation!"

—Richard Seume, *Shoes for the Road*

I HAVE A LITTLE RELIGIOUS LIST that goes in and out with me, And everything I don't or do I hope that God will see.

—Ray Stedman, "According to Light," sermon, January 11, 1976

WALTER MARTIN has done a real favor for us in writing *Screwtape Writes Again*. It's a book with the same flavor as C. S. Lewis's earlier book, *Screwtape Letters*. In this case, Screwtape writes his nephew, Wormwood, who is in training to be an emissary of the devil, to tell him how to handle the affairs of Satan and Satan's world so that the Christians and the world will be confused and stay lost. Everything is opposite from Christianity. For example, the book closes, "Glory to Lucifer in the lowest, Dragonslick."

But here's the paragraph that stands out. Remember everything's opposite. The enemy is Christ and the enemy's spirit is the Holy Spirit, because from the perspective down under, you know, everything is opposite.

Screwtape says to Wormwood, "If you can obscure these facts, there's a good chance that he will embrace what hell considers to be the perfect synonym for true religion—churchianity. In this marvelous imitation of the Enemy's church everything looks and sounds right and good, but the Enemy's Spirit is conspicuously absent. You must arrange to make him a devout Methodist or Anglican or Baptist or Presbyterian or what have you. Make him that. He must come to accept the church as a type of religious social club where people congregate. Nothing more. In a word, Wormwood, help him to become more religious, but for hell's sake, not more Christian!"

—Walter Martin, *Screwtape Writes Again*

REMORSE

A BANK HIRED a fellow to be a janitor. They closed early one day and he was in a hurry to get home like the others, so he quickly gathered up the trash. In this particular bank, all the trash was shredded. So he emptied all of what he believed to be trash, and sent it through the shredder. Just before he finished the last barrel, the closing cashier discovered he had shredded all the deposits of that day.

Well, two things happened. You can guess the first one. And after he was fired, they brought in a number of people early the next morning and seated them at a long series of tables. They tried to put together the shredded checks, attempting to match tiny, little pieces of signature, amounts of money, places, events, and so on. It made the headlines of the news with three words, "An impossible job." You could never put together thousands of checks that had been shredded, no matter how many people you hire. It's simply impossible. The remorse of the janitor could not change the outcome of this colossal mistake.

Sometimes

Across the fields of yesterday he sometimes comes to me,
A little lad just back from play, the boy I used to be.
He smiles at me so wistfully when once he's crept within,
It is as though he'd hoped to see the man I might have been.

—Thomas S. Jones, quoted in Donald T. Kauffman, *Baker's Pocket Treasury of Religious Verse*

REMORSE IS SORROW over being caught and the pain of consequences that follow. Repentance is not being concerned for ourselves but having a contrite heart.

REPENTANCE

REPENTANCE IS NOT like the person who sent the IRS a check for $150 with the remark, "If I can't sleep, I'll send you the rest."

—James Hewett, *Illustrations Unlimited*

There is a line by us unseen
That crosses every path,
The hidden boundary between
God's patience and his wrath.

O where is that mysterious bourne
By which our path is crossed,
Beyond which God himself has sworn
That he who goes is lost?

How far can one go on in sin?
How long will mercy spare?
Where does grace end and where begin
The confines of despair?

An answer from the sky is sent:
Ye who from God depart,
While it is called today repent,
And harden not your heart.

Anonymous, quoted in William Hendriksen, *Exposition of the Gospel according to Luke*

TRUE LIBERTY is not found without confession of our sins and the experience of divine forgiveness.

—Paul Tournier, *The Strong and the Weak*

Penitent

O God
You have driven me into a corner
Where I cannot escape.
I come to You penitently
For today I've sinned grieviously.
I have betrayed my highest ideals.
I have been false to my inner convictions.
I know I have broken Your heart.
Thank You for dealing with me
In the privacy of Your personal Presence
For my sin has been against You alone.
Cleanse me, Lord.
Change me.
Sin is so hideous, so outrageous!
Renew me until I am spiritually contagious.

—Ruth Harms Calkin, *Lord, It Keeps Happening and Happening*

RESCUE

G. K. CHESTERTON was once asked about what single book he would most like to have if he were stranded on a desert island. With typical wit, he replied, *Thomas' Guide to Practical Shipbuilding.*

—Bruce Larson, *Setting Men Free*

Some wish to live within the sound
Of church or chapel bell;
I want to run a rescue shop
Within a yard of hell.

—Norman Grubb, *C. T. Studd: Cricketeer and Pioneer*

I'm Drowning

Lord, I'm drowning
In a sea of perplexity.
Waves of confusion
Crash over me.
I'm too weak
To shout for help.
Either quiet the waves
Or lift me above them—
It's too late
To learn to swim.

—Ruth Harms Calkin, *Tell Me Again Lord, I Forget*

I ARRIVED ONE DAY at Pouletti, Persia, which is now Iran, on the shores of the Caspian Sea, to go up to the capital, Tehran. There was a man there in charge of transportation. He was having difficulty because there were more passengers than there were cars. Now I saw a car with only one passenger in it, so I said to the man in charge, "Why couldn't I go in that car? There's only one man in it."

"I'll see," he said.

Later he returned to me, crestfallen, "I'm sorry, sir. But the man in the car said he couldn't ride with you, for you see, he is a French diplomat and you're only a missionary."

Well, I suppose I could have felt squelched, but inwardly I straightened up and I said, "Hey, if he's a French diplomat, then he represents a shaky French kingdom which has had about twenty-six governments in thirty years. If he's a diplomat, I'm an ambassador of an unshakable kingdom which has had one government since the foundation of the world and will have only one government until the end of all time."

On the way across the Caspian Sea in the ship, the diplomat was caught by a treacherous lock in the ship's bathroom and he couldn't get out. So over the wall he raved frantically at me and said, "Please, sir, extricate me."

Ha! The ambassador of the kingdom of God extricated the diplomat from the kingdom of France. But then, isn't that what the ambassadors of the kingdom must do? Extricate the diplomats of this world who have boxed themselves up into the bathrooms of impossible ways of life and are saying—if they only knew it, "Please, sirs, extricate me!"

—E. Stanley Jones, *Growing Spiritually*

REMEMBER WHEN Paul and Silas were in prison singing? They were probably singing "How Great Thou Art" or "Praise God from Whom All 'Beatings' Flow." Personally, I'd be singing "Rescue the Perishing."

SOME OF US REMEMBER the heartache connected with the Lindbergh family when their son was kidnapped. They didn't know it, but the boy was murdered. They were required to give $50,000 ransom to get the boy back. They paid the money and they found the boy's corpse.

You may have read about the Weyerhaeuser family, timber tycoons from Washington State, who paid $200,000 for their nine-year-old son to be returned to them. That's a ransom for rescue.

Frank Sinatra, several years ago, paid a ransom to rescue his son, Frank Jr. back from the kidnapers for $240,000. Those people paid the price so as to gain rescue from bondage. That is what Christ did. He paid the price and rescued us from bondage.

A WORLD WAR II PILOT was hit by enemy fire and his plane began to lose altitude. At treetop level he lost part of his stabilizer, a section of his rudder, a tip of his wing, and the landing gear. Finally he came down in the top of the trees in his cockpit. He breathed a sigh of relief as he sat there in the cockpit as it rocked precariously back and forth. Enclosed in the cockpit all by itself he was saved, yet so as through fire. He was there intact, but he had very little to show for it. That is the message of 1 Corinthians 3:15.

A LITTLE HUNCHBACK BOY in Sunday school had memorized some Bible verses along with all the other kids in his class. One Sunday evening he was to come up to the front and recite the verses and then walk off the stage. One cruel youngster, seeing the hunchback boy stumbling onto the stage, yelled out, "Hey, cripple, why don't you get the pack off your back?" You could have heard a pin drop as this little boy stopped and just dissolved in tears.

All of a sudden, a man got up and walked down the aisle and came and stood by the boy and put his arm around him. He said, "I don't know what kind of person would say something like that, but I just want to say that the most courageous person in this room today is this little boy. You see, he's my son and

I'm proud of him." With that he reached down and picked up his son and carried him back to the seat.

And I thought as I read that account, that is exactly what God does for us. In the bruised, hunchback, broken fashion of our lives we do our best, and then we stumble and make a mess of things, as it were. The Lord Jesus says, "Oh, you're Mine. I'm proud of you. I love you."

—Ray Stedman, "The Way to Wholeness," sermon, September 5, 1971

TO THE ONLOOKERS, some things seem like an empty ritual, when to the person who is informed, they seem more significant than life itself. Take ol' Ed down in Florida. Every Friday evening about the time the sun is the size of a giant orange just about to dip into the water, ol' Ed comes strolling along the beach to find his way to his favorite pier. He's carrying in his bony hand a bucket full of shrimp. The shrimp are not for him. The shrimp are not for the fish. Strangely, the shrimp are for the sea gulls. Ed, alone with his thoughts, walks out to the end of the pier with his bucket, not saying a word. But that's where the ritual begins.

Before long the sky becomes a mass of little dots screeching and squawking, making their way to ol' Ed there on the end of the pier. They envelope him with their presence. Their fluttering wings sound like a roar of thunder. Ed stands there and sort of mumbles to them as they're feeding on the shrimp. In fact, he reaches in his bucket and he throws a few up to them. You can almost hear him say, "Thank you. Thank you." Within minutes, the bucket is empty. And Ed stands there, almost as if raptured, in his thoughts of another time and another place. Then, without a word being spoken, he quietly makes his way back home.

Who is ol' Ed anyway? His full name is Eddie Rickenbacker. He's was a captain in World War II. He flew a B-17 Flying Fortress. He and seven other men were sent on a mission across the Pacific to locate General MacArthur; however, their plane crashed in the water. Miraculously, they all made it out of the plane into a life raft.

Aboard their life raft, they fought the sun and the sharks. Most of all, they fought hunger, as all eight of these men ate and drank very little, until finally by the eighth day their rations ran out. No food. No water. They needed a miracle for them to survive.

After an afternoon devotional time, the men said a prayer and tried to rest. As Rickenbacker was dozing with his hat over his eyes, something landed on his head. It was a sea gull. That gull meant food . . . if he could catch it. And he did.

He tore the feathers off and they shared a morsel of it together. Then they used the intestines for fish bait. They were able to survive until they were found and rescued, almost at the end of their lives.

Later, Billy Graham asked Captain Rickenbacker about the story, because he heard that that experience had been used to lead him to a saving knowledge of Jesus Christ. Rickenbacker said to Billy, "I have no explanation except God sent one of His angels to rescue us."

Ol' Ed never forgot. He never stopped saying, "Thank you." Every Friday evening for years until he died, he would go to that old pier with a bucket full of shrimp and a heart full of gratitude for the rescue to say, "Thank you. Thank you. Thank you."

—Max Lucado, *In the Eye of the Storm*

MY HAPPIEST PRETEEN MEMORIES take me back to Mason Park swimming pool on the east side of Houston. Before I learned to swim on top of the water, I was diving into the deep end (which was against the rules) and swimming to the side, coming up for air next to the ladder.

I shall never forget on one frightening occasion, diving in, swimming the wrong way and getting into the traffic of those diving from the high diving board. Gasping for air, I swallowed water, couldn't scream for help and gagged. Teddy Muntz, the lifeguard on duty, dived into the pool, wrapped me in his big arms and saved me from danger and quite probably death. That day he was my savior and my rescuer.

DROWNING VICTIMS often fight their rescuers in the hysteria of that terrifying moment. The same is often true for those who are floundering spiritually because their faith has suffered shipwreck.

A young man who strayed from the Lord but was finally brought back by the help of a friend who really loved him. When there was full repentance and restoration, I asked this Christian how it felt while he was away from God. The young man said it seemed like he was out to sea, in deep water, in deep trouble, and all his friends were on the shoreline hurling accusations at him about justice, penalty, and wrong.

"But there was one Christian brother who actually swam out to get me and would not let me go. I fought him, but he pushed aside my fighting, grasped me, put a life jacket around me, and took me to shore. By the grace of God, he was the reason I was restored. He would not let me go."

—Howard G. Hendricks

MANY YEARS AGO, a man named Felix of Nola was escaping his enemies. He took temporary refuge in a rugged cave on a hillside. He had scarcely entered the opening of the cave before a spider began to weave its web across the small opening. With remarkable speed, the spider completely sealed off the mouth of the cave with its rather obvious web, giving the appearance that the cave had not been entered for many weeks. As Felix's pursuers passed by, they saw the web and didn't even bother to look in. Later, as the godly fugitive stepped out into the sunlight, he uttered these insightful words: "Where God is, a spider's web is as a wall; where He is not, a wall is but as a spider's web." God has never run out of ways to protect His own.

> The hosts of God encamp around
> The dwellings of the just.
> Deliverance He affords to all
> Who on His promise trust.

—Frank E. Gaebelein, ed., *The Expositor's Bible Commentary*

A MAN WAS DRIVING an old Ford on a lonely road when it chugged to a stop. He was at a loss about what to do since he didn't know much about cars. But he got out, put the hood up and began to tap here and there, jiggle this wire and that when he heard the roar of a car coming toward him. As it got closer, he saw it was a brand new Lincoln. And the fellow was nice enough to pull over. He stepped out, walked up and said, "What's the trouble?" "Oh," he said, "I can't get this old Ford to go." "Well," replied the Good Samaritan, "let me see." So he began to tinker inside and asked, "Do you have a screwdriver?" He adjusted something, then got inside, started it right up. "Say, thanks a lot! That's great. Who are you?" Putting his coat back on, the man said, "Well, I'm Henry Ford. I ought to know a little bit about that car we made."

—Billy Graham, *World Aflame*

IN 1989, an 8.2 earthquake almost flattened Armenia, killing over 30,000 people in less than four minutes.

In the midst of utter devastation and chaos, a father left his wife securely at home and rushed to the school where his son was supposed to be, only to discover that the building was flat as a pancake.

After the traumatic initial shock, he remembered the promise he had made to his son: "No matter what, I'll always be there for you." And tears began to fill his eyes. As he looked at the pile of debris that once was the school, it looked hopeless, but he kept remembering his commitment to his son.

He began to concentrate on where he walked his son to class at school each morning. Remembering his son's classroom would be in the back right corner of the building, he rushed there and started digging through the rubble.

As he was digging, other forlorn parents arrived, clutching their hearts, saying: "My son!" "My daughter!" Other well-meaning parents tried to pull him off of what was left of the school saying:

"It's too late!"

"They're dead!"

"You can't help!"

"Go home!"

"Come on, face reality, there's nothing you can do!"

"You're just going to make things worse!"

To each parent he responded with one line: "Are you going to help me now?" And then he proceeded to dig for his son, stone by stone.

The fire chief showed up and tried to pull him off of the school's debris saying, "Fires are breaking out, explosions are happening everywhere. You're in danger. We'll take care of it. Go home." To which this loving, caring Armenian father asked, "Are you going to help me now?"

The police came and said, "You're angry, distraught, and it's over. You're endangering others. Go home. We'll handle it!" To which he replied, "Are you going to help me now?" No one helped.

Courageously he proceeded alone because he needed to know for himself: "Is my boy alive or is he dead?"

He dug for eight hours, twelve hours, twenty-four hours, thirty-six hours, and then in the thirty-eighth hour, he pulled back a boulder and heard his son's voice. He screamed his son's name, "Armad!" He heard back, "Dad!?! It's me, Dad! I told the other kids not to worry. I told 'em if you were alive, you'd save me and when you saved me, they'd be saved. You promised, 'No matter what, I'll always be there for you!' You did it, Dad!"

"What's going on in there? How is it?" the father asked.

"There are fourteen of us left out of thirty-three, Dad: We're scared, hungry, thirsty, and thankful you're here. When the building collapsed, it made a wedge, like a triangle, and it saved us."

"Come on out, boy!"

"No, Dad! Let the other kids out first, 'cause I know you'll get me! No matter what, I knew you'll be there for me!"

—Jack Canfield, *Chicken Soup for the Soul*

RESURRECTION

(Also see *Easter*)

WHEN I WAS A BOY, I played sandlot football on a lot next door to a Methodist church at the end of our block in Houston. There was always a marshy puddle and lots of mud around it because of an outside leaky faucet. It was a place where locusts would come to find water. And once a year they would shed their skin.

If you've ever seen this sight, it's incredible. It looks exactly like a locust about an inch and a half long, but it's empty. You pick it up and it's light as a feather. It has its legs and it has its carcass, at least the shell about it, but if you squeeze it, there's nothing but air on the inside. Somehow, in the amazing way God has made insects, they have the ability to slip out of the shell.

IF YOU WANT TO STUDY a knotty problem of resurrection, study the life of Roger Williams—not the pianist, but the reformer of years ago. Roger Williams was buried not far from an apple tree. The root of the apple tree penetrated the coffin and made its way through the skull, down the spine, forking at the legs so that his body was inhabited by the roots of an apple tree. The nutrients of the body in the remains went into the apple tree and became part of the fruit. Are those who ate the apples eating Roger?

—Merrill Tenney, *The Reality of the Resurrection*

Christ Arose

Death cannot keep his prey, Jesus, my Savior!
He tore the bars away, Jesus, my Lord!
And up from the grave He arose,
With a mighty triumph o'er His foes.
He arose a Victor from the dark domain,
And He lives forever with His saints to reign,
He arose! He arose! Hallelujah! Christ arose!

—Robert Lowry

ONCE UPON A TIME I had a young friend named Philip. Philip was born with Downs Syndrome. He was a pleasant child—happy, it seemed—but increasingly aware of the difference between himself and other children. Philip went to Sunday school at the Methodist church. His teacher, also a friend of mine, taught the third-grade class with Philip and nine other eight-year-old boys and girls.

You know eight-year-olds. And Philip, because of his differences, was not readily accepted. But my teacher friend was creative, and he helped the group of eight-year-olds. They learned, they laughed, they played together. And they really cared about one another, even though eight-year-olds don't say they care about each other out loud. My teacher friend could see it. He knew it. He also knew that Philip was not really a part of that group. Philip did not choose nor did he want to be different. He just was. And that was just the way things were.

My friend had a marvelous idea for his class the Sunday after Easter last year. You know those things that pantyhose come in—the containers that look like great big eggs—my friend had collected ten of them. The children loved it when he brought them into the room. Each child was to get one. It was a beautiful spring day, and the assignment was for each child to go outside, find a symbol for new life, put it into the egg, and bring it back to the classroom. They would then open and share their new life symbols and surprises one by one.

It was glorious. It was confusing. It was wild. They ran all around the church grounds, gathering their symbols, and returned to the classroom. They put all the eggs on a table, and then the teacher began to open them. All the children stood around the table.

He opened one, and there was a flower, and they oohed and aahed. He opened another, and there was a little butterfly. "Beautiful," the girls all said, since it is hard for eight-year-old boys to say "beautiful." He opened another, and there was a rock. And as third graders will, some laughed, and some said, "That's crazy! How's a rock supposed to be like new life?" But the smart little boy who'd found it spoke up: "That's mine. And I knew all of you would get flowers and buds and leaves and butterflies and stuff like that. So I got a rock because I wanted to be different. And for me, that's new life." They all laughed.

My teacher friend said something to himself about the profundity of eight-year-olds and opened the next one. There was nothing there. The other children, as eight-year-olds will, said, "That's not fair—That's stupid!—Somebody didn't do it right."

Then my teacher friend felt a tug on his shirt, and he looked down. Philip was standing beside him "It's mine," Philip said. "It's mine."

And the children said, "You don't ever do things right, Philip. There's nothing there!"

"I did so do it," Philip said. "I did do it. It's empty. *The tomb is empty!*"

There was silence, a very full silence. And for you people who don't believe in miracles, I want to tell you that one happened that day last spring. From that time on, it was different. Philip suddenly became a part of that group of eight-year-old children. They took him in. He was set free from the tomb of his differentness.

Philip died last summer. His family had known since the time he was born that he wouldn't live out a full life span. Many other things had been wrong with his tiny body. And so, late last July, with an infection that most normal children could have quickly shrugged off, Philip died. The mystery simply enveloped him.

At the funeral, nine eight-year-old children marched up to the altar, not with flowers to cover the stark reality of death. Nine eight-year-olds, with their Sunday school teacher, marched right up to that altar, and laid on it an empty egg—an empty, old, discarded pantyhose egg.

—Harry Pritchett, Jr., *Leadership* magazine, Summer 1985

IN PAUL'S DAY a motto that hung in Athens read, "Once a man dies and the earth drinks up his blood, there is no resurrection." Paul hotly disagreed. Now, some may say, "Well, when Athens died, so died the doubt of resurrection." Are you kidding? As recently as the nineteenth century there was a poem spreading around England that has caught all kinds of people off guard. Charles Swinburne wrote it.

> From too much love of living,
> From hope and fear set free,
> We thank with brief thanksgiving
> Whatever gods may be
> That no life lives forever;
> That dead men rise up never;
> That even the weariest river
> Winds somewhere safe to sea.

It's a lie! Dead men rise up *ever!* And there is no safety at sea apart from Christ! The resurrection is our only hope.

—John Bartlett, *Bartlett's Familiar Quotations*

THE RESURRECTION is God's "Amen!" to Christ's statement, "It is finished."

—S. Lewis Johnson

REVENGE
(Also see *Anger*)

MAYBE YOU HEARD about the fellow who was told by his physician, "Yes indeed, you do have rabies." Upon hearing this, the patient immediately pulled out a pad and pencil and began to write.

Thinking the man was making out his will, the doctor said, "Listen, this doesn't mean you're going to die. There's a cure for rabies."

"I know that," said the man. "I'm makin' a list of people I'm gonna bite."

—Charles R. Swindoll, *Hope Again*

I SAW A CARTOON depicting a tiny baby only seconds after birth. The physician had the baby by the feet, holding him upside down, and slapping him on the fanny. Instead of crying, the kid was screaming angrily, "I want a lawyer!"

—Charles R. Swindoll, *Simple Faith*

SOME FELLOWS were stationed in Korea during the Korean War. While there, they hired a local boy to cook and clean for them. Being a bunch of jokesters, these guys soon took advantage of the boy's seeming naiveté. They'd smear Vaseline on the stove handles so that when he'd turn the stove on in the morning he'd get grease all over his fingers. They'd put little water buckets over the door so that he'd get deluged when he opened the door. They'd even nail his shoes to the floor during the night. Day after day the little fella took the brunt of their practical jokes without saying anything. No blame, no self-pity, no temper tantrums.

Finally the men felt guilty about what they were doing, so they sat down with the young Korean and said, "Look, we know these pranks aren't funny anymore, and we're sorry. We're never gonna take advantage of you again."

It seemed too good to be true to the houseboy. "No more sticky on stove?" he asked.

"Nope."

"No more water on door?"

"No."

"No more nail shoes to floor?"

"Nope, never again."

"Okay," the boy said with a smile, "no more spit in soup."

—Ray Stedman, "How to Hug," sermon, March 20, 1977

THERE WAS A GUY that could not get along with his wife and, on top of that, he couldn't get along with his mother-in-law. In frustration one day, he finally took a long walk. As he was about to return home, he got to the street corner and saw a hearse pull up to the stop sign. It had a big dog in it.

Behind that was another hearse. And then behind that second hearse, about fifty men were walking. He was seized with curiosity and walked up to the first hearse, knocked on the glass and a guy inside rolled his window down. "Yes?" he asked. "What is this?" asked the man.

"Well, in this casket is my wife. And in that casket in the other hearse is my mother-in-law. This big dog killed both of them."

"Hmm. Can I borrow that dog?"

And the guy inside said, "Get in line."

REVENGE is the greatest instinct in the human race.

—Friedrich Nietzsche

SEVERAL YEARS AGO, I drove my car into a busy shopping center and there was a small parking space just big enough for the compact car I was driving. I knew it would be a tight squeeze to get my ample frame in and out of the car without bumping the car next to me, but I was willing to try. Parking places were scarce.

My son, who was then small, was with me. He slipped out of his side with no problem, but I very gingerly pulled myself out and in the process, bumped the car a little bit. It bothered me, so I wiped off the side of his car to make sure it was okay. There wasn't a mark on it.

When I came up from that maneuver, the man inside his car wasn't smiling. I smiled and said, "I'm sorry, but there's no damage." He still wasn't smiling. So I closed the door and my boy and I started walking into the grocery store. Something told me to turn around and look, something was going to happen to my car. Sure as the world, when I turned around, he was already going around his car and he opened the back door of his car and he went smash, smash into my fender!

My first reaction was to separate his head from his body! That was my first reaction. But I thought, "Man, what a scandal this would create!" Pastor kills man in parking lot. He was bigger than I was, and I thought, "How much worse to read , 'Man kills pastor in parking lot.'" So I didn't do anything. My little boy had his hand in mine, and I thought, "Boy, it would just foul everything up if he saw his daddy out there get smeared all over the parking lot." So I didn't do anything.

Well, I did do something. I applied patience, a rare virtue in my life, and walked away. But you know what? That is a pleasant memory and a rare one in my mind right now. That day that I walked away from man's natural tendency toward revenge.

REVENGE IS a kind of wild justice; which the more man's nature runs to, the more ought the law to weed it out. . . . certainly, in taking revenge a man is but even with his enemy; but in passing over it, he is superior, for it is a prince's part to pardon.

—Sir Francis Bacon

I LIKE THE ATTITUDE of the preacher who refused to take revenge. He said, "I'm not going to get even. I'm going to tell God on you!"

RIGHTEOUSNESS

PEOPLE must be charmed into righteousness.

—Reinhold Niebuhr

EVER SMELLED old, rotten meat? Remember forgetting for several weeks something you put in the refrigerator? There is an odor that accompanies decay that's like nothing else. Down in Houston where I was raised, we were only fifty miles from the seaport city of Galveston. Delicious, fresh seafood was available in numerous restaurants in that area—and still is. But there were other ways we used to use seafood, especially shrimp. When a friend would get married, one of our favorite tricks was to secretly pull off the hubcaps of his getaway car and stuff them full of shrimp. It was great! Those shrimp wouldn't make any noise as they sloshed around hour after hour in the heat of South Texas. But the result was unreal. After two or three days of driving, parking in the sun, stop-and-go traffic, the bride (bless her shy heart) would slowly start sliding over closer to the door. She would begin to wonder if maybe her beloved groom had forgotten his Right Guard. As the day wore on, he would begin to wonder the same about her! All the while those little shrimp were doing their thing in each wheel. Finally (and sometimes they wouldn't discover the trick for over a week!), young Don Juan would pop off the hubcap—and I don't need to tell you the result. Old shrimp inside a hot hubcap for a week would make a skunk's spray seem like a shot of Chanel No. 5. It is gross! To keep shrimp, you must preserve them. If you don't, they perish. Years ago salt was used. Today we use ice more often.

Think of this earth as shrimp. The earth's inhabitants are in a continual state of perishing. We are "salt to the world" (NEB). R.V.G. Tasker, professor emeritus of New Testament exegesis at the University of London, is correct: "The disciples, accordingly, are called to be a moral disinfectant in a world where moral standards are low, constantly changing, or non-existent."

—R.V.G. Tasker, *The Gospel According to St. Matthew*

THE YEAR WAS 1977, and the month was September and the place was Moline, Illinois. That pre-Christmas season, Terry Schafer had a special gift she wanted to purchase for her husband, David. Her fear was that it might be too expensive. Oh, it wouldn't be too expensive for some families, but when you have to make ends meet on a policeman's salary, it could be too expensive. She kept it on her mind as she wandered along Fifth Avenue, hoping to find something like it or perhaps the very thing she had in mind.

Sure enough, she did. She slipped into the store and looked into the face of a kind shopkeeper and asked, "How much?" "$127.50." Ouch. Her anticipation turned to disappointment as she thought, "That's just too much for us. We can't afford it."

And then an idea popped into her mind. She said to him, "Though we don't know each other, perhaps you would allow me to put it on hold. I can pay a little now, and then about the end of October, I'll come back and pay you more. And, I promise you, by the time you have it gift-wrapped before Christmas, I'll pay the last amount."

A seasoned businessman, he knew a trusting soul when he saw one. So he smiled and said, "I'll tell you what. Since your husband is a police officer (as she had talked to him about that), I have every reason to trust you. Why don't you just give me the first payment? I'll gift wrap it and let you take it with you today." She was elated. She walked out with this wonderful gift she was so anxious to give him.

And like a lot of us, she wasn't able to keep the secret. So that night as David unwrapped the gift, Terry stood there beaming. He was thrilled at her thoughtfulness and covered her with hugs and kisses. Neither one of them realized, however, how significant that simple gift was. As a matter of fact, in the not-too-distant future, it would be the difference between David's life and death.

On October 1, that same year, Patrolman David Schafer was working the night shift and got a call on his police radio. A drugstore robbery was in process. Racing to the scene, he arrived just in time to observe the suspect getting into his car, starting the engine, and speeding away. Quickly David switched on his siren and began the pursuit. Three blocks later the getaway vehicle suddenly pulled over to the side of the road and stopped.

The suspect was still seated behind the wheel of his car as David cautiously approached the suspect. As he got about three feet from the driver's door, it flew open and the suspect fired an automatic pistol once, sending a .45-caliber slug toward David's stomach.

At seven o'clock the next morning, Terry answered the door of the Schafer's home. Carefully and calmly, the police officer explained David had been shot while trying to apprehend a robbery suspect. As the officer detailed what happened to David, he had bad news and good news. When she listened to the story, Terry Schafer was thinking how glad she was she didn't wait until Christmas to give her gift, how glad she was the shopkeeper had been willing to let her pay for it later. Otherwise, David Schafer, shot at point-blank range with a devastatingly deadly .45-caliber pistol, would surely have died. But the good news was that he was still alive and in the hospital—not with a gunshot wound but with a deep bruise in his abdomen.

Christmas had come early that year because David had with him the gift of life his wife could not wait to give: his brand-new bulletproof vest.

And that's why Christ came, to give us a vest of righteousness, to pay the price with His blood, that He might protect us with a shield that sin could never penetrate.

—Paul Aurandt, *More of Paul Harvey's The Rest of the Story*

_____

YEARS AGO Joe Bayly, the late *Eternity* magazine columnist, visited some German Christians who had been devoted soldiers in the German army during World War II. Two of them had been put up for promotion to become second lieutenants in the Nazi army. The commandant told them he would approve the promotion on one condition: that they join the Officers' Club. Being a member of the club would require them to attend some weekend dances. These young men believed that dancing was wrong because it could lead to immorality. Because of their convictions, they turned down the promotion.

Later in their military careers these same men were assigned to the death camps where thousands of Jews were stuffed into ovens and killed. Even though they did not directly participate in the slaughter, they knew what was going on. Yet they never voiced any protest.

When Joe Bayly talked to them many years after the war, they looked back on their experiences with no regret, convinced that they had made right decisions. For them, not conforming to social pressure and refusing to dance was an act of righteousness. And conforming to patriotic mass murder and remaining silent while thousands of Jews burned in ovens left them with no feelings of unrighteousness.

When we set our own standard of external righteousness, we are capable of any evil. When we are filled with His righteousness, no good is too great.

—Haddon Robinson, *What Jesus Said about Successful Living*

$\mathcal{S}s$

SALVATION
(Also see *Cross*)

DICK RUSSELL had a Bible study group. An unsaved man, at the urging of his wife, joined the group and discovered he really liked the acceptance he found there and especially the prayer time. He realized even Christian men had serious issues to deal with in their lives, and week after week there were praises to God for answered prayer. No stranger to family problems, the man told Dick as he called one night, "You know, my son was shot in the eye with a pellet gun. And the damage on the retina seems to be threatening his eyesight. I'd like for you to pray, Dick, that God would restore the sight." And so he agreed with him and they began to pray.

The next day, the doctor went in and discovered two cataracts, one on each eye, along with the damage in the retina. The fella was on his face before God as the doctor was doing his work. Then, lo and behold, when the gentleman came home from that surgery, their house had been burglarized. And things were in a turmoil. He called Dick. Again they prayed. The operation was a miraculous success. His son was fitted with contacts, and he had his eyesight back.

Before long the phone rang again. Dick was asked to pray about another need. The fella's daughter, hooked on heroin, was becoming destructive and breaking the windows and destroying pieces of furniture in the home. He said to Dick, "You have no idea what it's like to literally wrestle with your child and to pull her arms behind her back while the police snap the handcuffs on and take her out of the house." That, by the way, led to harassment from the drug crowd that she was running with—motorcycle gangs and obscene phone calls and again attempted damage to the home. Just one breaking experience after another.

And the fella stayed in this Bible study. Dick prayed with him about this impossible situation, growing in urgency, but unknown to the people he worked with. Just sort of a quiet burden he held ont o. Finally, this led to the ultimate.

There was one person in the family with whom he really felt close, his wife's mother. And would you believe it, she had a heart attack. Just sort of an ultimate climax—a final blow.

That evening, he came home from work, went upstairs to his room without a word, and closed the door. His wife, downstairs fixing supper, heard a noise, heard words. She went up and listened. She heard this man, broken, weeping, just dumping out to the Lord every ugly sin of his life and saying, "I'm spiritually bankrupt. I ask you now, Father, through Jesus Christ, to come into my life." And the wife, on the other side of the door, also wept, rejoicing at what God had done in this strange set of circumstances that broke that man to the place of submission and salvation. An answer to her own prayers for his salvation.

I DESERVED TO BE DAMNED in hell, but God interfered.

—Salvation Army Officer John Allen

THE BOY who held his little boat and said, "It's mine, I made it," suffered a keen disappointment. One day, with exuberant anticipation, he carried his boat to the shore of the lake and sailed it on the clear, blue water. The little boat skimmed along as the gentle breeze blew its sails across the rippling waves. Then suddenly, a gust of wind caught the little boat and snapped the string the boy was holding. Out farther and farther the little boat sailed until at last it vanished from sight. Sadly the boy made his way home—without his prized possession. It was lost.

The weeks and months went by. Then one day as the boy passed a toy shop, something caught his attention. Could it be? Was it really? He looked closer. It was. Yes, there in the display window was his own little boat. Overjoyed, the boy bolted into the store and told the owner about the boat on display. It really belonged to him. He had made it, hadn't he? "I'm sorry," the shopkeeper said, "but it's my boat now. If you want it, you'll have to pay the price for it."

Sad at heart, the boy left the store. But he was determined to get his boat back, even though it meant working and saving until he had enough money to pay for it.

At last the day came. Clutching his money in his fist, he walked into the shop and spread his hard-earned money on the counter top. "I've come back to buy my boat," the boy said. The clerk counted the money. It was enough. Reaching into the showcase, the storekeeper took the boat and handed it to the eager boy. The lad's face lit up with a smile of satisfaction as he held the little boat in his arms. "You're mine," he said, "twice mine. Mine because I made you, and now, mine because I bought you."

—Dale E. Galloway, *Rebuild Your Life*

THERE IS A MOVING STORY of Steinberg and a gypsy girl. Struck with her beauty, Steinberg took her to his studio and frequently had her sit for him. At that time he was at work on his masterpiece "Christ on the Cross." The girl used to watch him work on this painting. One day she said to him, "He must have been a very wicked man to be nailed to a cross like that." "No," said the painter. "On the contrary, he was a very good man. The best man that ever lived. He died for others." The little girl looked up at him and asked, "Did he die for you?" Steinberg was not a Christian, but the gypsy girl's question touched his heart and awakened his conscience, and he became a believer in Him whose dying passion he had so well portrayed. Years afterward a young Count chanced to go into the gallery at Dresden where Steinberg's painting of "Christ on the Cross" was on exhibition. The painting spoke so powerfully to him that it changed the whole tenor of his life. He was Count Nikolaus von Zinzendorf, founder of the Moravian Brethren.

—Clarence Macartney, *Preaching without Notes*

Chief of sinners though I be,
Jesus shed His blood for me;
Died that I might live on high,
Lives that I may never die.

—William McComb, quoted in William Hendriksen, *Exposition of the Gospel according to Luke*

My Captain

Out of the light that dazzles me,
Bright as the sun from pole to pole,
I thank the God I know to be
For Christ the conqueror of my soul.

Since His the sway of circumstance,
I would not wince nor cry aloud.
Under that rule which men call chance
My head with joy is humbly bowed.
Beyond this place of sin and tears
That life with Him! And His the aid,
Despite the menace of the years,
Keeps, and shall keep me, unafraid.

I have no fear, though strait the gate,
He cleared from punishment the scroll.

> Christ is the Master of my fate,
> Christ is the Captain of my soul.

—Dorothea Day, quoted in Hazel Felleman, *The Best Loved Poems of the American People*

ONE OF THE LARGEST DEPARTMENT STORES in our nation took on a commercial venture that proved to be disastrously unsuccessful. It was a doll in the form of the baby Jesus. It was advertised as being unbreakable, washable, and cuddly. It was packaged in straw with a satin crib and plastic surroundings, and appropriate biblical texts added here and there to make the scene complete.

It did not sell. The manager of one of the stores in the department chain panicked. He carried out a last-ditch promotion to get rid of those dolls. He brandished a huge sign outside his store that read:

> JESUS CHRIST—
> MARKED DOWN 50%
> GET HIM WHILE YOU CAN

—Charles R. Swindoll, *Growing Deep in the Christian Life*

None Other Lamb

> None other Lamb, none other Name,
> None other Hope in heaven or earth or sea,
> None other Hiding-place from guilt and shame,
> None beside Thee.
>
> My faith burns low, my hope burns low
> Only my heart's desire cries out in me
> By the deep thunder of its want and woe
> Cries out to Thee.
>
> Lord, Thou art Life tho' I be dead,
> Love's Fire Thou art, however cold I be:
> Nor heaven have I, nor place to lay my head,
> No home, but Thee.

—Christina Rossetti, quoted in Donald T. Kauffman, *Baker's Pocket Treasury of Religious Verse*

A BAZAAR WAS HELD in a village in northern India. Everyone brought his wares to trade and sell. One old farmer brought in a whole covey of quail. He had tied a string around one leg of each bird. The other ends of all the strings were tied to a ring which fit loosely over a central stick. He had taught the quail to walk dolefully in a circle, around and around, like mules at a sugarcane mill. Nobody seemed interested in buying the birds until a devout Brahman came along. He believed in the Hindu idea of respect for all life, so his heart of compassion went out to those poor little creatures walking in their monotonous circles.

"I want to buy them all," he told the merchant, who was elated. After receiving the money, he was surprised to hear the buyer say, "Now, I want you to set them all free."

"What's that, sir?"

"You heard me. Cut the strings from their legs and turn them loose. Set them all free!"

With a shrug, the old farmer bent down and snipped the strings off the quail. They were freed, at last. What happened? The birds simply continued marching around and around in a circle. Finally, the man had to shoo them off. But even when they landed some distance away, they resumed their predictable march. Free, unfettered, released, yet they kept going in circles as if still tied. . . . Salvation cuts the strings of sin. It's time to stop marching and start flying.

—Charles R. Swindoll, *The Finishing Touch*

SALVATION IS moving from living death to deathless life.

—Jack Odell, quoted in Lloyd Cory, *Quote Unquote*

O Lord God,
Teach me to know grace precedes, accompanies and follows my salvation,
    that it sustains the redeemed soul,
    that not one link of its chain can ever break.
From Calvary's cross wave upon wave of grace reaches me,
    deals with my sin,
    washes me clean,
    renews my heart,
    draws out my affection,
    kindles a flame in my soul,
    consecrates my every thought, word, work,
    teaches me thy immeasurable love.
How great are my privileges in Christ Jesus!
Without him I stand far off, a stranger, an outcast;
    in him I draw near and touch his kingly sceptre.

Without him I dare not lift my guilty eyes;
    in him I gaze upon my Father-God and friend.
Without him I hide my lips in trembling shame;
    in him I open my mouth in petition and praise.
Without him all is wrath and consuming fire;
    in him all is love, and the repose of my soul.
Without him is gaping hell below me, and eternal anguish;
    in him its gates are barred to me by his precious blood.
Without him darkness spreads its horrors in front;
    in him an eternity of glory is my boundless horizon.
Without him all within me is terror and dismay,
    in him every accusation is charmed into joy and peace.
Without him all things external call for my condemnation;
    in him they minister to my comfort,
    and are to be enjoyed with thanksgiving.
Praise be to thee for grace,
    and for the unspeakable gift of Jesus.

—Arthur Bennett, *The Valley of Vision*

_____

THE CONVERSION OF A SOUL is the miracle of a moment, but the making of a saint is the task of a lifetime.

—Alan Redpath, *The Making of a Man of God*

_____

A YOUNG MAN named Sinner once received from his Father a beautiful, bright-red convertible. He named it Salvation—sparkling, new, clean, modern, powerful.

It delighted the young man so much, especially because it was a gift. He could never have afforded it. So delighted, the boy even changed his name from Sinner to Saved.

He polished his car every week. Took pictures of it. Sent it to friends. Looked it over—front, back, under, top, bottom, inside out. Never—never tired of telling others about the gift. "My Father gave it to me. It was free!"

Some days later Saved was seen out on the highway, pushing Salvation. An individual named Helper walked up and introduced himself and asked if he could assist.

"Oh, no thanks. Just out enjoying my new car," as he wiped the sweat off his face. "Just had a little trouble because my bumper kept cutting my hands, especially on these hills. But then a nice man helped me. Showed me how to mount little rubber cushions right here, underneath the bumper, and now I can push this thing for hours without a blister. Also, I've been trying something new lately. They use it over in England. You put your back against the car, lift, and it works like a charm, especially on muddy roads."

Helper asked, "Have you pushed the car very far?"

"Well, about 200 miles altogether. It's been hard, but since it was a gift from my Father, that's the least I can do in return to thank him."

Helper opened the door on the right side and said, "Get in."

After hesitation, he decided it was worth a try and he slid in on the passenger side and rested for the first time since he'd been given the car. Helper walked around, opened the door, slid behind the wheel, and started the car.

"What's all that noise?" he said. Moments later they were moving down the highway quietly, at fifty, sixty miles an hour. He was taken aback. It all seemed to fall into place. It was even exciting. He knew he needed this Salvation Car to be admitted through the gate at the end of the highway. But somehow he felt that getting there was *his* responsibility.

—Larry Christenson, *The Renewed Mind*

WE HAD DINNER ONE EVENING with someone who interestingly enough had worked for a time with a magician, an illusionist. He told us, "You know, on the surface these things an illusionist does look very complicated. They saw women in two and they put the legs over here and head over there. You sit there in the audience and you think, 'Oh, how in the world can that happen? She didn't even scream. She's over there and she's over here—ten feet apart. How could it be?'" Then he said, "You know, when you're on the inside and you work with an illusionist, it is so simple. So simple! Once you have it explained to you, there's nothing to it. But the audience is amazed."

Salvation is like that. It seems incomprehensible how the sacrifice of one Man can secure the eternal salvation of all men who will believe—until you have it explained and see it with the eyes of faith.

HE IS NO FOOL who gives what he cannot keep to gain what he cannot lose.

—Jim Elliot, quoted in Sherwood Wirt, *Topical Encyclopedia of Living Quotations*

Nothing to pay! Yes, nothing to pay!
Jesus has cleared all the debt away.

Blotted it out with His bleeding hand!

Free and forgiven and loved you stand.

—Frances Havergal, quoted in William Hendriksen, *Exposition of the Gospel according to Luke*

DWIGHT L. MOODY made a mistake on October 8, 1871. He preached to his largest audience in the city of Chicago. The text had been, "What Will You Do Then with Jesus Who Is Called the Christ?" He said something he had never said before and, frankly, never said again. He was very fatigued and because of that he said to the audience after he presented the gospel, "Now I give you a week to think that over. And when we come together again, you will have opportunity to respond."

Then Ira Sankey came and began to sing. Even before he finished the song, you could hear the blare of the siren in the streets of Chicago as that great fire broke out and left 100,000 homeless. Hundreds of people died in that fire. And Dwight L. Moody rose to the occasion a few months later and he said, "I would give my right arm before I would ever give an audience another week to think over the message of the gospel. Some who heard that night died in the fire."

—Clarence Macartney, *Preaching without Notes*

SECOND COMING

(Also see *Future*)

A LITTLE-KNOWN FACT from the life of Christopher Columbus is that he predicted the end of the world. He wrote a volume called *The Book of Prophecies*, in which he prophesied that the world would end in the year 1656. He even stated very definitely that "there is no doubt that the world must end in one hundred fifty-five years."

—Paul Lee Tan, *Encyclopedia of 7,700 Illustrations*

I WORKED IN A MACHINE SHOP for four-and-a-half years alongside a fellow named George. His job was to sweep and clean out the shavings underneath the huge lathes and machines we were running. George was born again, and he loved the teaching of Scripture on prophecy. I remember hearing him sing hymns as he worked. Many of them had to do with the coming of Christ, such as "In the Sweet By and By" and "When the Roll Is Called Up Yonder."

Late one Friday afternoon about ten minutes to quitting time when we were all weary, I looked at George and said, "George, are you ready?" He said, "Uh–huh." But he was all dirty. He was just obviously not ready. In fact, he looked like he was ready to keep on working. I said, "Aren't you ready to go home?" He said, "Yeah, I'm ready." I said, "Look at you! Man, you're not ready. You've gotta go clean up." "No," he said, "let me show you something." So he unzipped his coveralls and underneath were the neatest, cleanest clothes you can imagine. He had them all ready. All he did when the whistle blew was just unzip and step out of that coverall, walk up, and punch his clock and he was gone. He said, "You see, I stay ready to keep from gettin' ready—just like I'm ready for Jesus!"

———————————————

THE GREAT YEAR of Millerite expectation was 1842. Between March of 1842 and March of 1843, Christ, however, was nowhere to be seen. You see, they had set the date: "Christ is coming back, 1842." They waited in vain. Miller was a disappointed man, aware that he had made a mistake and incapable of finding out why.

The Millerite hopes were down, but not out—1844 dragged on; meetings went on flatly. And in New Hampshire, on August 12, a camp meeting was dragging on, when rather suddenly, as if driven by the silent demand of a grieving multitude, one of the brothers stood up and announced the return of Christ would be on the seventh month of the current Jewish year. The proposal caught on. The fading hopes lived again. Excitement thrilled the place. A fixed date was set. And once again, more fervently than ever, the Millerites set out to warn the world. Only this time, Miller was to catch the fire rather than start it. October 22—the end of the world was announced.

In ten weeks the great day was at hand. In a Philadelphia store window the following sign was displayed: "This shop is closed in honor of the King of kings who will appear about the twentieth of October. Get ready, friends, to crown Him Lord of all." A group of 200 people left the city, as Lot had left Sodom before impending doom. Most of the Millerites gave up their occupations during the last days. Farmers left their crops in the fields, as they awaited the coming of Christ. October 22—He never came.

Hope seemed to spring eternal in the Millerite breast. Though they were no longer adjusting their timetable for the Lord's return, they did keep their hopes alive and set another date. But five years later, Christ did not come to Miller, but Miller went to Christ. His tombstone reads, "At the time appointed, the end shall be."

—John H. Gerstner, *The Theology of Major Sects*

MARCH 11, 1942, on Corregidor, a sixty-two-year-old Army officer, with his family, secretly slipped away from the Philippines and in a minor miracle made their way down to Australia. Before General MacArthur left the islands, he said, "I will return." Two-and-a-half years later, October 20, 1944, he stood again on the soil of the Philippines and said, "This is the voice of freedom. People of the Philippines, I have returned."

Now if you think a man can have that kind of credibility, and if you can appreciate that quality in a man, I'll tell you that Jesus Christ, the God-Man, has made the same promise far more credible than any human being will ever be. If you wrestle with the truth of Jesus' return, wrestle no longer. If you accept the historic fact of His ascension, then you have no room to doubt His historic, yet future, return. It will occur.

—John Bartlett, *Bartlett's Familiar Quotations*

SECURITY

SOMEONE ASKED AN ASTRONAUT, "How does it feel inside the space capsule?" The astronaut replied, "It really makes you think, when everything is done according to the lowest bidder. It really makes you think."

—Michael Green, *Illustrations for Biblical Preaching*

ON A BLUSTERY DAY a fellow was working on his roof, which had a sharp peak. So he decided to be safe he should somehow secure himself to something on the earth. He tied a rope around his waist, pulled it tight, climbed to the roof, and went over the peak. Then he threw the rope over the side and said to his boy, "Tie that to the tree." Well, the little kid thought, "That tree is rather small." So he tied it to the bumper of his dad's car.

Mom was busy in the house with chores of her own. She discovered, however, that she needed to make a quick trip to the store. She went out, put the car in reverse, and the guy came off the roof in fast order.

This guy's trusting in the rope, is just like those who hang on to religion for security. Religion is a curse. It isn't a cure.

I Should Really Like to Know

Said the robin to the sparrow
I should really like to know

Why those anxious human beings
Rush about and worry so.

Said the sparrow to the robin
Well, I think that it must be
That they have no heavenly Father
Such as cares for you and me.

—Elizabeth Cheney, quoted in Walter Knight, *Knight's Master Book of New Illustrations*

GUILLERMO VILAS, the Argentinean tennis pro, was interviewed in *Sports Illustrated* several years ago. In the interview he said, "Fervently I think that many times one feels oneself to be secure and suddenly one's world falls down like a pack of cards in a matter of seconds."

—*Sports Illustrated*, May 29, 1978

The Hiding Place

In a time of trouble, in a time forlorn,
There is a hiding place where hope is born.
There is a hiding place, a strong protective space,
    where God provides the grace to persevere;
For nothing can remove us from the Father's love,
Tho' all may change, yet nothing changes here.
In a time of sorrow, in a time of grief,
There is a hiding place to give relief.

In a time of danger, when our faith is proved,
There is a hiding place where we are loved.
There is a hiding place, a strong protective space,
    where God provides the grace to persevere;
For nothing can remove us from the Father's love
  Tho' all may change, yet nothing changes here.
  In a time of weakness, in a time of fear,
  There is a hiding place where God is near.

—Bryan Jeffery Leech

IN 1937 the great Golden Gate Bridge was completed. It cost $77 million. It was built in two stages: the first slowly, and the second rapidly. In the first stage, twenty-three men fell to their death. And the work ground to a halt because fear paralyzed the workmen as helplessly they watched their companions plummeting from the structure to the water far below. Finally, an ingenious person thought, "There needs to be a net." So they put together, for $100,000, the largest net ever built and hung that net beneath the workmen. When phase two began, ten were saved who fell into that net. The work proceeded twenty-five percent faster until the job was done.

—Walter Knight, *Knight's Master Book of New Illustrations*

SELF–ESTEEM
(Also see *Acceptance*)

WE ARE NOT WHAT WE ARE. We are not even what others think we are. We are what we think others think we are.

—James Dobson, *Hide or Seek*

IF I WERE TO DRAW A CARICATURE that would symbolize the millions of adults with low self-esteem, I would depict a bowed, weary traveler. Over his shoulder I would place the end of a mile-long chain to which is attached tons of scrap iron, old tires, and garbage of all types. Each piece of junk is inscribed with the details of some humiliation—a failure—an embarrassment—a rejection from the past. He could let go of the chain and free himself from the heavy load which immobilizes and exhausts him, but he is somehow convinced that it must be dragged throughout life. . . . Paralyzed by its weight, he plods onward, digging a furrow in the good earth as he goes. You can free yourself from the weight of the chain if you will but turn it loose.

—James Dobson, *Hide or Seek*

THE TAFT FAMILY was evidently good at pushing their children to cut their own swath and to find a specialty of which to be proud. When Martha Taft was in elementary school in Cincinnati, she was asked to introduce herself. She said, "My name is Martha Bowers Taft. My great-grandfather was president of the United States. My grandfather was United States senator. My daddy is ambassador to Ireland. And I am a Brownie."

—Alan Loy McGinnis, *Bringing Out the Best in People*

IT'S HIGH TIME we declare an all-out war on the destructive value systems. The destructive value systems of our society are: You must be either beautiful or you must be extremely intelligent. If you're pretty or handsome or if you are highly intelligent, you've got it made in our society. But God help you if you're dumb and ugly. . . . I think it's high time that we declare an all-out war on it. . . . I reject the notion that inferiority is inevitable. Although our task is more difficult for some children than for others, there are ways to teach a child of his genuine significance regardless of the shape of his nose or the size of his ears or the efficiency of his mind. Every child is entitled to hold up his head, not in haughtiness and pride, but in confidence and security.

—James Dobson, *Hide or Seek*

WHEN OUR CHILDREN WERE SMALL, three kids sat in the backseat of our car, and the youngest, Chuck Jr., sat between Cynthia and me. We had learned that was the safest place, so we could control his body. One day as we were driving along I said, "Hey, let's play what if? What if you could be anybody on earth, who would you like to be?"

One of the girls said, "I want to be the Bionic Woman." The others said who they would like to be, but Chuck never said a word. I pulled up to a stop sign. And as I stopped I looked at him and I said, "Chuckie?" "Yes sir?" "Who would you like to be?" "I'd like to be me." "Why do you want to be you?" "I like me." Boy, that is so good. You know, he was more settled than anybody in the family. He didn't want to be anybody else. He likes who he is. And you know what? He's the most refreshing of the whole bunch. He's just who he is.

SELF

(See *Ego*)

SENSITIVITY

A THOUGHTLESS PILOT got into an ill-equipped single-engine plane and took off. He didn't know much about how to handle the instruments—he just flew. The plane had no lights but he was flying up to a little country airstrip where he would land, he thought, before sunset. Unfortunately, he had strong winds against him and he didn't make it in time. The sun had already settled behind the western mountains and a haze was over the landing strip. Nearing the airstrip, he came down lower but he could not make out the boundaries of the runway. Panic seized him as he sensed he didn't have much fuel left. The runway was not equipped with lights, and he had no way of getting in touch with anyone. He began to circle. He realized one of those circling moments would be his last. He would crash to his death.

Down on the ground, a man was sitting on his porch and his sensitive ears were bothered by the drone of the engine as he kept hearing the plane going around and around and around. And he thought, "That guy's in trouble." Quickly he sped over to the runway and began to drive up and down the runway with his lights on bright, up and down, showing that young, inexperienced, foolish pilot how to find his way. The pilot turned. With a great breath of relief he began to land the plane. At the end of the runway the driver turned around and flashed his lights on the high beam and sat there, as if to say, "This is the end of the runway, and there are the lights." That pilot came right in and landed safely. A near tragedy was averted by sensitivity to need.

A LOVING CHRISTIAN COUPLE, sometime ago, read an account in a newspaper, which told of a woman, not able to drive too well, who pulled up to a wall to park. As she did, a person was walking in front of her. Intending to put her foot on the brake, the driver accidentally put her foot on the accelerator and drove the person into the wall. In a hurry, she thought she put the car in reverse, but she put it in low, and again drove into the person, causing multiple injuries. Terrible situation.

Everyone who read the article had tremendous feelings for the victim, and they should. But this couple that I mentioned also had feelings for the driver. They didn't know this woman from Eve, but they looked up her address and went to see her and encourage her. This, to me, was an illustration of some people who are able to see more than just the surface; they're able to feel for what is not making the headlines. The real need in Christian circles today is sensitivity to the needs of others.

SERVANTHOOD

NORMAN COUSINS, having spent considerable time with Albert Schweitzer at his little hospital at Lambarene in French Equatorial Africa, wrote of those days long after they had passed.

The biggest impression I had in leaving Lambarene was of the enormous reach of a single human being. Yet such a life was not without punishment of fatigue. Albert Schweitzer was supposed to be severe in his demands on the people who worked with him. Yet any demands he made on others were as nothing compared to the demands he made on himself. . . .

History is willing to overlook almost anything—errors, paradoxes, personal weaknesses or faults—if only a man will give enough of himself to others.

—Norman Cousins, *Albert Schweitzer's Mission*

I Wonder

You know, Lord, how I serve You
With great emotional fervor
In the limelight.
You know how eagerly I speak for You
At the women's club.
You know how I effervesce when I promote
A fellowship group.
You know my genuine enthusiasm
At a Bible study.

But how would I react, I wonder
If You pointed to a basin of water
And asked me to wash the calloused feet
Of a bent and wrinkled old woman
Day after day
Month after month
In a room where nobody saw
And nobody knew.

—Ruth Harms Calkin, *Tell Me Again, Lord, I Forget*

Unawares

They said, "The Master is coming
To honor the town today,
And none can tell at what house or home
The Master will choose to stay."
And I thought while my heart beat wildly,
What if He should come to mine,
How would I strive to entertain
And honor the Guest Divine!

And straight I turned to toiling
To make my home more neat;
I swept and polished and garnished,
And decked it with blossoms sweet.
I was troubled for fear the Master
Might come ere my work was done
And I hasted and worked the faster,
And watched the hurrying sun.

But right in the middle of my duties
A woman came to my door;
She had come to tell her sorrows
And my comfort and aid to implore,
And I said, "I cannot listen,
Nor help you any, today;
I have greater things to attend to."
And the pleader turned away.

At last the day was ended,
And my toil was over and done;
My house was swept and garnished—
And I watched in the dark—alone.
Watched—but no footfall sounded,
No one paused at my gate;
No one entered my cottage door;
I could only pray—and wait.

I waited till night had deepened,
And the Master had not come.
"He entered some other door," I said,
"And gladdened some other home!"
My labor had been for nothing,
And I bowed my head and I wept,
My heart was sore with longing—
Yet—in spite of it all—I slept.

Then the Master stood before me,
And his face was grave and fair;
"Three times today I came to your door,
And I craved your pity and care;
Three times you sent me onward,

Unhelped and uncomforted;
And the blessing you might have had was lost,
And your chance to serve has fled."
"O Lord, dear Lord, forgive me!
How could I know it was Thee?"
My very soul was shamed and bowed
In the depths of humility.
And He said, "The sin is pardoned,
But the blessing is lost to thee;
For, comforting not the least of Mine,
You have failed to comfort Me."

—Emma A. Lent, quoted in Hazel Felleman, *Poems That Live Forever*

LIKE MOST PHYSICIANS of great experience, Dr. Evan O'Neil Kane had become preoccupied with a particular facet of medicine. His strong feelings concerned the use of general anesthesia in major surgery. He believed that most major operations could and should be performed under local anesthetic, for, in his opinion, the hazards of a general anesthesia outweighed the risks of the surgery itself.

For example, Kane cited a surgical candidate who had a history of heart trouble. In some cases a surgeon may be reticent to operate, fearing the effects of the anesthesia on the heart of the patient. And some patients with specific anesthesia allergies never awakened. Kane's medical mission was to prove to his colleagues once for all the viability of local anesthesia. It would take a great deal of convincing.

Many patients were understandably squeamish at the thought of "being awake while it happens." Others feared the possibility of anesthesia wearing off in the middle of the surgery. To break down these psychological barriers, Kane would have to find a volunteer who was very brave, a candidate for major surgery who would be willing to accept local anesthesia.

In his distinguished thirty-seven years in the medical field, Kane had performed nearly four thousand appendectomies. So this next appendectomy would be routine in every way except one. Dr. Kane's patient would remain awake throughout the surgical procedure under local anesthesia.

The operation was scheduled for a Tuesday morning. The patient was prepped, wheeled into the operating room, and the local anesthesia was administered. Kane began as he had thousands of times before, carefully dissecting superficial tissues and clamping blood vessels on his way in. Locating the appendix, the sixty-year-old surgeon deftly pulled it up, excised it, and bent the stump under. Through it all, the patient experienced only minor discomfort. The operation concluded successfully.

The patient rested well that night. In fact, the following day his recovery was said to have progressed better than most postoperative patients. Two days later, the patient was released from the hospital to recuperate at home. Kane had proved his point. The risks of general anesthesia could be avoided in major operations. The potential of local anesthesia had been fully realized, thanks to the example of an innovative doctor and a very brave volunteer.

This took place in 1921. Dr. Kane and the patient who volunteered had a great deal in common. They were the same man. Dr. Kane, to prove the viability of local anesthesia, had operated on himself.

—Paul Aurandt, *More of Paul Harvey's The Rest of the Story*

BRUCE THIELEMANN, pastor of First Presbyterian Church in Pittsburgh, told of a conversation with a member of his flock who said, "You preachers talk a lot about 'do unto others,' but when you get right down to it, it comes down to basin theology."

Thielemann asked, "Basin theology? What's that?"

The layman said, "Remember what Pilate did when he had the chance to acquit Jesus? He called for a basin and washed his hands of the whole thing. But Jesus, the night before His death, called for a basin and proceeded to wash the feet of the disciples. It all comes down to basin theology: Which one will you use?"

—Craig Larson, *Illustrations for Preaching and Teaching from Leadership Journal*

I'll go where you want me to go, dear Lord,
    Real service is what I desire.
I'll sing You a solo any time, dear Lord,
    Just don't ask me to sing in the choir.

I'll do what you want me to do, dear Lord,
    I like to see things come to pass.
But don't ask me to teach boys and girls, O Lord.
    I'd rather just stay in my class.

I'll do what you want me to do, dear Lord,
    I yearn for Thy kingdom to thrive.
I'll give you my nickels and dimes, dear Lord.
    But please don't ask me to tithe.

> I'll go where you want me to go, dear Lord,
> I'll say what you want me to say;
> I'm busy just now with myself, dear Lord,
> I'll help you some other day.
>
> —Author unknown, quoted in Croft M. Pentz, *Speaker's Treasury of 400 Quotable Poems*

SIBLINGS

(Also see *Family*)

MY FAVORITE FOOD IS homemade chili con carne.

I remember the first time I ever tried to smoke. And as a matter of fact, it's directly related to chili, so I'll share it with you. Actually, I think it was the last time, also, I ever tried to smoke. It was my sister's idea. Let me set the record straight, to start with. We were both in a treehouse out back. And she got this novel idea that her little brother ought to try the taste of smoke. So she said, "Look, Babe, (she calls me Babe, affectionately, usually) go down to the cedar bark fence." We had a fence around our house. And she said, "Why don't you strip off several long strips of that cedar bark, because that really smokes good." So, like a dummy, I stripped off a fistful of that stuff, about 12 inches long, and rolled it up in three-holed notebook paper and stuck it in my mouth. And then she set fire to it. Well, it was kind of like gettin' hit in the face with a napalm bomb, if you can imagine such a thing.

That night my mother served for supper, what else? Homemade chili con carne, my favorite. She couldn't understand why I wasn't hungry that evening. I said as best I could with a tongue swollen almost as big as my fist, "Oh, I'm just not very hungry right now." Another page turned in the "live and learn" book of life.

ROBERT COLEMAN of Asbury College in Kentucky has written a book called *Written in Blood*. In it he includes the moving story of a little boy and his sister. The boy had had a dread disease and had been wonderfully delivered from death. He had been immunized against the disease. But the same immunization did not work on his sister and she was dying.

The physician, realizing she needed a transfusion of the boy's blood (a fair amount of it), called the boy aside and asked him if he would be willing to let that happen.

"Would you give your blood?" The little boy's lips trembled and he hesitated for a moment, looked out the window, and thought. Then he replied, "Yes, I'll do it." They took the brother and the sister into a room, and the blood began to be transferred. It was like a miracle. Life came to her body.

After a while the doctor came in and the little boy looked up and asked the doctor, "When do I die? When do I die?" The doctor understood why the boy's lips had trembled and why there was a moment of hesitation. He thought he would die, when all the doctor wanted was a little bit of his blood.

—Dennis DeHaan, *Windows on the Word*

SILENCE

A FRIEND OF MINE TOLD ME, "I seldom feel sorry for the things I did not say."

OVER THE LAST DECADES we have been inundated by a torrent of words. Wherever we go we're surrounded by words: words softly whispered, loudly proclaimed, angrily screamed; words spoken, recited, or sung; words on records, in books, on walls, in the sky; words in many sounds, many colors, many forms; words to be heard, read, seen, glanced at; words which flicker on and off, move slowly, dance, jump, wiggle. Words, words, words! They form the floor, walls, and ceiling of our existence.

Recently I was driving through Los Angeles, and suddenly I had the strange sensation of driving through a huge dictionary. Wherever I looked there were words trying to take my eyes from the road. They said, "Use me, take me, buy me, drink me, smell me, touch me, kiss me, sleep with me." In such a world who can maintain respect for words?

One of our main problems is that in this chatty society, silence has become a very fearful thing. For most people, silence creates itchiness and nervousness. Many experience silence not as full and rich, but as empty and hollow. For them silence is like a gaping abyss which can swallow them up. As soon as a minister says during a worship service, "Let us be silent for a few moments," people tend to become restless and preoccupied with only one thought: "When will this be over?"

—Henri Nouwen, *The Way of the Heart*

IN THE SILENCES I make in midst of the turmoil of life I have an appointment with God. From these silences I come forth with spirit refreshed, and with a renewed sense of power. I hear a Voice in the silences, and become increasingly aware that it is the Voice of God. O how comfortable is a little glimpse of God!

—David Brainerd, quoted in Charles R. Swindoll, *The Finishing Touch*

WHAT DOES SILENCE CREATE?
- It makes room for listening.
- It gives us freedom to observe.
- It allows time to think.
- It provides space in which to feel.
- It lets us broaden our awareness.
- It opens us to the entry of peace.
- It invites us to know our limitations and God's vastness.

SIMPLICITY

A MAN at the Los Angeles International Airport was worried about missing his plane. He had no wristwatch and could not locate a clock, so he hurried up to a total stranger and said, "Excuse me, could you give me the time, please?"

The stranger smiled and said, "Sure." He sat down the two large suitcases he was carrying and looked at the watch on his wrist. "It is exactly 5:09. The temperature outside is 73 degrees, and it is supposed to rain tonight. In London the sky is clear and the temperature is 38 degrees Celsius. The barometer reading is 29.14 and falling. And, let's see, in Singapore the sun is shining brightly. Oh, by the way, the moon should be full tonight here in Los Angeles, and . . ."

"Your watch tells you all that?" the man interrupted.

"Oh, yes, and much more. You see, I invented this watch, and I can assure you there's no other timepiece like it in the world."

"I want to buy that watch! I'll pay you two thousand dollars for it right now."

"No, it's not for sale," said the stranger as he reached down to pick up his suitcases.

"Wait! *Four* thousand. I'll pay you four thousand dollars, cash," offered the man, reaching for his wallet.

"No, I can't sell it. You see, I plan to give it to my son for his twenty-first birthday. I invented it for him to enjoy."

"Okay, listen—I'll give you *ten* thousand dollars. I've got the money right here."

The stranger paused. "Ten thousand? Well, OK. It's yours for ten thousand even."

The man was absolutely elated. He paid the stranger, took the watch, snapped it on his wrist with glee, and said "Thanks" as he turned to leave.

"Wait," said the stranger. With a big smile he handed the two heavy suitcases to the man and added, "Don't forget the batteries."

—Charles R. Swindoll, *Simple Faith*

THE CLASS AT SEMINARY was Old Testament Introduction. It was there I first met Merrill Unger. Now I thought it would be an introduction, a survey—learn a few verses in Genesis, see how it connects with Exodus, Leviticus. Getting into the prophets and learning how they thought and some of the things they taught. I thought, "This is the moment. Man, this will be great."

He was a surprise. I remember this little white-headed fellow standing there, about 110 pounds who blinked a lot. Had a little briefcase that looked like he had it on Noah's ark.

The first session he touched on numerous topics—the uniqueness of the Old Testament, theories of inspiration, the canonical credentials, the Apocrypha, the pseudoepigraphical texts, theories related to the critical concepts from the JEDP, the formation of the Masoretic text, the Black Obelisk of Shalmaneser III, myths and legends from Nabopalassar, and more. As he raced into rapid instruction he was writing all over the blackboard without erasing—just one thought on top of another. We all felt speechless. "Wait!" Some brave young theologian in the back (feeling as overwhelmed as I did) waved his hand, and said, "Dr. Unger, I thought this was Old Testament Introduction." Dr. Unger said, "Yes, that's why I'm keeping it simple."

A SIMPLE NOTE emerged from the brutal days of the Civil War. The communication came from a battle-weary President Lincoln to his general, Ulysses S. Grant. Only three lines, yet it was the written missile that ended the war. The date and the time appeared at the top:

> April 7, 1865
> 11 o'clock A.M.
>
> General Sheridan says, "If the thing is pressed, I think that Lee will surrender."
>
> Let the thing be pressed.
>
> A. Lincoln

Grant got the message and acted on it. He pressed it. Two days later at Appomattox, Robert E. Lee surrendered. The thing was pressed, and the bloodiest war in American history ended. Simplicity is indeed powerful.

—Carl Sandburg, *Abraham Lincoln, the War Years*

CHARLES JEHLINGER, former director of the American Academy of Dramatic Arts, used to instruct all apprentice actors with five words of advice: "Mean more than you say."

—Charles R. Swindoll, *Growing Strong in the Seasons of Life*

HIS DARK EYES darted from face to face. His lips were drawn tight across his teeth. His words sounded as if they were propelled from a jet engine. There was no monkey business with this coach. He was tough, determined as a steer in a blizzard. His job was a simple one—to build a championship team out of a rag-tag bunch of discouraged rookies and tired "has beens." But Vince Lombardi didn't know the word can't. And he refused to complicate a game that, when boiled down to the basics, consisted of blocking, tackling, running, passing, catching—all to be done with abandon. As he often said, "You do all those things right, you win. It's a matter of the basics. You gotta concentrate on the basics."

I will never forget this man's words to his Green Bay Packers on one occasion when he emphasized the basics. There they sat in a heap, tons of massive humanity hanging on the words of one man. Holding the pigskin high in the air, he shouted, "Okay, gentlemen, today we go back to the basics. You guys, look at this. This is a football!"

BENJAMIN HOFF, applying the principles and teaching of Lao–tzu to Winnie the Pooh, wrote a book called *Tao of Pooh.* In it he wrote, "The masters of life know the way. They listen to the voice within them, the voice of wisdom and simplicity, the voice that reasons beyond cleverness and knows beyond knowledge."

—Tom Haggai, *How the Best Is Won*

I HAVE A LITTLE SIGN that hangs in my study. It reads this way, "Idiosyncratically eccentric phraseology is the promulgator of terrible obfuscation." Doesn't that thrill you to hear that? And on the back is a translation, "Big words cause confusion."

One teacher I sat under put it in these words: "The one who says it most simply knows it best. Anybody can make the simple difficult, but it takes a gifted teacher to make the difficult understandable."

SIN

(Also see *Adultery, Immorality*)

THE LATE PRESIDENT Calvin Coolidge returned home from attending church early one Sunday afternoon. His wife had been unable to attend, but she was interested in what the minister spoke on in the service. Coolidge responded, "Sin." She pressed him for a few words of explanation. And being a man of few words with his wife, he responded, "Well, I think he was against it."

—Paul Lee Tan, *Encyclopedia of 7,700 Illustrations*

A CERTAIN MAN wanted to sell his house in Haiti for $2,000. Another man wanted to buy it, but because he was poor, he couldn't afford the full price. After much bargaining, the owner agreed to sell the house for half the original price with just one stipulation: he would retain ownership of one small nail protruding from just over the door.

After several years, the original owner wanted the house back, but the new owner was unwilling to sell. So the first owner went out, found the carcass of a dead dog, and hung it from the single nail he still owned. Soon the house became unlivable, and the family was forced to sell the house to the owner of the nail.

The moral of the parable is, "If we leave the devil with even one small peg in our life, he will return to hang his rotting garbage on it, making it unfit for Christ's habitation."

—*Leadership*, Spring 1983

SIN DOES NOT SERVE WELL as a gardener of the soul. It landscapes the contour of the soul until all that is beautiful has been made ugly; until all that is high is made low; until all that is promising is wasted. Then life is like the desert—parched and barren. It is drained of purpose. It is bleached of happiness. Sin, then, is not wise, but wasteful. It is not a gate, but only a grave.

—C. Neil Strait, quoted in Lloyd Cory *Quote Unquote*

THE GREATER THE MAN, the dearer price he pays for a short season of sinful pleasure.

—F. B. Meyer, *David*

BELIEVERS THROUGHOUT CHURCH HISTORY—the early church fathers, the Reformers, the Puritans—have been inspired by Scripture to reduce spirituality to two lists known as "the seven deadly sins and the seven virtues" of saintliness. The former includes pride, envy, anger, sloth, avarice, gluttony, and lust. The latter includes wisdom, justice, courage, temperance, faith, love, and hope.

Even though it finds its origin in one whose life was not centered on Christ our Lord, Mahatma Gandhi's own list of "seven deadly sins" in the form of contrasts deserves our attention: Wealth without work, pleasure without conscience, knowledge without character, commerce without morality, science without humanity, worship without sacrifice, politics without principle.

—Max DePree, *Leadership Is an Art*

THE GRASS ON THE OTHER SIDE is often not greener and often not even edible.

—James Dobson

THE FIRST and worst of all fraud is to cheat oneself. All sin is easy after that.

—Philip Bailey, nineteenth-century poet

LET'S SAY we were to get twenty of the best broad jump or long jump athletes in the world and take them to Huntington Beach pier and line them up. And let's say they were instructed, "We want you to jump as far as you can out into the water." Some could jump twenty-five feet. Some would come near the record and jump twenty-seven. Perhaps one could set a new record and jump twenty-nine or thirty feet. But nobody could jump to Catalina Island. It is humanly impossible. Every person would miss the mark because Catalina Island is twenty-six miles away. In Romans 3:23 there is the universal statement that God gives to all men when He says, "All have sinned and fall short of the glory of God."

All have missed the mark. All may have tried, but not one of them even came close to a spiritual Catalina, if you please. They all jump, they all tried all sorts of things, but by birth, by choice, by action, by nature, man constantly misses the mark, no matter how good his intentions may be.

—J. Vernon McGee, quoted in Paul Lee Tan, *Encyclopedia of 7,700 Illustrations*

DURING MY HITCH IN THE MARINES back in 1958, I was stationed on Okinawa where there was a leprosarium. At that time I was playing in the third division band in the Marine Corps and we were to do a performance on that north part of the island of Okinawa.

I had read about leprosy, but I had never seen a leper and I wasn't really prepared for what I saw. We went over a bridge or two and got into the interior of this compound. I saw stumps instead of hands. I saw clumps instead of fingers. I saw half faces. I saw one ear instead of two. I saw the dregs of humanity unable even to applaud our performances. I saw in the faces of men, women, and even some teenagers an anguish crying out. We could play music for them, but we could not cleanse them of their disease.

In Scripture leprosy is a picture of sin. And we see that it is cleansed rather than healed. Only Jesus' blood has the power to cleanse us of our condition of sinful corruption. Now I understand when Scripture says, "He was moved with compassion."

Because of sin, man has taken
>   the deity out of religion,
>   the supernatural out of Christianity,
>   the authority from the Bible,
>   God out of education,
>   morality and virtue out of literature,
>   beauty and truth out of art,
>   ethics out of business,
>   fidelity out of marriage.

SLAVERY

ON SEEING A LIVING SLAVE offered in New Orleans on a slave block: "There was a rising hatred inside of me against slavery, and I swore if someday I could do something about it, I would do something about it."

—Abraham Lincoln

AT ABRAHAM LINCOLN'S SECOND INAUGURAL, shortly before his assassination in 1865, he spoke of how both parties deprecated war, and yet war came. He continued, "Neither party expected the war, the magnitude, or the duration, which it has already attained. Each looked for an easier triumph. Both read the same Bible, and pray to the same God; and each invokes His aid against the other."

And with that, Lincoln let his own feelings show through as he spoke of how strange it was, "that any men should dare to ask a just God's assistance in wringing their bread from the sweat of other men's faces."

Ultimately, the black slaves were set free. Theoretically, it became legal as early as the first day of the year, 1863, in what has come to be known as the Emancipation Proclamation.

"The word spread," in the words of one historian, "from Capitol Hill out across the city, down into the valleys and fields of Virginia and the Carolinas, and even into the plantations of Georgia and Mississippi and Alabama. 'Slavery Legally Abolished!' read the headlines, and yet something amazing took place. The greater majority of the slaves in the South went right on living as though they were not emancipated. That continued throughout the Reconstruction Period."

"The Negro remained locked in a caste system of 'race etiquette' as rigid as any had known in formal bondage, and that every slave could repeat, with equal validity, what an Alabama slave had mumbled when asked what he thought of the Great Emancipator whose proclamation had gone into effect. 'I don't know nothin' 'bout Abraham Lincoln cep they say he sot us free. And I don't know nothin' 'bout that neither.'"

How tragic. A war was being fought. A document had been signed. Slaves were legally set free. The word is emancipated. And yet most continued to live out their years, and many of their children some of their years, in fear, saying, "I don't know nothin' 'bout that neither." In a context of freedom, slaves chose to remain slaves, though they were legally freed. Even though emancipated, they kept serving the same master throughout their lives.

—Shelby Foote, *The Civil War*

BACK IN OUR EARLIEST DAYS as a nation, a determined thirty-nine-year-old, radical-thinking attorney addressed the Virginia Convention. It was on March 23, 1775, a time of great patriotic passion, and his patriotism refused to be silenced any longer. Sounding more like a prophet of God than a patriot for his country, he announced:

"If we wish to be free we must fight! . . . I repeat it, sir, we must fight! An appeal to arms, and to the God of hosts, is all that is left in us. It is vain, sir, to extenuate the matter. The gentlemen may cry 'Peace, peace!'

but there is no peace. The war has actually begun! . . . Our brethren are already in the field. Why stand we here idle? . . . Is life so dear or peace so sweet as to be purchased at the price of chains and slavery? Forbid it, Almighty God. I know not what course others may take, but as for me, give me liberty or give me death!"

What a soul-stirring speech! We applaud the courageous passion of Patrick Henry to this day. Because of it he remains in our minds one of our national heroes.

Not quite ninety years later we were fighting one another in our country's worst bloodbath. And again I remind you, it was for the cause of liberty. The issue was slavery versus freedom. The black people of our nation were not free. It was the conviction of the United States government that they should be free, and if necessary we would take up arms against those who opposed their liberation from slavery.

Charles Sumner did a masterful job of summing up the issue of the Civil War in a speech made on November 5, 1864: "Where Slavery is, there Liberty cannot be; and where Liberty is, there Slavery cannot be."

—John Bartlett, *Bartlett's Familiar Quotations*

_____

IN 1824, Peru won its freedom from Spain. Soon after, Simón Bolívar, the general who had led the liberating forces, called a convention for the purpose of drafting a constitution for the new country.

After the convention, a delegation approached Bolivar and asked him to become their first president. Bolivar declined, saying that he felt someone else deserved the honor more than he did.

But the people still wanted to do something special for Bolivar to show their appreciation for all he had done for them, so they offered him a gift of a million pesos, a very large fortune in those days.

Bolivar accepted the gift and then asked, "How many slaves are there in Peru?" He was told there were about three thousand. "And how much does a slave sell for?" he wanted to know. "About 350 pesos for an able-bodied man," was the answer.

"Then," said Bolivar, "I will add whatever is necessary to this million pesos you have given me and I will buy all the slaves in Peru and set them free. It makes no sense to free a nation, unless all its citizens enjoy freedom as well."

I READ RECENTLY that the life cycle of a silkworm from egg to worm to moth includes the state at which the worm spins about itself a remarkable cocoon. This little sack is composed of 400 to 800 yards of silk fiber which seals it from the inside as it waits for metamorphosis. At the completion of the cycle, the adult moth will break the cocoon, tearing apart the fine silk cords that bind it, and fly free. But the silkworm farmer does not allow most to become adults. At a key point in the cycle, he steams the cocoons to keep the moths inside from maturing. If he didn't do this, they would go free, leaving a trail of broken threads which are useless to the exploiters. If they were allowed to mature and escape, by the way, the reproductive moth would lay up to 350 eggs. But they are not allowed to do so.

Could it be that many immature, caged Christians are kept from maturing because their ecclesiastical "captors" cannot fulfill selfish purposes in free people? Who wants their secure—though immature—traditions left behind in shambles? And we can't forget the hassle, either. Teaching people how to fly takes a lot more time and trouble than just allowing them to crawl.

A room full of moths is certainly a bigger challenge than a box full of worms.

—Charles R. Swindoll, *Growing Strong in the Seasons of Life*

SOLITUDE

IN SOLITUDE I get rid of my scaffolding: no friends to talk with, no telephone calls to make, no meetings to attend, no music to entertain, no books to distract, just me—naked, vulnerable, weak, sinful, deprived, broken—nothing. It is this nothingness that I have to face in my solitude, a nothingness so dreadful that everything in me wants to run to my friends, my work, and my distractions so that I can forget my nothingness and make myself believe that I am worth something. But that is not all. As soon as I decide to stay in my solitude, confusing ideas, disturbing images, wild fantasies, and weird associations jump about in my mind like monkeys in a banana tree. Anger and greed begin to show their ugly faces. . . .

The task is to persevere in my solitude, to stay in my cell until all my seductive visitors get tired of pounding on my door and leave me alone.

—Henri Nouwen, *The Way of the Heart*

AN INNER RESTLESSNESS grows within us when we refuse to get alone and examine our own hearts, including our motives. As our lives begin to pick up the debris that accompanies a lot of activities and involvements, we can train ourselves to go right on, to stay active, to be busy in the Lord's work. Unless we discipline ourselves to pull back, to get alone for the hard work of self-examination in times of solitude, serenity will remain only a distant dream.

—Charles R. Swindoll, *Intimacy with the Almighty*

Daffodils

I wandered lonely as a cloud
    That floats on high o'er vales and hills,
When all at once I saw a crowd—
    A host of golden daffodils
Beside the lake, beneath the trees,
Fluttering and dancing in the breeze.

Continuous as the stars that shine
    And twinkle on the Milky Way,
They stretched in never-ending line
    Along the margin of a bay:
Ten thousand saw I, at a glance,
Tossing their heads in sprightly dance.

The waves beside them danced, but they
    Outdid the sparkling waves in glee;
A poet could not but be gay
    In such a jocund company;
I gazed—and gazed—but little thought
What wealth the show to me had brought.

For oft, when on my couch I lie,
    In vacant or in pensive mood,
They flash upon that inward eye
    Which is the bliss of solitude;
And then my heart with pleasure fills,
And dances with the daffodils.

—William Wordsworth

SOLITUDE IS THE CULTIVATION OF SERENITY, a deliberate moving toward peacefulness and contentment within, which breeds a sense of security without.

SPEECH

(Also see *Advice, Communication, Tongue*)

AN ATTORNEY stood before a courtroom and made a great statement about denial. He had just heard this incredible presentation by the defense attorney and it was his turn to stand and do his final presentation. His rebuttal to the preposterous defense presented began like this: "Well, folks, denial is more than a river that runs through Egypt."

———————————————

MARK TWAIN was to deliver a lectureship in a small town in mid-America. Before the evening's speech he decided to have his mustache trimmed and get a shave and a haircut at a local barber shop. He dropped in rather unassumingly and waited his turn. The barber, a bit preoccupied with his work and the busy day, didn't notice him as the famous Mark Twain. As he began to trim Twain's hair, he said to his new customer, "You're new here. You've come to visit our city at a good time. Mark Twain is speaking tonight." The humorist responded, "Well, I guess so. That's what I hear." The barber asked, "Have you bought your ticket yet?" And he said, "Well, nope. Not yet." The barber said, "Well, it's all sold out. So you'll have to stand to hear him speak." "Just my luck," said Mark Twain. "I always have to stand when that fella lectures!"

—*The Little, Brown Book of Anecdotes*

———————————————

A MAN WAS LIVING in Atlanta, Georgia . . . or as they say down there "Atlaantnaa." He noticed not far from Atlanta was another town named Lafayette. But in Atlanta they pronounced it La-fay-ette. His daughters were beginning to pronounce it that way too.

Near where he was raised in Indiana there was also a town named Lafayette. So when he took his family on a vacation trip back to his hometown, he thought, "This would be a good chance for my kids to learn how to pronounce the name of that town correctly." As soon as they got into the city limits, they were all starving, and so they stopped off at a Burger King to eat a hamburger. "Now's my chance," he thought, "I'll ask someone who's a native of this town how to say the word Lafayette. So when the waitress served their hamburgers, he said to her, "Wait a minute. Before you leave, I want you to tell my daughters where we are. And I want you to say it very, very slowly. Pronounce it exactly as it's supposed to be pronounced." She looked rather puzzled and said, "Really?" He said, "Yeah." She said, "Okay. Bur-ger-King."

THERE USED TO BE A RESTAURANT in Dana Point, California that had a sign out front showing a woman with her head cut off. It was called *The Quiet Woman.*

MY TRAVELS have taken me to any number of large cities in the USA. And it's always interesting to see that life is not really so different from place to place. They may talk differently, but after a little time of language training, you can get along, even in Texas.

A fellow called me from Texas. And he said, "You probably can't tell it, but I'm from Texas." I said, "I can tell. I can tell. Believe me!"

We talked for a while, and I found out he went to school in Texas. And I said, "Where'd you go to school?" He said, "H'ard Pain." I said, "Howard Pain?" He said, "No, H'ard Pain." I said, "Oh, Howard Pain. What was your major?" He said, "Speech!"

A YOUNG SEVENTH-GRADER had the assignment of bringing Patrick Henry's great historic address at a PTA meeting. He stood up, trembling before all the parents, and everything went well until he got to his great line, where he said, "Give me puberty or give me death!"

IN THE ENGLISH LANGUAGE, the word *for* has a double meaning. *For* can mean "in order to" or it can mean "because of." If I say to my son, "Son, let's go to the barber shop for a haircut," it means "Let's go, not because we've already gotten the haircut, but in order to get one" But if you read of a man who was electrocuted for murder, he wasn't electrocuted "in order to" murder; he was electrocuted "because of" murder. Two different meanings.

It reminds me of a story I read as a teenager of a cowpoke in West Texas who rode into town and saw a sign on the sheriff's wall. It said, "Man Wanted for Robbery." And he went in the sheriff's office and said, "I've got two six-guns, I'll take the job." A man was wanted not in order to rob, but because there had been a robbery.

—W. A. Criswell, *Scott's Sermon Materials,* May 30, 1967

IT'S MUCH BETTER TO KEEP SILENT and let everybody think you're a fool, than to open your mouth and remove all doubt.

—Lewis Sperry Chafer, quoted in Ray Stedman, *Solomon's Secret*

I lost a very little word
    only the other day.
It was a very nasty word
    I really had not meant to say;
But then, it was not really lost
    as from my lips it flew,
My little brother picked it up
    and now he says it too.

—Guy King, *A Belief That Behaves*

ONE OF THE BIBLE TEACHERS who used to lecture at Dallas Seminary when I was a student there was as tough as nails, yet pure in heart. On one occasion while he was in the city to deliver a series of lectures, he went to a local barber shop to get a haircut. (A friend of mine happened to work there and overheard this conversation.) The barber, who didn't have the faintest idea who the man was, began talking about various issues of the day, giving his opinion, as barbers usually do. He peppered every phrase with an oath or a four-letter word. The teacher bit his lip as long as he could. Finally, he grabbed the barber's arm, pulled him around to the side of the chair, and looked the man right in the eye. Quietly but firmly he pulled on his own earlobe and said to the barber, "Does that look like a sewer?" The rest of the haircut was done in absolute silence.

—Charles R. Swindoll, *Hope Again*

THERE IS A NEW WORD for gobbledygook nowadays. That was one of my long time favorite words for verbiage and excess talk. The new word is called "bafflegab." Ever heard of that? Here's some bafflegab.

Bell Data ran an ad in the *Financial Times* of Canada that said: "This is a full-blown, state-of-the-art, fully integrated, user-friendly, multifunctional, omni-lingual, multi-tasking word and data processing system with advanced graphic generation capabilities." They were describing a pencil. I don't know why they didn't say, "We sell pencils."

A New York plumber didn't know whether he could use hydrochloric acid to unclog drains he was working on. He wanted to be assured that it was safe and so he wrote the National Bureau of Standards in Washington, D.C. And this was the answer they gave: "The efficacy of hydrochloric acid is indisputable, but the corrosive residue is incompatible with metallic substances." The plumber read the note and wrote them back and thanked them for the OK to use the acid. So the bureau panicked and they tried again with this note. "We cannot assume responsibility for the production of toxic and noxious residue which hydrochloric acid can produce; we suggest you use an alternate procedure." Well, he was flattered that they would write the second time to tell him it was OK. He was still a little confused about it. Finally, one of the bureau's top communicators grabbed the communication and wrote these lines, "Don't use the acid. It'll eat through pipes." Now that is good communication. That's simple, that's right to the point. No bafflegab, gobbledygook.

MY WIFE AND I enjoyed eating at a restaurant called La Tunisia. It was a lovely setting, full of atmosphere. It looked like a great, vast tent in the Tunisian area, Moroccan style. Delectable shish kebabs, and other delicious foods were served there. One evening after we had been seated, I saw the waitress coming. She had dark hair, olive-colored skin, and dark eyes, and I thought, "Wow! I bet she's from North Africa." She walked up and said, "Hi! Ya'll ordered ya'll's dranks yet?" Maybe southern Moroccan, but not what we expected. She told us later she was from Tyler, Texas. She had nothing to do with a North African area. You could tell by her speech.

MY SISTER went in to buy a lovely handkerchief at a very sophisticated store. The girl behind the counter who was selling these imported handkerchiefs looked like she was Miss Sophistication. Lucille looked in the counter and said, "That one's beautiful. It's lovely. I'd like to see it." And the girl reached in, pulled it out, and she said, "Yeah, and it's hand-did."

SPIRITUAL GIFTS

A YOUNG SCHOOLBOY was trying out for a part in the school play. His mother knew that he had set his heart on it, though she was afraid he would not be chosen. On the day the parts were awarded, she drove to school to pick him up. The young lad rushed up to her, eyes shining with pride and excitement. Then he said some words to her that should remain a lesson to us all: "I have been chosen to clap and cheer!" In the same way, God has lovingly chosen each of us for different and special tasks.

—Michael Green, *Illustrations for Biblical Preaching*

MY LIFE HAS BEEN CROSSED by men who have the gift of giving. Maybe yours has also. When I was at Dallas Seminary, God used a man in my life and in the lives of ten other fellows at the school at that time. Howard Kane chose to underwrite our tuition. Absolutely unsolicited. Each time tuition came due, there was a check in the mail.

I remember one time he came to Dallas and got all eleven of us together and said, "I want us to take a drive downtown." After a sandwich, he took us several blocks away to a men's store. Inside he suited us up in new suits, new sport coats, one fellow after another. He sat there and just beamed! He was happier than we were! He wasn't wealthy, but there was something inside of him (it's called a spiritual gift) that was not satisfied until there was an outlet for that gift.

SPORTS

AT A FOOTBALL GAME there are 70,000 people desperately in need of exercise watching twenty-two people desperately in need of rest.

—Howard G. Hendricks, *Say It with Love*

WE'RE AWFULLY HARD ON UMPIRES, but I'm told that's our right, since we paid to get into a ballgame. I've never quite figured out that logic. But I, for one, would like to see a little more courtesy shown to umpires, especially at Little League games, where nobody pays to get in. This is supposed to be a pleasant setting where boys have the opportunity to learn more about the game of life than the game of baseball. That was driven home to me recently when I read the words of Donald Jensen, who was struck in the head by a thrown bat while umpiring a Little League game in Terre Haute, Indiana. He continued to work the game, but later that evening was placed in the hospital by a physician. While being kept overnight for observation, Jensen wrote an eloquent letter to folks whose shenanigans make you cringe or bow your head in shame. At one point he said:

> The purpose of Little League is to teach baseball skills to young men. Obviously, a team which does not play well in a given game, yet is given the opportunity to blame that loss on an umpire for one call or two, is being given the chance to take all responsibility for the loss from their shoulders. A parent or adult leader who permits the younger player to blame his failures on an umpire . . . is doing the worst kind of injustice to that youngster. . . . This irresponsibility is bound to carry over to future years.

What Donald Jensen wrote that night in Indiana is absolutely right. Next time you're tempted to insult or mistreat an umpire, remember him—the late Donald Jensen. The following morning he died of a brain concussion.

—Charles R. Swindoll, *The Finishing Touch*

STEWARDSHIP

(Also see *Charity, Giving, Money, Wealth*)

Oh, God—
The bumper sticker says smile if you love Jesus;
So I smiled all day long . . .
And the people thought I worked for Jimmy Carter.
The bumper sticker said honk if you love Jesus;
So I honked . . . and a policeman arrested me
For disturbing the peace in a hospital zone.
The bumper sticker said wave if you love Jesus;
So I waved with both hands . . . but lost control of the car
And crashed into the back of a Baptist bus.
Oh, God—
If I cannot smile . . . or honk . . . or wave . . .
How will Jesus know I love Him?
If you love Jesus tithe . . . honking is too easy.

—Bruce Larson, *What God Wants to Know*

WHEN THE POSSESSOR OF HEAVEN and earth brought you into being and placed you in this world, He placed you here not as owner but as a steward.

—John Wesley

STEWARDSHIP IS the "use of God-given resources for the accomplishment of God-given goals."

—Ron Blue, *Master Your Money*

A MAN CALLED AT THE CHURCH and asked if he could speak to the Head Hog at the Trough. The secretary said, "Who?"

The man replied, "I want to speak to the Head Hog at the Trough!"

Sure now that she had heard correctly, the secretary said, "Sir, if you mean our pastor, you will have to treat him with more respect—and ask for 'The Reverend' or 'The Pastor.' But certainly you cannot refer to him as the Head Hog at the Trough!"

At this, the man came back, "Oh, I see. Well, I have ten thousand dollars I was thinking of donating to the Building Fund."

Secretary: "Hold the line—I think the Big Pig just walked in the door."

—James Hewett, *Illustrations Unlimited*

STRESS

ONE STRESSED-OUT SECRETARY told her boss: "When this rush is over, I'm going to have a nervous breakdown. I earned it, I deserve it, and nobody's going to take it from me."

—Billy Graham, *The Secret of Happiness*

IT DOESN'T MATTER how great the pressure is. What really matters is where the pressure lies, whether it comes between me and God or whether it presses me nearer His heart.

—Howard Taylor, *Hudson Taylor's Spiritual Secret*

Slow me down, Lord.
  Ease the pounding of my heart by the quieting of my mind.
  Steady my hurried pace with a vision of the eternal reach of time.
  Give me, amid the confusion of the day, the calmness of the everlasting
      hills.
  Break the tension of my nerves and muscles with the soothing music of
      the singing streams that live in my memory.
  Teach me the art of taking minute vacations—of slowing down to look at
      a flower, to chat with a friend, to pat a dog, to smile at a child, to read
      a few lines from a good book.
Slow me down, Lord, and inspire me to send my roots deep into the soil of
      life's enduring values, that I may grow toward my greater destiny.
Remind me each day that the race is not always to the swift; that there is more
      to life than increasing its speed.
Let me look upward to the towering oak and know that it grew great and
      strong because it grew slowly and well.

—Orin Crain, quoted in Charles R. Swindoll, *Three Steps Forward, Two Steps Back*

Pressed out of measure and pressed to all length;
Pressed so intently it seems beyond strength.
Pressed in body and pressed in soul;
Pressed in the mind till the dark surges roll;
Pressure by foes, pressure by friends;
Pressure on pressure, till life nearly ends.
Pressed into loving the staff and the rod;
Pressed into knowing no helper but God.

—Annie Johnson Flint, quoted in John R. Rice, *Poems That Preach*

THE LABORING MAN hasn't leisure for true integrity daily. No time for anything but to be a machine.

—Henry David Thoreau

Yes, yes we say
    without a thought for the day.
Running and fretting to make ends meet,
    rushing from Suzie to Joe and to Pete.
Our lives, in upheaval, have turned to a tizzy,
    never completing, because we're too busy.
All we must do for a tranquil soul,
    is employ a word, just one, called NO.

—Grant Howard, *Balancing Life's Demands*

Time of the Mad Atom

This is the age
Of the half-read page.
And the quick hash
And the mad dash.
The bright night
With the nerves tight.
The plane hop
With the brief stop.
The lamp tan
In a short span.
The Big Shot
In a good spot.

> And the brain strain
> And the heart pain.
> And the catnaps
> Till the spring snaps—
> And the fun's done.

—Virginia Brasier, quoted in Sara Brewton, *Of Quarks, Quasars, and Other Quirks*

I ARRIVED AT MY OFFICE unusually early one morning. Things were quiet, the sky was heavy and overcast, a normal California fall morning. My mind was on my schedule as I fumbled with the keys. In standard Swindoll fashion I pushed the door wide open in a hurry—only to be stopped in my tracks. A chill went up my back as I peered into the spooky study. The light switch is across the room, so I stood there at the door starting at the most startling reminder of reality imaginable! In the middle of the floor, sitting on rollers, was a *casket*—with a wilted spray of flowers on top along with a picture of ME! Now, my friend, if you want to know how to awaken someone from early morning slumber, *this routine will surely do it!* I suppose I stood there five minutes without moving a muscle as I blinked and gathered my senses. I checked my watch and was pleased to see the second hand still moving. All my reflexes responded correctly and my breath still brought a patch of fog to the mirror. "Praise God," I thought, "I'm still here." It was a grim reminder of the stress of overwork and the reality of death. We need to face it.

The Stress Diet

Breakfast
1/2 grapefruit
1 piece whole-wheat toast
8 oz. skim milk

Lunch
4 oz. lean broiled chicken breast
1 cup steamed zucchini
1 Oreo cookie
Herb tea

Mid-afternoon snack
Rest of the package of Oreo cookies

1 qt. rocky road ice cream
1 jar hot fudge

Dinner
2 loaves garlic bread
large mushroom and pepperoni pizza
large pitcher root beer
3 Milky Ways
Entire frozen cheesecake, eaten directly from the freezer

—Pamela Pettler, *The Joy of Stress*

A MAN WENT TO HIS PHYSICIAN, complaining of constant headaches. The physician asked him if he smoked.

"Yes, I do," said the fellow.

"Well, stop smoking," suggested the physician.

So he stopped, but the headaches persisted. He went back.

"Do you drink?"

"Yeah, I drink considerably."

So he stopped. The headaches persisted.

"Are you engaged in physical labor that would in some way put pressure on your back?"

"Yes, I am."

"Quit your job."

He quit his job and took another position, but his headaches persisted. Every day the pain pulsed through his head.

Finally, they discovered he was wearing a size 15 collar on a size 16 neck. No wonder he had a headache!

Superficial problems call for superficial solutions. But real life isn't like that; its headaches and stresses go deeper, right down to the bone. They touch the nerve areas of our security. But God says He is a present help in trouble. Go ahead, read Psalm 46. See God's strength through times of stress.

—Stuart Briscoe, *What Works When Life Doesn't*

SUBMISSION

(Also see *Surrender*)

WHEN GRACE CHANGES THE HEART, submission out of fear changes to submission out of love, and true humility is born.

—William Hendriksen, *Exposition of Philippians*

Christ Alone

Oh, the bitter shame and sorrow
    That a time could ever be
When I let the Saviour's pity
    Plead in vain; and proudly answered,
"All of self, and none of Thee!"

Yet He found me; I beheld Him
    Bleeding on the accursed tree;
Heard Him pray "Forgive them, Father!"
    And my wistful heart said faintly,
"Some of self, and some of Thee."

Day by day, His tender mercy,
    Healing, helping, full and free;
Brought me lower, while I whispered,
    "None of self and all of Thee."

—Theodore Monod, quoted in Croft M. Pentz, *Speaker's Treasury of 400 Quotable Poems*

A FELLOW was on top of the roof of his second-story home putting up a television antenna. It was large and tall, and he was trying to attach the guy wires from the antenna to a section of the roof. The wind was blowing making it even more difficult. Suddenly he began to slip, and he slid down that roof until he caught himself on the little metal rain gutter that went around the eaves of the second floor. In panic he held on and screamed up to heaven, "Isn't there anybody up there who can help me?"

And a voice from heaven came, "I can help you."

"Well, what shall I do?"

"Let go and I'll catch you."

"Is there anybody else up there who can help me?"

THE CAPTAIN OF THE SHIP looked into the dark night and saw faint lights in the distance. Immediately he told his signalman to send a message: "Alter your course 10 degrees south."

Promptly a return message was received: "Alter your course 10 degrees north."

The captain was angered; his command had been ignored. So he sent a second message: "Alter your course 10 degrees south—I am the captain!"

Soon another message was received: "Alter your course 10 degrees north—I am seaman third class Jones."

Immediately the captain sent a third message, knowing the fear it would evoke: "Alter your course 10 degrees south—I am a battleship!"

Then the reply came: "Alter your course 10 degrees north—I am a light-house."

—*Leadership* magazine, Spring 1983

OUR FAMILY has had several dogs during our years together. Some have been small and nervous, others large and placid. A few have gotten into fights with other dogs. I've noticed a curious "signal": When the dog being overpowered finally realizes it cannot win the fight, it finally submits and surrenders by lying down at the other dog's feet, baring its vulnerable throat and belly to the attacking dog above it. In this position it could get seriously hurt in an instant, but interestingly, that's how the dog is spared.

RECENTLY I HEARD Jack Hayford tell about a married couple who had attended a seminar taught by one of those male demagogues determined to show that Scripture teaches that the man is IN CHARGE at home. It was the kind of terrible teaching on submission that turns women into lowly doormats. Well, the husband just loved it! He had never heard anything like that in his life, and he drank it all in. His wife, however, sat there fuming as she listened to hour after hour of this stuff.

When they left the meeting that night, the husband felt drunk with fresh power as he climbed into the car. While driving home, he said rather pompously, "Well, what did you think about that?" His wife didn't utter a word, so he continued, "I think it was great!"

When they arrived home, she got out and followed him silently into the house. Once inside, he slammed the door and said, "Wait right there—just stand right there." She stood, tight-lipped, and stared at him. "I've been thinking about what the fellow said tonight, and I want you to know that from now on that's the way it's gonna be around here. You got it? That's the way things are gonna run in this house!"

And having said that, he didn't see her for two weeks. After two weeks, *he could start to see her just a little bit out of one eye.*

SUBSTITUTION

A PARTICULAR CHURCH recently received personal greetings from the Kejave Medical Center staff in Kenya and read of the following amazing story.

Eight-year-old Monica broke her leg as she fell into a pit. An older woman, Mama Njeri, happened along and climbed into the pit to help get Monica out. In the process, a dangerous black Mamba snake bit both Mama Njeri and Monica. Monica was taken to Kejave Medical Center and admitted. Mama Njeri went home, but never awoke from her sleep. The next day a perceptive missionary nurse explained Mama Njeri's death to Monica, telling her that the snake had bitten both of them, but all of the snake's poison was expended on Mama Njeri; none was given to Monica. The nurse then explained that Jesus had taken the poison of Monica's sin so that she could have new life. It was an easy choice for Monica. She then received Jesus as Savior and Lord on the spot.

BACK IN THE DAYS of the Great Depression a Missouri man named John Griffith was the controller of a great railroad drawbridge across the Mississippi River. One day in the summer of 1937 he decided to take his eight-year-old son, Greg, with him to work. At noon, John Griffith put the bridge up to allow ships to pass and sat on the observation deck with his son to eat lunch. Time passed quickly. Suddenly he was startled by the shrieking of a train whistle in the distance. He quickly looked at his watch and noticed it was 1:07—the Memphis Express, with four hundred passengers on board, was roaring toward the raised bridge! He leaped from the observation deck and ran back to the control tower. Just before throwing the master lever he glanced down for any ships below. There a sight caught his eye that caused his heart to leap poundingly into his throat. Greg had slipped from the observation deck and had fallen into the massive gears that operate the bridge. His left leg was caught in the cogs of the two main gears! Desperately John's mind whirled to devise a rescue plan. But as soon as he thought of a possibility he knew there was no way it could be done.

Again, with alarming closeness, the train whistle shrieked in the air. He could hear the clicking of the locomotive wheels over the tracks. That was his son down there—yet there were four hundred passengers on the train. John knew what he had to do, so he buried his head in his left arm and pushed the master switch forward. The great massive bridge lowered into place just as the Memphis Express began to roar across the river. When John Griffith lifted his head with his face smeared with tears, he looked into the passing windows of the train. There were businessmen casually reading their afternoon papers, finely dressed ladies in the dining car sipping coffee, and children pushing long spoons into their dishes of ice cream. No one looked at the control house, and no one looked at the great gear box. With wrenching agony, John Griffith cried out at the steel train: "I sacrificed my son for you people! Don't you care?" The train rushed by, but nobody heard the father's words, which recalled Lamentations 1:12: "Is it nothing to you, all who pass by?" (NIV)

—D. James Kennedy, "Is It Nothing to You?" March 19, 1978

I'LL CALL THIS YOUNG MAN Aaron, not his real name. Late one spring he was praying about having a significant ministry the following summer. He asked God for a position to open up on some church staff or Christian organization. Nothing happened. Summer arrived, still nothing. Days turned into weeks, and Aaron finally faced reality—he needed any job he could find. He checked the want ads and the only thing that seemed to be a possibility was driving a bus in southside Chicago—nothing to brag about, but it would help with tuition in the fall. After learning the route, he was on his own—a rookie driver in a dangerous section of the city. It wasn't long before Aaron realized just how dangerous his job really was.

A small gang of tough kids spotted the young driver, and began to take advantage of him. For several mornings in a row they got on, walked right past him without paying, ignored his warnings, and rode until they decided to get off. . . . all the while making smart remarks to him and others on the bus. Finally, he decided it had gone on long enough.

The next morning, after the gang got on as usual, Aaron saw a policeman on the next corner, so he pulled over and reported the offense. The officer told them to pay or get off. They paid but, unfortunately, the policeman got off. And *they* stayed on. When the bus turned another corner or two, the gang assaulted the young driver.

When he came to, blood was all over his shirt, two teeth were missing, both eyes were swollen, his money was gone, and the bus was empty. After returning to the terminal and being given the weekend off, our friend went to his little apartment, sank onto his bed and stared at the ceiling in disbelief. Resentful thoughts swarmed his mind. Confusion, anger, and disillusionment added fuel to the fire of his physical pain. He spent a fitful night wrestling with the Lord.

How can this be? Where's God in all of this? I genuinely want to serve Him. I prayed for a ministry. I was willing to serve Him anywhere, doing anything, and this is the thanks I get!

On Monday morning Aaron decided to press charges. With the help of the officer who had encountered the gang and several who were willing to testify as witnesses against the thugs, most of them were rounded up and taken to the local county jail. Within a few days there was a hearing before the judge.

In walked Aaron and his attorney plus the angry gang members who glared across the room in his direction. Suddenly he was seized with a whole new series of thoughts. Not bitter ones, but compassionate ones! His heart went out to the guys who had attacked him. Under the Spirit's control he no longer hated them— he pitied them. They needed help, not more hate. What could he do or say?

Suddenly, after there was a plea of guilty, Aaron (to the surprise of his attorney and everybody else in the courtroom) stood to his feet and requested permission to speak.

"Your honor, I would like you to total up all the days of punishment against these men—all the time sentenced against them—and I request that you allow me to go to jail in their place."

The judge didn't know whether to spit or wind his watch. Both attorneys were stunned. As Aaron looked over at the gang members (whose mouths and eyes looked like saucers), he smiled and said quietly, "It's because I forgive you."

The dumbfounded judge, when he reached a level of composure, said rather firmly: "Young man, you're out of order. This sort of thing has never been done before!" To which the young man replied with genius insight:

"Oh, yes, it has, your honor . . . yes, it has. It happened over nineteen centuries ago when a man from Galilee paid the penalty that all mankind deserved."

And then, for the next three or four minutes, without interruption, he explained how Jesus Christ died on our behalf, thereby proving God's love and forgiveness.

He was not granted his request, but the young man visited the gang members in jail, led most of them to faith in Christ, and began a significant ministry to many others in southside Chicago.

—Charles R. Swindoll, *Improving Your Serve*

CLIFF BARROWS, song leader of the Billy Graham Crusade ministry, tells a story about his children when they were younger. They had done something he had forbidden them to do. They were told if they did the same thing again they would have to be disciplined. When he returned from work and found that they hadn't minded, his heart went out to them. "I just couldn't discipline them," he said.

Any loving father can understand Cliff's dilemma. Most of us have been in the same position. He said, "Bobby and Bettie Ruth were very small. I called them into my room, took off my belt and then my shirt, with a bare back I knelt down at the bed. I made them both strap me with the belt ten times each. You should have heard the crying. From them, I mean. The crying was from them. They didn't want to do it. But I told them the penalty had to be paid and so through their sobs and tears they did what I told them.

"I smile when I remember the incident," he said. "I must admit I wasn't much of a hero. It hurt. I haven't offered to do that again. It was a once-for-all sacrifice, I guess we could say, but I never had to spank those two children again, because they got the point. We kissed each other. And when it was over we prayed together."

—Billy Graham, *How to Be Born Again*

SUCCESS

(Also see *Ambition, Achievement, Finish Line, Motivation*)

PEOPLE ARE WAITING for their ship to come in and they've never sent one out.

—*Wit and Wisdom*

A young man asked the older, "What's the secret of your success?"
"Good decisions," he replied.
"How do you learn to make good decisions?"
"You get that by experience."
"How do you get experience?"
"By making bad decisions."

—Tim Hansel, *Holy Sweat*

How do you measure success?
To laugh often and much;
To win the respect of intelligent people
      and the affection of children;
To earn the appreciation of honest critics
      and endure the betrayal of false friends;
To appreciate beauty;
To find the best in others;
To leave the world a bit better

whether by a healthy child,
a redeemed social condition,
or a job well done;
To know even one other life has breathed
because you lived—
this is to have succeeded.

—Ralph Waldo Emerson

SELF-DENIAL is the perennial challenge of humanity. A rampant selfishness is omnipresent in every generation, and the church of the eighties is not immune to me-ism. In fact, many declare our Zion has opted for a double dose. Clergy and parishioner alike calculate every move to maximize personal benefit. . . . Today, our bonfires of selfishness are fueled by the gasoline of affluence. . . . Today's self-centered churchgoer asks the same question of God, coupled with another one: "What will you do for me soon?" God is pictured as the dispenser (and withholder) of life's prizes—a television game-show host. . . . We conclude that such things as good health, fortune, and success are sure indicators of His approval for our lives. This is the Protestant ethic gone to seed.

Jon Johnston, "Growing Me-ism and Materialism," *Christianity Today,* January 17, 1986

SUCCESS IS NOT RARE. It is common. Very few miss a measure of it. It is not a matter of luck or of contesting, for certainly no success can come from preventing the success of another. It is a matter of adjusting one's efforts to overcome obstacles and one's abilities to give the service needed by others. There is no other possible success. Most people think of it in terms of getting; success, however, begins in terms of giving.

—Kenneth O. Gangel, *Thus Spake Qoheleth*

IF ONE ADVANCES CONFIDENTLY in the direction of his dreams, and endeavors to live a life he's imagined, he will meet with a success unexpected in common hours.

—Henry David Thoreau

THE TROUBLE WITH SUCCESS is that the formula is the same as the one for a nervous breakdown.

—*Executive Digest,* quoted in Lloyd Cory, *Quote Unquote*

THERE IS NEVER ENOUGH SUCCESS in anybody's life to make one feel completely satisfied.

—Jean Rosenbaum, quoted in Lloyd Cory, *Quote Unquote*

HERE'S THE SIMPLE FORMULA that will enable you to handle whatever success God may bring your way and will provide you with the relief you need while waiting:

SUBMISSION + HUMILITY – WORRY = RELIEF

A HUNTER was out in the woods when he met a bear. Accosting the man, the bear asked, "What do you want?" The hunter said, "I want a warm fur coat." The bear said, "That's fair enough. I, on the other hand, want a full stomach. Can't we talk about it and negotiate? Perhaps we can come up with a compromise." Half an hour later the bear got up and ambled away. On the ground was the hunter's gun. As you stop to think of what happened, you realize they both got their wish—the bear got his full stomach and the man got his fur coat.

—Erwin Lutzer, *When a Good Man Falls*

A MAN WAS BEING HONORED as his city's leading citizen. Called upon to tell the story of his life, he said, "Friends and neighbors, when I first came here thirty years ago, I walked into your town on a muddy dirt road with only the suit on my back, the shoes on my feet and all my earthly possessions wrapped in a red bandanna tied to a stick, which I carried over my shoulder. Today I'm the Chairman of the Board of the bank. I own hotels, apartment buildings, office buildings, three companies with branches in forty-nine cities, and I am on the boards of all the leading clubs. Yes, friends, your city has been good to me."

After the banquet a youngster approached the successful man and asked, "Sir, could you tell me what you had wrapped in that red bandanna when you walked into this town thirty years ago?" The man said, "I think, son, it was about a half million dollars in cash and $900,000 in government bonds."

—John C. Maxwell, *Be All You Can Be!*

SUFFERING

(Also see *Adversity, Pain, Trials*)

A LITTLE PIECE OF WOOD once complained bitterly because its owner kept whittling away at it, cutting it, and filling it with holes, but the one who was cutting it so remorselessly paid no attention to its complaining. He was making a flute out of that piece of ebony, and he was too wise to desist from doing so, even though the wood complained bitterly. He seemed to say, "Little piece of wood, without these holes, and all this cutting, you would be a black stick forever—just a useless piece of ebony. What I am doing now may make you think that I am destroying you, but, instead, I will change you into a flute, and your sweet music will charm the souls of men and comfort many a sorrowing heart. My cutting you is the making of you, for only thus can you be a blessing in the world."

—M. R. Dehaan, *Broken Things*

Gethsemane

Down shadowy lanes, across strange streams
Bridged over by our broken dreams;
Behind the misty caps of years,
Beyond the great salt fount of tears,
The garden lies. Strive as you may,
You cannot miss it in your way.
All paths that have been or shall be,
Pass somewhere through Gethsemane.

All those who journey, soon or late,
Must pass within the garden's gate;
Must kneel alone in darkness there,
And battle with some fierce despair.
God pity those who cannot say,
"Not mine but thine," who only pray,
"Let this cup pass," and cannot see
The purpose in Gethsemane.

—Ella Wheeler Wilcox, quoted in Clarence Macartney, *Great Nights of the Bible*

In the Morning

Today, Lord
I have an unshakable conviction
A positive resolute assurance

That what You have spoken
Is unalterably true.

But today, Lord
My sick body feels stronger
And the stomping pain quietly subsides.
Tomorrow . . .
And then tomorrow
If I must struggle again
With aching exhaustion
With twisting pain
Until I am breathless
Until I am utterly spent
Until fear eclipses the last vestige of hope
Then, Lord—
Then grant me the enabling grace
To believe without feeling
To know without seeing
To clasp Your invisible hand
And wait with invincible trust
For the morning.

—Ruth Harms Calkin, *Tell Me Again Lord, I Forget*

THERE IS NO PIT SO DEEP but He is not deeper still.

—Corrie Ten Boom, *The Hiding Place*

ALEKSANDR SOLZHENITSYN SAID, "It was only when I lay there on rotting prison straw that I sensed within myself the first stirrings of good. Gradually, it was disclosed to me that the line separating good and evil passes, not through states, nor between classes, nor between political parties either, but right through human hearts. So, bless you, prison, for having been in my life."

—Philip Yancey, *Where Is God When It Hurts?*

FEW MEN OF THIS CENTURY have understood better the inevitability of suffering than Dietrich Bonhoeffer. He seems never to have wavered in his Christian antagonism to the Nazi regime, although it meant for him imprisonment, the threat of torture, danger to his own family, and finally death. He was executed by the direct order of Heinrich Himmler in April 1945, in the

Flossenburg concentration camp, only a few days before it was liberated. It was the fulfillment of what he had always believed and taught: "Suffering, then, is the badge of true discipleship. The disciple is not above his master. Following Christ means *passio passiva* suffering because we have to suffer. That is why Luther reckoned suffering among the marks of the true Church, and one of the memoranda drawn up in preparation for the Augsburg Confession similarly defines the Church as the community of those 'who are persecuted and martyred for the gospel's sake' . . . Discipleship means allegiance to the suffering Christ, and it is therefore not at all surprising that Christians should be called upon to suffer."

—John R. Stott, *Christian Counter Culture*

THIS IS THE BITTEREST OF ALL—to know that suffering need not have been; that it has resulted from indiscretion and inconsistency; that it is the harvest of one's own sowing; that the vulture which feeds on the vitals is a nestling of one's own rearing. Ah me! this is pain!

—F. B. Meyer, *Christ in Isaiah*

IN A HOSPITAL where I was practicing, a little five-year-old boy was dying of lung cancer. His mother loved the Lord Jesus with all her heart, and painful as it was to watch her little boy suffering, she was right by his bed every day.

One night while she was gone home, there began to come sounds out of the room where this little boy was. He was saying, "I hear the bells. I hear the bells. They're ringing." He said that through the night. And nurses thought very little of it.

Next morning the mother came, walked into the nurses' station and asked, "How's my boy?" They said, "Well, he's hallucinating. He keeps talking about hearing bells. It's probably the medication." She stopped and pointed her finger at the nurse and said, "Now you listen to me. He is not hallucinating. He is not out of his head. I told my boy weeks ago that when the pain got so bad he couldn't breathe, when it got really bad, that he was going up to heaven to be with the Lord Jesus. And I said, when it got really bad, he was to look up in the corner of his room toward heaven and to listen for the bells. They'd be ringing. They'd be ringing for him."

She swept down the hall and turned into his room and saw her little boy. She picked him up and held him in her arms and rocked him. And he talked about the bells until they were just an echo.

—James Dobson

BRUCE WALTKE, one of my mentors in my student days at Dallas, tells a marvelous story about the day that he and his daughter were walking in the forest. They came upon something that you rarely see. It was an almost-born butterfly. The little cocoon was spinning and spinning and part of one fabulous wing was already out. This was right at the eye level of his daughter, so Waltke bent down and looked at that little cocoon at her level. She said, "Oh, Daddy, he's just struggling to get out." Bruce thought, "I'll just help it." And he said, "I reached down ever so carefully and gently and took the bottom of that cocoon and split it. And it all dropped in a blob and killed the butterfly." He said, "I learned a lesson—they need the struggle of emergence to survive."

MANY YEARS AGO a good friend of mine, Dr. Robert Lightner, who is a long-time member of the theology department faculty at Dallas Seminary, was involved in a terrible plane crash. He was in a single-engine plane that flipped over during takeoff. He was badly injured and bruised beyond recognition. His wife, Pearl, said when she first saw him, "I looked at this black mass of flesh, and I didn't even know who he was." Thankfully, he did recover, and today he is a living testimony of the grace of God through that ordeal. "I learned things I didn't know I needed to learn," I heard him say on one occasion. Isn't that the way it usually is?

—Charles R. Swindoll, *Hope Again*

SURRENDER

(Also see *Submission*)

FATHER, I WANT TO KNOW THEE, but my coward heart fears to give up its toys. I cannot part with them without inward bleeding, and I do not try to hide from Thee the terror of the parting. I come trembling, but I do come. Please root from my heart all those things which I have cherished so long and which have become a very part of my living self, so that Thou mayest enter and dwell there without a rival. Then shalt Thou make the place of Thy feet glorious. Then shall my heart have no need of the sun to shine in it, for Thyself wilt be the light of it, and there shall be no night there. In Jesus' name, Amen.

—A. W. Tozer, *The Pursuit of God*

Take Over

At first, Lord, I asked You
To take sides with me.
With David the Psalmist
I circled and underlined:
"The Lord is for me . . ."
"Maintain my rights, O Lord . . ."
"Let me stand above my foes . . ."
But with all my pleading
I lay drenched in darkness
Until in utter confusion I cried
"Don't take sides, Lord,
Just take over."
And suddenly it was morning.

—Ruth Harms Calkin, *Tell Me Again, Lord, I Forget*

Lord, what I had done with youthful might,
Had I been from the first true to truth,
Grant me, now old, to do—with better sight,
And humbler heart, if not the brain of youth;
So wilt thou, in thy gentleness and truth,
Lead back thy old soul, by the path of pain,
Round to his best—young eyes and heart and brain.

—George MacDonald

Man a Nothing

O Lord,
I am a shell full of dust,
    but animated with an invisible rational soul
    and made anew by an unseen power of grace;
Yet I am no rare object of valuable price,
    but one that has nothing and is nothing,
    although chosen of thee from eternity,
        given to Christ, and born again;
I am deeply convinced of the evil and misery of a sinful state,
    of the vanity of creatures,
    but also of the sufficiency of Christ.

When thou wouldst guide me I control myself,
When thou wouldst be sovereign I rule myself.
When thou wouldst take care of me I suffice myself.
When I should depend on thy providings I supply myself,
When I should submit to thy providence I follow my will,
When I should study, love, honour, trust thee, I serve myself;
   I fault and correct thy laws to suit myself,
Instead of thee I look to man's approbation,
     and am by nature an idolater.
Lord, it is my chief design to bring my heart back to thee.
Convince me that I cannot be my own god, or make myself happy,
     nor my own Christ to restore my joy,
     nor my own Spirit to teach, guide, rule me.
Help me to see that grace does this by providential affliction,
     for when my credit is god thou dost cast me lower,
     when riches are my idol thou dost wing them away,
     when pleasure is my all thou dost turn it into bitterness.
Take away my roving eye, curious ear, greedy appetite, lustful heart;
Show me that none of these things
     can heal a wounded conscience,
     or support a tottering frame,
     or uphold a departing spirit.
Then take me to the cross and leave me there.

—Arthur Bennett, *The Valley of Vision*

MAYBE YOU HAVE TO ADMIT that you've been far too proud, lived much too secretly. When I decided to let down my guard a number of years ago, I wrote out this simple prayer to God. It helped break down my resistance to the counsel of others.

Lord, I am willing
To receive what You give
To lack what You withhold
To relinquish what You take
To suffer what You inflict
To be what You require.
And, Lord, if others are to be
Your messengers to me,

> I am willing to hear and heed
> What they have to say. Amen.
>
> —Nelson Mink, *Pocket Pearls*

WHEN OUR OLDER DAUGHTER, Charissa, was in high school, she was on the cheerleading squad. One day at the church office I got an emergency call from her school. She had accidentally fallen from the top of a pyramid of the other cheerleaders during practice and landed on the back of her head. To her amazement and everyone else's, she couldn't move. It took me about fifteen minutes to drive from my study at the church to the school campus. I was praying all the way, "Lord, You are in charge of this situation. I have no idea what I'm going to face. You be the Lord and Master. I am trusting You in all this."

When I got to the school, they already had Charissa immobilized on a wraparound stretcher. I slipped to my knees beside her.

"Daddy, I can't move my fingers. My feet and legs are numb," she said. "I can't feel anything in my body very well. It's kind of tingling."

At that moment, I confess I had feelings of fear. But I leaned closer to Charissa and whispered in her ear, "Sweetheart, I will be with you through all of this. But more important, Jesus is here with you. He is Lord over this whole event."

Her mother and I were totally helpless. We had no control over the situation or over the healing of our daughter's body. She was at the mercy of God. I can still remember the deliberatness with which I acknowledged Christ as Lord in my heart and encouraged her to do the same. Cynthia and I waited for hours in the hospital hallway as extensive X-rays were taken and a team of physicians examined our daughter. We prayed fervently and confidently.

Today, Charissa is fine physically. She recovered with no lasting damage. She did have a fracture, but thankfully it wasn't an injury that resulted in paralysis. Had she been permanently paralyzed, we would still believe that God was in sovereign control. He would still be Lord!

Christ's Bondservant

> Make me a captive, Lord,
> And then I shall be free;
> Force me to render up my sword,
> And I shall conqueror be.

I sink in life's alarms
When by myself I stand;
Imprison me within Thine arms,
And strong shall be my hand.

My heart is weak and poor
Until its master find;
It has no spring of action sure—
It varies with the wind:
It cannot freely move
Till Thou hast wrought its chain;
Enslave it with Thy matchless love,
And deathless it shall reign.

My power is faint and low
Till I have learned to serve:
It wants the needed fire to glow,
It wants the breeze to nerve;
It cannot drive the world
Until itself be driven;
Its flag can only be unfurled
When Thou shalt breathe from heaven.

My will is not my own
Till Thou hast made it Thine;
If it would reach a monarch's throne
It must its crown resign:
It only stands unbent
Amid the clashing strife,
When on Thy bosom it has leant
And found in Thee its life.

—George Matheson, quoted in Donald T. Kauffman, *Baker's Pocket Treasury of Religious Verse*

When I panic, I run.
When I run, I lose.
When I lose, God waits.
When I wait, He fights.
When He fights, I learn.

I HAVE LEARNED TO HOLD EVERYTHING LOOSELY. That way it doesn't hurt when God takes them from me.

—Corrie Ten Boom

_____

BACK WHEN I WAS A LITTLE BOY, we worshipped in a church in East Houston that had a big white sign with broad black letters that read, "Let go and let God." I remember sitting there as a child and as a young adolescent looking at those words. In fact, I looked at them every Sunday for several years. "Let go and let God." They sounded real great, and I'm sure whoever put them up there wanted them to speak to everybody there.

It's a little dubious whether this is the origin, but it seems to be rather well documented: A college student back in the nineteenth century took six postcards and wrote a large letter on each one of the postcards: L–E–T–G–O–D. He then put them on the mantelpiece in his room where he was living at school. One evening a draft blew through the window and the "D" blew away. As he picked it up, what he saw seemed to be a message from God, the secret of the Christian life. Only by letting go can you let God carry out His will in your life.

—Paul Lee Tan, _Encyclopedia of 7,700 Illustrations_

𝒯𝓉

TALENT (See *Ability*)

TEAMWORK

A GIRAFFE is a horse put together by a committee.

WHEN I WAS IN HIGH SCHOOL, a gifted young man named Donald Carpenter could play football like few people I've ever seen. His sophomore year he made the all-city team of Houston. His junior year he made all-state—unanimous choice. And it was obvious by his senior year that he was going to turn the place upside down—he was home free.

But the coach made a tragic mistake. In our summer practice before our senior year he changed all the plays so that they keyed on Donald Carpenter. The team virtually was to revolve around Carpenter.

Everything went great for five games. We were hardly scored upon.

And then suddenly, in the sixth game, first play from scrimmage, Carpenter broke his ankle. Needless to say, the latter part of our season was not much to brag about. We lost everything. Why? Because we didn't have a team; we had a one-man show.

THE BIG NAME WAS DENNIS CONNORS. In the twelve-meter sailboat race held in Australia, America's Cup was won by America 4 to 0. We were thrilled with that, at least those of us who are sports enthusiasts. We didn't say much about it several years ago when we lost 4 to 3, but when we won it back everybody was excited. And Dennis Connors was the one with all the glory, the one holding the trophy. He's the one, of course, who led the project. He's the one who knows the sailing, the one in the middle of the ticker-tape parade, the hero of the yacht club. He's the one who put that trophy back on the shelf.

Connors, of course, was not alone. A whole crew of people were working around him as he skippered the boat. A television documentary did a whole piece about this project. It showed people on the crew, aside from Connors. In fact, one particular person on the crew stood out in my mind, because he never sees the water, though he goes on every one of those races. He never enjoys watching where the other boat is and how close they are to the finish line. In fact, he's continually drenched by the ocean waves. He works down in what's called the sewer of the boat. Doesn't that sound exciting? He's down underneath. He never feels anything but the water pouring over him. But whatever he does down there, according to Connors himself, makes that race possible for that boat. He makes it possible for them to win.

———————————————

How Important Are You?

More than
you think.
A rooster
minus a hen
equals
no baby chicks.
Kellogg minus
a farmer
equals
no corn flakes.
If the nail
factory closes,
what good is the
hammer factory?
Paderewski's
genius wouldn't have
amounted to much
if the
piano tuner
hadn't showed up.
A cracker maker
will do better
if there's a
cheesemaker.

The most skillful
surgeon needs
the ambulance driver
who delivers the
patient.
Just as Rogers
needed Hammerstein
you need someone
and someone
needs you.

—Charles R. Swindoll, *Come Before Winter*

SUPER BOWL SUNDAY the television camera panned up above, far away from the field. We saw an individual who does nothing but study the opponents and every play. This person is away from the emotion of the field. He's away from the excitement of the crowd. His work is the technical work of studying the eleven men who are the defensive team fighting against his team to keep them from winning. He punches it into the computer. He studies it. He watches it through his binoculars. He puts it in his head. He works it over. Then he's the one who sends the signal down to the head coach who wears the headphone (if he hasn't jerked it off, thrown it on the ground, and stomped on it). If he is listening, he's listening to the man who is way up there, away from all the fun and games, doing the hard work of technical strategy in football. He's conveying to that coach what the opposition is doing to keep them from scoring—continually in contact with the head coach.

When they win, they never go upstairs and grab the guy out of the press box area and bring him down and put him on the shoulders of the players. But the coach will tell you quickly that he himself didn't win that game. It was his staff of men working behind the scenes to give him the strategy needed to win the game and the players themselves who really won it.

JOHN STEMMONS, a well-known Dallas businessman, was asked to make a brief statement on what he considered to be foundational to developing a good team. His answer was crisp and clear: "Find some people who are comers, who are going to be achievers in their own field, and people you can trust. Then grow old together."

—Charles R. Swindoll, *Quest for Character*

WHAT ARE SOME QUALITIES of people who are a valuable asset to any endeavor? Let me suggest at least eight:

Initiative—being a self-starter with contagious energy.

Vision—seeing beyond the obvious, claiming new objectives.

Unselfishness—releasing the controls and the glory.

Teamwork—involving, encouraging, and supporting others.

Faithfulness—hanging in there in season and out.

Enthusiasm—providing affirmation, excitement to a task.

Discipline—modeling great character regardless of the odds.

Confidence—representing security, faith, and determination.

—Charles R. Swindoll, *The Finishing Touch*

TEMPTATION

I CAN RESIST EVERYTHING but temptation.

—Oscar Wilde

RATTLESNAKES ARE FAIRLY COMMON where I live. I encounter one almost every summer. It is a frightening experience to see a rattlesnake coiled, looking at you, ready to strike. He's lightning-quick and accurate. I have a simple two-point program for handling rattlesnakes: shun and avoid. It's as simple as that. You don't need much insight to figure out what to do with something as dangerous as a diamondback rattler. You don't mess around.

—LeRoy Eims, *Be the Leader You Were Meant to Be*

SOMETIMES YOU GET GIFTS in the strangest ways. My friend, Ray Stedman, was ministering at a place back East. One morning he was having breakfast alone. There in front of him was a beautiful pewter salt and pepper set and a little creamer. In a moment of weakness, he thought, "Now that would fit neatly in my suitcase. I could take that home and this place would never miss it." Then the more he thought about it and the scandal he would create as a minister stealing these things, he thought, "I can't do that."

So the next Sunday while he was preaching, he was on the subject of stealing and he admitted this to everyone. He said, "I want you to know that even I can be tempted to do that."

The following Sunday morning, at his study there was a little package. He unwrapped it to find a lovely pewter salt and pepper shaker and creamer.

Someone in the congregation heard his story and called back there and thought, "If he wants it that much, I'll send it to him."

Next Sunday he told about receiving the gift and said, "I also noticed this lovely color television set." But, he added, "You know what? I didn't get a color television set."

AN ATTORNEY I KNOW works in conjunction with the Federal Reserve bank in another city where stacks and stacks of paper money are counted. One afternoon he invited me to go with him. As we walked in together, we were checked all over, and at the end of a narrow hallway we were checked again. And, of course, television cameras were everywhere. Behind a bulletproof glass in the secured room are people who do nothing but count.

I said, "How can the workers resist the temptation to steal some of the money?" My attorney friend answered, "Everything is fine until they begin to realize what they're doing and then we have problems. As long as they're just counting slips of paper, that's fine. But when they suddenly realize, 'Hey, this is a hundred dollar bill I have in my hand,' then we have problems."

A MAN WAS TRAVELING in a foreign city and was alone on a street that had an X-rated theater. No one was there who knew him. Silently he stood in front of the marquee and read the words and he looked at a few of the pictures and he was tempted to go in. As he backed away toward the curb, he remembered, "I would be true for there are those who trust me. I would be true for there are those who care." The old hymn that they sang in the church back home came to his rescue. He turned and went on.

—Gordon MacDonald, *The Effective Father*

THE FOLLOWING IS a sequential series of percentages that tells some interesting facts about Americans. For example:

1% of Americans read the Bible more than once a day;

15% of American married men they say do most of the cooking in the household;

30% of Americans smoke cigarettes;

42% of Americans cannot name a country near the Pacific Ocean;

60% of Americans do not spend a lot of time on their personal appearance;

67% of Americans believe files are being kept on them for unknown reasons;

70% of Americans own running shoes but don't run;

74% of Americans say if they had their life to live over, they'd continue with their formal education;

76% of American owners of small businesses do not have a college degree;

83% of American companies have fewer than twenty employees;

84% of Americans believe heaven exists;

94% of American men would change something about their looks if they could;

96% of American school children can identify Ronald McDonald (who is second only to Santa Claus);

99% of American women would change something about their looks if they could.

—Daniel Weiss, *One Hundred Percent*

IN A "FRANK AND ERNEST" CARTOON the two characters are standing before a priest and Frank asks, "How come opportunity knocks once, but temptation beats at my door every day?"

Few would argue that the percentage of occasions when we face life's temptations is terribly high—dare I say 98 percent? Or how about 100 percent? And I have yet to meet anyone who denies ever having been tempted.

MARC ANTHONY was known as the silver-throated orator of Rome. He was a brilliant statesman, magnificent in battle, courageous, strong. He was handsome. He had all the qualities of becoming a ruler of the world. However, he had the vulnerable flaw of moral weakness. On one occasion his personal tutor shouted in his face, "O Marcus, O colossal child, able to conquer the world but unable to resist a temptation."

ON OKINAWA I would take a little bus to the place where we had our Bible study, I would get off the bus at a particular corner. I had to walk down about four blocks and then uphill about two. Okinawa has more bars per mile than any island in the South Pacific. I discovered that the answer to temptation was to keep on looking straight ahead. I looked neither to the right nor to the left.

And I've discovered that what works in Okinawa works here at home. When your eyes turn to the right or to the left, you're on your way to grabbing the bait. Usually it isn't that first glance; it's that second stare that leads into sin.

BACK IN 1958 a small community in northeastern Pennsylvania built a little red brick building that was to be their police department, their fire department, and their city hall. They were proud of that building; it was the result of sacrificial giving and careful planning. When the building was completed, they had a ribbon—cutting ceremony, and more than six thousand people were there— nearly all the town's residents. It was the biggest event of the year!

Within less than two months, however, they began to notice some ominous cracks on the side of this red brick building. Sometime later, it was noticed that the windows would not shut all the way. Then it was discovered that the doors wouldn't close correctly. Eventually, the floor shifted and left ugly gaps in the floor covering and corners. The roof began to leak. Within a few more months, it had to be evacuated, to the embarrassment of the builder and the disgust of the taxpayers.

A firm did an analysis shortly thereafter and found that the blasts from a nearby mining area were slowly but effectively destroying the building. Imperceptibly, down beneath the foundation, there were small shifts and changes taking place that caused the whole foundation to crack. You couldn't feel it or even see it from the surface, but quietly and down deep there was a weakening. A city official finally had to write across the door of that building, "Condemned. Not fit for public use." Ultimately, the building had to be demolished.

There is a moral there. Erosion goes unnoticed when you play with temptation until your character is permanently damaged.

—Charles R. Swindoll, *Hand Me Another Brick*

A MAN I KNEW through my ministry was going with a girl who, some of us thought, was not at all worthy of him. We breathed a sigh of relief when he went away into the army for two or three years (this was during the war). The girl drifted around with other fellows, and, most happily, the young man met a worthy girl in a distant city. He fell in love with her and married her. When the war was over and he had returned to his home with his bride, the first girl drove by the house one evening and dropped in to see her old flame and meet his wife. But the wife was not there. The first girl made no attempt to hide her affection and moved in such a voluptuous way that the young man realized that he had but to reach out his hand and she was his. He told me about it afterwards. There was within him all that goes with male desire. There was something much more within him and he began to talk about what a wonderful girl he had married. He showed the pictures of his wife to the first girl and praised his wife to the skies, acting as though he did not understand her obvious advances. It was not long before she left, saying as she went, "Yes, she must be quite a girl if she can keep you from reaching." The young man was never more joyful in his life. He said that in that moment all of the love between him and his wife was greater and more wonderful than ever; he could think of his wife in a clean, noble way. A philanderer might have scoffed at him, deriding him for "sacrificing" his pleasure. But there was not the slightest hint of sacrifice in the generally accepted sense of the word. There was however every sacrifice in the sense of the heart. The turning of his heart and mind and soul, yes, and body, to the love of his true wife was the living sacrifice which praised her and made him all the more noble because of it. It is in this sense the believer in Christ presents his body a living sacrifice to his Lord.

—Donald Barnhouse, *Romans*, Vol. 4

OSCAR WILDE, the Irish wit of the past century, author and playwright, was not only a good writer. He was a student of human nature. He loved stories. And he liked to tell the story about the day the devil was traveling across the Libyan Desert and happened upon a pack of his imps who were in the midst of giving fits to a rather holy hermit, but without much success. The sainted man shook off all their temptations and suggestions. Lucifer stood back only so long. Finally, after rubbing his chin and coming to certain conclusions about their approach, he said to them, "What you do is too crude. Step back." Then he whispered in the man of God's ear, "Your brother has just been made Bishop of Alexandria." All of a sudden the hermit's countenance changed and a malignant presence of jealousy clouded the once serene face of the saint. "I mean, the very idea that my brother would be chosen over me." The devil looked at his demons and said, "Now that is the sort of thing I'd recommend."

—W. E. Sangster, *The Craft of Sermon Illustration*

WHEN TEMPTED to plunge into the old life: "Thou fool, dost not thou know that thou art carrying God around with thee."

—Augustine

THE WAY an Eskimo kills a wolf is grizzly, yet it offers fresh insight into the consuming, self-destructive nature of sin.

First the Eskimo coats his knife blade with animal blood and allows it to freeze. Then he adds another layer of blood, and another, until the blade is completely concealed by frozen blood.

Next, the hunter fixes his knife in the ground with the blade up. When a wolf follows his sensitive nose to the source of the scent and discovers the bait, he licks it, tasting the fresh frozen blood. He begins to lick faster, more and more vigorously, lapping the blade until the keen edge is bare. Feverishly now, harder and harder, the wolf licks the blade in the Arctic night. So great becomes the craving for blood that the wolf does not notice the razor sharp sting of the naked blade on his own tongue nor does he recognize the instant at which his insatiable thirst is being satisfied by his own warm blood. His carnivorous appetite just craves more— until the dawn finds him dead in the snow!

—Paul Harvey, quoted in Chris T. Zwingelberg, "Sin's Peril," *Leadership* magazine, Winter 1987

THINK, FATHERS, THINK; think, mothers, think; think, young men, so much is at stake—think what the temptations and the dangers and the almost sure issues of this and that choice in life must be. All our trades, professions, occupations in life have, each one, its own perils and temptations and snares to the soul; as well as its own opportunities of gain and honour, and praise, and service. The ministry, teaching, law, medicine, the army, political life, newspaper life, trades of all kinds, the money-market of all kinds, and so on. Open your eyes. Count the cost. Are you able? Will you venture? Take that line of life which you are just about to choose. Take time over it. Look all around it. Imagine yourself done with it. Look at this man and that man who are done with it. Would you like to be like them? Study well the successes and the failures in that line of life. Read the thirteenth and the nineteenth chapters of Genesis, and then take those two chapters with you to your knees, and so make your choice.

—Alexander Whyte, *Old Testament Bible Characters*

LONG WOODEN SHOOTS had been built in the forest to slide tree trunks down the slope to the valley and into the river. They were hundreds of yards long, smooth and polished inside, and the foresters used them as well. They would sit on the floor of the shoot or on an axe-handle, and go tobogganing down to save themselves the trouble of walking. Well, a workman caught his foot in a hole in the shoot and couldn't get it free, and at that moment he heard a shout of warning, which meant that a trunk was on its way down. He saw the thing coming, and as he still couldn't free his foot, he hacked it off with an axe and jumped clear just in time. He was crippled for life, but at least he was alive.

Oh, God, give me the courage to cut out of my life that liaison which is threatening my family's happiness, that indulgence which is sapping my strength of purpose, that doubt which is leading me to disobey You, that disobedience which is causing me to doubt You. Oh, God, *heal my faithlessness* and restore me to health.

—Robert Raines, *Creative Brooding*

IN OUR MEMBERS there is a slumbering inclination towards desire which is both sudden and fierce. With irresistible power, desire seizes mastery over the flesh. All at once a secret, smouldering fire is kindled. The flesh burns and is in flames. It makes no difference whether it is sexual desire or ambition or vanity or desire for revenge or love of fame and power or greed for money or, finally, that strange desire for the beauty of the world, of nature. Joy in God is ... extinguished in us and we seek all our joy in the creature. At this moment God is quite unreal to us, he loses all reality, and only desire for the creature is real; the only reality is the devil. Satan does not fill us with hatred of God, but with forgetfulness of God. . . . The lust thus aroused envelops the mind and will of man in deepest darkness. The powers of clear discrimination and of decision are taken from us.

—Dietrich Bonhoeffer, *Temptation*

TEN COMMANDMENTS
(See *Bible*)

TERRITORY

MAN NEEDS A PLACE, and this need is vital to him. . . . Life is not an abstraction. To exist is to occupy a particular living-space, to which one has a right. This is true even of animals. The zoologist, Professor Portmann, of Basle, pointed out to me that the seagulls on the railings . . . always stand at least twelve inches apart. If another gull comes down between them, they fly away at once. All respect the law, that each has a right to a minimum living space.

Architects and sociologists ought to give thought to this, because man is less conscious of his vital needs, and more ready to disregard them. He allows himself to be herded into compact masses, without realizing that he loses his individuality as a person in a society that is too compact. To exist is to have a place, a space that is recognized and respected by others.

—Paul Tournier, *A Place for You*

A CARTOON showed a singer about to perform. He addressed the audience, "I'd like to share a song with you that the Lord gave me a year ago . . . and even though He did give it to me, any reproduction of this song in any form without my written consent will constitute infringement of copyright laws which grants me the right to sue [you] . . . praise God."

—*The Wittenberg Door*

EVER WATCH PEOPLE at the grocery store checkout jockey their carts to get ahead in line—to such extremes at times that it leads to an argument a hair this side of a fistfight? All for the sake of saving sixty, maybe ninety seconds. It's like, "This is my space and nobody is going to squeeze me out of it. I'll sue, if necessary!"

This selfish attitude is also alive and well on airplanes. I remember one in particular: I was sitting on a 727 about halfway back in the coach section (three-plus-three configuration) when a family of three came aboard. Apparently they had purchased their tickets late and were unable to secure reserved seating in the same row. The airline attendant assured them that there were several empty seats, and surely someone would be willing to swap.

My row on the right side was full, as were several others, but just in front of me were two empty seats, middle and window, and on the other side, same row, the middle and aisle seats were open.

The family—all of them friendly and courteous—asked the gentleman on the aisle if he would be willing to move from the right side aisle seat to the left side aisle seat. That's all—just stand up, take two steps to the left, then sit back down. Just swap seat 17D for seat 17C.

Do you think he'd do it? No way. He wasn't even courteous enough to answer verbally. Just stared straight ahead as he shook his head firmly. And when a flight attendant tactfully tried again, he unloaded a piece of his mind he couldn't afford to lose. I mean the guy absolutely refused to budge. This was his "space," ladies and gentlemen. He had paid good money for it, and there was no way he was going to let anybody, for any reason, take it away from him. Small world, small mind.

THEOLOGY

I THINK I LEARNED my first theology at my mother's knee. She said, "Lord help you if you ever do that again!"

Credo

Not what, but *Whom,* I do believe,
    That, in my darkest hour of need,
    Hath comfort that no mortal creed
    To mortal man may give;—
Not what, but *Whom!*
    For Christ is more than all the creeds,
    And his full life of gentle deeds
    Shall all the creeds outlive.
Not what I do believe, but *Whom!*
    Who walks beside me in the gloom?
    Who shares the burden wearisome?
    Who all the dim way doth illume,
    And bids me look beyond the tomb
    The larger life to live?—
Not what I do believe,
    But *Whom!*
    Not what
    But *Whom!*

—John Oxenham, quoted in Thomas Curtis Clark, *Christ in Poetry*

A GROUP OF THEOLOGIANS were discussing predestination and free will. When the argument became heated, the dissidents split into two groups. One man, unable to make up his mind which group to join, slipped into the predestination crowd. Challenged as to why he was there, he said, "I came of my own free will." The group reacted, "Free will? You can't join us!" And he retreated to the opposing group and met the same challenge. "What are you doing here?" "I was sent here." "Get out!" they stormed. "You can't join us unless you come of your own free will."

—Leslie Flynn, *Great Church Fights*

CHARLES SCHULZ, in one of his "Peanuts"cartoons, shows Lucy and Linus looking out the window, watching it rain. Lucy begins the conversation:

Lucy:	Boy, look at it rain . . . what if it floods the whole world?
Linus:	It will never do that . . . In the ninth chapter of Genesis, God promised Noah that this would never happen again, and the sign of that promise is the rainbow.
Lucy:	You've taken a great load off my mind . . .
Linus:	Sound theology has a way of doing that!

—Robert L. Short, *Parables of Peanuts*

THERE ARE TWO THINGS you cannot save: saints and seats.

—H. A. Ironside

I DON'T KNOW ANYONE who would build a summer home at the base of Mount Vesuvius, and it would be tough trying to get campers to pitch their tents where Big Foot has been spotted. No family I know is interested in vacationing in a houseboat up the Suez Canal. Or swimming in the Amazon near a school of piranhas. Or building a new home on property that straddles the San Andreas fault.

I mean, some things make no sense at all. Like lighting a match to see if your gas tank is empty. Or stroking a rhino to see if he's tame. They've got a name for nuts who try such stunts. Victims. Or, if they live to tell the story, just plain stupid.

And yet there are Christians running loose today who flirt with risks far greater than any of the above. And they do so with such calm faces you'd swear they had ice water in their veins. You'd never guess they are balancing on the tightwire of disaster without a net.

Who are they? They are the ones who rewrite the Bible to accommodate their lifestyle. We've all met them. Outwardly they appear to be your basic believer, but down inside, operation rationalization transpires daily. They are experts at rephrasing or explaining away the painful truth of texts.

Here is a sampling of accommodating theology:

God wants me happy. I can't be happy married to her. So I'm leaving—and I know He will understand.

There was a time when this might have been considered immoral. But not today. The Lord gave me this desire and wants me to enjoy it.

Look, nobody's perfect. So I got in deeper than I planned. Sure, it's a little shady, but what's grace all about, anyway?

Hey, life's too short to sweat the small stuff. We're not under law, you know.

Whenever they run across Scripture verses or principles that attack their position, they alter them to accommodate their practice. That way, two things occur: (1) all desires (no matter how wrong) are fulfilled, and (2) all guilt (no matter how justified) is erased.

That way everybody can do his own thing and nobody has any reason to question another's actions. If he does, call him a legalist and plow right on. . . .

The consequences of sin may not come immediately—but they will come eventually. And when they do, there will be no excuses, no rationalization, no accommodation.

—Charles R. Swindoll, *The Finishing Touch*

TWO CONGREGATIONS of differing denominations were located only a few blocks from each other in a small community. They thought it might be better if they would merge and become one united body, larger and more effective, rather than two struggling churches. Good idea, but both were too petty to pull it off. The problem? They couldn't agree on how they would recite the Lord's Prayer. One group wanted "forgive us our trespasses" while the other demanded "forgive us our debts." So the newspaper reported that one church went back to its trespasses while the other returned to its debts!

—Leslie Flynn, *When the Saints Come Storming In*

TWO MAJOR MISTAKES are commonly found in the family of God. One is giving lost people too much theology; two is giving saved people too much of the gospel. Saved people don't grow if all they're told is the cross and the tomb. Lost people won't understand if what they are told is the deep subjects of theology.

CHARLES HADDON SPURGEON for decades held the attention of the people of London in the great Metropolitan Tabernacle where he preached. And though he died in his mid-fifties, he altered the city of London with his influence. On his deathbed he said, "My brethren, my theology has become very simple. It consists of four words: Jesus died for me." And he died.

—Donald Kauffman, *Baker's Pocket Treasury of Religious Verse*

INSTRUCTION IN SOUND THEOLOGY will help the suffering. It is a reminder that God has chosen them for salvation; they are still firmly in the family of God; and God has not moved.

TIME

TIME IS SIGNIFICANT because it is so rare. It is completely irretrievable. You can never repeat it or relive it. There is no such thing as a literal instant replay. That appears only on film. It travels alongside us every day, yet it has eternity wrapped up in it. Although this is true, time often seems relative, doesn't it? For example, two weeks on a vacation is not at all like two weeks on a diet. Also, some people can stay longer in an hour than others can in a week! Ben Franklin said of time, " . . . that is the stuff life is made of." Time forms life's building blocks. The philosopher William James once said, "The great use of life is to spend it for something that will outlast it."

—Lloyd Cory, *Quote Unquote*

YESTERDAY IS A CASHED CHECK; tomorrow is a promissory note. Today is cash in hand so use it—invest it.

—John Haggai, *How to Win over Worry*

I'D LIKE TO PLAY DEVIL'S ADVOCATE and tell you how to waste your time. Five proven ideas come immediately to mind:

First, worry a lot. Start worrying early in the morning and intensify your anxiety as the day passes.

Second, make hard-and-fast predictions. For example, one month before his July 1975 disappearance, Jimmy Hoffa announced: "I don't need bodyguards."

Third, fix your attention on getting rich. You'll get a lot of innovative ideas from the secular bookshelves (I counted fourteen books on the subject last time I was in a bookstore), plus you'll fit right in with most of the hype pouring out of entrepreneurial seminars and high-pressure sales meetings.

Fourth, compare yourself with others. Now, here's another real time-waster. If it's physical fitness you're into, comparing yourself with Arnold Schwarzenegger or Jane Fonda ought to keep you busy.

Fifth, lengthen your list of enemies. If there's one thing above all others that will keep your wheels spinning, it's perfecting your skill at the Blame Game.

Put these five surefire suggestions in motion and you will set new records in wasting valuable time.

—Charles R. Swindoll, *The Finishing Touch*

THERE IS A LEGEND about Satan and his imps planning their strategy for attacking the world that's hearing the message of salvation. One of the demons says, "I've got the plan, master. When I get on the earth and take charge of people's thinking, I'll tell them there's no heaven."

The devil responds, "Ah, they'll never believe that. This Book of Truth is full of messages about the hope of heaven through sins forgiven. They won't believe that. They know there's a glory yet future."

On the other side of the room another says, "I've got the plan. I'll tell 'em there's no hell."

"No good," he says. "Jesus, while He was on earth, talked more of hell than of heaven. They know in their hearts that their wrong will have to be taken care of in some way. They deserve nothing more than hell."

And one brilliant little imp in the back stood up and said, "Then I know the answer. I'll just tell them there's no hurry." And he's the one Satan chose.

—C. S. Lewis, *The Screwtape Letters*

OUR GOAL, then, is not to *find more time* but to *use time more wisely*. Make an honest appraisal of your week. If there are leaks in your time dike, why not plug them?

If your priorities should be sifted more clearly from the trivia, that would be to your advantage.

If a simple plan would help to organize your day, that's only playing it smart.

If you should give a kind but unqualified, unexplained "No" more often, do it.

It's easy to forget that time is our slave, not our sovereign, isn't it?

I READ OF AN OLD NORWEGIAN who had kept very careful notes of his life in a series of notebooks he kept on the shelf of his business. On his eightieth birthday he went to the store and pulled the books from the shelf and began to compute his life. He was surprised to find that he had spent five of his eighty years waiting for people. He had spent six months tying neckties, three months scolding children, eight days telling dogs to lie down and be quiet.

I don't know if the old fellow was a Christian or not, but if he had been, in his eighty years he would probably have spent about six thousand hours (one hundred hours a year, based on forty-minute sermons) attending Sunday morning and evening church services and some midweek services and some Bible conferences.

FOR NINE LONG YEARS the record of the mile hovered just above four minutes. As early as 1945, Gunder Haegg had approached the barrier with a time of 4:01.4. But many people said the limits of physical capacity had been reached; it was impossible to break the four-minute barrier. But in 1954 Roger Bannister broke the tape at 3:59.4. And what was the result? Well, as soon as the myth of the "impossible barrier" was dispelled, the four-minute mile was attacked and pierced by many with apparent ease. In almost no time the four-minute achievement was bettered sixty-six times by twenty-six different runners! If one dismisses this as merely the power of competition, the point is missed. There was just as much competition before the four-minute mile was broken. The succeeding runners discovered from Bannister that it can be done.

—Alan Loy McGinnis, *Bringing Out the Best in People*

TONGUE

(Also see *Advice, Communication, Speech*)

NONE WAS BETTER at insults than Winston Churchill, who had no love affair with Lady Astor. Actually, the feeling was mutual. On one occasion she found the great statesman rather obviously inebriated in a hotel elevator. With cutting disgust she snipped, "Sir Winston, you are drunk!" to which he replied, "M'lady, you are *ugly*. Tomorrow I will be sober." That may be a classic example of how *not* to handle an insult.

—*The Little, Brown Book of Anecdotes*

ON ANOTHER OCCASION Winston Churchill and Lady Astor engaged in verbal sparring when she told him, "If I were your wife, I'd put arsenic in your tea." He responded, "If I were your husband, I'd drink it."

—*The Little, Brown Book of Anecdotes*

MY DIET IS BALANCED. My food is the best.
But it's the words I have eaten that I cannot digest.

_____

> If your lips would keep from slips,
> Five things observe with care:
> To whom you speak; of whom you speak;
> And how, and when, and where.
>
> —William Norris

_____

AT LEAST ONCE EVERY DAY one ought to hear a song, read a good poem, see a fine painting and, if possible speak a few reasonable words.

—Johann von Goethe

_____

THE TONGUE is the only tool that grows sharper with constant use.

—Washington Irving

_____

NO MEMBER OF OUR BODY needs so great a number of muscles as our tongue, for this member exceeds all the rest in the number of its movements.

—Leonardo da Vinci

_____

A CARTOON SHOWS a line of pews and the same sentence is being passed verbally from one pew to the other.

First pew:	"My ear kind of hurts."
Second pew:	"The pastor has an earache."
Third pew:	"The pastor got a hearing aid."
Fourth pew:	"The pastor is having trouble hearing."
Fifth pew:	"The pastor got a double earring."
Last pew:	An old lady with a cane is walking out and says, "That does it, I'm outta here! The pastor's got a double earring."

—*Leadership* magazine, Winter 1990

_____

WHAT PEOPLE SAY about us is never quite true; never quite false; they always miss the bull's-eye, but rarely fail to hit the target.

—Lloyd Cory, *Quote Unquote*

PERHAPS LIKE ME you've received a phone call from someone who says, "I want to tell you about so-and-so." And I'll say, "Wait a minute. May I quote you?" There's usually a long pause. And then they'll say, "Well, I'm not sure that would be a good idea." Invariably my answer would be, "Then I'm not interested in hearing what you have to say. If you're not interested in putting your name on it, if you're not interested in being there when we confront the individual, I'm not interested in listening to what you've got to say." Gossip and rumor have ruined many a soul, haven't they?

XANTHUS, THE PHILOSOPHER, once told his servant that the next day he was going to have some friends for dinner and that he should get the best thing he could find in the market. The philosopher and his guests sat down the next day at the table. They had nothing but tongue—four or five courses of tongue—tongue cooked in this way, and tongue cooked in that way. The philosopher finally lost his patience and said to his servant, "Didn't I tell you to get the best thing in the market?" The servant said, "I did get the best thing in the market. Isn't the tongue the organ of sociability, the organ of eloquence, the organ of kindness, the organ of worship?"

Then Xanthus the philosopher said, "Tomorrow I want you to get the worst thing in the market." And on the morrow the philosopher sat at the table, and there was nothing but tongue—four or five courses of tongue—tongue in this shape and tongue in that shape. The philosopher lost his patience again and said, "Didn't I tell you to get the worst thing in the market?" The servant replied, "I did; for isn't the tongue the organ of blasphemy, the organ of defamation, the organ of lying?"

—Spiros Zodhiates, *The Behavior of Belief*

TRAVEL

(Also see *Adventure*)

BRENT LAMB told a funny story. He'd gotten caught in an American Airlines strike. He was trying to fly from Tennessee to southern California, and he had to take a circuitous route to get there.

"I bought one of those $10 sandwiches in the airport," he began. "I ate one-half and stuck the other one in the little bag that's on the back of the airline seat. You know, those little vomit bags?" And he said, "I rolled up the bag and decided I'd hang on to it because I probably would need it later. We were to have a long layover. As I was getting off the plane, one of the flight attendants said to me, 'Can I take that for you?' I replied, 'No, I'm gonna eat it later.'"

ONE FORWARD-THINKING PROPHET SAID, "Can you imagine the time your great grandchildren will have at their senior prom? In the twenty-first century it'll probably be common for proms to be held in foreign countries like Australia. 'We're going to Australia tonight.' That'll be a popular choice. It'll be only a half-orbital shuttle run in twenty-nine minutes with a shuttle busload of formally attired space travelers enjoying the spectacular view—a panorama of the hemispheres. On the way home they'll stop by a McDonald's for a spaceburger in Hong Kong and tell about how times were in Australia."

—Denis Waitley, *Seeds of Greatness*

A LOST MOTORIST asked a farmer for directions.

"Where is the main highway to Quincy?"

"I don't know."

"Well, where is the highway to Hannibal?"

"I don't know."

"Where does this highway go?"

"I don't know."

"You don't know much do you?"

"No, but I ain't lost."

—Tim Timmons, *Maximum Living in a Pressure Cooker World*

TO ARRIVE is better than to travel hopefully.

—Robert Louis Stevenson

WILLIAM LEAST HEAT MOON, an Indian by blood, decided after he'd lost his job at a college in Missouri that he would strike out in his Ford van and know what the rest of the world was like. His wife had recently left him and he decided there had to be a better way and a better world out there.

So he took off following the blue lines on the map—the blue highways. The better maps have the big highways in gold and in bold red, but the blue roads are the roads that interested Moon. He wanted to go places like Dime Box, Texas; Scratch Ankle, Alabama; Remote, Oregon; Simplicity, Virginia;

Nameless, Tennessee; Whynot, Mississippi; Igo, California just down the road from Ono, California; and hundreds of other little holes in the road. He would travel, ultimately, the distance of about half the world's circumference as he went across and around the cycle of America.

By his own admission, he left "an age that carries with it its own madness and futility." And he set out "to the open road in search of places where change didn't mean ruin and where time and men and deeds connect."

—William Least Heat Moon, *Blue Highways*

ABOUT OVERSEAS TRAVEL: "You need a great sense of humor and no sense of smell."

—Ken Bemis

A MAN DISCOVERED 80 percent of all accidents occur within two miles of home, so he moved.

A CHRISTIAN PHYSICIAN was traveling in Korea. He was on one of those busy, crowed trains making its way through the northern part of South Korea. Across from him sat an older gentleman with a large white package of cloth. The Korean kept smiling at the doctor and the doctor smiled back. The Korean gentleman struck up a conversation. Unfortunately, the only line of Korean the physician knew was, "I do not know how to speak Korean." Having heard that, nonetheless, the man continued the dialogue, or attempted to, only to hear again in Korean, "I do not know how to speak Korean." More words were spoken and the doctor, as he started to say again, "I do not know how to speak Korean," thought he heard a word that triggered the picture of something else in his mind—*Jesu*. He raised his eyebrows and he pointed to the man's chest, toward his heart, and said, *"Jesu? Jesu?"* Oh, the Korean just almost exploded, *"Jesu! Jesu! Jesu!"* And though they couldn't speak the same language, for the rest of the train ride there was the "communion of the saints."

JUST LISTEN to the jingles: "Get away from it all . . . ," "Fly our friendly skies . . . ," "We're ready when you are . . . ," "Doing what we do best . . . " Sure sounds like a good time.

While all that may be true, believe me, there's another side of traveling that never gets much press. Like being bumped to standby because they overbooked your flight, and then arriving at the hotel only to discover they gave your room to another party because you didn't get there before six o'clock. Like having your luggage go on to Berlin for the week and you're caught in a March blizzard in Toronto with only sneakers and a sweater and have to borrow some shaving gear from the guy next door whose face is broken out with terminal acne. Like being stuck on an elevator between floors 14 and 12 with an older woman who was taking her two nervous poodles out for their evening break, and she tends to faint in close places. Like being served a toadstool omelet for breakfast and spending the next two days cramped up in the fetal position, wondering if your will is in order and how the wife and kids are going to get along without you. Like anticipating a nice relief in your schedule only to discover you're expected to speak fourteen times in three days—plus an all-day seminar with two hundred discouraged pastors and several depressed couples whose marriages are on the rocks. And the television doesn't work, so you miss the final NCAA championship basketball game that evening. And you run out of clean shorts. And you step on your glasses getting out of the shower. And you're driven to the airport by a guy who grins a lot and says "Praise the Lord" forty-one times. And you come back to Los Angeles on a five-hour flight in a jam-packed 747, holding a box of Pampers for the mother of twins who have colic. And one just kicked your coffee over. And your briefcase handle pulls loose. And your in-box at the office looks like the Leaning Tower. And the first five people you see the next day ask cutely, "Well—how was the vacation?"

TRIALS

(Also see *Adversity, Pain, Suffering*)

DO YOU REMEMBER Harold Kushner's book titled *When Bad Things Happen to Good People?* R. C. Sproul had a great answer for that. Someone asked him on one occasion, "Why do bad things happen to good people?" His answer was classic. He said, "I haven't met any good people yet, so I don't know."

—R. C. Sproul, *Doubt and Assurance*

WHEN I SEE the magnificent Golden Gate Bridge, I remember that an engineer must take into account three loads, or stresses, while designing bridges. These are: the dead load, the live load, and the wind load.

The dead load is the weight of the bridge itself. The live load is the weight of the daily traffic that the bridge must carry. The wind load is the pressure of the storms that beat on the bridge. The designer plans for bracings that will enable the bridge to bear all these loads.

In our lives, too, we need bracings which make it possible to carry the dead load of self, the live load of daily living, and the wind load of emergencies. When we place our trust in Christ, He gives us the strength we need to withstand these various stresses. He thus gives our lives usefulness, stability, and durability.

—Wilbur Nelson, *Anecdotes and Illustrations*

FOUR GUYS DECIDED to go mountain climbing one weekend. In the middle of the climb, one fella slipped over a cliff, dropped about sixty feet and landed with a thud on the ledge below. The other three, hoping to rescue him, yelled, "Joe, are you OK?"

"I'm alive . . . but I think I broke both my arms!"

"We'll toss a rope down to you and pull you up. Just lie still!" said the three.

"Fine," answered Joe.

A couple of minutes after dropping one end of the rope, they started tugging and grunting together, working feverishly to pull their wounded companion to safety. When they had him about three-fourths of the way up, they suddenly remembered he said he had broken BOTH his arms.

"Joe! If you broke both your arms, how in the world are you hanging on?"

Joe responded, "With my TEEEEEEEEEEEETH. . . ."

—Charles R. Swindoll, *Standing Out*

WHEN I WORKED IN A MACHINE SHOP, we had a department that was called a heat treat department. Some of the metal was heated so hot it became white. And across the top of that white-hot liquid surface came portions of what is called slag or dross that needed to be wiped away by a worker in an asbestos suit. The purpose of removing the slag was to make the metal as nearly pure as possible. The heat of our trials brings to the surface the dross that binds us. Jesus is the One who wipes it clean.

A SOUTHERN PREACHER SAID, "When the Lord sends tribulation, He 'spects us to tribulate."

—Paul Lee Tan, *Encyclopedia of 7,700 Illustrations*

THE CHANCELLOR of the University of Glasgow introduced one day to the young men of that university, God's missionary, David Livingstone. When Livingstone stood up and walked to the front of the platform to speak to the group of university men, the students looked at him earnestly. They saw his hair burned crisp under the torrid tropical sun. They saw his body wasted and emaciated from jungle fever. They saw his right arm hanging limp at his side, destroyed by the attack of a ferocious African lion. When the students looked at Livingstone, they stood up with one accord in awe and in silence before God's missionary.

—W. A. Criswell, *Expository Sermons on Galatians*

ON SEPTEMBER 22, 1967, the late V. Raymond Edman, president of Wheaton College, had been ill but got up to give an address in chapel. He died while speaking on the subject "An Invitation to Visit a King." Earlier, he had written these words:

> They took them all away—my toys—
> Not one of them was left;
> They set me here, shorn, stripped of humblest joys,
> Anguished, bereft.
> I wondered why. Ah, the years have flown.
> Unto my hand
> Cling weaker, sadder ones who walk alone—
> I understand, I understand.

—V. Raymond Edman, *The Disciplines of Life*

Praise God for the Furnace

It was the enraptured Rutherford who could shout in the midst of serious and painful trials, "Praise God for the hammer, the file, and the furnace."

The hammer is a useful tool, but the nail, if it had feeling and intelligence, could present another side of the story. For the nail knows the hammer only as an opponent, a brutal, merciless enemy who lives to pound it into submission, to beat it down out of sight and clinch it into place. That is the nail's view of the hammer, and it is accurate except for one thing: The nail forgets that both it and the hammer are servants of the same workman. Let the nail but remember that the hammer is held by the workman and all resentment toward it will disappear. The carpenter decides whose head shall be beaten next and what hammer shall be used in the beating. That is his sovereign right. When the nail has surrendered to the will of the workman and has gotten a little glimpse of his benign plans for its future it will yield to the hammer without complaint.

The file is more painful still, for its business is to bite into the soft metal, scraping and eating away the edges till it has shaped the metal to its will. Yet the file has, in truth, no real will in the matter, but serves another master as the metal also does. It is the master and not the file that decides how much shall be eaten away, what shape the metal shall take, and how long the painful filing shall continue. Let the metal accept the will of the master and it will not try to dictate when or how it shall be filed.

As for the furnace, it is the worst of all. Ruthless and savage, it leaps at every combustible thing that enters it and never relaxes its fury till it has reduced it all to shapeless ashes. All that refuses to burn is melted to a mass of helpless matter, without will or purpose of its own. When everything is melted that will melt and all is burned that will burn, then and not till then the furnace calms down and rests from its destructive fury.

—A. W. Tozer, *The Root of the Righteous*

Treasures

One by one God took them from me
All the things I valued most
Till I was empty handed
Every glittering toy was lost.
And I walked earth's highways
Grieving in my rags and poverty
Until I heard His voice inviting,
"Lift those empty hands to me."

And I turned my hands toward heaven
And He filled them with a store
Of His own transcendant riches
Till they could contain no more.
And at last I comprehended
With my stupid mind, and dull,
That God could not pour His riches
Into hands already full.

—Martha Snell Nicholson, *Ivory Palaces*

I thank God for bitter things;
   They've been a "friend to grace";

They've driven me from paths of ease
    To storm the secret place.
I Thank Him for the friends who failed
    To fill my heart's deep need;
They've driven me to the Savior's feet,
    Upon His love to feed.
I'm grateful too, through all life's way
    No one could satisfy,
And so I've found in God alone
    My rich, my full supply!

—Florence Willett, quoted in V. Raymond Edman, *The Disciplines of Life*

CONTRARY TO WHAT MIGHT BE EXPECTED, I look back on experiences that at the time seemed especially desolating and painful with particular satisfaction. Indeed, I can say with complete truthfulness that everything I have learned in my seventy-five years in this world, everything that has truly enhanced and enlightened my existence, has been through affliction and not through happiness. In other words, if it ever were to be possible to eliminate affliction from our earthly existence by means of some drug or other medical mumbo jumbo, as Huxley envisaged in *Brave New World,* the result would not be to make life delectable, but to make it too banal and trivial to be endurable. This, of course, is what the Cross signifies. And it is the Cross, more than anything else, that has called me inexorably to Christ.

—Malcolm Muggeridge, *A 20th Century Testimony*

Guests

Pain knocked upon my door and said
That she had come to stay,
And though I would not welcome her
But bade her go away,
She entered in. Like my own shade
She followed after me,
And from her stabbing, stinging sword
No moment was I free.

And then one day another knocked
Most gently at my door.
I cried, "No, Pain is living here,
And there is not room for more."

And then I heard His tender voice,
"Tis I, be not afraid."
And from the day He entered in—
The difference it has made!

For though He did not bid her leave,
(My strange, unwelcome guest),
He taught me how to live with her.
Oh, I had never guessed

That we could dwell so sweetly here,
My Lord and Pain and I,
Within this fragile house of clay
While years slip slowly by!

—Martha Snell Nicholson, quoted in John R. Rice, *Poems That Preach*

ARTHUR GORDON RELATES a story of a man who had been stricken with polio at age three, and his parents, probably Depression-poor and overwhelmed, had abandoned him at a New York City hospital. Taken in by a foster family, he was sent to stay with their relatives in Georgia when he was six, in hopes that the warmer climate would improve his condition. What improved his condition, though, was Maum Jean, an elderly, black woman who took that "frail, lost, lonely little boy" into her heart. For six years, she daily massaged his weak legs; administering her own hydrotherapy in a nearby creek; and encouraged him spiritually with her stories, songs, and prayers. Gordon writes,

Night after night Maum Jean continued the massaging and praying. Then one morning, when I was about twelve, she told me she had a surprise for me.

She led me out into the yard, placed me with my back against an oak tree; I can feel the rough bark of it to this day. She took away my crutches and braces. She moved back a dozen paces and told me that the Lord had spoken to her in a dream. He had said that the time had come for me to walk. "So now," said Maum Jean, "I want you to walk over to me."

My instant reaction was fear. I knew I couldn't walk unaided; I had tried. I shrank back against the solid support of the tree. Maum Jean continued to urge me.

I burst into tears. I begged. I pleaded. Her voice rose suddenly, no longer gentle and coaxing but full of power and command. "You can walk, boy! The Lord has spoken! Now walk over here."

She knelt down and held out her arms. And somehow, impelled by something stronger than fear, I took a faltering step, and another, and another, until I reached Maum Jean and fell into her arms, both of us weeping.

It was two more years before I could walk normally, but I never used the crutches again. . . .

Then the night came when one of Maum Jean's tall grandsons knocked on my door. It was late; there was frost in the air. Maum Jean was dying, he said; she wanted to see me.

The old cabin was unchanged: floors of cypress, windows with wooden shutters—no glass, roof of palm thatch mixed with pitch. Maum Jean in bed, surrounded by silent watchers, her frail body covered by a patchwork quilt. From a corner of the room, a kerosene lamp cast a dim saffron light. Her face was in shadow, but I heard her whisper my name. Someone put a chair close to the bed. I sat down and touched her hand.

For a long time I sat there. . . . Now and then Maum Jean spoke softly. Her mind was clear. She hoped I remembered the things that she had taught me. Outside, the night stirred with a strong wind. In the other room the fire snapped, throwing orange sparks. There was a long silence; she lay with her eyes closed. Then the old voice spoke, stronger suddenly, "Oh," said Maum Jean, with surprising gladness. "Oh, it's so beautiful!" She gave a little contented sigh, and died. . . .

All that happened a long time ago. I now live in another town. But I still think of Maum Jean often, and the main thing she taught me: nothing is a barrier when love is strong enough. Not age. Not race. Not disease. Not anything.

—Arthur Gordon, *A Touch of Wonder*

Free Me, Lord

> Lord, just today I read
> That Paul and Silas were
> Stripped and beaten
> With wooden whips.
> "Again and again the rods
> Slashed across their bared backs"
> But in their desolate dungeon
> Their feet clamped in stocks
> They prayed.

They sang.
They praised.
In this musty midnight of my life
Imprisoned in a dungeon of confusion
Bound by chains of anguish
Help me, please help me
To pray
To sing
To praise
Until the foundation shakes
Until the gates fling open
Until the chains fall off
Until I am free
To share the Good News
With other chain-bound prisoners.

—Ruth Harms Calkin, *Tell Me Again, Lord, I Forget*

A BAR OF STEEL worth $5, when made into ordinary horseshoes, is then worth $10. If this same $5 bar is manufactured into needles, the values rises to $350. And yet if it's made into delicate springs for expensive watches, it is worth more than $250,000. The same bar of steel is made more valuable by being cut to its proper size, passed through one blast furnace after another, again and again, hammered and manipulated, beaten and pounded, finished and polished until it's ready for those delicate tasks.

—M. R. DeHaan, *Broken Things*

IN 1659, a Puritan writer wrote:

"God, who is infinite in wisdom and matchless in goodness, hath ordered our troubles, yea, many troubles to come trooping in upon us on every side. As our mercies, so our crosses seldom come single; they usually come treading one upon the heels of another; they are like April showers, no sooner is one over but another comes. It's mercy that every affliction is not an execution, every correction not a damnation. The more the afflictions, the more the heart is raised heavenward."

—Thomas Brookes, *The Mute Christian under the Smarting Rod*

Day by Day

Day by day and with each passing moment,
Strength I find to meet my trials here.
Trusting in my Father's wise bestowment,
I've no cause for worry or for fear.
He whose heart is kind beyond all measure
Gives unto each day what He deems best—
Lovingly, its part of pain and pleasure,
Mingling toil with peace and rest.

—Linda Sandell

TRUST

A HUGE CROWD was watching the famous tightrope walker, Blondin, cross Niagara Falls one day in 1860. He crossed it numerous times—a 1,000-foot trip 160 feet above the raging waters. He not only walked across it; he also pushed a wheelbarrow across it. One little boy just stared in amazement. So after completing a crossing the fellow looked at that little boy and he said, "Do you believe I could take a person across in the wheelbarrow without falling?" "Yes, sir. I really do." The fellow says, "Well then, get in, son."

—Paul Lee Tan, *Encyclopedia of 7,700 Illustrations*

LET'S SAY A BEGINNING PIANIST is practicing one Saturday afternoon in the church sanctuary. Suddenly Van Cliburn walks in the back door and listens to the struggling musician. He says, "I have the ability to come into and give my gift and genius to those who will depend on me. Now tomorrow, if you want to play for the church service, I promise you that if you depend on me, and I'll sit very near you, you will play beautiful piano." So the musician agrees.

Sunday morning, he is there as promised. As the pianist sits down, he tells himself, *Right now I'm going to depend totally on that man's gift.* But when he takes his eyes off Van Cliburn and starts thinking, *Everybody's watching me,* the performance falls apart.

The Road of Life

AT FIRST, I saw God as my observer, my judge, keeping track of the things I did wrong, so as to know whether I merited heaven or hell when I die. He was out there sort of like a president.

But later on when I met Christ, it seemed as though life were rather like a bike ride, but it was a tandem bike, and I noticed that Christ was in the back helping me pedal.

I don't know just when it was that He suggested we change places, but life has not been the same since. When I had control, I knew the way. It was rather boring, but predictable . . . It was the shortest distance between two points.

But when He took the lead, He knew delightful long cuts, up mountains, and through rocky places at breakneck speeds, it was all I could do to hang on! Even though it looked like madness, He said, "Pedal!"

I worried and was anxious and asked, "Where are you taking me?" He laughed and didn't answer, and I started to learn to trust.

I forgot my boring life and entered into the adventure. And when I'd say, "I'm scared," He'd lean back and touch my hand.

He took me to people with gifts that I needed, gifts of healing, acceptance and joy. They gave me gifts to take on my journey, my Lord's and mine.

And we were off again. He said, "Give the gifts away; they're extra baggage, too much weight." So I did, to the people we met, and I found that in giving I received, and still our burden was light.

I did not trust Him, at first, in control of my life. I thought He'd wreck it; but He knows bike secrets, knows how to make it bend to take sharp corners, knows how to jump to clear high rocks, knows how to fly to shorten scary passages.

And I am learning to shut up and pedal in the strangest places, and I'm beginning to enjoy the view and the cool breeze on my face with my delightful constant companion, Jesus Christ.

And when I'm sure I just can't do any more, He just smiles and says, "Pedal."

—Tim Hansel, *Holy Sweat*

TRUTH

IT'S BETTER NOT TO KNOW so much than to know so many things that ain't so.

—Josh Billings, quoted in John Bartlett, *Bartlett's Familiar Quotations*

WHEN TRUTH UNMASKS WRONG, those who are exposed get very nervous, like the two brothers in a story I heard recently.

These brothers were rich. They were also wicked. Both lived a wild, unprofitable existence, using their wealth to cover up the dark side of their lives. On the surface, however, few would have guessed it, for these consummate cover-up artists attended the same church almost every Sunday and contributed large sums to various church-related projects.

Then the church called a new pastor, a young man who preached the truth with zeal and courage. Before long, attendance had grown so much that the church needed a larger worship center. Being a man of keen insight and strong integrity, this young pastor had also seen through the hypocritical lifestyles of the two brothers.

Suddenly one of the brothers died, and the young pastor was asked to preach his funeral. The day before the funeral, the surviving brother pulled the minister aside and handed him an envelope. "There's a check in here that is large enough to pay the entire amount you need for the new sanctuary," he whispered. "All I ask is one favor: Tell the people at the funeral that *he was a saint.*" The minister gave the brother his word; he would do precisely what was asked. That afternoon he deposited the check into the church's account.

The next day the young pastor stood before the casket at the funeral service and said with firm conviction, "This man was an ungodly sinner, wicked to the core. He was unfaithful to his wife, hot-tempered with his children, ruthless in his business, and a hypocrite at church. . . . but compared to his brother, *he was a saint.*"

—*Leadership* magazine, Fall 1995

MRS. FISHER WAS RECOVERING FROM SURGERY and got a card from her fourth-grade class: "Dear Mrs. Fisher, Your fourth-grade class wishes you a speedy recovery by a vote of 15–14."

—Howard G. Hendricks, *Say It with Love*

SHORTLY AFTER THE COMMUNIST REVOLUTION, a spokesman for the party visited one of the peasant villages and began to promote communism. He said, "Thanks to the party, we have increased wheat production by 100 percent." One little man stood up in the back and said, "My name is Menski, and I would like to know where all that wheat is."

The next year the same official returned to the same village and began the same litany of propaganda, except in this case he said, "I want you to know by now we have increased the wheat production 200 percent." Little man in the back stood up and said, "My name is Menski, and I have one question. Where is all that wheat?"

Third year came. Same official approached these people and began his same talk. And he said, "The communist party has increased the wheat production

300 percent." Little fellow stood up in the back. And the official says, "I know, you're Menski, and..." The fellow responded, "No, my name is Polaski and I have a question. Where is Menski?"

—Leslie Flynn, *Humorous Incidents and Quips*

TO WALK IN THE TRUTH is more than to give assent to it. It means to apply it to one's behavior. He who "walks in the truth" is an integrated Christian in whom there is no dichotomy between profession and practice. On the contrary, there is in him an exact correspondence between his creed and his conduct. Such conformity of life to the truth on the part of his children brought John greater joy than anything else. To him truth mattered.

—John R. W. Stott, *The Epistles of John*

GOD FORBID that we should traffic in unlived truth.

—H. A. Ironside

WHEN I WAS mustering out of the Marine Corps in the Berkeley area, I didn't have a car, and I wanted to go to church. So I walked to an area where there were several churches and I chose one by name. It was a great stone structure. I walked inside, great massive doors, and there was a vast narthex, and in it were huge pictures, portraits of people—great people in panorama. There was Mahatma Ghandi and Abraham Lincoln. There was Jesus of Nazareth. There was one of the philosophers, I believe it was Socrates. There was President Eisenhower. And above them on a great, bronze engraving were the words, "You are all the sons of God . . ." Dot, dot, dot, an ellipses, meaning, it's not complete but that's enough for you to read. Galatians 3:26 was the reference. I turned to a Testament and I read it. and The verse says, "You are all the sons of God by faith in Christ Jesus." They weren't all sons of God unless they were IN CHRIST JESUS, excluding no one. You need the *whole* truth!

WHEN ALEKSANDR SOLZHENITSYN was awarded the Nobel Prize in literature, he concluded his speech by quoting a Russian proverb: "One word of truth outweighs the whole world." If I could change a couple of words in that proverb, I would say, "One person of truth impacts the whole world."

IN HIS EARLY DAYS a famous evangelist, Brownlow North, had lived a life that was anything but Christian. Once, just before he was to enter the pulpit in a church in Aberdeen, he received a letter that recalled a shameful series of events he had been engaged in. And North's stomach turned. It concluded by saying, "If you have the gall to preach tonight, I'll stand and expose you." North took that letter and went to his knees. A few minutes later he was in the pulpit. He began his message by reading the letter from start to finish. And he said, "I want to make it clear that this letter is perfectly true. I am ashamed of what I have read and what I have done. And I come tonight, not as one who is perfect, but as one who is forgiven." God used that letter and the balance of his ministry almost as a magnet to bring people to Jesus Christ.

—William Barclay, *The Acts of the Apostles*

AFTER A MORNING CHURCH SERVICE a man stopped me and said, "I've waited till the end to talk to you, because I've got a question that may take a long time to answer. I want to know from you, what is the truth? I've heard you talk and I've listened to you preach. What do you mean when you refer to the truth?"

He was standing with his arms folded hugging a Bible to his chest. I punched the cover of his Bible and said, "Everything within the covers of that Book, and nothing else." I don't think I had ever answered that question like that before. He expected a long answer, but to his surprise, and a little to mine, it wasn't very long at all. Scriptural truth is what we need.

KING CHARLES told Oliver Cromwell on one occasion to pose for a portrait. He didn't want to, didn't believe in that kind of vain stuff, but he did, because the king said to. He sat down before a rather diplomatic artist who began to put his thoughts together as the man was posing. And the artist noticed that Cromwell had a rather sizable wartlike growth on the side of his nose, near his cheek. He carefully suggested that Cromwell turn his face the other side to the canvas so that there might be a little better pose. Cromwell responded, "Mr. Lely, I desire you would use all your skill to paint my picture truly like me, and not flatter me at all; but remark all these roughnesses, pimples, warts, and everything you see; otherwise I will never pay a farthing for it."

—George Sweeting, *Great Quotes and Illustrations*

THE BEST WAY TO SHOW that a stick is crooked is not to argue about it or to spend time denouncing it, but to lay a straight stick alongside it.

—D. L. Moody, quoted in George Sweeting, *Great Quotes and Illustrations*

Uu

UNBELIEF

A NUMBER OF YEARS AGO there appeared in the *New Yorker* magazine an account of a Long Island resident who ordered an extremely sensitive barometer from a respected company, Abercrombie and Fitch. When the instrument arrived at his home he was disappointed to discover that the indicating needle appeared to be stuck pointing to the sector marked "Hurricane." After shaking the barometer vigorously several times—never a good idea with a sensitive mechanism—and never getting the point to move, the new owner wrote a scathing letter to the store, and, on the following morning, on the way to his office in New York City, mailed it. That evening he returned to Long Island to find not only the barometer missing but his house as well! The needle of the instrument had been pointed correctly. The month was September, the year was 1938, the day of the terrible hurricane that almost leveled Long Island.

—Adapted from *Bits and Pieces*, quoted in Lloyd Cory, *Quote Unquote*

UNDERSTANDING

AN USHER AT OUR CHURCH who had been involved with counting the morning offering met me as I was leaving the church. He smiled as he walked up to me, stuck out his hand, and said, "I've got something for you. It came in the offering."

Here was a little hand-scribbled note from a child who had been in our worship service. It read:

> TO PASTER CHUCK SWINDOL
> I don't think you know me, but I shure know you. You are a very good speeker for Jesus Christ, I think your neet.
> I even understand what you are saying and that's how it should be.
> I LOVE YOU!

Guess what was attached to the note. A chocolate sucker, all wrapped in cellophane ready to be enjoyed.

DONALD BARNHOUSE used to hold an open forum in his church in Philadelphia on Sunday evenings. With just a microphone and a Bible in his hand he would answer questions from the congregation which was usually packed with students and young intellectuals as well as people from the church.

One young man stood up in the balcony and said, "I'd like to know how those children of Israel could walk around the wilderness for forty years and their shoes never wear out and their clothes never wear out." Barnhouse looked at him, blinked a time or two, and he said, "God!" The guy up there said, "Oh, now I understand," and sat down. Barnhouse said, "No, you don't, Son. Nobody understands."

UNEXPECTED

FIND A PIECE OF PAPER and get your pen or pencil handy.

> Pick a number between 1 and 10 and write it down.
> Multiply your number by 9.
> If you have a number with two digits, add the first and second digits together.
> Subtract 5.
> Pick the letter of the alphabet that corresponds to your number. (A is 1, B is 2, etc.)
> Think of a country in the world that begins with that letter.
> Take the next letter in the alphabet and think of an animal that begins with that letter.

Of all the countries and animals in the world, do you think I can guess which ones you wrote down? Your answers are Denmark and elephant. Was I right? Pretty amazing, isn't it?

A BURGLAR STALKED the neighborhood watching for homes left unguarded by people leaving for vacation. He watched as a family loaded their suitcases into their car and departed. He waited until dark and then approached the front door and rang the bell. There was no answer. The burglar neatly picked the lock and let himself in. He called into the darkness, "Is anybody home?" He was stunned when he heard a voice in reply, "I see you, and Jesus sees you." Terrified, the burglar called out, "Who's there?" Again the voice came back, "I see you, and Jesus sees you." The burglar switched on his flashlight and aimed it in the direction of the voice. He was instantly relieved when his light revealed a caged parrot reciting the refrain, "I see you, and Jesus sees you." The burglar laughed out loud and switched on the lights. Then he saw it. Beneath the parrot's cage was a huge Doberman pinscher. Then the parrot said, "Attack, Jesus, attack!"

—R. C. Sproul, *Pleasing God*

THE WELL-KNOWN MISSIONARY to the New Hebrides, John G. Paton, had aroused the enmity of the local native chief by his success in preaching the gospel, so the chief hired a man to kill the missionary. The man went to the missionary's house, but instead of murdering Paton he returned in terror, saying he had seen a row of men, dressed in white, surrounding the missionary's home. The chief thought the man had drunk too much whiskey and encouraged him to try again. The next time others of the tribe accompanied him. That night they all saw three rows of men surrounding Paton's house. When the chief asked the missionary where he kept the men in the daytime who surrounded his house at night, Paton, knowing nothing of what happened, disclaimed the whole idea. When the chief, in amazement, told his story, the missionary realized the natives had seen an angelic company which God had sent to protect him.

—Paul Little, *Know What and Why You Believe*

I HAVE A GREAT FRIEND down in Montgomery, Alabama, and a few years ago he told me an unforgettable story of a summer vacation he planned for his wife and children. He was unable to go himself because of business, but he helped them plan every day of a camping trip in the family station wagon from Montgomery all the way to California, up and down the West Coast, and then back to their home.

He knew their route exactly and the precise time they would be crossing the Great Divide. So, my friend arranged to fly himself out to the nearest airport (without telling his family) and hire a car and a driver to take him to the very place where every car must pass by. He sat by the side of the road several hours waiting for the sight of that familiar station wagon. When it came into view, he stepped out on the road and put out his thumb to hitchhike a ride with his family who assumed that he was three thousand miles away.

I said to him, "Coleman, I'm surprised they didn't drive off the road in terror or drop dead of a heart attack. What an incredible story. Why did you go to all that trouble?" I love the answer.

"Well, Bruce," he said, "someday I'm gonna be dead and when that happens I want my kids and my wife to say, "'You know, Dad was a lot of fun.'"

Wow, I thought. Here is a man whose whole game plan is to make fun and happiness for other people.

It made me wonder what my family will remember about me. I'm sure they will say, "Well, Dad was a nice guy but he worried a lot about putting out the lights and closing the windows and mowing the lawn and picking up around the house." I'd also like them to be able to say that Dad was the guy who made life a whole lot of fun.

—Bruce Larson, *The One and Only You*

UNITY

NO MAN IS AN ISLAND, entire of itself; every man is a piece of the continent, a part of the main; if a clod be washed away by the sea, Europe is the less, as well as if a promontory were, as well as if a manor of thy friends or of thine own were; any man's death diminishes me, because I am involved in mankind; and therefore never send to know for whom the bell tolls, it tolls for thee.

—John Donne, cited in John Bartlett, *Bartlett's Familiar Quotations*

Hezekiah 6:14

"The reason mountain climbers
are tied together
is to keep the sane ones from going home."

I don't know who said it,
or when, or where,
but I've chuckled over it,
thought about it, and quoted it, too.

With a mountain of mercy behind me
and a mountain of mission ahead,
I need you, my sister, my brother,
I need to be tied to you,
and you need me, too.

We need each other . . .
to keep from bolting,

fleeing in panic, and returning
to the "sanity"of unbelief.

Wise words, whoever said them;
I've placed them in my "bible";
they are my Hezekiah 6:14.

—Gerhard E. Frost, *Blessed Is the Ordinary*

USING THE ANALOGY OF THE HUMAN BODY, there are some diseases that can spread infection throughout the body of Christ. The mind can become swollen with pride. The heart can grow cold and indifferent because of sin. The digestive system can get clogged by sterile theory and unapplied theology, so the body can't digest what needs to be turned into energy or eliminate what needs to be released. When that occurs we start to fight among ourselves or we lose our equilibrium and find ourselves unable to stay balanced. . . .

Sometimes a dreaded thing occurs in the body—a mutiny—resulting in a tumor. . . .

A tumor is called benign if its effect is fairly localized and it stays within membrane boundaries. But the most traumatizing condition in the body occurs when disloyal cells defy inhibition. They multiply without any checks on growth, spreading rapidly throughout the body, choking out normal cells. White cells, armed against foreign invaders, will not attack the body's own mutinous cells. Physicians fear no other malfunction more deeply: it is called cancer. For still mysterious reasons, these cells—and they may be cells from the brain, liver, kidney, bone, blood, skin, or other tissues—grow wild, out of control. Each is a healthy, functioning cell, but disloyal, no longer acting in regard for the rest of the body.

Even the white cells, the dependable palace guard, can destroy the body through rebellion. Sometimes they recklessly reproduce, clogging the bloodstream, overloading the lymph system, strangling the body's normal functions—such is leukemia.

Because I am a surgeon and not a prophet, I tremble to make the analogy between cancer in the physical body and mutiny in the spiritual body of Christ. But I must. In His warnings to the church, Jesus Christ showed no concern about the shocks and bruises His Body would meet from external forces. "The gates of hell shall not prevail against my church," He said flatly (Matthew 16:18). He moved easily, unthreatened, among sinners and criminals. But He cried out against the kind of disloyalty that comes from within.

—Paul Brand and Philip Yancey, *Fearfully and Wonderfully Made*

FEW DOCTRINES are more important than this one. Because the church is under constant attack, we need to be good students of the subject. Because we are fellow members of the body, we need to apply ourselves to mutual harmony. And because disease can diminish the effectiveness of the body, we must maintain habits of health and a consistent program of exercise in harmony with God's body-building program.

IN ESSENTIALS, unity. In nonessentials, liberty. In all things, charity.

—Philip Melanchthon, quoted in Leslie Flynn, *When the Saints Come Storming In*

No East or West

In Christ there is no East or West,
In Him no South or North,
But one great Fellowship of Love
Throughout the whole wide earth.

In Him shall true hearts everywhere
Their high communion find.
His service is the golden cord
Close-binding all mankind.

Join hands then, Brothers of the Faith,
Whate'er your race may be!—
Who serves my Father as a son
Is surely kin to me.

In Christ now meet both East and West,
In Him meet South and North,
All Christly souls are one in Him,
Throughout the whole wide earth.

—John Oxenham, quoted in Donald T. Kauffman, *Baker's Pocket Treasury of Religious Verse*

Believe as I believe, no more no less
That I am right and no one else, confess;
Feel as I feel, think as I think,
Eat as I eat and drink as I drink;

Look as I look, do as I do
Then I'll have fellowship with you.

—Leslie Flynn, *Great Church Fights*

UNION HAS AN AFFILIATION with others but no common bond that makes them one in heart. *Uniformity* has everyone looking and thinking alike. *Unanimity* is complete agreement across the board. *Unity*, however, refers to a oneness of heart, a similarity of purpose, and an agreement on major points of doctrine.

—Charles R. Swindoll, *Hope Again*

PICTURE A COUPLE OF COMIC STRIP CHARACTERS. One is sitting alone, watching television. In storms the other, demanding that he change the channel to show the one she wants to watch, threatening him with her fat little fist in his face. Rather meekly he asks her what makes her think she can walk in and take over. She blurts out: "These five fingers!" which she tightens into a fist. It works. Without a word the little guy responds by asking which channel she prefers.

Naturally, she gets to watch any channel she wants. Slowly, he slips out of the room, feeling like a wimp. He looks at his own five fingers and asks, "Why can't you guys get organized like that?"

—Charles R. Swindoll, *The Grace Awakening*

WITHIN THE CHURCH of historic Christianity there have been wide divergences of opinion and ritual. Unity, however, prevails wherever there is a deep and genuine experience of Christ; for the fellowship of the new birth transcends all historical and denominational boundaries. Paul of Tarsus, Luther of Germany, Wesley of England, and Moody of America would find deep unity with each other, though they were widely separated by time, by space, by nationality, by educational background, and by ecclesiastical connections.

—Merrill C. Tenney, *John: The Gospel of Belief*

IN THE CHURCH there is the bond of family, yet room for variety. The devil tries to disrupt unity. Two chickens tied at the legs and thrown over a clothesline may be united, but they do not have unity.

—Leslie Flynn, *Great Church Fights*

Vv

VICTORY

IF SATAN CAN WIN VICTORY over a significant Christian, he has won victory over those who have impacted your life.

HOW CAN YOU STAND YOUR GROUND when you are weak and sensitive to pain, when people you love are still alive, when you are unprepared?

What do you need to make you stronger than the interrogator and the whole trap?

From the moment you go to prison you must put your cozy past firmly behind you. At the very threshold, you must say to yourself: "My life is over, a little early to be sure, but there's nothing to be done about it. I shall never return to freedom. I am condemned to die—now or a little later. But later on, in truth, it will be even harder, and so the sooner the better. I no longer have any property whatsoever. For me those I love have died, and for them I have died. From today on, my body is useless and alien to me. Only my spirit and my conscience remain precious and important to me."

Confronted by such a prisoner, the interrogation will tremble.

Only the man who has renounced everything can win that victory.

—Aleksandr Solzhenitsyn, *The Gulag Archipelago*

WILMA WAS BORN PREMATURELY. This produced complications that resulted in her contracting double pneumonia (twice) and scarlet fever. But the worst was a bout with polio which left her with a crooked left leg and a foot twisted inward. Metal leg braces, stares from neighborhood kids, and six years of bus rides to Nashville for treatments could have driven this young girl into a self-made shell. But she refused.

Wilma kept dreaming. And she was determined not to allow her disability to get in the way of her dreams. Maybe her determination was generated by the faith of her Christian mother who often said, "Honey, the most important thing in life is for you to believe it and keep on trying."

By age eleven, Wilma decided to "believe it." And through sheer determination and an indomitable spirit to persevere, regardless, she forced herself to learn how to walk without the braces.

At age twelve she made a wonderful discovery: Girls could run and jump and play ball just like boys! Her older sister Yvonne was quite good at basketball, so Wilma decided to challenge her on the court. She began to improve. The two of them ultimately went out for the same school team. Yvonne made the final twelve, but Wilma didn't. However, because her father wouldn't allow Yvonne to travel with the team without her sister as a "chaperone," Wilma found herself often in the presence of the coach.

One day she built up enough nerve to confront the man with her magnificent obsession—her lifetime dream. She blurted out, "If you will give me ten minutes of your time every day—and only ten minutes—I'll give you a world-class athlete."

He took her up on the offer. The result is history. Young Wilma finally won a starting position on the basketball squad; and when that season ended, she decided to try out for the track team. What a decision!

In her first race, she beat her girlfriend. Then she beat all the girls in her high school, then, *every* high school girl in the state of Tennessee. Wilma was only fourteen, but already a champion.

Shortly thereafter, although still in high school, she was invited to join the Tigerbelle's track team at Tennessee State University. She began a serious training program after school and on weekends. As she improved, she continued winning short dashes and the 440-yard relay.

Two years later she was invited to try out for the Olympics. She qualified and ran in the 1956 games at Melbourne, Australia. She won a bronze medal as her team placed third in the 440-meter relay. It was a bittersweet victory. She had won—but she decided that next time she would "go for the gold."

Wilma realized that the victory would require an enormous amount of commitment, sacrifice, and discipline. To give her "the winner's edge" as a world-class athlete, she began a do-it-yourself program similar to the one she had employed to get herself out of those leg braces. Not only did she run at six and ten every morning and three every afternoon, she would often sneak down the dormitory fire escape from eight to ten o'clock and run the track before bedtime. Week after week, month in and month out, Wilma maintained the same grueling schedule for over twelve hundred days.

Now we're ready for Rome. When the sleek, trim, young black lady, only twenty years old, walked out onto the field, she was ready. She had paid the price. Even those eighty thousand fans could sense the spirit of victory. It was electrifying. As she began her warm-up sprints, a cadenced chant began to emerge from the stands: "Vilma . . . Vilma . . . VILMA!" They were as confident as she that she could win.

And win she did! She breezed to an easy victory in the 100-meter dash. The she won the 200-meter dash. And finally, she anchored the U.S. women's team to another first-place finish in the 400-meter relay. Three gold medals—she was the first woman in history ever to win three gold medals in track-and-field. I should add that each of the three races was won in world-record time.

—Denis Waitley, *Seeds of Greatness*

Thou Art My Victory

I prayed for help, I prayed for strength,
    I prayed for victory:
I prayed for patience and for love,
    For true humility
But as I prayed, my dying Christ
    By faith I seemed to see,
And as I gazed my glad heart cried,
    "All things are mine, thro' Thee!"

If He doth dwell within my heart,
    Why need I strength implore?
The Giver of all grace is mine,
    And shall I ask for more?
And need I pray for victory,
    When He who conquered death
Dwells in my very inmost soul,
    Nearer indeed than breath?

Oh help me, Lord, to realize
    That Thou are all in all;
That I am more than conqueror
    In great things and in small
No need have I but Thou hast met
    Upon the cruel tree.
Oh precious, dying, risen Lord,
Thou are my victory!

—Avis B. Christiansen, quoted in Charles R. Swindoll, *Victory*

SOMETIME AGO the Fighting Irish of Notre Dame playing on their own home court had the audacity to whip the Bruins of UCLA. Digger Phelps, the coach of that Notre Dame team, said, "The victory is sweet, but unfortunately in a short period of time we will have to go to Pauley Pavilion and battle them on their own court." And everybody in California shouted "Amen" when he made that statement. And sure enough, in a very short time, every sports fan in the area watched UCLA on their home court soundly defeat the Fighting Irish. You may win the battle, but there is always another one to fight another day.

VISION

A PREACHER saved up enough money to buy a few inexpensive acres of land. A little run-down, weather-beaten farmhouse sat on the acreage, a sad picture of years of neglect. The land had not been kept up either, so there were old tree stumps, rusted pieces of machinery, and all sorts of debris strewn here and there, not to mention a fence greatly in need of repair. The whole scene was a mess.

During his spare time and his vacations, the preacher rolled up his sleeves and got to work. He hauled off the junk, repaired the fence, pulled away the stumps, and replanted new trees. Then he refurbished the old house into a quaint cottage with a new roof, new windows, new stone walkway, new paint job, and finally a few colorful flower boxes. It took several years to accomplish all this, but finally, when the last job had been completed and he was washing up after applying a fresh coat of paint to the mailbox, his neighbor (who had watched all this from a distance) walked over and said, "Well, preacher—looks like you and the Lord have done a pretty fine job on your place here."

Wiping the sweat from his face, the minister replied, "Yeah, I suppose so, but you should have seen it when the Lord had it all to Himself."

—Ted Engstrom, *Pursuit of Excellence*

THE FOUR-WORD QUESTION must have made both men smile later on when they thought about it: "Do you see anything?" It was asked by an aide whose name has not found its way into the history books, but the one who was asked the question is known by many—Dr. Howard Carter, a well-known British archaeologist who at the time had his head poked into an ancient Egyptian tomb. For six uninterrupted years the man had been digging. There were trenches all around the area, endless trenches, tons of sand and rock that had been moved aside and made into mounds, big boulders, as well as smaller rocks. Mounds of worthless debris were all over the area and nothing for six years had been discovered until this most unusual history-making day in 1922.

You see, everyone else had dug into the Royal Valley and said by the time they finished combing the area there was nothing else to be discovered, nothing else to be found. Which made the question all the more interesting as Dr. Carter stared in disbelief into this ancient tomb, soon to discover in the minds of many archaeologists the most significant discoveries in the history of that particular discipline.

Peering into silent darkness, Howard Carter saw wooden animals, statues, chests, gilded chariots, carved cobras, unguent boxes, vases, daggers, jewels, a throne, a wooden figure of the goddess Sekhmet, and a hand-carved coffin of a teenaged king. In his own words, he saw "strange animals, statues, and gods— everywhere the glint of gold." It was, of course, the priceless tomb and treasures of King Tutankhamen, the world's most exciting archaeological discovery up to that time. More than three thousand objects in all, taking Carter the next ten years to remove, catalog, and restore. "Exquisite!" "Incredible!" "Elegant!" "Magnificent!" "Aah!" were all words and phrases used by Dr. Carter and his aide, who had earlier asked, "Do you see anything?"

—Charles R. Swindoll, *Come Before Winter*

ON THOSE FROSTY MORNINGS when I grab my camera and tripod, and head out into the meadow behind the house, I quickly forget about me. I stop thinking about what I'll do with the photographs, or about self-fulfillment, and lose myself in the sheer magic of rainbows in the grass. Letting go of self is an essential precondition to real seeing. When you let go of yourself, you abandon any preoccupations about the subject matter which might cramp you into photographing in a certain predetermined way. As long as you are worried about whether or not you will be able to make good pictures, you are unlikely to take the best photographs you can. When you let go, new conceptions arise from your direct experience of the subject matter, new ideas and feelings will guide you as you make pictures."

—Freeman Patterson, *Photography and the Art of Seeing*, cited in *Preaching*, November/December 1991

ON MAY 24, 1965, a thirteen-and-a-half-foot boat slipped quietly out of the marina at Falmouth, Massachusetts. Its destination? England. It would be the smallest craft ever to make the voyage. Its name? *Tinkerbelle*. Its pilot? Robert Manry, a copyeditor for the *Cleveland Plain Dealer*, who felt that ten years at the desk was enough boredom for a while. So he took a leave of absence to fulfill his secret dream.

Manry was afraid—not of the ocean, but of all those people who would try to talk him out of the trip. So he didn't share it with many, just some relatives, and especially his wife, Virginia, his greatest source of support.

The trip? Anything but pleasant. He spent harrowing nights of sleeplessness trying to cross shipping lanes without getting run down and sunk. Weeks at sea caused his food to become tasteless. Loneliness, that age-old monster of the deep, led to terrifying hallucinations. His rudder broke three times. Storms swept him overboard, and had it not been for the rope he had knotted around his waist, he would never have been able to pull himself back on board. Finally, after seventy-eight days alone at sea, he sailed into Falmouth, England.

During those nights at the tiller, he had fantasized about what he would do once he arrived. He expected simply to check into a hotel, eat dinner alone, then the next morning see if perhaps the Associated Press might be interested in his story. Was he in for a surprise! Word of his approach had spread far and wide. To his amazement, three hundred vessels, with horns blasting, escorted *Tinkerbelle* into port. And forty thousand people stood screaming and cheering him to shore.

Robert Manry, the copyeditor turned dreamer, became an overnight hero. His story has been told around the world. But Robert couldn't have done it alone. Standing on the dock was an even greater hero—Virginia. Refusing to be rigid and closed back when Robert's dream was taking shape, she encouraged him on, willing to take risk, allowing him the freedom to pursue his dream.

—Charles R. Swindoll, *The Quest for Character*

VISION IS ESSENTIAL for survival. It is spawned by faith, sustained by hope, sparked by imagination, and strengthened by enthusiasm. It is greater than sight, deeper than a dream, broader than an idea. Vision encompasses vast vistas outside the realm of the predictable, the safe, the expected. No wonder we perish without it!

—Charles R. Swindoll, *Make Your Dream Come True*

I HAVE A DREAM that one day on the red hills of Georgia the sons of former slaves and the sons of former slaveowners will be able to sit down together at the table of brotherhood.

I have a dream that my four little children will one day live in a nation where they will not be judged by the color of their skin, but by the content of their character.

When we let freedom ring, when we let it ring from every village and every hamlet, from every state and every city, we will be able to speed up that day when all of God's children, black men and white men, Jews and Gentiles, Protestants and Catholics, will be able to join hands and sing in the words of the old Negro spiritual, "Free at last! Free at last! Thank God Almighty, we are free at last!"

—Martin Luther King, August 28, 1963

Renascence

The world stands out on either side
No wider than the soul is wide;
Above the world is stretched the sky,—
No higher than the soul is high.
The heart can push the sea and land
Further away on either hand;
The soul can split the sky in two,
And let the face of God shine through.
But East and West will pinch the heart
That cannot keep them pushed apart;
And he whose soul is flat—the sky
Will cave in on him by and by.

—Edna St. Vincent Millay, quoted in Andrew Blackwood, *Preaching from Prophetic Books*

VISION IS LOOKING AT LIFE through the lens of God's eye.

Ww

WEALTH
(Also see *Charity, Giving, Money, Stewardship*)

TWO WOMEN met at a cocktail party after a separation of many years. After the initial delighted exchange of greetings, the first woman noticed that her friend was wearing an extraordinary diamond. She couldn't help commenting, "That's the most beautiful and enormous diamond I've ever seen!" "Yes, it's an unusual diamond," was the reply. "It's the Calahan Diamond. And it comes complete with the Calahan curse."

"What's the Calahan curse?"

"Mr. Calahan!" she said.

—Bruce Larson, *There's a Lot More to Health Than Not Being Sick*

WEALTH sometimes brings us to a fork in the road, a turning-point decision. Remember Lot and Abraham? H. C. Leupold reminds us "wealth is not incompatible with holiness of life." Don't think for a moment that all who are rich are carnal. But then again some do make bad decisions. As Leupold says of Lot, "The gradual degeneracy of a relatively good character begins at this point."

—H. C. Leupold, *Exposition on Genesis*

Yuppie Prayer
(Young Upwardly Progressive Professionals)

Now I lay me down to sleep.
I pray my Cuisinart to keep.
I pray my stocks are on the rise,
and that my analyst is wise,
that all the wine I sip is white
and that my hot tub's watertight,
that racquetball won't get too tough,

that all my sushi's fresh enough.
I pray my cordless phone still works,
that my career won't lose its perks,
my microwave won't radiate,
my condo won't depreciate.
I pray my health club doesn't close
and that my money market grows.
If I go broke before I wake,
I pray my Volvo they won't take.

DURING THE GREAT DEPRESSION, poverty swept across America like a whirling tornado, ripping up dreams and scattering hopes to the wind. One such poverty twister hit a small part of Texas where a man named Yates ran a sheep ranch. Struggling even to keep food on the table, Yates and his wife did all they could to survive. Finally, they had to accept a government subsidy or lose their home and land to the creditors.

One day, in the midst of this bleakness, a geologic crew from a large oil company came knocking. With Yates's permission, they wanted to drill a wildcat well on his property, promising him a large portion of the profits if they struck oil. "What could I lose?" thought Yates, and he signed all the papers.

The oil crew immediately set up the machinery and began drilling. Five hundred feet down, they came up dry. Eight hundred feet, still dry. One thousand feet they sunk the shaft, and no oil. Finally, at a little over eleven hundred feet, they tapped into one of the richest oil reserves in Texas. The hole sprayed its black wealth high into the air, and soon the well was pumping eighty thousand barrels of oil a day.

Overnight, Yates and his family became millionaires. His property, once called Yates's Field, became known as Yates's Pool. And soon hundreds of oil wells dotted the land where once only sheep grazed.

—Bill Bright, *How You Can Be Filled with the Holy Spirit*

PICTURE YOURSELF as an impoverished prospector, tirelessly searching for fortune on your small farm in South Africa during the 1930s. After a heavy storm, you walk up and down your land to see if the rain washed up anything. Eventually, you come across an unusual stone the size of a hen's egg. As you wipe away the mud from its surface, it begins to look like a diamond in the rough. Trembling with excitement, you rush home to show the stone to your family. A few days later you sell the "rock"—a 726-carat diamond—for $315,000. Sound incredible? Yes, but it actually happened to a poor prospector named Jacobus Jonker.

—Victor Argenzio, *Diamonds Eternal*

HERE'S ONE PHILOSOPHY: "Get all you can; can all you get; then sit on the can."

A WOMAN in West Palm Beach, Florida, died alone at the age of 71. The coroner's report was tragic. "Cause of death: *Malnutrition.*" The dear old lady wasted away to 50 pounds. Investigators who found her said the place where she lived was a veritable pigpen, the biggest mess you can imagine. One seasoned inspector declared he'd never seen a residence in greater disarray.

The woman had begged food at her neighbors' back doors and gotten what clothes she had from the Salvation Army. From all outward appearances she was a penniless recluse, a pitiful and forgotten widow. But such was not the case.

Amid the jumble of her unclean, disheveled belongings, two keys were found which led the officials to safe-deposit boxes at two different local banks. What they found was absolutely unbelievable.

The first contained over seven hundred AT&T stock certificates, plus hundreds of other valuable certificates, bonds, and solid financial securities, not to mention a stack of cash amounting to nearly $200,000. The second box had no certificates, only more currency—lots of it—$600,000 to be exact. Adding the net worth of both boxes, they found that the woman had in her possession well over A MILLION DOLLARS. Charles Osgood, reporting on CBS radio, announced that the estate would probably fall into the hands of a distant niece and nephew, neither of whom dreamed she had a thin dime to her name. She was, however, a millionaire who died a stark victim of starvation in a humble hovel many miles away.

I conducted a funeral several years ago for a man who died without family or friends. All he had was a fox terrier . . . to whom he left his entire estate: around $76,000.

—Charles R. Swindoll, *Improving Your Serve*

WISDOM
(Also see *Education, Knowledge*)

WE TRY TO HIDE our lack of wisdom. Like the man who bought a yacht. His wife was nervous because he had no experience in sailing. But he knew he could handle it and so for weeks he practiced in the harbor before taking it out to sea. Finally, he talked his nervous wife into going on the yacht with him. Gingerly she stepped aboard. Out into the harbor they headed and he tried to put her at ease. He said, "Honey, look, I practiced enough in this harbor to know where every rock, every reef, every sand bar is." At that very moment a huge hidden rock beneath the surface made a large crunching sound from stem to stern. "There," he said with a sheepish grin, "is one of them going by now."

Unless I learn to ask no help
    From any other soul but Him,
To seek no strength in waving reeds
    Nor shade beneath the straggling pine,
Unless I learn to look at grief,
    Unshrinking from her tear-blind eyes,
And take from pleasure fearlessly
    Whatever gifts will make me wise,
Unless I learn these things on earth,
    Why was I ever given birth?

Wisdom

When I have ceased to break my wings
    against the faultiness of things;
And learned that compromises wait
    behind each hardly opened gate;
When I can look life in the eyes,
    grown calm and very coldly wise;
Life will have given me the truth
    and taken in exchange my youth.

—Sara Teasdale, quoted in Charles R. Swindoll, *Living on the Ragged Edge*

MAY NOT THE INADEQUACY of much of our spiritual experience be traced back to our habit of skipping through the corridors of the Kingdom like children through the marketplace, chattering about everything, but pausing to learn the true value of nothing?

—A. W. Tozer, *The Divine Conquest*

WISDOM IS THE ABILITY to see with discernment, to view life as God perceives it.

Understanding is the skill to respond with insight.

Knowledge is the rare trait of learning with perception—discovering and growing.

—Charles R. Swindoll, *The Strong Family*

WISDOM IS the God-given ability to see life with rare objectivity and to handle life with rare stability.

—Charles R. Swindoll, *Living on the Ragged Edge*

WHAT COMES FROM THE LORD because it is impossible for humans to manufacture it? Wisdom. What comes from humans because it is impossible for the Lord to experience it? Worry. What is it that brings wisdom and dispels worry? Worship.

—Charles R. Swindoll, *The Quest for Character*

ONCE THERE WAS AN OLD MAN who lived in a tiny village. Although poor, he was envied by all, for he owned a beautiful white horse. Even the king coveted his treasure. A horse like this had never been seen before—such was its splendor, its majesty, its strength.

People offered fabulous prices for the steed, but the old man always refused. "This horse is not a horse to me," he would tell them. "It is a person. How could you sell a person? He is a friend, not a possession. How could you sell a friend?" The man was poor and the temptation was great. But he never sold the horse.

One morning he found that the horse was not in the stable. All the village came to see him. "You old fool," they scoffed, "we told you that someone would steal your horse. We warned you that you would be robbed. You are so poor. How could you ever hope to protect such a valuable animal? It would have been better to have sold him. You could have gotten whatever price you wanted. No amount would have been too high. Now the horse is gone, and you've been cursed with misfortune."

The old man responded, "Don't speak too quickly. Say only that the horse is not in the stable. That is all we know; the rest is judgment. If I've been cursed or not, how can you know? How can you judge?"

The people contested, "Don't make us out to be fools! We may not be philosophers, but great philosophy is not needed. The simple fact that your horse is gone is a curse."

The old man spoke again. "All I know is that the stable is empty, and the horse is gone. The rest I don't know. Whether it be a curse or a blessing, I can't say. All we can see is a fragment. Who can say what will come next?"

The people of the village laughed. They thought that the man was crazy. They had always thought he was a fool; if he wasn't he would have sold the horse and lived off the money. But instead, he was a poor woodcutter, an old man still cutting firewood and dragging it out of the forest and selling it. He lived hand to mouth in the misery of poverty. Now he had proven that he was, indeed, a fool.

After fifteen days, the horse returned. He hadn't been stolen; he had run away into the forest. Not only had he returned, he had brought a dozen wild horses with him. Once again the village people gathered around the woodcutter and spoke. "Old man, you were right and we were wrong. What we thought was a curse was a blessing. Please forgive us."

The man responded, "Once again, you go too far. Say only that the horse is back. State only that a dozen horses returned with him, but don't judge. How do you know if this is a blessing or not? You see only a fragment. Unless you know the whole story, how can you judge? You read only one page of a book. Can you judge the whole book? You read only one word of a phrase. Can you understand the entire phrase?

"Life is so vast, yet you judge all of life with one page or one word. All you have is a fragment! Don't say this is a blessing. No one knows. I am content with what I know. I am not perturbed by what I don't."

"Maybe the old man is right," they said to one another. So they said little. But down deep, they knew he was wrong. They knew it was a blessing. Twelve wild horses had returned with one horse. With a little bit of work, the animals could be broken and trained and sold for much money.

The old man had a son, an only son. The young man began to break the wild horses. After a few days, he fell from one of the horses and broke both legs. Once again the villagers gathered around the old man and cast their judgments.

"You were right," they said. "You proved you were right. The dozen horses were not a blessing. They were a curse. You only son has broken his legs, and now in your old age you have no one to help you. Now you are poorer than ever."

The old man spoke again. "You people are obsessed with judging. Don't go so far. Say only that my son broke his legs. Who knows if it is a blessing or a curse? No one knows. We only have a fragment. Life comes in fragments."

It so happened that a few weeks later the country engaged in war against a neighboring country. All the young men of the village were required to join the army. Only the son of the old man was excluded, because he was injured. Once again the people gathered around the old man, crying and screaming because their sons had been taken. There was little chance that they would return. The enemy was strong, and the war would be a losing struggle. They would never see their sons again.

"You were right, old man," they wept. "God knows you were right. This proves it. Your son's accident was a blessing. His legs may be broken, but at least he is with you. Our sons are gone forever."

The old man spoke again. "It is impossible to talk with you. You always draw conclusions. No one knows. Say only this: Your sons had to go to war, and mine did not. No one knows if it is a blessing or a curse. No one is wise enough to know. Only God knows."

—Max Lucado, "The Woodcutter's Wisdom," In the Eye of the Storm

WITNESSING
(Also see *Evangelism*)

I DECIDED ONE DAY I would present the gospel to a doctor friend as we had lunch together. I drew a simple little chart that had on one side of the page a circle—God—and wrote under it *holy*. Then on the other side of the page I drew a circle representing the world—mankind—and under it the word *unholy*. And then I built a bridge between God and mankind with a cross and wrote the name of Christ across the horizontal bar of the cross. I was so careful to keep it simple.

After lunch I slid it across the table at that restaurant. My heart was just in my throat. I thought, He's gonna believe. He's gonna love this! He looked at that, studied it for a few seconds, and he smiled and he said, "In a thousand years I could never believe that." Couldn't have been more clear or simple, but he couldn't have been further from interest in that truth. And I said, "Have you ever seen that before?" He said, "No. Never in my life. Never. Never seen it and I'm not interested."

JACK COOPER in Dallas is an ophthalmologist. Instead of the trite "Now is the time for all good men to come to the aid of their country" flip chart standard for eye examinations, he made one that says, "God loves you and has a wonderful plan for your life."

He would do his cataract surgery, giving his patients eyesight again. Then when they would come in for a checkup, he would say, "Let's see how you're doing." He would have them read, "God loves you and has a wonderful plan for your life." "Wow! I can read! 'God loves me and has a wonderful plan for my . . . What does this mean?"

—Howard G. Hendricks, *Say It with Love*

SO LIVE that you wouldn't be ashamed to sell the family parrot to the town gossip.

—Will Rogers

THE PASTOR, dressed in a comfortable pair of old blue jeans, boarded a plane to return home. He settled into the last unoccupied seat next to a well-dressed businessman with a *Wall Street Journal* tucked under his arm. The minister, a little embarrassed over his casual attire, decided he'd look straight ahead and, for sure, stay out of any in-depth conversation. But the plan didn't work. The man greeted him, so, to be polite, the pastor asked about the man's work. Here's what happened:

"I'm in the figure salon business. We can change a woman's self-concept by changing her body. It's really a very profound, powerful thing."

His pride spoke between the lines.

"You look my age," I said. "Have you been at this long?"

"I just graduated from the University of Michigan's School of Business Administration. They've given me so much responsibility already, and I feel very honored. In fact, I hope to eventually manage the western part of the operation."

"So you're a national organization?" I asked, becoming impressed despite myself.

"Oh, yes. We are the fastest growing company of our kind in the nation. It's really good to be a part of an organization like that, don't you think?"

I nodded approvingly and thought, "Impressive. Proud of his work and accomplishments. Why can't Christians be proud like that? Why are we so often apologetic about our faith and our church?"

Looking at my clothing, he asked the inevitable question, "And what do you do?"

"It's interesting that we have similar business interests," I said. "You are in the body-changing business; I'm in the personality-changing business. We apply 'basic theocratic principles to accomplish indigenous personality modification.'"

He was hooked, but I knew he would never admit it. (Pride is powerful.)

"You know, I've heard about that," he replied, hesitantly. "But do you have an office here in the city?"

"Oh, we have many offices. We have offices up and down the state. In fact, we're national: we have at least one office in every state of the union, including Alaska and Hawaii."

He had this puzzled look on his face. He was searching his mind to identify this huge company he must have read or heard about, perhaps in his *Wall Street Journal.*

"As a matter of fact, we've gone international. And Management has a plan to put at least one office in every country of the world by the end of this business era."

I paused.

"Do you have that in your business?" I asked.

"Well, no. Not yet," he answered. "But you mentioned management. How do they make it work?"

"It's a family concern. There's a Father and a Son, and they run everything."

"It must take a lot of capital," he asked, skeptically.

"You mean money?" I asked. "Yes, I suppose so. No one knows just how much it takes, but we never worry because there's never a shortage. The Boss always seems to have enough. He's a very creative guy. And the money is, well, just there. In fact those of us in the Organization have a saying about our Boss, 'He owns the cattle on a thousand hills.'"

"Oh, he's into ranching too?" asked my captive friend.

"No, it's just a saying we use to indicate his wealth."

My friend sat back in his seat, musing over our conversation. "What about with you?" he asked.

"The employees? They're something to see," I said. "They have a 'Spirit' that pervades the organization. It works like this: the Father and Son love each other so much that their love filters down through the organization so that we all find ourselves loving one another too. I know this sounds old-fashioned in a world like ours, but I know people in the organization who are willing to die for me. Do you have that in your business?" I was almost shouting now. People were starting to shift noticeably in their seats.

"Not yet," he said. Quickly changing strategies, he asked, "But do you have good benefits?"

"They're substantial," I countered, with a gleam. "I have complete life insurance, fire insurance—all the basics. You might not believe this, but it's true: I have holdings in a mansion that's being built for me right now for my retirement. Do you have that in your business?"

"Not yet," he answered, wistfully. The light was dawning.

"You know, one thing bothers me about all you're saying. I've read the journals, and if your business is all you say it is, why haven't I heard about it before now?"

"That's a good question,"I said. "After all, we have a 2,000-year-old tradition."

"Wait a minute!" he said.

"You're right," I interrupted. "I'm talking about the church."

"I knew it. You know, I'm Jewish."

"Want to sign up?" I asked.

—Jeffrey Cotter, *Eternity* magazine, March 1981

AS AMBASSADORS for Christ, we need to have an ethical standard which guides our appeal, regardless of how people respond.

I believe there is such a standard. And, simply stated, it is this: Any persuasive effort which restricts another's freedom to choose for or against Jesus Christ is wrong.

—Em Griffin, *The Mind Changers*

IN A CARTOON a crusader is riding a horse and carrying a big shield with a cross on it. He is thrusting a spear down on the throat of this guy on the ground who's saying, "Tell me more about this Christianity. I'm terribly interested."

—Em Griffin, *The Mind Changers*

I COULD FILL A BOOK with amazing stories of stuff people have done and said shortly after they learned I was in the ministry. One fella sitting next to me on a plane during the mealtime nervously changed his request from a Bloody Mary to a ginger ale, whispering to me in a sweat that he really meant to order that in the first place. I told him not to worry, I didn't mind at all what he drank, which he thought was a hint, and in a panic he ordered *me* a Bloody Mary. When I declined, he decided to change seats. In his hurry, he spilled his meal all over me. Sometimes it is easier to just tell folks I'm an author. But then they want to know what kind of books I write, and that leads to another Bloody Mary-ginger ale episode.

I will never forget the time I was walking down a long corridor, preparing to make a hospital call. As I approached the parishioner's room, her husband was just leaving. On his way out the door he lit up a cigarette, then glanced down the hall and suddenly recognized me from a distance. I smiled and waved. He nervously waved back and was absolutely at a loss to know how to hide the cigarette from me. Still holding the lighted cigarette, he slid his hand into his pants pocket! I decided to act as though I hadn't seen it and engaged him in a lengthy conversation. It became hilarious. The more we talked the shorter the cigarette got in his hand and the more he looked like a chimney. There was smoke swirling out of his pants pocket and curling up behind his coat collar. Unable to restrain myself any longer, I asked him why he didn't go ahead and finish his cigarette. Would you believe it? He denied even having a cigarette. Within seconds he dashed to the elevator and fled, which is probably good. Had we talked much longer, the poor man would have become a living sacrifice.

—Charles R. Swindoll, *The Bride*

DR. BORIS KORNFELD was a Jew who lived in Russia. And for some reason, (maybe a slip of the tongue where he referred to Stalin as finite), he was dumped in the Gulag and was to live there the rest of his life.

Since he was a medical doctor, he was to keep practicing medicine and keep the slaves alive so they could die with all the right things said on their records. Dr. Kornfeld was to rewrite the records to say, "This person is healthy," whether he was or not. The slave was then put back into the slave block and expected to do the work. If slaves died out there of starvation, that was fine—but they were not to die in the hospital.

Slowly, the physician began to see through all of his misapplied politics and philosophy of life. He finally decided there must be another way. And through the influence of a fellow inmate, he heard of Jesus Christ and ultimately came to know the Messiah—Dr. Boris Kornfeld personally received Jesus Christ into his life.

The transformation was slow but steady. On one occasion he worked on the very guard who had beaten slaves. He had a chance to tie an artery loosely so the man could bleed to death and no one would know it. But now that Christ lived in his life and he found himself unable to kill. He even mumbled to himself on occasions, "Forgive us our trespasses as we forgive those who trespass against us."

Strange words to come from the lips of a Jew in a Russian prison camp! I'm sure he didn't realize what a model he was and I'm sure he didn't think very much about the cycle. But on one occasion he was working with another inmate who had cancer of the intestines. The man looked like he wouldn't live.

Boris Kornfeld was so concerned for that man's faith that he leaned over and spoke quietly to him as the patient drifted in and out of the anesthesia. He told the man about Christ and explained God's love which was demonstrated in the Savior's death and resurrection. When the man would come to, he would tell him more. At one point, the patient awoke, and in his groggy state, he heard a noise down the hall. His surgeon, Dr. Kornfeld, was being brutally murdered.

When the patient finally did regain consciousness, he realized what it meant for Dr. Kornfeld to have given his life for a cause, and the patient himself personally received Christ as well.

Because Boris Kornfeld had a vision of the cycle, he used hs influence to shape a life that did not die, but lived on to challenge and exhort the thinking of prosperous and materialistic western America. His patient's name: Aleksandr Solzhenitsyn.

—Charles Colson, *Loving God*

THOMAS AQUINAS, who knew a great deal about education and a bit about motivation, once said that when you want to convert a person to your view, you go over to where he is standing, take him by the hand, and guide him. You don't stand across the room and shout at him. You don't order him to come over where you are. You start where he is and work from that position. He said that's the only way to get people to budge.

—Alan Loy McGinnis, *Bringing Out the Best in People*

SOMETIME AGO I had an evening with Dick and Mary Chase. It was delightful. I'd missed them since their days at Biola. And I met a new member of their family. Her name is Mindy. She has beautiful black, curly hair and a little stubby tail. Now Mindy listens to Christian radio all day long. And when I walked in and I looked over there, they said, "Meet Mindy." And I said, "Hi, Mindy." You know, she heard my voice, she remembered "Insight for Living." That's the voice. And she just began to shake all over. I roughed up her hair and we were having a great time.

Mary has a terrific sense of humor. She said, "You know, this dog really, really knows the gospel. She hears Christian radio all day long. There are conversations in this room between Dick and the faculty members, and they get into serious subjects, and Mindy just sits there, just listens. There are songs and there are prayers. And she hears us talking with students on into the wee hours of the morning. Mindy has been exposed to the gospel for all of her life. But she's never led one person to the Savior. And she never will, even if she wanted to, 'cause she isn't equipped. That's our job. We gotta do it."

—Charles R. Swindoll, *Growing Deep in the Christian Life*

AIM AT HEAVEN you will get earth "thrown in": aim at earth and you get neither.

—C.S. Lewis, *Christian Behavior*

WORK
(See *Jobs*)

WORKAHOLICS

THE ONLY MAN who got all of his work done by Friday was Robinson Crusoe.

—Mrs. M. M. Reeve, quoted in Lloyd Cory, *Quote Unquote*

MOST MIDDLE-CLASS AMERICANS tend to worship their work, to work at their play, to play at their worship. As a result, their meanings and values are distorted. Their relationships disintegrate faster than they can keep them in repair, and their lifestyles resemble a cast of characters in search of a plot.

—Gordon Dahl, quoted in *Leadership* magazine, Fall 1982

> Pussy cat, pussy cat, where have you been?
> I've been to London to look at the queen.
> Pussy cat, pussy cat, what did you there?
> I frightened a little mouse under her chair.

Stupid cat. She had the chance of a lifetime. All of London stretched out before her. Westminster Abbey. The British Museum. Ten Downing Street. Trafalgar Square. The House of Parliament. The Marble Arch in Hyde Park. She could've heard the London Philharmonic or scrambled up an old wooden lamp post to watch the changing of the guard. I doubt that she even cared she was within walking distance of St. Paul's Cathedral. She probably didn't even realize it was the historic Thames rushing by beneath that big rusty bridge she scampered across chasing more mice.

After all, she didn't even scope out the queen as Her Majesty stood before her. Not this cat. She is such a mouseaholic, she can't stop the same old grind even when she's in London. What a bore!

There is an old Greek motto that says:

> YOU WILL BREAK THE BOW
> IF YOU KEEP IT ALWAYS BENT.

Which, being translated loosely from the original means, "There's more to being a cat than tracking mice." Or, "There's more to life than hard work."

—Charles R. Swindoll, *Growing Strong in the Seasons of Life*

POSSIBLY THE GREATEST MALAISE in our country is our neurotic compulsion to work.

—William MacNamara

WORLD

IT'S A WONDERFUL WORLD. It may destroy itself, but you'll be able to watch it on TV.

—Bob Hope

I SAW A CARTOON that said, "The rat race is over—the rats won."

EVER WONDER what archaeologists will dig up from our civilization? McDonald's signs—Michael Jackson's "Thriller" albums—football goals—nuclear subs—religious artifacts from the People's Temple and books like *Give Me That Prime Time Religion*. Pornography, alcohol, drugs, music, films—all will show what a crazy generation we are.

PHILOSOPHERS HAVE ONLY interpreted the world differently. The point is to change it.

—Karl Marx

I CAN IMAGINE a cartoon that might appear in some business magazine, showing a tired businessman late one evening—tie pulled loose after a busy day—watching a business report. Only this time things are much more realistic. Imagine his startled look as he hears:

Closing averages in the human scene were mixed today:
- Brotherly Love—down a couple of points.
- Self-interest—up a half.

- Vanity showed no movement.
- Guarded Optimism—slipped a point in sluggish trading.
- Over all, nothing really changed.

—Charles R. Swindoll, *Growing Deep in the Christian Life*

Nurses' Duties in 1887

In addition to caring for your fifty patients, each nurse will follow these regulations:

1. Daily sweep and mop the floors of your ward, dust the patient's furniture and window sills.
2. Maintain an even temperature in your ward by bringing in a scuttle of coal for the day's business.
3. Light is important to observe the patient's condition. Therefore, each day fill kerosene lamps, clean chimneys, and trim wicks. Wash the windows once a week.
4. The nurse's notes are important to aiding the physician's work. Make your pens carefully; you may whittle nibs to your individual taste.
5. Each nurse on day duty will report every day at 7 A.M. and leave at 8 P.M., except on the Sabbath, on which day they will be off from 12 noon to 2 P.M.
6. Graduate nurses in good standing with the director of nurses will be given an evening off each week for courting purposes or two evenings a week if you go regularly to church.
7. Each nurse should lay aside from each payday a goodly sum of her earnings for her benefits during her declining years so that she will not become a burden. For example, if you earn $30 a month, you should set aside $15.
8. Any nurse who smokes, uses liquor in any form, gets her hair done at a beauty shop, or frequents dance halls will give the director of nurses good reason to suspect her worth, intentions, and integrity.
9. The nurse who performs her labors and serves her patients and doctors faithfully and without fault for a period of five years will be given an increase by the hospital administration of five cents a day, providing there are no hospital debts that are outstanding.

—Charles R. Swindoll, *The Quest for Character*

ONE HISTORIAN SAYS that the average age of the world's great civilizations is a duration of about two hundred years each. Almost without exception, each civilization passed through the same sequence. From bondage to spiritual faith, from spiritual faith to great courage, from great courage to liberty, from liberty to abundance, from abundance to leisure, from leisure to selfishness, from self-ishness to complacency, from complacency to apathy, from apathy to depen-dence, from dependence to weakness, from weakness back to bondage. Makes sense, doesn't it? Starts and stops at bondage. Why? Because it is rotating on the axis of depravity.

—Lloyd Cory, *Quotable Quotes*

TWO THOUSAND YEARS AGO, it's estimated that Jesus spoke to perhaps twenty thousand to thirty thousand people in His entire lifetime. Today, if He were liv-ing, in one address He could speak to over one billion, thanks to the satellite, in one moment of time.

—Ben Armstrong, *The Electric Church*

I SMILE when I read this from the newspaper. "The world is too big for us. Too much going on, too many crimes, too much violence. Try as you will you get behind in the race. It's an incessant strain to keep pace. You still lose ground. Science empties its discoveries on you so fast you stagger beneath them in hopeless bewilderment. The political world is news seen so rapidly you're out of breath trying to keep pace with who's in and who's out. Everything is high pressure. Human nature can't endure it much more!"

Now it wasn't that that made me smile. It was that it appeared June 16, 1833—150 or more years ago. That was the "good old days." And you don't have any idea, nor did I, what the *Boston Globe* had as its headlines November 13, 1857—three words: "ENERGY CRISIS LOOMS." That's *1857*. The subheading said: "World May Go Dark since Whale Blubber So Scarce!"

You're smiling, aren't you? You can't help but smile, because everything has to do with perspective. For some, the "good old days" means what was simple and uncomplicated and beautiful and free of the horrors of our present times. Or was there ever a time like that?

My "good old days" take me back to a world war where there were little markers on windows up and down the little street where I lived in Houston. And grieving parents peeled those little markers off when their son died in that war.

The "good old days" would take you back to the time when, horses died in the streets of New York because of cholera. The "good old days" were times in my father's era when cars couldn't be started from inside. You had to go out-side and crank them. And you had to walk in rainy days on boggy streets because back then there weren't hard surfaces and beautiful freeways and road-ways.

One news commentator said it very well. It was Paul Harvey. "Had the first product using electricity been the electric chair, we would all be afraid to plug in our toasters in the morning!" It's how you look at it, isn't it?

—Denis Waitley, *Seeds of Greatness*

WORRY
(Also see *Anxiety, Fear, Stress*)

I HAVE NEVER SEEN a gravestone that reads, "He died of worry." But some of them ought to read that way. How many illnesses are directly connected with our worries, our anxieties, trying to take the responsibility that was designed for God to handle. If you can't handle it, why are you trying to handle it? If you can't change it, why are you worrying about it? But we do, don't we?

In fact, I have a friend who worries when she doesn't have something to worry about. She has to have that security. I think she keeps a mental list of those reserved areas, then when she runs out of the conscious ones she draws on the unconscious. And she just brings them on, just like ammunition in a machine gun, just to fire them into her life.

CORRIE TEN BOOM, for the last two years of her life, spent it in our congregation in Fullerton, California. It was a wonderful experience to have this godly woman in our midst during that extended period of time as we literally watched her die. She said on one occasion, "Worry does not empty tomorrow of sorrows; it empties today of strength."

A WOMAN WORRIED for forty years that she would die of cancer. She finally died of pneumonia at age seventy. She wasted thirty-three years worrying about the wrong thing.

—John Haggai, *How to Win over Worry*

WHOEVER ISN'T SCHIZOPHRENIC these days isn't thinking clearly.

—*LIFE* magazine, January 1981

WORSHIP

(Also see *Church*)

CHRISTIANS CAN BE GROUPED into two categories—marbles and grapes. Marbles are "single units that don't affect each other except in collision." Grapes, on the other hand, mingle juices: each one is a "part of the fragrance" of the church body.

The early Christians didn't bounce around like loose marbles, ricocheting in all directions. Picture them as a cluster of ripe grapes, squeezed together by persecution, bleeding and mingling into one another.

Fellowship and worship, then, is genuine Christianity freely shared among God's family members. It's sad to think of how many Christians today are missing that kind of closeness. Sermons and songs, while uplifting and necessary, provide only part of a vital church encounter. We need involvement with others too. If we roll in and out of church each week without acquiring a few grape juice stains, we really haven't tasted the sweet wine of fellowship.

—Anne Ortlund, *Up with Worship*

WHAT, THEN, IS THE ESSENCE OF WORSHIP? It is the celebration of God! When we worship God, we celebrate Him: We extol Him, we sound His praises, we boast in Him.

Worship is not the casual chatter that occasionally drowns out the organ prelude; we celebrate God when we allow the prelude to attune our hearts to the glory of God by the means of the music.

Worship is not the mumbling of prayers or the mouthing of hymns with little thought and less heart; we celebrate God when we join together earnestly in prayer and intensely in song.

Worship is not self-aggrandizing words or boring clichés when one is asked to give a testimony; we celebrate God when all of the parts of the service fit together and work to a common end.

Worship is not grudging gifts or compulsory service; we celebrate God when we give to Him hilariously and serve Him with integrity.

Worship is not haphazard music done poorly, not even great music done merely as a performance; we celebrate God when we enjoy and participate in music to His glory.

Worship is not a distracted endurance of the sermon; we celebrate God as we hear His Word gladly and seek to be conformed by it more and more to the image of our Savior.

Worship is not the hurried motions of a "tacked-on" Lord's Table; we celebrate God preeminently when we fellowship gratefully at the ceremonial meal that speaks so centrally of our faith in Christ Who died for us, Who rose again on our behalf, and Who is to return for our good.

As a thoughtful gift is a celebration of a birthday, as a special evening out is a celebration of an anniversary, as a warm eulogy is a celebration of a life, as a sexual embrace is a celebration of a marriage—so a worship service is a celebration of God.

—Ronald Allen, *Worship: Rediscovering the Missing Jewel*

MARY BROKE HER VASE.

Broke it?! How shocking. How controversial. Was everybody doing it? Was it a vase-breaking party? No, she did it all by herself. What happened then? The obvious: all the contents were forever released. She could never hug her precious nard to herself again. . . .

The need for Christians everywhere (nobody is exempt) is to be broken. The vase has to be smashed! Christians have to let the life out! It will fill the room with sweetness. And the congregation will all be broken shards, mingling together for the first time. . . .

If you know one another as broken people, you're ready to get on with a church service.

—Anne Ortlund, *Up with Worship*

CONSIDER THIS when it comes to worship:
- Draw near and listen well, because God is communicating.
- Be quiet and stay calm, because God hears the inaudible and sees the invisible.
- Make a commitment and keep it, because God doesn't forget.
- Don't decide now and deny later, because God doesn't ignore decisions.

WHEN I WAS OVERSEAS, I was working with a man who was under great stress and great pressure. He was a maverick sort of a missionary. He didn't fit the pattern or the mold of what you think of as a missionary. His ministry was in great part to the soldiers, who happened to be on the island of Okinawa by the thousands—in fact, it might be safe to say tens of thousands.

I went to his home one evening to visit with him, and his wife said he wasn't there but was probably down at the office. The office was downtown in a little alley area off of the streets of Naha. It was a rainy night. And I decided that I would get on the bus and travel down to be with Bob. She'd mentioned his stress and pressure, so I expected to find the man folded up in despondency, discouragement, and depression, and just ready to finish it off.

I got off that little bus and I walked down the alley about a block and a half and I turned right, down a little smaller alley, to a little hut with a tatami mat inside. As I got away from the street noise, I heard singing, "Come, Thou fount of every blessing, / Tune my heart to sing Thy grace." And then that next stanza, "Prone to wander—Lord, I feel it, / Prone to leave the God I love."

Quietly I eavesdropped on his private praise service. As I stood in the rain and looked through the walls of that little cheap hut, I saw a man on his knees with his hands toward heaven giving God praise, with his Bible on one side and an InterVarsity Christian hymnal on the other side, his little spiral notebook, worn from use. And I saw him turn from page to page, where he would read it to God, then he would find a hymn and he would sing it to God.

And the remarkable thing is that that pressure that he was under did not leave for perhaps another two weeks, it seems. But that praise service alone before God absolutely revolutionized his life.

WRITING

WE CHRISTIAN AUTHORS must confess to having bored plenty of people. So far the evangelical reading public has been tolerant, buying millions of books of uneven quality each year. But a saturation point is inevitable. If Christian writing is not only to maintain interest in the forgiving Christian audience, but also to arouse interest in the skeptical world beyond the Christian subculture, then it must grow up.

If we need models of how to do it well, we need only look as far as the Bible. Only ten percent of the Bible's material, the epistles, is presented in a thought-organized format. The rest contains rollicking love stories, drama, history, poetry, and parables. There, humanity is presented as realistically as in any literature.

Why else do the paired books of Samuel, Kings, and Chronicles exist, if not to give a detailed context to the environment in which angry prophets were told to deliver their messages? Can we imagine a more skillful weaving of nature and supernature than the great nature psalms, the theological high drama of Job, and the homespun parables of Jesus? What literary characters demonstrate a more subtle mixture of good and evil than David or Jeremiah or Jacob? And, from the despair of Ecclesiastes to the conversion narratives of Acts, is any wavelength on the spectrum of faith and doubt left unexpressed on the Bible's pages?

C. S. Lewis once likened his role as a Christian writer to an adjective humbly striving to point others to the Noun of truth. For people to believe that Noun, we Christian writers must improve our adjectives.

—Philip Yancey, "The Pitfalls of Christian Writing," *Open Windows*

ALL ORIGINALITY AND NO PLAGIARISM makes for dull preaching.

—Charles H. Spurgeon

I THINK ALL ORIGINALITY and no quoting of other sources makes for dull reading.

ZEAL

JOHN KNOX is one of my favorites—thirty-two years younger than Martin Luther, but every bit as zealous. A history book said, "He was a stern man for a stern age in the midst of a violent people." Luther is described by some as the thunderclap of the Reformation. If so, then John Knox was the lightning bolt. Queen Mary once said, "I fear his pulpit more than the armies of England put together." John Knox hit the floor running, three-fourths gristle and the rest bone. The man was an unbelievable giant. He took the message to Scotland and they accepted it freely, quickly. One wag said, "Why, of course the Scots were ready to receive it. It was free, wasn't it?"

—Herbert Lockyer, *All the Prayers of the Bible*

WHAT WILL YOU BE LIKE as a Christian ten years from now? Many will be walking with Christ and serving Him in various capacities around the world, but for others there will be a tragedy because ten years from now they will have lost their burning zeal and love for Christ. Not necessarily because they wanted to or because they set their heart in rebellion against God's will, but because they set their life by the world's agenda. Then Christ and His Great Commission gradually dims.

—Billy Graham, The Urbana Conference, 1984

RICHARD BAXTER, Reformed pastor of the seventeenth cetury, said, "O sirs, how plainly, how closely, how earnestly should we deliver a message of such moment as ours, when everlasting life or everlasting death of our fellow-men is involved in it! . . . There is nothing more unsuitable to such a business, than to be slight and dull. What! speak coldly for God, and for men's salvation? Can we believe that our people must be converted or condemned, and yet speak in a drowsy tone? In the name of God, brethren, labour to awaken your own hearts, before you go to the pulpit, that you may be fit to awaken the hearts of sinners. . . . Oh, speak not one cold or careless word about so great a business as heaven or hell. Whatever you do, let the people see that you are in good earnest. . . . A sermon full of mere words, how neatly soever it be composed, while it wants the light of evidence, and the life of zeal, is but an image or a well-dressed carcass."

—*Christianity Today*, February 20, 1992

w. e. sangster of Westminster Central Hall was once a member of a group responsible for interviewing applicants for the Methodist ministry. A rather nervous young man presented himself before the group. The candidate said he felt he ought to explain that he was rather shy and was not the sort of person who would ever set the Thames River on fire, that is, create much of a stir in the city.

"My dear young brother," responded Sangster with insightful wit and wisdom, "I'm not interested to know if you can set the Thames on fire. What I want to know is this: If I picked you up by the scruff of your neck and dropped you into the Thames, would it sizzle?"

Acknowledgments

Dear Lord by Bill Adler. Reprinted by permission of Thomas Nelson Publishers. ©1982.

Secrets to Inner Beauty: Transforming Life through Love by Joe Aldrich. Reprinted by permission of Vision House. ©1977.

Light on the Gospels by Abel Ahlquist. Reprinted by permission of The United Lutheran Publication House. ©1929.

The Battle for Your Faith by Willard M. Aldrich. Published by Multnomah Press. ©1975 by Willard M. Aldrich.

Joyful Living in the Fourth Dimension by Charles L. Allen. Reprinted by permission of Fleming H. Revell, a division of Baker Book House Company. ©1983.

You Are Never Alone by Charles L. Allen. Reprinted by permission of Fleming H. Revell, a division of Baker Book House Company. ©1978.

The Secret of Abundant Living by Charles L. Allen. Reprinted by permission of Fleming H. Revell, a division of Baker Book House Company. ©1980.

Worship: Rediscovering the Missing Jewel by Ronald Allen. Reprinted by permission of Multnomah Publishers, Inc. copyright ©1982 by Multnomah Press.

Great Quotes from Great Leaders by Peggy Anderson. Reprinted by permission of Great Quotations. ©1989.

Snappy Steeple Stories by Oren Arnold. Reprinted by permission of Kregel Publications.

Diamonds Eternal by Victor Argenzio. Reprinted by permission of David McKay Company. ©1974.

More of Paul Harvey's the Rest of the Story by Paul Aurandt. Reprinted by permission of William Morrow and Company. ©1980.

The Freedom of Forgiveness: Seventy Times Seven by David Ausburger. Copyright ©1970, Moody Bible Institute of Chicago. Moody Press. Used by permission.

"Festus" by Philip Bailey from *Handbook of Preaching Resources from Literature* edited by James D. Robertson. Copyright ©1962. Reprinted by permission of Baker Book House.

The Daily Study Bible, The Acts of the Apostles by William Barclay. Reprinted by permission of The Saint Andrews Press. ©1953.

The Gospel of John by William Barclay. Reprinted by permission of The Saint Andrews Press. ©1955.

The Gospel of Luke by William Barclay. Reprinted by permission of The Saint Andrews Press. ©1953.

The Gospel of Mark by William Barclay. Reprinted by permission of The Saint Andrews Press. ©1954.

The Letters of James and Peter by William Barclay. Reprinted by permission of The Saint Andrews Press. ©1958.

The Letters of John and Jude by William Barclay. Reprinted by permission of The Saint Andrews Press. ©1958.

The Letters to Timothy, Titus, and Philemon by William Barclay. Reprinted by permission of The Saint Andrews Press. ©1956.

The Letter to the Hebrews by William Barclay. Reprinted by permission of The Saint Andrews Press. © 1957.

The Letters to the Corinthians by William Barclay. Reprinted by permission of The Saint Andrews Press. ©1954.

The Letters to the Galatians and Ephesians by William Barclay. Reprinted by permission of The Saint Andrews Press. ©1954.

The Letters to the Thessalonians by William Barclay. Reprinted by permission of The Saint Andrews Press. ©1954.

The Revelation of John by William Barclay. Reprinted by permission of The Saint Andrews Press. ©1959.

The King and the Kingdom by William Barclay. Reprinted by permission of Baker Book House Company. ©1968.

Let Me Illustrate by Donald Barnhouse. Reprinted by permission of Fleming H. Revell, a division of Baker Book House Company. ©1967.

Romans by Donald G. Barnhouse. Reprinted by permission of William B. Eerdmans Publishing Co. ©1952 1964.

One Life by Christian Barnard. Reprinted by permission of Macmillan Publishing Co., Inc. ©1969.

Bartlett's Familiar Quotations by John Bartlett. Reprinted by permission of Little, Brown, and Company, Inc. ©1980.

The Collected Works of Abraham Lincoln by Roy Basler. Reprinted by permission of Rutgers Univeristy Press. ©1953.

A View from the Hearse by Joseph Bayly. Copyright ©1973 by Joseph Bayly. Published by ChariotVictor Publishing. Used with permission.

The Last Thing We Talk About by Joseph Bayly. Copyright ©1969 by Joseph Bayly. Published by ChariotVictor Publishing. Used with permission.

Psalms of My Life, by Joseph Bayly. Reprinted by permission of Tyndale House Publishers, Victor Books. ©1981.

The Valley of Vision: A Collection of Puritan Prayers and Devotions by Arthur Bennet. Reprinted by permission of The Banner of Truth Trust. ©1975.

Laughter in the Walls by Bob Benson. Reprinted by permission of Impact Books. ©1969.

Preaching from Prophetic Books by Andrew Blackwood. Reprinted by permission of Abingdon-Cokesbury Press. ©1951.

The Poetry and Prose of William Blake by William Blake. Reprinted by permission Doubleday & Company, Inc. ©1965.

Master Your Money by Ron Blue. Reprinted by permission of Thomas Nelson Publishers. ©1986.

The Best Loved Hymns and Prayers of the American People by John E. Bode.

Temptation by Dietrich Bonhoeffer. Reprinted by permission of Macmillan Publishing Co. ©1953.

A Casket of Cameos by F. W. Borham.

Fearfully & Wonderfully Made by Paul Brand and Philip Yancey. Copyright ©1980 by Paul Brand and Philip Yancey. Used by permission of Zondervan Publishing House.

Braude's Handbook of Stories for Toastmasters and Speakers by Jacob M. Braude. Reprinted by permission of Prentice-Hall, Inc. ©1957.

Speaker's Encyclopedia of Stories, Quotations and Anecdotes by Jacob M. Braude. Reprinted by permission of Prentice-Hall, Inc. ©1955.

Pursuit of Holiness by Jerry Bridges. Reprinted by permission of NavPress. ©1978.

How You Can Be Filled with the Holy Spirit by Bill Bright. Reprinted by permission of Campus Crusade for Christ, Inc. ©1969.

Revolution Now by Bill Bright. Reprinted by permission of Campus Crusade for Christ. ©1969.

Bound for Joy: Philippians—Paul's Letter from Prison by Stuart Briscoe. Copyright ©1975 by Stuart Briscoe. Published by Regal Books. Used with permission.

Spiritual Stamina by Stuart Briscoe. Copyright ©1988 by Stuart Briscoe. Published by Multnomah Press. Used with permission.

What Works When Life Doesn't by Stuart Briscoe. Used by permission of ChariotVictor Publishing. ©1976.

The Golden Treasure of Puritan Quotations by Thomas Brookes. Copyright ©1975, Moody Bible Institute of Chicago. Moody Press. Used by permission.

The Mute Christian Under the Smarting Rod of God by Thomas Brookes. Reprinted by permission of Royal Exchange. ©1659.

Expository Discourses on 1 Peter by John Brown. Reprinted by permission of Banner of Truth. ©1848.

Of Quarks, Quasars, and Other Quirks: Quizzical Poems for the Suupersonic Age by Sara Brewton, John E. Brewton, and John Brewton Blackburn. Reprinted by permission of Thomas Y. Crowell Co. ©1977.

Skillful Hands: Studies in the Life of David by Raymond Brown. Reprinted by permission of Christian Literature Crusade. ©1972.

Illustrations for Preaching by Benjamin P. Browne. Reprinted by permission of Broadman Press. ©1977.

Better than Medicine by Leroy Brownlow. Reprinted by permission of Brownlow Publishing Company.

Sourcebook of Poetry by Al Bryant. Reprinted by permission of Kregel Publications. ©1968.

Pilgrim's Progress by John Bunyan. Reprinted by permission of The Heritage Press. ©1942.

"Pastoral Transitions" by Don Bubna. *Leadership Magazine.* ©Fall 1983.

Where Have I Been? by Sid Caesar.

"Penitent" from *Lord It Keeps Happening and Happening* by Ruth Harms Calkin. Pomona, CA. Copyright ©1976. Used by permission.

"Spiritual Retreat" *Lord, You Love to Say Yes* by Ruth Harms Calkin. Pomona, CA. Copyright ©1976. Used by permission.

Tell Me Again, Lord, I Forget by Ruth Harms Calkin. Reprinted by permission of David C. Cook Publishing. ©1974.

Who Switched the Price Tags? by Anthony Campolo. Reprinted by permission of Word Books. ©1986.

Chicken Soup for the Soul: 101 Stories to Open the Heart and Rekindle the Spirit by Jack Canfield and Marc Victor Hansen. Reprinted by permission of Health Communications, Inc. ©1993.

If by Amy Carmichael. Copyright ©1980 by The Zondervan Corporation. Used by permission of Zondervan Publishing House.

Rose from Brier by Amy Carmichael. Reprinted by permission of Christian Literature Crusade. ©1973.

Toward Jerusalem by Amy Carmichael. Reprinted by permission of Christian Literature Crusade. ©1936.

God Is No Fool by Lois A. Cheney. Reprinted by permission of Abigdon Press. ©1969 by Lois A. Cheney.

The Renewed Mind by Larry Christenson. Reprinted by permission of Bethany House Publishers. ©1974.

Christ in Poetry, by Thomas Davis Clark and Hazel Davis Clark. Reprinted by permission of Association Press. ©1952.

The Master Plan of Evangelism by Robert Coleman. Reprinted by permission of Fleming H. Revell, a division of Baker Book House Company. ©1964.

Loving God by Charles Colson. Copyright ©1983, 1987 by Charles W. Colson. Used by permission of Zondervan Publishing House.

Making It Happen by Charles Paul Conn. Reprinted by permission of Fleming H. Revell, a division of Baker Book House Company. ©1981.

"Light for the Blind" presentation by Jack Cooper. May 6, 1967 to International Academy of Opticians, Dallas, TX.

Popular Quotations for All Uses by Lewis Copeland. Reprinted by permission of Garden City Publishing Company. ©1942.

10,000 Jokes, Toasts, and Stories by Lewis and Fay Copeland. Reprinted by permission of Garden City Publishing. ©1940.

Quote Unquote by Lloyd Cory. Used by permission of ChariotVictor Publishing. ©1977.

"Talking Business" by Jeffrey Cotter. *Eternity Magazine*. © March 1981. Used with permission.

Albert Schweitzer's Mission: Healing and Peace by Norman Cousins. Copyright ©1985 by Norman Cousins. Reprinted by permission of W.W. Norton & Company.

Abiding Hope by W. A. Criswell.

Expository Sermons on Galatians by W. A. Criswell. Copyright ©1973 by The Zondervan Corporation. Used by permission of Zondervan Publishing House.

Why I Preach That the Bible Is Literally True by W. A. Criswell. Reprinted by permission of Broadman Press. ©1969.

Stay in the Game: It's Too Soon to Quit by Van Crouch. Reprinted by permission of Honor Books. ©1989.

Windows on the Word by Dennis DeHaan. Reprinted by permission of Radio Bible Class. ©1984.

Broken Things: The Ministry of Suffering by M. R. DeHaan. Reprinted by permission of Zondervan Publishing. ©1976.

Men Sent from God by Richard W. DeHaan. Reprinted by permission of Radio Bible Class. ©1966.

Windows, Ladders and Bridges by Dudley Dennison, Jr. Copyright ©1976 by Zondervan Publishing House. Used by permission of Zondervan Publishing House.

Leadership Is an Art by Max DePree. Reprinted by permission of Dell Publishing. ©1987.

Hide or Seek by James Dobson. Reprinted by permission of Fleming H. Revell, a division of Baker Book House Company. ©1974.

Love Must Be Tough by James Dobson. Reprinted by permission of Word Books. ©1983.

The Strong-Willed Child by James Dobson. ©1978 by Tyndale House Publishers, Inc. All rights reserved.

Straight Talk to Men and Their Wives by James Dobson. Reprinted by permission of Word Books. ©1980.

What Wives Wish Their Husbands Knew About Women by Dr. James Dobson. ©1975 by Tyndale House Publishers, Inc. Used by permission. All rights reserved.

The Effective Executive by Peter Drucker. Reprinted by permission of Harper & Row Publishers. ©1966.

Your Erroneous Zones by Wayne W. Dyer. Reprinted by permission of Avon Books. ©1976.

The Disciplines of Life by Raymond V. Edman. Copyright ©1948 by Raymond V. Edman. Published by ChariotVictor Publishing. Used with permission.

In Quietness and Confidence by Raymond V. Edman. Reprinted by permission of Scripture Press. ©1953.

Be the Leader You Were Meant to Be by LeRoy Eims. Used by permission of ChariotVictor Publishing. ©1975.

Temptations Men Face by Tom L. Eisenman. Reprinted by permission of InterVarsity Press. ©1990.

Shadow of the Almighty by Elisabeth Elliot. Reprinted by permission of Zondervan Publishing House. ©1958.

Through Gates of Splendor by Elisabeth Elliot. Reprinted by permission of Harper & Brothers. ©1957.

Popular Quotations for all Ages by George Eliot.

A Time for Commitment by Ted W. Engstrom with Robert C. Larson. Reprinted by permission of Daybreak Books, Zondervan Publishing House. ©1987.

Integrity by Ted W. Engstrom with Robert C. Larson. Reprinted by permission of Word Books. ©1987.

The Making of a Christian Leader by Ted Engstrom. Copyright ©1976 by The Zondervan Corporation. Used by permission of Zondervan Publishing House.

Motivation to Last a Lifetime by Ted Engstrom and Robert Larson. Copyright ©1984 by The Zondervan Corporation. Used by permission of Zondervan Publishing House.

The Pursuit of Excellence by Ted W. Engstrom. Copyright ©1982 by The Zondervan Corporation. Used by permission of Zondervan Publishing House.

"The Power Abusers" by Ronald M. Enroth. *Eternity Magazine.* © October 1979. Used with permission.

Dictionary of Humorous Quotations by Evan Escar. Reprinted by permission of The Crown Publishing Group. ©1949.

The Little, Brown Book of Anecdotes edited by Clifton Fadiman. Reprinted by permission of Little, Brown and Company. ©1985.

Standing Tall by Steve Farrar. Reprinted by permission of Questar Publishing, Multnomah Books. ©1994.

The Best Loved Poems of the American People by Hazel Felleman. Reprinted by permission of Garden City Books. ©1936.

Poems That Live Forever by Hazel Felleman. Published by Doubleday. ©1965.

Between Walden and the Whirlwind by Jean Fleming. Reprinted by permission of NavPress. ©1985.

The Second Greatest Commandment by William M. Fletcher. Reprinted by permission of NavPress. ©1984.

Rebirth of America by Robert Flood. Reprinted by permission of Arthur S. Demoss Foundation. ©1986.

Did I Say That? by Leslie B. Flynn. Used by permission of ChariotVictor Publishing. ©1986.

Great Church Fights by Leslie B. Flynn. Copyright ©1976 by Leslie B. Flynn. Published by ChariotVictor Publishing. Used with permission.

Now a Word from Our Creator by Leslie B. Flynn. Used by permission of ChariotVictor Publishing. ©1976.

When The Saints Come Storming In by Leslie B. Flynn. Used by permission of ChariotVictor Publishing. ©1988.

You Don't Have to Go It Alone Leslie B. Flynn. Reprinted by permission of Accent Books. ©1981.

Humorous Incidents and Quips for Church Publications by Leslie B. and Bernice Flynn. Copyright ©1972, 1979. Published by Baker Book House. Used with permission.

God's Will: You Can Know It by Leslie F. and Bernice Flynn. Used by permission of ChariotVictor Publishing. ©1979.

The Civil War, A Narrative by Shelby Foote. Reprinted by permission of Vantage Books. ©1986.

Money, Sex, and Power by Richard J. Foster. Reprinted by permission of Harper & Row Publishers. ©1985.

Great Words of the New Testament by J. B. Fowler, Jr. Reprinted by permission of Broadman Press. ©1991.

Man's Search for Meaning by Victor Frankl. Reprinted by permission of Pocket Books. ©1980.

Blessed Is the Ordinary by Gerhard Frost. Reprinted by permission of Winston Press. ©1980.

The Complete Poems of Robert Frost by Robert Frost. Reprinted by permission of Buccaneer Books. ©1983.

The Expositor's Bible Commentary, Vol. 4 edited by Frank Gaebelein. Copyright ©1988 by Zondervan Publishing House. Used by permission of Zondervan Publishing House.

Rebuild Your Life: How to Survive a Crisis by Dale Galloway. Reprinted by permission of 20/20 Vision, Lexington, KY. ©1975 by Dale Galloway.

You Can Win with Love by Dale Galloway. Published by Harvest House. ©1976 by Dale Galloway.

Thus Spake Qoheleth by Kenneth O. Gangel. Reprinted by permission of Christian Publications, Inc. ©1978.

100 Portraits of Christ by Henry Gariepy. Used by permission of ChariotVictor Publishing. ©1987.

Our Christian Heritage by Stuart P. Garver. Reprinted by permission of Christ's Mission, Inc. ©1973.

Book of Anecdotes by Daniel George. Reprinted by permission of Folcroft Publishers, ©1957.

The Theology of Major Sects by John H. Gerstner. Copyright ©1960. Published by Baker Book House. Used with permission.

A Touch of Wonder by Arthur Gordon. Reprinted by permission of Fleming H. Revell, a division of Baker Book House Company. ©1974.

"Call to Commitment" by Billy Graham, ©1960 (copyright renewed 1988), 1994 Billy Graham Evangelistic Association, used by permission, all rights reserved.

The Holy Spirit by Billy Graham. Reprinted by permission of Word Books. ©1978.

How To be Born Again by Billy Graham. Reprinted by permission of Word Books. ©1977.

The Secret of Happiness by Billy Graham. Reprinted by permission of Word Books. ©1955.

Till Armageddon: A Perspective on Suffering by Billy Graham. Reprinted by permission of Word Books. ©1981.

World Aflame by Billy Graham. Reprinted by permission of Word Publishing. ©1965.

Illustrations for Biblical Preaching by Michael P. Green. Reprinted by permission of Fleming H. Revell, a division of Baker Book House Company. ©1982.

The Mind Changers by Em A. Griffin. Copyright ©1976 by Em Griffin. Published by Tyndale House Publishers, Inc.

C.T. Studd: Cricketeer and Pioneer by Norman P. Grubb. Reprinted by permission of Christian Literature Crusade. ©1948.

God, But I'm Bored by Eileen Guder. Reprinted by permission of Doubleday. ©1971.

How to Win over Worry by John Haggai. Copyright ©1987 by Harvest House Publishers, Eugene, Oregon, 97402. Used by permission.

How the Best Is Won by John Haggai. Reprinted by permission of Thomas Nelson Publishers. ©1987.

Samuel Logan Brengel by C. W. Hall. Reprinted by permission of Salvation Army. ©1933.

2,500 Best Modern Illustrations by G. B. F. Hallock. Reprinted by permission of Harper & Brothers. ©1935.

Markings by Dag Hammarskjold. Reprinted by permission of Alfred A. Knopf. ©1964.

Greater Men and Women of the Bible by James Hastings. Reprinted by permission of T. & T. Clark. ©1915.

The Best of Vance Havner by Vance Havner. Reprinted by permission of Baker Book House. ©1980.

Living by the Book by Howard G. and William D. Hendricks. Copyright ©1991, Moody Bible Institute of Chicago. Moody Press. Used by permission.

Taking a Stand: What God Can Do Through Ordinary You by Howard G. Hendricks. Reprinted by permission of Multnomah Press. ©1972.

Say It With Love by Howard G. Hendricks. Used by permission of ChariotVictor Publishing. ©1973.

A Woman for All Seasons by Jeanne W. Hendricks. Reprinted by permission of Thomas Nelson Publishers. ©1977.

Afternoon by Jeanne W. Hendricks. Reprinted by permission of Thomas Nelson Publishers.©1979.

New Testament Commentary, Exposition of Philippians by William Hendriksen. Reprinted by permission of Baker Book House. ©1979.

New Testament Commentary, Exposition of the Gospel according to Luke by William Hendriksen. Reprinted by permission of Baker Book House Company. ©1978.

Illustrations Unlimited edited by James S. Hewett. ©1988. Used by permission of Tyndale House Publishers, Inc. All rights reserved.

1000 Years of Irish Poetry: The Gaelic & Anglo-Irish Poets from Pagan Times to Present by Kathleen Hoagland. Reprinted by permission of Devin. ©1982.

Snappy Stories That Preachers Tell by Paul E. Holdcraft. Reprinted by permission of Abingdon-Cokesbury Press. ©1932.

Balancing Life's Demands by J. Grant Howard. Reprinted by permission of Multnomah Press. ©1983.

Beyond Futility by David Allan Hubbard. Reprinted by permission of William B. Eerdmans Publishing Co. ©1976.

Dictionary of Humorous Quotations by Elbert Hubbard. Reprinted by permission of The Crown Publishing Group. ©1949.

Grace is not a Blue-Eyed Blond by R. Loft on Hudson. Reprinted by permission of Word Books. ©1968.

Liberating the Ministry from the Success Syndrome by Kent and Barbara Hughes. Reprinted by permission of Tyndale House Publishers. ©1987.

Podium Humor by James C. Humes. Reprinted by permission of Harper & Row Publishers. ©1975.

"Acceptance" by Gladys M. Hunt. *Eternity Magazine.* © October 1969. Used with permission.

One Church's Answer to Abortion by Bill Hybels. Copyright ©1986, Moody Bible Institute of Chicago. Moody Press. Used by permission.

Quality Friendship by Gary Inrig. Copyright ©1981, Moody Bible Institute of Chicago. Moody Press. Used by permission.

Iacocca: An Autobiography by Lee Iacocca and William Novak. Reprinted by permission of Bantam. ©1986.

Act Like Men by H. A. Ironside. Reprinted by permission of Loizeau Brothers, Inc.

Timothy, Titus, and Philemon by H. A. Ironside. Reprinted by permission of Loizeau Brothers, Inc. ©1947.

No Other Foundation by Jeremy Jackson. Reprinted by permission of Cornerstone Books. ©1980.

Crowded Peas and Lonely People by Marion Leach Jacobsen. Reprinted by permission of Tyndale House Publishers. ©1972.

God's Trombones by James Weldon Johnson. Reprinted by permission of The Viking Press, Penguin Books. Reprint 1976.

"Growing Me-ism and Materialism" by Jon Johnson. *Christianity Today.* ©January 17,1986 by Jon Johnson.

A Song of Ascents: A Spiritual Autobiography by E. Stanley Jones. Abingdon Press. ©1968.

Growing Spiritually by E. Stanley Jones. Reprinted by permission of Abingdon Press. ©1953.

The Epistles of St. Peter by John Henry Jowett. Reprinted by permission of Hodder and Stoughton. ©1906.

Baker's Pocket Treasury of Religious Verse by Donald Kauffman. Published by Baker Book House. ©1980.

A Testament of Devotion by Thomas Kelly. Reprinted by permission of Harper & Row Publishers. ©1941.

Being Holy, Being Human by Jay Kesler. Reprinted by permission of Word Books. ©1988.

A Belief That Behaves by Guy H. King. Reprinted by permission of Marshall, Morgan & Scott, Ltd. ©1941.

Knight's Master Book of New Illustrations by Walter B. Knight. Reprinted by permission of William B. Eerdmans Publishing Co. ©1956.

"Tender Loving Heart" by James K. Krames. *Living Free*, No. 35–75.

Reprinted by permission of Penguin Putnam Inc. from *On the Road with Charles Kuralt* by Charles Kuralt. Copyright ©1985 by CBS Inc.

When Bad Things Happen to Good People by Harold S. Kushner. Copyright ©1981, 1989 by Harold S. Kushner. Reprinted by permission of Schocken Books, distributed by Pantheon Books, a division of Random House, Inc.

"The Day I Stopped Being Ashamed" by Joseph Lahey. *Guideposts* Magazine. ©1976.

Ask Me to Dance by Bruce Larson. Reprinted by permission of Word Books. ©1972.

Believe and Belong by Bruce Larson. Reprinted by permission of Fleming H. Revell, a division of Baker Book House Company. ©1982.

The One and Only You by Bruce Larson. Reprinted by permission of Word Books. ©1974.

Setting Men Free by Bruce Larson. Reprinted by permission of Zondervan Publishing House. ©1967.

There's a Lot More to Health Than Not Being Sick by Bruce Larson. Reprinted by permission of Word Books. ©1981.

What God Wants to Know by Bruce Larson. Reprinted by permission of Harper San Francisco. ©1993.

Illustrations for Preaching and Teaching from Leadership Journal by Craig Brian Larson. Reprinted by permission of Baker Books. ©1993.

Life's Choices: Discovering the Consequences of Sowing and Reaping by John W. Lawrence. Published by Multnomah Press. ©1975 by John W. Lawrence.

The World's Best Loved Poems by James Gilchrist Lawson. Reprinted by permission of Harper & Row Publishers. ©1927.

Articles from *Leadership Magazine*. ©Summer 1981, ©Fall 1982, ©Spring 1983, ©Fall 1985, ©Winter 1986, ©Spring 1990, ©Winter 1990.

The Task of Adam by John Leax. Reprinted by permission of Zondervan Publishing House. ©1985.

The Sacrament of the Broken Seed by John Leax. Reprinted by permission of Zondervan Publishing House. ©1985.

How to Win Customers and Keep Them for Life by Michael LeBoeuf. Reprinted by permission of Berkley Books. ©1987.

Sourcebook of 500 Illustrations Robert G. Lee. Copyright ©1964 by Zondervan Publishing House. Used by permission of Zondervan Publishing House.

Exposition on Genesis by H. C. Leupold. Copyright ©1965. Published by Baker Book House. Used with permission.

You Don't Have to Be in Who's Who to Know What's What by Sam Levenson. Reprinted by permission of Simon & Schuster, Pocket Books. ©1979

Christian Behavior by C. S. Lewis. Reprinted by permission of HarperCollins Publishers Ltd. ©1945.

Mere Christianity by C. S. Lewis. Reprinted by permission of HarperCollins Publishers Ltd. ©1970.

The Problem of Pain by C. S. Lewis. Reprinted by permission of HarperCollins Publishers Ltd. ©1962.

The Screwtape Letters by C. S. Lewis. Reprinted by permission of HarperCollins Publishers Ltd. ©1959.

The Weight of Glory and Other Addresses by C. S. Lewis. Reprinted by permission of Macmillan Co. ©1949.

Gift from the Sea by Anne Morrow Lindbergh. Reprinted by permission of Random House. ©1955.

Know What and Why You Believe by Paul Little. Used by permission of ChariotVictor Publishing. ©1980.

Fatherlove: Learning to Give the Best You've Got by Bruce Lockerbie. Reprinted by permission of Doubleday & Company. ©1981.

All the Prayers of the Bible by Herbert Lockyer. Reprinted by permission of Zondervan Publishing House. ©1959.

If I Should Die before I Live by Joe LoMusio. Reprinted by permission of R. C. Law & Co. ©1989.

In the Eye of the Storm by Max Lucado. Reprinted by permission of Word Publishing. ©1991.

No Wonder They Call Him Savior by Max Lucado. Reprinted by permission of Multnomah Press. ©1986.

UpWords by Max Lucado. Reprinted by permission of Max Lucado and UpWords Radio Ministry.

1,500 Inspirational Quotes and Illustrations by M. Lunn. Published by Baker Book House. ©1974.

Failure: The Back Door to Success by Erwin W. Lutzer. Copyright ©1975, Moody Bible Institute of Chicago. Moody Press. Used by permission.

When a Good Man Falls by Erwin W. Lutzer. Used by permission of ChariotVictor Publishing. ©1985.

Great Nights of the Bible by Clarence Macartney. Reprinted with permission of Abingdon-Cokesbury Press. ©1943.

Peter and His Lord by Clarence Macartney. Reprinted with permission of Cokesbury Press. ©1937.

Preaching without Notes by Clarence Macartney. Reprinted with permission of Abingdon Press. ©1946.

Chasing the Wind by William MacDonald. Copyright ©1975, Moody Bible Institute of Chicago. Moody Press. Used by permission.

The Grace of God by William MacDonald. Reprinted with permission of Walterick Publishers. ©1960.

Cyclopedia of World Authors by Frank N. Magill. Reprinted with permission of Salem Press. ©1974.

"Victory through Christ" article by Walter A. Maier. *Decision Magazine,* November, 1989. Used with permission.

Lion and Lamb by Brennan Manning. Reprinted with permission of Fleming H. Revell, a division of Baker Book House Company. ©1986.

John Doe, Disciple: Sermons for the Young in Spirit by Peter Marshall. Reprinted with permission of McGraw-Hill ©1963.

The Light and the Glory by Peter Marshall and David Manuel. Reprinted with permission of Fleming H. Revell, a division of Baker Book House Company. ©1977.

Mr. Jones, Meet the Master by Peter Marshall. Reprinted by permission of Fleming H. Revell, a division of Baker Book House Company. ©1950.

Screwtape Writes Again by Walter Martin. Reprinted by permission of Vision House Publishers. ©1975.

The Quotable Lewis by Wayne Martindale and Jerry Root. Reprinted by permission of Tyndale House Publishers. ©1989.

Be All You Can Be! by John C. Maxwell. Used by permission of ChariotVictor Publishing. ©1995.

"Envy Went to Church" by Elva McAllaster. *Christian Life* Magazine. ©January 1970.

Matthew by Vernon J. McGee. Reprinted by permission of Thru The Bible Books. ©1973.

Bringing Out the Best in People by Alan Loy McGinnis, copyright ©1985 Augsburg Publishing House. Used by permission of Augsburg Fortress.

The Friendship Factor by Alan Loy McGinnis. Reprinted by permission of Augsburg Publishing House. ©1979.

12,000 Religious Quotations by Frank S. Mead.

The Christian Circle by Henrietta Mears.

Abraham by F. B. Meyer. Reprinted by permission of Creative Publishing. ©1979.

Christ in Isaiah by F. B. Meyer. Reprinted by permission of Christian Literature Crusade.

David: Shepherd, Psalmist, King by F. B. Meyer. Reprinted by permission of Christian Literature Crusade. ©1977.

Expository Preaching by F. B. Meyer. Reprinted by permission of Christian Literature Crusade. ©1954.

John the Baptist by F. B. Meyer. Reprinted by permission of Christian Literature Crusade. ©1983.

William Carey: The Father of Modern Missions by Basil Miller. Reprinted by permission of Bethany House Publishers. ©1952.

The Edge of Adventure by Keith Miller and Bruce Larson. Reprinted by permission of Word Books. ©1974.

The Best Loved Hymns and Prayers of the American People by Harold Vincent Milligan. Reprinted by permission of Garden City Publishing Co. ©1942.

Pocket Pearls by Nelson Mink. Copyright ©1987 by Nelson Mink. Tyndale House Publishers, Inc. Used with permission.

The Christian in Business by John E. Mitchell, Jr. Reprinted by permission of Fleming H. Revell, a division of Baker Book House Company. ©1962.

Memoirs of Field Marshall Montgomery by Bernard L. Montgomery. Reprinted by permission of Quality Paperback Ser. ©1982.

A Drink at Joel's Place by Jess Moody. Reprinted by permission of Word Books. ©1967.

The Crises of the Christ by G. Campbell Morgan. Reprinted by permission of Fleming H. Revell, a division of Baker Book House Company. ©1936.

The Gospel of Matthew by G. Campbell Morgan. Reprinted by permission of Fleming H. Revell, a division of Baker Book House Company. ©1929.

The First Epistle of Paul to the Corinthians by Leon Morris. Reprinted by permission of William B. Eerdmans Publishing Co. ©1978.

Man Does Not Stand Alone by A. Cressy Morrison. Reprinted by permission of Fleming H. Revell, a division of Baker Book House Company. ©1944.

Masterpieces of Religious Verse by James Dalton Morrison. Reprinted by permission of Harper & Brothers. ©1948.

A 20th Century Testimony by Malcolm Muggeridge. Reprinted by permission of Thomas Nelson Publishers. ©1988.

Jesus Rediscovered by Malcolm Muggeridge. Reprinted by permission of Tyndale House Publishers. ©1971.

A Treasury of Humor by Clyde Murdock. Reprinted by permission of Zondervan Publishing. ©1967.

2,400 Outlines, Notes and Quotes by Archibald Naismith. Reprinted by permission of Baker Book House. ©1967.

Anecdotes and Illustrations by Wilbur Nelson. Copyright ©1971. Published by Baker Book House. Used with permission.

Freedom for Ministry by Richard J. Neuhaus. Reprinted by permission of Harper & Row, Publishers. ©1956.

"Sharing the Family." *Newsweek.* ©May 15,1978. Used by permission.

"All Shook-Up." *Newsweek.* ©August 29,1977. Used by permission.

Ivory Palaces by Martha Snell Nicholson. Reprinted by permission of Martha Snell Nicholson. ©1946.

Character Above All by Peggy Noonan. Reprinted by permission.

The Way of the Heart by Henri J. Nouwen. Reprinted by permission of The Seabury Press. ©1981.

Drumbeat of Love by Lloyd John Olgive. Reprinted by permission of Word Books. ©1976.

Outdoor Survival Skills by Larry Dean Olseon. Reprinted by permission of Brigham Publishers. ©1976.

Disciplines of a Beautiful Woman by Anne Ortlund. Reprinted by permission of Word Books. ©1977.

Up with Worship by Anne Ortlund. Copyright ©1975. Regal Books, Ventura, CA 93003. Used with permission.

101 Hymn Stories by Kenneth Osbeck. Reprinted by permission of Kregel Publications. ©1982.

The Art of Understanding Your Mate by Cecil Osborne. Reprinted by permission of Zondervan Publishing House. ©1970.

Abraham to the Middle East Crisis by G. Frederick Owen. Reprinted by permission of William B. Eerdmans Publishing Company. ©1939.

Knowing God by J. I. Packer. Reprinted by permission of Intervarsity Press. ©1973.

The Grand Essentials by Ben Patterson. Reprinted by permission of Word Books. ©1987.

Waiting, Finding Hope When God Seems Silent by Ben Patterson. Copyright ©1989 by Ben Patterson. Used by permission of InterVarsity Press, PO Box 1400, Downers Grove, IL 60515.

The Day America Told the Truth by James Patterson and Peter Kim. Reprinted by permission of Prentice-Hall Press. ©1991.

The Vindication of Tradition by Jaroslav Pelikan. Reprinted by permission of Yale University Press. ©1984.

Prophecy for Today by Dwight J. Pentecost. Reprinted by permission of Zondervan Publishing House. ©1961.

Things Which Become Sound Doctrine by Dwight J. Pentecost. Reprinted by permission of Fleming H. Revell, a division of Baker Book House Company. ©1955.

The Speaker's Treasury of 400 Quotable Poems by Croft M. Pentz. Reprinted by permission of Zondervan Publishing House. ©1963.

Peter's Quotations by Laurence J. Peter. Reprinted by permission of Bantam Books. ©1977.

The Myth of Greener Grass by J. Allan Petersen. Reprinted by permission of Tyndale House Publishers. ©1983.

The Marriage Affair by J. Allan Petersen. Reprinted by permission of Tyndale House Publishers. ©1971.

How to Be a Saint While Lying Flat on Your Back by William Petersen. Reprinted by permission of Zondervan Publishing House.

A Long Obedience in the Same Direction by Eugene Peterson. Reprinted by permission of InterVarsity Press. ©1980.

The Joy of Stress by Pamela Pettler. Reprinted by permission of William Morrow and Company. ©1984.

Phillips' Book of Great Thoughts and Funny Sayings by Bob Phillips. Reprinted by permission of Tyndale House Publishers. ©1993.

The World's Greatest Collection of Heavenly Humor by Bob Phillips. Copyright 1982 by Bob Phillips. Published by Harvest House Publishers. Used with permission.

Making Men Whole by J.B. Phillips. Reprinted by permission of Collins. ©1955.

Leisure: The Basis of Culture by Joseph Pieper. Reprinted by permission of The New American Library.

The Incomplete Book of Failures by Stephen Pile. Reprinted by permission of E.P. Dutton. ©1979.

Set Forth Your Case by Clark Pinnock. Copyright ©1967. Published by Craig Press.

What Luther Says: An Anthology by Ewald M. Plass. Reprinted by permission of Concordia Publishing House. ©1959.

Happiness Is an Inside Job by John Powell. Reprinted by permission of the publisher. Copyright ©1989 by John Powell. Published by Thomas More, 200 East Bethany Drive, Allen, Texas 75002.

"Footprints" by Margaret Rose Powers. *Guideposts Magazine.* ©July 1992.

Articles from *Preaching Magazine,* © March–April 1988; ©circa early 1989; © May–June 1989; © July–August 1989; © May–June 1990; © March–April 1991; © May–June 1991; © March–April 1993. Used with permission.

"Philip" by Harry Pritchett, Jr. *Leadership* Magazine. ©Summer 1985.

"Learning the Bicycle" by Wyatt Prunty. *The American Scholar* Magazine. Used with permission.

Quote Magazine, vol. 51, no. 7, ©July 1991. Used with permission.

Can We Trust the Bible? by Earl Radmacher. Reprinted by permission of Tyndale House Publishers. ©1979.

You and Your Thoughts: The Power of Right Thinking by Earl Radmacher. ©1977 by Earl Radmacher. Reprinted by permission of Tyndale House Publishers, Inc. All rights reserved.

Creative Brooding by Robert A. Raines. Reprinted by permission of Macmillan Publishing Co. ©1966.

Lord, Could You Make It a Little Better? by Robert A. Raines. Reprinted by permission of Word Publishing. ©1976.

"No Lover" by Natalie Ray. *Eternity Magazine.* ©Fall 1975. Used with permission.

Jesus Makes Me Laugh with Him by David A. Redding. Senior Minister, Liberty Presbyterian Church, Delaware, OH 43015. Copyright ©1977 by David A. Redding. Published by Zondervan Publishing. Used with permission.

The Bible Speaks to Our Times by Alan Redpath. Reprinted by permission of Fleming H. Revell, a division of Baker Book House Company. ©1993.

The Making of a Man of God by Alan Redpath. Reprinted by permission of Fleming H. Revell, a division of Baker Book House Company. ©1962.

Victorious Christian Service: Studies in Nehemiah by Alan Redpath. Reprinted by permission of Fleming H. Revell, a division of Baker Book House Company. ©1958.

Faith Is by Pamela Reeve. Reprinted by permission of Multnomah Publishers, Inc. copyright ©1994 by Pamela Reeve.

Relationships: What It Takes to Be a Friend by Pamela Reeve. Reprinted by permission of Multnomah Press. ©1982.

Poems That Preach by John R. Rice. Reprinted by permission of Sword of the Lord Publishers. ©1952.

How to Be a Christian without Being Religious by Fritz Ridenour. Reprinted by permission of Tyndale House Publishers. ©1971.

Can Christians Love Too Much? by Margaret J. Rinck. Reprinted by permission of Zondervan Publishing. ©1989.

Word Pictures in the New Testament by Archibald Thomas Robertson. Reprinted by permission of Broadman Press. ©1930.

Biblical Preaching, The Development and Delivery of Expository Messages by Haddon Robinson. Reprinted by permission of Baker Book House. ©1980.

What Jesus Said about Successful Living by Haddon Robinson, ©1991. Used by permission of Discovery House Publishers, Box 3566, Grand Rapids, Michigan 49501. All rights reserved.

We Prepare and Preach by Clarence Roddy. Copyright ©1959, Moody Bible Institute of Chicago. Moody Press. Used by permission.

Time Out, Ladies by Dale Evans Rogers. Reprinted by permission of Fleming H. Revell, a division of Baker Book House Company. ©1966.

The Strength of a Man by David Roper, ©1989. Used by permission of Discovery House Publishers, Box 3566, Grand Rapids, Michigan 49501. All rights reserved.

A Pictorial Biography of C. H. Spurgeon by Bob L. Ross. Reprinted by permission of Pilgrim Publishing. ©1974.

Abraham Lincoln, the War Years by Carl Sandburg. Reprinted by permission of Harcourt, Brace & Company. ©1939.

For Believers Only by J. Oswald Sanders. Reprinted by permission of Bethany Fellowship. ©1976.

Robust in Faith by J. Oswald Sanders. Copyright ©1965, Moody Bible Institute of Chicago. Moody Press. Used by permission.

Spiritual Manpower by J. Oswald Sanders. Copyright ©1965, Moody Bible Institute of Chicago. Moody Press. Used by permission.

Spiritual Leadership by J. Oswald Sanders. Copyright ©1969, Moody Bible Institute of Chicago. Moody Press. Used by permission.

The Craft of Sermon Illustration by W. E. Sangster. Reprinted by permission of The Epworth Press. ©1946.

Pocket Smiles by Robert Savage. Reprinted by permission of Tyndale House Publishers. ©1984.

How Should We Then Live? by Francis Schaeffer. Reprinted by permission of Good News Publisher. ©1983.

Tough Times Never Last by Tough People Do by Robert Schuller. Reprinted by permission of Thomas Nelson Publishers. ©1983.

Self-Love: The Dynamic Force of Success by Robert H. Schuller. Copyright ©1969 by Robert H. Schuller. Used by permission of Dutton, a division of Penguin Putnam Inc.

Scott's Sermon Material. ©May 30, 1967, ©July 30, 1967. All rights reserved.

The House on the Rock by Charles Sell. Used by permission of ChariotVictor Publishing. ©1987.

Shoes for the Road by Richard H. Seume. Copyright ©1974, Moody Bible Institute of Chicago. Moody Press. Used by permission.

Winning over Uncertainty by Robert R. Shank. Reprinted by permission of Priority Living, Inc. ©1987.

Listen to the Green by Luci Shaw. Reprinted by permission of Harold Shaw Publishers. ©1971.

Letters to Karen by Charles W. Shedd. Reprinted by permission of Abingdon Press. ©1965.

The Parables of Peanuts by Robert L. Short. Reprinted by permission of Harper and Row, Publishers. ©1968.

Rich Christians in an Age of Hunger by Ronald J. Sider. Reprinted by permission of InterVarsity Press. ©1977.

Growing through Divorce by Jim Smoke. Reprinted by permission of Bantam Books. ©1986.

The Gulag Archipelago by Aleksandr Sozhenitsyn. Reprinted by permission of Harper and Row, Publishers. ©1973.

One Day in the Life of Ivan Denisovich by Aleksandr Sozhenitsyn, translated by Ralph Parker, Translation copyright ©1963 by E. P. Dutton and Victor Gollancz, Ltd. Copyright renewed ©1991 by Penguin USA and Victor Gollancz, Ltd. Used by permission of Dutton, a division of Penguin Putnam Inc.

Fanfare: A Celebration of Belief by Nancy Spiegelberg and Dorothy Purdy. Reprinted by permission of Multnomah Press. ©1981.

Doubt and Assurance by R. C. Sproul. Reprinted by permission of Baker Book House. ©1992.

Pleasing God by R. C. Sproul. ©1988 by R. C. Sproul. Used by permission of Tyndale House Publishers, Inc. All rights reserved.

Lectures to My Students by Charles H. Spurgeon. Reprinted by permission of Zondervan Publishing House. ©1954.

Metropolitan Tabernacle Pulpit by Charles H. Spurgeon. Reprinted by permission of Banner of Truth Trust. ©1971.

The Treasury of the Bible by Charles H. Spurgeon. Reprinted by permission of Zondervan Publishing House. ©1968.

Treasury of David by Charles H. Spurgeon. Reprinted by permission of Associated Publishers and Authors. ©1970.

Principles of Spiritual Growth by Miles J. Stanford. Reprinted by permission of Back to the Bible. ©1977.

Birth of the Body by Ray Stedman. Reprinted by permission of Vision House Publishers. ©1974.

From Guilt to Glory by Ray Stedman. Reprinted by permission of Word Books. ©1978.

Solomon's Secret: Enjoying Life, God's Good Gift by Ray Stedman. Published by Multnomah Press. ©1985 by Ray Stedman.

What More Can God Say? by Ray Stedman. Copyright ©1974. Regal Books, Ventura, CA 93003. Used with permission.

The Home Book of Proverbs, Maxims, and Familiar Phrases by Burton Stevenson. Reprinted by permission of Macmillan. ©1961.

Sourcebook of Poetry by Dale Martin Stone. "The Reaper" by Robert Louis Stevenson reprinted by permission. ©1942.

The Message of the Sermon on the Mount by John R. W. Stott. ©1978 by John R. W. Stott. Used by permission of InterVarsity Press. PO Box 1400, Downers Grove, IL 60515.

The Epistles of John by John R. W. Stott. Reprinted by permission of William B. Eerdmans Publishing Co. ©1964.

The Preacher's Portrait by John R. W. Stott. Reprinted by permission of William B. Eerdmans Publishing Co. ©1961.

Great Quotes and Illustrations by George Sweeting. Reprinted by permission of Word Books. ©1985.

Wide My World, Narrow My Bed: Living and Loving the Single Life by Luci Swindoll. Reprinted by permission of Multnomah Press. ©1982.

Encyclopedia of 7,700 Illustrations by Paul Lee Tan. Copyright ©1990 by Paul Lee Tan. Reprinted by permission of Assurance Publishers.

G. W. Target, "The Window," in *The Window and Other Essays,* published by Pacific Press Publishing Association, Inc. Nampa ID, USA.

Hudson Taylor and the China Inland Mission by Howard Taylor. Reprinted by permission of China Inland Mission. ©1918.

Hudson Taylor's Spiritual Secret by Howard and Mary G. Taylor. Copyright ©1958, Moody Bible Institute of Chicago. Moody Press. Used by permission.

The Art of Leadership by Ordway Tead. Reprinted by permission of McGraw-Hill. ©1935.

The Hiding Place by Corrie Ten Boom. Reprinted by permission of Bantam Books, Inc. ©1974.

John: The Gospel of Belief by Merrill C. Tenney. Reprinted by permission of William B. Eerdmans Publishing Co. ©1948.

The Reality of the Resurrection by Merrill C. Tenney. Reprinted by permission of Harper & Row, Publishers. ©1963.

Greek-English Lexicon of the New Testament by Joseph Henry Thayer. Reprinted by permission of Zondervan Publishing House. ©1962.

Christianity is Christ by W. H. Griffith Thomas. Reprinted by permission of InterVarsity Christian Fellowship. ©1981.

The Saving Life of Christ by Major W. Ian Thomas. Reprinted by permission of Zondervan Publishing House. ©1961.

Thoreau: Walden and Other Writings by Henry David Thoreau. Reprinted by permission of Bantam Books. ©1981.

Born to Win by Lewis Timberlake.

A Place for You by Paul Tournier. Reprinted by permission of Harper & Row Publishers. ©1968.

The Strong and Weak by Paul Tournier. Reprinted by permission of The Westminster Press. ©1963.

To Understand Each Other by Paul Tournier. Reprinted by permission of John Knox Press. ©1967.

Man's Concern with Death by Arnold Toynbee. Reprinted by permission of McGraw-Hill. ©1968.

The Divine Conquest by A. W. Tozer. Reprinted by permission of Christian Publications. ©1950.

God Tells the Man Who Cares by A. W. Tozer. Reprinted by permission of Christian Publications, Inc. ©1970.

The Knowledge of the Holy by A. W. Tozer. Reprinted by permission of Harper & Brothers. ©1961.

Man, the Dwelling Place of God by A. W. Tozer. Reprinted by permission of Christian Publications. ©1966.

Of God and Man by A. W. Tozer. Reprinted by permission of Christian Publications. ©1960.

The Pursuit of God by A. W. Tozer. Reprinted by permission of Christian Publications. ©1982.

The Root of the Righteous by A. W. Tozer. Reprinted by permission of Christian Publications. ©1986.

The Misunderstood Man by Walter Trobisch. Copyright ©1983. Quiet Waters Publications. PO Box 4955, Springfield, MO 65808. Used with permission.

Sacred Stories by Ruth A. Tucker. Reprinted by permission of Zondervan Publishing House. ©1989.

"What's Happening to American Morality?" Copyright ©October 13, 1975. *U. S. News & World Report.* Used with permission.

Demons in the World Today by Merrill Unger. ©1971 by Tyndale House Publishers, Inc. All rights reserved.

Seeds of Greatness by Dennis Waitley. Reprinted by permission of Fleming Revell. ©1983.

The Winner's Edge: Best Kept Secrets of Total Success by Dennis Waitley. Reprinted by permission of Berkley Publishing. ©1986.

How to Talk with Practically Anybody about Practically Anything by Barbara Walters. Reprinted by permission of Dell Publishing. ©1979.

Thoughts of a Christian Optimist by William Arthur Ward. Reprinted by permission of Drake House Publishers. ©1968.

Courage of a Conservative by James Watt. Reprinted by permission of Simon and Schuster. ©1985.

One Hundred Percent by Daniel Weiss.

Baker's Pocket Book of Religious Quotes by Albert M. Wells, Jr. Reprinted by permission of Baker Book House.

"Bus Ride" by Olga Wetzel. *Eternity Magazine.* ©February 1977. Used with permission.

1,010 Illustrations, Poems, and Quotes by Glen Wheeler. Reprinted by permission of Standard Publishing. ©1967.

Honesty, Morality, and Conscience by Jerry White. ©1978. Used by permission of NavPress/Pinon Press. All rights reserved. For copies call 1-800-366-7788.

The Fight by John White. ©1989 by John White. Used by permission of InterVarsity Press, PO Box 1400, Downers Grove, IL 60515.

Old Testament Bible Characters by Alexander Whyte. Reprinted by permission of Zondervan. ©1952.

Be Alert by Warren Wiersbe. Reprinted by permission of ChariotVictor Publishing. ©1984.

Be Hopeful by Warren Wiersbe. Reprinted by permission of ChariotVictor Publishing. ©1982.

Lonely People by Warren Wiersbe. Reprinted by permission of Back to the Bible. ©1983.

Making Sense of the Ministry by Warren and David Wiersbe. Reprinted by permission of Baker Book House. ©1983.

Walking with the Giants by Warren Wiersbe. Reprinted by permission of Baker Book House. ©1971.

The Morning After by George F. Will. Reprinted by permission of Collier Macmillan Publishers. ©1986.

The Spirit of the Disciplines: Understanding How God Changes Lives by Dallas Willard. Reprinted by permission of Harper and Row, Publishers. ©1988.

Topical Encyclopedia of Living Quotations by Sherwood E. Wirt. Reprinted by permission of Bethany House Publishers. ©1982.

Jesus, Man of Joy by Sherwood E. Wirt. Copyright ©1991 by Sherwood E. Wirt. Published by Here's Life Publishers. Used with permission.

Your Churning Place by Robert Wise. Copyright ©1977. Regal Books, Ventura, CA.93003. Used with permission.

Great Leaders of the Christian Church by John Woodbridge. Copyright ©1988, Moody Bible Institute of Chicago. Moody Press. Used by permission.

They Call Me Coach by John Wooden.

Romans in the Greek New Testament by Kenneth Wuest. Reprinted by permission of William B. Eerdmans Publishing Company. ©1955.

A Musician Looks at the Psalms by Don Wyrtzen. Reprinted by permission of Zondervan Publishing House. ©1991.

Open Windows by Philip Yancey. ©1982 by Philip Yancey. Used by permission.

Where Is God When It Hurts? by Philip Yancey. Reprinted by permission of Zondervan Publishing House. ©1977.

Behavior of Belief by Spiros Zodhiates. Reprinted by permission of William B. Eerdmans Publishing Company. ©1959.

"Sins Peril" by Chris T. Zwingelberg. *Leadership Magazine.* ©Winter 1987.